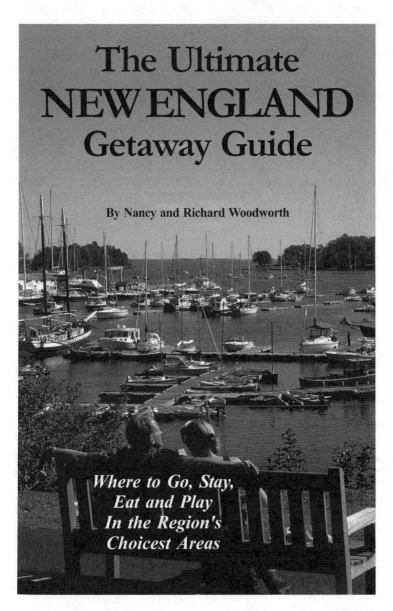

The Ultimate
NEW ENGLAND
Getaway Guide

By Nancy and Richard Woodworth

Where to Go, Stay,
Eat and Play
In the Region's
Choicest Areas

Wood Pond Press
West Hartford, Conn.

The authors value their reputation for credibility and personally visit the places recommended in this book. They do not rely on researchers or field inspectors who come and go with varying perspectives and loyalties to do their leg work. Nor do they ask the owners to fill out information forms or to approve the final copy. They make their recommendations based on their experiences and findings. No fees are charged for inclusion.

Prices and hours, especially in restaurants and lodging establishments, change seasonally and with business conditions. Those reported in this book were correct at presstime and are subject, of course, to change. They are offered as a relative guide to what to expect. Lodging rates are for double occupancy and include breakfast, unless specified to the contrary, except for hotels and motels. EP (European Plan) means no meals. MAP (Modified American Plan) means breakfast and dinner. AP (American Plan) includes breakfast, lunch and dinner.

For updates between editions, check out the Wood Pond Press web site at www.getawayguides.com. Favorite inns, B&Bs, resorts and attractions from this book and from others by the authors are detailed there.

The authors welcome readers' comments and suggestions.

Cover Photo: Camden Harbor, Camden, Me.

Contents

To Our Readers

Location. Location. Location. The realtors' mantra applies to the traveler, too. When you want a break, a getaway from everyday life, usually you think first of the destination. How about the shore? The mountains? The lake? The country? The city?

Then you consider the specifics. Do you want a place to relax and chill out? Or to be active and on the go?

Do you want to see the sights? Visit museums and galleries? Go shopping? Hike or ski? Play tennis? Hang out around the pool or at the beach?

Probably you'll want to indulge. Eat some good food. Perhaps treat yourself to some spa services. Bask in a luxurious guest room or suite with all the comforts of home, and then some.

If you're like many of today's getaway goers on the go, you'll want to go first class. You will want a room with an oversize canopy bed, a fireplace and a whirlpool tub. And probably a TV/DVD player, a decanter of wine and some bedside chocolates.

Where do you turn to find out the options? The ads and brochures, the broadcasts and websites may help. But their litany of come-ons may exaggerate or confuse.

The best recommendations are often "word of mouth." That's where we can help. As journalists and frequent travelers who live and work in New England, we have spent years exploring our home region. What we've found and experienced, we report here. We tell it like it is, so you can separate the wheat from the chaff.

New England is perfect for getaways and quick respites from the daily routine. It's compact enough that, depending on location, you can get almost anywhere in the region for a day trip, a weekend, or a longer break. Yet it is diverse enough to offer a veritable world of activities and opportunities like no other region around.

You want recreation? History? Culture? Scenery? Mountains? Lakes? The ocean? Cosmopolitan cities? Luxury accommodations? Fine dining? Great shopping? New England has them all.

After all these years of traveling throughout and writing about New England, we know not only the best getaway destination areas, but also the best places to go and things to do in each area. Each of the 30 destinations we write about here has a variety of attractions for anyone seeking a getaway. Rather than stressing a different theme for each destination, we select those that are best all-around, to serve a variety of interests. Each also has a number of comfortable lodgings in which to stay and good places to eat. And within each getaway destination, we've tried to provide getaways within a getaway, places where you can retreat for privacy or peace and quiet. So that at the conclusion of your getaway, you return rejuvenated.

Here, then, are 30 special New England destinations, each suitable for a terrific getaway.

Nancy and Richard Woodworth

About the Authors

Nancy Webster Woodworth began her travel and dining experiences in her native Montreal and as a waitress in summer resorts across Canada during her McGill University years. She worked in London and hitchhiked through Europe on $3 a day before her marriage to Richard Woodworth, whom she met while skiing at Mont Tremblant. She started writing her "Roaming the Restaurants" column for the West Hartford (Conn.) News in 1972. That led to half of the book, *Daytripping & Dining in Southern New England,* in 1978. She since has co-authored *Inn Spots & Special Places in New England, Getaways for Gourmets in the Northeast, Waterside Escapes in the Northeast, New England's Best, Inn Spots & Special Places / Mid-Atlantic, Best Restaurants of New England* and *Inn Spots & Special Places in the Southeast.* She and her husband have two grown sons and live in West Hartford.

Richard Woodworth has been an inveterate traveler since his youth in suburban Syracuse, N.Y., where his birthday outings often involved adventures by train with friends for the day to nearby Utica or Rochester. After graduation from Middlebury College, he was a reporter for newspapers in Syracuse, Jamestown, Geneva and Rochester before moving to Connecticut to become editor of the West Hartford News and eventually executive editor of Imprint Newspapers. With his wife and sons, he has traveled to the four corners of this country, Canada and portions of Europe, writing their findings for newspapers and magazines. With his wife, he has co-authored three editions of *Inn Spots & Special Places* for New England, the Mid-Atlantic and the Southeast, *Getaways for Gourmets in the Northeast, Best Restaurants of New England, Waterside Escapes in the Northeast* and their newest book, *New England's Best.* He also was co-author and editor of *Celebrate!West Hartford, An Illustrated History* for the town's Sesquicentennial. Between travels and duties as proprietor of Wood Pond Press, he tries to find time to ski or head south in the winter and weed the garden or head north in the summer.

Excerpts from the authors' books are on line at www.getawayguides.com. The authors may be reached by e-mail at woodpond@ntplx.net.

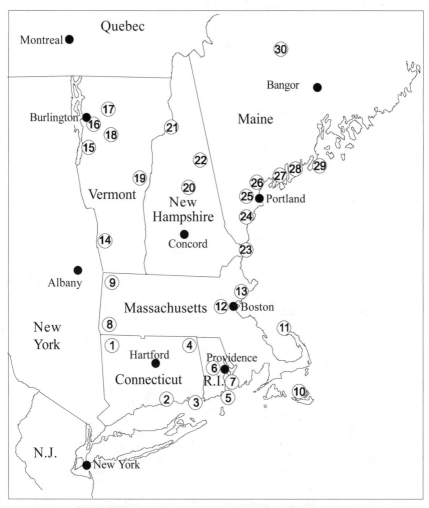

THE ULTIMATE NEW ENGLAND GETAWAY GUIDE

1. Northwest Connecticut
2. Lower Connecticut River Valley
3. Mystic/Stonington, CT
4. Northeast Connecticut
5. Newport, RI
6. Providence, RI
7. Bristol, RI
8. Southern Berkshires, MA
9. Williamstown/North Adams, MA
10. Nantucket, MA
11. Provincetown, MA
12. Boston, MA
13. Salem, MA
14. Manchester, VT
15. Middlebury, VT

16. Burlington, VT
17. Stowe, VT
18. Mad River Valley, VT
19. Woodstock, VT
20. Lake Winnipesaukee, NH
21. Franconia/Bethlehem, NH
22. Mount Washington Valley, NH
23. Portsmouth, NH
24. Kennebunkport, ME
25. Portland, ME
26. Freeport/The Harpswells, ME
27. Camden/Rockland, ME
28. Blue Hill/Deer Isle, ME
29. Mount Desert Island, ME
30. Moosehead Lake, ME

Couple strolls toward picnic area at foot of waterfall in Kent Falls State Park.

Connecticut's Northwest Corner

A Patchwork Country Sampler

"The Hidden Corner," New York magazine once called it, touting the virtues of the Northwest Corner as a place for city people to make their second homes.

And hidden it is, this rural panoply called the Northwest Corner by its residents and the legions of Sunday drivers who have headed here for years from across Connecticut and adjacent New York.

Less than two hours' drive from the nation's largest metropolitan area are the Litchfield Hills, which seem to have a corner on the state's hidden treasures. Here is an unspoiled, forested countryside with more state parks and public lands than any other area in Southern New England.

Much of the land not in the public domain is owned by wealthy residents, celebrities and visiting New Yorkers, who have made this their weekend retreat or second home. The state parks and forests are relatively uncrowded and so are many of the inns, restaurants and shops that are frequented by travelers. This is a place for those who cherish nature, quiet times and a subdued sophistication.

Northwest Connecticut doesn't shout its assets. You'll find few of the kinds of major attractions that beckon visitors elsewhere in New England. The area simply presents itself, quietly and quaintly, for anyone to enjoy.

The Northwest Corner is a mosaic of many things and many places, too many to cover in a short getaway. It's the estates of gentlemen farmers in Sharon and Salisbury, the covered bridges and country stores along the Housatonic River in Cornwall and Kent, the Alpine inns around Lake Waramaug, the Indian ties of old Washington and the historic firsts of Litchfield. It's country shops, the Appalachian Trail, whitewater canoeing, chamber music concerts and sports-car races at Lime Rock.

Be advised that the Northwest Corner is rather spread out – a collection of four "pockets" that extend about 25 miles from end to end. Because even the residents seldom go between them, each pocket is best dealt with individually. The whole makes up a patchwork country sampler.

Sharon, Salisbury and the Cornwalls

The homes are larger, the shops swankier and the restaurants more expensive the farther you delve into the Northwest Corner. In this northwesternmost area, cultural attractions and the Hotchkiss and Salisbury preparatory schools have drawn residents and visitors for the good life. Salisbury has a country-perfect Main Street flanked by white clapboard neoclassical estates, small shops and bakeries, and the country's oldest library.

Just a few miles away is Cornwall, considered by some the most photogenic of Northwest Corner towns. Each of its sparsely populated hamlets grew separately among the hills along the Housatonic River. Skiers bound for Mohawk Mountain pass near charming Cornwall Center, unaware of its existence. The covered bridge at the mountain hamlet of West Cornwall is a focus for river explorations.

Sharon epitomizes the region's quiet affluence. The homes of the Buckley family and other "Tories" from Revolutionary days line Route 41 south of town, giving the town a Yankee aristocratic flavor. More than 300 houses are a century or more old. The Clock Tower heads the long village green, where the marker says the land is "still much as it was laid out in the wilderness in 1739."

Seeing and Doing

Sharon Audubon Center, Route 4, Sharon.

Explore the countryside at this, one of five National Audubon Society centers in the country. It's as marvelous for its abundant trees and pristine lakes as it is for wildlife (Canada geese, deer, beavers, otters and an occasional bear). The Clement R. Ford Home, a handsome large old summer place, houses a fine interpretive museum, a good shop and varied workshops. But "most visitors come to walk and to learn about the land and its inhabitants," reports the director. Half of the 860 acres form a natural sanctuary; the other half contain most of the eleven miles of self-guiding trails, two ponds and an herb garden.

(860) 364-0520. www.audubon.org/local/sanctuary/sharon. Center open Tuesday-Saturday 9 to 5, Sunday 1 to 5; trails open dawn to dusk. Adults $3, children $1.50.

Music Mountain, off Route 7, Falls Village (Box 738, Lakeville 06039).

Founded in 1930 as the permanent home of the Gordon String Quartet, this is the oldest continuous chamber music festival in the United States. The performance hall and musicians' residences were built by Sears, Roebuck and are listed in the National Register of Historic Places. The acoustically perfect Gordon Hall, the centerpiece of the 132-acre campus, provides views of the gardens, grounds and hills from all 335 seats and from the lawn, permitting listeners to savor music and nature as one. Various string quartets from around the world present weekend concerts Sunday afternoons and some Saturday evenings in summer. Jazz concerts are staged most other Saturday evenings. Amazingly, the venture remains perhaps the only one of its importance to be managed by volunteers.

(860) 824-7126. www.musicmountain.org. Concerts, Saturdays at 8 and Sunday at 3, mid-June into September. Tickets, $20, students $10.

Lime Rock Park, 497 Lime Rock Road (Route 112) in Lime Rock, (800) 722-3577, is billed as "the road racing center of the East," staging sports car races on summer holidays and other weekends through mid-October. The track weaves through 350 acres around grassy knolls on a plateau beneath the hills. It's truly a park, with a natural amphitheater in which spectators watch the racing from blankets and lawn chairs on the grassy hillsides. Access to the race paddocks allows fans to get up-close to both cars and drivers. Actor Paul Newman races here. If that and the scenery aren't enough, there sometimes are vintage race cars and NASCAR stock cars doing their thing.

TOURING. Mount Riga is the generic name for a series of peaks stretching northwest from Salisbury to the Connecticut-Massachusetts-New York junction. Here you can hike the Appalachian Trail, swim or camp at South Pond, visit a restored stone iron furnace from the days when Salisbury was a major producer of iron, climb Bald Peak or Bear Mountain, or drive (on dirt roads) across the scenic heights of Connecticut's highest area to Mount Washington in the Berkshires. The state and Mount Riga Inc., an association of 90 old-line Salisbury families who summer there, own most of the land, which you reach from Washinee Street, west of Route 44 at the Salisbury Town Hall.

Twin Lakes, just northeast of Salisbury off Route 44, is one of the most scenic places imaginable and one we've often passed without realizing it was there. Mount Riga and Canaan Mountain are backdrops for these two beautiful lakes dotted with homes and, on the east side off Twin Lakes Road, a public beach and boating area. A drive along Between-the-Lakes Road or an afternoon boat ride are good ways to enjoy the area.

Cathedral Pines, a centuries-old stand of gigantic pines near the foot of the Mohawk Mountain ski area, was reduced nearly to rubble by a tornado some years back. Drive along winding Essex Hill Road from the ski area access road to see the devastation, just as nature left it, and the new growth. You come out of the spiked forest into an open field where cows graze; just beyond is Marvelwood School and Cornwall Center. An historic marker advises that writer Mark Van Doren "enriched many lives from his Cornwall home."

Mohawk State Forest atop 1,683-foot Mohawk Mountain in Cornwall is perfect for foliage viewing. Drive in from Route 4, past a couple of scenic overlooks with sweeping vistas to the west. About two and a half miles in is a wooden observation tower with 35 steep steps, which you can climb for a panoramic view in all directions.

River Expeditions. Increasingly popular pastimes on the Housatonic River are canoeing, kayaking and rafting, both whitewater and flatwater varieties. On weekends from March through October, more than 400 canoes and kayaks have been counted in the 45-mile stretch from Sheffield, Mass., south to Kent – most concentrated in the twelve miles between Falls Village and Cornwall Bridge. Jennifer Clarke of Clarke Outdoors at 163 Route 7 in West Cornwall, one mile south of the covered bridge, says there's no better way to experience the area than from a canoe going down the river. Many canoeists take picnic lunches; family outings are popular, and you can get instruction, hire guides and obtain shuttle service back to your car. The standard trip takes three or four hours and canoes or kayaks can be rented by the day. Fishermen and campers find all they need at Housatonic River Outfitters, 24 Kent Road, Cornwall Bridge.

SHOPPING. Salisbury offers a variety of shopping in a small area, which is fine for ambling around on a pleasant afternoon. Classic gifts and home furnishings are on display on two floors of an 1832 house called **Perfect Pear,** a fabulous shop near the White Hart Inn. **Riga Traders** is an amazing ramble of whimsical themed rooms carrying items related to golf, fly-fishing and children, among others – everything from home accents to folk art to sweaters and ties. Antiques and jewelry are featured at **Passports.** Check out the marvelous variety of handcrafted items at **Creative Hands Gallery & Gifts,** 15 Academy St. **Habitant,** a good kitchen store, is down another side street at 10 Library St.

Tea connoisseurs are in their element at **Harney & Sons,** which sells exotic teas by the bag or tin at the packing factory at 11 Brook St. John Harney, former innkeeper at the White Hart Inn, started a mail-order tea business in his family home across from the inn and now has an esteemed enterprise with a retail shop and sophisticated tasting room, open daily 10 to 5 and Sunday noon to 5. For more than a taste, stop for traditional tea service at **Chaiwalla,** Mary O'Brien's tea house at 1 Main St. She offers homemade soups, tomato pie and open-face sandwiches as well as tea.

Shops seem to come and go in Lakeville, a mile away along Route 44. **Corner Clothiers** has suave apparel and the **Iron Rooster Boutique & Gift Shop** is worth a stop. **April 56 Extreme Cookery** carries a potpourri of gourmet foods, Junior League cookbooks and original gifts.

In Cornwall, stop **at Cornwall Bridge Pottery,** Route 7, a half mile south of Cornwall Bridge. Todd Piker works with a 35-foot-long climbing kiln that he fires six times a year to produce three tons worth of pots each time. His showroom is lined with honest, mostly functional stoneware pottery, from tiny creamers to lamps and pots that seem too big to use for anything. Many are decorated with birds and fish. The pottery behind his home is open daily and features seconds. His retail showroom in West Cornwall has a furniture showroom and a Barn Gallery upstairs.

Lodging and Dining

Interlaken Inn, 74 Interlaken Road (Route 112), Lakeville 06039.

Built in 1973, this modern resort and conference center in a rural setting is situated down the hill from the Hotchkiss School between Long Pond and Lake Wononskopomuc, which give the inn and the village their names. The 30-acre property includes frontage on the lovely clear lake, where guests may swim or take out a canoe or rowboat; there's also a large heated pool. The main inn is contemporary with a slate floor and leather sofas in the lobby. The 55 deluxe motel-style rooms are crisply decorated. Sunnyside, a shingled rear building that is all that is left of the original New England inn on the site, has twelve rooms with brass beds and Victorian antiques. The English Tudor-style house called Countryside has eight rooms with king or queen beds. Contemporary buildings contain eight one-bedroom townhouse suites, each with fireplace, kitchen, dining area, loft bedroom with two double beds and one and a half baths. Tennis, a sauna, a game room and golf privileges at Hotchkiss's nine-hole course are available. Breakfast is offered buffet-style.

Morgan's Grille, a rattan-filled dining area renovated from the former cocktail lounge in the rear overlooking the pool, serves lunch and dinner. The menu ranges from light fare to grilled beef tenderloin . Start with salmon gravlax and warm blinis. Typical main courses are grilled tuna with ginger-shiitake mushroom sauce and herb-roasted chicken with cider sauce. Warm chocolate cake is the signature dessert.

(860) 435-9878 or (800) 222-2909. Fax (860) 435-9878. www.interlakeninn.com. Eighty-three rooms and suites with private baths. Doubles, $139 to $339 EP. Entrées, $17 to $27. Lunch daily, 11:30 to 2. Dinner nightly, 5:30 to 9 or 10.

The White Hart, The Village Green, Box 545, Salisbury 06068.

A wide white porch full of wicker and chintz fronts the venerable White Hart Inn, several times abandoned and recently restored but still subject to the vagaries of a succession of owners, most famously Edsel Ford, who bought it in 1935 when his children were at the Hotchkiss School. Today the White Hart is owned by Scott Bok, a long-time weekend resident. The accommodations are recommendable following recent upgrades. Three are suites, six contain two double beds and most of the rest have queensize canopy four-poster beds. Mahogany reproduction or country pine furniture, TV sets in armoires and Waverly floral wallpapers with matching comforters are the norm. On the main floor, the clubby Hunt Room has a library, small bar and piano.

Meals are served in the Garden Room, a sunny place with trellised wallpaper, botanical prints and brass chandeliers, and in the fireplaced Colonial-era Tap Room, dating to 1806 when the inn opened. In season, lunch and dinner also are served on the front porch overlooking the village green. The short menu of updated American tavern fare runs from baked salmon fillet with morel-dill sauce to juniper-rubbed venison tenderloin with Umbrian game sauce.

(860) 435-0030 or (800) 832-0041. Fax (860) 435-0040. www.whitehartinn.com. Twenty-three rooms and three suites with private baths. Doubles, $150 to $300, off-season $130 to $200. Entrées, $20 to $26. Lunch daily, 11:30 to 3, Saturday to 4. Dinner nightly, 5 to 9 or 9:30. Sunday brunch, 10 to 4.

Cornwall Inn & Lodge, 270 Kent Road (Route 7), Cornwall 06754.

A variety of lodgings and a restaurant are found in this refurbished 1821 inn on three rural acres surrounded by forests. Both aspects have been enhanced by new owners Stacey Marcin and Mark Hampson, who moved from Philadelphia to raise their young family in a house behind the inn. The main inn holds four B&B rooms and a two-bedroom suite upstairs. Across the parking lot is the lodge, a motel-style building with eight rooms, cedar post beds and rustic furnishings typical of a mountain lodge. All rooms have feather beds with down comforters, television, telephone and data port. The inn has a common room off the restaurant. Outside are a swimming pool and hot tub. The property abuts the Appalachian Trail and contains a mountain stream emptying in the Housatonic River 300 yards away. Continental breakfast is included in the rates.

The restaurant is on the upswing under executive chef Stefan Kappes, a Culinary Institute of America-trained chef whose classic country cooking style meshes with two small country-style dining rooms and a large tavern. His signature dishes are roast duckling and rack of lamb, but you'll likely also find crab cakes, cajun-spiced pork tenderloin and New York strip steak with port wine and green peppercorn sauce. The fish of the day might be roasted tautog (blackfish) with braised fennel and tomatoes. Typical appetizers are fried calamari with a spicy tomato sauce, pot stickers with soy-ginger sauce and baked brie in puff pastry. Dessert could be warm apple-cranberry bread pudding with cinnamon-laced vanilla bean ice cream.

(860) 672-6884 or (800) 786-6884. www.cornwallinn.com. Twelve rooms and one two-bedroom suite with private baths. Doubles, $139 to $189. Suite, $209. Entrées, $15 to $24.50. Dinner, Thursday-Sunday 5 to 10.

Inn at Iron Masters, 229 Main St. (Route 44), Lakeville 06039.

This attractive 28-unit motel is set back from the highway over the old Davis Ore Mine, which furnished iron for the Salisbury cannons that helped outgunned colonists win the Revolutionary War. Each carpeted unit has two double beds, sitting area, TV and telephone. All rooms have been refurbished with Ethan Allen furniture, Laura Ashley wallpaper and fabrics, and new bathroom fixtures. The stone fireplace in the lobby dates to the 18th century and is usually ablaze for a complimentary continental-plus breakfast, which is served at tables nearby. Guests enjoy swimming in a pool in a nicely landscaped garden area.

(860) 435-9844. Fax (860) 435-2254. www.innatironmasters.com. Twenty-eight rooms. Doubles, $115 to $195.

┌─ *Peak Experience* ─────────────────────────────

Hilltop Haven Bed & Breakfast, 175 Dibble Hill Road, West Cornwall 06796.

For a romantic getaway on top of the world, escape to this charmer perched at bluff's edge, almost 800 feet straight above the Housatonic River. Everett Van Dorn, a former Navy budget analyst whose parents built this as their summer home, offers two comfortable, paneled bedrooms, each with a double bed and private bath. The common facilities make the place: a huge, cathedral-ceilinged library with walls and floors of fieldstone and windows on three sides; a living room with grand piano, TV and another fireplace; a sun porch, and a wraparound stone veranda from which you can see New York's Catskill Mountains. Everett, who occupies a cabin on the forested 63-acre property, puts out decanters of sherry at night and prepares a lavish breakfast of shrimp and cheese strata or grand marnier french toast. This is a much lived-in home, reflecting the furnishings and tastes of the owner's late parents.

(860) 672-6871. www.hilltopbedandbreakfast.com. Two rooms with private baths. Doubles, $145 to $160.

└──

Pastorale Bistro & Bar, 223 Main Street, Lakeville.

This handsome white house dating to 1765 has housed many an upscale restaurant. One that should last was opened in 2003 by French chef-owner Frederic Faveau and his wife Karen Hamilton. Frederic's masterful cooking impressed us first at Litchfield's West Street Grill and later at the Birches Inn on Lake Waramaug. His food here is every bit as brilliant but less contrived – "more bistro-like, with a more laid-back presentation," he says. The emphasis is on local and organic ingredients.

The main floor houses an atmospheric bar/lounge with booths for dining and a small dining room. Up a staircase passing a window onto the kitchen is the main dining area, a mix of booths and tables covered with white linens and white butcher paper. An outside patio is popular in season. Starters entice, from the shrimp and scallop ravioli to seared sweetbreads with polenta cake and mesclun greens. The watercress and duck confit salad is a classic of its genre. Gallic accents embellish entrées like mussels marinière, beef bourguignonne and steak frites. The menu also offers a cheeseburger with Irish cheddar and the specialty grilled leg of lamb in a port wine reduction, served perhaps with mustard greens and a casserole of flageolet beans, roasted tomatoes, roasted garlic and preserved lemon. Desserts reflect the owner's French heritage as well: the specialty cherry clafoutis from Burgundy, tarte tatin and chocolate marquise. The crème brûlée might bear an Asian accent of ginger and lemongrass.

(860) 435-1011. Entrées, $16.50 to $22. Dinner, Tuesday-Saturday 5 to 9 or 9:30. Sunday, brunch noon to 3:30, dinner noon to 8.

The Woodland, 192 Sharon Road (Route 41), Lakeville.

A lounge with an ornate silver pressed-tin ceiling and curved greenhouse windows adds to this classy-looking establishment known for good, reasonably priced food in a wooded area south of Lakeville. Beehive lights hang over the smart red booths in a dining room striking for the artworks on the walls (done by the talented sisters of owner Carol Peters), woven placemats and a profusion of fresh flowers. For lunch, choose from a variety of sandwiches and salads, a steak dish from tacos to tartare or perhaps an item from the extensive sushi and sashimi menu offered by a sushi chef working out of sight in the kitchen. At night, there is more of the same, from burgers to quesadillas, plus entrées from sole meunière or amandine and herb-roasted chicken to sliced hanger steak on garlic toast and steak au poivre. The heart of the menu is the specials, one night's including lobster ravioli with wild mushrooms and arugula, cajun blackened tuna, veal scaloppine with dark beer and whole grain mustard, and rainbow sushi with crab, avocado and the works. Finish with such delectable homemade desserts as cranberry linzer torte, chocolate fudge cake with kahlua sauce, pear custard cake or kiwi sorbet.

(203) 435-0578. Entrées, $15 to $28. Lunch, Tuesday-Saturday 11:30 to 2:30. Dinner, Tuesday-Saturday 5:30 to 9 or 10.

Kent

If you arrive in the area from the south, the sign along Route 7 at the town line identifies a scenic highway for the next 28 miles. The road slices along the Housatonic River through a bucolic valley flanked by hills bereft of much besides forests and wildlife. On your left you will spot sheep, goats, chickens and belted galloway cows grazing at the **Rainwater Farm Project,** a twelve-acre organic farm at 170 Kent Road, designed to revive the town's rural heritage. If you stop at the farm shop or to explore the property, you might startle geese resting beneath a bench at the entrance to the Kent Land Trust's new **Kent River Walk.** Later, on the right is a hillside lawn populated by the life-size steel and bronze animal sculptures of Denis Curtiss, lately titled "The Dog Show." If there are no dogs, you might want to take home a giraffe, rhino or elephant.

Welcome to Kent, an up-and-coming town where the largest presence, other than the Kent School campus, are the shops, galleries and restaurants interspersed among historic homes along Main Street (Route 7). The **Kent Historical Society** opens a large house, Seven Hearths, built in the 1750s in the Flanders historic district north of the village, as a modest museum and art gallery in summer. Beyond is **Kent Falls State Park,** a 200-foot cascade ending in an open meadow. A little covered bridge leads from the parking lot to the meadow with picnic tables scattered about. Visitors may take a winding but wide pathway to the head of the falls, a short hike from the parking area.

Sloane-Stanley Museum, U.S. Route 7 North, Kent.

When artist-writer Eric Sloane died in 1985, he left an enormous legacy, including the museum that bears his name and displays a collection of his beloved early American tools made by hand. He designed the barn-like structure for the purpose. Wooden shovels and bowls, baskets and pitchforks, axes and scythes are grouped in ambient settings. Horse-drawn sleighs and other artifacts are shown along with Sloane paintings in the gallery. A wing houses a reproduction of the artist's studio from nearby Warren. Adjacent is a cabin that Sloane built in two weeks when a TV film was being made of his book, *The Diary of an American Boy.* Below the museum are the remains of the Kent Iron Furnace, which produced pig iron in the 1800s.

(860) 927-3849. Open Wednesday-Sunday and holidays, 10 to 4, mid-May through October. Adults, $4, children $2.50.

Museum of Industrial & Agricultural Machinery, Kent-Cornwall Road, Kent.

Just north of the Sloane-Stanley Museum and sharing a common entrance are seven exhibit buildings housing antique farm and factory machinery under the auspices of the volunteer Connecticut Antique Machinery Association. A couple of steam engines on a narrow-gauge railroad track mark the site. Esoteric collections of early tractors, farm implements, internal combustion engines and steam engines are housed in the Agricultural and Industrial halls. The Mining Museum chronicles aspects of the area's early iron industry and displays Connecticut minerals.

(860) 927-0050. www.ctamachinery.com. Open May-October, Wednesday-Sunday 10 to 4.

SHOPPING. Antiquing is big around here, and the **Kent Antiques Center** in a restored 160-year-old farmhouse at Kent Station Square is a multi-dealer shop. On two floors **The Heron American Craft Gallery** offers one of the finest collections of contemporary crafts in New England. **Foreign Cargo** carries distinctive clothing and jewelry, home accessories and antiques, along with Asian and African art and artifacts. Outdoor gear and apparel are stocked at the large **Backcountry Outfitters,** which also serves through-hikers on the Appalachian Trail. Fine art is shown at the sophisticated **Paris-New York-Kent Gallery. Country Clothes** shows casual clothing and gifts in a 19th-century house. Women's clothing is paired with antiques at **B. Johnstone & Co.** and with artsy household accessories at **Terston Home Accents.** At **Strobel Baking Co.,** Patsy Strobel makes everything from scratch; her breads and pies are said to be the best around.

Lodging and Dining

The Inn at Kent Falls, 107 Kent-Cornwall Road (Route 7), Kent 06757.

Located in the historic Flanders section between the village and Kent Falls State Park, this sprawling, good-looking 1741 house is surrounded by 2.5 tranquil acres.

Ira Goldspiel, an escapee from the New York fashion industry, and his cousin, Glen Sherman, renovated the old Flanders Arms B&B and reopened in 2003. They offer six guest quarters, five fireplaces, and an all-white living room, a cheery den and a screened porch for common areas. Decor is crisp and contemporary, with Frette linens and fluffy down duvets on the oversize beds and Aveda toiletries in the bathrooms. Every room has TV, CD, phone and internet access and the plump, oversize furniture of today, although many retain historic touches such as wide-board floors and indoor window shutters. Three guest rooms come with queen beds, one with a fireplace. Three suites have kingsize beds. The premier Falls suite offers a fireplace in the bedroom, an adjoining library alcove, a clawfoot soaking tub and rainforest shower. The Lakes Suite has two fireplaces, one in the bedroom and another in the bathroom. A continental-plus breakfast including quiche or smoked salmon is served in the dining room or on the screened porch. The porch looks out onto a gorgeous angular swimming pool.

(860) 927-3197. Fax (860) 927-3239. www.theinnatkentfalls.com. Three rooms and three suites with private baths. Doubles, $155 to $245. Suites, $295 to $325.

Restaurant Moosilauke, 23 Maple St., Kent.

They named the place after their favorite New Hampshire hiking mountain, incorporated a moose on their logo and offer a specialty drink called a moose passion martini (vodka and passion fruit sorbet). But otherwise there's nothing particularly moose-like in this inviting, ultra-hot New American restaurant that chef James Nunzig and Christine Reynolds opened in 2003 in a charming 1730s house beside the Kent-Warren road. Unless it's the chocolate color of the striking high-back leather chairs that flank white-clothed tables in two main-floor dining rooms and an upstairs bar and lounge. Dining is by candlelight and the glow of a central fireplace flickering into each beamed dining room, or out back on a honeysuckle-bordered patio. The ambitious menu beckons as much as the ambiance: perhaps pan-roasted shoyu-marinated salmon with a sesame-miso vinaigrette, a confit of duck leg over white bean cassoulet with smoked pork and sausage, or a duo of pancetta-wrapped lamb tenderloin and grilled leg of lamb. The select wine list is particularly strong on reds to accompany such robust fare. Autumn appetizers were lighter, perhaps a roasted red beet carpaccio with warm goat cheese crouton or crisp squash blossom rellenos stuffed with crab and corn. Dessert could be rum mocha-walnut layer cake, a lemon-lime tart with raspberry coulis or a cheese plate with panini crisps, olives and dried white figs.

(860) 927-4145. www.restaurantmoosilauke.com. Entrées, $17 to $26. Dinner, Tuesday-Sunday 5 to 9 or 10.

Fife 'n Drum, 53 North Main St., Kent.

An updated continental menu, an atmospheric taproom with fireplace, a candlelit dining room with pewter service plates and signed Eric Sloane prints on the walls, and owner Dolph Traymon at the piano. That's the formula that draws patrons to this legendary establishment, which includes eight motel rooms and a gift shop. Tableside preparation of caesar salad, roast duckling, rack of lamb, filet mignon au poivre and châteaubriand for two is featured. Recent appetizers supplement the traditional clams casino and fried calamari with more contemporary offerings like a smoked salmon and shrimp wrap with sesame-orange dipping sauce. Besides the signature steak dishes, expect such entrées as scallop and shrimp sauté provençal, grilled jerk spice-crusted pork loin with mango chutney-rum sauce, and shrimp and chicken piccata. A tavern menu is available as well. The owner's piano repertoire is as wide-ranging as the food. The 1,000-selection wine list carries a Best of Award of Excellence from Wine Spectator.

(860) 927-3509. www.fifendrum.com. Entrées, $14.95 to $29.95. Lunch, 11:30 to 3. Dinner, 5:30 to 9:30 or 10. Closed Tuesday.

Patisserie-Plus, Extraordinaire

Belgique Salon de Thé, Main Street, Kent.

Pierre Gilissen, a former embassy chef from Belgium, and his wife Susan turned a rundown property at the main intersection of Routes 7 and 341 into a destination for gourmands. They first opened Belgique Patisserie & Chocolatier, featuring exquisite (and incredibly decorated) European desserts, baguettes, breads and Belgian chocolates made on site. The Belgian hot chocolate alone made it a stop not to be missed, but the couple captured more hearts with their Salon de Thé, "a European tea room serving gastronomic delights, desserts and wines" in an elegant, mustard-yellow Queen Anne Victorian house. Don't expect a typical meal. The menu offers no appetizers or entrées but rather savories, and you pick and choose among them. How about smoked salmon crêpes or duck confit and frisée salad, foie gras au torchon, bouillabaisse, venison stew or beef Wellington? The charcuterie plate offers a good taste of the exotic meat offerings. Indulge in one of the fabulous sweets, perhaps coconut dacquoise or a chestnut papilotte. Accompany with tea, Belgian beer, one of the 150 wines or even an aged cognac. Raved a Hartford restaurant critic: "It has won my vote for best espresso, along with my votes for best dessert, best beer, best service, and overall, best place I've ever eaten in the state." Due to limited seating, there is a $30 average minimum per person per table.

(860) 927-3681. Lunch savories, $8 to $19. Dinner savories, $8 to $28. Desserts, $9.75 to $14. Lunch and afternoon tea, seatings Thursday-Sunday 1 to 2:30. Dinner, Friday and Saturday 6 to 8. Sunday champagne brunch, noon to 2:30.

Lake Waramaug's Alpine Country

Nothing in the area seems quite so European as sitting on the terrace of the Hopkins Inn for lunch or a pre-dinner cocktail and gazing down the hillside on Lake Waramaug. The lake reminds some of those in Austria and Switzerland, and the surrounding inns capitalize on it. Off in worlds unto themselves east of the lake are quaint New Preston, a hamlet that seems to consist primarily of exotic shops, and picturesque Washington Depot and Washington, the former nestled in a valley and the latter perched on a hilltop.

Hills rise sharply above the boomerang-shaped Lake Waramaug, and a scenic, nine-mile-long shore road winds slowly around. Its sylvan shoreline is flanked by substantial summer homes on manicured lawns. Three country inns sit not far from water's edge. At the west end of the lake is **Lake Waramaug State Park,** a wonderfully picturesque site, its picnic tables scattered well apart along the tree-lined shore, right beside the water. The lake's Indian name means "good fishing place." It's also good for swimming and boating, and is mercifully uncrowded. On the lake's north and east sides are the forested Above All and Mount Bushnell state parks.

Mount Tom State Park in nearby Woodville is often overlooked. Right beside Route 202 is a 60-acre spring-fed pond for swimming; the excellent beach facilities include individual changing rooms. Picnic tables are smack dab on the shore and scattered along the hillside. A mile-long trail rises 500 feet to a tower atop Mount Tom. The hilltop village green in the postcard-perfect community of **Washington** is as classic as any in Connecticut. Large houses and prominent churches surround it, and off to one side is the Gunnery School's interesting campus. The **Gunn Historical Museum,** housed in a 1781 wooden structure near the green, is open Thursday-Saturday 10 to 4 and Sunday noon to 4, free. It has a fine thimble collection, dollhouses, spinning wheels and western Indian baskets.

The Institute for American Indian Studies, 38 Curtis Road, Washington.

Dedicated to Indian relics and archeological digs, this establishment made history some years back when a team uncovered a fluted "clovis" spear point, which they say confirms Indians at the spot 10,000 years ago. A mastodon skeleton inside the contemporary museum shows the type of animal they would have hunted. There are arrowheads, very early Indian pottery, sandstone dishes and dioramas of early Indian life. Also on the premises are an Indian longhouse, a simulated dig site and an unusual, specialized museum shop with handcrafted copies of items in the collection. A twenty-minute habitat trail takes the visitor through stages of geological and botanical development in Connecticut.

(860) 868-0518. www.birdstone.org. Open Monday-Saturday 10 to 5, Sunday noon to 5, April-December. Monday and Tuesday in winter. Adults $4, children $2.

Hopkins Vineyard, 25 Hopkins Road, New Preston.

A hillside location with a good view of Lake Waramaug marks this family operation personally run by Bill and Judy Hopkins, dairy farmers turned winemakers, and their offspring. The rustic red barn provides a quick, self-guided tour, an attractive showroom and tasting area, and the country-sophisticated Hayloft Wine Bar upstairs, where on weekends you can order a cheese and pâté board and wines by the glass and savor a view of the lake. The gift shop sells wine-related items like baskets, grapevine wreaths and stemware. The winery's cat may be snoozing near the wood stove, upon which a pot of mulled wine simmers on chilly days. On nice days, sip one of the eleven varieties of award-winning wines – perhaps a hearty cabernet franc or an estate chardonnay – in a small picnic area overlooking the lake.

(860) 868-7954. www.hopkinsvineyard.com. Open Monday-Saturday 10 to 5, Sunday 11 to 5, May-December; Wednesday-Sunday in March and April, Saturday-Sunday in January and February.

Lodging and Dining

The Huckleberry Inn, 219 Kent Road, Warren 06754.

One of New England's more sumptuous, charming and personality-driven B&Bs fills a void in the Litchfield Hills – the gap between the small, makeshift B&B in someone's house and the larger, high-end inn staffed for the purpose. That's the way Andrea DiMauro planned it. After twelve years as a personal chef for affluent families in suburban New York, the perky, 33-year-old blonde and her contractor husband restored a 1779 farmhouse to create three plush bedrooms and three distinctive common areas, all decorated with great style. They also gutted a former blacksmith shop/garage into an idyllic, two-level cottage in which celebrities have chosen to hide out. The handsome yellow house came with the patina of age: hand-hewn beams, wide-plank chestnut floors, intricate woodwork and warming fireplaces. The couple created luxurious baths with whirlpool tubs, tumbled marble showers and heated marble floors. They furnished with plump, oversize beds, pressed linens and goose down comforters, TV/VCRs, exotic toiletries and showy art. Guests watch Andrea cook organic breakfasts, while sipping espresso and cappuccino made with the special Huckleberry blend from her shiny Capresso "coffee center" machine on a sideboard in the dining room. The blackboard menu posts the morning's offerings: at our visit, citrus fruits with cardamom glaze and pomegranate seeds, cranberry-pumpkin bread, baby bella and fontina omelets with sausage links, and the grand finale – a smidgen of ginger crème brûlée. The four-course repast is taken at tables in the dining room or the adjacent stone-floored sun porch, both as country chic as the rest of the house. Guests find complimentary Hopkins Vineyard wine in their rooms and an array of liqueurs stashed in a remarkable mahogany liquor cabinet (made during Prohibition to look like a radio) in the fireplaced living room.

(860) 868-1947 or (866) 868-1947. Fax (860) 868-6014. www.thehuckleberryinn.com. Three rooms and one cottage with private baths. Doubles, $205 to $285. Cottage, $365.

The Boulders Inn, Route 45, New Preston 06777.

This venerable inn across the road from Lake Waramaug has been grandly refurbished in Adirondack lodge style under new ownership to appeal to a more sophisticated, moneyed clientele. The new look is evident in the main-floor public rooms that sprawl across the front of the substantial Dutch Colonial residence built in 1890. The luxurious living room has been redecorated in cool taupe and beige, with six oversize lodge chairs facing windows onto the lake. Boulders remain integral to the decor, comprising the massive fireplace chimney and jutting out from the walls of the inner dining room. Five accommodations with king or queen beds are upstairs in the main house. Three rooms facing the lake offer large, cushioned window seats to take in the view. The most luxurious are seven rooms (four of which may be joined to become a pair of suites) in a rear carriage house with plush chintz seating in front of stone fireplaces. Favored for romantic getaways are eight more contemporary rooms with fireplaces in four hillside duplex cottages called guest houses. Renovated and upgraded with king or queen four-poster beds, the guest houses have new decks in front and back facing woods and lake, and five have whirlpool tubs. The Boulders added a state-of-the-art fitness facility and spa program in 2004. A full breakfast is included in the rates.

The six-sided Lake Dining Room with windows onto Lake Waramaug, the intimate inner dining room with walls of boulders, and three tiered patios for outdoor dining are the varied settings for some of the area's more sophisticated meals. One recent night's main courses ranged from grilled black pearl salmon with aged balsamic butter to New York strip steak au poivre. Cassoulet provençal and venison steak with sherry demi-glace also tempted from the short contemporary American menu. Among appetizers were a scallop and blue crab terrine with coconut emulsion and Thai-spiced lobster oil. Desserts were an ethereal cheesecake with candied ginger crust and white and dark chocolate mousse in a tuile cup.

(860) 868-0541 or (800) 455-1565. Fax (860) 868-1925. www.bouldersinn.com. Seven rooms, three suites and eight cottages with private baths. Doubles, $350 to $595. Suites, $395 to $875.

Entrées, $28 to $39. Dinner, Wednesday-Saturday 6 to 9, Sunday 5 to 8.

A Premier Country-House Hotel

Mayflower Inn, Route 47, Washington 06793. A country-house hotel that is a home away from home – warm, emotional, stylishly informal, full of sensibility and lavish enough to spoil the soul. The words are from the inn's magazine of a brochure and accurately reflect a singular inn that defines Relais & Chateaux in America. Well-traveled New Yorkers Robert and Adriana Mnuchin spared no expense in producing accommodations that are the ultimate in comfort and good taste. Fifteen rooms are upstairs on the second and third floors of the main inn. Ten more are in two guest houses astride a hill at the side. Each room is full of comfort and flair. Typical is Room 24 with a kingsize canopy four-poster feather bed awash in pillows, embroidered Frette linens, a feather duvet and a chenille throw. An angled loveseat faces the fireplace, the TV hides in an armoire and oversize wicker rockers await on the balcony overlooking the sylvan property. The bathroom, bigger than most people's bedrooms, is wainscoted in mahogany and has marble floors, double vanity, tub and large walk-in shower. Fine British, French and American antiques and accessories, prized artworks and elegant touches of whimsy – like the four ancient trunks stashed in a corner of the second-floor hallway – dignify public and private rooms alike. Opening off the lobby, an intimate parlor with plush leather sofas leads into the ever-so-British gentleman's library. On the garden level is a state-of-the-art fitness center. Outside are 28 acres of horticultural Eden, including exotic specimen trees and terraced Shakespeare and rose gardens, plus a tennis court and a swimming pool.

Across the back of the inn are three handsome dining rooms serene in white and mauve, and along one side is an English-style piano bar. Chef Jamie West from California's San Ysidro Ranch changes the menu seasonally. A recent autumn visit produced the likes of pancetta-wrapped monkfish osso buco, roasted free-range chicken with madeira jus and rosemary-crusted Colorado rack of lamb with black currant sauce. Specialty starters are house-smoked salmon with tomato-caper relish and togarashi-seared ahi tuna sashimi with Chinese mustard sauce. Desserts are extravagant, from maple crème brûlée to the "chocolate symphony" – a chocolate mousse pyramid, chocolate-caramel tart, chocolate truffle and white chocolate ice cream. Or settle for the signature plate of Mayflower cookies. Some of the dinner appetizers and pastas turn up on the lunch menu. The outdoor terrace with its view of manicured lawns and imported specimen trees is an idyllic setting in season.

(860) 868-9466. Fax (860) 868-1497. www.mayflowerinn.com. Seventeen rooms and eight suites with private baths. Rates, EP. Doubles, $400 to $600. Suites, $650 to $1,300. Entrées, $21 to $36. Lunch daily, noon to 2. Dinner nightly, 6 to 9.

The Birches Inn, 233 West Shore Road, New Preston 06777. This formerly faded lakefront inn has been renovated, offering comfortable accommodations – some right at water's edge – and a restaurant whose fortunes rise and fall with changing chefs. The inn's second floor offers five handsome guest rooms. The lakeview Room 7, the largest, has a king bed, two armchairs, an impressive armoire, TV, telephone and hand-painted bureau. In the Birch House behind are four new accommodations with TV and telephone, including two with king beds and whirlpool tubs. But the getaways of choice remain three rooms in the

Lake House across the road. They're smaller but share an extended deck beside the water, and the views are spectacular. "You can almost fish from the porch," one chef said wistfully as he led a tour. The best has a king bed with a brass headboard, a sofabed, a refrigerator and a whirlpool tub. Guests enjoy continental breakfast in the main inn in a sunny room overlooking the front deck. Wine and cheese are put out in the afternoon in a small parlor with a fireplace.

The spacious dining room, painted coral with eucalyptus green trim, seats 70 at well-spaced tables draped in white over floral undercloths. Big windows look down the lawn toward Lake Waramaug. The formerly cutting-edge cuisine has been toned down a bit and made more affordable lately through a succession of chefs. A recent autumn menu featured pan-seared wild Atlantic salmon crusted with pesto and pine nuts and oven-roasted Long Island duck with white peach-brandy sauce. Appetizers included a grilled portobello mushroom tower and crispy fried calamari with lemon-caper aioli. The dessert feature was apple tart with caramel and spiced rum hard sauce.

(860) 868-1735 or (800) 525-3466. Fax (860) 868-1815. www.thebirchesinn.com. Eleven rooms and one suite with private baths. Doubles, $150 to $375 May to mid-November, $125 to $325 rest of year.

Entrées, $20 to $30. Dinner, Wednesday-Monday 5:30 to 9, May-October; Thursday-Monday, rest of year.

The Hopkins Inn, 22 Hopkins Road, New Preston 06777.

This landmark yellow Federal structure astride a hill above Lake Waramaug is known far and wide for its European cuisine, and we often recommend it when asked where to take visitors for lunch in the country. But it does have eleven guest rooms (nine with private baths) and a couple of apartments, unexceptional but light and airy and furnished with country antiques as befits its origin as a summer guest house in 1847.

On a warm day or evening, few dining spots are more inviting than the inn's large outdoor terrace, shaded by a giant horse-chestnut tree and distinguished by striking copper and wrought-iron chandeliers and lanterns. Inside, two dining rooms stretch around the lakeview side of the inn; the overflow goes to a paneled Colonial-style taproom up a few stairs. One dining room is Victorian, while the other is rustic with barn siding and ships' figureheads on the walls. The fare reflects chef Franz Schober's Austrian heritage. The menu always includes wiener schnitzel and sweetbreads Viennese, dishes that we remember fondly from years past. Other possibilities might be trout meunière, backhendl with lingonberries, chicken cordon bleu, loin lamb chops and filet mignon with béarnaise sauce. The roast pheasant with red cabbage and spaëtzle is especially popular in season. For vegetables, you may get something unusual like braised romaine lettuce. Appealing desserts are baba au rhum (rich, moist and very rummy), white chocolate mousse, strawberries romanoff and grand marnier soufflé glacé. Finish with a flourish with cappuccino or liqueured coffees.

(860) 868-7295. Fax (860) 868-7464. www.thehopkinsinn.com. Nine rooms with private baths, two rooms with shared bath and two apartments. Doubles, $85 to $110 EP. Apartments, $160 EP.

Entrées, $18.75 to $24.75. Lunch, Tuesday-Saturday noon to 2, Saturday only in April, November and December. Dinner, 6 to 9 or 10, Sunday 12:30 to 8:30. Closed January-March.

Oliva, 18 East Shore Road (Route 45), New Preston.

Chef Riad Aamar moved from Doc's up the road to take over this ground-level café, a snug, grotto-like setting with stone walls, bleached barnwood and a huge, warming fireplace for chilly evenings. In summer, folks spill out from the 30-seat interior to tables on a jaunty, flower-bedecked front terrace nurtured by his wife, Joanna Lawrence. Here, in a kitchen even smaller than at Doc's, the Moroccan-born chef produces dynamite pizzas, super appetizers and a dozen robust pastas and Mediterranean entrées. Among the latter are linguini with garlicky shrimp, scallops and gorgonzola, Chilean sea bass served over roasted vegetables with saffron-lemon cream, roasted stuffed Moroccan chicken and Moroccan lamb tagine. You might start with the house antipasto (roasted vegetables, mixed cheeses and often prosciutto), seared sea scallops wrapped in grape leaves or the grilled wild mushroom and truffle pecorino cheese polenta. Many choose one of the thin-crust pizzas, perhaps the artichoke with prosciutto and olives or the portobello with spinach and sundried tomatoes. Pizzas are served in small and large sizes, and like the appetizers can be ordered "assaggi" style (a sampler of any two). Desserts could be a caramelized pear marzipan tart, pot de crème or hazelnut biscotti.

(860) 868-1787. Entrées, $13.25 to $23.75. Lunch, Thursday-Sunday noon to 2:30. Dinner, Wednesday-Sunday 5 to 9. BYOB.

Thomas Moran's Petite Syrah, 223 Litchfield Turnpike (Route 202), New Preston.
After cooking for six years at the Mayflower Inn nearby, chef Thomas Moran's name carried weight locally when he and his wife embarked in 2003 on their first solo venture, an intimate bistro in a small white dormered house that formerly housed the French restaurant Le Bon Coin in the Woodville section of New Preston. The chef claims "a love affair with the California wine country," which accounts for his naming the restaurant for a wine indigenous to California. His small lounge with a copper-topped bar is painted a wine red, in contrast to the beamed dining room appointed in white and brown. His theme is "California Meets New England," a reference to the light, creative California style with Asian accents he imparts to local ingredients. Appetizers like Maine jonah crab spring roll and a duck confit quesadilla with spicy Chinese sambal are examples. Main courses typically range from Maine diver scallops with steamed cockles, shrimp wontons, Thai noodles and ponzu soy broth to venison medallions with sautéed potato cake and cranberry-chestnut essence. Dessert could be a classic crème brûlée or chocolate decadence cake with praline ice cream.

(860) 868-7763. Entrées, $22 to $29. Lunch, Saturday and Sunday 11:30 to 3. Dinner, Thursday-Monday 6 to 11.

─ *Perfect Pantry* ──────────────
The Pantry, Titus Road, Washington Depot.
There's no better chic-country spot for late breakfast, lunch or tea than this specialty food and gift shop for gourmets. At tables tucked amidst high-tech shelves displaying everything from American Spoon preserves to red currant or green peppercorn vinegars, cooking gadgets and serious equipment, you can lunch on innovative fare. A counter displays and a blackboard lists the day's offerings from an extensive repertoire. At one visit the chef was dishing up a muffuletta sandwich, that New Orleans favorite done up inside a loaf of bread, plus salads of tuna and swordfish niçoise and entrées of torta rustica, salmon cakes and a vegetarian chili with watercress cabbage slaw. Soups like curried cauliflower and celery-leek are heavenly, and desserts are to sigh over: among them, pecan tart with ginger ice cream, linzer torte and grapefruit soufflé.

(860) 868-0258. Entrées, $6.50 to $8.95. Open Tuesday-Saturday 10 to 6. Lunch. 11:30 to 3:30. Tea, 3:30 to 5.

G.W. Tavern, 20 Bee Brook Road, Washington Depot.

This restaurant of many changing names has seen several big-bucks renovations over the years. But none more so than the latest that transformed the late Bee Brook, a highly rated fine-dining establishment, into a downscaled pub and tavern whose initials stand for George Washington – this is, after all, another of those towns named for the first president. The main dining room with vaulted skylight is now a tavern with an elegant Colonial look, oriental carpets on the floors and wonderful murals of surrounding towns on the walls. The rear porch beside the stream has been enclosed for year-round casual dining. The outdoor terraces are popular in summer. Chef-owner Robert Margolis features "good, simple pub food." At a recent autumn visit, the changing menu opened with stuffed potato skins and Buffalo-style chicken wings as well as crispy fried oysters with homemade tartar sauce and salmon cakes with curried mango chutney. Main courses are equally varied. Go basic with burgers, meat loaf, chicken pot pie or fish and chips. Or splurge on Maryland crab cakes, filet mignon with brandied cream sauce or the daily special, perhaps braised lamb shank bordelaise or prime ribeye with Yorkshire pudding. Desserts include blueberry cobbler and triple chocolate cake.

(860) 868-6633. Entrées, $12.50 to $30. Lunch daily, 11:30 to 5:30. Dinner nightly, 5:30 to 10 or 11. Saturday and Sunday brunch, 11:30 to 2:30.

SHOPPING. The hilly hamlet of New Preston at the southeast end of Lake Waramaug is gaining small retailers of note. **J. Seitz & Co.** has broadened its original emphasis on the Southwest into a two-floor paradise of "spirited style for you and your home." Antiques, accessories and interior design are the focus of a changing lineup of shops with names like **Betsey & Duane, Déjà Vu Antiques, City House-Country House** and **The Village Barn and Gallery.** Interspersed amid them all you'll find select cookware at **New Preston Kitchen Goods.** Across the street, New York-based **Lou Marotta & Friends** carries antiques plus new furniture, jewelry, baby clothes, men's wear, bath products and what have you.

Washington Depot has a large and well-stocked bookstore, the **Hickory Stick Bookshop.** Authors, many of whom have homes in the area, are occasionally on hand to autograph their books. Orchids grow in pots and are pictured in frames at **The Orchid Gallery.** Find Canadian antiques, porcelain, painted boxes and such at the **Tulip Tree Collection,** women's sportswear at **Finula's** and gifts at **Fancy That!** Check out the **Green Hill Trading Co.** and its annex for home and garden.

Litchfield

Connecticut's finest example of a late 18th-century New England village, Litchfield is the place to which we take first-time visitors to the region (we have relatives who make a beeline there almost every time they visit). You should, too, if you're anywhere in the area.

The entire center of the village settled in 1720 is a National Historic Landmark. While Williamsburg had to be restored, Litchfield simply has been maintained by its residents as a living museum. Most of the old homes and buildings are occupied. Some are opened to the public on Open House Day one Saturday in July.

The **Litchfield Historic District** is clustered around the green and along North and South streets (Route 63). The statuesque, gleaming white Congregational Church is said to be the most photographed in New England. Where else do a bank and a jail share a common wall as they do at North and West streets? The young attendant pointed them out proudly from the information center on the green. South Street is a broad, half-mile-long avenue where three governors, five state chief justices, six congressmen and two U.S. senators have lived. Landmarks include the birthplaces of Ethan Allen, Henry Ward Beecher and Harriet Beecher Stowe, plus Sheldons Tavern, where George Washington slept (he visited town five times). Sarah Pierce opened the first academy for the education of women in America on North Street in 1792. Here too is the **Tapping Reeve House & Law School** (1773), the first law school in the country. The house with its handsome furnishings and the tiny school with handwritten ledgers of students long gone, including Aaron Burr, John C. Calhoun and 130 members of Congress. It's open Tuesday-Saturday 11 to 5 and Sunday 1 to 5, April through mid-November; adults $5, students $3. The fee also includes admission to the **Litchfield History Museum,** which has seven galleries of early American paintings, decorative arts, furniture, textiles and local history exhibits.

White Memorial Conservation Center and Nature Museum, 80 Whitehall Road, Litchfield.

Just west of Litchfield are 4,000 acres of nature sanctuary bordering Bantam Lake, the state's largest natural lake. Thirty-five miles of woodland and marsh trails are popular with hikers, horseback riders and cross-country skiers. This is a great place for observing wildlife, birds and plants in a variety of habitats. Almost every outdoor activity is available, including bird-watching from a unique observatory in which groups can watch birds undetected, and swimming at Sandy Beach along Bantam Lake. For the more sedentary, dioramas, giant hand-painted and photo murals and mounted animals in the recently expanded nature museum depict the natural diversity found outside. The state-of-the-art facility has good collections of Indian artifacts, an unusual exhibit on the art of taxidermy, a working honeybee hive, a lifesize beaver lodge, a fluorescent rock cave, 3,000 species of butterflies, live animals and an excellent nature library and gift shop.

(860) 567-0857. www.whitememorialcc.org. Grounds open free year-round. Museum, Monday-Saturday 9 to 5, Sunday noon to 5, April-October; Monday-Saturday 8:30 to 4:30, Sunday noon to 4, rest of year. Adults $4, children $2.

White Flower Farm, Route 63, Litchfield.

This institution three miles south of Litchfield is a don't-miss spot for anyone with a green thumb. In fact, people come from across the country to see the place made famous by its catalog, wittily written by the owner under the pen name of Amos Pettingill. Ten acres of exotic display gardens are at peak bloom in late spring; twenty acres of growing fields reach their height in late summer. Greenhouses with indoor plants, including spectacular giant tuberous begonias, are pretty all the time.

(860) 567-8789. www.whiteflowerfarm.com. Shop and grounds open daily 9 to 5:30, April-Christmas.

Topsmead State Forest, Buell Road, Litchfield.

Little known but a great destination for a tranquil outing in the country is this 511-acre preserve atop a knoll a mile east of Litchfield Center, the onetime summer estate of an heiress to the Chase brass fortune of Waterbury. It offers scenic views, picnic sites and trails for hiking and cross-country skiing. An ecology trail is marked by interpretive signs. The finely crafted English Tudor mansion that was once Miss Edith Chase's summer home is opened occasionally for guided tours.

(860) 567-5694. House tours, Saturday and Sunday noon to 5, second and fourth weekend of month, June-October. Grounds open year-round. Free.

SHOPPING. Tony Litchfield, which clings to a vision of Connecticut more in keeping with its Colonial past than its sophisticated present, offers elements of both in its shopping area facing the broad green. (Only here would a proposal for a Talbots chain store generate months of controversy, the proposal finally winning and **Talbots** now a dignified presence among the locally owned stores and restaurants.) Also facing the green is **Workshop Inc.**, a boutique with updated women's apparel and accessories and a downstairs gallery of home furnishings, **Hayseed** stocks a great selection of cards along with jewelry, sweaters and clothing for the country lifestyle. **Kitchenworks** has expanded its kitchenware and gourmet shop. Others of appeal to specific interests are **Jeffrey Tillou Antiques,** the **Thomas McKnight Gallery, Bella Cosa** for Italian ceramics and **R. Derwin Clothiers.** In an historic carriage house in a quaint courtyard behind the village green is **Cobble Court** with "a new breed" of home furnishings on two floors.

Lodging and Dining

Toll Gate Hill, 571 Torrington Road (Route 202), Litchfield 06759.

This ancient-feeling inn actually is of relatively recent vintage, having opened in 1983 with six guest rooms, three dining rooms, a small tavern and a ballroom in a rural 1745 landmark house northeast of town. It's situated back from the road in a stand of trees, its red frame exterior dimly illuminated at night and appearing to the traveler much as it must have more than two centuries ago. Four rooms and suites opened in 1986 in an adjacent "school house," and another building with ten more rooms and suites and a reception area was added to the rear of the property in 1990. The bedrooms are handsomely done in custom fabrics and antiques with queensize canopy beds, upholstered chairs and loveseats, and TVs. Fireplaces are attractions in three rooms and five suites; the latter also have mini-refrigerators and VCRs. Balconies off rooms in the newer building overlook the woods. Innkeeper Alicia Fecora serves a continental breakfast for overnight guests.

Meals are served in two small, charming dining areas on the old tavern's main floor and upstairs in a ballroom complete with a fiddler's loft for piano and other musical entertainment. Tall booths are featured in the tavern with its dark wood and wide-plank floors. The more formal room, dressed with peach linens and Villeroy & Boch china, is enhanced by wall murals of 18th-century Litchfield painted by a local artist. Chef Carlton Rogers presents an ambitious menu more in keeping with the 21st century than the 18th. Dinner might start with flounder carpaccio or tea-smoked duck summer rolls with a lychee salsa. Steamed fillet of red snapper, quail escabèche, maple-lacquered pork porterhouse and dried fruit-crusted rack of lamb with madras curry sauce are typical main courses. Desserts might be caramelized apple crêpe, pineapple-white chocolate bread pudding or chocolate ravioli with hazelnut gelato.

(860) 567-1233 or (866) 567-1233. Fax (860) 567-1230. www.tollgatehill.com. Fifteen rooms and five suites with private baths. Mid-April through December: doubles $115 to $170, suites $195. Winter: doubles $95 to $135, suites $160.

Entrées, $18 to $24. Lunch daily, noon to 2. Dinner, 5:30 to 9:30 or 10:30. Closed Monday and Tuesday in off-season.

West Street Grill, 43 West St., Litchfield.

The trendoids who pack this place at lunch and dinner seven days a week agree with the restaurant critics; the food is intensely flavorful and the sleek black and white digs quite stylish. We thought our first lunch – comprised of a rich butternut-squash and pumpkin bisque, the signature grilled peasant bread with parmesan aioli, an appetizer of grilled country bread with a brandade of white beans and marinated artichokes, a special of grilled smoked-pork tenderloin with spicy Christmas limas, an intense key lime tart and an ethereal crème brûlée – could not be surpassed. But Irish owner James O'Shea and his chef outdid themselves at dinner, when we got to taste much of the menu. Beet green soup, corn cakes with crème fraîche and chives, roasted beet and goat cheese napoleons with a composed salad, and nori-wrapped salmon with marinated daikon, cucumbers and seaweed salad were masterful beginnings. A passion-fruit sorbet cleared the palate for the entrées: tasting portions of pan-seared salmon with roasted fennel and kohlrabi, spicy shrimp cake with ragout of black beans and corn, grilled ginger chicken with polenta and ginger chips, and grilled leg of lamb with marinated eggplant, potato galette and a tomato-olive compote. Next came a parade of desserts: a plum tart in a pastry so tender as not to be believed, a frozen passion-fruit soufflé, a hazelnut torte with caramel ice cream and a sampling of sorbets (raspberry, white peach and blackberry). It was suggested that we return in three weeks to sample the new menu, but we begged off, thinking we never could eat that well (or that much) again. Now after a few years? Well, maybe.

(860) 567-3885. Entrées, $22 to $37. Lunch daily, 11:30 to 3, weekends to 4. Dinner, 5:30 to 9:30 or 10:30.

3W & the Blue Bar, 3 West St., Litchfield.

Traditionalists don't know quite what to make of this new establishment with the odd name (for its address and the color of its bar in back) and its specialty of sushi. Chef Erly Gallo and partner Jennifer Hallock transformed the prime corner space facing the Litchfield green into an urbane, salon-style setting for dining at blond pine tables amid brick walls, hardwood floors and a pressed-tin ceiling. There's a small sushi bar in front. In back, screened from the two-level dining area by a wide curtain/partition of bamboo, is the blue bar with stone counter tops. Chef Erly rolls the sushi, including one of tempura-style lobster. But his Asian-inspired fare goes far beyond. Look for starters like crab dumplings, tuna carpaccio and a crunchy Thai salad. Main dishes range from mahi mahi en papillote and sautéed tiger shrimp and mussels with crunchy plantain to scotch-marinated sirloin with a brown sugar and soy demi-glace. Less adventurous palates are appeased with grilled sirloin steak topped with gorgonzola cheese. The winter menu even offers a "traditional" beef stew. Desserts come from the in-house bakery.

(860) 567-1742. www.3wandthebluebar.com. Entrées, $20 to $27. Lunch, Monday-Friday 11:30 to 3. Dinner nightly, 5:30 to 9:30 or 10:30, Sunday 5 to 8.

FOR MORE INFORMATION: Litchfield Hills Visitors Bureau, Box 968, Litchfield, CT 06759, (860) 567-4506. www.litchfieldhills.com.

Connecticut River and Goodspeed Opera House are seen from Gelston House River Grill.

Lower Connecticut River Valley

One of the 'Last Great Places'

As it nears the end of its 400-mile journey from the Canadian border, New England's longest river wends and weaves between forested hillsides and sandy shores. Finally it pauses, almost delta-like, in the sheltered coves and harbors of Essex, Old Saybrook and Old Lyme before emptying into Long Island Sound.

A sand bar blocked the kind of development that has urbanized other rivers where they meet the ocean. Indeed, the Connecticut is the nation's biggest waterway without a major city at its mouth.

Its unspoiled nature, its verdant and steep banks, and the small towns that grew up beside it make the lower Connecticut River estuary a national treasure. Indeed, it is one of 40 areas in the world that the Nature Conservancy included on its list of "Last Great Places" worth protecting.

Protected it always has been, fortunately. You can tell from the lack of development along the lower river where you might otherwise expect it. At the mouth of the river on one side is the borough of Fenwick, an old-Yankee enclave of substantial summer homes and a small golf course that occupies the choicest piece of real estate in Connecticut. On the other side are the tidal marshlands that serve as a refuge for wildlife and inspired the late resident birder Roger Tory Peterson.

Geography and the powers-that-be have protected the lower river valley since it was settled in the 17th century. Historic Essex was founded in 1635, its harbor a haven for shipbuilding long ago and for yachting in modern times. Touted by the New Yorker magazine as "a mint-condition 18th-century town," it lately was named "the best small town in America." Essex relives its past in the Connecticut River Museum at Steamboat Dock, in the boatworks and yacht clubs along its harbor, in the lively Tap Room at the historic Griswold Inn, and in the lovely old homes along Main Street and River Road.

Across the river from Essex is Old Lyme, which has less of a river feel but exudes a charm of its own. In a pastoral area that is now part of an historic district, artists gathered at the turn of the last century in the mansion of Florence Griswold, daughter of a boat captain. Thus began the American Impressionist movement , and the arts are celebrated and flourish here to this day.

Upriver are Deep River, Chester and East Haddam, unspoiled towns steeped in history.

The attractions for visitors include a Victorian opera house producing top musicals, a hillside medieval castle reminiscent of those along the Rhine, a vintage railroad and an ancient car ferry, maritime and art museums, good restaurants and choice places to stay.

The artists who founded the Lyme Art Colony a century ago came to the area seeking rest and renewal as well as inspiration. Visitors will find similar rewards today.

Seeing and Doing

Most of the area's attractions and activities are alongside or near the river. Casual visitors are likely to miss them as they travel by on north-south Route 9 or east-west Interstate 95. You have to know what and where they are.

For this guide, we occasionally hopscotch back and forth across the Connecticut River as we head south from the mid-valley toward Long Island Sound. You can cross the river on bridges only on State Route 82 from Haddam to East Haddam and on I-95 and U.S. Route 1 between Old Saybrook and Old Lyme.

Another way across is aboard the tiny **Chester-Hadlyme ferry,** which has plied the river between Chester and Hadlyme since 1769. The second oldest continuously operating ferry service in the country, it carries up to nine cars and 49 passengers on each four-minute trip and operates "on demand," April-November. Vehicles $3, passengers $1.

For the visitor, the lower part of the valley begins at Haddam and East Haddam, twin hamlets on either side of the river, linked by an antiquated bridge. East Haddam is particularly quaint, stuck in a time warp from the 19th century.

Sightseeing and specialized excursions along the Connecticut River on a 400-passenger boat are offered from Goodspeed Landing by **Camelot Cruises Inc.,** 1 Marine Park, Haddam, (860) 345-8591 or (800) 522-7463. Brunch buffet cruises are scheduled from noon to 2:30 Sundays from May-October for $29. Camelot also offers three-hour murder mystery dinner cruises Fridays and Saturday nights from 7 to 10 for $59.75 each. New Orleans luncheon cruises are available on selected Thursdays in summer. Fall foliage lunch cruises are offered in the fall.

Goodspeed Musicals, Goodspeed Landing, East Haddam.

The past is present at this restored 1876 Victorian confection built by shipping magnate William Goodspeed on the east bank The opera house – a national treasure – produces uplifting musicals, revivals and new tryouts. Each is top flight – 43 have been world premieres and sixteen have gone on to Broadway, including "Annie," "Man of La Mancha" and "Shenandoah." The three shows each season run for about three months each. You climb endless flights to reach your seat in tiered intimacy. At intermission, munch popcorn from the old-fashioned machine and sip champagne by the glass in the Victorian bar or on the veranda high above the river. You'll think you've died and gone to the 19th century. Since 1984, Goodspeed has developed three new musicals annually and fostered emerging artists on a second stage, Goodspeed-at-Chester/The Norma Terris Theatre.

(860) 873-8668. www.goodspeed.org. Shows are Wednesday at 2 and 7:30, Thursday at 7:30, Friday at 8, Saturday at 4 and 8:30 and Sunday at 2 and 6:30, April-December. Tickets, $24 to $53.

Gillette Castle State Park, 67 River Road, East Haddam.

A fieldstone castle that looks to be straight out of Europe is the centerpiece of this picturesque, 164-acre park on the former estate of William Gillette. The actor and playwright known for his stage portrayal of Sherlock Holmes designed the house of his dreams after medieval castles in Germany and had it built starting in 1914 on the last of a series of seven hills at a bend in the Connecticut River, with a spectacular view from a stone patio that awes visitors to this day. Gillette's vivid imagination is revealed in each of the 24 rooms of the castle, which took a crew of twenty men five years to complete. No two of the 47 doors within the structure are alike; their external door latches are intricately carved of wood, as are the light switches. Gillette designed the furniture, including built-in couches and a dining room table that moves on metal tracks on the floor. He even rigged a liquor cabinet with locks and strategically placed mirrors allowing views of the front door and the libations from his bedroom.

Other than the intriguing castle, his chief legacy was a three-mile-long narrow-gauge railroad he designed and operated through tunnel and across trestle around his property. The train has been moved and most of the tracks dismantled, but his "Grand Central Station" survives as a depot in a picnic area; the state planned to restore a small loop of the railroad. Gillette's own walking paths were constructed with near-vertical steps, stone-arch bridges, and wooden trestles spanning up to forty feet. Other outdoor attractions include a vegetable cellar and Gillette's goldfish pond. A guided walk through the castle takes about a half hour. You can enjoy stunning views of the water below, walk along the river and picnic at tables scattered throughout the park.

(860) 526-2336. Park open daily, 8 to dusk; free. Castle open daily 10 to 4:30, Memorial Day to Columbus Day. Castle tours $5, children $3.

Essex Steam Train & Riverboat, 1 Railroad Ave., Essex.

With its whistle tooting and smokestack spewing, the Valley Railroad Company's marvelous old steam train runs from the depot in the Centerbrook section of Essex through woods and meadows to the Connecticut River landing at Deep River. There it connects with the three-deck Mississippi-style riverboat MV Becky Thatcher for an hour's cruise up past Gillette Castle to the Goodspeed Opera House and back. Narration highlights the history, folklore, flora and fauna along the way. The two-hour trip into the past is rewarding for young and old alike. Railroad buffs enjoy the working railroad yard, vintage rail cars and exhibits gathered around the National Register landmark depot. For hikers, the railroad on its first two excursions of the day offers a connection to Gillette Castle – you get off at the Ferry Road landing in Chester, board the Chester-Hadlyme Ferry and take a moderately strenuous hike up to the castle. The Essex Clipper dinner train runs two-hour excursions on weekends in a vintage luxury dining car, Friday at 7:30, Saturday at 7 and Sunday at 4, June-October.

(860) 767-0103 or (800) 377-3987. www.essexsteamtrain.com. Train and Riverboat trips run at 11, 12:30, 2 and 3:30, daily in summer, Wednesday-Sunday in October and Friday-Sunday in late spring and early fall. Train and boat, adults $24, children $12. Train only, adults $16, children $8. Dinner train, $60.

Connecticut River Museum, 67 Main St., Essex.

Restored in 1975 from an 1878 steamboat warehouse, this interesting, cupola-topped structure at Steamboat Dock is living testimony to the maritime, economic and cultural heritage of the lower Connecticut River Valley. The site has been significant for nearly 400 years. It is where Native Americans pulled their dugout canoes ashore, where Colonial shipbuilders debated revolution, and where travelers boarded steamboats on the way to Hartford or New York. The river's story is highlighted in changing exhibits on the main floor. A recent one focused on "Fenwick-on-the-Sound: From Public Playground to Private Borough" and paid tribute to the late actress Katharine Hepburn, the borough's "most famous" resident. Another consisted of small boats from the museum's collection, including a shad boat that worked on the river and a birch bark canoe owned by the late newsman Charles Kuralt, who lived in Essex. Upstairs, where windows on two sides and a balcony afford sweeping views of the river, is the permanent shipbuilding exhibit. The highlight is a full-size replica of the first American warship, David Bushnell's strange-looking Turtle, built here in 1776 as a secret weapon to win the Revolutionary War. There's also a model of a Dutch explorer ship that sailed up the river in 1614. Boats built and used on the river are displayed in the boathouse. The foundation property also includes a small waterfront park with benches and the 1813 Hayden Chandlery, now the Thomas A. Stevens maritime research library.

(860) 767-8269. www.ctrivermuseum.org. Open Tuesday-Sunday, 10 to 5. Adults $6, children $3.

Connecticut River Expeditions, Steamboat Dock, Essex.

Newly berthed at Steamboat Dock, the 60-passenger environmental research vessel R/V River Quest gives afternoon and sunset cruises for the public. The 75-minute narrated tours of Essex Harbor and the lower river are offered twice daily, pointing out historical and ecological attractions along the way. Early sunset evening cruises for adults (bring your own beverages and picnic baskets) are offered Monday-Friday at 6:30 in summer and Friday-Sunday at 4:30 in fall.

(860) 662-0577. www.ctriverexpeditions.org. Daytime cruises at 1 and 3 daily in summer, weekends in early spring and late fall; adults $12, children $8. Sunset cruises, $15.

The Essex Waterfront. As a living and working yachting and shipbuilding town, the Essex waterfront is a center of activity, and you'll find marinas all around. Just south of Steamboat Dock along Novelty Lane are the century-old Dauntless Club, the Essex Corinthian Yacht Club and, on a watery point between the river and Middle Cove, the posh Essex Yacht Club. The historic structures here and elsewhere in town are detailed in a walking map, available at the Connecticut River Museum.

Uptown Essex. Besides the waterfront area, Methodist Hill at the other end of Main Street has a cluster of historic structures. Facing tiny Champlin Square is the imposing white Pratt House (circa 1732), restored and operated by the Essex Historical Society to show Essex as it was in yesteryear (open June-Labor Day, weekends 1 to 4, $2). The period gardens in the rear are planted with herbs and flowers typical of the 18th century. The society also operates the adjacent Hill Academy Museum (1833), an early boarding school that now displays historical collections of old Essex. Next door in the academy's former dormitory is the Catholic Church and, next to it, the Baptist Church, one of only two Egyptian Revival structures in this country.

Old Saybrook, a busy commercial and residential community, grew inland from the point where in 1614 the Dutch explorer Adriaen Block became the first white man to enter the river Quonitocutt, or "Long Tidal River." Fort Saybrook, Connecticut's first military fortification, was built near the river's mouth in 1636 by the British. What once served as protection from the Pequot Indians is now an eighteen-acre historical park created by the Fort Saybrook Monument Park Association. Shore portions yield panoramic views of the river and storyboards depict the history of the original Saybrook colony, one of Connecticut's first.

Old Lyme. In one of New England's prettiest towns beside an inlet at the mouth of the Connecticut River, American Impressionist artists found refuge a century ago from the trials of city life in New York and Boston. Much of the character that drew them remains to this day. Lyme Street, over the years the home of Connecticut governors and chief justices, is a National Historic District. The long main street is lined with gracious homes from the 18th and 19th centuries, including one that is particularly handsome called Lyme Regis, the English summer resort after which the town was named. The First Congregational Church pictured in Childe Hassam's paintings stands at the end of the street.

Florence Griswold Museum, 96 Lyme St., Old Lyme.
The opening of a striking riverfront gallery has doubled the attendance as well as the size of this museum that's the home of the American Impressionist movement. The museum in Miss Florence Griswold's pillared 1817 mansion interprets its status as a boarding house that became America's most famous summer art colony. The interior walls reveal the fascinating saga of a seafaring family's financial rise and fall, how Miss Florence decided in 1899 to take in boarders to save her house, and how artists who gravitated there found a kindred spirit who lent them respectability. Part of their legacy is the unique panels the visiting artists painted on the walls and doors in every room. Especially prized is the dining room, where 40 paintings by more than 30 artists constitute what the museum calls a complete chronicle of the art colony movement in America. Across the mantel the artists left a delightful caricature of themselves for posterity. The art colony thrived for twenty years and its works are on permanent display. They include major works by Childe Hassam and John Henry Twachtman, and the largest collection of Willard Metcalf paintings in the world. Also on view are selections from the priceless Hartford Steam Boiler Collection of American Art, recently donated to the museum by the insurance company.

Changing exhibitions are produced in the new Krieble Gallery, a modernist, white and silvery series of barn-like buildings overlooking Miss Florence's garden backing up to the Lieutenant River, where many of her boarders set up easels to paint the gardens and the marshy shoreline. Three soaring, skylit galleries were showing variations of a world-class exhibit called "The American River" at a recent visit. With the completion of the 10,000-square-foot gallery, the Griswold House was undergoing restoration and refurbishing in 2005 to better interpret its former role as a boarding house for the Lyme Art Colony.

(860) 434-5542. www.flogris.org. Open Tuesday-Saturday 10 to 5 and Sunday 1 to 5; Griswold House closed Sunday January-March. Adults $7, children $4.

The **Lyme Art Association Gallery,** 90 Lyme St., next door to the Florence Griswold Museum and built in 1918 on land donated by Miss Florence, is headquarters of the Lyme Art Association. Founded in 1902, it is said to be the nation's oldest summer art group to have held continuous exhibitions in its own gallery. Many of the Lyme Impressionists showed here in its early days. It continues to exhibit the work of some of the region's finest and newest representational artists in seven major shows each season (Tuesday-Saturday noon to 4:30, Sunday 1 to 4:30, most of year; admission $4).

At 84 Lyme St. is the handsome, Federal-style **Lyme Academy College of Fine Arts,** with changing exhibits by local artists and academy students and faculty (Tuesday-Saturday 10 to 4 and Sunday 1 to 4; donation). Works of the Lyme Impressionists also are hung in the Town Hall, and the public library often has exhibits. The Cooley Gallery at 25 Lyme St. is a nationally recognized dealer of American art.

Escape to Nature's Refuge

Ferry Point State Park, Ferry Road, Old Lyme.

If you crave peace and quiet alongside the water, head for this little-known park. Leave your car in the parking lot beside the state Department of Environmental Protection's Marine Headquarters and enjoy one of the handful of picnic tables and a gazebo beside the Connecticut River. Follow the boardwalk south underneath the railroad bridge and leave the busy marinas and the roar of I-95 behind. Walk alongside the river and marshlands a few hundred yards to a twenty-foot-high observation platform. You're in another world, with scarcely a sign of civilization in your panoramic vista. Here you can see the marshland reclamation project and peer across a channel to an osprey nest on the Great Island Wildlife Management Area. Look past the mouth of the river and across the Sound to the North Fork of Long Island. Plaques along the way identify ducks, herons and anadromous fish, among others. You may be joined by fishermen, birders and a kayaker or two.

Park open daily, dawn to dusk.

SHOPPING. The choicest shopping opportunities for visitors are in Essex and Chester.

The **Talbots** store confronting visitors head-on as they enter the downtown section of Essex sets the tone. Also fashionable in different ways are **Silkworm, J. Alden Clothier, Stonewear Clothing** and a colorful place called **Equator. A Pocketful of Posies** bills itself as a shabby chic boutique. Pillows and tableware are featured among home accessories at **Portabella. Fenwick Cottage** stocks unusual gifts and decorative accessories. Jewelry, incense, candles and gifts are the specialty of **Scensibles.** Another concentration of stores is farther down Main Street at Griswold and Essex squares. **Red Balloon** offers precious clothes for precious children. Lilly Pulitzer is featured at **The Yankee Palm. Red Pepper** carries items not seen anywhere else, among them interesting glasses and goblets in all kinds of colors made in

Upstate New York, and cat pins by a woman who lives on a farm with seven cats. The shop carries clothing from small designers, almost all made in this country – which is unusual these days. **Hattitudes** stocks more kinds of hats than we ever expected to see. **The Essex Coffee & Tea Company** dispenses fancy beverages. Behind it is **Sweet P's,** a candy and ice cream shop. Also here is the **Essex Mariner** with model boats, carved shore birds and nautical brass. Nearby is **Olive Oyl's** for carry-out cuisine and specialty foods.

Lately, Chester has become a destination for shoppers, especially those with an interest in the esoteric. We like the colorful Italian tableware and pottery at **Ceramica** and the French-inspired fabrics and pottery at **Souleiado en Provence.** Traditional and contemporary local crafts are exhibited at **Connecticut River Artisans.** All things herbal are featured at **R.J. Vickers Herbery.** Leif and Katherine Nilsson show their contemporary paintings at Nilsson Spring Street Studio & Gallery. Kathryne Wright's **Hammered Edge Studio & Gallery** specializes in unusual jewelry and wearable art. Special interests are served at **The Willow Tree** (vintage clothing), **Dino Varano** (crafted artware) and **One of a Kind Antiques.**

Where to Stay

As with the attractions above, lodging establishments are detailed geographically from north to south.

Inns and Hotels

The Inn & Vineyard at Chester, 318 West Main St., Chester 06412.

The Inn at Chester, a hostelry built in 1983 around the historic 1776 John B. Parmelee House on twenty rural acres west of town, has a new name and a new look. Edward Safdie, the nationally known restaurateur, hotelier, spa innovator and cookbook author, came out of retirement in 2003 to purchase the fading Inn at Chester. He and his wife Carlene, an Old Lyme antiques dealer, remade it in the image of his former Norwich Inn & Spa in eastern Connecticut and his famed Sonoma Mission Inn & Spa in California. Carlene Safdie decorated the guest rooms and suites in a minimalist, country elegant look with mostly queensize pencil-post beds, Eldred Wheeler furniture, French toile and Schumacher fabrics, and Berber carpeting. French doors were added to sixteen rooms on the main floor to open onto private decks and patios. Each room has a flat-screen TV, data port and cordless telephone. Newly tiled baths contain pedestal sinks, massage showerheads and quite an array of spa-quality toiletries. The inn's restaurant was reborn (see Where to Eat), the tavern redecorated and an enormous outdoor dining terrace added. Guests have continental breakfast in the tavern. Although the man called the father of the American spa movement didn't want another spa, he planned exercise trails for walking or jogging, a tennis court and wellness treatment rooms for relaxation or deep tissue massage services. And, yes, he planted vidal blanc grapes – "the first organic vineyard in New England," he said – to make wine for on-premises consumption.

(860) 526-9541. Fax (860) 526-1607. www.innatchester.com. Thirty-nine rooms and five suites with private baths. Doubles, $135 to $295. Suites, $250 to $450.

Copper Beech Inn, 46 Main St., Ivoryton 06442.

Upgraded accommodations are offered at this venerable establishment in the Ivoryton section of Essex, both in an imposing white mansion shaded by the oldest copper beech tree in Connecticut and in a nicely secluded carriage house out back. Innkeepers Ian and Barbara Phillips started renovating with the guest quarters upstairs above the noted restaurant (see Where to Eat), refurbishing three period rooms and a kingsize suite overlooking the rear gardens. The most deluxe is the sumptuous front master bedroom, big enough to include a kingsize carved mahogany poster bed, a couple of sitting areas and a new gas fireplace. Its redone bath has been tiled in marble and boasts a hydro-massage tub and a heated floor. We still like best the nine rooms in the carriage house. Each has a jacuzzi or hydro-massage tub and french doors onto a deck or balcony overlooking the gardens. Second-floor rooms retain their original vaulted ceilings with exposed beams. Mahogany queensize or kingsize beds, club chairs, TVs and telephones are the norm. Guests relax in an elegant, wraparound atrium/solarium in the front of the inn. A continental-plus breakfast buffet has been augmented lately with a couple of prepared egg dishes such as quiche or coddled eggs.

(860) 767-0330 or (888) 809-2056. www.copperbeechinn.com. Twelve rooms and one suite with private baths. Doubles, $150 to $350.

Griswold Inn, 36 Main St., Essex 06426.

The Griswold Inn has historic appeal matched by few inns in this country. The floors in some of the guest rooms list to port or starboard, as you might expect of an inn dating to 1776, when it was built as Connecticut's first four-story structure. When commandeered by the British during the War of 1812, the inn was found to be long on charm but short on facilities. Today, all 31 guest accommodations in the main inn, the annex and in houses across the street come with private baths, air conditioning and telephones, and all but nine in the annex have been enhanced cosmetically of late. That means updated bath fixtures, fabric window treatments and wide-plank hardwood floors with oriental rugs. Rooms upstairs in the inn range from standard facing the street (twin beds and a small bathroom with shower) to a suite with queen bed and a sitting alcove with a convertible loveseat lit by a lamp so dim as to be useless for anything but romance. Six suites with fireplaces across the street in a retail complex known as Griswold Square are the most deluxe, in a comfortable and historic way. A complimentary continental breakfast buffet is put out in the Steamboat Room section of the atmospheric restaurant (see Where to Eat).

(860) 767-1776. Fax (860) 767-0481. www.griswoldinn.com. Fourteen rooms and sixteen suites with private baths. Doubles, $100 to $220. Suites, $160 to $370.

Old Lyme Inn, 85 Lyme St., Old Lyme 06371.

New owners have upgraded the venerable Old Lyme Inn and added sumptuous B&B accommodations in their historic home down the street. Eight guest rooms in a wing off the elegant 1850s mansion are decorated in plush Empire or Victorian style. Marblehead mints are perched atop the oversize pillows on the canopy and four-poster beds, comfortable sofas or chairs are grouped around marble-top tables, and gleaming white bathrooms are outfitted with herbal shampoos and Dickenson's Witch Hazel made in nearby Essex. Five rooms in the older part of the inn are similarly equipped but smaller. All rooms have televisions and telephones. Continental breakfast is included in the rates. Lunch and dinner are available in the inn's restaurant (see Where to Eat). Owners Keith and Candy Green also offer four B&B rooms in their 1895 landmark home surrounded by 25 Ionic columns at 2 Lyme St. Called Rooster Hall and grand as can be, it comes with 2,000 square feet of porches and terraces overlooking parterre gardens, a dining room set for sixteen and a third-floor recreation center with fitness equipment, billiards table and ping-pong table. A rear suite is equipped with a kitchenette and a whirlpool tub. The enormous master suite has two stunning bathrooms – hers white and frilly with a whirlpool tub and his, dark and clubby with a central shower enclosed in glass.

(860) 434-2600 or (800) 434-5352. Fax (860) 434-5352. www.oldlymeinn.com. Thirteen rooms with private baths. Doubles, $165 to $185 weekends, $135 to $165 midweek. B&B, four rooms with private baths, doubles $175 to $235.

Bee and Thistle Inn, 100 Lyme St., Old Lyme 06371.

Stately trees, gardens all around and a flower-bedecked entrance welcome visitors to this cheery yellow inn, set on five acres bordering the Lieutenant River in the historic district of Old Lyme. Built in 1756 with subsequent additions and remodeling, the structure is a charming ramble of parlors and porches, dining rooms and guest rooms. Eleven upstairs rooms come with period country furnishings. They vary widely in size from small with double or twin beds to large with queensize canopy beds and loveseats. Room 2 with a queen bed has a new gas fireplace and Room 3 has a new kingsize bed. Four-poster, fishnet canopy and spool beds are covered with quilts or afghans. Nooks are full of games and old books are all around. Breakfast in the inn's restaurant (see Where to Eat) is complimentary for inn guests. It's taken on the inn's sunny dining porches, a great place to start the day.

(860) 434-1667 or (800) 622-4946. Fax (860) 434-3402. www.beeandthistleinn.com. Eleven rooms and one cottage with private baths. Doubles, $130 to $239.

Saybrook Point Inn & Spa, 2 Bridge St., Old Saybrook 06475.

This glamorous resort hotel and marina is nicely situated on a point near where the Connecticut River meets Long Island Sound. Developer Louis Tagliatela Sr. sank $25 million into rebuilding the old and rather infamous Terra Mar resort from the ground up, and recently added more luxury rooms and a destination spa. On three floors, the hotel now has 81 sumptuous rooms and suites, most quite a bit larger than the industry norm and two-thirds with water views across the busy marina. Most have small Juliet balconies, some so cramped you can barely stand on them. Fifty come with fireplaces and sixteen have jacuzzis. All are outfitted with kingsize or two double beds, 18th-century reproduction mahogany furniture, wet bars and ahead-of-their-time bedside consoles that "do everything but send faxes," says operations director Stephen Tagliatela, the owner's son. They control the lights and air conditioning, display directions in several languages and tell the current times around the world. Italian marble glistens in the bathrooms as well as in a lobby bearing hand-loomed carpets from England. An indoor pool looks through a wall of glass onto an outdoor pool near the water. Beside the indoor pool are a jacuzzi, steam room and a well-equipped health club facility. Twelve spa rooms and a dedicated lounge area were added in 2000. At the other end of the U-shaped hotel is the Terra Mar Grille, an elegant waterside dining room and lounge (see Where to Eat).

(860) 395-2000 or (800) 243-0212, Fax (860) 388-1504. www.saybrook.com. Seventy-six rooms and four suites. Doubles, $219 to $389. Suites, $449 to $799.

Bed and Breakfasts

Bishopsgate Inn, Goodspeed Landing, Box 290, East Haddam 06423.

Situated down a long driveway a block from the Goodspeed Opera House, this

1818 Colonial house was built by an Essex shipbuilder and once was occupied by a Goodspeed. Now it's lovingly run by energetic Colin and Jane Kagel, and their son Colin, his wife Lisa and their young son. "Ours is a real family enterprise," says Jane. And a winning one, at that. The house is full of books, artworks and family collections, including Jane's silver urns and Colin's canvas-backed working decoys. The six guest rooms with featherbeds and antique furnishings are decorated with character. Four have working fireplaces. The most dramatic is the Director's Suite, with a beamed cathedral ceiling, a kingsize brass and iron bed, a private balcony and a dressing area off a theatrical bathroom that has lights around the mirror of the double vanity and its own sauna. Jane and Lisa cook full breakfasts in the 1860 kitchen, which has a small fireplace and baking oven. Their crustless spinach quiche is a favorite, as are the stratas and waffles. All are served by candlelight at a long table in a beamed dining room.

(860) 873-1677. Fax (860) 873-3898. www.bishopsgate.com. Six rooms with private baths. Doubles, $110 to $145. Suite, $175.

Riverwind, 209 Main St. (Route 9A), Deep River 06417.

A sense of history pervades this charming, atmospheric B&B, which has been nicely redecorated in a country Shaker look by new owners Roger and Nicky Plante. They offer eight guest rooms and an equal number of common areas that afford space for mingling or privacy. The heart of the house is the beamed keeping room and dining room with a huge fireplace. In front, the Plantes brightened up the living room and rejuvenated the library and game room, as well as an upstairs sitting room with a fireplace. The formerly enclosed front porch has been opened to the outside and made more welcoming with a lineup of white rocking chairs. Bedrooms on two floors vary in configuration and style. Most have queen beds and all are appointed with period antiques and stenciling. The rear Champagne and Roses Room comes with a queensize half-tester canopy bed, fireplace, a Japanese steeping tub and a private balcony nestled in the treetops. The new, third-floor Moonlit Suite has a mission-style queen bed (with an extra sleigh bed in an alcove), a brick fireplace, double whirlpool tub and satellite TV. From a twelve-foot stone cooking fireplace in the atmospheric keeping room comes a variety of fancy breakfast treats.

(860) 526-2014. Fax (860) 526-0875. www.riverwindinn.com. Six rooms and two suites with private baths. Doubles, $135 to $210. Suites, $165 to $225.

Deacon Timothy Pratt House B&B, 325 Main St., Old Saybrook 06475.

Listed on the National Register, this 1746 center-chimney Colonial once was the home of the deacon at the pillared Congregational meetinghouse across the street. It served five generations of Pratts and now houses an expanding B&B. Former electrical engineer Shelley Nobile opened with four guest quarters and in 2003 added three more rooms in the former James Pharmacy building next door. Each room has a queensize canopy or poster bed, working fireplace, bath with whirlpool tub, TV, telephone and stereo/CD player. A fishnet canopy bed is angled from the corner in the Sunrise Room, which has two Queen Anne wingback recliners and an oversize jacuzzi. The premier accommodation in the main house is a suite with a carved four-poster rice bed, working fireplace, french doors opening onto a TV room with a day bed and an extra-large bathroom with a double jacuzzi. A pleasant living room is furnished with period pieces and decorative accents characteristic of the rest of the house. A full breakfast is served by candlelight on weekends in a formal dining room with an extra-long table for sixteen. A continental breakfast buffet is offered on weekdays. Next door, Shelley continues to operate the James Gallery, a gift shop and an old-fashioned ice cream parlor and soda fountain. *(860) 395-1229 or (800) 640-1190. Fax (860) 395-4748. www.pratthouse.net. Five rooms and two suites with private baths. Doubles, $170 to $220 weekends, $110 to $130 midweek.*

Where to Eat

The Best for Food

Restaurant du Village, 59 Main St., Chester.

Here's as provincial French a restaurant as you will find in this country, from its canopied blue facade with ivy geraniums spilling out of flower boxes to the sheer white-curtained windows and french doors opening onto the side brick entryway. The 40-seat dining room is charming in its simplicity: a few French oil paintings, white linens, carafes of wild flowers and a votive candle on each table. Alsatian chef Michel Keller and his Culinary Institute-trained American wife Cynthia run the highly rated establishment with T.L.C. A third-generation pastry chef, Michel bakes perhaps the best French bread you will taste in this country. Among his appetizers, standouts are the cassoulet, a small copper casserole filled with sautéed shrimp in a light curry sauce; the croustade with grilled vegetables, and escargots with wild mushrooms in puff pastry. We also like the baked French goat cheese on herbed salad greens with garlic croutons. Entrées might be pan-seared tuna steak topped with tapenade, rabbit flamande, roast duck with kumquats and Cynthia's specialty, a stew of veal, lamb and pork with leeks and potatoes. Desserts change daily and are notable as well. Michel might prepare an open fruit tart with blueberries and peaches in almond cream, a gratin of passion fruit and paris-brest, in addition to his usual napoleons, soufflés glacé and crème brûlée.

(860) 526-5301. Entrées, $27 to $32. Dinner, Tuesday-Saturday 5 to 9, Sunday 5 to 8.15. Closed Tuesday in winter.

Copper Beech Inn, 46 Main Street, Ivoryton.

Surrounded by gardens and shaded by the largest copper beech tree in Connecticut, this venerable inn offers high-style dining in three elegant, refurbished dining areas. The chandeliered main Ivoryton Room conveys a rich, sumptuous Victorian motif. The paneled and beamed-ceilinged Comstock Room retains the look of the billiards parlor that it once was. Between the two is a pretty garden porch with a handful of romantic tables for two. The formal, contemporary French fare has been refreshed by executive chef William Von Ahnen and his wife Jacqueline, the pastry chef, who moved to the Copper Beach after a long tenure at the famed Chantecleer in Nantucket. The menu ranges widely from fillet of gray sole stuffed with a scallop mousse and served with a lobster claw and a lobster-ginger sauce to roasted rack of Colorado lamb with a rich red wine sauce. Indeed, all the food tends to be rich here, from the house-made lobster and sole sausage with truffle beurre blanc to the sautéed foie gras with a caramelized blackberry-chardonnay sauce. The lobster française, a house specialty deglazed with madeira, brandy and cream and garnished with black truffle risotto, is fabulous. So is the magret and confit of duck with armagnac-laced dried plums and the grilled veal chop with marchand du vin sauce. Finish with one of Jacqueline's spectacular desserts, perhaps the chocolate tasting for two, a creamy mixed-fruit tart or a light and ethereal tarte tatin with cinnamon ice cream.

(860) 767-0330 or (888) 809-2056. Entrées, $26 to $38. Dinner, Tuesday-Sunday 5:30 to 9:30.

Gabrielle's, 78 Main St., Centerbrook.

This Victorian-era house with a gazebo-like front porch has been a culinary landmark in the area since 1979. A trio of new owners tore down walls of what had been Steve's Centerbrook Café and created more open dining areas that are suave in ecru with white trim, accented by stunning art works and greenery. It's a stylish setting for the contemporary and artistic American fare created by talented chef Daniel McManamy, veteran of many an area restaurant. A perfect lunch here brought the signature mussels and frites, incredibly thin fries that were addictive when paired with the tarragon aioli dip, and cornmeal-crusted fried oysters with chipotle aioli. These and other mainstays on the lunch menu turn up as appetizers and small plates at night. The fairly extensive dinner menu also offers salads, thin-crust pizzas and fifteen entrées from grilled brook trout with shiitake mushrooms in a carrot-ginger sauce to grilled New York sirloin steak with roasted walnut-gorgonzola butter. A dish called lobster in vatapa (simmered with shrimp and scallops and served in a spicy sauce over rice), Indian-spiced breast of duckling and chicken in green mole indicate the kitchen's range. Desserts might be white and dark chocolate mousse, crème brûlée, linzer torte and apple-almond tart with french vanilla ice cream.

(860) 767-2440. www.gabrielles.net. Entrées, $18 to $25. Lunch, Tuesday-Friday and Sunday 11:30 to 3. Dinner, Tuesday-Sunday from 5 to 9 or 9:30.

Café Routier, 1353 Boston Post Road, Old Saybrook.

This lovable bistro began as a truck stop, but you'd never know that from its current location. Co-owners Rob Rabine and Jeffrey Renkl moved into a stylish space more than double the size of the original, giving more kitchen space for Jeff and the pastry chef to work their magic, and allowing Rob to expand his wine cellar. The new quarters seat about 100 at black dining tables, a zinc dining counter and a communal table, plus another 30 outside on the patio. The first-rate fare continues to be Yankee bistro with a pronounced French accent, although no one involved is French. Although some people never stray far from the French classics, others mix and match the regional and seasonal offerings. Crusty bread, served with flavorful olive oil, staved off hunger before our party dug into the likes of fried oysters with a chipotle mustard dipping sauce, a zesty Asian duck salad, an endive and arugula salad dressed with too much gorgonzola, and a rather paltry clams and chorizo dish to start. No one could fault the second courses, an Alsatian tarte, the signature "camp-style" grilled trout with whole-grain mustard sauce and lyonnaise potatoes, the sautéed calves liver with balsamic jus and sweet roasted onions, and the steak frites, a flavorful strip steak with house-made fries and a wilted watercress salad. Desserts included crème brûlée flavored with lavender picked just outside the door, double chocolate torte, profiteroles, and homemade ice creams and sorbets – ginger and lemon-crème fraîche at our visit.

(860) 399-8700. www.caferoutier.com. Entrées, $18 to $25. Dinner nightly, from 5:30.

River Tavern, 23 Main St., Chester.

Here's a chic city bistro in the country, as fashioned by chef-owner Jonathan

Rapp, who made a name with his brother Tom at the restaurant Etats-Unis on New York's Upper East Side. Freestanding candles top butcher-block tables set side by side in big-city style in the long and narrow storefront room. At the far end is a wall of etched glass framing bamboo trees in a planter, backlit for all to see. The minimalist decor is what Jonathan calls "comfortable modern." So is the short contemporary American menu, printed daily. Appetizers might be grilled scallops with a grapefruit beurre blanc, blue cheese soufléed pudding with poblano cream sauce, and handmade spaghetti with baked artichoke ragu. Recent main courses ranged from homemade pappardelle with local wild mushrooms and chicken ragu to grilled swordfish with hot pepper puree and slow-roasted tomatoes, roast chicken stuffed with herbs and roasted pears and served with macaroni and cheese, and cassoulet of pork and beef cooked with wine, tomatoes, peppers, smoked chiles and beans. Typical desserts are lemon-coconut cake, peach croustade, chocolate pot de crème and a warm apple and concord grape crumble. More choices are listed on the café menu, which included at our visit a charcuterie plate, a bowl of mussels and a dish called "two eggs baked with smoked bacon, thyme and cream."

(860) 526-9417. Entrées, $18 to $25. Dinner nightly except Tuesday, from 5:30. Also closed Monday in winter.

The Inn & Vineyard at Chester, 318 West Main St., Chester.

New owner Edward Safdie has run twenty celebrity restaurants from California to Monaco, so he knows good food – and demands it. That's why he devoted much of his early effort here to expanding and enhancing the restaurant operation. The 50-seat tavern was totally refashioned in a modern, drop-dead red motif, with leather banquettes, windsor chairs and upholstered chairs at a polished wood bar. The main post and beam dining room in the 200-year-old barn retains its rough-hewn walls, fieldstone fireplace, wrought-iron chandeliers and soaring windows. Outside beneath a century-old maple tree is a new, three-tiered deck seating 150 diners overlooking a pond and a fountain. The herb-seared ahi tuna in a spicy Thai vegetable broth and the rosemary-scented Pennsylvania free-range chicken roasted on the rotisserie quickly became chef Michael Fichtel's signature dinner dishes. Other entrées could be grilled swordfish with caper-dill cream and filet mignon with a cabernet reduction. Featured dessert at our visit was a fall apple sampler: a mini-apple pie, caramelized apple bread pudding, apple crisp and a dollop of vanilla bean ice cream. Meat loaf with truffled mashed potatoes and vegetables was the hit of the season in Jack's Tavern. Both the dining room and tavern menus are available seasonally on the Maple Terrace, which also has a barbecue menu.

(860) 526-9541. Entrées, $17.95 to $25.95, tavern $10.50 to $14.95. Lunch, Tuesday-Saturday 11:30 to 2:30. Dinner, Tuesday-Sunday 5:30 to 9:30. Sunday brunch, 11 to 2.

Bee and Thistle Inn, 100 Lyme St., Old Lyme.

This cheery yellow inn's restaurant consistently wins statewide awards for "romantic dining" and "best desserts." Dining is in country-pretty enclosed porches on either side of the inn as well as in a room linking the two in back. Luncheon choices are generally of the brunch and dinner variety. Instead of soups and sandwiches expect substantial salads and entrées from mushroom strudel and seafood stew to fillet of sole and grilled tournedos of beef. In the traditional inn style, regulars like to start with cocktails in the living room as they peruse the menu proposed by innkeeper Philip Abraham, the Culinary Institute of America-trained chef. His short dinner menu ranges widely from grilled yellowfin tuna with apple-beet salsa to seared venison medallions with gin-juniper gravy. Our crab cakes with chipotle rémoulade and the filet mignon were sensational, their simple names failing to do justice to the complexities of their preparation or that of their accompaniments. We also enjoyed the thin-sliced, rare breast of duck served on a passion-fruit puree with a spiced pear beggar's purse. You might start with the cured salmon napoleon, the breast of turkey terrine studded with sundried cherries and pistachios or the pan roast of oysters with minced root vegetables in puff pastry. Finish with a triple-nut bourbon tartlet, a ginger-scented pear dumpling or one of the homemade ice creams and sorbets.

(860) 434-1667 or (800) 622-4946. Entrées, $26 to $34. Lunch, Wednesday-Saturday 11:30 to 2. Dinner, Wednesday-Sunday from 5:30. Sunday brunch, 11 to 2.

Old Lyme Inn, 85 Lyme St., Old Lyme.

The restaurant at this venerable inn has been in transition under new ownership. Keith and Candace Green banished Victoriana in favor of a stylish Federal decor they felt more appropriate for Old Lyme. They produced The Grill, casual but smart, white-tablecloth dining areas that are open daily, and turned the vast and formerly austere restaurant into the smaller and warmer Winslow Dining Room and Lounge, open weekends for dinner and live piano music. The kitchen offers what Keith calls "hearty American food," from apricot chicken to roasted prime rib au jus, as well as a prime steak menu. The format continues to evolve as the Greens try to find their niche. Recent summer offerings ranged from blackened Stonington sea scallops over a watercress nage to veal milanaise and four versions of lobster. Lump crab and corn cake with mango salsa was offered as both an appetizer and an entrée. Typical desserts are crème caramel, chocolate mousse and mocha buttercrunch pie.

(860) 434-2600 or (800) 434-5352. www.oldlymeinn.com. Entrées, $24.50 to $37.50. Lunch, Monday-Saturday noon to 2. Dinner nightly, 6 to 9 or 10. Sunday, brunch 11 to 3, dinner 4 to 9.

Sherlock's 221, 9 Halls Road, Old Lyme Marketplace, Hall's Road, Old Lyme.

This wine bar and grill in the Old Lyme Marketplace strip plaza took its new name following a contest among customers who linked the name of owner Lynne Sherlock with the address of detective Sherlock Holmes. The dining room bears a stylish Mediterranean bistro look in earth colors and is open to a wine bar in back. A few tables are outside for sidewalk dining in season. The menu offers an eclectic variety of Mediterranean-inspired fare, from caramelized scallops drizzled with white truffle oil on roasted beet risotto to rack of lamb with mango mint slaw. Favorite appetizers are the crab cake with rémoulade sauce and grilled corn relish and the lobster and scallop sausage simmered in a lobster sauce. The signature pasta choice is sautéed lobster and crab with shiitake mushrooms and black truffles on fresh rolled fettuccine. Specialty cakes and desserts come from the grill's bakery adjunct.

(860) 434-9837. www.sherlocks221grille.com. Entrées, $19 to $24. Lunch, Monday-Saturday 11:30 to 2:30. Dinner Monday-Saturday 5 to 9 or 10.

Jack's American Bistro and Wine Bar, 286 Main St., Old Saybrook.

"Global comfort food" is featured in this convivial bistro opened in 2004 by Jack Flaws, once a chef at the celebrated Max Downtown restaurant in Hartford. He and his parents transformed a former restaurant space into a sophisticated setting in gold and ruby red, with an L-shaped banquette along two walls at the rear of the dining room. Tables are covered with pale yellow cloths and set with shiny gold service plates. A separate room houses the wine bar. Typical starters are Rhode

Island calamari with hot pepper rings, steak carpaccio and tuna tartare. Early favorites among entrées were sesame-crusted tuna, honey-roasted swordfish with chardonnay-mustard sauce and cornish game hen prepared in the peking duck style and rolled in a butternut squash crêpe. A griddle in the kitchen produces desserts like beignets with espresso syrup and hot chocolate dipping sauce.

(860) 395-1230. Entrées, $15 to $26. Lunch, Tuesday-Friday 11:30 to 4. Dinner, Tuesday-Sunday, 5 to 10 or 11. Sunday brunch, 11:30 to 2.

Food with a Water View

Terra Mar Grille, Saybrook Point Inn, 2 Bridge St., Old Saybrook.

There may be no more glamorous dining room on the Connecticut waterfront than this L-shaped room wrapping around an interior bar, with windows onto the mouth of the river beyond a marina. Cushioned rattan chairs are at generally well-spaced tables dressed in heavy cream-colored cloths and lit by shaded gas lamps. It's a formal, special-occasion place, although the outdoor tables appear more casual. The food here generally measures up to the view. For lunch, the breast of chicken stuffed with spinach, roasted peppers and mushrooms and topped with a whole-grain mustard and garlic sauce proved exceptional. The whole wheat pasta primavera with a julienne of vegetables seemed dull only in comparison. The dinner menu yields about a dozen main courses, from seafood paella, blackened escolar and tilapia meunière to chicken breast stuffed with wild mushrooms and goat cheese, grilled pork chop with cabernet demi-glace and filet mignon with port wine demi-glace. The seafood crêpe and the grilled shrimp wrapped in pancetta are good starters. Dessert could be warm apple napoleon, chocolate bourbon cake or a trio of crème brûlées.

(860) 395-2000. Entrées, $21.95 to $33.95. Lunch daily, 11:30 to 2. Dinner nightly, 6 to 9 or 10. Sunday brunch, 11 to 2.

Gelston House River Grill, 8 Main St. (Route 82), East Haddam.

The Carbone family of Hartford restaurant fame took over this landmark white confection at Goodspeed Landing and succeeded where others have failed. With a sensational riverside location and a captive audience from the Goodspeed Opera House next door, the re-christened River Grill has not only survived but has added a dining room off the lounge. The new room lacks the view of the elegant main dining room, a huge enclosed porch with big windows on all sides overlooking the river. But the food is the same, and generally praised – no mean feat for a busy place subject to the demands of theater-goers. Recent starters on the short contemporary menu were two salads, a wild mushroom risotto, salmon cake with spicy rémoulade and mussels provençal. The six entrées ranged from salmon fillet with tomato aioli to New York strip steak with compound butter. The lunch menu is twice as extensive. In season, the outdoor Beer Garden is popular for lunch and casual suppers. On the second and third floors are two guest rooms and two suites with private baths, renting for $100 and $225 respectively a night.

(860) 873-1411. Entrées, $19 to $27. Lunch, Wednesday-Saturday 11:30 to 2:30. Dinner, Wednesday-Saturday, 5:30 to 9. Sunday, brunch 11 to 2:15, dinner 4 to 8.

The Blue Oar, 16 Snyder Road, Haddam.

Who'd ever think a former snack bar at river's edge overlooking a marina would dispense good, innovative fare? Third-generation restaurateur Jim Reilly saw the possibilities for the one-room shack at the Midway Marina off Route 154 north of

Tylerville. He painted picnic tables in rainbow colors on the grounds, installed chairs at a counter running around the perimeter of a wraparound porch, hung blue oars overhead and built a makeshift pavilion outside. You bring your own bottle, review the blackboard menu, place your order and find a table. Jim cooks "whatever's fresh that day" on a six-foot industrial grill on the porch with sauces he prepares ahead. The five-item menu at a recent visit listed the likes of braised tilapia with roasted tomatoes, artichoke hearts and saffron rice; grilled salmon with white wine sauce over a warm black bean and corn salad, and grilled rosemary pork loin with orange-cranberry sauce and mashed potatoes. Starters are simple: chowders, potato-cheddar-bacon soup and steamers. Desserts, displayed in a pastry case at the counter, might be key lime mousse, white and dark chocolate mousse tower and strawberry-rhubarb tart. The snack bar heritage is evident in burgers, deli sandwiches and hot dogs, available day or night. Dinner is by candlelight, and the setting by the river, though very much weather-dependent, is pleasantly rustic and refreshing.

(860) 345-2994. Entrées, $15.95 to $18.95. Lunch, Tuesday-Sunday 11:30 to 5. Dinner nightly, 5 to 9. Closed Columbus Day to Mother's Day. BYOB. No credit cards.

Happy Hubbub of History

Griswold Inn, 36 Main St., Essex.

The immensely popular Gris is an experience in Americana, and has been since 1776. The always-crowded Tap Room is a happy hubbub of banjo players and singers of sea chanteys, and everyone loves the antique popcorn machine. There's much to see in four dining rooms: the important collection of Antonio Jacobsen marine oils in the dark paneled Library, the Currier and Ives steamboat prints in the Covered Bridge Room, the riverboat memorabilia in the Steamboat Room, the musket-filled Gun Room with 55 pieces dating to the 15th century. Together, they rank as one of the outstanding marine art collections in America. A new chef was upgrading the menu, a mixed bag of seafood, meat and game. Choices range from pesto-crusted sea bass to chicken pot pie, prime rib and New York strip steak with house-made worcestershire sauce. Three versions of the inn's patented 1776 sausages are served as a mixed grill with sauerkraut and German potato salad at dinner. They're in even more demand for lunch, when you also can get eggs benedict or Welsh rarebit, a goat cheese and arugula salad or yankee pot roast. At our latest lunch, a wicker swan full of packaged crackers helped sustain us as we waited (and waited) for our orders of crostini and shepherd's pie. The oil lamps were lit at noon, the place was hopping and the atmosphere was cheery on a dank autumn day. That we remember, more than the food. The ever-popular Sunday hunt breakfast ($16.95) is an enormous buffet of dishes ranging from baby cod and creamed chipped beef to scrambled eggs and a soufflé of grits and cheddar cheese.

(860) 767-1776. Entrées, $18.50 to $28. Lunch, Monday-Saturday 11:45 to 3. Dinner, 5:30 to 9 or 10. Sunday, hunt breakfast 11 to 2:30, dinner 4:30 to 9.

FOR MORE INFORMATION: Central Regional Tourism District – Connecticut's Heritage River Valley, 31 Pratt St., Hartford, CT 06103, (860) 244-8181 or (800) 793-4480. www.enjoycentralct.com.

More localized information may be found at www.essexct.com, www.chesterct.com and www.oldsaybrookct.com.

Old and new mix at Cannon Square in front of Inn at Stonington.

Mystic/Stonington, Conn.

Connecticut by the Sea

The southeastern corner of Connecticut is relatively small, like the rest of the state, but it has left its mark. For years, its maritime heritage and attractions have made it the state's biggest draw for tourists, a getaway destination for nearby city-dwellers who want to be close to the ocean.

Only in recent years has its traditional appeal been overshadowed by another kind of draw. Just inland from the shore, two Indian-run casinos that quickly became the biggest and most profitable in the world have become latter-day meccas for visitors from afar.

The traditional and the nouveau co-exist in uneasy tension, the historic shoreline section leery of the lure of their powerful neighbors to the north and their increasing impact on the territory. And yet, the traditional visitor – as opposed to the casino-goer – finds the shore area relatively unchanged.

Long may it remain so, for here is Connecticut's piece of New England by the sea. It's a place for beaching and boating and all the other attributes of life along the shore, of course. It's also a place for rediscovering and reliving the nation's seafaring days. From the mid-1600s to the battles of the American Revolution, from the whaling and shipbuilding eras to the early submarines and nuclear Tridents, this is maritime country with all its trappings.

At its apex is Mystic, far better known than its population of 2,600 would suggest. Although a mere village and a post-office address straddling the Mystic River – a political nonentity enveloped in the larger towns of Groton and Stonington – Mystic is important beyond its size. A center for shipbuilding since the 17th century, Mystic produced more than 1,000 sailing vessels, more noted captains and more important sailing records than any place its size in the world. Much of its legacy is wrapped up in one engaging package at Mystic Seaport, the nation's premier maritime museum. To the west is Groton, "Submarine Capital of the World." The huge U.S. Naval Submarine Base keeps alive a tradition dating from before the Revolution, when the colonies launched the first naval expeditions here. Beneath old Fort Griswold, site of the bloody Revolutionary massacre where the traitor Benedict Arnold did Groton in, the Electric Boat Division of General Dynamics builds the nation's nuclear subs.

On either side of Mystic along the shore, the pace is considerably quieter and the signs of tourism, if any, quite different. Contemporary life has almost passed by the fishing hamlet of Noank, Mystic's quaint neighbor to the southwest.

To the southeast lies the charming borough of Stonington – as historic a seaside enclave as you'll find along the East Coast. Here, on a picturesque peninsula facing the Rhode Island resort of Watch Hill, Long Island Sound begins to meld into the open Atlantic. The home port of Connecticut's last surviving commercial fishing fleet, Stonington is still living a history that helps put Mystic Seaport into perspective.

Seeing and Doing

Mystic

Mystic has been a center for shipbuilding since the 17th century. In the mid-1800s, the village of 1,500 owned eighteen whalers and the boatyards produced 22 clippers, some of which set sailing records that have never been equaled. Later, many of the nation's fastest sailing yachts and schooners were built here.

Mystic's ties with the water are epitomized by its unusual bascule bridge. Its picturesque downtown is the only place where Main Street/U.S. Route 1 traffic is stopped every hour as the 80-year-old drawbridge over the Mystic River lifts to let sailboats pass on their way to and from Long Island Sound.

From the drawbridge, walk south along the boardwalk on the east bank and enjoy the new Mystic River Park. Another favorite walk is along Gravel Street on the west bank north of downtown. It passes the gleaming white homes of 18th- and 19th-century sailing captains along the river across from Mystic Seaport.

Mystic Seaport Museum, 75 Greenmanville Ave. (Route 27), Mystic.

From a local marine historical museum with one building in the old Greenman family shipyard in 1929, Mystic Seaport has evolved into the nation's largest maritime museum. The seventeen-acre site along the Mystic River contains more than 60 historic buildings, hundreds of boats, a planetarium and significant collections of maritime artifacts and nautical photography. Together they create a mix of a working 19th-century seafaring community and a museum of massive proportions. You can poke through the old bank and print shop, watch shipbuilders and craftsmen at work, view early gardens, board three sailing vessels and visit the hardware store, schoolhouse, the drugstore and doctor's office, and the delightful little Fishtown Chapel. Guides cook on the open hearth of the Buckingham House kitchen, sing chanteys and demonstrate sail-setting, whaleboat rowing and fish salting. Climb aboard the Charles W. Morgan (1841), the last of America's wooden whaleships afloat, the full-rigged training ship Joseph Conrad (1882), and the 1921 fishing schooner L.A. Dunton. View more than 400 small wooden craft, the largest such collection in the country, on display in the Small Boat Exhibit and North Boat Shed or afloat along the seaport's docks. This is a low-key place where craftsmen answer questions and exhibit interpreters at major sites spin their tales; in between, you wander at will.

Sailors love the seaport and can spend hours in each building. For others, all the exhibits and boats may start to overwhelm after half a day. But don't miss the Seaport's signature exhibition, "Voyages: Stories of America and the Sea." It fills all three floors of the Stillman Building with art, artifacts and interactive multi-media presentations illustrating how Americans have been and still are connected to the sea. And there's plenty more: the Seamen's Inne for food and drink, the steamboat Sabino for river excursions, and the vast Mystic Seaport Museum Stores for gifts, contemporary marine art and a book shop with the best commercial collection of maritime volumes around.

(860) 572-0711 or (888) 973-2767. www.visitmysticseaport.com. Open daily, 9 to 5 April-October, 10 to 4 rest of year. Adults $17, children $9.

Mystic Aquarium & Institute for Exploration, 55 Coogan Blvd., Mystic.

A $52 million expansion has turned the Mystic Marinelife Aquarium into one of the best anywhere. Only the exhibit building and theater remain from days gone by, and they sport a new look. Now you will marvel at the deep-sea explorations and shipwrecks of Challenge of the Deep, home base of ocean explorer Robert Ballard's Institute for Exploration. You'll linger at the spectacular outdoor Alaskan Coast habitat where beluga whales and harbor seals swim about or bathe and bark, as the case may be. Watch penguins pass by like so many little fish in an aquarium in the Roger Tory Peterson Exhibit. Touch a cownose ray as it swims past your fingertips in the new Ray Touch Pool. Follow the Marsh Walk between the fur seals and Steller sea lions of the Pribilof Islands section and the stranded mammals undergoing rehabilitation in the Seal Rescue Clinic. The original exhibit building, now called Sunlit Seas, features 40 new fish and invertebrate exhibits. The colorful Coral Reef stars 500 varieties of exotic fish, sharks, stingrays and moray eels.

Open the doors of the R/V Discovery for an eight-minute theater presentation to prepare for the high-tech multimedia exhibits and interactive displays in the Challenge of the Deep. Among its fascinating deep-sea findings are Ballard's discovery of the sunken Titanic and his most recent archaeological expeditions, including one in 2000 to the Black Sea. In the new Immersion Theater, you might see an interactive show like one called "Dolphin Sense" or watch Ballard's 2003 expedition to the Titanic wreck.

Emerge from the dark into the open and a manmade pond, flanked by outdoor tables beside the Waterfront Café. You'll never again think of Mystic as just another aquarium. The atmosphere and experience are more like something you'd expect of a Disney Epcot Center transferred up north.

(860) 572-5955. www.mysticaquarium.org. Open daily, 9 to 6; weekdays 10 to 5, December-March. Adults $16, children $11.

WATER TRIPS. Schooner excursions are available through **Voyager Cruises,** 15 Holmes St., Mystic, (860) 536-0416. The 81-foot, gaff-rigged schooner Argia gives scenic half-day sails daily at 10:20 and 2:20, May-October, and sunset cruises nightly from 5:30 to 7:30; adults $36, children $26. Shorter tours around Mystic harbor and the Mystic Seaport Museum complex are offered daily at 1:30; adults $25, children $15.

Mystic River Tours, 31 Water St., Mystic, (860) 536-9980, offers scenic 90-minute tours of the Mystic Harbor aboard for up to six passengers aboard electric boats that are both quiet and environmentally friendly. Tours leave hourly from 10 to 5 for $25 per person. Sunset cocktail cruises may be arranged at night. **Mystic River Kayak Tours,** 15 Holmes St., Mystic, (860) 536-8381, rents kayaks, bicycles and mopeds. Kayak rentals and tours and moonlight paddles are offered by **King Cove Marina,** 926 Stonington Road, Stonington (860) 599-4730.

An Old-Time River Cruise

S.S. Sabino, South Gate, Mystic Seaport, Mystic.

For a trip into the past, board the 57-foot, two-deck Sabino, the last coal-fired passenger steamboat operating in the country. Built in 1908 in East Boothbay, Me., and long used on Maine's Damariscotta River, it was acquired in 1974 by Mystic Seaport for passenger excursions. Half-hour river cruises are available for up to 100 Seaport visitors on the half hour from 10:30 to 3:30; adults $5.25, children $4.25. The Sabino is at its best after hours when it gives 90-minute evening cruises down the Mystic River past Noank and Masons Island to Fishers Island Sound. Along the way, you'll wait for the Mystic bascule bridge to rise and pass the place in Noank where workers built the original engine, which you can see for yourself in the boat's exposed engine room.

(860) 572-5731. Evening cruises, daily at 4:30, also Friday and Saturday at 6:30, mid-May to mid-October. Adults $10.25, children $8.75.

ART. Explore regional art at its best at the **Mystic Art Association Galleries and Studios,** 9 Water St. Beside the Mystic River, it features changing exhibitions and special events in the summer. The **Mystic Seaport Museum Store** has an art gallery and a variety of nautical arts and crafts. Mystic hosts the annual **Mystic Outdoor Art Festival,** scheduled the second weekend in August and considered one of the best in the East.

SHOPPING. Mystic has an uncommon concentration of interesting stores. **Olde Mistick Village,** Route 27 at I-95, offers 60 shops in a landscaped, built-to-look-old complex. Here is a catch-all of boutiques, gift shops and such designed to appeal to tourists. The carillon music from its Anglican chapel lends a happy air and the ducks in a pond beside the water wheel keep restless youngsters amused.

Downtown Mystic. Stores here are increasingly upscale and of appeal to residents as well as visitors. **Whyevernot** has unique items, from jewelry to fabrics to clothing. **McMonogram for Kids** has children's clothes. **Mark, Fore & Strike** offers fine clothing. **The Bermuda Shop** shows classic, elegant apparel for women. **Jackeroos** sells men's and women's clothes from Australia, New Zealand and the South Sea Islands. **Mildly Wild Sportswear** has "original Mystic designs created, printed and stitched by us." **Peppergrass & Tulip** offers a potpourri of things for the boudoir, apparel, preserves, wood carvings and such. **Comina** has exotic international furnishings and accessories. **The Finer Line Gallery/Framers of the Lost Art** is one of several galleries, and we like almost everything at **The Company of Craftsmen.** **Bank Square Books** is a well-stocked bookstore. **Good Hearted Bears and More** has them in all guises, even in reindeer outfits at Christmas. Jewelry inspired by the sea is featured at **Mermaid's Cove Jewelers.** The best ice cream in town is dispensed at the **Mystic Drawbridge Ice Cream Shoppe.**

A Slice of Pizza

Mystic Pizza, 56 West Main St., Mystic.

When does a hole-in-the-wall pizzeria become a tourist attraction? When it catches the eye of a Hollywood screenwriter and is the subject of a movie starring the then-unknown Julia Roberts. Amy Jones, who was summering in the area, chose the place as the setting for her story of the lives and loves of three young waitresses. The 1988 hit "Mystic Pizza" was filmed in Mystic and neighboring towns, and suddenly Mystic Pizza in the little downtown storefront could not keep up with demand, customers lining the sidewalks for a "slice of heaven" and stopping traffic to take pictures. So the Zelepos family branched out, opening Mystic Pizza II at the Route 2 rotary in North Stonington and doubling their original size by expanding into a laundromat next door. The place now has separate rooms for eating in and taking out. But the waitresses still wear their "A Slice of Heaven" T-shirts, and movie photos and press clippings jazz up the walls. They sell Mystic Pizza T-shirts, caps and mugs and send frozen pizzas across the country. Oh, yes, they still make pizza dough in small batches. They also compliment their vast selection of toppings with soups, salads, burgers, grinders, calzones and half a dozen dinner entrées from veal parmesan to steak and shrimp.

(860) 536-3700. www.mysticpizza.com. Entrées, $11.95 to $17.95. Pizzas, $5.25 to $9.45 small, $9.75 to $17.25 large.

Enjoy Nature, Find History

Denison Pequotsepos Nature Center, 109 Pequotsepos Road, Mystic.

Here's a change of pace: 200 wooded acres of wildlife sanctuary, a wonderfully quiet place to walk, hike or jog on eight miles of trails. The newly renovated indoor natural history museum contains woodland, wetland and meadow displays depicting southeastern Connecticut's habitats and wildlife, many of which are found throughout the sanctuary. A broad-winged hawk, a peregrine falcon and three kinds of owls live in large outdoor aviaries. More than 150 species of birds have been identified within the sanctuary. A sign explains one of the many stone walls winding through the sanctuary (be on the lookout throughout the area for the thousands of miles of stone walls made by pioneer farmers near the sea as a windbreak to prevent farmland from disappearing and to keep cattle out of the crops – the sign here tells that they also were a way to dispose of all the rocks removed from the soil).

Across the road from the nature center is the 1717 **Denison Homestead Museum,** a brown-shingled house with a curving stone wall out front. The interior is authentically furnished with heirlooms from six generations of Denisons who lived here until 1941. The wildlife sanctuary was the bulk of a land grant given to Capt. George Denison in 1654 by the King of England. The homestead built by Denison's grandson was the working farm for the family, who as frugal Yankees rarely threw out anything and saved their possessions in the attic and barn. Billed as the only New England home restored in the style of five eras, it has a Colonial kitchen with fireplace, a Revolutionary era bedroom with poster bed, a Federal parlor, a Civil War bedroom with ornate franklin stove and a 1930 living room with fine Dutch china.

(860) 536-1216. www.dpnc.org. Nature center open Monday-Saturday 9 to 5, Sunday noon to 4. Adults $6, children $4.

(860) 536-9248. www.denisonsociety.org. Homestead open mid-May to mid-October, Thursday-Monday 11 to 5. Adults $5, children $2.

Groton

History and submarines vie for the visitor's attention in this bustling town. On the east bank of the broad Thames River, Groton is the "submarine capital of the world." The vast U.S. Navy Submarine Base keeps alive a tradition dating from before the Revolution, when the colonies launched the first naval expeditions here. The Electric Boat Division of General Dynamics pioneered here in the production of nuclear submarines. From Groton, the Long Island Sound shoreline wraps around Groton Long Point, an early summer colony, and around quaint Noank to Mystic.

Historic Ship Nautilus/Submarine Force Museum, Naval Submarine Base, 1 Crystal Lake Road, Groton.

The storied Nautilus, the world's first nuclear-powered submarine, was built at Groton's General Dynamics Electric Boat Division shipyard in 1954. Returned to its birthplace, it has been opened to visitors after cruising faster, deeper, farther and longer than any craft in history. A recent $4 million expansion has doubled the size of the submarine museum, which contains the world's finest collection of submarine artifacts. It traces the history of underwater navigation, showing a submarine control room, working periscopes and models depicting submarine style and development. Films of submarines past and present are shown in a 70-seat theater. The expansion includes a museum store, a cut-away model of a 688 Los Angeles Class sub, a ballistic missile, Cold War exhibits and a library with sitting-area views of the Thames River. Outside are four mini-submarines. The highlight for most remains a self-guided tour of portions of the 519-foot-long Nautilus, berthed beside a dock in the Thames. The lines may be long, but you get to see the control room, torpedo room, attack center, officers' and crew's quarters and dining areas.

(860) 694-3174 or (800) 343-0079. www.ussnautilus.org. Open Wednesday-Monday 9 to 5 and Tuesday 1 to 5, mid-May through October; Wednesday-Monday 9 to 4, rest of year; closed first full week of May and the third full week of October. Free.

Fort Griswold Battlefield State Park, 57 Fort St., Groton Heights.

A 135-foot-high obelisk on the hilltop of this seventeen-acre park commemorates one of the bloodiest battles of the American Revolution, the 1781 massacre of 88 Colonists by British troops under the infamous turncoat Benedict Arnold. It provides a good view of the waterfront. At its base is a free **Monument House Museum** with historic displays from the era. Downhill is the 1750 **Ebenezer Avery House,** which sheltered the wounded after the battle. The center-chimney Colonial with period furnishings is open summer weekends from 1 to 5, free. The remains of the fort are worth a look.

(860) 449-6877. Park open daily 8 to dusk, year-round; monument and museum, daily 10 to 5 Memorial Day to Labor Day, weekends to Columbus Day. Free.

Project Oceanology, 1084 Shennecossett Road, Groton.

The public may participate in two-and-one-half-hour educational cruises from mid-June through Labor Day aboard a 55-foot research vessel departing from the University of Connecticut campus at Avery Point. EnviroLab expeditions teach passengers how to identify fish, measure lobsters, examine bottom mud and collect water samples. They're scheduled daily at 10 and 1, mid-June through August. Harbor tours to the landmark New London Ledge Lighthouse, which is explored inside and out, leave Tuesday, Thursday and Saturday at 4, mid-June to late

September. Seal watch tours for the public are scheduled weekends in February and March.

(860) 445-9007 or (800) 364-8472. www.oceanology.org. Adults $19, children $16. Reservations recommended.

NEW LONDON. Across the Thames River from Groton is New London, a seaport dating to 1646 and later a whaling center of note. The area's largest city and commercial center, it's the home of Connecticut College and the U.S. Coast Guard Academy, as well as the headquarters of Pfizer, the pharmaceutical company. All back up to the Thames River – pronounced locally "Thames," not "Tems," despite the city founders' ties with old London.

Of interest to visitors are the **Lyman Allyn Art Museum,** with a collection of more than 30,000 paintings and decorative arts, and the **Connecticut College Arboretum,** which grows 300 varieties of native trees and shrubs. Also open to the public is **Monte Christo Cottage,** the boyhood home of playwright Eugene O'Neill. Nearby in Waterford is the **Eugene O'Neill Memorial Theater Center,** which gives summer visitors a front-row seat on the newest works in American theater.

The 231-acre **Harkness Memorial State Park** beside Long Island Sound in Waterford is a quiet refuge for beachcombers, picnickers and garden enthusiasts. The 42-room Harkness Mansion, an Italian-style villa, is open summer weekends for tours. Beatrix Farrand, garden architect for the rich and famous, designed the extravagant plantings in the restored gardens around the mansion.

Stonington

The historic "borough" of Stonington is Connecticut's most captivating seaside community, a living anachronism jutting into the Atlantic and cut off from the mainstream by a railroad track spanned by a viaduct. The picturesque peninsula is a curious blend of early fishing village, lively arts colony and an increasingly tony, year-round residential enclave. The rural countryside north of the borough is called North Stonington.

"Take a walk," advises the historical society's guide to the borough. Indeed, that's the best way to see and savor the tight little community full of old houses hugging the sidewalks and each other. The architecture is an intriguing mix of gambrel roofs, old Cape Cod and pillared Greek Revival styles. The two main roads through the borough are narrow (and partly one-way); they and their cross streets are crammed with history dating back to 1649. Sea captains sailed the Seven Seas from Stonington, which became known as the "Nursery of Seamen." Around 1800, this was Connecticut's most populated town and the Wadawanuck Hotel could sleep 1,300 guests – that's long-gone and the only accommodations now are at a couple of B&Bs. The last commercial fishing fleet in Connecticut is manned by the resident Portuguese community, which stages a Blessing of the Fleet festival annually in late July.

The Stonington Historical Society, founded in 1910 and one of the first around, has marked with signs many structures from the 18th and 19th centuries. One is the 1780 Col. Amos Palmer House at Main and Wall, where artist James McNeil Whistler once lived; it was later the home of poet Stephen Vincent Benet and since was occupied by his granddaughter. On Harmony Street is the 1786 Peleg Brown House, birthplace of Capt. Nathaniel Palmer, who at age 22 discovered Antarctica. The appeal of the old houses is enhanced by all the garden courtyards and glimpses of the harbor with its fishing trawlers. On Cannon Square are two "18-pounders" that repulsed the British in the War of 1812; beside the square, the old Ocean Bank is a replica of the Athenian Treasury at Delphi, Greece. From Stonington Point you can see across Long Island Sound to Fishers Island, N.Y., and east to Watch Hill, R.I., and the open Atlantic.

Palmer House, 40 Palmer St., Stonington.

The majestic, sixteen-room Victorian mansion that Capt. Nathaniel Palmer and his seafaring brother Alexander built in 1853 was saved by the historical society from demolition in 1994 and opened to the public as a fine example of a prosperous sea captain's home. Several rooms contain memorabilia from the brothers' adventures, family portraits and local artifacts. The piano in the parlor is the only original piece remaining in the house, but rooms are appointed with period pieces. The craftsmanship by local shipwrights is evident in the sweeping staircases and built-in cabinetry. The cupola yields a view of the surrounding countryside and sea.

(860) 535-8445. www.stoningtonhistory.org. Open May-October, Tuesday-Sunday 10 to 4. Adults $4, children $2.

Old Lighthouse Museum, 7 Water St., Stonington.

The first government-operated lighthouse in Connecticut is perched on a rise above Stonington Point, where the villagers turned back the British. Opened in 1927, the museum is a tiny storehouse of Stonington memorabilia. In six small rooms on two floors are displayed the Stonington Historical Society's collection of photos of old Long Island Sound lighthouses, an ice-harvesting exhibit, whaling and fishing gear, articles from the Orient trade and an exquisite dollhouse. Climb the circular stone staircase to the top of the tower for a panoramic view of three states and Long Island Sound.

(860) 535-1440. Open May-October, daily 10 to 5 in July and August, Tuesday-Sunday 10 to 5 rest of season. Adults $4, children $2.

SHOPPING. Water Street in Stonington is home to several special shops, with more opening every year. Fine antiques are the specialty at such places as **Grand & Water, Orkney & Yost** and **Devon House Antiques.** At the **Hungry Palette,** silk-screened and hand-printed fabrics can be purchased by the yard or already made up into long skirts, wrap skirts, sundresses and colorful accessories like Bermuda bags. **Quimper Faience** has firsts and seconds of the popular hand-painted French china at this, its flagship store and world administrative headquarters. **Findings** offers fine home furnishings and accessories. **Cumulus** carries handcrafted jewelry and gifts. **Solomon's Mines** also purveys fine jewelry. High fashion apparel and accessories are offered by New York fashion designer Narua Barraza at her new store, **Barraza. Luli** advertises beautiful wordly clothes. The expanding **Fun! Company** went from one to three Water Street outlets before consolidating at 71 Cutler St. with room after room of closeouts of clothing, home accessories and toys.

Between expeditions, stop at **Stonington Vineyards,** 523 Taugwonk Road, where Nick and Happy Smith run a growing winery operation. Among their premium vinifera wines are a fine chardonnay and a cabernet franc. The less expensive Seaport white and blush wines reflect the winery's proximity to the historic Stonington and Mystic Seaport areas. The first crop of local grapes was scheduled for harvesting in 2005 at the new, state-of-the-art **Jonathan Edwards Winery,** successor to the Crosswoods Vineyards at 74 Chester Maine Road in North Stonington.

┌─ *Cool Casinos* ───

The rise of the native-American casinos and related development just north of this area in little more than a decade borders on the incredible.

The **Foxwoods Resort Casino,** Route 2, Ledyard, (860) 885-3000 or (800) 752-9244, run by the Mashantucket Pequots, is a hugely profitable enterprise hulking out of the rural forests north of Mystic. Tastefully done (surprisingly so, given its nature), the six casinos are open 24 hours a day year-round and attract more than 40,000 visitors on an average day. The nearly 6,500 slot machines are the major draw for those who, like us, can't part with more than a quarter at a time. Also draws are the 3,200-seat high-stakes bingo hall (the world's largest, which launched Foxwoods on its way), a performance theater and arena hosting big-name entertainers and boxing matches, 24 restaurants and three hotels with more than 1,400 rooms, including the eighteen-story Grand Pequot Tower. For other interests, Foxwoods offers a spa, a shopping concourse, an eighteen-hole golf course and a museum.

The **Mohegan Sun Casino,** 1 Mohegan Sun Blvd., Uncasville, (860) 646-5682 or (888) 226-7711, is close on the heels of Foxwoods as the world's second largest casino and, suddenly, one of its most spectacular. Compared with Foxwoods, the Mohegan tribe's nicely themed casino is more urban, looking at the start rather like a shopping mall with its direct-access highway, five-story parking garage and giant food court. Its gaming began in the Casino of the Earth, a huge circular room patterned on the four seasons, each distinguished by different native-American designs, traditions and imagery. Recent additions include the world's largest planetarium atop the new Casino of the Sky, celebrity-name restaurants (think Jasper White, Michael Jordan, Todd English), a 10,000-seat arena and a glitzy, 34-story, 1,200-room luxury hotel – Connecticut's largest – beside the Thames River.

└──

Mashantucket Pequot Museum & Research Center, 110 Pequot Trail, Ledyard.

Hailed as the most ambitious new museum in New England, this remarkable place just south of the Foxwoods casino is a destination on its own. The state-of-the-art museum includes a half-acre indoor re-creation of a 16th-century coastal Indian settlement called Pequot Village – complete with twelve wigwams and 51 life-like figures posed in daily activities. Four acres of permanent exhibits, six computer interactive programs and more than a dozen films in various theaters help bring the story of America's native people into perspective. There are two research libraries (one for children), a gallery, a gift shop and a restaurant featuring native American cuisine.

(860) 396-6800 or (800) 411-9671. www.pequotmuseum.org. Open daily, 9 to 5. Adults $15, children $10. www.pequotmuseum.org.

Where to Stay

Creature Comforts Galore

The Inn at Mystic, Route 1, Mystic 06355.

If it's romance you're after, follow the lead of privacy-seeking Lauren Bacall and Humphrey Bogart. The movie stars are said to have honeymooned here in what is now the heart of a thirteen-acre complex beside Pequotsepos Cove. The inn that began as a motor inn takes its name from the 1904 white-pillared mansion atop the hill, which has five large and antiques-decorated guest rooms, some with fireplaces and all with whirlpool tubs. Behind the mansion is a secluded gatehouse with three attractive fireplaced accommodations for two done in a Ralph Lauren country look. In summer on a wicker rocker on the inn's spacious veranda, gazing out over English gardens and orchards toward Long Island Sound, or in winter sitting deep in a chintz-covered sofa by a fire in the drawing room with its 17th-century pine paneling, you may feel like a country squire, if not a movie star. Rooms down a hill in the motor inn area vary from good to spectacular. Twelve deluxe units in the renovated East Wing come with queensize canopy beds, wing chairs and fireplaces, plus balconies or patios with water views. Six rooms here have huge jacuzzis in the bathrooms with mirrors all around. In yet another building on the property is the inn's **Flood Tide Restaurant** (see Where to Eat). Complimentary tea and pastries are offered in the afternoon. A tennis court, a small pool, two putting greens and use of canoes, kayaks and rowboats in the cove are other pluses here.

(860) 536-9604 or (800) 237-2415. Fax (860) 572-1635. www.innatmystic.com. Sixty-seven rooms with private baths. Rates, EP. Doubles, $115 to $295, May to mid-November; $85 to $285, rest of year.

The Inn at Stonington, 60 Water St., Stonington.

From the ashes of the fire-ravaged Harborview Restaurant rose this luxury B&B facing the waterfront. Owner Bill Griffin spared no expense in producing a handsome gray and white-trimmed, three-story inn up against the sidewalk in front, with docks and water behind. Four guest rooms on the first floor and eight on the second come with fireplaces and ten have jacuzzi tubs. Beds are queensize except for two kings. English-style fruitwood furniture, rich fabrics, upholstered club chairs and built-in shelves around the fireplaces are the norm. Six open onto private balconies overlooking the water. The best view may be from the cheery yellow third-floor sitting room with a common balcony outfitted with Parisian-style bistro chairs. Six larger rooms with high ceilings are available in a new brick annex next door. All come with jacuzzi tubs and five have kingsize beds and fireplaces. On the main floor of the main inn are a living room/dining area where a substantial continental breakfast is served. Wine and cheese are complimentary in the afternoon. The inn includes a basement exercise area and has kayaks and bicycles for guests to use.

(860) 535-2000. Fax (860) 535-8193. www.innatstonington.com. Eighteen rooms with private baths. Doubles, $175 to $395 weekends, $175 to $295 midweek. Off-season: doubles, $155 to $295 weekends, $135 to $265 midweek.

Stonecroft, 515 Pumpkin Hill Road, Ledyard 06339.

Ten deluxe guest accommodations and an acclaimed restaurant are the hallmarks of this inn on six rural acres surrounded by 300 acres of Nature Conservancy woodlands and stone walls northwest of Mystic. Joan Egy and her late husband began by renovating the handsome yellow 1807 Georgian Colonial residence into a B&B. Country French furnishings lend a comfortable, elegant look to the four downstairs common rooms – from the Snuggery library that once was a "borning" room to a luxurious rear great room with a nine-foot-wide fireplace. The premier Stonecroft Room here comes with a kingsize four-poster bed, loveseat and a wraparound mural depicting a day in the life of Stonecroft about 1820. The Egys finished off a rear three-story barn with a fieldstone tavern and dining room on the ground floor and six deluxe guest rooms upstairs. Rooms and suites in the barn are more upscale than those in the main house. Each has a sitting area, a gas fireplace with a built-in TV overhead, and a large bath with double whirlpool tub and separate shower. They're elegantly furnished in country French or English styles, plus one in Colonial decor for Yankee purists. All open onto private or shared wraparound balconies overlooking the rural scene. Our room was named for Orlando Smith, discoverer of Westerly granite, whose portrait and granite samples were framed above the bureau. That distinguishing bit of trivia seemed not of great interest to previous occupants, whose guest book entries revealed details of romance in words and sketches. Terrycloth robes, bath sheets rather than towels, Crabtree & Evelyn toiletries and soft music throughout the common areas help provide a serene, therapeutic stay. Breakfast is a four-course event.

(860) 572-0771. Fax (860) 572-9161. www.stonecroft.com. Eight rooms and two suites with private baths. Weekends: doubles $200 to $245, suites $300. Midweek: doubles $150 to $195, suites $250.

Steamboat Inn, 73 Steamboat Wharf, Mystic 06355.

You're so close to the water, you feel as if you're on board ship at this luxurious B&B beside the Mystic River (indeed you are, if you stay on owner John McGee's new Valiant "boat and breakfast" moored outside). All ten inn rooms have whirlpool baths and televisions hidden in cupboards or armoires. Six on the second floor contain fireplaced sitting areas facing the river. They're outfitted in lavish style: mounds of pillows and designer sheets on the queensize canopy or twin beds, loveseats or sofas and a plush armchair in front of the fireplace, and mantels and cabinet work that make these rooms look unusually homelike. Four rooms on the ground floor are suite-size in proportion and come with double whirlpool tubs and wet bars with microwaves, but are on view to the constant stream of passersby on the wharf unless the blinds are drawn. Guests have little reason to leave their rooms, but there's a common room on the second floor. It has all the right magazines as well as glass tables for continental breakfast. Homemade breads and muffins are put out each morning, and tea and sherry in the evening.

(860) 536-8300. Fax (860) 536-9528. www.steamboatinnmystic.com. Ten rooms with private baths. Doubles, $235 to $300 summer and fall weekends, $195 to $270 summer midweek, $165 to $225 fall midweek. Rest of year: $185 to $245 weekends, $125 to $175 midweek.

Mystic Marriott Hotel and Spa, 625 North Road (Route 117), Groton 06340.

The glamorous Mystic Marriott isn't even in Mystic. The big, six-story, cream-colored hotel with Greek temple-like pediments overlooks a reservoir in a once-sleepy corner of Groton. It's geared to the corporate and resort crowd, what with 285 rooms and suites equipped with the latest equipment for business travelers and public facilities like the Elizabeth Arden Red Door Spa and a Starbucks Coffee Bar in the lobby. An indoor pool, fitness center, whirlpool and sauna are among the offerings. Guest rooms come with the usual hotel amenities, such as in-room coffeemakers, hair dryers, irons and the morning newspaper at the door. Beds are generally one or two queensize. Twenty-two deluxe rooms with whirlpool tubs have kingsize beds. Concierge level rooms include upgraded amenities and evening hors d'oeuvres in the lounge. Three meals a day are served in the hotel's stylish **Octagon** restaurant, where award-winning executive chef John Trudeau features "the art of steak" at night.

(860) 446-2600 or (866) 449-7390. Fax (860) 446-2696. www.mysticmarriott.com. Two hundred eighty-one rooms and four suites. Doubles, $169 to $309.
Entrées $17 to $32. Lunch daily, 11:30 to 2:30. Dinner nightly, 5:30 to 10.

The Whaler's Inn, 20 East Main St., Mystic 06355.

The folks from the luxury Steamboat Inn across the Mystic River acquired and upgraded this venerable inn and motel in the heart of town. There are 41 rooms in the older main building and nearby houses, and two newer motel buildings surrounding a courtyard. The newest accommodations are eight upscale rooms with whirlpool tubs, fireplaces and partial water views in a building called the Hoxie House on the river side of the property. It was nicknamed the Jimmy Carter Wing after the former president and his party booked it in 2004 during christening ceremonies in Groton for a new nuclear-powered submarine bearing his name. Rooms throughout the complex vary. All come with TVs and phones. Motel units in the Noank House have one or two double beds and showers; those in the Stonington House, bathtubs. Rooms in the inn and the 1865 House next to it are decorated traditionally and most have queen beds. These and the new luxury rooms are the higher-priced accommodations. The small lobby is nicely outfitted with wing chairs and oriental carpets. Continental breakfast is offered in a common hospitality room.

(860) 536-1506 or (800) 243-2588. Fax (860) 572-1250. www.whalersinnmystic.com. Forty-nine rooms with private baths. Doubles, $149 to $249 in summer, $89 to $199 rest of year.

Small and Charming

House of 1833, 72 North Stonington Road, Mystic 06355.

Romance is the theme at this pillared, Greek Revival mansion on three hillside acres in Old Mystic – from the fireplaced bedrooms to the live music the pianist-host plays at breakfast. Owners Carol and Matt Nolan offer five large queensize guest rooms, all with fireplaces and some of them quite spacious and unusual. The front part of the double parlor, furnished in Greek Revival, opens into a Victorian section notable for a crystal chandelier, a grand piano and an antique pump organ. A heavy door off the front parlor leads to the Peach Room, the former library, now outfitted with a mahogany canopy bed draped in peach fabric, a plush settee with matching chair on an oriental rug, a wicker-furnished porch, and a bathroom with a walk-in shower through which one passes to get to the double whirlpool tub. Upstairs are four more guest rooms with thick carpeting and fine fabrics. The rear Verandah Room comes with a queen bed enclosed in wispy sheer curtains, a ladyslipper clawfoot tub on a platform beside the fireplace and a little wicker balcony. The secluded third-floor Cupola Room has a four-poster bed draped from the ceiling, a potbelly stove and a double whirlpool tub. The stairs rise to a cupola with two seats from which to observe the sunset. Matt Nolan plays light contemporary music on the grand piano during breakfast, which might be baked custard french toast or eggs florentine in puff pastry. Guests enjoy a tennis court, swimming pool and use of eighteen-speed bicycles.

(860) 536-6325 or (800) 367-1833. www.houseof1833.com. Five rooms with private baths. Memorial Day to mid-November: doubles, $179 to $249 weekends, $129 to $179 midweek. Rest of year: $129 to $179 weekends, $99 to $149 midweek.

The Old Mystic Inn, 52 Main St., Box 733, Old Mystic 06372.

Great aromas and tastes are part of the inn experience offered by innkeeper Michael Cardillo Jr., a Culinary Institute of America grad who was private chef for a Fairfield County family before deciding it was time to move on. He bought this historic hostelry near the head of the wide Mystic River, where he treats guests to afternoon cakes, brownies and popcorn. They bed down for the night in four antiques-furnished guest rooms in a red and white 1794 Colonial house up against the road and four newer rooms in a blue carriage house built out back in 1988. All have queen beds, and three in the main house have working fireplaces. Two larger rooms in the carriage house come with canopy beds, gas fireplaces and whirlpool tubs. The main house has pleasant sitting rooms upstairs and down, a front porch and an atmospheric front dining room for a gourmet breakfast. The main course might be herbed scrambled eggs in puff pastry with smoked gouda mornay sauce and steamed asparagus. The deep back yard includes perennial gardens and a gazebo.

(860) 572-9422. www.oldmysticinn.com. Eight rooms with private baths. Doubles, $145 to $185 May-October, $115 to $175 rest of year.

Randall's Ordinary, Route 2, North Stonington 06359.

Hark back to the old days at this secluded ordinary (British definition: a tavern or eating house serving regular meals) in the midst of 27 acres at the end of a dirt road lined with stone walls. This one is anything but ordinary, from its hearth-cooked meals (see Where to Eat) to its overnight accommodations in a 1685 farmhouse or in a restored 1819 barn that was dismantled and moved to the site from upstate New York. Anyone cherishing the past would enjoy the three rooms upstairs in the ancient main house with queensize beds and hand-loomed coverlets, decorative fireplaces and baths with whirlpool tubs. They are spacious and, except for modern comforts, look much as they would have in the 18th century. Twelve newer-feeling rooms and suites are located in the rear barn. Designed in what might be called a rustic contemporary style, they retain their original beams, barn siding and bare floors. Most have queensize canopy beds, baths with whirlpool tubs and heat lamps, TVs and telephones. Four have loft bedrooms with skylights and spiral staircases from the sitting rooms. The getaway treat here is the enormous Silo Suite, complete with domed jacuzzi loft above a circular silo bedroom and a skylit loft living room. Guests are served a continental breakfast in the lobby of the barn.

(860) 599-4540 or (877) 599-4540. Fax (860) 599-3308. www.randallsordinary.com. Ten rooms and five suites with private baths. Weekends: doubles $169, suites $195 and $350. Midweek: doubles $149, suites $165 and $300. Closed November-April.

Antiques & Accommodations, 32 Main St., North Stonington 06359.

The name of this attractive yellow house, built in 1861 with the gingerbread trim of its era, is appropriate. For owners Ann and Thomas Gray are antiques dealers who sell many of the furnishings in their B&B near the center of the quaint hamlet of North Stonington. Memories of traveling in England inspired the Grays to furnish their home in the Georgian manner with formal antique furniture and accessories. Three rooms and suites are named after English towns where their favorite B&Bs are, among them Broadway and Tetbury. Besides a parlor with TV, their house offers a downstairs guest room with a queen bed, working fireplace and a stereo system. Upstairs is another guest room with canopied bed and a bridal room filled with photographs of honeymooners who have stayed there. The Grays serve a four-course breakfast by candlelight in the formal dining room or on the flower-bedecked front porch. "Breakfast goes on for hours," says Ann. "One Sunday, the last people got up from the table at 12:30." These hospitable hosts also have been known to dispense wine late into the evening while everyone lingers on the patio. Behind the house are exotic gardens, mostly herbs and greens laid out in meticulous quadrants.

(860) 535-1736 or (800) 554-7829. www.antiquesandaccommodations.com. Three rooms and suites with private baths. Doubles, $129 to $189.

—A Seaside Hideaway—

Orchard Street Inn, 41 Orchard St., Stonington 06378.

Three plush and private accommodations are offered in this new seaside B&B, a bright yellow cottage along the ocean marsh. Richard Satler and Regina Shields gutted the interior of the old Lasbury Guest House to produce a seaside B&B. Each section of the cottage has its own entrance off a private patio, a queensize bed, all-new bath, TV with DVD player, mini-refrigerator and loveseat. The spiffy, summery decor is best in the rear Delphinium Room, with vaulted ceiling, high queensize poster bed, wicker loveseat and a large patio facing the wetlands. Regina offers a full breakfast – fruits, muffins, croissants and perhaps an omelet – at bistro tables in the reception area in the main house.

(860) 535-2681. www.orchardstreetinn.com. Three rooms with private baths. Doubles, $160 to $175 April-December, $130 to $145 in winter.

Another Second Penny Inn, 870 Pequot Trail, Stonington 06378.

Guests at this atmospheric, 1710 Colonial home on five rural acres enjoy large accommodations with updated amenities, gourmet breakfasts and a distinct feeling of times gone by. The house had been a tavern at one time and retains a big old kitchen that innkeepers Jim and Sandra Wright use for hearthside cooking as well as an upstairs suite with a swinging partition in the middle that could be raised to make enough space for a dance hall. On one side is a queensize poster bed, gas fireplace and a bath with jetted clawfoot tub. On the other is a sitting room with a day bed. The Denison Room has a queensize poster bed, gas fireplace and a bathroom so big it holds not only a jetted clawfoot tub but also a small refrigerator, a dressing table and a yellow slipper chair in the middle. The front Noyes Room comes with two twin beds that can be joined as a king, an electric fireplace and a full bath. All rooms have TV/VCRs and are decorated in Colonial style with oriental rugs and handmade quilts employed as wall hangings. Guests gather in a cozy front library and in the dining room for a breakfast to remember. The morning of our visit brought vanilla poached pears, maple-oatmeal-walnut muffins, a garden vegetable quiche and the usual "dessert," a selection of Jim's homemade sorbets, including apple, kiwi, peach and mulled cider. The B&B's name comes from an obscure parable cited by the president of Mills College when colleague Jim had second thoughts about having splurged to buy an old yacht: "If you have two pennies, with the first buy bread for your stomach, and with the second buy hyacinths for your soul." Jim named the boat "Second Penny," and the B&B when he retired became another.

(860) 535-1710. Fax (860) 535-1709. www.secondpenny.com. Two rooms and one suite with private baths. Doubles, $155 to $185 weekends, $115 to $139 midweek. Children over 8.

Where to Eat

Dining with a View

The Grange at Stonecroft, 515 Pumpkin Hill Road, Ledyard.

A pastoral scene is on view from the expansive, granite-walled dining room in the restored barn at the Stonecroft inn. Floor-to-ceiling, multi-paned windows yield a grand view of a landscaped stone terrace for outdoor dining, a grapevine-covered pergola and a water garden. The interior is furnished like that of an English country manor, with a lounge area of high-back couches facing a fireplace and well-spaced tables set with cream-colored linens and Villeroy & Boch china. It's a thoroughly delightful setting for sensational fare prepared by European-trained chef de cuisine Drew Egy, the innkeeper's son. Dinner begins with an amuse-bouche, usually a couple of morsels – perhaps a spring roll with apricot-fennel filling, a shumai dumpling or a mushroom tart – that hint of treats to come. We were pleased with a couple of sensational starters, baja-style scallop ceviche with cucumber and a grilled tortilla and the trio of exotic shrimp: curry-coconut with spiced banana chutney, spicy rangoon with ginger-hoisin sauce, and chile-cilantro grilled over cucumber. Asian grilled tuna and rack of New Zealand lamb are signature main courses. We liked the paupiette of veal paillard stuffed with artichokes and bel paese cheese and wrapped in prosciutto, and the pan-roasted duck breast and confit with bing cherry glaze and a fabulous brie and wild rice risotto. The dessert specialty is the night's chocolate trio, at our visit a little pot of intense chocolate mousse, three homemade truffles and a chocolate fudge brownie, plus a bonus, chocolate ice cream with a stick of white chocolate. An equal triumph was the banana and Bailey's Irish cream cheesecake with bruléed bananas and chocolate sauce.

(860) 572-0771 or (800) 772-0774. Entrées, $20 to $36. Dinner by reservation, nightly except Tuesday 5 to 9.

Skipper's Dock, 66 Water St., Stonington.

The folks who made the Harborview into one of the great restaurants in the state returned to its last remaining adjunct, the Skipper's Dock on the water at pier's end in Stonington harbor. Ainslie Turner and her late husband Jerry turned the place into a cheery, year-round restaurant and tavern with fireplaces ablaze in cool weather and an expansive deck right out over the water. The result is a happy cross between the haute Harborview (since destroyed by fire and rebuilt as the Inn at Stonington) and the casual Skipper's Dock of old. The food reflects the Harborview's creative side. You can still get a mug of creamy clam chowder and cherrystone clams on the half shell. You also can get stuffed quahogs Portuguese and the specialty oysters Ainslie, toasted with garlic aioli and panko crumbs. Main dishes include the Harborview's classic Marseilles-style bouillabaisse, a savory array of choice seafood in a tomato-fennel-saffron broth, panko-crusted ahi sesame tuna and an old specialty, coquilles St. Jacques and grilled filet mignon with gorgonzola and garlic butter. The dessert list might feature the Harborview's signature grasshopper pie. The fried oysters with french fries and slaw and the Grand Central pan roast, a seafood sauté with an addictive sauce, were first-rate treats at our latest lunch. Much of the fare is offered day and night in the Harbar, a high-style pub with framed magazine covers on the walls and boating gear hanging overhead.

(860) 535-0111. Entrées, $16.95 to $25.95. Lunch daily, 11:30 to 4. Dinner nightly, 4 to 9:30 or 10. Closed Tuesday in winter and month of January.

Flood Tide, Route 1, Mystic.

This hillside restaurant in front of the Inn at Mystic serves up some of the area's fanciest food along with a view of Pequotsepos Cove looking toward Long Island Sound. A new exhibition kitchen with a clay-pit brick oven along one side may take some diners' eyes off the view in the formal dining room, whose refurbished setting is one of updated nautical elegance. The $15.95 daily luncheon buffet at one visit yielded everything from ceviche, caviar, seafood salad, eggs benedict, seafood crêpes and fettuccine with lobster alfredo to bread pudding and kiwi tarts. You can also order à la carte. In the evening, the brick oven is put into play with entrées categorized as wood grilled, wood-burning oven roasted and on the wood-burning turn spit. Expect things like grilled Stonington fluke with lime butter, lobster pot au feu, bouillabaisse, orange-honey brined chicken with thyme jus, cinnamon-rubbed pork rack with calvados demi-glace, filet mignon, even a roasted vegetable mille-feuille. Châteaubriand is finished tableside for two. Start with oven-roasted mussels basted with hazelnut-garlic butter, fried oysters with roasted garlic aioli, lobster cappuccino or one of the Tuscan brick-oven tarts. Lavender crème brûlée, bananas foster and flamed mango parfait are extravagant endings. A small outdoor patio is popular in summer.

(860) 536-8140. Entrées, $22 to $35. Lunch, Monday-Saturday, 11:30 to 2:30. Dinner nightly, 5:30 to 9:30 or 10. Sunday brunch, 11 to 2.

Boom, 194 Water St., Stonington.
This trendy establishment occupies a prime harborfront location in the Dodson Boatyard, with a view of the marina's boats and booms from which it takes its name. Tables in the dining room with wraparound windows are topped by nautical charts covered with glass. A noisy bar is a focal point. Chef-owner Jean Maude Fuller-Gest's menu is short but sweet and her food has been well received of late. For lunch, our party of four sampled the Carolina clam chowder (a bit odd with diced sweet potatoes) and roasted tomato soup. The fried oyster sandwich and the scallop taco were better than the bland portobello mushroom and grilled chicken sandwiches. The BOAT sandwich (bacon, olive tapenade, arugula and tomato) is a better choice these days. Chocolate ganache, key lime pie and mango sorbet were good desserts. At night, look for main courses like pan-seared salmon with artichoke hearts and diced tomatoes, Stonington scallops with roasted red pepper curry sauce, native flounder with a tomato-basil coulis and kalamata olive tapenade, and black angus sirloin with house-made steak sauce on the side.

(860) 535-2588. www.boomrestaurant.net. Entrées, $17.50 to $22.50. Lunch, Tuesday-Saturday 11:30 to 2:30. Dinner, Tuesday-Sunday 5 to 9. Sunday brunch, 11 to 2.

The Up River Café, 37 Main St., Westerly, R.I.
Just across the Rhode Island state line is this stylish bistro in a restored woolen mill, with great food and a terrific waterside setting along the Pawcatuck River at the edge of downtown Westerly. Owners Daniel and Jennifer King from California added fireplaces in the casual, brick-walled River Pub as well as in a couple of the white-clothed dining rooms with large windows overlooking the water. They also added a large and perfectly idyllic dining patio beside the river on a peninsula with water on two sides. The regional American menu is so enticing that decisions are difficult. Typical main courses are Atlantic salmon marinated in miso and sake, seared Stonington sea scallops bearing a white truffle sauce on lobster-mushroom risotto, fire-roasted lamb chops with aged goat cheese and medallions of beef tenderloin with green peppercorn sauce. A burger on a baguette with house-made pickles and fries is among the offerings. So are such appetizers as a jonah crabmeat, spinach and artichoke gratin with house-made pita chips; Asian fried calamari with wasabi aioli, and a grilled pizza that changes daily. The lobster nachos with spicy homemade guacamole were sensational but more than one of us could finish for lunch. The other liked the signature crab cake sandwich with chipotle rémoulade on a house-made burger roll, a hefty, spilling-over-the-sides affair that leaves competitors in the dust. Neither of us had room for such desserts as guava crêpes with hot

passion fruit sauce, warm chocolate and banana bread pudding with Dan's drunken bourbon sauce, the Chickie's root-beer float or even the assorted cookie plate.

(401) 348-9700. Entrées, $18 to $28. Lunch daily, 11:30 to 5. Dinner nightly, 5 to 10.

Seafood Siblings by the Shore

Abbott's Lobster in the Rough, 117 Pearl St., Noank.

For more than 50 years, this old lobstering town has been the home of a lobster pound like those you dream of and too seldom find. People from all over manage to find their way to the hard-to-find spot at the mouth of the Mystic River, partly because of the delectable lobsters and partly because of the setting overlooking Fishers Island and Long Island Sound, with a constant parade of interesting craft in and out of Mystic Harbor. You sit outside at gaily colored picnic tables placed on ground strewn with mashed-up clam shells. You order at a counter and get a number – since the wait is often half an hour or more and the portions to come are apt to be small, bring along drinks and appetizers to keep you going. A 1¼-pound lobster (about $14.95) comes with coleslaw, a bag of potato chips and a paper bib. Also available are steamers, clam chowder, mussels, shrimp in the rough, lobster or crab rolls and a complete lobster feast. Adjacent shacks dispense desserts and shellfish from a raw bar. If lobsters aren't your thing, head to **Costello's Clam Shack,** just beyond in the Noank Shipyard, an open-air place beneath a blue and white canopy right over the water. Now owned by Abbott's (they're Abbott's and Costello's, in friendly competition with each other), it's smaller and less crowded. Most folks go there for the fried clams and fried scallops, served with french fries and coleslaw. Burgers, hot dogs and chicken sandwiches also are available.

(860) 536-7719. www.abbotts-lobster.com. Entrées, $15 to $23. Open daily, noon to 9, May to Labor Day; Friday-Sunday noon to 7, Labor Day to Columbus Day. BYOB.

Costello's: (860) 572-2779. Open daily, noon to 9, Memorial Day to Labor Day. BYOB.

Other Choices

Water Street Café, 143 Water St., Stonington.

City slickers and old salts pack former New York hotel chef Walter Hoolihan's hot spot, so much so that it traded spaces with Walter's Market & Deli across the street. The move produced larger quarters in an arty and funky, bright red and black dining area in front of a curving solid mahogany bar on one side and more tables in front of an old lunch counter on the other. From his somewhat larger new kitchen, Walter fulfills a with-it, contemporary, all-day menu, supplemented by specials that change nightly. Typical starters are lobster spring rolls with soy sauce, crab fritters with rémoulade sauce, tuna tartare, escargot pot pie, a prosciutto quesadilla and a warm duck salad with asparagus and sesame-orange dressing. London broil and sweet and sour spareribs conclude the all-day menu. Evening yields up to fifteen blackboard specials, usually including seared yellowfin tuna and the specialty duck and scallops with oyster mushrooms. Others could be pepper-seared halibut with roast corn-shiitake salsa, pan-roasted venison steak with crab cream sauce and rack of lamb with tequila-goat cheese sauce. Desserts vary from coconut-walnut-chocolate cake to crème caramel and poached pears with ginger ice cream.

(860) 535-2122. Entrées, $16.95 to $24.95. Breakfast, Friday and Monday 7 to 11:30 and Saturday and Sunday 8 to 2. Lunch, Thursday-Monday 11:30 to 2:30. Dinner nightly, 5:30 to 10 or 11.

Captain Daniel Packer Inne, 32 Water St., Mystic.

Once a stagecoach stop on the New York to Boston route, this shingled gray building with red door dating to 1756 is across the road from the river. Everyone enjoys the crowded tavern downstairs, where a light pub menu is served amid the original walls of brick and stone and a fire blazes in the huge fireplace three seasons of the year. The main floor exudes history in a couple of handsome dining rooms with working fireplaces and bare tables topped by formal mats portraying sailing ships. In the pub, longtime owners Richard and Lulu Kiley offer a varied lunch menu of chowders, salads, burgers, grilled pizzas and seafood, beef, poultry and pasta entrées. The dinner menu upstairs adds some twists, especially in terms of seafood: baked codfish with grilled pineapple chutney, roasted Atlantic salmon with basil sauce and red pepper confit, and grilled swordfish stacked with caramelized onions and fennel and finished with roasted red pepper coulis. Other entrées are more traditional: veal homard, sliced lamb with a raspberry-veal demi-glace and angus strip steak with a truffle demi-glace. All come with garden salad, baguettes and roasted garlic. Bailey's cream cheese cheesecake, turtle pie, double chocolate mousse and gelatos are favored desserts. A pub menu similar to that offered at lunch is available in the pub at dinnertime.

(860) 536-3555. www.danielpacker.com. Entrées, $19.95 to $29.95. Lunch daily, 11 to 4. Dinner, 5 to 10. Pub daily from 11.

Noah's, 113 Water St., Stonington.

This endearing restaurant – long known for good food, casual atmosphere and affordable prices – has been gussied up a bit lately. The once-funky double storefront now has fine art on the walls of the main dining room, where cherry booths beneath paddle fans and a tin ceiling draw the locals for three meals a day. A front room with a handsome horseshoe-shaped mahogany bar offers a bar menu. Owners Dorothy and John Papp post contemporary international specials daily to complement traditional dinners on the order of broiled flounder, cod Portuguese and grilled chicken. The night's numerous specials have been upscaled lately and are a tad pricier, as you'd expect for dishes like prosciutto-wrapped monkfish with chianti sauce, spice-rubbed mako shark, grilled bluefish with mango-lime relish, grilled rare salmon with wasabi and pickled ginger, and lobster and monkfish sauté. Seafood is featured, but you might find grilled brace of quail with chardonnay cream sauce or veal flank steak with pinot noir sauce. Save room for the scrumptious homemade desserts, perhaps chocolate-yogurt cake, bourbon bread pudding, or what one local gentleman volunteered was the best dessert he'd ever had: fresh strawberries with Italian cream made from cream cheese, eggs and kirsch.

(860) 535-3925. www.noahsfinefood.com. Entrées, $12.25 to $23.95. Breakfast, 7 to 11, Sunday to noon. Lunch, 11:15 to 2:30. Dinner, 6 to 9 or 9:30. Closed Monday.

Restaurant Bravo Bravo, 20 East Main St., Mystic.

Contemporary Italian fare is delivered with flair at this 50-seat restaurant with a new martini bar on the main floor of the Whaler's Inn. The extensive menu overseen by chef-owner Carol Kanabis rarely changes but offers plenty of excitement, especially among the specials. For dinner, grilled shrimp wrapped in prosciutto with skewered artichokes, seafood sausage stuffed with lobster and scallops, and sirloin carpaccio make good starters. Pastas include fusilli with shrimp in a sundried tomato-vodka sauce and black pepper fettuccine with grilled scallops, roasted tart apples and a gorgonzola alfredo sauce. Typical entrées are crab cakes topped with lobster-chive sauce, a saffron-seasoned seafood stew, osso buco and braised lamb shanks. Grilled local ostrich with a sweet corn sauce was a special at one visit. The lengthy dessert roster includes the obligatory tiramisu as well as tartufo, fruit napoleon with mascarpone cheese and ricotta cheesecake with grand marnier sauce.

(860) 536-3228. Entrées, $16.95 to $24.95. Lunch, Tuesday-Saturday 11:30 to 2:30, also Sunday in summer. Dinner, Tuesday-Sunday 5 to 9 or 10.

Seamen's Inne Restaurant & Pub, 65 Greenmanville Ave. (Route 27), Mystic.

Enormous numbers of people eat inside or out at this popular old warhorse, which keeps things humming in a variety of venues beside Mystic Seaport. The replica of a sea captain's house has two main dining rooms in front, both properly historic, and the casual Samuel Adams Pub at the side. In season, the place to be is the canopy-covered riverside terrace out back. We've always found the pub a fetching place for lunch or supper with its pressed-tin ceiling, bare wood floors and tables, and a side greenhouse window filled with plants. We liked a lunch of New England clam chowder (thick and delicious for $4.95 a bowl), the steamed mussels in a wine garlic sauce and shrimp and oyster pasta with a spicy cajun sauce (both $9.25). The dinner menu blends traditional New England fare with continental accents, from basic fish and chips to chicken saltimbocca and pepper-crusted filet mignon with gorgonzola cheese and port wine demi-glace. Baked codfish, Stonington fishermen's stew, seafood pot pie and baked stuffed lobster are among specialties.

(860) 572-5303. Entrées, $14.99 to $28.99. Lunch daily, 11:30 to 2:30. Dinner, 4:30 to 9 or 10.

┌─ *Hark to the Hearthside* ─────────

Randall's Ordinary, Route 2, North Stonington.

Relive the old days with a hearthside meal in this 1685 farmhouse secluded in the midst of 27 rural acres. The atmospheric restaurant offers Colonial-style food, cooked as it was 200 years ago and served by waitresses in period garb in three spartan dining rooms. For dinner, up to 75 patrons gather at 7 o'clock in a small taproom where they pick up a drink, popcorn, crackers and cheese. Then they watch cooks preparing their meals in antique iron pots and reflector ovens in an immense open hearth in the old keeping room. Dinner is prix-fixe with a choice of four or five entrées, perhaps roast capon with wild rice stuffing, roast ribeye beef, roast pork loin, hearth-grilled salmon and Nantucket scallops with scallions and butter – a signature dish that is truly exceptional. The meal includes soup (often onion or Shaker herb), anadama or spider corn bread, squash or corn pudding, a conserve of red cabbage and apples, and desserts like apple crisp, Thomas Jefferson's bread pudding or pumpkin cake. Lunch, with similar food but less fanfare, is à la carte.

(860) 599-4540 or (877) 599-4540. Prix-fixe, $39. Breakfast, Friday-Sunday, 7 to 11. Lunch, Friday-Sunday noon to 2 or 3. Dinner nightly, 5:30 to 9. Closed November-April.

FOR MORE INFORMATION: Mystic Chamber of Commerce, 14 Holmes St., Box 143, Mystic, CT 06355, (860) 572-9578 or (866) 572-9578. www.mysticchamber.org.

Mystic and Stonington are part of the Connecticut East Convention & Visitor's Bureau, 470 Bank St., New London, CT 06320, (860) 444-2206 or (800) 863-6569.

Information also is available from the Mystic Depot Welcome Center, 2 Roosevelt Ave., Mystic, (860) 572-1102.

Bucolic campus of Pomfret School typifies charm of the Quiet Corner.

Northeastern Connecticut

The Quiet Corner

When Northeastern Connecticut's tourism advocates were trying to decide what to call their region of rural hill towns and mill villages, someone suggested "The Quiet Corner." The name stuck.

This is indeed the quiet corner, a land of rolling hills and fertile farms, languishing towns and tranquil villages, and timeworn stone walls stretching endlessly into the distance. It's Connecticut's forgotten corner, in time and spirit far removed from the Hartford, Worcester and Providence metropolitan areas that threaten to encroach like triple pincers upon its country charms.

The Quiet Corner wasn't always quiet. Back in the 19th century, it was a fashionable resort area on the order of Lenox and Watch Hill. "Newport without the water," some called it. Wealthy New Yorkers and Bostonians summered in Pomfret and Woodstock on vast country estates with dreamlike names like Gwyn Careg, Courtlands and Glen Elsinore. Hard-scrabble mill towns prospered along the rivers, as did the mill owners who lived in the hill villages.

The 20th century took its toll on some of the area's inherent wealth. So did the move to the South of the textile mills upon which the local economy had been based. The quiet corner became the neglected corner.

But not for long. Area officials and the National Park Service turned their efforts toward forming a National Heritage Corridor to preserve "the last green valley" in the crowded Boston-to-Washington megalopolis. Pomfret and Woodstock and Brooklyn managed to retain their timeless pace and sense of place.

Meanwhile, sleepy Putnam, the county seat and once the area's leading mill town, reinvented itself. What had been a collection of empty downtown storefronts became the antiques center of New England. The change stimulated the locale's economy and its psyche. Newcomers with means and taste have followed in the footsteps of their 19th-century predecessors, imbuing the area with pockets of affluence.

But the changes that some lament locally are relative. The Quiet Corner remains the state's least-developed area – "classic New England without traffic or kitsch," as the New York Times once described it. "The Street" in Pomfret carries much of the grace of a century ago. A low-key sophistication is lent by Pomfret, the Rectory, Hyde and Marianapolis preparatory schools and the headquarters of firms like Crabtree & Evelyn, one of the area's largest employers.

The visitor has an opportunity to share in the good life here. You can stay in a gracious inn or a B&B brimming with history. Old-fashioned hospitality will be dispensed by your host – perhaps an artist, a chef, a furniture maker, a music lover, an architect or a teacher.

Activities and sightseeing come quietly here. You might want to venture north into Massachusetts to visit Old Sturbridge Village, the region's leading tourist attraction and a restored New England village of the 1830s. But outside the museum grounds within earshot of the Mass Pike, you will be accosted by 21st-century commercialism. You'll want to return to the Quiet Corner, if only for another day or two. Here the essence of old New England lives on, quietly and for real.

Seeing and Doing

Weathered barns and ancient stone walls in farm fields border the roads, evidence of the agricultural character of the region. The biggest annual events are the Brooklyn Fair the last weekend in August and the Woodstock Fair on Labor Day Weekend. Both are among the nation's longest-running agricultural fairs. A new tradition are the Walking Weekends staged every October to promote regional greenways and preserve "the last green valley" from encroaching development.

Enjoying the Countryside

Quinebaug-Shetucket Rivers Valley National Heritage Corridor, 107 Providence St., Putnam.

Much of the Quiet Corner is part of this National Heritage Corridor designated in 1994. The area's 25 towns are cooperating with the National Park Service to save "this relatively undeveloped rural island in the midst of the most urbanized region in the nation." Forests and farmland make up nearly three-fourths of the corridor's 695,000 acres, an area half the size of the Grand Canyon. Yet it is being squeezed, lying only an hour from three of New England's four largest metropolitan areas.

To show off this "resource of local, regional and national importance," the corridor committee schedules innovative **Walking Weekends** on the first two long weekends in October. Walk leaders include historians, college professors, foresters, authors, park rangers, archeologists, farmers and naturalists. They guide several thousand people on a total of more than 120 free walks, visiting mill towns, highlands, forests, farms, parks and more at the height of fall foliage season. One year there were even a bird walk, a fisherman's walk, a riverside botanical walk, a candlelight walk and a dog's walk (with adults on leash). Another year they took in a dairy farm, a bison herd, a tree farm, a corn maze, an old graveyard and a "lost village." The heritage corridor also publishes maps and guides for 32 choice outings on your own.

(860) 963-7226 or (866) 363-7226. www.lastgreenvalley.org.

Hill Towns and Mill Villages. A booklet of this name, prepared by the Association of Northeastern Connecticut Historical Societies, is a helpful adjunct for touring rural Woodstock, Pomfret, Brooklyn and Canterbury as well as the nearby mill towns of Thompson, Putnam, Killingly and Plainfield. We particularly enjoy "The Street" lined with the Pomfret School's academic buildings, churches and gracious homes in Pomfret and the stunning Thompson Hill common on, yes, a hilltop in Thompson. Woodstock is the area's ultimate hilltop village. Instead of a main street its chief feature is the Woodstock Hill green with a sweeping three-state view available behind the 1865 Woodstock Academy. The green is surrounded by an 1821 meetinghouse, a graveyard and fine old homes including the landmark Roseland Cottage (see below), with the large Woodstock Fairgrounds spreading out nearby.

The spine of the Quiet Corner is traversed by one of the prettiest roads in the country. Poke along **Scenic Route 169,** which meanders north-south from Woodstock to Canterbury, to discover the region's past. Buildings and land along both sides have been placed on the National Register. The 32-mile stretch is the longest officially designated scenic road in Connecticut and one of the only thirteen National Scenic Byways as designated by Congress.

Bicycling is popular in this area, and a local brochure has maps for ten distinct self-guided bicycle tours. Among the areas covered are Putnam Heights, Thompson, Pomfret-Woodstock, Canterbury-Scotland and Eastford-Ashford.

The **Air Line State Park Trail** is a National Recreation Trail on the abandoned Air Line Railroad bed from East Hampton through Pomfret and on to Putnam and the Putnam River Trail, a paved two-mile-long trail along the Quinebaug River. The Air Line Trail offers 30 miles of walking or biking in summer and cross-country skiing in winter.

Off scenic Route 169 is the **Connecticut Audubon Society Center at Pomfret,** 189 Pomfret St., (860) 928-4948. Its new nature center offers guided bird walks, wildlife programs and more. It adjoins Connecticut Audubon's little-known, 700-acre **Bafflin Sanctuary,** a vast expanse of meadows, forests, wetlands and grassland habitats and ten miles of nature trails. Bird watchers are in their element with red-tailed hawks, pileated woodpeckers, meadowlarks, bobolinks and such. The sanctuary is open daily, dawn to dusk. Center is open Wednesday-Saturday, noon to 4.

Mashamoquet Brook State Park, Route 44, Pomfret.

The 1,000-acre park offers picnicking, swimming, camping and a trail to the park's most famous feature, the **Wolf Den,** a cave into which local Revolutionary War hero Israel Putnam crept in 1742 and killed the last she-wolf that had preyed on sheep and poultry in northeastern Connecticut. A 4.7-mile trail leads to rock formations known as **Table Rock** and **Indian Chair,** the last atop a twenty-foot cliff with a view of the entire valley. At the entrance to the park is the **Brayton Grist Mill & Marcy Blacksmith Museum.** This example of a one-man mill operation survives from a time when water-powered grain mills were integral to every town. The milling equipment employed until 1928 remains in its original location. The fine blacksmithing tool collection belonged to three generations of the Marcy family.

(860) 928-6121. Trails open daily, dawn to dusk, free. Parking, $7 to $10 weekends in summer. Grist mill and museum open Saturday and Sunday 2 to 5, May-September. Free.

Historic Sites

Roseland Cottage, 556 Route 169, Woodstock.

If the Quiet Corner has an "attraction," this 1846 house may be it. And its thrusting gables and vivid pink facade stand in colorful contrast to the otherwise Colonial character of the attractive New England village. Woodstock native Henry C. Bowen, a New York merchant and publisher, was into roses and the Fourth of July. So he planted a formal garden with roses outside his summer house, upholstered much of its furniture in pink and named it Roseland Cottage. To his wild pink Gothic Revival mansion trimmed in gingerbread for his famous Independence Day celebrations came the day's luminaries, among them Ulysses S. Grant, Benjamin Harrison, Rutherford B. Hayes and William McKinley. Facing the village green, the house and its Gothic furnishings remain much as they were in the 19th century. The parterre garden, with 600 yards of dwarf boxwood edging, has survived since it was laid out in 1850. In the rear barn is the oldest extant bowling alley in a private residence; balls of varying sizes line the chute.

(860) 928-4074. Tours on the hour, Friday-Sunday 11 to 5, June to mid-October. Adults $8, children $4.

The Prudence Crandall Museum, Routes 14 and 169, Canterbury.
The site of New England's first academy for African-American girls has a fascinating history to reveal. Asked to educate their children, Prudence Crandall ran afoul of townspeople when she admitted such a girl in 1833. They withdrew their children, so she ran a boarding school for "young ladies and misses of color" until she was hounded out of town. Now a museum, the house is interesting for its architecture and three first-floor period rooms with exhibits on 19th-century Canterbury, African-Americans, Miss Crandall and women's history.

(860) 546-9916. Open Wednesday-Sunday 10 to 4:30, April to mid-December. Adults $2.50, children $1.50.

Churches and Schools. The spireless **Old Trinity Church** in Brooklyn, the oldest Episcopal church (1771) now standing in the oldest diocese in the country, is open some summer afternoons but is used only once a year on All Saints Day. Modeled after Trinity Church in Newport and King's Chapel in Boston, it is a favorite of photographers. The gem of an interior is all bare wood, which remains unpainted. Other little treasures are the Pomfret School chapel and the Tiffany windows in Pomfret's Christ Church. Also peek into the brick one-room **Quassett School** in Woodstock. The Pomfret and Rectory private schools offer pleasant campuses.

Daniel Putnam Tyler Law Office, Route 169, Brooklyn.
Amid the classic churches and homesteads of the Brooklyn Green historic district stands a statue of Israel Putnam, the local Revolutionary War hero ("he dared to lead where any dared to follow") who led the charge at Bunker Hill. Hidden behind is the one-room country lawyer's office where Putnam's great-grandson practiced from 1822 to 1875. It is maintained by the Brooklyn Historical Society.

(860) 774-7728. Open Memorial Day to Labor Day, Wednesday and Sunday 1 to 5. Free.

Putnam Elms, 191 Church St., Brooklyn
A side road from the green leads past the historic Trinity Church to the rambling house built in 1784 by Col. Daniel Putnam, son of Israel Putnam, and occupied by the Putnam family until 1953. Still maintained by Putnam descendants and open for tours, the house tells the story of a leading New England family from the Colonial era to this day. It holds antique furnishings, costumes and fine art.

(860) 774-3059 or 774-1567. www.putnamelms.org. Open Wednesday, Saturday and Sunday 1 to 4:30, July to mid-October. Adults $5, students $3.

Antiquing

Antiquing around the Quiet Corner has long been popular in pockets like Coventry and Eastford, but a major concentration has emerged in downtown Putnam, which now proclaims itself "The Antiques Capital of the Northeast."

It started in 1991 when Jerry Cohen subdivided the old Bugbee's department store at Main and Front streets into the **Antiques Marketplace,** renting space to 250 dealers on three floors and producing the largest group showroom in Connecticut. More than a dozen antiques stores quickly followed, and scores of antiquarians sell everything from tag-sale trinkets to fine furniture. Word spread that here was the antiques center of New England, if not the entire Northeast, stocking an incredible array of goods from antique clocks to lawn ornaments to railroad-crossing signals. The entire scene draws noted collectors and designers as well as dealers and common folk. On one floor of the 22,000-square-foot marketplace, Jerry Cohen shows the largest selection of antique Stickley furniture in New England at his **Mission Oak Shop.**

Down the street, the 30,000-square-foot **G.A. Renshaw Architecturals** features architectural antiques, furniture, salvage items and other major pieces in a variety of period rooms. **The Great Atlantic Auction Company** offers bars, fountains and statues for restaurant interiors. A former drug store has been turned into **Jeremiah's,** a large multi-dealer shop, now full of odds and ends. A former bank building has been transformed into the suave **Antiques Unlimited,** purveyor of quality furniture, accessories and silver, some at rather substantial prices. A camera shop became **The Little Museum Company.** A former A&P supermarket is now **Pink House Antiques,** crammed to the rafters with tag-sale schlock. Poke around town and you'll find your own discoveries.

There's no Starbucks here, but a prime corner spot in town was taken in 2004 by **Victoria Station Café,** 75 Main St. It's not yet a café but rather a full-scale coffee house that serves pastries, croissants, soups and light lunch, with tables outside beside a bucking horse statue, open daily from 7 a.m. to 9 or 11 p.m. More substantial fare, including full breakfast and lunch, is available at the **Pickled Pepper Café,** 172 Main St., open daily 6 to 2. Still more substantial family fare is offered at **The Courthouse Bar & Grille,** 121 Main St., open daily for lunch and dinner.

Live community theater performances are scheduled at the **Bradley Playhouse,** a restored century-old vaudeville theater at 30 Front St., (860) 928-7887.

A Bit of Britain

Mrs. Bridges' Pantry, 136 Main St., Putnam.

British antiques and books, yarns and such hard-to-find foods as haggis, bridies and salad cream are crammed into this expanding enterprise, which began as a weekend pantry in a multi-dealer antiques shop and now is a destination for those British in blood or spirit. For an afternoon pick-me-up during your antiquing rounds, know that it operates a snug tearoom serving everything British the British way. You can order elevenses (a pot of tea with biscuits), tea sandwiches, baked beans on toast, mini-cakes or a ploughman's lunch. The tearoom has expanded lately to provide more table space, or you can relax at a table on the sidewalk out front.

(860) 963-7040 or (888) 591-5253. www.mrsbridgespantry.com. Tea, $3 to $7.50. Open daily except Tuesday, 11 to 5.

SHOPPING. Until the Putnam Antiques District emerged, shopping was centered in South Woodstock. **Scranton's Shops,** a ramble of rooms in an 1878 blacksmith shop, is full of country wares from more than 90 local artisans. The array is mind-boggling, and we defy anyone to get out without a purchase. Nearby, **The Livery Shops** and **Garden Gate Florist** offer more small rooms given over to floral arrangements and local artisans who show their wares on consignment. At one visit, the impressive, one-of-a-kind items included an amusing picnic dish set with flies and ants painted on, the striking dishes of Majilly Designs, and the watercolors of innkeeper Tom McCobb, one of which inspired a surprised "hey, that's my house" from our tour guide. Other shoppers like **Coco's Cottage** for clothing and gifts, the **Flying Carpet Studio** for handcrafted rugs and canvases, and **Resourceful Judith** for garden ornaments. The **Gathering Basket** is a fresh food market and deli, and **Java Jive** offers lunch as well as coffee and music.

Garden-Related Endeavors

Farms and gardens flourish in the last green valley.

Horticulturalists will want to seek out **Logee's Greenhouses,** 141 North St., Danielson, (860) 774-8038 or (888) 774-8038. Push your way through the narrow paths past a jungle of greenery on all sides. On a chilly day, seeing all the orchids and begonias among 2,000 kinds of exotic indoor plants in thirteen greenhouses will warm your innards. Although this is a thriving commercial container-gardening enterprise, it's low-key and no one may know you're there. Joy Logee Martin, owner of the 100-year-old family business, is considered one of the great horticulturalists in the country. Open daily, 9 to 4.

In the center of Pomfret is **Martha's Herbary,** 589 Pomfret St., (860) 928-0009. Martha and Richard Paul have herb gardens outside, and devote much of the main floor of their historic house to a shop offering herbal gifts and "accessories in and out of the garden." Unusual varieties of herbs, perennials, heirloom vegetables and flowers are featured. Martha conducts workshops in herbal lore and decorating plus gourmet cooking classes in her demonstration kitchen.

Another kind of garden product is featured at **Sharpe Hill Vineyard,** 108 Wade Road, Pomfret. Steven Vollweiler, a New York business owner of German and French parentage, scoured the Northeast to find a microclimate perfect for wine grapes. He found it here on a 100-acre hill in the back of beyond. He and his wife Catherine planted 25 acres of vinifera grapes and built a big rust-colored barn to hold winemaking equipment and an 18th-century-style taproom furnished with antiques for tastings. Next came an outdoor wine garden for lunch and an attached tavern for gourmet meals (see Where to Eat). Winemaker Howard Bursen's wines have upstaged California's in blind tastings. After finally reaching the place, few visitors can leave without acquiring at least a bottle of chardonnay.

A new winery in the area is **Taylor Brooke Winery,** 848 Route 171, Woodstock. Richard Auger received a book on winemaking one Christmas, started making wine for friends, planted 2,000 vines and built a small barn to house his winery and shop.

On a 200-acre farm tucked in the highest hills of Ashford is **Westford Hill Distillers,** 196 Chatey Road, (860) 429-0464. Margaret and Louis Chatey set out to produce eau de vie, the prized brandy translated from the French for "water of life," from locally grown fruit as a way of preserving the family's rural homestead. Although not licensed for public sales or tours, Connecticut's first artisan distiller schedules open houses throughout the year.

An Excursion into Yesteryear

Old Sturbridge Village, 1 Old Sturbridge Village Road, Sturbridge, Mass.

One of New England's most popular attractions lies just across the Massachusetts state line, and most visitors to northeastern Connecticut take advantage. With great emphasis on authenticity, this 200-acre outdoor history museum re-creates a New England farming village of the 1830s. More than 40 restored buildings were relocated from various sections of New England, and a small house – the most common type of dwelling in early New England, but the originals now almost vanished from the landscape – was being erected on site in 2005. Throughout the village, costumed interpreters demonstrate life as it used to be. The meetinghouse dominates the common, around which are craft shops, homes, a bank, a law office and a country store. Paths lead to an area where grist and sawmills operate by water power. Nearby are a blacksmith and cooperage and a working historical farm. With a new focus on heritage breeds of farm animals, the village is now home to rare native pigs, cattle, sheep and chickens. Although Old Sturbridge is special any time, it's at its best in the fall, particularly around Thanksgiving, the traditional New England holiday. The shoemaker and his apprentice turn out low black boots in the shoe shop, their Shaker-style wood stove offering a pleasant blast of warmth on a chilly day. The preacher in Richardson Parsonage polishes up his Sunday sermon, while a teacher in felt top hat and black cape gives lessons at the schoolhouse. Tinners are at work on small coffee pots and pepper boxes that ultimately wind up in the village's large gift shop. You can eat at Bullard Tavern, where a cafeteria dispenses chowder, chicken pot pie and sandwiches, or order a snack on the patio at Nooning or the sweet shop Little Cakes in season. Or get a full meal at the new Oliver Wight Tavern, located next to the shops at the museum's entrance.

(508) 347-3362 or (800) 733-1830. www.osv.org. Open daily, 9:30 to 5 May-October and 9:30 to 4 in April, November and December; Wednesday-Sunday 9:30 to 4, January-March. Admission (valid for two consecutive days), adults $20, children $5. January-March, adults $12, children $5.

Where to Stay

The Inn at Woodstock Hill, 94 Plaine Hill Road, Box 98, South Woodstock 06267.

The 1816 Christopher Wren-style home of Henry Bowen, whose landmark shocking-pink summer cottage is up the road, imparts the atmosphere of an English manor house to this handsome country inn. The main living room, a library, the morning/TV room and a small dining room are a kaleidoscope of chintz fabrics, fine paintings, plush oriental rugs and tiled fireplaces. More Waverly floral chintz accents the prevailing peach, pink and blue color scheme in the 22 guest rooms. All are sleek and comfortable with reproduction antiques and wicker furniture, chairs and loveseats, TVs, thick carpeting and modern baths, some with double marble sinks. Six rooms have fireplaces and six have four-poster beds. An outside entrance leads to a cozy lounge, where colorful wine labels under glass top the bar. Here in a wing connected to a barn are two dining rooms that form the heart of the inn's restaurant (see Where to Eat). Warm mulled cider or lemonade and a decanter of sherry await guests in the afternoon. A continental-plus breakfast is served in the morning.

(860) 928-0528 or (866) 365-0002. Fax (860) 928-3236. www.woodstockhill.com. Twenty-two rooms with private baths. Doubles, $130 to $195.

The Mansion at Bald Hill, 29 Plaine Hill Road, Box 333, South Woodstock 06267. The 1892 shingled and stucco mansion that served as a summer cottage for the Bowen family has been opened to B&B guests by Peter and Sharon Cooper, who own the Harvest Restaurant in Pomfret, successor to their original restaurant known as Harvest at Bald Hill nearby. Off by itself on Bald Hill amid several acres of gardens, terraces and grounds, the 21-room mansion is a throw-back to the Gilded Age. The main floor with its ten-foot-high ceilings, plaster cornices and crown molding is a treasure trove of grand public areas: foyers and a music room paneled in hazelwood, a library of olive wood and a formal dining room of stained oak with floor-to-ceiling cabinets stocked with Bowen family china, silver and glassware. A parlor with one of the mansion's thirteen fireplaces opens onto both library and dining room as well as a wide stone terrace along the back of the house. While the public areas remain much as they have for more than a century, the Coopers have refurbished and updated the guest quarters on the second and third floors. They offer eight bedrooms and suites with private baths, and five smaller rooms with shared baths in the former servants' wing. Among the largest is Mrs. Bowen's Suite, with a majestic kingsize poster bed, a huge window seat in the bay window, TV hidden in the armoire, and a couple of wing chairs beside the fireplace. A tad smaller is Mr. Bowen's Room, with a kingsize sleigh bed, two wing chairs by the window and, beside the fireplace a plump white chair and a half with ottoman, which Sharon calls "a sweetheart chair" for two. Other rooms vary from the kingsize Wentworth – hard to believe it served as Mrs. Bowen's dressing room – to the smallest Garden Room, cheerful in coral tones with a queen bed and a modern bathroom. The Coopers prepare the likes of omelets, eggs benedict, Swedish pancakes and crème brûlée french toast for breakfast. Before or after, guests enjoy the formal gardens and grounds in a tranquil wooded setting.

(860) 974-3456. www.mansionatbaldhill.com. Four rooms and four suites with private baths and five rooms with shared baths. Doubles, $120 to $165, ($95 for shared bath). Suites, $150 to $200.

Celebrations Inn, 330 Pomfret St., Pomfret 06259.
An 1885 Queen Anne Victorian that was once a private school for girls is now "a festive B&B," as billed by owners Jean and Bill Barton. The couple were in corporate management and consulting and knew well how people need to "step back from the crazed corporate life," in Jean's words. "We provide a respite so they can celebrate the everyday pleasures." Here those pleasures begin on a wraparound porch that opens into a grand foyer with antique furnishings along the sides. Off one side of the foyer is a library with books and board games. Off the other side are a large parlor and an elaborate dining room, which opens past a sunny, plant-filled area onto a side deck overlooking restored gardens. Each of the common rooms has a working fireplace, as do two of the five upstairs guest accommodations. One is the Far East Suite with a canopied queensize iron bed, a few Asian treasures and a small sitting room. The other is the front-corner Sweet Celebrations, "our romance room," says Jean. It has a kingsize sleigh bed and the polished wood floors and colorful Thibault wallpapers characteristic of the house. The Lady Slipper Suite down its own side hallway offers a carved mahogany queen bed, a collection of whimsical footwear and a large sitting room with windows on three sides. Jean has fun decorating the house seasonally – at our visit she was changing the theme from Valentine's to St. Patrick's Day. She also treats guests to afternoon tea and her

homemade herbal cordials. Breakfast culminates in a main course like pepperoni breakfast pie or irish cream french toast.

(860) 928-5492 or (877) 928-5492. Fax (860) 928-3306. www.celebrationsinn.com. Three rooms and two suites with private baths. Doubles, $125 to $200. Suites, $175.

Friendship Valley, 60 Pomfret Road (Route 169), Box 845, Brooklyn 06234.

Prudence Crandall, the Canterbury educator who was hounded out of town for teaching African-American girls in her academy in the 1830s, named this Georgian-style country house Friendship Valley when it was occupied by one of her benefactors, abolitionist William Lloyd Garrison, who married Helen Benson in the living room. Now the antiques-filled guest rooms are named for the five families to which the house has belonged over its illustrious 200 years. Architect Charles Yates and his wife Beverly, transplanted Texans, bought the house to run as a B&B full of Southern hospitality in a bucolic valley of twelve wooded acres and wetlands near what passes for the center of tiny Brooklyn. The prime accommodation is the Prince Suite, transformed from a wood shed at the rear of the main floor, with a cathedral ceiling, queen mahogany rice poster bed, a jacuzzi tub and a private entrance. Four more bedrooms, three with fireplaces, are located upstairs in the main house. They convey a decidedly historic but comfortable feeling, from the antique twin beds from France in the Wendel Room to the step-up queensize four-poster in the Benson. Guests enjoy two small front parlors, one a library and the other a fireplaced living room with TV hidden in a cabinet. Beyond are a formal dining room and a lovely sun porch overlooking the gardens. These are the settings for a hearty breakfast culminating in eggs, quiche, pancakes or baked french toast. Beverly also offers tea and dessert in the afternoon or evening.

(860) 779-9696. www.friendshipvalleyinn.com. Four rooms and one suite with private baths. Doubles, $140 to $170.

Cobbscroft, 349 Pomfret St. (Route 169), Pomfret 06258

This rambling white house almost up against the road is home to artists Janet and Tom McCobb as well as a gallery for the works of watercolorist Tom, who has a studio in the rear barn, and those of artist-friends. The McCobbs receive guests in a library with a gorgeous needlepoint rug and deep shelves full of books and a TV. Beyond is a large gallery/living room hung with a variety of art, all for sale and all very enticing. Some is by Janet, who paints furniture, decorative objects and frames in a faux style. Tom's watercolors adorn the white walls of an airy gallery/parlor. Off the library are a double and a single guest room joined by a bathroom, rented as a family suite. Upstairs are three more guest rooms. One with twin beds has lacy white spreads and curtains, a sofa and knickknacks including little dolls. Janet's charming stenciling enhances a front corner room with a four-poster bed, a chaise lounge and a most unusual oval clawfoot tub. Over the living room is the bridal suite, a wondrous affair with windows on three sides, a working fireplace, loveseat, dressing table and a bed covered in frilly white linens. Two wooden chickens and a collection of lambs are among the country touches in the dining room, where guests breakfast on eggs, quiche or strata at a long table. In the afternoon, the McCobbs serve tea with cinnamon toast or fruit bread and offer a drink. Guests help themselves to brandy in the living room after dinner.

(860) 928-5560. www.cobbscroft.com. Three rooms and a two-room family suite with private baths. Doubles, $90. Suite, $125.

Daniel Trowbridge House, 193 Hampton Road (Route 97 North), Pomfret Center 06259.

More than most, this distinctive B&B on an 80-acre working farm lives up to the cliché, "a step back in time." Chickens are apt to join furniture maker Tom Campbell as he emerges from the barn to lead guests into the antiques-filled house that he and his wife, Cris Cadiz, share with overnight guests in three atmospheric guest quarters. Tom's carpentry talents are everywhere evident in the 1730s Colonial house that the couple, barely out of college, turned into a welcoming home. The dining room holds his fabulous chestnut farm table for eight, a side table and a corner cupboard. The bedrooms harbor his handmade beds. There's a queensize poster bed in the front-corner Rufus Porter Room, in which a local artist painted an antique wrap-around mural bearing all the original elements of the 19th-century itinerant artist. A friend painted a primitive yet realistic mural of the rural scene outside the window in the front-corner Colonial Room, which has a queensize turned-post bed and the original pumpkin pine floor. The entire back of the second floor is given over to the spacious North Suite, where a new bath with shower goes off the queen bedroom and a sitting room across the foyer has a murphy-style bed. Guests hang out in a charming living room with a woodstove. The couple's chickens furnish fresh eggs for breakfast. Cris employs the bounty from her gardens to prepare omelets with fresh herbs, fruit crêpes and blueberry pancakes. She offers beverages and local wines in the evening. The back yard descends to a farm pond, and Tom has cut walking paths so guests can explore the rolling countryside.

(860) 974-3622. www.danieltrowbridgehouse.com. Two rooms and one suite with private baths. Doubles, $135. Suite, $165. Two-night minimum required.

B&B at Taylor's Corner, 880 Route 171, Woodstock 06281.

The inside of this restored 18th-century center-chimney Colonial is ever so historic, and the five acres outside are awesome. Walk out the rear of what once was the front of the house and you're greeted by stunning perennial gardens and even a pet cow. Owners Peggy and Doug Tracy offer B&B guests a rural experience. Inside the house, which is listed on the National Register of Historic Places, are eight working fireplaces and two beehive ovens, one in the front keeping room. Beyond is a formal parlor with TV; on a wall the Tracys have framed a mysterious confession found hidden between bricks in the chimney and written by someone seeking forgiveness in 1795. Across the hall is a large, fireplaced dining room with hooked rugs on the floors and Hitchcock chairs at a table for six. Here Peggy serves breakfast on her collection of fine Danish porcelain – continental on weekdays, supplemented by entrées like oven omelets, french toast or Finnish pancakes on weekends. Up creaky stairs are two spacious rear bedrooms with queensize beds angled from the corners. A third bedroom in front has a queen and a twin bed. All have fireplaces and telephones. Stuffed animals are on each bed, and colorful comforters, antique chairs, bedside candies and fresh flowers are the norm.

(860) 974-0490 or (888) 503-9057. Fax (860) 974-0498. www.taylorsbb.com. Three rooms with private baths. Doubles, $125 to $140 weekends, $95 midweek.

Elias Child House, 50 Perrin Road, Woodstock 06281.

This rambling house began as one room in 1714 and grew into a handsome center-hall Colonial, surrounded by 40 bucolic acres. Nine fireplaces, including two walk-in cooking hearths in which the innkeepers prepare snacks and dinners, are original. So are twelve-over-twelve windows with the original wavy glass, wide-board floors, paneling and wainscoting. The old indoor privy, a mark of wealth in the 18th century, is still part of a screened porch. Upstairs is the rambling Aimee suite, which begins with a queen bed and a twin bed and offers an antique crib in an alcove between bed chamber and sitting room, both of which have fireplaces. Across from the suite is Polly's Room, again with a fireplace and a queen bed topped with a quilt. Caroline's Room on the main floor has a queen bed and a three-quarter bed plus a fireplace. Innkeepers Tony and MaryBeth Gorke-Felice serve a hearty country breakfast and optional dinners by reservation. The Felices employ 18th-century recipes for their hearth-cooking demonstrations. Guests help prepare their meal, which might consist of onion soup, roast chicken or turkey, garlicked potatoes, carrots with ginger root and Colonial lavender cake.

(860) 974-9836 or (877) 974-9836. Fax (860) 974-1541. www.eliaschildhouse.com. Two rooms and one suite with private baths. Doubles, $105 and $110. Suite, $135.

Feather Hill Bed & Breakfast, 151 Mashamoquet Road (Rte 44), Pomfret 06258.
Birds abound in on this eight-acre property that abuts the Mashamoquet State Park and the Air Line Rail Trail. That attracted Angela and Fred Spring to purchase the 1936 center-hall Colonial house and turn it into a B&B with accommodations named for birds. They share their large house with guests in three country-frilly bedrooms with queen beds, one with a whirlpool tub, and the Dove Nest suite, also with whirlpool tub. A large swimming pool area separates the main house from the Feather Nest Cottage, which has a queen bedroom, living room with sofabed, fireplace and TV, kitchen and dining room. Its deck overlooks the pool, which also is on view from the four-season Pavilion porch off the fireplaced parlor in the main house. Baked fruit compote is the signature dish at breakfast, when guests sometimes spot turkey or deer running in the fields.

(860) 963-0522 or (866) 963-0522. www.featherhillbedandbreakfast.com. Three rooms, one suite and one cottage with private baths. Doubles, $100 to $148. Suite, $175. Cottage, $200.

Where to Eat

The Harvest, 37 Putnam Road, Pomfret.
The Harvest at Bald Hill, a longtime local favorite, is better than ever in its large and stylish quarters at a prime Pomfret location. Peter Cooper, a former chef at the Brown University faculty club in Providence, took over a 1765 house and built a substantial addition. The establishment focuses on an open lounge with a cherry wood bar and several dining tables in the center, a semi-open kitchen and a floor-to-ceiling wall of wines showcasing the Harvest's award-winning wine cellar at the entry. Around the periphery are a grill room with a fireplace, a couple of handsome fireplaced dining rooms, two dining porches, a cocktail terrace and a banquet facility. The menu changes seasonally to reflect the harvest. Main courses vary widely from cedar-planked roast salmon with ginger butter and seared yellowfin tuna with a pineapple-teriyaki glaze to roast duckling with orange-raspberry sauce, tenderloin of pork au poivre, the signature grilled lamb with rosemary and garlic, and eight versions of steaks and chops. The emphasis on the harvest shows up spectacularly in the vegetable and bean sauté, the Pacific Rim vegetable grill and the roasted vegetable roulade Santa Fe. An extensive menu of Japanese cuisine, including

sushi by a Japanese chef, is offered with the regular menu Sunday-Thursday. A bistro menu is offered weekdays in the Black Cat Lounge.

(860) 928-0008. www.harvestrestaurant.com. Entrées. $17.95 to $27.95. Dinner, Tuesday-Saturday 5 to 8:30 or 9. Sunday, brunch 11 to 1:45, dinner 3 to 8.

The Inn at Woodstock Hill, 94 Plaine Hill Road, South Woodstock.

Hearty continental/American fare is offered by German chef-owner Richard Naumann in the inn's restaurant in a carriage house beside the 1816 Christopher Wren-style home of the Bowen family that founded Woodstock. The carriage house contains a cozy lounge, a small dining room with banquettes draped in chintz and a long and narrow main dining room with windows onto fields and woods. The extensive menu features dishes like blackened tuna steak with spicy creole sauce, pecan-encrusted red snapper with cranberry salsa, grilled duck breast with a cognac-bordelaise sauce, roast pork tenderloin with cranberry-peach chutney, and baked rack of lamb dijon. A few sandwiches and salads supplement a dinner-like luncheon menu, with main courses ranging from oriental chicken stir-fry to filet mignon with green peppercorn sauce. One of us ordered the day's pasta off the appetizer list, a fine dish of ravioli stuffed with mushrooms and a sundried tomato sauce. The other sampled the chicken dijon sandwich topped with mushrooms, bacon and cheese, an ample plateful that proved too much to finish. Desserts included Dutch hazelnut cake, white amaretto mousse and chocolate-almond torte laced with grand marnier.

(860) 928-0528. www.woodstockhill.com. Entrées, $18 to $35. Lunch, Tuesday-Saturday 11 to 2, April-December. Dinner, Monday-Saturday 5 to 9. Sunday, brunch 11 to 2, dinner 3:30 to 7.

A Taste of the French Countryside

Sharpe Hill Vineyard, 108 Wade Road, Pomfret.

Meals of distinction are offered in a part-time restaurant at this small, emerging winery owned by New Yorkers Steven and Catherine Vollweiler. After sampling wines in a tasting room that looks like a taproom of the 1700s, the serious adjourn by reservation to eat inside in a twelve-table fireside tavern attached to the winery or outside in an idyllic, umbrella-tabled wine garden, beside vineyards climbing 700 feet up Sharpe Hill. Catherine, the executive chef, is known for definitive cuisine, including a superior ratatouille, curried chicken salad and hearth-cooked winter stews. Lunch is served her way – that is to say, the big meal of the day – at seatings at noon and 3. "You can't get a sandwich but rather a beautiful meal to experience what wine is really for," says she. If you want something light, she might suggest grilled sea bass with a boiled white potato drizzled with virgin olive oil, paired with a glass of chardonnay and followed by a green salad. Want something heartier? How about smoked trout, followed by Jamaican-jerked chicken with papaya salsa or wood-grilled lamb chops, and perhaps a fruit and cheese platter or one of the desserts delivered fresh from a New York bakery. The choice of eight entrées on the à la carte menu changes weekly. On Friday nights in summer, the winery offers weekly theme dinners. Dinner is served weekends the rest of the year. Day or night, the experience is a taste of the French countryside in northeastern Connecticut.

(860) 974-3549. www.sharpehill.com. Lunch by reservation, Friday-Sunday in summer, Sunday in winter, seatings at noon and 3. Entrées, $22 to $28.

Dinner by reservation, Friday at 6:30 or 7, second Friday of the month in summer, every Friday and Saturday in winter. Entrées, $26 to $34.

The Vine Bistro, 85 Main St., Putnam.

This contemporary American bistro and martini bar is a favorite of shoppers in the heart of Putnam's burgeoning antiques district. Lisa Cassettari oversees a stark white space accented with blond wood tables (dressed with white linens at night) and large, colorful paintings done by a local artist. The name reflects her aim to serve fresh fare, as in the vineyard proverb: "The grape is most delightful when first picked from the vine." At lunch, things get off to a fine start when plates puddled with olive oil, garlic and rosemary arrive for soaking up the good, crusty bread. There is quite a selection of soups, sandwiches and salads, including a caesar salad served with Maryland crab cakes. The specialty vodka rigatoni is first-rate. Others in our party sampled an appetizer of portobello mushrooms sautéed with spinach, roasted peppers, tomatoes, garlic and olive oil, and a generous sandwich of turkey, swiss and whole berry cranberry sauce. A sensational finale was tangerine sorbet, served in a frozen tangerine on a big white plate squiggled with raspberry puree. Pumpkin cheesecake laced with cognac was another winner. Much the same fare is available at dinner, minus the sandwiches and plus half a dozen specials. Expect treats like vodka rigatoni with jumbo shrimp, sautéed salmon with a velvety dill sauce, "chicken d'vine" with artichoke hearts, veal marsala and locally raised duckling.

(860) 928-1660. Entrées, $17.95 to $27.95. Lunch, Tuesday-Sunday 11 to 4. Dinner, Tuesday-Saturday 5 to 9, Sunday 5 to 7.

The Vanilla Bean Café, 450 Deerfield Road (Junction of Routes 169, 44 and 97), Pomfret.

A popular little café in a 150-year-old yellow barn, this is a "true" place run by Barry Jessurun and siblings Eileen (Bean) and Brian, with occasional appearances by the rest of the family. You order at a counter and your choice is delivered to one of the butcher-block tables with bentwood chairs inside or, on nice days, to the patio out front, where outdoor grill items may be available. The eclectic menu includes an award-winning chili, hearty soups, great sandwiches, Brian's signature fish cakes and blackboard specials like gumbo, buffalo burger, beef stew and quiche. We enjoyed the turkey sandwich which, the menu advised, is not "that awful turkey roll but the real thing," along with the half and half, a mug of assertive sausage and turkey gumbo and half a roast beef sandwich with the works. The desserts are rich: brownies and hot fudge sundaes, perhaps, or even a milk shake. The dinner menu might add a large bean burrito, a tasso ham and andouille sausage quesadilla, chicken teriyaki with vegetables, smoked mozzarella and basil ravioli, even grilled swordfish with a fennel-daikon citrus salad or grilled ribeye steak with mushroom pan sauce. Beer, wine and espresso also are available at this fun-loving, unpretentious place, where everyone from students to farmers in pickup trucks seems to hang out. There's live musical entertainment after dinner on Fridays and Saturdays, starting about 8.

(860) 928-1562. www.vanillabeancafe.com. Entrées, $11 to $19. Open Monday and Tuesday 7 to 3, Wednesday-Friday 7 to 8, weekends 8 to 8, later on music nights and in summer.

Jessica Tuesday's, 35 Main St., Putnam.

The specials are in particular demand at Jessica Jellison's casual café and deli situated in an endearing adjunct to the old Putnam railroad station. We learned the hard way, arriving late for a Friday lunch when all the soups and enticing blackboard specials were gone. We settled for a chicken caesar wrap, which was okay, and a chef's salad that was a travesty in a bowl. The assorted cakes, cookies and Italian pastries are baked daily, but again the pickings near the end of the day were slim. The setting at bistro tables amid antique décor and the outdoor deck are quite appealing, which accounts for the loyal patronage.

(860) 928-5118. www.jessicatuesdays.com. Salads and sandwiches, $4.50 to $6.95. Open Tuesday-Friday 7:30 to 3:30, Saturday 9 to 3.

— A Mid-Summer Night's Dream

The Golden Lamb Buttery, Hillandale Farm, 499 Wolf Den Road, Brooklyn.

For more years than we can remember, this has been our most cherished restaurant. We love it for summer lunches, when the surrounding fields and hills look like a Constable painting. We love it for weekend evenings, when we have cocktails on a hay wagon driven by a tractor through the fields and listen to the pure voice of a folksinger who plays her guitar. We love fall lunches and dinners ensconced beside the glowing fireplace in the barn. We especially love the Elizabethan madrigal dinners served in December, when a group of renaissance singers carol through the rooms and pork tenderloin is a festive main course. And everyone loves Jimmie and Bob Booth, the octogenarian owners of the farm on which the restaurant stands – she the wonderful chef and he the affable host at this, his family farm. Weekend dinners are the main deal, and you can tell as you enter through the barn, where a 1953 Jaguar convertible is displayed among such eclectic items as a totem pole and a telephone booth, that you are in for an unusual treat. Step out on the back deck and gaze over the picturesque scene as waitresses in long pink gingham skirts show the blackboard menu ($65 prix fixe) and take your order. When you are seated following the hayride, the table is yours for the evening. The leisurely meal starts with some knockout soups that Jimmie makes with herbs from her garden. There's a choice of four entrées, always duck and often salmon, châteaubriand and lamb. These are accompanied by six to eight vegetables served family style and, for us, almost the best part of the meal. Marinated mushrooms and cold minted peas are forever among them and, depending on the season, you might find celery braised with fennel, carrots with orange rind and raisins, tomatoes with basil and lime juice, or a casserole of zucchini and summer squash with mornay sauce. Dessert could be lemon or grand-marnier mousse. Add classical music or folksongs and a bottle of wine from Bob's choice selection for a fantasy-like experience. Weekday lunch offers a sampling of Jimmie's cooking (entrées, $13 to $18, like seafood crêpes, salmon quiche, the delicious Hillandale hash and Londonderry pork stew) without the evening magic, but with a charm all its own.

(860) 774-4423. Prix-fixe, $65. Lunch, Tuesday-Saturday noon to 2:30. Dinner, Friday and Saturday, one seating at 7:30. Dinner reservations required far in advance. Closed January-March. No credit cards.

FOR MORE INFORMATION: Eastern Connecticut Regional Tourism District, 470 Bank St., New London, CT 06320, (860) 444-2206 or (888) 628-1228. www.ctquietcorner.org.

Cornelius Vanderbilt's Breakers is largest oceanfront mansion along Newport's Cliff Walk.

Newport, R.I.

A Wealth of History

History combines with water and wealth to make Newport probably the single most varied town in New England. Here in one roughly ten-square-mile area are seashore, history, architecture, culture, affluence, hotels and inns, shops and restaurants in both quantity and variety that are the envy of cities many times its size.

As an early and prosperous seaport dating to 1639, Newport contains more pre-Revolutionary buildings than any other in America – more than New York, Boston and Philadelphia combined. The quaint Point and Historic Hill sections hold an unrivaled array of Colonial houses. Most are restored, signed and lived-in, some are open to the public, and all are a delight to view on walking tours as you literally step back in time.

There are some of the nation's oldest public buildings and edifices as well: the 1763 Touro Synagogue, the oldest house of Jewish worship in the country; the Christopher Wren-inspired Trinity Church (1726), which has the second oldest organ in the country; the 1739 Old Colony House, locally believed to be the real Independence Hall (Rhode Island was the first colony to separate from Britain and the Declaration of Independence was read from its balcony); the 1748 Redwood Library, oldest in the country, and the 1741 Newport Artillery Company Armory and Museum, headquarters of the oldest militia organization in America. The Old Stone Mill in Touro Park is believed by some to have been built by Norsemen in the 11th century.

Newport's wealth of history was crowned during its second heyday following the Civil War. The Astors, Vanderbilts, Morgans and others of America's 400 built summer "cottages" near the ocean along Bellevue Avenue, creating a society resort unmatched for glitter and opulence. Now opened to the public, America's largest collection of what Europeans would call palaces draws visitors by the thousands.

What links both eras of Newport's history and makes it so engaging for today's visitor is, of course, the ocean. Newport is at the southern tip of Aquidneck Island, surrounded by water on three sides. The restored waterfront areas off America's Cup Avenue and Lower Thames Street are great for browsing, shopping and viewing yachts. Out Ten-Mile Drive are today's mansions – large homes (some strikingly contemporary) showing that Newport hasn't lost its luster. The road connects with Bellevue Avenue to give walkers, bikers and motorists a front-door view of mansions and ocean. Walk the Cliff Walk for even better views.

There's a wealth of things to keep you busy. Tour the mansions along Bellevue Avenue, bicycle the Ten-Mile Drive, visit the old Newport Casino that's now the International Tennis Hall of Fame, see the legacies of the America's Cup races. Explore the old Touro Synagogue and the Green Animals topiary garden, take the self-guided history tours, savor the seafood, browse through the shops, ogle the yachts, swim in the ocean and revel in all that is Newport. There's something for everyone here. That 's what makes it such a great getaway destination.

Seeing and Doing

The Mansions

Nowhere else in this country can such a concentration of Gilded Age mansions be found. Created by America's leading architects for America's wealthiest families, the best are open for tours and few visitors fail to take in at least one. Most are strung along leafy **Bellevue Avenue,** which is paved with concrete and lined with brick sidewalks, gas lights and utility poles with a period look. Some are illuminated by floodlights at night.

MANSION TOURS. The Preservation Society of Newport County, 424 Bellevue Ave., offers guided tours of its nine mansions and a topiary garden. All are open daily in summer, and most in spring and fall (details below).

The Breakers, 44 Ochre Point Ave., is the 72-room seaside summer home of Cornelius Vanderbilt II, patriarch of America's wealthiest family. It is the most opulent of Newport's "cottages" and the most visited. Architect Richard Morris Hunt modeled it after a northern Italian palazzo with a vast lawn stretching down to the Cliff Walk. Built in a mere two years (1893-95), it was an extravagant place for a man described as quiet, kind and a pillar of his church – ironically, he was disabled by a stroke in 1896, was unable really to enjoy his summer home, and died in 1899. Tour highlights are the lower and upper loggias (from the upper on a clear day you can see the Elizabeth Islands far out to sea), the 45-foot-high Great Hall, an immense tapestry on the landing of the grand staircase (softly illuminated by a stained-glass ceiling), a magnificent 42-by-58-foot dining room, and a music room totally executed in Paris and shipped to this country. Upstairs, the bedrooms are comparatively modest, but the bathtubs had a choice of fresh or salt water. Also on view are the kitchens and butler's pantries, an area bigger than most houses. The **Breakers**

Stable and Carriage House shows Vanderbilt family memorabilia, including several horse carriages and a model train exhibit.

Rosecliff, 548 Bellevue Ave. Rosecliff's reputation as the most romantic mansion wasn't hurt by the fact that "The Great Gatsby" wooed Mia Farrow here. The house was designed by Stanford White to resemble the Grand Trianon of Louis XIV in Versailles, and finished in 1900 for Mrs. Hermann Oelrichs, an heiress whose father made his fortune in Virginia City as one of a partnership that struck the Comstock Lode. She was considered one of the three great hostesses of Newport and is said to have spent $25,000 each summer on perfume to fill the light fixtures. The living room could double as a ballroom – at 80 by 40 feet, it was the largest in Newport and was the scene of many lavish balls. The grand staircase is graceful, heart-shaped and appropriately romantic looking. Rosecliff is sometimes rented for various functions; we enjoyed cocktails on the terrace during a New England press convention some years ago and felt elegant indeed.

The Elms, 367 Bellevue Ave. Built in 1901 for coal baron Edward J. Berwind by Philadelphia architect Horace Trumbauer in the classical style of 18th-century France, this palatial structure is considered one of the finest homes in America, partly because of its balanced architectural plan. It doesn't exactly have a lived-in look; in fact, the Elms is more like a museum, with some furniture on loan from the Metropolitan Museum. The large proportions of the rooms, especially the entrance hall and ballroom, are awesome. Yet the conservatory is perfectly charming, bright and cheerful, with a marble fountain, statues in the corners and a gigantic marble urn. As befits a coal baron, Mr. Berwind had tracks for a coal car under his house; the car could be pushed out to the road where it would be filled with coal, thus ensuring no unsightly coal delivery on the property. He also generated his own electricity. The grounds are thought to be the finest of the Newport mansions, with specimen trees, a sunken garden, marble teahouses, statuary, fountains, and labeled trees and shrubs.

Marble House, 596 Bellevue Ave. Considered the most sumptuous of the "cottages," Marble House was completed in 1892 for William K. Vanderbilt, younger brother of the Vanderbilt who built the Breakers. Architect Richard Morris Hunt modeled it after the Petit Trianon at Versailles. The cost was reported in press accounts at the time to be $11 million, of which $7 million was spent on marble alone. Vanderbilt gave it as a 39th birthday present to his wife Alva, who envisioned it as her "temple to the arts" in America. All the original Louis XIV furnishings are here, and the ballroom is practically covered in gold. The society hostess once gave a ten-course dinner party for more than 100 of her best friends' dogs, which came to dinner in party dress. Later she had a Chinese tea house built on the seaside cliff, where she hosted rallies for women's right to vote.

Chateau-sur-Mer, 474 Bellevue Ave. The original villa, built in 1852 and the most palatial Newport residence until the Vanderbilt mansions came along, was extensively redone by Richard Morris Hunt twenty years later. William Wetmore, who made a fortune in the China trade, was the first owner. His son, George Peabody Wetmore, a Rhode Island governor and senator, inherited it, and his daughter Edith lived here until her death in 1968. It is considered a fine example of lavish Victorian architecture. Light streams into the galleried, three-story-high entrance hall through a stained glass skylight. Although much of the interior is quite dark, at least it feels lived in. A collection of Victorian toys enchants younger visitors.

Kingscote, 253 Bellevue Ave. A picturesque cottage by architect Richard Upjohn in the Gothic Revival style, Kingscote is one of the very early summer residences remaining, having been built in 1839. A McKim, Mead and White dining room was added in a new wing in 1881. It's one of the nicest rooms of all the mansions, decorated with Tiffany glass tiles and stained-glass panels of dahlias. Since one of the two owners of the house was in the China trade, there's a fabulous collection of Chinese export ware. The house was left to the Preservation Society in 1972 with most of its furnishings intact. It looks lived-in and thoroughly livable.

Also opened by the Preservation Society are the 1860 Italianate villa **Chepstow** designed by local architect George Champlin Mason, the shingle-style 1881 **Isaac Bell House** (a restoration work in progress), the 1748 **Hunter House** in the historic Point section and the **Green Animals** topiary garden in nearby Portsmouth (see below).

(401) 847-1000. www.newportmansions.org. Mansion schedules vary: all open daily 10 to 5 (Breakers 9 to 5), mid-June to mid-September; major mansions open daily mid-April to mid-November; Breakers, Elms and Marble House open daily, mid-November to Jan. 2; Rosecliff open daily and Breakers and Elms open weekends, January to mid-April. Admission: Breakers (including Stables), adults $15, children $4. Any other single property, adults $10, children $4. Combination tickets to five properties, adults $31, children $10.

Several other mansions are open to visitors under private auspices:

The Astors' Beechwood, 580 Bellevue Ave., is the most extravagant. Built in 1857 as an Italian seaside villa, this was purchased in 1880 by the William Backhouse Astors, at the time the richest family in America. Mrs. Astor coined the phrase "the 400," because that's how many her ballroom in New York could hold. In 1890 she took $2 million, went to the Continent and had sent back to her mansion a music room from France, a dining room from an English manor house, and a ballroom that is a replica of one in a Viennese palace. Insisting upon being called "*The* Mrs. Astor," she had 281 diamonds in her stomacher and looked like a walking chandelier, according to our tour guide. The house is one of the most recent to be restored and opened to the public; the owners have tracked down many of the original furnishings. Beechwood Theater Company actors portray Mrs. Astor's family, friends and domestic staff at the height of the Victorian Era.

(401) 846-3772. www.astors-beechwood.com. Open daily 10 to 5, mid-May through October; special Victorian Christmas hours, early November to mid-December; Friday-Sunday 10 to 4, rest of year. Adults $15, children $10.

Belcourt Castle, 657 Bellevue Ave. The summer home of Oliver Hazard Perry Belmont and his wife, the former Mrs. William K. Vanderbilt, was built in 1891 at a cost of $3 million by (who else?) Richard Morris Hunt in the style of Louis XIII's palace. Since 1956, the castle has been the home of the Tinney family and a place to display their 2,000 art treasures and antiques from 33 countries. There's a fine collection of stained glass and a golden coronation coach that weighs four tons – imagine what that would be worth these days! Costumed guides take you around, and Mrs. Tinney leads a special owner's tour Tuesday and Friday at 2:30. Candlelight or ghost tours are given nightly except Tuesday for $15.

(401) 846-0669. www.belcourtcastle.com. Open daily except Tuesday, noon to 5. Adults $10, children $5.

Rough Point, 680 Bellevue Ave.
This impressive mansion on a windswept oceanfront promontory near the far end of the Cliff Walk was left by her father in 1925 to twelve-year-old Doris Duke,

his only child and considered the richest heiress in the world. It became one of her private retreats and the public was never allowed inside until 2000. Now it's open for 90-minute guided tours under auspices of the Newport Restoration Foundation, founded and funded in 1968 by Doris Duke. The foundation eventually preserved 84 houses and now administers the Samuel Whitehorne House Museum and Prescott Farm. Unchanged since Miss Duke's death in 1993, the huge mansion remains a time capsule, reflecting her extraordinary collections of fine and decorative arts and furniture, displayed in their original setting. Rough Point is not accessible by auto. A courtesy shuttle bus departs every twenty minutes from the Gateway Visitor Center, where tickets are obtained

(401) 847-2448 or (401) 849-7300. www.newportrestoration.com. Tours, Tuesday-Saturday 10 to 3:20, April to early November. Admission, $25.

The Samuel Whitehorne House, 416 Thames St.
Built in 1811, this restored Federal-style mansion is the only one of its era in Newport open to the public. It features a hipped roof, circular entry portico, a grand center hall and a formal garden, but is of most interest as the home of Doris Duke's wide-ranging collection of early Newport furniture. She gathered it together because she felt too little was on display in the city of its origin. Excellent examples of richly carved handcrafted furniture from the workshops of cabinetmakers like the Townsends and Goddards, who lived and worked in the town's Point section, are shown in period settings.

(401) 847-2448. Open late April through October, Thursday-Monday 11 to 4, weekends from 10. Adults $10, children $4.

Historic Sites

Newport has more than 400 structures dating from the Colonial era, most of them on Historic Hill and the Point, and others of later vintage around town. A few places not to miss:

The Museum of Newport History, 127 Thames St.
Much of Newport's history and culture are on display in this newish interactive museum in the 1772 Brick Market. The three-story museum of the Newport Historical Society provides an overview of varied aspects of local history and makes a good starting place for the history-minded Newport visitor. Pick up a telephone speaker to hear about religious history. View the locally made Goddard and Townsend furniture on display in a middle-class parlor, not far from a printing press that belonged to Benjamin Franklin's brother, James. Climb aboard the reproduction Ocean House omnibus for a nine-minute video tour down turn-of-the-century Bellevue Avenue, accompanied by the clip-clops of horses' hooves. The museum sponsors guided walking tours of the Historic Hill section Thursday-Saturday at 10, May-September, for $8.

(401) 841-8770. www.newporthistorical.org. Open daily except Tuesday, 10 to 5, Sunday 1 to 5, to 4 November-March. Adults $5, children $3.

Fort Adams, Fort Adams State Park, off Harrison Avenue.
Named for President John Adams, the fort was begun during the Revolution and is one of the largest seacoast fortifications in the country. Near the start of Ocean Drive, the hilly point juts into Narragansett Bay and provides as good a vantage point today for yacht-watching as it did for soldiers defending their country. The

fort has been reopened for scheduled tours, and garrison drills and camp reenactments are given at times. Tours of the fort are offered in the summer. Also in the 80-acre state park is Eisenhower House, the summer White House of President Eisenhower (not open for tours). The park offers picnicking, swimming and fishing.

(401) 847-0707. www.fortadams.org. Guided fort tours on the hour, daily 10 to 4, mid-May through Columbus Day; adults $6, children $3 to $5. Park open daily from sunrise to sunset; parking $2.

The Museum of Yachting, Fort Adams State Park.

Housed in a 19th-century granite building on a point at the end of Fort Adams in Newport Harbor, this museum showcases the history of yachting and yacht racing. Costumes, memorabilia, photos, paintings and models trace the history of sailing inside what was once an Army mule barn. The photo exhibit called "The Mansions and the Yachts" focuses on the sailing roles of the Vanderbilts, Astors and Morgans ("while the women were here for the social life, this is what the men did," our guide explained). The Small Craft Gallery displays old wooden boats beneath a model of the boat that won the first America's Cup perched near the ceiling. Located in the museum's boat basin are classic yachts dating from the late 1800s to 1965, restored by the museum and actively sailed by volunteers throughout the summer. Among them are the flagship Courageous, winner of the America's Cup in 1974 and 1977, and Dennis Connor's Freedom (1980). The museum is small, but appeals to laymen as well as sailors and you'll get a feel for part of Newport's heritage.

(401) 847-1018. www.museumofyachting.org. Open daily 10 to 5, mid-May through October. Adults $5, children $4.

International Tennis Hall of Fame and Museum, 194 Bellevue Ave.

A gracious Victorian air lingers around the historic Newport Casino, built in 1880 by Stanford White and considered the cradle of American lawn tennis. The U.S. Lawn Tennis Men's Singles and Doubles Championships were held here from 1881 to 1914, when the event moved to Forest Hills, N.Y., and later became the U.S. Open. Major tournaments are still held on the grass courts each summer. The world's largest tennis museum chronicles the sport's history and includes the Davis Cup Theater, where old tennis films are shown. Visitors can test their tennis trivia in new interactive video displays and, for a fee, play tennis on thirteen grass courts or three indoor courts.

(401) 849-3990 or (800) 457-1144. www.tennisfame.com. Open daily, 9:30 to 5. Adults $8, children $4.

Touro Synagogue National Historic Site, 27 Touro St.

A home of worship for Congregation Jeshuat Israel, this is the oldest place of Jewish worship in the United States. Built in 1763 in classic Georgian style, the simple but beautifully proportioned exterior – cream brick with a trim of dark brown – hides an ornate interior in which twelve Ionic columns, representing the tribes of Israel, support a gallery where women in this Orthodox congregation sit. The Holy Ark at the end of the sanctuary contains the Torah scrolls dating from 1658. Above the ark is a representation of the Ten Commandments in Hebrew painted by Newport artist Benjamin Howland. The synagogue has a fascinating history, which you can learn from guided tours.

(401) 847-4794. www.tourosynagogue.org. Tours every half hour, Sunday-Friday 10 to 5, July to Labor Day; Monday-Friday 1 to 3 and Sunday 11 to 3, May-June and September-October; Friday at 1 and Sunday 1 to 3, rest of year. Donation.

Two churches are of note. **Trinity Church** at Church and Spring streets is a white-spired landmark nicely framed by the spruced-up Queen Anne Square rising from America's Cup Avenue. Rhode Island's first Anglican church was built in 1726 from designs by Christopher Wren. It has the second oldest organ in the country, two Tiffany windows and a triple-deck wineglass pulpit. It's open daily in summer 10 to 4, admission $2. **St. Mary's Church,** at Spring Street and Memorial Boulevard, is the oldest Catholic parish in Rhode Island. Work was begun on the Gothic-style red stone church in 1848. The church is most famous as the site of the 1953 wedding of Jacqueline Bouvier to John F. Kennedy. The Kennedys summered in Newport in 1961, attending Mass on Sundays. A brass marker on the tenth pew, right side facing the altar, designates it as theirs. Open Monday-Friday 7 to 11:30.

Hunter House, 54 Washington St. Restored by the Preservation Society of Newport County, Hunter House is an outstanding example of Georgian architecture and is considered one of the ten finest Colonial homes in America. Beside the harbor, it was built for a wealthy merchant family in 1748, and its collection of early Rhode Island furniture crafted by the famous Goddard and Townsend families in mahogany and walnut is priceless.

(401) 847-1000. Open daily 10 to 6, mid-June to mid-September. Adults $10, children $4.

Newport Colony House, Washington Square. Built in 1739 in the style of an English manor house, this handsome brick building was the center of governmental affairs for 160 years. Rhode Island was the first colony in 1776 to declare its independence and in May, the Declaration of Independence was read from its balcony. The building, still used for public ceremonies, displays the famous full-length portrait by Rhode Islander Gilbert Stuart of George Washington, who met here with Rochambeau during the Revolutionary War.

(401) 846-0813. Tours every half hour, Thursday-Saturday 10 to 3:30, mid-June to late August; rest of year by appointment. Adults $4, children free.

Redwood Library and Atheneum, 50 Bellevue Ave. Designed in 1748 by the architect who did Touro Synagogue, this is the nation's oldest lending library. It contains countless valuable books and a fine collection of early American paintings, including six by Gilbert Stuart. Almost across the street in **Touro Park** is the **Old Stone Mill,** a 26-foot-high landmark that some think is a Viking church tower predating Columbus's voyage. Others think it is the remains of Gov. Benedict Arnold's 17th-century windmill.

(401) 847-0292. Library open Monday-Saturday, 9:30 to 5:30. Free.

Oceanside Attractions

Ten-Mile Drive. Formerly known as the Ocean Drive, this is the East Coast's version of California's Seventeen-Mile Drive in Carmel. It meanders along Newport's southern shore past rocky points with crashing surf, spectacular scenery that provides an awesome setting for equally spectacular mansions and contemporary homes. As it nears Bellevue Avenue it passes a couple of beach clubs, including the fabled Bailey's Beach where society's 400 sun, swim and socialize. Brenton Point State Park is along the drive and a favorite of sunset-watchers. Benches are placed strategically all along a bluff for contemplating the ocean and stairs lead down to the rocks, where you can sunbathe and picnic.

The Cliff Walk. For an intimate look at the ocean and the backs of the mansions, the 3.5-mile Cliff Walk along Newport's southeastern shore is a must. The walk begins off Memorial Boulevard at the western end of Easton's Beach (Newport's First Beach). Although you can get onto the walk at several points, we like to start at the foot of Narragansett Avenue, where you walk down to the ocean on the Forty Steps. The first couple of miles are well-maintained and quite easy; the last part past Marine Avenue and around the point near East Bailey's Beach requires good shoes and a stout heart since the path disappears and the going is rocky. You also must pass through a couple of dark, damp tunnels. The faint-hearted might want to take the first half of the walk and retrace their steps.

Nature by the Sea

Green Animals, 380 Cory's Lane off Route 114, Portsmouth.

The topiary is terrific in these gardens run by the Preservation Society just north of Newport. On view are 80 trees and shrubs sculpted into shapes of a camel, giraffe, lion and elephant at the corners of the original garden, plus a donkey, ostrich, bear, horse and rider, dogs, birds and more. The animals are formed of California privet; the geometric figures and ornamental designs of golden and American boxwoods. The charming small estate that slopes toward Narragansett Bay also includes dahlia and vegetable gardens, espaliered fruit trees, a grape arbor, and a gift and garden shop where you can buy forms to make your own topiary.

(401) 847-1000. Open daily 10 to 6, mid-April to mid-September. Adults $10, children $4.

The Norman Bird Sanctuary, 583 Third Beach Road, Middletown.

Here is a sleeper, offering the region's best birding and wildlife viewing possibilities. The 450-plus-acre wildlife refuge harbors more than seven miles of hiking trails. Visitors can enjoy a leisurely stroll through fields and woods or hike over craggy ledges to the top of Hanging Rock for a good view of the ocean, Second Beach, marshlands and Gardiner's Pond. A trailside natural history museum and the Barn Owl Gift Shop are available for browsing.

(401) 846-2577. Open daily, 9 to 5. Adults $4, children $2.

BEACHES. Most of the Ocean Drive beaches are private, but you can sunbathe in Brenton Point State Park. Those in the know also go to **Gooseberry Beach,** a privately owned beach open to the public on Ocean Drive just west of Bailey's Beach; this family-oriented place with little surf charges $10 for parking. For surf swimming, head for **Easton's Beach** (also known as First Beach), a wide and sandy three-quarter-mile strand along Memorial Boulevard from the Cliff Walk to the Middletown line. The surf action lures surfers from far and wide in the off-season. There are boardwalks, an amusement rotunda and the Newport Aquarium, and cabanas may be rented. Parking costs $8 on weekdays, $15 on weekends. Beyond Easton's Beach in Middletown are **Second Beach** (where surfing is permitted) and **Third Beach,** parking at both, $10 on weekdays, $15 on weekends). **King Park** along Wellington Avenue in Newport is on a sheltered harbor with pleasant lawns, a pier, a beach, a raft with slides and a bathhouse. **Fort Adams State Park** has a free beach with a small roped-off area for swimming; parking $2. At all beaches, lifeguards work weekends starting Memorial Day, and daily from mid-June to Labor Day.

Shopping

Innumerable and oft-changing stores line Thames Street, the Brick Market Place, and Bannister's and Bowen's Wharves. Lately, the hot spots are along Lower Thames Street, where shops are burgeoning out to Wellington Square and beyond, and Spring Street, home of exotic galleries and boutiques that seem to come and go. Bellevue Avenue near Memorial Boulevard is where the 400 used to shop and some still do.

The fun begins outside the Gateway Information Center, where a store called **Kelly & Gillis,** a.k.a. Signs of Intelligent Life.com, advertises ridiculous gifts, accessories and home furnishings. Other downtown favorites are **Collage** for jewelry and gifts, **Primavera** for unusual gifts and garden accessories, **Scrimshanders** with scrimshaw and Nantucket lightship baskets, and **Rue de France** for French country decor and accessories. **Mark Fore & Strike** carries men's and women's sportswear, while **The Narragansett** offers fine clothing for men and women. **Irish Imports** carries gorgeous wool things, and **Michael Hayes** carries designer men's and women's fashions. Look for resort wear at the **Sail Loft** and the **Upperdeck Clothing Co.,** and handcrafted furniture at **The Ball & Claw,** the showroom of Jeffrey P. Greene, specialist in Newport's famed Goddard and Townsend designs. **Onne van der Wal Gallery** shows award-winning nautical photography. The **Museum Store** of the Preservation Society of Newport County stocks local books, jewelry, gifts and nautical memorabilia.

Of special interest along Lower Thames Street are places like **Tea & Herb Essence,** which offers a little of everything from passion fruit teas to herbal remedies and handmade soaps. At **Thames Glass,** you can watch owner Matthew Buechner and his fellow glass blowers create fabulous fish, flowers, vases and ornaments. Potter-in-residence Bridget Butlin shapes wonderful stoneware at **Thames Street Pottery.** We were particularly taken by all the fish-shaped clocks and dinner plates. On Spring Street, check out **Edna Mae's Millinery Store,** which carries unique hats made exclusively for the owner. Sweet pillows, quilts and prints are among the offerings at **Sarah Elizabeth's.**

Up on Bellevue Avenue, check out more Michael Hayes stores (including one for children) and the posh **Newport Gallery of World Art** for paintings that appeal to those who still live in Newport's "cottages." **Runcible Spoon,** an outstanding kitchen shop, displays gaily colored pottery amid the lobster platters and garlic salsas. **Cadeaux du Monde** bills itself as a museum where all the exhibits (art and handicrafts) are for sale.

Where to Stay

Newport has an incredible number of accommodations from large hotels, motels and time-share resorts to more than 200 inns and B&Bs at last count. For a getaway break, the oceanside resorts and some of the smaller, more personalized B&Bs are good choices.

Oceanside Resorts for a Splurge

The Chanler at Cliff Walk, 117 Memorial Blvd., Newport 02840.

A boutique hotel and restaurant, the reborn Chanler occupies Newport's most dramatic oceanside location and makes the most of it. The extravagant French

Empire-style showplace, enveloped in lush landscaping behind a sweeping stone entry identified only by a plaque, is situated on four acres at the terminus of the Cliff Walk and overlooks Easton's Beach and the open Atlantic. Built in 1865 as the summer home of Congressman John Winthrop Chanler of New York, it was renovated to the tune of $10 million plus by John and Jean E. Shufelt, who undertook a similar renovation earlier at the Mission Point Resort on Michigan's Mackinac Island. Twenty sumptuous guest rooms are furnished and decorated to different eras, among them Renaissance, Greek Revival, English Tudor, Louis XIV, Colonial, Federal, French Provincial, Victorian and Mediterranean. All have plump king or queensize beds and jacuzzi baths and all but two have gas fireplaces. Most come with crystal chandeliers, fine paintings, flat-screen TVs, DVD players and wet bars. The best for views are the largest (Renaissance) with a rooftop deck in the main house and three villas in the east wing with ocean-facing decks with hot tubs and a casual New England island theme. Three garden villas in front with floral names and themes have both baths with jacuzzis and garden courtyards with hot tubs under pergolas and two sitting areas to compensate for their smaller size and lack of ocean views.

Three meals a day come with a spectacular view in **The Spiced Pear,** the hotel's luxurious restaurant. From an exhibition kitchen, chef Richard Hamilton delivers inspired regional American fare with a nod to his Southern heritage. The bill of fare is exotic and complex, as in appetizers of peeky toe crab on green papaya puree and diver scallops with ossetra caviar and champagne. The signature lamb loin with tomato-mint relish proved excellent, but the real hit of our meal was the buttery poached lobster paired with "macaroni and cheese," actually a creamy orzo rice laced with mascarpone cheese and truffle oil. Desserts included a tarte tatin prepared with mango rather than apple and a trio of chocolate, vanilla and hazelnut ice creams. As the chef fiddled with the format, the original à-la-carte dinner menu was changed to a variety of prix-fixe tasting menus, each with several choices and some bearing substantial surcharges. The mahogany paneled lounge and the adjoining outdoor terraces overlooking the ocean also provide food and drink.

(401) 847-1300. Fax (401) 847-3620. www.thechanler.com. Twenty rooms with private baths. Doubles, $895 to $1,095 in summer, $295 to $1,095 rest of year.

Spiced Pear, (401) 847-2244. www.spicedpear.com. Prix-fixe, $59. Lunch daily in season, 11:30 to 2:30, weekends in off-season. Dinner nightly in season, 5:30 to 10, Wednesday-Sunday in off-season.

Castle Hill Inn & Resort, 590 Ocean Drive, Newport 02840.

The old Inn at Castle Hill has a new name, deluxe accommodations and a new vitality to go with its grand hilltop setting overlooking Narragansett Bay. Traditionalists and romantics might opt for the eight Victorian guest rooms and three suites in the main inn or adjacent Swiss-style chalet, the former laboratory of original owner Alexander Agassiz, the Harvard marine biologist. All recently refurbished, most have king or queen beds, double whirlpool marble baths, fireplaces and original antiques. The opulent 30-foot-high Turret Suite includes a deep soaking tub beside the window on the main bedroom level, which is joined by a winding mahogany staircase to a loft sitting area with a 360-degree view. More private are six outlying Harbor House units overlooking the bay from a cliff about 30 feet from the mansion, each with porch, kingsize bed, gas fireplace, whirlpool bath and TV. The ultimate place for escape is one of the eight enlarged and refurbished Beach House rooms that rank with the best beachside cottage accommodations in southern New England. Elegant with vaulted ceilings, gleaming hardwood floors and beachy decor, each has a kingsize bed, TV/VCR, sofabed in the sitting area, fireplace, granite-counter galley kitchen, double whirlpool tub and separate shower, and an outdoor deck facing the ocean. From the whirlpool tub in several, you can look out onto the beach – and be there in no time. An extravagant breakfast, perhaps eggs benedict or lobster omelet, is complimentary in the mansion.

Dining for guests and the public is in the oval Sunset Room, a windowed porch just across from the mahogany bar and lounge and jutting out toward the bay. Redecorated with a billowing cream-colored taffeta canopy on the ceiling, this is the place for Castle Hill's long-popular Sunday brunch. The kitchen is under the tutelage of Casey Riley, who transferred here after opening Agora at the Westin Hotel in Providence. His food aspires to the heights. Recent examples were wild coho salmon grilled with toasted coriander and lemon in a lemongrass-ginger broth and roasted Colorado rack of lamb with garlic-parsley crust, acorn squash bread pudding, toasted chanterelles and imported Devon cream. You might start with the foie gras of duck, pan roasted with dried fruit flapjacks, toasted pecans, balsamic syrup, micro greens and Normandy butter. Dessert could be banana-walnut soufflé with espresso crème anglaise, an "autumn fancy" assortment of three desserts or the chocolate signature, an assortment of five. A grill menu is offered from 3 until sunset in summer on the bay-view cabana terrace with an outdoor bar.

(401) 849-3800 or (888) 466-1355. Fax (401) 849-3838. www.castlehillinn.com. Fourteen rooms, three suites and eight cottages with private baths. Doubles, $395 to $850. Suites, $850 to $1,450. Cottages, $5,075 weekly in summer.

Entrées, $24 to $39. Lunch, 11:30 to 3 Monday-Saturday in summer, Friday-Saturday in off-season. Dinner nightly, 5:45 to 9:30; jackets requested. Sunday brunch, 11 to 3.

Inns/B&Bs

Cliffside Inn, 2 Seaview Ave., Newport 02840.

Based in an 1880 summer villa built by a Maryland governor, this Victorian charmer is among the most luxurious of Newport's upscale B&Bs, although it may be upstaged by its over-the-top sibling, the Abigail Stoneman Inn. As restored by late owner Winthrop Baker, Cliffside's bedrooms became places in which to linger – not from which to escape, as may be the case with museum-piece Victorian inns. Each of the thirteen accommodations in the main house has one or two working fireplaces. Their "bathing salons" – eleven with whirlpool tubs and two with steam baths – are some of America's most glamorous. The entire lower floor of the six-sided Tower Suite is devoted to a wood-paneled bathroom, including whirlpool tub, marble shower and bidet. Upstairs is a bed-sitting room beneath an octagonal cathedral ceiling, with Eastlake queen bed, fireplace and bay window. The newest and most luxurious accommodations are in the Cliffside Cottage, a onetime ranch house near the Cliff Walk at the foot of the property. Each of its three suites comes with three fireplaces and sound-system bathrooms. The Seaview on the lower floor is a stone-walled hideaway with an antique French kingsize bed and wood-burning fireplace. Its plush sitting room shares a see-through gas fireplace with the marble bathroom, which has an Allure bath, shower and sound system to end all systems. Upstairs, the queensize Atlantic enjoys an ocean view as well as a sitting room with a media center sporting LCD TV, DVD, VCR, CD and multi-room stereo system. The kingsize Cliff has "his and her" sitting rooms, one a living room and the other a study. Besides offering every amenity one could want, Cliffside pampers guests with exotic afternoon tea service in the inn's formal parlor or on the wide front veranda. In the morning, the staff serves up a lavish breakfast, which culminated at our visit in eggs benedict with a subtle hollandaise sauce. There's food for thought here, too, in the more than 100 paintings of reclusive artist Beatrice Turner, onetime owner of the house, whose life story and background are full of mystery.

(401) 847-1811 or (800) 845-1811. Fax (401) 848-5850. www.cliffsideinn.com. Eight rooms and eight suites with private baths. Doubles, $245 to $425. Suites, $375 to $575. Add $50 weekends, May-October.

Abigail Stoneman Inn, 102 Touro St., Newport 02840.

"Menus" for pillows, bath toiletries and tea, and a "water bar." These one-of-a-kind luxury amenities distinguish this deluxe small B&B opened by the Cliffside Inn and its expanding Legendary Inns of Newport group. The 1866 Renaissance-style Victorian is notable not so much for the five accommodations, sumptuous as they are, what with high-style Victorian antique furnishings and art, kingsize beds, fireplaces, marble baths with two-person whirlpool tubs, steam baths and extravagant media centers concealed behind mirrors or in armoires. But rather for the complimentary "amenities menus" that take personalized room service to a higher level. Even guests who have – and expect – everything probably don't have some of these. The pillow menu offers guests twenty styles of pillows from a collection worth more than $10,000. For bathing in some of the most glamorous whirlpool-tub settings you'll ever find, the bath menu offers a choice of 30 imported soaps, bath salts, foams and oils from halfway around the world, and the leftovers go home in a soap "doggy bag." The inn's J.B. Finch Pub is a water bar, offering 25 of the world's best bottled waters – a selection of which you'll also find in the entry hall and in your room. And then there are the teas, an exceptional offering of 35 kinds, available around the clock and sometimes taken in a cozy Tea for Two Room off the entry hall. The amenities upstage even the inn's third-floor suite, 1,500 square feet of luxury appropriately named Above and Beyond. It has two kingsize bedrooms, a kitchen/dining area and a sitting room/library that has secret panels leading to a huge "bathing salon." Ensconced in a dormer window is a wood-paneled whirlpool tub for two amidst an array of plants, a chandelier and a wall-sconce lighting system with sixteen individual lights on dimmers. Breakfast is a gourmet event, taken at individual tables in the parlor or, by most guests, in bed.

(401) 847-1811 or (800) 845-1811. www.abigailstonemaninn.com. Two rooms and three suites with private baths. Doubles, $425. Suites, $525 and $625. Add $50 weekends May-October.

The Francis Malbone House, 392 Thames St., Newport. 02840.

Elegant guest rooms, commodious common rooms and a large rear courtyard and lawn make this an exceptional B&B choice for those who want to stay in downtown Newport. It bears the name of the shipping merchant for whom the house was built in 1760. The main house holds eight corner bedrooms on the second and third floors plus a main-floor suite, six with fireplaces. The four front rooms are bigger and have harbor views. All are handsomely furnished with antique queen beds covered by monogrammed duvet comforters. A nine-bedroom rear addition offers larger rooms, each with a kingsize bed, fireplace, jacuzzi and bigger vanities and closets – "all the things we wanted but couldn't have in the old house," according to innkeeper Will Dewey. The four rear rooms in the addition share two private garden courtyards. The most luxurious are two suites in the 1710 Mason House at the rear of the property. The downstairs holds a living room, dining room, kitchen and sunroom with a courtyard. Upstairs are two spacious bedrooms, each with king bed, fireplace, and double jacuzzi tub and TV in the bathroom. Occupants join other guests for tea and breakfast in the main inn. All guests enjoy a fountain courtyard between the buildings, and share a couple of elegant, high-ceilinged front parlors and a library with TV. The newer wing also holds a 40-seat breakfast room, where guests partake of a gourmet breakfast, from eggs benedict to belgian waffles.

(401) 846-0392 or (800) 846-0392. Fax (401) 848-5956. www.malbone.com. Sixteen rooms and four suites with private baths. Mid-April to mid-November: doubles $245 to $345, suites $395 to $475. Rest of year: doubles $99 to $260, suites, $200 to $345.

Admiral Fitzroy Inn, 398 Thames St., Newport 02840.

The interior of this plain, shingled box-like structure masks its not-so-distant status as the St. Mary's Church convent. Newly billed as "a European-style hotel in the heart of Newport" by the Newport Harbor Corp., also owner of the posh Castle Hill Inn & Resort, the seventeen-room B&B is quite appealing inside, especially the striking hand-painted decorative touches everywhere. Done for the former innkeeper by a young artist, they vary from borders to murals and entire walls and are worthy of a gallery. One guest room's large mural of an apricot tree in a clay pot is so realistic it even shows bugs and a butterfly. An elevator serves rooms on three floors, most of them quite spacious by Newport standards and artfully furnished with antique queensize or king beds, white duvet comforters, and upholstered or wicker loveseats and chairs. All have TVs and small refrigerators, some hidden in hand-stenciled armoires. A European-style continental breakfast is taken at individual tables in the cheery main-floor dining room, its walls highlighted by hand-painted garlands of flowers.

(401) 848-8000 or (866) 848-8780. Fax (401) 848-8006. www.admiralfitzroy.com. Sixteen rooms and one suite with private baths. Doubles, $165 to $305 mid-June through mid-September; $75 to $265 rest of year.

Hydrangea House Inn, 16 Bellevue Ave., Newport 02840.

A garden oasis in the middle of Newport is one of the draws at this Victorian townhouse decorated to the hilt by antiques dealers Dennis Blair and Grant Edmondson. Their B&B expanded into an adjacent building and was renovated in 2004 to produce nine reconfigured rooms, some enlarged into split-level affairs and all now with fireplaces and jacuzzi tubs. The ultimate is the 50-foot-long Hydrangea room on the third floor. Furnished with Edwardian antiques, it has a kingsize canopy bed, a fireplace, a skylit double whirlpool tub encased in Italian marble in the room, a steam bath in the bathroom, and a TV/VCR and stereo system. Four second-floor guest rooms go off a wide second-floor hallway with stippled gold walls painted with a pastry brush to look like marble. Each is decorated with splashy draperies and wallpapers that match; the fabrics may be repeated on the bed headboards or, in one case, a valance over the shower. The rear of the second floor opens onto a spacious plant-filled veranda, overlooking a showplace garden, complete with a spreading bamboo tree. The third floor opens onto a sundeck formed by the roof for the veranda below. The latest renovation also produced a basement spa with a massage table, steam bath and sauna. An elegant breakfast is served at a table for fourteen in the chandeliered dining room or seasonally on the veranda, which lends a more residential, verdant feeling than you'd suspect from the building's storefront facade up against the street.

(401) 846-4435 or (800) 945-4667. Fax (401) 846-6602. www.hydrangeahouse.com. Nine rooms with private baths. Doubles, $250 to $425 Memorial Day through October, $225 to $385 rest of year.

Ivy Lodge, 12 Clay St., Newport 02840.

A mansion-like, three-story entry hall, 33 feet high and paneled in carved oak, awaits guests at this attractive B&B, tucked away at the end of a residential street behind Bellevue Avenue. Eight guest rooms and suites are available in a house that was described by an 1886 newspaper as "one of the prettiest cottages in Newport." A particularly appealing room, fashioned from the former library on the main floor, has a queensize mahogany sleigh bed, a Delft-tiled fireplace and a double jacuzzi and separate shower. Upstairs bedrooms go off galleries, supported by fluted and carved columns, around the richly paneled hall. Six have gas fireplaces and three have jacuzzi tubs. Each room now has TV and telephone, a small refrigerator in the closet, a steam iron and hair dryer. The most-requested room, the stately yet cheery yellow Turret with kingsize bed, comes with a flat-screen TV with VCR/DVD, two-person jacuzzi and double vanity. The paneling in the common areas is awesome and there's "no plaster in any part of the hall," as the 1886 newspaper article put it. A small reception parlor, pretty in pink, wicker and chintz, is enhanced by a fireplace and floral prints. Beyond is a large and elegant living room. The 21-foot-long table in the chandeliered dining room is set for breakfast for sixteen, with room to spare. There's a choice of main courses, perhaps tomato-basil cream cheese frittata or gingerbread pancakes with lemon sauce. A wraparound veranda is fine for lounging beside the tranquil grounds, where there are lawn games and a goldfish pond.

(401) 849-6865 or (800) 834-6865. Fax (401) 849-0704. www.ivylodge.com. Eight rooms with private baths. Doubles, $139 to $399 May-October, $99 to $319 rest of year.

The Old Beach Inn, 19 Old Beach Road, Newport 02840.

Unusual touches prevail in this romantic, intimate B&B run by Luke and Cyndi Murray. One is the old anchor embedded in the third-story turret of the home built as the Anchorage in 1879. Another is the ornate wedding bed with lace draped in the center in the Forget-Me-Not bedroom. How about the palladian arch leading into the jacuzzi bathroom off the Ivy Room, with a faux book case along one wall and an antique wood-burning fireplace? Cyndi's eclectic decorating styles are reflected in the English country decor in the guest rooms, named after flowers and full of whimsical touches. Ever upgrading, the Murrays added two rooms with separate entrances in the rear carriage house. These have TVs and a more contemporary air. Guests gather in a small front parlor or a larger Victorian living room. Here, two plush chairs and a couch face a glass cocktail table held up by four bunnies. The room holds a rabbit fashioned from moss, a tiled fireplace and a copper bar in the corner. The Murrays serve an expanded continental breakfast in the dining room or outside on the porch or a brick patio overlooking a pleasant back yard with a gazebo and fishpond.

(401) 849-3479 or (888) 303-5033. www.oldbeachinn.com. Seven rooms with private baths. Doubles, $135 to $300 May-October, $85 to $225 rest of year.

Architects Inn, 31 Old Beach Road, Newport 02840.

The 1873 Woodbine Cottage in which local architect George Champlin Mason resided has been turned into one of Newport's nicest B&Bs. Harlan and Sheila Tyler offer three elegant guest rooms, each spacious with queensize bed, working fireplace, sitting area and TV/VCR. The most popular is the Redwood Room with majestic canopy bed and a clawfoot soaking tub. Two suites with king or queensize beds have sitting rooms with new fireplaces. The premier Perry Suite also has a jacuzzi tub. Guests enjoy the large main-floor living room and library, each with fireplace and eleven-foot-high ceiling. A fireplace also enhances the dining room, where breakfast begins with a buffet of cereal, muffins, yogurt, fresh fruit and juices. A plated seasonal fruit, perhaps warm apple compote or bananas foster, follows. The main event could be eggs benedict, breakfast casserole or french toast made with Portuguese sweet bread. The side porch is employed for breakfast and afternoon refreshments in season.

(401) 847-7081 or (888) 834-7081. Fax (401) 847-5545. www.architectsinn.com. Three rooms and two suites with private baths. Doubles, $175 to $275 May-October, $99 to $185 rest of year.

An 'Island' Resort

Hyatt Regency Newport Hotel & Spa, 1 Goat Island, Newport 02840.

You want to stay on an island, close to downtown but away from the crowds? You won't be alone, but this may be the next best thing. The rejuvenated Hyatt is Newport's all-around large resort hotel, from its indoor and outdoor pools, tennis courts, spa and health club to its banquet room, conference center and underground garage. Most of the rooms on six floors of a brick structure that looks at first glance like a grain elevator afford views of the water. For head-on views, choose the newer Captain's Quarters, where nearly half the 47 more deluxe rooms open right onto the bay. The hotel's spa offers a variety of treatments and packages. In 2004, the hotel completed a major facelift to its **Windward Grille** to show off its waterfront location. Light fare is available in the **Auld Mug Lounge.**

(401) 851-1234. Fax (401) 851-3201. Two hundred forty-six rooms and eighteen suites. Doubles, $189 to $365 May to late October, $99 to $199 rest of year.

Hotels and Motels

Newport Marriott, 25 America's Cup Ave., Newport 02840.

Newport's biggest hotel is on Long Wharf, next to the Gateway Center transportation and information complex and with the harbor across the street. Billed as one of the Marriott chain's top resort hotels, it has 319 guest rooms arranged around a five-story atrium. They tend to be on the small side; the place was started as a Holiday Inn Crowne Plaza, and the rooms are not as large as Marriott would have built. Best are those with harbor or city views; others look over the atrium or the parking garage. The top floor is a deluxe concierge level. Facilities include an indoor pool, sauna, whirlpool, fitness center and four racquetball courts. Dine in **Fathoms,** lately refurbished in sea colors with fanciful sculptures of fish around the room and curved panels that impart the sensation of being on a ship. Window tables and the eye-catching bar and lounge afford views of the harbor.

(401) 849-1000 or (800) 458-3066. www.newportmarriott.com. Three hundred twelve rooms and seven suites. Doubles, $145 to $350.

Long Wharf Resort, 5 Washington St., Newport 02840.

The newest in a growing roster of time-sharing resort properties headquartered in Newport, this is quite a spread. – built in the shingle style with a circular tower to resemble the landmark Newport Casino and facing the harbor across the street. This one is all small condo-style units of two and three bedrooms, nicely furnished with everything families or two couples might need for a week's vacation. Half the units on the L-shaped structure's second, third and fourth floors get water or courtyard views; the rest face a parking lot or the Marriott. The master bathrooms contain single whirlpool tubs. The main floor includes a lounge area with a fireplace and a small pool in which any swimmers are on full view with a trickling waterfall as a backdrop. The pool opens through plastic flaps to a much larger pool area outdoors, and a third pool was under construction in 2004. There's also a small theater in which movies are shown nightly at 7. There's no meal service, but guests can prepare their own.

(401) 847-7800 or (800) 225-3522. Fax (401) 845-0127. Eighty-two suites. Rates, $335 to $460 May-October, $120 to $350 rest of year.

Seaview Inn, 240 Aquidneck Ave. (Route 138A), Middletown 02842.

A good view of Easton's Pond and the ocean from a hilltop back from the road commends this motel of 1950s vintage, which dropped the motel from its name and fancied itself as an inn under new owners. It's the only one of the Newport area's many standard motels that's close to the ocean – others farther out Routes 138 or 114 in Middletown could be in Anytown, but the prices are lower than in Newport proper. This has accommodations on two floors, all with balconies or patios to enjoy the view. Adirondack chairs are placed strategically around the lawn. Rooms have paneled walls, two double beds, color TV and a couple of wood and leather motel chairs. Continental breakfast is served to guests in the coffee shop.

(401) 846-5000 or (800) 495-2046. Fax (401) 848-0873. www.seaviewnewport.com. Thirty-nine rooms and two suites with private baths. Doubles, $129 to $219 June-September, $59 to $179 rest of year.

Where to Eat

The Black Pearl, Bannister's Wharf.

Our favorite all-around restaurant in Newport – and that of many others, judging from the crowds day and night – is the informal tavern, the outdoor deck with umbrella-topped tables and the elegant Commodore Room that comprise the Black Pearl. The Commodore Room, whose small-paned windows overlook the harbor, dispenses contemporary continental cuisine (dinner entrées from gray sole meunière and grilled swordfish with tomato-beurre blanc to breast of pheasant with perigeux sauce and dry-aged sirloin steaks obtained from a New York butcher). More casual is the cozy and noisy tavern, where people line up at lunch time for the great clam chowder (thick and dill-laced and seemingly better every time we order it), crab benedict, a tarragon chicken salad and the famous pearl burger in pita bread with mint salad. Most popular in summer is the outdoor patio on the wharf, where you sit beside the water under colorful umbrellas and watch the world go by. You can get most of the tavern fare outside, with heartier entrées (baked cod with pepper jack cheese, 21 Club chicken hash and grilled calves liver) available inside at both lunch and dinner. Desserts are few but scrumptious. Although the service may be so fast as to make you feel rushed (the world's smallest kitchen serves up to 1,500 meals a day in summer), we've never been disappointed by the fare.

(401) 846-5264. Entrées, $19 to $38; tavern, $15.50 to $28. Dinner nightly in Commodore Room, from 6; jackets required. Tavern and outdoor café open daily from 11. Closed six weeks in winter.

White Horse Tavern, Marlborough and Farewell Streets.

Established in 1673, this imposing burgundy structure is the oldest operating tavern in the country. It has elegant Colonial decor in a warren of small rooms on two floors with wide-board floors, exposed beams, small-paned windows and big fireplaces. The historic charms appeal particularly in the off-season, when the fireplaces are lit. They made a pleasant backdrop for a lunch that included an interesting yogurt-cucumber-walnut soup, baked marinated montrachet cheese, halibut in a brandy-grapefruit sauce and a somewhat bland chicken salad resting in half an avocado. At night, the tuxedoed staff offers a fancy menu and prices to match. Expect main courses like chargrilled tuna au poivre, butter-poached lobster in puff pastry over truffle-scented orzo, cognac-cider glazed duck breast, individual beef wellington and herb-crusted Colorado rack of lamb. Starters could be baked escargots en croûte, oysters rockefeller or confit of duck and chèvre raviolis. For most, this is special-occasion dining, topped off by such masterful desserts as lavender crème brûlée or a trio of chocolate truffles on a bed of raspberry purée.

(401) 846-3600. www.whitehorsetavern.com. Entrées, $28 to $40. Lunch, Wednesday-Saturday 11:30 to 2:30. Dinner nightly, 5:30 to 9:30 or 10, jackets required. Sunday brunch, 11 to 2.

The Place, 28 Washington Square.

This wine bar and grill adjunct of Yesterday's, a pubby Washington Square institution, was opened by owners Maria and Richard Korn as a showcase for their longtime chef, Alex Daglis. He obliges with the most exciting cuisine in Newport, served stylishly at white-clothed tables on two levels of a long, narrow dining room with brass rails, oil lamps, Victorian lights and sconces. Folks rave about the changing entrées, from the fennel-encrusted tuna with mandarin-ginger vinaigrette to the mustard-crusted rack of lamb with apple-honey demi-glace. We never got beyond the appetizers, so tempting that we shared and made a meal of five. The shrimp and corn tamales, the exquisite scallops with cranberries and ginger, the gratin of wild mushrooms, and raviolis of smoked chicken and goat cheese were tasty warmups for a salad of smoked pheasant with poached pears and hazelnuts. An apple crêpe with apple sorbet was a crowning finale. To accompany, you can sample "flights" of wine or "schooners" of microbrews (four seven-ounce pilsner glasses ensconced in a handmade wooden schooner). More casual fare is served day and night in the original Yesterday's, rechristened an Ale House to differentiate it from the wine bar and grill.

(401) 847-0116. www.yesterdaysandtheplace.com. Entrées, $20.95 to $29.95. Dinner nightly, 5:30 to 10 or 11, fewer nights in off-season.

Restaurant Bouchard, 505 Thames St.

After sixteen years as executive chef at the famed Le Chateau in New York's Westchester County, Albert J. Bouchard III struck out on his own. The French-trained chef and his wife sought out a small establishment where he could exercise "total artistic control," which turned out to be the former tea room in a 1785 Georgian-style house. Their restaurant is a beauty in celadon and cream, with well spaced tables dressed in floor-length cloths. A small bar in the front room looks to be straight out of Provence, and a landscaped brick patio is pleasant for drinks and hors d'oeuvres in summer. The food is classic French with contemporary nuances. Typical entrées run from seafood gratin in a gruyère and boursin cheese sauce to crispy veal sweetbreads in a tarragon sauce. Dover sole, salmon persille, coffee-crusted magret of duck sauced with balsamic and brandy, and pheasant with truffle sauce illustrate the range. Starters like asparagus and lobster in puff pastry, house-smoked salmon wrapped around goat cheese and confit of duck with oriental sauce earn acclaim. So do the chocolate crêpes and individual soufflés for dessert.

(401) 846-0123. www.restaurantbouchard.com. Entrées, $23.50 to $28. Dinner nightly except Tuesday, 6 to 9:30 or 10. Sunday brunch, 11 to 2.

The West Deck, 1 Waite's Wharf.

Exciting bistro cuisine at refreshing prices draws those in the know to this waterside spot beside the harbor, a century-old structure that once served as a garage for an oil company. Here, in an airy, garage-like space that's one-third cooking area, 30 diners can be seated at tables dressed in white. Ten more cozy up to an L-shaped eating bar facing the open kitchen. A long sun porch alongside nearly doubles the capacity, and more can be accommodated seasonally on a super outside patio where there's a wood grill. The menu is printed nightly, and at our latest visit offered a dozen entrées from sesame-crusted mahi mahi with coconut-curry sauce and banana chutney to grilled filet mignon with stilton cheese and port wine sauce. The night's terrine of duck, rabbit, quail and foie gras with hazelnuts and port wine glaze proved fabulous. So was a superior leg of venison with sundried cherry sauce, served with thyme-mashed potatoes, although a couple of elements in the signature mixed grill of petite filet, lamb chop, chicken and andouille sausage proved surprisingly tough. A couple of the rich desserts – grand marnier crème brûlée and cappuccino-praline mousse with espresso sauce – compensated. In season on the waterfront deck, the outdoor grill furnishes the bulk of the dishes on a simpler, all-day menu that ranges from burgers and a fish sandwich to teriyaki steak and lobster.

(401) 847-3610. Entrées, $22 to $32. Lunch menu outside in summer, noon to 9. Dinner nightly, 5:30 to 10 or 11. Off-season, dinner Wednesday-Sunday, 5:30 to 9 or 10.

Asterisk, 599 Lower Thames St.

One of Newport's more trendy and eclectic restaurants is run by the scion of a family of Danish restaurateurs. John Bach-Sorenson alighted from Copenhagen in Newport – "it reminded me of home" – and looked for a restaurant site. He found it in a working auto-repair garage, now transformed into a airy and colorful space with a part-open rear kitchen and a remarkable handcrafted bar along one side. A romantic, dimly lit salon look is conveyed by shaded gas lamps flickering on close-together white-linened tables beneath a high, industrial-look ceiling. Garage doors open onto an enclosed, canopied sidewalk café out front. The continental-Asian menu ranges widely from potato-wrapped grouper and sole meunière to pork chops with melted brie and peaches, veal scaloppini and steak au poivre. You can opt for mussels marinière with frites or "le petite asterisk:" one-half lobster, ten oysters, four shrimp, and eight clams and mussels ($42). Frozen tiramisu parfait, raspberry crème brûlée and profiteroles are favorite desserts. The place is named for one of John's favorite French comic-strip characters, known for fighting the bureaucracy, which he had to do to win a wine and beer license. John also runs Boulangerie, a bakery and sandwich shop at 382 Spring St., and lately took on La Petite Auberge, a classic French restaurant at 19 Charles St.

(401) 841-8833. Entrées, $19 to $32. Dinner nightly, from 5.

The Mooring, Sayer's Wharf.

Ensconced in a building that once served as the New York Yacht Club station house, this has arguably the best harborfront location in town. An outside patio right by the water and window tables in the dining room as well as a new bar/lounge created by enclosing an upper deck take advantage of the view. That the food is so good is a bonus. We've been pleasantly surprised by the quality every time we've eaten here. For a late lunch on a summer Saturday, our party of four had to wait only ten minutes for a table on the breezy patio as we eyed the entrée salads and hefty sandwiches passing by. We sampled the warm salmon salad, the seafood quiche with coleslaw, steamed mussels with garlic bread, half a dozen littlenecks, and a terrific scallop chowder we deemed even better than the award-winning clam chowder. A recent winter lunch produced aforementioned clam chowder, better than ever, as well as an open-faced, knife-and-fork concoction that lived up to its billing as the ultimate grilled cheese sandwich. We also were smitten by the day's blue-plate special ($12.95): a cup of chowder, succulent grilled salmon with tomato-basil sauce, french fries and coleslaw. Dinner choices are as basic as fish and chips, fried clams and baked haddock and as elevated as charbroiled swordfish with lemon-tarragon butter, flame-grilled tiger shrimp, seafood mixed grill and a rich seafood pie. The interior décor is nautical with old photographs and prints, and the dark tables are bare. The Mooring's more casual annex, the seasonal **Smokehouse Café,** is known for its smoked foods, chowders and barbecued ribs and wings that, the manager proclaimed, are out of this world.

(401) 846-2260. Entrées, $14.95 to $29.95. www.mooringrestaurant.com. Lunch and dinner daily, 11:30 to 10 or 11.

The Clarke Cooke House, Bannister's Wharf.

Long considered one of Newport's fanciest and with an attitude to match, the venerable Clarke Cooke House converted its downstairs dining rooms into the **Candy Store** café, a summer sushi bar and a porch with water view, as well as a mid-level Grille, a middle-of-the-road bistro offering lunch and dinner with the Candy Store menu. The result is more space for casual fare at somewhat more down-to-earth prices. Upstairs is a formal dining room called the **Skybar,** colorful in green and white, with banquettes awash in pillows beneath a beamed ceiling. In summer it opens to a breezy but elegant canopied upper deck called the **Porch** with a great view of the waterfront. Chef Ted Gidley's take on contemporary French fare ranges from fillet of sole lyonnaise and native halibut embellished with caviar vin blanc and lobster vinaigrette to molasses-cured breast of magret duck, steak au poivre and roast rack of lamb persillade. Carpaccio of yellowfin tuna, raviolis of lobster and morels with champignon sauce and pan-seared breast of squab with foie gras "au torchon" are typical appetizers. Dessert might be vanilla crème brûlée, hazelnut, chocolate and caramel nougatine mousse cake, and a chocolate-studded triumph called "snowball in hell."

(401) 849-2900. www.clarkecooke.com. Entrées, $27 to $39. Dinner nightly in season, 6 to 10 or 10:30, weekends in off-season. Candy Store and Grille, entrées $17.95 to $32.95. Lunch daily, 11:30 to 5, weekends in winter; dinner nightly from 5, Wednesday-Sunday in winter.

Scales and Shells, 527 Thames St.

Plain and exotic seafood items are simply but assertively prepared in what retired sea captain Andy Ackerman bills as Newport's only "only fish" restaurant, with deliveries unloaded straight from the docks out back. The well-spaced tables are covered with black and white checked cloths, the floors are bare and, but for a few models of fish on the walls, the decor is stark. A second-floor addition called **Upscales,** a smaller and quieter room, is open from May-September with a more sophisticated menu. The blackboard menu offers an enormous range of seafood, and you've got to walk up front and face it head-on to take everything in. Monkfish, scallops, shrimp, swordfish, snapper, scrod – you name it, it comes in many variations, wood-grilled, broiled or tossed with pasta. Shrimp or clams fra diavolo are served right in their own steaming-hot pans. Pick and choose from a raw bar near the front entrance. There also are appetizers like calamari salad, grilled clam pizza and Sicilian mussels. Desserts include Italian gelatos and tarts.

(401) 846-3474. www.scalesandshells.com. Entrées, $10.95 to $19.95. Dinner, Monday-Saturday 5 to 9 or 10, Sunday 4 to 9. No credit cards.

Café Zelda, 528 Thames St.

Newporters consider this old-timer one of their favorite restaurants – a neighborhood kind of place that's comfortable, unpretentious and enjoyable any time of day or night. Its food fortunes rise and fall with the executive chef, but have been on a roll lately under John Philcox, a veteran on the Newport scene. He offers a reprise of some of the specialties we enjoyed with he owned Le Bistro on Bowen's Wharf, from steak tartare to bouillabaisse. That place hasn't been the same since his departure, but Zelda fans are the richer for it, both in terms of good food and pleasant prices. His international dinner menu includes comfort foods like the popular Zelda burger with Vermont cheddar and onions, steak frites and herb-roasted chicken breast with Zelda's mac 'n cheese. You'll also find entrées like seared ahi tuna, braised lamb shanks and Portuguese-style pork chops with littleneck clams. Start with mussels Brittany, escargots bourguignonne or smoked chicken spring rolls with sweet chile dipping sauce. Eggs Copenhagen is a brunch favorite.

(401) 849-4002. www.cafezelda.com. Entrées, $18.95 to $25.95. Lunch, daily 11:30 to 3, Friday-Sunday winter. Dinner nightly, 5 to 10.

Repast and Romance

Tucker's Bistro, 150 Broadway.

For romance, there's no more idyllic place in Newport than this newish Mediterranean bistro in the heart of the out-of-the-way restaurant row beloved by locals along Broadway. Co-owners Tucker Harris and Ellen Coleman have fashioned a 1920s deco bistro in a double storefront. The bar is in a small room with a library look. Most of the dining takes place in couple of larger rooms with white-clothed tables holding antique shaded lamps amidst red lacquered walls hung with impressionist paintings and a ceiling draped in vine branches, rhinestone strands and twinkling white lights. Tucker likens the decor to a cross between art gallery and bordello. The partners tweak their printed menu with a trio of daily specials, including soft-shell crab tempura and baked striped bass fillet with gorgonzola sauce at our visit. Otherwise, expect about a dozen entrées, from lobster and scallop stew or grilled chipotle-glazed Atlantic salmon fillet to five-spiced duck, pork shanks braised in bourbon and molasses, and veal pot-au-feu. Appetizers go international, as in Thai shrimp nachos, sautéed pierogis, escargots crostini, grilled pizzas and beef carpaccio. The dessert specialty is a signature banana pudding.

(401) 846-3449. www.tuckersbistro.com. Entrées, $20.95 to $27.95. Dinner nightly, from 6.

FOR MORE INFORMATION: Newport County Convention & Visitors Bureau, Gateway Visitor Information Center, 23 America's Cup Ave., Newport, RI 02840, (401) 845-9123 or (800) 976-5122. www.gonewport.com.

Singing bonfires light up river in outdoor sculpture event called WaterFire Providence.

Providence, R.I.

Renaissance City

New England's second largest city is a city on the move. The most ambitious renewal project in America has uncovered the downtown waterfront. The Providence River – for years obscured by the world's widest bridge – now flows like a canal beneath graceful Venetian-style spans and past cobblestone riverwalks, parks and an amphitheater. The celebrated WaterFire "singing bonfires" blaze in the middle of the river on many an evening. A gleaming convention center and the huge Providence Place shopping mall draw people "downcity" day and night. Providence even spawned several movies and became the setting for a hit television drama.

While the downtown renaissance steals the show, there's much of enduring interest to visitors just beyond, particularly along College Hill on the East Side and Federal Hill, the city's Little Italy on the West Side.

College Hill – a steep, tree-lined neighborhood of Colonial streets with providential names like Benefit, Hope, Benevolent and Power – is a lively mix of historic residences and institutions, including top-ranked Brown University with its world-class libraries and the Rhode Island School of Design with its outstanding art museum. Benefit Street's remarkable "Mile of History" harbors the most impressive collection of original Colonial homes and structures in America. At the foot of College Hill are the restored South Main and North Main Street areas, where the city was born along the Providence River.

While the Yankee colonists settled the East Side, later immigrants settled west of downtown. Their ethnic ties remain strong to this day. The Italian neighborhood known as Federal Hill in particular possesses a foreign air that lures visitors to its restaurants and markets.

All this is on a compact, human scale. Providence is unusual in that most of its historic, cultural and sightseeing attractions are within walking distance of downtown.

Everywhere there are churches, whose spires give the heart of the city a classic New England look. They reflect a religious heritage dating to the city's founding in 1636 by Roger Williams, who fled the tyranny of Massachusetts Puritanism and named his settlement at the head of Narragansett Bay "in commemoration of God's providence." The city is the birthplace of religious freedom in America.

Its renaissance makes it providential for the visitor today.

Seeing and Doing

The views of the skyscrapers through the ivied gates of Brown University give it something of the look of Boston. The spotlighted State Capitol dome could be Washington's. The restored townhouses, close-in mansions, gaslight-type lanterns and statued squares lend the air of Philadelphia. The East Side's nearly perpendicular hills could be San Francisco's. The parks, promenades and bridges along the revived downtown riverfront lend the cosmopolitan air of Venice or Amsterdam.

This is the rejuvenated Providence, a lively blend of old and new.

The 'New' Providence

While "old" Providence reigns on its flanks, the new Providence is centered "downcity," a local term coined to erase the connotations of a downtown that had been almost abandoned in the latter half of the last century.

Much of the credit for Providence's renaissance goes to its ebullient mayor for 21 years, Vincent A. "Buddy" Cianci Jr. Before he was convicted in 2002 on a federal corruption charge, he led the transformation of the mob capital of New England into an American Venice – a model of urban renaissance and the setting for the hit NBC show entitled "Providence."

You can see and sense the new Providence in its restaurants and hotels, its theaters and galleries, and its festivals and activities focused "downcity."

Waterplace Park and Riverwalk. The jewel in the crown of revitalized downtown Providence is this four-acre plaza at the foot of State Capitol hill, an open, pedestrian-friendly link between the Providence Place Mall, downtown and College Hill/East Side. This is Providence's New England "green," although it substitutes promenades and waterways for trees and green. The landscaped park surrounds a tidal basin joining the Providence, Woonasquatucket and Moshassuck rivers that had been covered over by the "world's widest bridge." A terraced plaza rises around a one-acre pond with a spouting fountain, forming an outdoor amphitheater where concerts, plays, art shows and WaterFire events are staged. Joining the park to the east is Riverwalk, more than a mile of cobblestone and brick walkways, Venetian-style footbridges and gardens beside the river. They will connect eventually with the soon-to-be-renovated Old Harbor area on Narragansett Bay near India Point Park. The schedule of performances in the amphitheater is available at an information center in the Boat House clock tower, 2 American Express Way.

Gondola rides along the river are offered nightly by **La Gondola,** (401) 421-8877. Authentic Venetian-style gondolas, each powered by a gondolier, take up to six passengers on 30- to 40-minute rides, Friday and Saturday from 4 to midnight and Sunday-Thursday from 5 to 11. The price is $79 for the first two persons and $15 each additional for those with reservations. Walk-ons may be accommodated on excursions of 15 to 20 minutes, $40 for two and $10 each additional.

Splash Duck Tours, 10 Dorrance St., (401) 421-3825. Hour-long tours aboard an amphibious vehicle cruise the streets of downtown and plunge into the Providence River for a quick trip to Narragansettt Bay. The narrator points out the city's major sites. Tours daily, mid-May through September. Adults $20, children $12.

In winter, the center of town turns into an outdoor skating rink. The **Bank of America Skating Center** at 2 Kennedy Plaza, (401) 331-5544, is almost twice the size of New York's Rockefeller Center rink. Skate rentals and concession stands are available in a 3,500-square-foot pavilion across from the Biltmore Hotel. Public skating sessions are scheduled Monday-Friday 10 to 10, Saturday and Sunday 11 to 10. Adults $5, children $3.

A Moving Experience

WaterFire Providence. In a unique evening attraction that draws more than 500,000 visitors annually, 100 floating bonfires light up the waters of three rivers in an "outdoor sculpture" that runs for nearly two-thirds of a mile through Waterplace Park and Riverwalk. Fires on 100 braziers dance atop the waters, accompanied by music that reflects a variety of cultures and rhythms, as orchestrated by outdoor sculptor Barnaby Evans. The crackling flames, the flickering firelight on the arched bridges, the scent of flaming cedar and pine, the silhouettes of black-clad fire tenders floating by in their torch-lit boats and the music bouncing off walkways and bridges and interacting with sounds of blazing bonfires – all combine to create a powerful work of art and a moving symbol of the city's renaissance. Spectators stroll along cobbled walkways and over the Venetian-style footbridges, dance on a cobblestone circle on Westminster Street or listen to jazz on an outdoor stage, as the occasion or mood demands. WaterFire occurs several times a month from May to October, usually on weekend evenings. The fires are tended from dusk to past midnight.

SHOPPING. Downtown Providence received a retail shot in the arm with **Providence Place,** an upscale, 150-store mall built atop a 4,000-car parking garage between the Westin Hotel, the State Capitol and I-95 and facing Waterplace Park. The three-floor mega-mall includes three big-name anchors, Filene's, Lord & Taylor and Nordstrom, as well as an IMAX theater, a sixteen-screen cinema, a Dave & Buster's adult arcade, chain restaurants and a food court. Retail tenants range from Brooks Brothers and Banana Republic to Borders Books & Music, Bed, Bath & Beyond, and Bailey, Banks & Biddle. And that's just some of the B's. Validate your parking ticket with a $10 purchase and get up to three hours for $1. The mall is open daily 10 to 9:30, Sunday noon to 6.

Providence Place is the contemporary counterpart to **The Arcade** at 65 Weybosset St., built in 1828 as the nation's first indoor shopping mall. The arcade reopened in 1980 with three floors of specialty shops and restaurants connected by balconies with cast-iron railings and topped by a block-long skylight. Shops have come and gone, and the main floor is now mostly fast-food eateries, where much of Providence seems to line up for a quick weekday lunch.

On the East Side, Thayer Street near the Brown University campus is lined with college-type shops, galleries and bookstores. Beyond is Wayland Square, a neighborhood center of old-line shops. More contemporary stores are found along South Main Street. Art galleries and antiques shops are proliferating along four blocks of nearby Wickenden Street.

ARTS AND ENTERTAINMENT. Providence claims more artists per capita than any city in the country. It has made a home for them in the downcity arts and entertainment district, where a new tax incentive program exempts them from state income taxes. Their growing presence is noted in **Gallery Night Providence,** a free tour of nearly 30 galleries and museums. The event is staged the third Thursday of every month from March through November. A free ArTrolley runs between the sites. Also on Gallery Nights, two guided **Art and the City walking tours** leave the John Brown House at 52 Power St., (401) 438-0463; tickets, $5. One tour explores how Providence's status as a center for the arts began. The other looks at the contemporary art scene.

risd/works, 10 Westminster St., (401) 277-4949, is an innovative hybrid of a retail store, gallery and design showroom showcasing the works of Rhode Island School of Design alumni and faculty in a variety of media. The collection covers a wide range of items from $1 greeting cards to $50 flatware patters to $5,000 artworks. It's open Monday-Saturday 10 to 6 and until 9 on the third Thursday monthly for Gallery Night Providence. Evening hours are extended for special events including WaterFire Providence.

The performing arts are represented by the Tony Award-winning **Trinity Repertory Company,** whose resident company performs in two venues at the Lederer Theater Center, 201 Washington St., (401) 351-4242. Touring Broadway shows and entertainers light up the marquee at the restored **Providence Performing Arts Center,** 220 Weybosset St.

The 'Old' Providence

The oldest section of town is the riverfront area along North and South Main streets. Roger Williams and his 17th-century colonists built their homes, shops and churches on the hill rising sharply up the east bank, an area now known variously as College Hill and the East Side. In the 18th century, the town's leading citizens were the four Brown brothers (John, Joseph, Nicholas and Moses), merchants and entrepreneurs whose funds helped build Brown University and one of the nation's most powerful business dynasties.

The early legacy has been preserved by the Providence Preservation Society, founded in 1956 by John Nicholas Brown. The National Register has designated 26 historic districts in Providence, which claims more intact Colonial and early Federal buildings than any city in America.

History and Architecture

Benefit Street "Mile of History," College Hill. One block above Main Street, Benefit Street's Mile of History contains notable homes dating back to early Providence, when this was *the* street (it still is). It is an extraordinary, lived-in mix of 18th- and 19th-century residential and institutional treasures – more than 200 on tree-lined Benefit Street with its imitation gaslights and brick sidewalks, and more on cross streets. One of America's most distinctive thoroughfares, Benefit Street is eminently walkable – and that's the best way to see and savor it.

Summer Walks. Guided walking tours from mid-June to mid-October are conducted by the Rhode Island Historical Society from the John Brown House, 52 Power St., (401) 331-8575 Ext. 34 or (401) 438-0463. The main 90-minute Benefit Street Mile of History tour departs Tuesday through Saturday at 11 and Sunday at noon, with extra tours Tuesday and Saturday at 2. A Women's History Walk leaves Wednesday at 2. A Providence Artwalk departs Friday at 2. A Providence Riverwalk tour leaves Wednesday and Saturday at 10 from the Rhode Island Convention Center, 1 Sabin St. Tour fees: adults $10, children $5.

For a self-guided tour, start at the Roger Williams National Memorial for orientation purposes, walk south on Benefit Street, with occasional detours along side streets, and return via South Main Street.

Roger Williams National Memorial, 282 North Main St.
This four-and-a-half-acre plot is the site of the original 1636 settlement, birthplace of religious freedom in America. National Park Service rangers preside over a small visitor center with exhibits and a brief slide show describing the life of the city's founder. Outside are a park with gardens and a shrine around the site of the spring that supplied Williams's water and was the true beginning of the colony. Several blocks east and almost straight up on Congdon Street is Prospect Terrace, site of the Roger Williams memorial statue. It yields a panoramic view of downtown Providence.
(401) 521-7266. Open daily, 9 to 4:30. Free.

Governor Stephen Hopkins House, 15 Hopkins St. at Benefit St.
Owned by the state and administered by the National Society of Colonial Dames, this is the dark red clapboard home of the ten-times governor of Rhode Island, first chancellor of Brown University and a signer of the Declaration of Independence. Governor Hopkins added the main part of the house in 1743 to the original two 1707 rooms. He became a Quaker after he married his second wife and the home reveals his simplicity of heart. Here is the four-poster in which George Washington slept, the wig stand on which he rested his wig and a decanter set he presented to his host. On display are the owner's spectacles, his baby cap and shoe buckles. Guides point out the children's room with a trundle bed, an old cradle with a cloth doll, a tiny chair used by tots to learn to walk as they held onto the back, and the weasel (a wool winder that popped every 40th revolution – hence "Pop Goes the Weasel"). Beside the house is a typical 18th-century parterre garden designed by a Hopkins descendant and centered by a sundial with a Hopkins quote: "A garden that might comfort yield."
(401) 884-8337. Open April-December, Wednesday and Saturday 1 to 4, and by appointment. Free.

John Brown House, 52 Power St.
The first great mansion in Providence was built in 1786 for John Brown, China trade merchant, slave trader, privateer and patriot. John Quincy Adams called it "the most magnificent and elegant private mansion that I have ever seen on this continent." An outstanding example of late Georgian architecture, it is now a house museum with nine rooms and a priceless collection of Rhode Island cabinetmakers' furniture. The most prized piece is Joseph Brown's Goddard-made nine-shell desk and bookcase. Visitors see a video show giving a good overview of early life in Providence before they are guided on hour-long tours through the three-story

museum, now owned by the Rhode Island Historical Society. You can tell that John Brown really weighed 300 pounds in his later years by his capacious waistcoat spread on one of the beds. The third floor displays collections of early dolls, silver and pewter, most of it the family's, as well as goods brought back from the Orient by neighbor Edward Carrington. The carriage house garage contains John Brown's robin's-egg-blue chariot, the earliest coach made in America (1782).

(401) 331-8575. www.rihs.org. Open Tuesday-Saturday 10 to 5 and Sunday noon to 4, April-December; Friday-Saturday 10 to 5 and Sunday noon to 4, rest of year. Adults $7, children $3.

Gov. Henry Lippitt House Museum, 199 Hope St.
A red-brick Italianate mansion built in 1865, this is considered one of the most complete, authentic and intact Victorian houses in the country. The two-term governor made a fortune selling textiles during the Civil War and spared no expense in building his Renaissance Revival home. The high-Victorian interior includes richly carved woodwork, meticulously detailed stenciling, faux marble and stained-glass windows. The floor of the billiards room is inlaid with nine types of wood and the neoclassical chandeliers are cast in bronze.

(401) 453-0688. www.preserveri.com. Open Friday 11 to 3 and by appointment. Adults $5, children $2.

The **Nightingale-Brown House,** 357 Benefit St., (401) 272-0357, was home to five generations of the Nicholas Brown family until 1985. The house on the Brown University campus is open for guided tours Thursday and Friday from 1 to 4; adults, $3.

The emerging **Heritage History Museum,** 350 Eddy St., is Rhode Island's first statewide history museum and multi-cultural center. Nineteen historical and cultural organizations worked together to renovate a former Narragansett Electric Co. power plant on the Providence River to tell their stories in an interwoven manner. The only New England affiliate of the Smithsonian Institution, the museum will have a huge gallery space to display borrowed Smithsonian artifacts and accommodate traveling exhibits to enhance the telling of Rhode Island history and place it in a regional and national context. The building, with 90-foot ceilings and floor space equivalent to two football fields, will have gallery space on four floors when its much-delayed phased opening begins, scheduled for 2006.

Arts and Letters

The educational heritage of Brown University and the creative influence of Rhode Island School of Design (RISD, locally called Riz-Dee) have left their marks on Providence, particularly on College Hill.

Brown University, head of College Street, College Hill, (401) 863-2378. The nation's seventh oldest (1764), Brown was the Baptist answer to Congregationalist Yale and Harvard, Presbyterian Princeton and Episcopalian Penn and Columbia. Graduates still process down the hill to the First Baptist Meeting House for commencement exercises, although the university shed its Baptist ties in 1938 and then entered a period of rapid expansion. The original **University Hall,** patterned by Joseph Brown after Princeton's Nassau Hall, houses the administration at the head of College Street today. The admissions office is located in the 19th-century Italian villa-style **Corliss-Brackett House** at Prospect and Angell streets, where students start guided campus tours on most weekdays and Saturday mornings from September to December.

Brown University Libraries. The huge **John D. Rockefeller Jr. Library** at 10 Prospect St. houses the university's general collections. Next door at 20 Prospect is the old **John Hay Library,** now home of the university archives and special collections. Foremost here is the McLellan Collection of Abraham Lincoln memorabilia – two small upstairs rooms with 700 Lincoln manuscripts, busts, portraits and even a lock of his hair. The curator considers the collection one of the finest in the country. The Lownes History of Science Collection is said to be the largest botanical collection anywhere. The beaux arts **John Carter Brown Library** across the quadrangle is a world-renowned repository of early Americana. It's furnished like a "gentleman's library" with huge hanging tapestries at either end. The scholar will find such national treasures as Thomas Paine's original manuscripts for *Common Sense* and eight editions of Christopher Columbus's 1493 letters.

Museum of Art – Rhode Island School of Design, 224 Benefit St.

One of the nation's outstanding small art museums is operated by one of its leading art and design schools. From mosaics and other treasures of ancient Greece and Rome to a fine collection of oriental art (don't miss the exquisite robes donated by Lucy Truman Aldrich) to an outstanding selection of works by French artists (Monet, Degas, Manet, Cezanne and Matisse, among many) to changing exhibits, there is a bit of everything among the nearly 80,000 works here. The famous bronze of Balzac by Rodin is one of the museum's prized possessions, as is its Gorham silver collection. The holdings, displayed in 45 galleries on three floors, trace the history of art from antiquity to the 21st century. The adjoining Pendleton House (1906), housing American furniture and decorative arts, is the earliest example of an "American wing" in an American museum. It includes examples from the Townsend and Goddard circle of Colonial Newport craftsmen, plus the Lucy Truman Aldrich collection of 18th-century porcelain figures, wonderfully displayed in cabinets lighted from inside. Paintings by American masters such as Gilbert Stuart, John Singleton Copley and John Singer Sargent hang on the walls. The 1994 Daphne Farago wing contains two large galleries for contemporary works in all media.

(401) 454-6500. www.risd.edu/museum. Open Tuesday-Sunday 10 to 5 (also third Thursday of month 5 to 9). Adults $8, children $2. Free Sunday 10 to 1 and Friday noon to 1:30.

The Providence Art Club, 11 Thomas St.

This 1790 brick-veneered house within easy walking distance of the RISD Museum has harbored the nation's second oldest art club (1880) with its parlors and private dining rooms for more than 100 years. A spacious upstairs gallery holds changing exhibits by a membership involved in everything from oils to photography. Two buildings down the street is the unusual 1866 Norman-Breton Fleur de Lys Building, former studio of Sidney R. Burleigh, dean of Rhode Island artists in the early 1900s. The Greek Revival building at 5 Thomas St. was long the headquarters of the Providence Water Color Club.

(401) 331-1114. Open Monday-Friday 11 to 4, Saturday-Sunday 2 to 4, September-June; Monday-Friday 11 to 3 in July and August; free.

Providence Athenaeum, 251 Benefit St.

One of America's oldest subscription libraries is housed in this 1838 Greek-Doric temple-style building, which was the center of Providence's early intellectual and literary life. Many valuable books are shelved in its alcoves, within which Edgar Allan Poe wooed local poet Sarah Helen Whitman. The rare book wing has original Audubon elephant folios and changing art exhibits. Books are for members only, but the rare book displays and art exhibits are open to all.

(401) 421-6970. Monday-Friday 8:30 to 5:30, Saturday 9:30 to 5:30, Sunday 1 to 5; closed weekends in summer. Free.

Where to Stay

Chain motels are concentrated south of Providence in the Warwick area and east of the city (a shorter drive) in Seekonk, Mass. For a city weekend, however, you probably will want accommodations in or near downtown.

Downcity Hotels

The Westin Providence, 1 West Exchange St., Providence 02903.

New England's fanciest downtown hotel outside Boston is part of the Rhode Island Convention Center complex. From the striking, 25-story-high gabled roof that denotes its Neoclassic presence on the Providence skyline to the majestic four-story lobby rotunda with its marble floor and columns, the Westin defines class. Each of the 364 handsomely appointed rooms and suites comes with kingsize or two double beds, at least one easy chair with ottoman, a spacious writing desk, a TV hidden in an armoire, two telephones, a mini-bar and a coffeemaker stocked with Starbucks coffee. Our quiet cocoon of a deluxe corner room had a triple-sheeted kingsize bed topped with six big pillows, two upholstered chairs and large windows that opened. The contemporary European decor in champagne tones supposedly reflects the interior of a Newport mansion. The more memorable Newport touch was the immense bathroom, where for some reason the rack with hand towels was clear across the room from the washstand. Chocolates and a weather forecast arrived at nightly turndown, and the day's newspaper was at the door in the morning. Guests enjoy the hotel's fitness center with an indoor pool beneath the dome atop the rotunda building. The Library Bar & Lounge off the lobby rotunda is the ultimate in plush surroundings and a refuge for creative appetizers, single-malt scotches and cigars. The elegant **Agora** restaurant was an early favorite of the national food media, but a change in chefs coincided with a switch to a new look and a steakhouse menu. **CitiPerk** offers less lofty fare for breakfast and lunch.

(401) 598-8000. Fax (401) 598-8200. www.westin.com/providence. Three hundred sixty rooms and four suites. Doubles, $189 to $399. Suites, $494 to $1,700.

Providence Biltmore, 11 Dorrance St., Providence 02903.

An early feather in Providence's cap, this historic downtown hotel appears a bit dated lately in comparison with its all-new neighbor across the plaza and gets mixed reviews, except for rooms on its concierge floors. The brick dowager opened in 1922 to a special trainload from New York, a 50-piece band and a sea of roses as it recreated the high standards of living enjoyed at the Vanderbilt Biltmore Estate in North Carolina. After falling on hard times and closing in 1973, it reopened following a $15 million renovation in 1979. It later was taken over by the Omni chain and since has become a Grand Heritage hotel. At the top of the three-story lobby you can see the wonderfully ornate, original gilt ceiling, and the crystal chandelier and palm trees remind some of the Plaza in New York. A glass elevator shoots from the lobby up the side of the building. The original 500 bedrooms have been converted into 290 larger accommodations, done in soft and soothing colors. Most have kingsize or two double beds, plus armchairs and sofas in elegant sitting areas, with TVs hidden in armoires. Some suites have kitchenettes. Amenities include a new fitness center and a Paul Mitchell Salon and Spa. The hotel claims the largest and most elegant **Starbucks** in America, as well as fine dining in the renowned **McCormick & Schmick's** seafood restaurant.

(401) 421-0700 or (800) 294-7709. Fax (401) 455-3050. www.providencebiltmore.com. Two hundred fifty-eight rooms and 32 suites. Doubles, $169 to $269. Suites, $289 to $319.

The Hotel Providence, 311 Westminster St., Providence 02903.

Providence's first European-style boutique hotel opened in 2005 in the heart of the downcity arts and entertainment district. Two late 19th-century brick buildings were joined with a newer structure to provide 64 rooms and sixteen suites, plus a first-rate restaurant and piano bar. All rooms have pillow-top king or queensize beds with down comforters, armoires, oversize desks and large-screen TVs. Sumptuous fabrics and antiques from the owner's personal collection convey a turn-of-the-last-century flavor. The Dunfey Hotel Group is managing the hotel that was built by local developer Stanley Weiss. He persuaded friends Tom and Rozann Buckner to relocate their acclaimed **L'Epicureo** restaurant from Federal Hill to larger quarters on the hotel's main floor (see Where to Eat).

(401) 861-8000 or (800) 861-8990. Fax (401) 861-8002. www.thehotelprovidence.com. Sixty-one rooms and nineteen suites. Doubles, $159 to $359. Suites, $249 to $529.

Providence Marriott Hotel, Charles and Orms Streets (Exit 23 off I-95), Providence 02904.

A multi-million-dollar renovation created a new entrance, expanding the lobby and upgrading guest rooms at this motor hotel built in 1974. Like others of the chain, it's good for families, with a large indoor-outdoor pool, game room, sauna, whirlpool and exercise equipment. The 351 rooms on six floors are ordinary size, nicely decorated and have queen or kingsize beds. Some have a view of the nearby State Capitol or face onto the landscaped pool area. The lobby is especially welcoming. **Bluefin Grille** restaurant offers three meals a day. It's a long walk to downtown, but buses pass every fifteen minutes.

(401) 272-2400 or (800) 937-7768. Fax (401) 273-2686. www.marriottprovidence.com. Three hundred forty-six rooms and five suites. Doubles, $169 to $249.

Bed & Breakfasts

The Old Court, 144 Benefit St., Providence 02903.

You can stay on historic Benefit Street and relive the Providence of yesteryear, thanks to the conversion of an 1863 Episcopal church rectory into a B&B. Owners Jon and Carol Rosenblatt, who also own a series of small East Side restaurants, spared no expense in the restoration. Italianate in design, the Old Court has ornate mantelpieces, plaster moldings and twelve-foot-high ceilings. Each of the ten guest rooms is decorated differently, if rather sparely. Some have brass beds, some four-poster, and most have exotic wallpapers. All beds are queen or kingsize except for one with two doubles and another with twins. The large Eastlake Room is done with Eastlake furniture and offers a sofa and wet bar. Lace curtains and old clocks convey a feeling of the past. Air conditioning, telephones and televisions are concessions to the present. Because there is no common room, the Old Court seems rather like a small urban hotel. A full breakfast is served in a pleasant pink breakfast room.

(401) 751-2002. www.oldcourt.com. Ten rooms with private baths. March-November: Doubles, $135 to $175 weekends, $115 to $145 midweek. Rest of year: Doubles $115 to $145 weekends, $95 to $115 midweek.

State House Inns, 43 Jewett St., Providence 02908.

What began as a modest ten-room B&B has become two B&B inns and a B&B hotel in the Smith Hill residential neighborhood overlooking the State Capitol across Interstate 95. All go under the umbrella name of the original. Two are one house apart from each other and about a block from the Shaker-style State House Inn opened in 1990 by Monica and Frank Hopton. They added two larger properties in 2003 in partnership with her parents, former Nantucket innkeepers Kenneth and Phyllis Parker.

The Christopher Dodge House at 11 West Park St., a majestic three-story 1858 Italianate brick mansion that had been converted into an apartment house, is the largest and most deluxe of the three. Now restored as "a B&B hotel," it has fifteen elegant, high-ceilinged bedrooms with ornate plaster moldings, tin ceilings, polished wide-board pine floors and white or light-colored painted walls. Crisply appointed in Shaker, Colonial or Mission style, a typical room has a king or queen bed, a TV concealed in an armoire, a gas fireplace beneath a marble mantel, a comfortable armchair, a desk and a view of the State House dome through the rippled panes of the inn's tall antique windows. Guests meet for breakfast near the fireplace in a brick-walled dining room, where the sideboard holds a continental buffet that's mere preliminary to a main course of perhaps baked apple french toast, quiche or eggs benedict – the same kind of fare served at the related B&Bs. Doubles here range from $149 to $159.

Newest is the 13-room **Mowry-Nicholson House** at 57 Brownell St., an 1865 Victorian converted into a B&B from a condemned boarding house. Its eight rooms and five family suites are furnished in simpler early American style that complements its wide wraparound front porch. Doubles here are $129 to $139 and suites, $139 to $149.

The original **State House Inn,** a bit farther removed from the interstate highway, has a loyal following who like its nicely furnished rooms, each with king or queensize bed topped with quilt or comforter, TV, telephone and an overstuffed chair. Two rooms have fireplaces. Hooked rugs or carpets cover the maple floors that are original to the house. The main floor harbors a small guest parlor and a bigger, fireplaced dining room where breakfast is served. Doubles here are $129 to $149.

(401) 351-6111. Fax (401) 351-4261. www.providence-inn.com. Thirty-three rooms and five suites with private baths. Doubles, $129 to $159.

The Cady House, 127 Power St., Providence 02906.

The owner's eclectic collections of folk art are everywhere evident in this imposing 1839 residence with pillared entrance on College Hill. Anna Colaiace and her husband Bill, a radiologist, offer three much-decorated Victorian guest quarters with queen beds. A side suite contains a daybed with trundle bed in the living room and a sturdy armoire and dresser in the bedroom. A rear bedroom has a luxurious settee in a windowed alcove and a giant bathroom with clawfoot tub, separate shower and a circular stand holding a multitude of plants. Guests enter a front bedroom through the bathroom to find a spacious room with sofa and tiled fireplace. The wild wallpapers throughout "are my interpretation of Victorian," says Anna, who did the decorating herself. A former caterer, she serves an ample breakfast on the weekends (continental during the week) in a formal dining room opening onto a delightful screened porch. The porch overlooks a curved terrace and showy gardens on a triple lot. Folk art and sculptures continue in the lower garden. Along with their growing collections, the couple's two dogs are much in evidence.

(401) 273-5398. www.cadyhouse.com. Two rooms and one suite with private baths. Doubles, $110.

C.C. Ledbetter Bed & Breakfast, 326 Benefit St., Providence 02903.

There is artistry in Clare "C.C." Ledbetter's laid-back B&B, which occupies an historic house with a big side yard and garden in the heart of the East Side historic district, across from the John Brown House. The artistry is reflected in C.C.'s amazing collection of paintings and photographs, her choice of colors (vivid green and apricot for the guest living room), and in the dhurrie rugs, Delft tiles and handmade quilts gracing four guest rooms sharing two baths. A new bedroom created from storage areas at the rear of the third floor has a private bath, king bed and view of the downtown skyline. The spacious third-floor front room running the width of the house contains a queen bed and an exercise machine, typical of the home-like touches in this much-lived-in house. Each room is decorated in eclectic style and has a small television. C.C., who raised three children in Montana before moving back East and deciding to settle in Providence sight unseen, serves a continental-plus breakfast of fruit, cheese, bagels, homemade breads or English muffins.

(401) 351-4699. Two rooms with private baths and three rooms with shared bath. Doubles, $85 to $115. No credit cards.

Where to Eat

Providence, home of the Johnson & Wales University College of Culinary Arts, has an inordinate number of restaurants. Some rank among the best and most interesting in New England.

Fine Dining

Al Forno, 577 South Main St.

Food at its gutsiest is served at this widely honored restaurant, a bustling yet comfortable establishment on two floors of a renovated 19th-century stable near the waterfront. Rhode Island School of Design graduates Johanne Killeen and George Germain applied their artistic talents to northern Italian cooking, generating national publicity and developing a cult following for Al Forno, which literally means "from the oven." Their followers love the pizzas done over the open fire with ever-changing toppings. They love the salads dressed with extra-virgin olive oil and balsamic vinegar. They love the pastas bearing such goodies as grilled squid and spicy peppers. And they love the grilled items done on the wood grill using fruitwoods and even grapevines from nearby Sakonnet Vineyards. They also don't seem to mind long waits for a table. Pizza done over the grill in the main-floor kitchen open to the bar is the signature dish. With a crackly thin crust and different toppings every day (ours had tomato, onion, gorgonzola, chicken, tarragon and tomato coulis), it is sensational. We also loved a starter of cool vermicelli with five little salads (cucumber, jîcama, carrot, red pepper and Egyptian beans). The menu is tweaked daily, but you might find a clam roast with hot spicy sausage and endive in a tomato broth, pepper-grilled chicken with arugula and parmigiana, and grilled veal tenderloin with roasted crimini and portobello mushrooms on grilled polenta. Our choucroute garni included three of the fattest sausages ever topping mild sauerkraut, accompanied by wide noodles sparked with fresh coriander. The skirt steak, seared right on the coals, came with wilted watercress and a green chile sauce. Dessert, which must be ordered with the main course, is the icing on the cake. We'd try any of Johanne's special tarts – the lemon soufflé version is ethereal. Another masterpiece is a sourdough waffle with caramel-walnut ice cream and chocolate. The "grand cookie finale" has been widely imitated. A tray on a pedestal holds two kinds of chocolate cookies, ricotta fritters, pinwheels, ginger molasses cookies and chocolate truffles – a mix-and-match play on textures and flavors that's heaven for cookie lovers.

(401) 273-9760. www.alforno.com. Entrées, $23.95 to $39.95. Dinner, Tuesday-Friday 5 to 10, Saturday 4 to 10.

New Rivers, 7 Steeple St.

The intimate space where Al Forno got its start is now the setting for nationally honored chef Bruce Tillinghast, who had been chef in executive dining rooms in Boston before returning to his hometown to open his own operation, happily unpretentious and lacking in attitude. New Rivers tucks tables for 40 and a small bar into a pair of rooms in an 1870 building at the base of College Hill, near the confluence of the two recently uncovered rivers for which the restaurant is named. A striking picture of six red pears glistening against a dark green wall sets the theme in the main dining room, where white butcher paper covers pale yellow tablecloths beneath a rust-colored ceiling. The smaller side dining room has more pale yellow, from cloths to walls, and a yellow-tiled bar at which some folks like to perch and eat. The fare is the most diverse in Providence, reflecting a multi-cultural mix of Mediterranean and Middle Eastern cuisines with Asian influences. Nime chow spring rolls combining lobster meat, julienned vegetables, sprouts and pungent basil rolled in cool Thai rice wrappers, served with a gingery dipping sauce, are the specialty appetizer. Or you could start with grilled shrimp on sugarcane skewers with spicy pineapple salsa and crispy cassava. Move on to one of the small meals or pastas, as basic as a half-pound burger on a Portuguese sweet roll or as exotic as sundried tomato and artichoke tortellini with Tuscan sausage, roasted fennel, olives and mint. Heartier appetites are well served by items from the grill and oven: perhaps baked sand dab with crab and corn stuffing, grilled Atlantic halibut on Thai purple rice, and bulgogi (Korean beef with spicy pickle and shiitake mushrooms over rice and soy sprouts). A made-to-order lemon tartlet, garnished with blueberries or other seasonal fruit, is the specialty dessert. Other standouts are homemade ice creams like huckleberry or rum-spiked praline and a cookie plate bearing eight New Rivers favorites.

(401) 751-0350. Entrées, $21 to $26. Dinner, Tuesday-Saturday 5:30 to 10.

L'Epicureo, 311 Matthewson St.

From a humble start in her late father's butcher shop, Rozann and Tom Buckner built a hugely successful Federal Hill restaurant that moved in 2005 into grand quarters in the Hotel Providence. The move was not only a feather in the new hotel's cap but provided a larger arena for Tom Buckner's much-acclaimed cooking skills. Beyond a glamorous lounge and piano bar is a 150-seat, Renaissance-style dining room with crystal chandeliers and gilt-framed paintings hung on rich burgundy walls. Vintage wine bottles are on display in a wall of glass and stainless steel. The Buckners' sophisticated style and polished service continued in their new digs, as did their signature contemporary Italian dishes and exemplary desserts. The opening menu ranged widely from an open-face Maine lobster pot pie with truffle sauce to a classic veal osso buco over risotto milanese. An artichoke and bacon tartlet, an oyster sampling and a potato and truffle frittata are among the starters, but knowing diners go for the chef's antipasto sampler for the table to share. And everyone goes for the desserts, be they the special tiramisu over espresso creme anglaise, the rustic apple crostada or the trio of exotic ice creams with a shortbread cookie.

(401) 521-3333. Entrées, $20 to $39. Dinner, Monday-Saturday 5 to 10 or 11, Sunday noon to 9.

Café Nuovo, One Citizens Plaza.
This dramatic restaurant along the revived downtown riverfront epitomizes the city's renaissance. The large and airy interior off the lobby rotunda of the Citizens Bank tower is spectacular in gray, white and red, with fabulous views of water and skyline from soaring windows. For a ringside seat on the Providence River, the gondolas and WaterFire, the best tables in town are those for 60 lucky diners on the outdoor terrace. The setting matches the trendy food that's architectural as well as unusual. Ex-Manhattan chef Timothy Kelly, who has been with owner Dimitri Kriticos since Café Nuovo opened, calls the cuisine fusion. At lunch, we devoured a couple of appetizers: the nime chow shrimp rolls with cellophane noodles, tiny vegetables and a lemongrass dipping sauce, and a chopped salad of cucumbers, tomatoes, asparagus, snap peas and more, standing tall in a radicchio cup. Both were as exciting to taste as to look at. Against these high-rise theatrics the low-rise smoked salmon club sandwich with side potato and tossed salads looked mundane, though it proved excellent. Dessert was a crystal bowl filled with fruit sorbets and ice creams, studded with a candy stick. For dinner, the chef traverses the world to produce the likes of Szechwan-seared Hawaiian ahi tuna, ginger-crusted salmon with key lime beurre blanc, dover sole meuniere, Hudson Valley duck with pickled cherries and rack of lamb crusted with chèvre and macadamia nuts. Café Nuovo's innovative pasta and risotto dishes give new meaning to the genre: perhaps a lemon risotto with caramelized sea scallops or lobster-stuffed raviolis with half a lobster tail over Narragansett succotash. The pastry chef's desserts are the talk of the town. Consider the "chocolate chocolate" (chocolate custard, chocolate-caramel leaves, hazelnut pralines, milk chocolate ganache and chocolate-chambord ice cream) or the "pot o'mousse (dark and white chocolate mousses served in a chocolate pot with cappuccino-tartufo ice cream).

(401) 421-2525. Entrées, $20.95 to $33.95. Lunch, Monday-Friday 11:30 to 3. Dinner, Monday-Saturday, 5 to 10:30 or 11.

Neath's, 262 South Water St.
West meets East in Cambodian chef-owner Neath Pal's stylish New American bistro in a restored warehouse along the river. The main floor holds an angular bar, but the culinary action is upstairs in a high-ceilinged space with bold yellow and red walls. White cloths, votive candles and small vases with fresh flowers top the widely spaced tables seating 75, some next to big windows overlooking the developing parkland along the river. In the rear kitchen he fuses New England ingredients with French and Asian preparations for a highly personalized cooking style. It showed up in an appetizer of shrimp and shiitake-mushroom dumplings, steamed and then grilled and served with a shoyu dipping sauce, wood-grilled

baguette slices lathered with a coconut and scallion sauce, and a bowl of extra dipping sauce for good measure. The star of our dinner was a special salad of chilled Maine crab with diced cucumbers and tomatoes and delicate potato gaufrettes, the crabmeat stunningly pure and the wafers so thin and intricately latticed as not to be believed. Signature main dishes are lobster with snow peas and shiitake mushrooms, simmered in coconut milk with red curry and served over chow foon noodles; grilled pork loin chop with stir-fried Asian broccoli, and pan-roasted Hudson Valley duck breast and confit with a subtle ginger glaze over sweet-potato gratin and wilted spinach. We were pleased with the oven-roasted Chilean sea bass, succulent and of the melt-in-the-mouth variety, teamed with a cool cucumber salad. The chicken breast rubbed with lemongrass was wood-grilled and served with a Thai basil salad. Ginger ice cream accompanies the signature dessert of crunchy fried wontons filled with molten chocolate. Passion-fruit crème brûlée served in an almond lace cookie is another favorite.

(401 751-3700. www.neaths.com. Entrées, $20 to $27. Dinner, Tuesday-Sunday 5:30 to 10 or 10:30.

Mill's Tavern, 101 North Main St.

A four-foot-long silver fork placed horizontally on the wall above the stone-framed kitchen sets the culinary theme at this updated, 21st-century tavern specializing in wood-fired, modern American cooking. Little remains of the converted 1850s mill for which the place is named. Instead, picture a blend of timeless Manhattan steakhouse and modern New England tavern: high ceilings, wrought-iron candle chandeliers, planked oak floors, wood paneling and white-clothed tables flanked by leather banquettes or dark wood chairs upholstered in black and cream. A rotisserie, wood oven and grill impart a smoky, outdoorsy flavor to chef-owner Jaime D'Oliveira's eclectic fare. Typical are the crispy sweet salmon with a counterpoint of tart tomato-citrus jam and the veal chop with a bold portobello vinaigrette. Two of the more intriguing entrées are rabbit stew and spit-roasted suckling pig. "From the pantry" come such appetizers as the signature "Mill's sandwich:" a tower of currant-studded biscuit filled with duck confit and rich foie gras, with a sweet, tea-braised fig on the side. An artisan cheese plate is a fitting ending to such a procession of taste treats. So are desserts like roquefort cheesecake with pear confit and port-thyme elixir and the Mill's sundae with ginger ice cream, roasted pears, butterscotch and spiced pecans.

(401) 272-3331. Entrées, $17 to $28. Dinner nightly, 5 to 10 or 11.

XO Steakhouse, 125 North Main St.

"Life is uncertain, order dessert first," begins the menu at this unconventional restaurant. It then proceeds to list the sweets, prior to the caesar "the way it should be" salad and the tuna ceviche cones and braised duck leg appetizers. John Elkhay, executive chef and co-owner, has always been in the vanguard – at In-Prov, Angels, Atomic Grill and now at the XO Café renamed XO Steakhouse. The current arena is an avant-garde fantasy in ivory, gold and black, augmented by pop art and mirrors. The food measures up in the Elkhay tradition of on-the-edge style, innovation and presentation – no longer fusion to the max, but rather cutting-edge steakhouse. Still the favorite starter is the bento box sampler, a shiny black Japanese box yielding four of the best: crunchy, rice flour-battered calamari rings with smoked jalapeño mayonnaise and chopped hot peppers, warm oysters with leeks and bacon cream, tempura mushroom fries and teriyaki beef on a stick. The rest of the menu is comprised mainly of prime steaks and chops with a choice of sauces, culminating in the XO filet topped with sliced seared scallops and macadamia nut butter on a bed of roasted asparagus. Lobster mashed potatoes, red pepper parmesan spaëtzle and truffle fries are among the sides. The crème brûlée tray is a selection of three tiny pots of caramelized custards whose flavors could be banana, ginger, mango, coconut, maple, clove or rosewater. The pineapple upside-down cake with guava sorbet appealed at our autumn visit. The café is named for a zesty Asian sauce, but also plays on the word extraordinary. That's just how Elkhay fans describe it.

(401) 273-9090. www.xocafe.com. Entrées, $18 to $35. Dinner nightly, 5 to 10 or 11.

10 Steak and Sushi, 55 Pine St.

Call it exotic, funky, sexy, sophisticated, as the ads and reviewers do. Cutting-edge chef John Elkhay calls it "the next evolution in food," as served at another of his new Providence restaurants. Here he joined the most unlikely of dining trends – healthful, low-fat cuisine and prime red meat – in one improbable combination and pulled it off. Designed with a capital D, the high-ceilinged interior is a palette of blues on blue. It's also sinewy and curvy, from a pair of nudes on the walls to the prime tables positioned around a circular banquette in the front window and the curving sushi bar in back. Pulsating Latin music plays in the background to complement the sensuousness of the ambiance as well as the menu terminology ("fore play" and "entrées we love"). The left side of the oversize menu lists nigiri and sashimi, sushi rolls "for beginners," "designer rolls" and large samplers called "love boats for party animals." The right-hand side details a few fish and other entrées. The heart of the menu is titled the $1010°$ Fahrenheit Grill. It includes the signature aged prime steaks as well as breast of chicken, Colorado lamb chops and veal chop Tuscan style. Four sauces are available, as are ten sides. The dessert menu is presented with three-D glasses for greater impact. Up pop the goodies, ranging from the specialty chocolate soufflé to mango-papaya carpaccio with coconut sorbet. Martinis, margaritas and mojitos are featured in the lively bar.

(401) 453-2333. www.tenprimesteak.com. Entrées, $18 to $33. Lunch, Tuesday-Friday 11:30 to 5. Dinner, Monday-Saturday 5 to 10 or 11.

Moda, 525 South Water St.

The view of the Providence River is terrific and so is the food at this chic, ultra-modern bistro living up its Spanish-Portuguese name for "style." The main floor is a clubby dining area around a bar, mostly black quilted walls, a cool tile floor and windows onto the water. Upstairs is quieter and seems even closer to the water with the sunset and city lights reflected in floor-to-ceiling windows and mirrors. Progressive American food is offered up by hotshot local chef Jules Ramos. He offers a fresh take on such appetizers as lump crab rangoons, Kobe beef tataki, open-face duck ravioli and a treat called "hazelnut duck french toast" starring sliced rare duck on a tiny piece of French toast, topped with foie gras mousse and surrounded by grape preserves. Entrées are equally "progressive," from pan-roasted halibut alantejana with chourico sausage and clams to hazelnut-crusted rack of lamb with rosemary-fig chutney. Braised rabbit stew over truffled pappardelle was a robust winter dish. Warm chocolate valrhona cake with green tea ice cream and a white chocolate flan with blueberry coulis and crystallized ginger are stellar sendoffs.

(401) 331-2288. Entrées, $20 to $30. Dinner, Monday-Saturday 5 to 10 or 11.

Raphael Bar Risto, 1 Union Station.
This sleek, sensuous place on the ground level of the old Union Station is just the ticket for those addicted to Raphael Conte's "progressive Italian" cuisine. Looking onto Waterplace Park, the restaurant's streamlined, retro-modern interior features blond maple, travertine marble, big windows and white walls with deco curves and dramatic art. An armless and headless Venus de Milo is backed by a crackled glass wall with cascading water at the entry. Ahead lie the Tunnel Bar and two dining rooms that could be a modern art museum: an eclectic mix of original pop art, a trio of Warholesque portraits of Marilyn Monroe and a 24-foot-long mural. A fisherman, Ralph (short for Raphael) Conte often adds his morning catch to that supplied by his purveyors. He imparts an innovative, sometimes flamboyant spin on traditional pastas such as black ravioli stuffed with crabmeat and vodka-flashed shrimp. A wood grill in the open kitchen produces a with-it roster of pizzas. Besides the signature lobster fra diavolo, look for entrées like roasted whole red snapper with capers and lemon, crispy duck with port wine-plum sauce and grilled veal chop with porcini sauce. Desserts include an acclaimed tiramisu with espresso bean sauce and a refreshing lemon napoleon – lemony cream custard layered with lemon shortbread and lemon anglaise.
(401) 421-4646. www.raphaelbarristo.com. Entrées, $17 to $30. Dinner, Monday-Saturday from 5.

The Gatehouse, 4 Richmond Square.
This chic East Side restaurant occupies a restored gatehouse on the banks of the Seekonk River. At night, the darkened interior of one of southern New England's prettiest restaurants shimmers with the moon reflecting off the river and the glow of rich wood and brick walls, candlelight and charming paintings of old Providence scenes all around. Diners at window tables on the enclosed porch feel they are on a cruise ship. Executive chef Nat Hughes's dinner menu entices with the likes of blackened ahi tuna with creamy mustard sauce, wood-grilled swordfish with smoked shrimp garlic butter, cioppino, Portuguese pork and clams alentejana, and wood-grilled veal tenderloin with chimichurri sauce. There's a New Orleans accent to starters like seafood gumbo, creole caesar salad with fried oysters and wood-grilled andouille sausage with a crispy jambalaya cake and creole mustard sauce. Desserts follow suit, perhaps warm apple crisp with homemade praline-pecan ice cream, espresso crème brûlée or caramelized banana cream tart.
(401) 521-9229 or (888) 333-4283. www.thegatehouse.com. Entrées, $18 to $27. Dinner, Tuesday-Sunday 5 to 10 or 11. Sunday brunch, 11 to 3.

Pot au Feu, 44 Custom House St.
No less an authority than the late Julia Child was partial to Bob and Ann Burke's long-running success – 33 years in 2005 and the first five-star rating granted by Rhode Island Monthly magazine reviewers. A country French bistro in the basement contains old dark beams, brick and fieldstone walls, steel tables and a zinc bar. Here you order typical bistro food – omelets, onion soup, pâtés (one of duck foie gras), salmon gravlax, quiche and salade au chèvre, all at reasonable prices. The twenty or so dinner entrées might include shrimp provençal, broiled salmon with a citrus-ginger butter, roasted chicken with a pecan and maple syrup glaze, and the namesake pot au feu, the traditional French "pot on fire" of braised meats and vegetables.
Upstairs in the **Salon,** amid crisp white linens, lacquered black chairs and wall panels painted black with gold, the haute menu is traditional, except perhaps for a

recent offering of grilled medallions of ostrich with a caramelized onion and madeira sauce. Dinner is à la carte, and the three-course table d'hôte dinners for an extra $10 represent good value. On the night we dined we were celebrating a double birthday. Fond memories of escargots bourguignonne and clams épinard dance in our heads, as do thoughts of the mushroom soup, the salad with fresh mushrooms and cherry tomatoes, the French bread served from a huge basket with sweet butter, the pink roast lamb, the tournedos with blue cheese, the crisp vegetables, the crème brûlée, the mousse au citron, the espresso. Memories are a bit blurred by a couple of the best martinis we've had and a bottle of La Cour Pavillon Medoc – well, it was a birthday! We can't wait to go back before too many more roll around.

(401) 273-8953. Salon: Entrées, $19.50 to $29. Lunch, Tuesday-Friday noon to 1:30. Dinner, Thursday-Saturday 6 to 9 or 9:30.
Bistro: Entrées, $13.95 to $20.95. Lunch, Monday-Friday 11:30 to 2. Dinner, Monday-Saturday 5:30 to 9 or 10.

Rue de L'Espoir, 99 Hope St.

Originally a Left Bank-type bistro, this favorite of the College Hill crowd has changed to an international menu, and now is French more in name than in fact. Over 30 years it has evolved into a contemporary American bistro with a loyal following who cherish its comfortable country ambiance. Longtime owner Deb Norman offers a with-it dinner menu featuring such entrées as clam roast pomodori, roasted salmon with pistachio-orange crust, a "duet" of duck breast and sea scallops served with two sauces, and wood-grilled filet mignon dusted with espresso, cinnamon and coriander and served with a shallot-madeira demi-glace. Mix and match some of the small plates: perhaps lobster madeira crêpe, Thai crab cakes, grilled chiles rellenos with mango salsa or cognac-laced chicken liver pâté served on a cheese board with toasts of Portuguese sweet bread. Some of the specialty salads, among them niçoise, roasted salmon or duck, and caesar with grilled chicken or shrimp, are meals in themselves. For lunch, the grilled scallops and tomatoes on a bed of greens has a nippy citrus-thyme vinaigrette, pan-sautéed mussels are served with a champagne sauce on a bed of wilted greens, and from the dessert tray we recall a memorable charlotte malakoff (lady fingers, whipped cream, nuts, kirsch and strawberry preserves). A large selection of beers is available, as are interesting and affordable wines. This remains a great place for breakfast. Although famous for its honey oat bread french toast with yogurt and fruit, we could only manage the $4.95 special: two eggs, coffee, corn muffin and crispy home fries. The fries were so addictive that most were snitched by the person who had come in only for fresh orange juice and caffe au lait.

(401) 751-8890. Entrées, $18.95 to $27.95. Breakfast, Tuesday-Friday 7:30 to 11, weekends 8:30 to 2:30. Lunch, Tuesday-Sunday 11:30 to 2:30. Dinner nightly, 5 to 9 or 10:30.

Adesso, 161 Cushing St.

The best and most enduring of the ever-changing eateries on College Hill is this chic café in a converted garage just off Thayer Street. Adesso means "now" in Italian, and this is a now place. Casual and noisy, it's done up crisply in grays and mauve, with heavy European cutlery rolled up inside gray napkins atop charcoal gray oilcloths, neon signs on the walls and changing pots of flowering plants on the tables year-round. Skylights and huge windows make the rear room an oversize greenhouse, while the dark interior dining room yields a view of the open mesquite grill. Celebrated for its flashy "Cal/Ital" cuisine, the kitchen with an open grill and wood oven features a broad range of pasta dishes, entrée salads and grill items. Consider tagliatelle with sliced sirloin strips and mushrooms in a merlot sauce, baked salmon with a smoked salmon and horseradish crust or grilled sirloin with steak frites. Highlights of several meals here over the years included grilled squid with a salsa of red peppers, onions and black olives; swordfish with a relish of cucumber, red apple and onion; sesame-crusted tuna with a garlic-ginger-soy sauce, and Canadian pheasant served on wild rice with a madeira and black truffle sauce. Worthy endings were warm chocolate-bourbon truffle cake with french vanilla ice cream and a chocolate terrine capped with white chocolate ganache and served with raspberry sauce. The sleek chrome and glass salt and pepper grinders were so handsome that we bought a pair to take home.

(401) 521-0770. Entrées, $19.95 to $27.95. Dinner, Monday-Saturday 5 to 10:30 or 11:30, Sunday 4:30 to 10:30.

Country Charm in the City

Olga's Cup and Saucer, 103 Point St.

Coffee with the best artisan breads and pastries in town is the hallmark of this small café with a bakery of great note. It's the offspring of the much-loved Olga's Cup and Saucer in Little Compton, which baker Olga Bravo runs with Rebecca Wagner, an Al Forno alumnus who's known for her soups. They added a year-round bakery in a charming English-style cottage in the India Point section just south of downtown Providence. Their summer following expected lunches as well as breads, so the partners obliged. The thin-crust corn and tomato pizzas, sandwiches, pastas, tempting entrées and delicious desserts pack in the noonday crowds. Morning coffee, enormous muffins, scones and breads for toasting are so popular that you can barely get in the door. There's a handful of tiled tables made by the owners, who also are artists. Most choice are those outside beneath apricot trees beside a showplace little English garden, full of raised and potted beds bursting with flowers, vines and herbs. It's a touch of country in the midst of the city.

(401) 831-6666. Entrées, $6 to $9. Open Monday-Friday, 7 to 6, Saturday 8 to 5. Lunch, 11 to 3.

Changes of Pace

CAV, 14 Imperial Place.

What to make of a place whose name is an acronym for Coffee, Antiques and Victuals, and also alludes to a French wine cellar (cave, pronounced cahv)? Egyptian owner Sylvia Moubayed, former executive director of the Providence Atheneum, not only makes the coffeehouse cum restaurant cum antiques shop a happening place. She sells the decor to help pay the bills. The former warehouse with a fourteen-foot-high ceiling near the waterfront is rather overwhelming, what with chairs and rugs hanging from the rafters, dining tables tucked between glass cases of art objects and displays of Asian bronzes and carved wooden masks, a staff clad in black, and people emerging here, there and everywhere. The tables are set with kilim rugs, a couple of booths are topped with hoods and the enormous menu comes in an album. It runs to at least eight typewritten pages, not counting specials of the day and night. This is much more than an ambient pause for coffee or tea and pastries. It's a lunch stop for ladies who shop, a celebratory venue for a special-occasion dinner, and a club with live jazz or blues on weekends. The eclectic, international menu covers all the bases and all price ranges. The food, though upstaged by the ambiance, is quite good. Sit back, watch the scene and enjoy.

(401) 751-9164. Entrées, $13.50 to $23.95. Lunch daily, 11:30 to 4. Dinner nightly, 4 to 10 or 11.

L'Elizabeth, 285 South Main St., is a romantic spot for a tête-à-tête coffee or drink. It has a true European feeling, with the look of a salon where there are different groupings of sofas and chairs, and is very dimly lit at night. No meals are served, but stop here in the afternooon for tea and Elizabeth Mahoney's torte cake with raspberry, apricot and chocolate. Espresso, cappuccino, international coffees, hot toddies and a large selection of single-malt scotches and liqueurs are available. Open daily, 3 to midnight, weekends to 1 a.m.

Union Station Brewery, 36 Exchange Ter., produces specialty ales, lagers and stout in a section of the old Union Station, along with snacks and light fare to go with. More award-winners emanate from **Trinity Brewhouse**, across from the Providence Civic Center at 186 Fountain St.

Wickenden Street, just southeast of downtown, offers a panoply of food: Z Bar and Grille, Café Zog (coffee, sandwiches and juices), the Coffee Exchange, I-Scream, O-Cha Thai cuisine and sushi bar, and Taste of India. It's a funky street that USA Today dubbed bohemian in a feature highlighting how a wave of movies and the hit TV show helped turned Providence into a getaway destination for the young and hip.

A Taste of Federal Hill

No trip to Providence is complete without a look at Federal Hill. The tight little enclave of ethnic eateries along Atwells Avenue just west of downtown out-Italians Boston's famed North End for authenticity. The traditional stress on heavy Neapolitan cuisine has been considerably broadened with the likes of **Mediterraneo** and **Pane e Vine.** Not to mention the sleek **Eclectic Grille, Gracie's Bar & Grille, Aquaviva Restaurant & Tapas Bar, Providence Oyster Bar, Providence Prime,** the Caribbean **Montego Bay on the Hill, Mia Sushi Bar & Grille, Don Jose Tequila's** and the **Bombay Club.** Traditionalists still dote on the **Blue Grotto, Cassarino's** and **Camille's.**

The heart of the area is DePasquale Square, a charming cobblestone plaza with a fountain, pots of flowers, tiny white lights in the trees, and outdoor tables and benches. Here you can order a sandwich and a fine imported dessert at **Caffe Dolce Vita,** or take out a lunch to go from the marvelous deli cases at glamorous **Venda Ravioli.**

Around the corner at 92 Spruce St. is **Pastiche,** a bakery and gourmet dessertery par excellence. Partake of an exotic homemade dessert (perhaps toffee-walnut torte or a fabulous looking fruit tart) with cappuccino or café au lait in stylish digs beside the fireplace.

The natives are right when they say there's a touch of Europe – make that the world – here.

FOR MORE INFORMATION: Providence/Warwick Convention & Visitors Bureau, One West Exchange Street, Providence, RI 02903, (401) 274-1636 or (800) 233-1636. www.goprovidence.com.

Bristol, R.I.

The 'Quintessential' Waterfront Town

What – all of a sudden Bristol is a getaway destination in Southern New England? A two-bit town that few outside Rhode Island had heard of and that most bypassed on their way to Newport or New Bedford, if they passed it at all? A place that had little claim to fame other than staging the nation's oldest Fourth of July parade every summer? An aging town on the far side of the East Bay, where there was little reason to visit, hardly a decent place to eat and scarcely a place to stay, if anybody wanted to?

Yes, Bristol. How times have changed in less than a decade for a town that had been insular and introverted. A preservation group called Save Blithewold rescued a struggling garden estate and turned it into one of Rhode Island's leading tourist attractions. Other museums followed or raised their profiles, as did parks and recreation activities. Inns and B&Bs emerged in historic structures. Restaurants popped up across town. Boutiques and shops revived a dormant downtown.

And now, outsiders are discovering that there's far more to Bristol than a great parade. They are beating a path to the town of 22,500 squeezed on a narrow strip between Mount Hope and Narragansett bays.

Although tourism came lately to Bristol, history did not. With a street plan laid out in 1680, Bristol has outstanding examples of architecture spanning three centuries from Federal and Greek Revival homes to 19th-century country garden estates to modern showplaces outside the historic district. Some of the most imposing are schools and museums.

With a protected harbor on Narragansett Bay, the town became an early shipbuilding and maritime center. The fruits of its prosperity are evident throughout the stately historic district and along the waterfront, in town and along the posh Poppasquash peninsula accessed by a causeway.

Bristol proper has no fewer than 35 parks and public places along the water. The best is Colt State Park, 464 acres of play areas and scenery on the peninsula. Besides the revived Blithewold Mansion, Gardens and Arboretum, attractions are as diverse as the Herreshoff Marine Museum and America's Cup Hall of Fame, Brown University's Haffenreffer Museum of Anthropology, an Audubon Society environmental education center, the 17th-century Mount Hope Farm and majestic Linden Place, an 1810 Federal mansion.

All this prompts visitors to agree with those who tout Bristol as "the quintessential New England waterfront town."

They tell docents at the Blithewold mansion that they would like to live there. They stop at local real estate offices to check out the listings. They tell shopkeepers, restaurateurs, innkeepers, fellow tourists – almost anybody they encounter – what a wonderful town it is.

Although off the beaten path, Bristol has a way of showing people a good time.

Seeing and Doing

The red, white and blue center stripes down the middle of Hope Street mark the route of the nation's oldest and largest Fourth of July parade, an event staged

Poppasquash peninsula is viewed across harbor from pub deck at Thames Street Landing.

annually since 1785 with considerable pomp and flair. Scores of historic houses are decked out in patriotic regalia for the occasion, a phenomenon equaled only by the myriad tiny white lights twinkling everywhere as if by local edict for the Christmas season.

Flag-waving Bristol people, it seems, like to show off their town. And there's much to show off.

WALKING TOURS. Three walking tours are outlined in the Discover Bristol guide. One, the Cultural Wood Street Walk, covers parts of State and Thames streets and highlights Wood Street, an eclectic neighborhood full of Portuguese bakeries, fisheries and markets, settled by those who immigrated from Portugal and the Azores to work in Bristol's mills and factories and who today represent about a third of the population. A longer walk covers historic buildings and homes along Hope and High streets. A third walk focuses on the Thames Street waterfront.

Bristol is the southern terminus of the new East Bay Bicycle Path, a cyclist's dream that extends fourteen miles along Narragansett Bay from Providence to Bristol. It's a scenic route for biking, walking, running or rollerblading.

Blithewold Mansion, Gardens & Arboretum, 101 Ferry Road, Bristol.
New England's finest seaside garden estate was saved from private development in 1999 by a private friends group called Save Blithewold. Its revival coincided with and even inspired the rebirth of Bristol, drawing visitors from afar.

Built of stone in 1908 as a summer residence by Pennsylvania coal baron Augustus Van Wickle, the 45-room English-style manor house is surrounded by 33 acres of landscaped grounds, gardens and exotic plants beside Narragansett Bay. With the help of a landscape architect (family friend John DeWolf), his wife Bessie, a horticulturalist, and their daughter Marjorie developed an arboretum and extensive gardens that were left to the citizens of Bristol following Marjorie's death on the estate in 1976 at age 93. A 100-foot giant sequoia (the biggest east of the Rockies and so tall that it wears a lightning rod for protection) is a highlight of the arboretum. A bamboo grove the size of a tennis court grows 30 feet high. A rose garden with century-old climbers, perennial gardens, water and rock gardens, and more than 300 species of trees and shrubs (especially Asian) are viewed along self-guiding trails. One leads across a stone bridge over a pond to a century-old rock garden with salt-tolerant plants nestled beneath trees right beside the shore. Others lead to the expanded display gardens, a showcase for new annuals and tender perennials in striking combinations, many grown in the Blithewold greenhouse. More than 50,000 daffodils burst into bloom in the Bosquet woodland in April.

The stone and stucco mansion, listed on the National Register, is furnished much as it was early in the last century, with most of the original wallpaper and prized possessions from antiques to clothing still intact. Twelve rooms on two floors are open for self-guided tours. Included are a daughter's bedroom with Stickley furniture and the cozy maid's room. The master bedroom, with twin canopy Dutch marquetry beds and hand-painted wallpaper depicting a Dutch village scene, opens onto a sun porch bigger than most bedrooms. Many pieces were handcrafted for the family in Renaissance style, among them several chairs in the dining room made of oak from the Blithewold gardens. Printed sheets in the rooms point out Tiffany lamps, Baccarat crystal, Gorham silver, more than 30 sets of fine china, hand-embroidered linens, family photographs and postcards from their world travels. Visitors remark favorably that the house looks more lived-in and livable than the mansions in Newport.

(413) 253-2707. www.blithewold.org. Self-guided tours of mansion and grounds, Wednesday-Sunday 10 to 4, mid-April to Columbus Day; adults $10, children free. Christmas at Blithewold, Thanksgiving through December, Wednesday-Sunday 1 to 8, adults $10, children $6. Grounds open year-round, daily 10 to 5, adults $5.

Herreshoff Marine Museum/America's Cup Hall of Fame, 1 Burnside St., Bristol. Bristol's reign as the yacht-building capital of the world is evident at Rhode Island's most important maritime site, bordering Narragansett Bay at the southern end of Hope Street. From 1863 to 1945, the Herreshoff Manufacturing Co. on this site produced the world's finest yachts with cutting-edge design and engineering. The first U.S. Navy torpedo boats and mammoth schooners were among its output. The Herreshoff family designed and built a record eight consecutive successful defenders of the America's Cup from 1893 to 1934. The museum displays more than 60 classic sailing and power yachts, some of which can be boarded. The Nathanael G. Herreshoff Room holds a unique collection of 535 study models that he, his son Sidney and grandson Halsey used to create the designs. In addition, it showcases hundreds of artifacts and memorabilia from the Herreshoff legacy, including steam engines, photos, correspondence, silver and china, tools and even the notes and spectacles of Nathanael, the famed naval architect. The museum operates the America's Cup Hall of Fame here, detailing the history of the world's oldest international sporting trophy. The property encompasses the old family homestead, seven former company buildings and a large portion of the company waterfront.

(401) 253-5000. www.herreshoff.org. Open May-October, daily 10 to 5. Adults $8, children $2.

Linden Place, 500 Hope St., Bristol.

The most prominent landmark in the heart of town is the columned 1810 Federal mansion built for Gen. George DeWolf of the seafaring Rhode Island family, a merchant who made his fortune in the slave-trading business and fled the town in 1825 when forced into bankruptcy following the failure of his Cuban sugar crop. The grand house was occupied by his descendants, including grandson Samuel Pomeroy Colt (founder of U.S. Rubber Co., now Uniroyal, and director of 26 leading corporations). The mansion hosted four American presidents, served as a summer home for actress Ethel Barrymore and was featured in the movie, "The Great Gatsby." The interior holds a dramatic Honduras mahogany spiral staircase as well as artworks and furnishings from five generations who occupied the house until 1989, when it was saved from possible demolition by a friends group. The Bristol Art Museum is based in the house and presents changing exhibits. The two-acre property features a summerhouse, a carriage house, 19th-century sculptures, gazebos and rose gardens.

(401) 253-0390. www.lindenplace.org. Open Thursday-Saturday 10 to 4, Sunday and holidays noon to 4, May-October and December. Adults $5, children $2.50.

Haffenreffer Museum of Anthropology, 300 Tower St., Bristol.

Relics from native peoples around the world are preserved here on the land where Metacom, the mighty war chief King Philip, held court over the Wampanoags. They're the legacy of beer baron Rudolf F. Haffenreffer, who purchased 375 acres of Metacom's land for a dairy farm in 1916. Haffenreffer collected Native American and Inuit artifacts and by 1928 his collections had become so extensive that he opened them to the public as King Philip Museum. In 1955 he donated the land and artifacts to Brown University, which now runs the museum and opens the property to the public. The main building is a treasure trove of nearly 100,000 rare artifacts from the native peoples of the Americas, Africa, Asia and the Pacific, only one-tenth of which can be displayed at one time. Four galleries show a range of exhibits from Native American clothing and weapons to Hopi kachina dolls, African masks, and Taoist paintings from the Mien Hill Tribe of northern Thailand. The wetu and tipi exhibits feature life-size replicas of 17th-century Native American dwellings. The grounds are favored for picnics, woodland walks and bird watching. The site looks across Mount Hope Bay to Fall River, Mass.

(401) 253-8388. www.haffenreffermuseum.org. Open Tuesday-Sunday 11 to 5, June-August; Saturday-Sunday 11 to 5, rest of year. Adults $3, children $1.

Mount Hope Farm, 250 Metacom Ave., Bristol.

Here is a great place to walk, picnic, fly a kite or just get away from it all. The grounds at this historic farm dating to the 1680s, a landmark on the National Register of Historic Places, are open to the public. Walking trails wind around the 200-acre hilltop property past meadows, woodlands, ponds and streams to Cove Cabin, an Adirondack-style log cabin beside Mount Hope Bay. The outsize cabin was built by Rudolf Haffenreffer as a base for Boy Scouts from the Wampanoag tribe to canoe and sail out onto Narragansett Bay. Although no longer a working farm, you may see a variety of pheasants, Rhode Island Reds, Scottish Highlanders and other livestock in residence. You also can see a soaring 1860 barn and visit the 1745 Governor Bradford House, named for the senator and deputy governor who entertained George Washington for a week here during his presidency. (The house was used more recently in the filming of Stephen Spielberg's *Amistad).* These days it is used for functions, takes in B&B guests as a country inn (see Where to Stay) and is open for house tours. Overnight guests and tour participants also enjoy the colorful gardens, where a children's playhouse is a replica in miniature of the Bradford House. The Haffenreffers sold the farm in 1999 to the local Mount Hope Trust, which opened it to the public.

(401) 254-1745. www.mounthopefarm.com. House open for tours, daily May-October, adults $6. Grounds open daily, 8 to 7:30 or dusk, whichever is earlier. Free.

Paradise by the Bay

Colt State Park, Colt Drive, Route 114, Bristol.

What a fabulous state park to have in your back yard. Bristol is the fortunate benefactor of local industrialist Samuel Pomeroy Colt's largesse, a 464-acre recreational paradise on the former Colt farm along Narragansett Bay. It's considered the "gem" of the state parks system – and that could apply nationally, rather than just to little Rhody. A three-mile loop drive is Bristol's condensed answer to Newport's Ten-Mile ocean drive. It hugs the Narragansett Bay shoreline and weaves around pastures, tidal ponds, ornamental statues, groomed fruit trees, manicured lawns and thick woods. Along the way you pass open bay vistas, hiking trails and bicycle paths, a saltwater fishing pier, boat launch, picnic groves (more than 400 picnic tables at 45 scattered sites), ten large playfields, an open-air Chapel-By-the-Sea and the huge stone barn that housed Colt's herd of prized Jersey cows. Colt, the nephew of Hartford's Samuel Colt of revolver fame, bought and combined three farms on Poppasquash Neck in the early 1900s to breed what he hoped would be the world's best Jersey herd. He designed a system of roads that linked them together and built the fanciful stone bridge over the Mill Gut salt marsh that is part of the elaborate trail network. On a brilliant Columbus Day afternoon, we encountered countless strollers and picnickers, kite flyers, a man with a walking stick exercising his pet goats, and a family outing of Hassidic Jews playing baseball. All were enjoying the legacy left by Samuel Colt on marble gates at the entrance, inscribed "Private Property, Samuel P. Colt, Open to the Public."

(401) 253-7482. Open daily year-round, sunrise to sunset. Free.

Audubon Society of Rhode Island's Environmental Education Center, 1401 Hope St. (Route 114 North), Bristol.

Near the Bristol-Warren town line is a 25-acre wildlife refuge on a former farm where wildlife thrived and corn and other crops were grown. Willed to the society in 1992, the center includes Rhode Island's largest aquarium with wildlife exhibits, touch tanks and a tidal pool with a rare blue lobster. A replica of a 35-foot-long right whale is suspended from the ceiling to allow a view of its inner structure. Interactive exhibits reveal the bay shoreline and a cornfield at night. A new half-mile long boardwalk curves through a freshwater swamp and salt marshes to the Narragansett Bay shoreline, where it intersects with the East Bay Bike Path.

(401) 245-7500. www.asri.org. Open daily 9 to 5 (Sunday from noon, October-April). Adults $5, children $3.

SHOPPING. The most interesting boutiques and shops are spread out along Hope Street, in the vicinity of State Street. Antiques is a common denominator of many, including **Alfred's, Robin Jennings Antiques, Muzzi's Attic** and **Jesse-James Antiques. Paper, Packaging and Panache** is one of the best card and stationery shops we've seen. **Kate & Company** has specialty foods, gifts, clothing and home accents, while **European Kitchen** mixes cookware from France and Italy. **A Novel Idea** is an interesting new bookstore. **The Potted Garden** is a small plant store with colorful ideas displayed on its side deck.

The new Thames Street Landing offers a variety of boutiques, including **The Claddagh Connection, Old China Trader** and **Chatelaine** for women's clothing and shoes. Our favorite Gray's Ice Cream of Tiverton has a branch here, **Gray's on the Dock.**

Where to Stay

Bristol Harbor Inn, 259 Thames St., Bristol 02809.

Comfortable accommodations near the harbor in downtown Bristol are available in this new boutique hotel located in three restored buildings stretching from Thames Street to the waterfront. It's the centerpiece of a multi-use retail, restaurant and residential complex called Thames Street Landing developed by local innkeeper Lloyd Adams and two Syracuse University classmates from afar. The hotel has a two-story lobby and 40 guest rooms off central corridors on three floors. Eight snug "historic" rooms in the former 1797 Bank of Bristol edifice closest to the street come with queen beds, gas fireplaces and reproduction Federal mahogany furniture and brass chandeliers. Their red and brown decor gives way to beachy light browns and tans as rooms with more contemporary furnishings proceed through the 1800 DeWolf Rum Distillery toward the water. Water-view suites with ample sitting rooms and queensize bedrooms offer more space. Some rooms have kingsize or two double beds. About half have water views. TVs, telephones and hair dryers are among the hotel amenities. A complimentary continental breakfast is offered in the main-floor Counting Room. In 2004, the owners teamed with a restaurateur to add the **DeWolf Tavern** restaurant (see Where to Eat) in an adjacent lumber company warehouse along the harbor.

(401) 254-1444 or (866) 254-1444. Fax (401) 254-1333. www.bristolharborinn.com. Twenty-eight rooms and twelve suites with private baths. May-October: doubles $119 to $209, suites $169 to $209. November-April: doubles $89 to $109, suites $119 to $129.

Point Pleasant Inn, 333 Poppasquash Road, Bristol 02809.

This sumptuous waterfront B&B reflects the vision of Trish Hafer, co-owner with her husband Gunter, semi-newcomers to town who think "the best place in the world is Bristol." The Hafers have the means to live anywhere – he commutes between five residences across the country – but this is the grandest, "and meant to be shared." They undertook a year of renovations to the 33-room English country manor house known variously as Rockwell Manor and Point Pleasant Farm, reconfiguring a number of bedrooms on the second floor into five deluxe B&B rooms and suites, the maximum that zoning in this prime waterfront peninsula jutting into Narragansett Bay would allow. Our quarters in the master suite were sumptuous indeed: a living-room-size space with a king poster bed dressed in Italian linens, TV in a built-in cabinet, two leather chairs and a desk facing the harbor through the rear window, and not one but two bathrooms at opposite corners of the room – his with a walk-in shower, hers with a dressing room, shower with multiple heads and whirlpool tub. Trish, a Southern belle whose background was in culinary and hotel management, had thought of everything and then some, stocking the room with terry robes, a Bose radio, luxurious toiletries, chocolates and the latest magazines. Other rooms are smaller but similarly equipped. A second suite with jacuzzi occupies a far corner of the house, and one of three bedrooms opens through french doors onto a large rear balcony overlooking the harbor. All rooms have tubs and separate showers, telephones and TVs. A TV room/den on the second floor is whimsically decorated with oars on the walls and an airplane propeller between art works. Coffee, juice and banana bread are put out here for guests in the morning, before they move to the formal dining room for the main course, perhaps french toast stuffed with cream cheese and marmalade, accompanied by bacon and a fruit smoothie. The Hafers greet guests with cocktails and hors d'oeuvres in the huge living room, and maintain an open bar off the dining room. Gunter, one of the biggest contractors in Colorado, may show some of his construction handiwork here in the music room, the wine cellar, the downstairs billiards and game room, the sauna and exercise room, and his handyman's dream of a workshop at the back of the five-car garage. Outside on their 25 acres of waterfront paradise are terraces, a swimming pool, hot tub and a quarter-mile of water frontage facing Bristol across the harbor.

(401) 253-0627 or (800) 503-0627. Fax (401) 253-0371. www.pointpleasantinn.com. Four rooms and two suites with private baths. Doubles, $300 to $495. Closed November-April.

Rockwell House Inn, 610 Hope St., Bristol 02809.

Built in the Federal style in 1809 by the first marshal of Bristol's famous Fourth of July parade, this imposing house now exhibits Georgian, Greek Revival, Italianate and Victorian features – so much so that it was noted in the Smithsonian magazine for its eclectic architecture and decorative pieces. It was a private residence until 1991, when Debra and Steve Krohn purchased it for Bristol's first B&B. They share their home with guests in four bedrooms and several common areas furnished in traditional style. Two large front-corner bedrooms, one on the ground floor and the other upstairs, come with kingsize beds and gas fireplaces. Another large corner bedroom on the second floor has a king bed. There's a queen bed in a smaller room in back. Terrycloth robes, hair dryers, lighted makeup mirrors and irons are among the room amenities. The high-ceilinged main floor is notable for inlaid hardwood floors, eight-foot pocket doors and hand stenciling. Guests enjoy two parlors with TV/VCR and an extensive video collection, including the latest movies forwarded by Steve's mother, who is in the entertainment business and nominates for the Academy Awards. A decanter of sherry awaits on the bar in the "courting corner" of the rear parlor. Debra is known for her breakfasts, which start with a "Victoria sundae" of fresh fruit topped with homemade granola and vanilla yogurt and may culminate in walnut-raisin bread french toast stuffed with cream cheese and strawberry preserves. The meal is taken in the candlelit dining room, on an enclosed back porch or on a backyard patio beside a trickling fishpond, overlooking an unexpectedly deep back yard. Debra calls it "our secret garden."

(401) 253-0040 or (800) 815-0040. www.rockwellhouseinn.com. Four rooms with private baths. Doubles, $199 to $229.

Bradford-Dimond-Norris House, 474 Hope St., Bristol 02809.

Across from the imposing Linden House, this majestic white house with an Ionic-columned veranda topped by Chinese Chippendale balustrade stands at the town's main intersection. Dating to 1792, the house gained a third floor and enough embellishments following the Civil War to warrant its nickname, "The Wedding Cake House." Suzanne and Lloyd Adams opened it as a B&B in 1995 after a year's renovations. They furnished it with four-poster beds, antiques and paintings in elegant Colonial style. A guest room at the rear of the main floor has a fishnet canopy bed, fainting couch and Victorian sofa, opening to a second room with a twin bed. The other bedrooms are on the second floor, including a prized front corner room with canopy bed and wide-board floor. All rooms have queensize beds and TVs. The formal front parlor contains a baby grand piano. An expanded continental breakfast is served at a table for eight in the chandeliered dining room or on the rear veranda.

(401) 253-6338 or (888) 329-6338. Fax (401) 253-4023. www.bdnhouse.com. Four rooms with private baths. Doubles, $110 to $140.

The Governor Bradford House at Mount Hope Farm, 250 Metacom Ave. (Route 136), Bristol 02809.

The home of some of Bristol's most illustrious families for more than 300 centuries, the 127-acre Mount Hope Farm estate is now operated by a local trust as a venue for weddings and corporate retreats and as a country inn taking overnight guests year-round. The largest and most popular rooms are four in the 1745 manor house named for William Bradford, the U.S. senator and deputy governor of Rhode Island, who purchased it in 1783 and hosted George Washington for a week. Not only did George Washington sleep here, he and the senator made the rounds of taverns in town, according to innkeeper John Paul Smith. The Washington Room and others are shown on public house tours. Three guest rooms that look much as they did in the past have working fireplaces. The queen-bedded Nathaniel Byfield is named for the farm's first owner, one of the four original Bristol proprietors who purchased the lands from the Plymouth Colony in 1680. Also with a working fireplace is the kingsize Rudolf Haffenreffer Room, named for the family that last owned the farm and whose brewery made the beer that made Narragansett famous. One other room has two double beds, and the fourth has twin beds. Four more rooms with a variety of bed configurations are available in a section known as the North Pasture. One is a single with a twin bed. Three rooms with double beds have been opened recently in the pool house next to the swimming pool. Complimentary breakfast features fresh eggs from the farm's heritage breed of Rhode Island Reds, a flock of nine hens and a rooster named Netop, a Narragansett word for friend that is associated with Rhode Island founder Roger Williams.

(401) 254-1745. Fax (401) 254-1270. www.mounthopefarm.com. Eleven rooms with private baths. Doubles, $175 to $275 May-October, $100 to $175 rest of year.

1808 William's Grant Inn, 154 High St., Bristol 02809.

A mural of Bristol harbor in the front hall welcomes guests to this five-bay Colonial/ Federal house first granted by Deputy Governor William Bradford to his grandson in 1808. The mural is one of several plus countless cupboard-door designs hand-painted by the mother of a former innkeeper and retained by former Army officer Warren Poehler and his wife Diane, who added abundant collections from their own travels to the B&B. They offer five fairly ample guest rooms, each with queensize bed and gas fireplace. Each is themed in decor according to its name. The front-corner Sturbridge Room on the ground floor is properly historic, with bath facilities in former closets on either side of the brick chimney. The premier room is on the side toward the rear off the dining area, with understated antique nautical decor and a whirlpool tub. Antique equestrian decor graces the front-corner Middleburg Room upstairs. The other front-corner upstairs room has been turned into a guest parlor, with TV set, piano and a tray of complimentary liqueurs in a corner. Two tables in a dining area open to the kitchen are the setting for a breakfast of perhaps Portuguese french toast or New Zealand egg and bacon pie. In season, guests enjoy a back porch and a leafy backyard with a koi pond whose occupants not only thrive but also multiply each winter.

(401) 253-4222 or (800) 596-4222. Fax (401) 254-0987. www.wmgrantinn.com. Five rooms with private baths. Doubles, $139 to $159 April-October, $99 to $119 rest of year.

Hearth House, 736 Hope St., Bristol 02809.

The ten fireplaces in this 1798 Colonial house make the new name a natural for the former Parker Borden House B&B, as orchestrated by Angie and Tony Margiotta. The former New York City teachers found Bristol the perfect place for realizing Angie's dream of operating a B&B. Thanks to Angie's background as a high school drama teacher who had her own cabaret act, the place has something of a theatrical flair. Facing the waterfront across a busy intersection, the dark red house smack up against the sidewalk has three guest accommodations, each with kingsize bed and a fireplace or wood-burning stove and each appointed in dramatic colors, especially fiery reds. Roses are the theme on the comforter and the rose-colored walls in Victorian Rose Room, whose lace-curtained windows yield a glimpse of the harbor. The Skylight Garden Room, colorful in vivid green, has a skylight above the bed and an enclosed sitting porch looking onto the rear garden. The Harbor View Suite comes with two fireplaces and a bath/sitting room with a tiled jacuzzi tub. A second-floor common room contains a fireplace and satellite TV/VCR. Both Margiottas are into cooking, and the fruits of their labors are served for breakfast at a table for six in the dining room. Guests relax two at a time in the glider swing in the back yard.

(401) 253-1404. www.hearthhouse.com. Two rooms and one suite with private bath. Doubles, $150. Suite $175. Two-night minimum weekends. Children over 12.

Where to Eat

DeWolf Tavern, 259 Thames St., Bristol.

The area's most exciting dining emanates from this new restaurant along the Bristol harborfront, run by the owners of the Bristol Harbor Inn in partnership with restaurateur Melicia Phillips. It's exciting for its setting, elegant yet historic as all get-out with wide-plank floors of yellow pine and exposed-truss ceilings in the restored DeWolf Warehouse. And it's exciting for its cuisine, as dished up by chef Sai Viswanath. He prepares contemporary cuisine with accents from his native India, such as charcoal tandoor oven-roasted lobster basted with garlic-herb butter, or roast quail stuffed with mushroom biryani and served on truffled soubise sauce. His opening menu ranged incredibly widely from seafood goulash with crabmeat pilaf wrapped in cabbage and a fricassee of swordfish with white wine, grapes and mushrooms to grilled baby veal chops over fettuccine with tomatoes, olives, roasted red peppers and herbs. There was even a hearty entrée salad featuring grilled lamb steak with watercress, pea shoots, black olives, grilled zucchini and potatoes with a rosemary vinaigrette and lavender-lemon chutney. To start, how about oyster chowder, a lobster popover or tandoor oven-roasted jumbo shrimp on a coconut lentil bisque with ginger-carrot slaw? Finish with chocolate lava cake with a kirsch-cherry center or a warm chocolate chip-banana bread sandwich with rum-raisin ice cream and butterscotch sauce. All this good eating takes place on two floors of dressed-up early American warehouse decor – a tavern with a casual menu on the main floor and fine dining upstairs. In summer, diners move outside to a patio off the tavern and a deck upstairs, both with harbor views.

(401) 254-2005. www.dewolftavern.com. Entrees, $23 to $36. Lunch daily, 11:30 to 2:30, May-October. Dinner nightly, 5 to 10.

Hotpoint, 31 State St., Bristol.

The antique neon sign outside the entrance has been around longer than this stylish bistro. Chef-owner Jim Reardon thought it represented a cool name for the restaurant he established in a former appliance store. So Hotpoint it is, a reference to the cutting-edge cuisine that's some of the most innovative and most consistent in town. White-clothed tables covered with strips of butcher paper are dressed with flowers in the beige and taupe bistro dining room with a couple of tables beside the front window and a three-stool bar with an espresso machine in back. Votive candles flicker as you savor treats from shrimp scampi and lobster cardinale to chicken marsala and steak au poivre. Among the more creative possibilities are wasabi pea-crusted salmon with lemongrass-ginger, sea scallops around blue cheese polenta, and molasses-marinated pork tenderloin glazed with bourbon and maple syrup. Kangaroo salad, ostrich au poivre and venison tenderloin with juniper berry demi-glace might be specials during game season. Start with the superior saffron-scented seafood chowder or a lobster bisque redolent with basil and brandy. How about a sesame shrimp salad, margarita-cured gravlax or Maine crab cake topped with smoked jalapeño mayonnaise? Finish with banana cheesecake, mocha crème brûlée or flourless chocolate cake.

(401) 254-7474. www.hotpointbistro.com. Entrées, $17.99 to $28. Dinner, Tuesday-Sunday 5 to 9 or 10. Sunday brunch, 10:30 to 2:30 October-May.

Redlefsen's Rotisserie & Grill, 444 Thames St., Bristol.

European visitors come here for "a taste of home," in the words of proprietor Walter Guertler. He and his wife Sally took over a popular establishment from its Swedish founders, keeping the name but relocating to expanded quarters in a former truck garage on the waterfront. A large, high-ceilinged, skylit dining room with yellow walls and well-spaced, sturdy wood tables is separated from a convivial bar/lounge by a large fireplace open to both sides. A cuckoo clock and trompe-l'oeil murals of Bavarian villages convey a foreign air. A small front patio with a harbor view is popular in summer. From an open kitchen chef David Reniere prepares some of the European favorites the Guertlers brought with them, although these have been updated lately to appease American tastes. That may be fortunate, because the specialty wiener schnitzel that two in our party ordered was so like cardboard as to be nearly inedible. The baked scallops and the roasted half chicken were much better. The options, which rarely change, ranged from panko-crusted scrod rémoulade and grilled rainbow trout with mustard-dill sauce to lobster pot pie, rotisserie pork loin rubbed with molasses and grilled ostrich tournedos. Regulars praise the grilled bauerwurst and bratwurst, served with sauerkraut. Lightly grilled gravlax, chicken liver pâté and deep-fried oysters are typical appetizers. A "daisy crêpe" containing vanilla ice cream and topped with chocolate sauce and nuts is the signature dessert. Walter encourages diners to adjourn to a plush sitting area by the fire in the lounge for coffee and after-dinner drinks.

(401) 254-1188. www.redlefsens.com. Entrées, $17 to $28. Dinner, Tuesday-Saturday from 5. Brunch, Saturday and Sunday 11 to 3.

Roberto's, 301 Hope St., Bristol.

First-rate pastas and other Italian dishes are the hallmarks of this cozy restaurant opened by chef Robert Myers, who cooked earlier at Puerini's in Newport, and manager Robert Vanderhoof. The pair tweaked their first names for the venture to reflect the Italian-oriented menu. There are a handful of starters such as black angus beef barley soup, portobello mushrooms sautéed with plum tomatoes and shallots in dry madeira wine and homemade polenta that changes daily. But almost everyone starts with the fabulous bread salad, a medley of vegetables sautéed with shallots, cannellini beans, Italian bread and rosemary. The rest of the menu is split between pastas and main dishes. The shrimp piccata over fettuccine and the mixed seafood possillipo over linguini come highly recommended. Chicken and veal dishes may be prepared in any of twelve styles, from carbonara to piccata. Tournedos with a roasted garlic demi-glace is a favorite among beef offerings. All these treats and more are served in a cozy front room, where tables seating 28 are appointed with white linens, candles and fresh flowers. A second dining room with four tables and a small bar area is in back.

(401) 254-9732. www.robertosonline.com. Entrées, $17 to $24. Lunch, Monday-Friday 11:30 to 2:30. Dinner nightly, 5 to 9 or 9:30.

The Lobster Pot, 119 Hope St., Bristol.

Although it's been around since 1929, the Lobster Pot has never been better than since New York jewelry manufacturer Jeffrey Hirsh took over and upgraded both decor and cuisine. A vast place with equally vast windows onto the harbor, it has one of the better water views of any restaurant – you almost feel as if you're on a boat. A tiled fireplace, photos from Mystic Seaport, and white linens and china on the tables enhance the setting. Dining is by candlelight with traditional Yankee fare – lobster, of course, but also all kinds of seafood, steaks, poultry and veal, including veal oscar. Lobster comes in bisque, stew, ravioli, newburg, sauté, salad, fried and in clambake, as well as in sizes up to three pounds. There's little unusual, although in this area bouillabaisse and welsh rarebit, served with caesar salad, might qualify. More of the same is available at lunch, as are seven salads and things from lobster club sandwich to eggs oscar. Desserts tend to be liqueur parfaits, ice cream puffs and Indian pudding.

(401) 253-9100. Entrées, $15.50 to $25.95. Lunch, Tuesday-Saturday 11:30 to 3:30. Dinner, Tuesday-Saturday 3:30 to 10, Sunday noon to 9.

S.S. Dion, 520 Thames St., Bristol.

"Seafood and sunsets" are the specialties of Sue and Steve Dion, who combined the initials of their names for this restaurant with a clamshell logo, a nautical setting and a water view across the street. Tropical fish entertain in a large aquarium as classical music plays and candles flicker in hurricane chimneys at well-spaced tables. A round enamel Scandinavian fireplace warms the dining room in winter. There's outside dining under an awning in summer. Steve is the host and Sue the head chef, preparing stylish seafood and pasta fare – things like scrod classico, baked stuffed shrimp, seafood casserole, shrimp scampi on capellini and seafood fra diavolo. Grilled fish choices are available with any of five sauces. There are the usual suspects among chicken, veal and beef entrées. Lately, Sue has added oriental twists as in poached scrod with ginger and soy, oriental linguini and chicken teriyaki. Brownie pie and strawberry shortcake are favorite desserts.

(401) 253-2884. Entrées, $13.95 to $19.95. Dinner, Monday-Saturday 5 to 9.

Aidan's Pub & Grub, 5 John St., Bristol.

The Irish-born owner covers the outdoor deck for St. Patrick's Day festivities at this popular Irish pub known locally as an adult hangout for authentic food and ale. The formula proved successful for Aidan Graham, a sometime drummer who hails from County Westmeath in the midlands of Ireland. He opened a second, more formal Aidan's in Newport and, more recently, added the Judge Roy Bean Saloon at the foot of State Street in Bristol. Locals consider his original the real thing, a lively space with a noisy bar at one end and low round tables elsewhere. At the far end, attractively on view from the street, is a large and appealing dining deck with a glimpse of the harbor. Regulars rave about the awesome burgers and the traditional fish and chips. They also go for the Irish specialties, among them bangers and mash, Dublin pot pie, the Irish mixed grill (limerick bacon, Irish sausage and pork chops), and shepherd's pie topped with mashed potatoes – the delectable potatoes worth eating just on their own. Order the sirloin steak rare, for it's sautéed in Irish whisky and arrives sizzling on a platter so hot it keeps on cooking at the table. Accompany with a pint of ale or two. And finish with the Bailey's Irish cream pie.

(401) 254-1940. Entrées, $7.50 to $15.95. Open daily, 11:30 to 10 or 11.

J.F. Goff's Pub, 251 Thames St., Bristol.

If you want food with a view, consider this casual newcomer at the foot of the Thames Street Landing complex. The spacious outdoor deck is on the wharf at water's edge, with waves lapping almost underfoot. The rooftop deck, employed at busy times as a bar or for private parties, affords a panoramic view. An extensive all-day menu of burgers, sandwiches, wraps and salads at rather hefty prices is offered inside and out, around the bar and in a casual dining area. A blackboard posts more substantial specials, changing weekly but typified by crab claws, pork chops, turkey dinner, mixed grill and a game platter. They were out of the caesar salad with jonah crab when we stopped for lunch, but the clam chowder was good, the burger was burnt and hard as a rock, and the clam cakes were at least filling if bland. The folks at the next table ordered a platter of nachos so big that most of it went home in a styrofoam container. The setting remains etched in memory more than the food.

(401) 253-4523. Entrées, $8 to $16. Lunch and dinner daily, 11:30 to 9 or 10.

Quito's, 411 Thames St., Bristol.

There's a small seafood store in front, so you know the fish is fresh as can be in Al Quito's no-nonsense restaurant next to a park at water's edge. The emphasis is family casual at booths and tables inside. In season, the tables of choice are outside on a canopied patio. Fried seafood is featured, served with coleslaw and fries ("no substitutes") and available for takeout. Rather unexpected, from the looks of the place, is the variety of other dishes, from scrod oregano and scallops florentine to grilled swordfish or tuna and pan-seared scallops, served with potato and vegetables. There are chowders and stews, pastas, caesar salads (with lobster or sirloin) and seafood casseroles. The variety extends to the sandwich menu, with options from an "all-natural, low-fat garden burger" to a crab cake sandwich on a homemade roll.

(401) 253-4500. Entrées, $13.95 to $22.95. Open daily except Tuesday, 11:30 to 9, Sunday to 8. Closed Monday and Tuesday in March-April and October-December. Closed January and February.

FOR MORE INFORMATION: East Bay Tourism Council, (401) 245-0750 or (888) 278-9948. www.eastbayritourism.com.

Relaxation with a tranquil Berkshires view is order of the day at Bartholomew's Cobble.

The Southern Berkshires, Mass.

Culture and Beauty

Ah, the Berkshires! The word conjures up thoughts of New England to anyone west of the Hudson River, of Tanglewood to the knowledgeable music lover, of quaint villages and country inns to generations of travelers, of scenic beauty that has inspired the artists and authors who have called the Berkshires home.

The Berkshires means different things to different people: at least three mountains worthy of the name, small lakes and streams, culture and arts, classic New England villages and hamlets, palatial "cottages" and historic homes, and places and names associated with the best of Americana.

For the visitor, the number of attractions is mind-boggling – enough to keep one busy for a week, if not longer. And yet the lesser known, unexpected discoveries in almost every nook and cranny of the mountain mosaic that is the Berkshires account for much of their unfolding appeal, even to those who know them well.

Summer simply wouldn't be summer in New England without a Sunday afternoon at Tanglewood. We make it a day-long outing, stopping for a morning swim in a secluded stream and then spreading our blanket on the lawn outside the music shed for a picnic and an afternoon with the Boston Symphony, Beethoven and the New York Times.

And New England simply wouldn't be New England without a visit to picturesque Stockbridge and the scenic countryside of the southern Berkshires. This is the inland route we take with visitors from afar who want to see and sense New England in a short tour.

Few places in the world offer as vast a spectrum of the arts and as scenic a setting.

The arts are centered in Lenox and Stockbridge, which attracted literati of such name and number in the mid-1800s that the area became known as "America's Lake Country." Herman Melville, Nathaniel Hawthorne, Henry Adams, Edith Wharton and Henry Wadsworth Longfellow all lived here. Today, the Berkshires are an unrivaled summer cultural center with the foremost in music, theater and dance festivals.

The sophistication of Lenox and Stockbridge stands in contrast with the Berkshires of yesteryear, much of which still slumbers off the beaten path a few miles away. The natural beauty prompted Oliver Wendell Holmes's quote: "There's no tonic like the Housatonic," a reference to the river that snakes through the southern Berkshires. Waterfalls, ponds and hidden lakes abound. The flora of Naumkeag, Bartholomew's Cobble and the Berkshire Botanical Garden attract visitors in season.

The Berkshires' mix of scenic beauty and culture make for a stimulating yet calming getaway.

Seeing and Doing

The Culture

Nowhere else is so much music, art and theatrical activity concentrated in one area in the summer. Among the offerings:

Performing Arts

Tanglewood, West Street (Route 183), Lenox.

The summer home of the Boston Symphony Orchestra and its Berkshire Music Center programs, Tanglewood is synonymous with music and the Berkshires. The 210-acre estate, with the waters of Stockbridge Bowl shimmering in the distance, is a perfect setting for the BSO, which began presenting nine weekends of concerts each summer back in 1936. The 5,000 seats in the open-air Koussevitzky Music Shed are reserved far in advance for Friday and Saturday evening and Sunday afternoon concerts. It's the place for the connoisseur who wants to see or be seen. Up to 10,000 more can be accommodated at $14 to $18 each on the lawn (bring your own chairs, blankets, picnics and wine, or pick up something from the cafeteria). On the lawn you can't see but can hear just fine. We try to arrive when the gates open two hours prior to the performance and pick a spot under the biggest tree just outside the shed to ward off sunstroke or showers. The grounds are made for strolling, and you can view the replica of Nathaniel Hawthorne's Little Red Shanty across Hawthorne Road from the Friends of Tanglewood tent. Special events feature visiting performers many weekdays in season in the Shed or in the acoustically spectacular Seiji Ozawa Hall, which seats 1,200 inside and another 200 on sloping lawns so situated that you can see right onto the stage. The hall is used for chamber music concerts and student recitals most weeknights in summer and for community events in spring and fall. Free open rehearsals for the Sunday concerts are scheduled Saturday mornings at 10:30 in the Shed – an excellent and intimate way for budget-watchers to get up close.

(413) 637-1940 or (800) 274-8499. www.bso.org. Concerts, Friday and Saturday at 8:30, Sunday at 2:30, last weekend of June through August. Tickets, $14 to $90.

Berkshire Theatre Festival, Main Street, Stockbridge.

The area's oldest summer institution has been described by the New York Times as "one of the most adventurous and exciting theaters in the country." Dedicated exclusively to the American repertoire, the festival brings top talent and four shows each summer to the 440-seat playhouse and four more to the decade-old Unicorn Theatre for new or experimental works. The Main Stage Playhouse, designed in 1886 by Stanford White as the Stockbridge casino, was the social center of the community until it became the nation's second summer theater in 1928.

(413) 298-5576 or (866) 811-4111. www.berkshiretheatre.org. Main Stage performances, late June to Labor Day, Monday-Saturday at 8, matinees Thursday and Saturday at 2; tickets, $45 to $60. Unicorn performances, early June to Labor Day, Monday-Saturday at 8; tickets $25 to $35.

Shakespeare & Company, 70 Kemble St., Lenox.

The 63-acre campus of the former Lenox School for Boys is the new home for one of America's largest Shakespeare festivals. Moving from Edith Wharton's Mount, where the company had rented space for 25 years, the company gradually started work on a center for Shakespeare performance and studies, with plans for the world's only accurate reconstruction of the Elizabethan-era Rose Playhouse, Shakespeare's first theater. Meanwhile, Shakespearean plays are presented in the 100-seat salon of the Spring Lawn Mansion, one of the original Berkshire Cottages, and in the Founders' Theater, a scaffold-and-canvas arena fashioned from an old gymnasium and seating 418 people in movable chairs and cushion-backed benches on three sides. Josie's Place, a lobby dining area and bar, is open before and after all performances. Playgoers may picnic on the grounds and explore walking trails where they might come across an impromptu outdoor performance.

(413) 637-3353. www.shakespeare.org. Performance schedules vary, generally Tuesday-Sunday afternoons and evenings late June to Labor Day and Friday-Sunday in October. Tickets, $34 to $56.

Jacob's Pillow Dance Festival, 358 George Carter Road off Route 20, Becket,

What Tanglewood is to music, the "Pillow" is to dance. The oldest and foremost summer dance festival in America offers nine weeks of everything from classic ballet to folk dancing and is known for its 300-plus world premieres. The rural 100-acre wooded setting includes two theaters, the main 620-seater named for dance pioneer Ted Shawn, who launched the full-fledged festival in 1933 and performed for years with dancer and choreographer Martha Graham, one of his early disciples. Leading troupes perform there, while lesser lights dance Thursday-Sunday in the not-so-formal Doris Duke Studio Theatre; tickets, $18 to $20. You can bring your own food for a picnic on the lawn prior to the performance, or dine under the tent at the Pillow Café, casually in the Pillow Pub or snack in the Tea Garden. Before the main events, free performances are presented on the Inside/Out outdoor stage Wednesday-Saturday at 6:30.

(413) 243-0745. www.jacobspillow.org. Main performances, Wednesday-Saturday at 8:30, Saturday and Sunday at 2. Tickets, $45 to $55.

STILL MORE PERFORMANCES: The **Aston Magna Festival,** the oldest summer festival in America devoted to early chamber music performed as the composers imagined it on period instruments, presents five concerts Saturdays at 6 from early July to early August, in Great Barrington, generally in St. James Church. (A new winter series offers periodic concerts roughly monthly in the Mahaiwe Performing Arts Center, Great Barrington.) Chamber music emanates to national notice from a barn-like shed on a wooded slope off Route 7 south of Pittsfield during **South**

Mountain Concerts, scheduled five Sundays at 3 in September and early October. The **Berkshire Choral Festival** features conductors and choristers from across the country Saturdays at 8 in its concert shed at the Berkshire School in Sheffield. The **Berkshire Opera Company** presents three operas each summer at its new home, the 700-seat Mahaiwe Performing Arts Center in Great Barrington, and other Berkshire sites. **Stockbridge Chamber Concerts** offers summer concerts featuring world-class artists in the opulent Searles Castle in Great Barrington.

The Visual Arts

Norman Rockwell Museum at Stockbridge, 9 Glendale Road (Route 183), Stockbridge.

The world's largest collection of original art by America's favorite illustrator is on display here. The museum moved from the Old Corner House in town to a $5 million building on the 36-acre Linwood estate along the Housatonic River in the Glendale section. Nine galleries display more than 570 original paintings and drawings by the artist, who lived his last 25 years in Stockbridge and made its scenes and people his subjects. Highlights include 322 Saturday Evening Post covers ranging from celebratory to nostalgic and poignant. Both guided and unguided tours are scheduled. The artist's studio was moved to the site from the center of Stockbridge and was re-created as he left it. The museum also includes changing exhibits of Stockbridge memorabilia and a gift shop that does a land-office business, including the sale of some 30,000 reproductions annually of Rockwell's painting of Stockbridge's Main Street at Christmas.

(413) 298-4100. www.nrm.org. Open daily 10 to 5, May-October; Monday-Friday 10 to 4 and weekends 10 to 5, rest of year. Adults $12, children free.

Chesterwood Estate & Museum, 4 Williamsville Road, Stockbridge.

The secluded estate of sculptor Daniel Chester French, famed for the Minute Man in Concord and the Seated Lincoln in Washington, has been open to the public since his daughter donated it in 1969 to the National Trust for Historic Preservation. Visitors start at a gallery in the old cow barn, where many of French's sculptures are shown. But the house and studio are the gems of Chesterwood. The 30-room Colonial Revival built in 1900 is where French spent six months a year until he died there in 1931. Gracious rooms flank the wonderfully wide, full-length hall in which a summer breeze cools the visitor. One interesting item among many is a rose from Lincoln's casket. In the 22-foot-high studio you can see French's plaster-cast models of the Seated Lincoln and a graceful Andromeda, which he was working on at his death. It's placed on a flatcar on a 40-foot-long railroad track and wheeled outdoors occasionally so students can see, as French did, how a sculpture looks in natural light. The front of the studio with a corner fireplace, couch and piano is where he entertained frequent guests; in back is a piazza with wisteria vines and concord grapes framing a view of Monument Mountain. Chesterwood's gift shop is worth a visit. You also may stroll along easy trails in a hemlock forest carpeted with needles. A picnic area overlooks a large cutting garden.

(413) 298-3579. www.chesterwood.org. Open daily 10 to 5, May-October. Adults $10, children $5.

Frelinghuysen Morris House & Studio, 92 Hawthorne St., Lenox.

Set back down a ten-minute walk on 46 acres next to Tanglewood is this relatively new cultural prize. It was the summer home of opera singer Suzy Frelinghuysen and painter George L.K. Morris, both key members of the American Abstract Artists Group, who championed Cubism long after it went out of style. Morris designed the striking, Bauhaus-inspired structure. Preserved as it was in the early 1940s, the tiered white house harbors paintings, murals and sculptures by Picasso, Braque, Léger and Gris as well as the late owners' own works and those of American Cubist friends. Guides lead hourly tours to help immerse the visitor into the artists' pre-World War II world, when championing abstract art was highly controversial. Walking trails in the woodlands surrounding the house museum lead past a monumental sculpture, "The Mountain," a reclining woman on a raised platform that Morris commissioned from his friend Gaston Lachaise.

(413) 637-0166. www.frelinghuysen.org. Tours hourly, Thursday-Sunday 10 to 4, July 4 to Labor Day, Thursday-Saturday through Columbus Day. Adults $10, children $3.

Santarella Museum and Gardens, 75 Main Road, Tyringham.

It's worth the trip just to look at the outside of this fairytale place, once the home and studio of Sir Henry Kitson, sculptor of the Minute Man in Lexington. Called the Gingerbread House and looking as if it's straight from Hansel and Gretel, it is certainly the most unusual gallery in an area that has many. The roof, fashioned to resemble an English thatched roof, is itself a sculpture, weighing 80 tons and resting on a frame of chestnut beams. Go inside – you'll marvel at the stained-glass windows, stone floors and some very interesting works by Berkshire artists. Out back, you can wander around a sculpture garden with surprises at every turn. Sit beside an idyllic pond and admire the wildflowers and birds.

(413) 243-3260. Open daily 10 to 5, Memorial Day to Columbus Day. Adults, $4.

Berkshire Center for Contemporary Glass, 6 Harris St., West Stockbridge.

You can see glassblowers at work in this large co-op studio and gallery, the centerpiece of what is billed as the premier working artists' community in the Berkshires. Watch up close as artists form hot molten glass into whimsical vases, sculptures, elegant perfume bottles and more. The beautiful products are artfully displayed in a gallery, where we were amused by a platter of glass donuts. Classes in making paperweights and the like are offered to the public. Nearby, contemporary sculptures stand outside the **Waterside Gallery.** A brochure detailing "The Art of West Stockbridge" guides visitors to various studios.

(413) 232-4666. Open daily, 10 to 6, to 4:30 in off-season. Free.

Nature's Beauty

The wealth of the Southern Berkshires is not all in its arts. Residents know it best, perhaps, for its beautiful and varied natural attractions. They range from wildlife preserves to mountain vistas, from gardens to waterfalls.

The Mount Estate & Gardens, 2 Plunkett St., Lenox.

The Mount – an icon of American architecture and landscape design – is the creation of one of America's greatest authors. Like Jefferson's Monticello, novelist Edith Wharton's Mount is an "autobiographical house." It was designed by its owner – a Renaissance woman whose grace in the art of living made her the Martha Stewart of her day – as a compelling reflection of her storied life and work. She designed and built the 42-room Georgian Revival mansion based on the principles outlined in her best-selling 1897 book *The Decoration of Houses,* which is still in print. The 50-acre estate combines English, French and Italian elements in a classic New England setting above Laurel Lake. It includes three acres of formal gardens in the Italian style, a stable, a bookstore and the Terrace Café, which is open seasonally for light lunch and refreshments on the same terrace where the novelist entertained the likes of Henry James and the Vanderbilts. "It is an exquisite and marvelous place," James wrote, a precursor to what visitors find today. Restored to the tune of $9 million so far, the estate is on display as never before. Seven top designers have furnished the stunning public rooms "in the style of Edith Wharton," as if she were their client today. Lately, the bedroom suite – the private sanctum where the first woman to win the Pulitzer Prize for fiction wrote each morning – has been restored and opened to public view.

(413) 637-1899. www.edithwharton.org. Open May-October, daily 9 to 5. Adults, $16.

Naumkeag, 5 Prospect Hill Road, Stockbridge.
The interior of this 44-room, shingle-style gabled "summer cottage" designed in 1886 by McKim, Mead and White for Joseph H. Choate, lawyer for the Rockefeller family and ambassador to the Court of St. James, is much admired. Chinese export porcelain, rare Persian rugs, Murano glass and family portraits by John Singer Sargent are part of the Choate family collection found throughout the house, one of the few Berkshire Cottages open to the public. We like it best, however, for the eight acres of lavish hillside landscaping and gardens surrounded by 40 acres of woodlands and meadows stretching to the Housatonic River valley. Choate's daughter Mabel worked with Fletcher Steele, the preeminent landscape architect, to produce a private world of terraces, walkways, sculpted topiary, fountains and even a Chinese pagoda in twelve distinct garden areas. In a cool Venetian garden, water trickles from a tiny fountain; a stream cascades beside the steps in a grove of birch trees. The sculpture in the gardens reflects Mabel Choate's interest in the arts.

(413) 298-3239. Open Memorial Day to Columbus Day, daily 10 to 5. Adults $10, children $3. Gardens only, $8.

Berkshire Botanical Garden, Junction of Routes 102 and 183, Stockbridge.
"Horticulture – the Berkshires' other culture" is the theme at this fifteen-acre, mostly outdoor botanical showplace. It features spectacular display gardens that are among the oldest in the country, a terraced herb garden, a pond, shrubs, trees, perennial borders, a wildflower meadow, annuals, experimental plantings and more. More than 3,000 varieties that thrive in the Berkshires are displayed in an informal country setting. Display gardens laid out on a residential scale inspire the home gardener. So do the spectacular window boxes brimming with begonias, impatiens, geraniums and more. The solar greenhouse attracts special attention, and we liked the maple syrup house, the magnificent rose garden and the prolific vegetable garden with its own weather station. Inside are a small library and gift shop, both with a stress on things botanical. Picnickers are welcome on the grounds.

(413) 298-3926. www.berkshirebotanical.org. Open May-October, daily 10 to 5. Adults $7, students $5.

Pleasant Valley Wildlife Sanctuary. 472 West Mountain Road off Route 7, Lenox.
Up a mountain road atop Lenox Mountain next to Yokun Brook is a 1,314-acre preserve established in 1929 by the Massachusetts Audubon Society. Seven miles of nature trails wind through upland hardwood forests, meadows and wetlands.

Note the beaver "lodges" of tree branches and mud where nocturnal beavers spend their time along the brook. A trailside nature center contains live and stuffed animals.

(413) 637-0320. Nature center open Tuesday-Friday 9 to 5, Saturday-Sunday 10 to 4, also Monday late June through Columbus Day. Trails open dawn to dusk. Adults $4, children $3.

—Away-from-It-All Outings—

Mount Washington. On a plateau 2,000 feet above sea level is the curious little town of Mount Washington, which dwells in isolation alongside Mount Everett, the second highest mountain in Massachusetts. The town is a veritable treasure of scenery acknowledged by few other than its 130 or so year-round residents. Start your driving tour near South Egremont at the junction of Routes 23 and 41 next to **Smiley Pond,** a busy bird refuge and wildlife preserve. Following signs for Bash Bish Falls, you start the climb, passing an occasional house or an abandoned inn along the way. Eight miles up is the 1,100-acre **Mount Everett State Reservation,** with Guilder Pond and its showy June display of mountain laurel, which blooms all over the mountain; it takes fifteen minutes to hike to the summit from the upper parking lot. Continue past the 1876 Town Hall and the 1874 Church of Christ down a road through a 400-foot-deep gorge to **Bash Bish Falls,** an 80-foot plunge that is the Berkshires' most dramatic. A good trail leads from a parking lot to the top of the falls. Cable fences on both sides of the crystal-clear creek keep one from seeing much of the falls, but the view through the gorge toward the Catskills is rewarding. Farther down the road, just before the New York State line, is a short road leading to the base of the falls. The state park at the falls is part of the much larger **Mount Washington State Forest,** which offers 30 miles of hiking trails. Several other waterfalls and mountain peaks in Massachusetts's southwesternmost town lure lovers of the wild and remote, with numerous hiking trails awaiting. The high-bush blueberries that make Blueberry Hill Farm the town's commercial livelihood sometimes go begging for lack of pickers.

New Marlborough-Monterey-Tyringham. These sparsely populated towns offer scenery and history in a choice package. Poke along back roads or follow a Circle Tour map provided by the Berkshire Visitors Bureau. We enjoyed the abandoned mills in the Mill River area and the Bucks County look of the Clayton area. Umpachene Falls, if you persevere long enough to find it, has a lovely park and a falling stream that you'll likely have to yourself. York Lake in Sandisfield State Forest offers delightful picnic groves on both sides of a small beach. The hamlets of Southfield, New Marlborough and Monterey are particularly quaint. An enchanting valley cutting between hills in Tyringham reminds some of the Austrian Tyrol. Mark Twain and Grover Cleveland summered here, and Sir Henry Kitson built his fantastic "Gingerbread House" in the valley. Follow not only the Tyringham Main Road but the parallel side road along the hillside past Shaker Pond and beside some colorful old Shaker buildings, the last remnants of the once-thriving Shaker community overlooking Tyringham Cobble. These really are back roads – some of them dirt and most bumpy. Don't go without a detailed map.

Bartholomew's Cobble, Rannape Road off Route 7A, Ashley Falls.

Cobble is an old Yankee word for a limestone outcropping above a meadow and this one straddles two rocky knolls rising above the Housatonic River. The tranquil setting of meadow and woods offers 277 acres of natural rock gardens, where no fewer than 500 species of wildflowers, 100 species of trees, shrubs and vines, and 40 species of ferns have been catalogued. All over the cobble you can follow five miles of hiking trails and rest on rustic benches. The small natural history museum displays local flora and fauna, plus Indian artifacts. On Sunday mornings in summer, naturalists guide canoe trips along the river to spot wildlife.

(413) 229-8600. Grounds open year-round, daily dawn to dusk. Museum and visitor center open daily 9 to 4:30, April-November; closed Sunday and Monday rest of year. Adults $5, children $1.

Shopping

Lenox offers the area's toniest shops and galleries. On Walker Street you'll find **Talbots** for classic clothes and **Evviva!** for contemporary by designers with a background in the arts. **Tanglewool** sells English cashmeres and other hand knits, Italian bags, Arche shoes from France, creative jewelry, and imported yarns and knitting patterns; everything here has flair. **Mary Stuart Collections** at 81 Church St. purveys exquisite accessories for bed and bath, fine china and glass, plus gifts and children's clothing fit for royalty. For contemporary crafts and wearable art, visit the **Hoadley Gallery.** Italian ceramics and other contemporary art are featured at **Cose D'Argilla.** Huge crinkled glass sculptures caught our eye at the **Wit Gallery**, as did the colorful metal art and ceramics at **Hotchkiss Mobiles Gallery.** Handsome weavings, from pillows to coats, are displayed at **Weaver's Fancy.** The works of 400 artisans are shown at the **Hand of Man** crafts gallery in the Curtis Shops.

In Stockbridge, don't miss the changing little shops in the Mews, a skip over from the Red Lion Inn – from the **American Craftsman Gallery** in front to the **Origins Gallery** in back. **Williams & Sons Country Store** is a true, jumbled-up country store operating since 1795 – amble in and enjoy the aromas. Nearby are **Vlada Boutique,** full of clothing, gifts and jewelry, and **Holsten Galleries** with stunning contemporary glass sculpture.

Great Barrington is where much of the interesting shopping action has focused of late, especially along Railroad Street. Expect to find surprises from **Byzantium Crystal Essence** to **Gatsby's,** an old-time department store. Billing itself as "Provence in the Berkshires," **Mistral's** offers an attractive selection of bed and bath accessories, perfumes and kitchenware. Along Main Street are **Evergreen Contemporary Crafts,** where we were struck by the flamingo birdhouses among all the neat American pottery, clothing and gifts, and **T.P. Saddle Blanket and Trading Co.,** a colorful store stocking rugged mountain and Western apparel, turquoise jewelry, hot sauces, rugs and even furniture on two fascinating floors. A mile north of Great Barrington on Route 7 is the **Jenifer House Commons,** a collection of markets primarily involving antiques.

Great Barrington Pottery, actually at 391 North Plain Road (Route 41) in Housatonic, is worth a visit to see the Richard Bennett pottery that merges East and West, the first authentic Japanese wood-burning kiln built in the United States, and a collection of beautiful silk flowers that can be custom-arranged. Tea is served daily from 1 to 4 in a ceremonial tea house amid formal Japanese gardens.

ANTIQUING is big business in the Berkshires, and all the Berkshires towns contain antiques stores. The biggest concentration is around Sheffield, where every second house seems to have an antiques sign in front of it. One place not to miss is **Twin Fires** on Berkshire School Road at Route 41, Sheffield. Seemingly more antiques than are carried by all the rest of the dealers around are grouped in two barn structures with three floors each. One section is a recreated arcade with shops from 18th-century London.

Where to Stay

Large and small country inns, B&Bs, motels and resorts are dotted across the area. Many are booked far in advance for Tanglewood. Most require stays of three or four nights on peak weekends, and some insist on prepayment of the entire bill. Rates vary widely, highest on summer and foliage weekends, often lower weekdays and much lower out of season.

Inns and B&Bs

The Red Lion Inn, 30 Main St., Stockbridge 01262.

The granddaddy of them all, this big white wood structure immortalized by Norman Rockwell in his painting of Main Street is the essence of an old New England inn. For more than two centuries, it has dominated Stockbridge's Main Street, its guests rocking on the wide front porch – which seems a block long – or sipping cocktails in the homey parlor. Antique furniture and china fill the public rooms, and the Pink Kitty gift shop is just the ticket for selective browsers. Also here is **Country Curtains,** the original in the retail chain launched by Jane Fitzpatrick, who took over the inn in the late 1960s with her state-senator husband and has restored it with taste. Rooms and suites in the rambling inn and seven nearby guest houses are furnished in period decor. Rooms with private baths have a double or two twin beds, television and telephone. Thirty rooms that share baths have one double or twin beds and television. Continental breakfast is included. Twenty-six suites come with a queen bed or two twins and a separate sitting area with TV/VCR. A deluxe suite in the former firehouse has a kingsize poster bed and jacuzzi bath upstairs and an open sitting room with dining area and kitchen downstairs. The Red Lion also rents a two-bedroom apartment called Meadowlark, part of sculptor Daniel Chester French's summer studio at Chesterwood, for $350 a night, May-October.

The dining room is enormously popular with visitors and pleasant in an old hotel kind of a way, and the food situation has been enhanced by new executive chef Brian Alberg. He launched five-course regional tasting menus ($85) on weekends in the off-season, and imparted new takes to regional favorites on the regular menu. Entrées run the gamut from roast turkey with the trimmings and prime rib with a popover to – don't these sound au courant? – a jumbo lump crab martini with crispy wonton chips and citrus-grilled swordfish with basil-fennel relish. Traditionalists can still start with New England clam chowder and finish with apple pie à la mode for a meal from yesteryear. More intimate dining takes place in the dark-paneled **Widow Bingham Tavern,** everyone's idea of what a Colonial pub should look like. In season, the shady outdoor courtyard lined with spectacular impatiens is a colorful and cool retreat for a drink, lunch or dinner. The same menu is served inside and out. A smaller menu is available downstairs in the **Lion's Den,** which offers entertainment at night.

(413) 298-5545. www.redlioninn.com. Fifty-four rooms and 26 suites with private baths and 30 rooms with shared baths. Rates, EP. Mid-June to late October: doubles $100 to $220, suites $285 to $430. Rest of year: doubles $89 to $220, suites $185 to $395.

Entrées, $22 to $32. Lunch daily, noon to 2:30, Sunday to 4. Dinner nightly, 5:30 to 9 or 10.

The Gables Inn, 103 Walker St., Lenox 01240.

One of the original Berkshires cottages built in 1885 in the heart of Lenox, this was the home of the mother-in-law of Edith Wharton, the writer who lived here while her own cottage, The Mount, was under construction. The Queen Anne Victorian has been upgraded and expanded by Frank and Mary Newton, who offer some of Lenox's finest accommodations. The Jockey Club Suite offers a brass bed in a niche, an ample sitting area with two sofas facing a big-screen TV, and a private entrance from the back-yard pool area. Also in demand are two large second-floor suites bearing the names of Teddy and Edith Wharton. Both have cathedral ceilings, working fireplaces and TVs. The queen-canopied bedroom in the Tanglewood Suite opens onto a garden patio and the walls of its sitting room are hung with old framed Boston Symphony Orchestra programs. The Show Business Room is full of signed photos of old stars and a library of showbiz volumes, with which to curl up on the chintz loveseat in front of the fireplace. Frank likes to show guests the eight-sided library where Edith Wharton wrote some of her short stories and the enclosed, solar-heated swimming pool with a whirlpool in the back yard. There's a tennis court as well. A full breakfast is served in the spectacular dining room. In summer, Mary Newton pampers B&B guests in six spacious rooms at their home down the street, built by a cousin of Edith Wharton and called **The Summer White House.**

(413) 637-3416 or (800) 382-9401. www.gableslenox.com. Thirteen rooms and four suites with private baths. Mid-May through October: doubles $190 to $210, suites, $250. Rest of year: doubles $99 to $130, suites $160.

Summer White House, (413) 637-4489. Six rooms with private bath. Doubles $210, July and August only.

Stonover Farm Bed & Breakfast, 169 Undermountain Road, Lenox 01240.

Los Angeles record producer Tom Werman and his wife Suky returned to their East Coast roots to restore a 110-year-old stone "cottage" that served as the farmhouse to the Stonover Estate. It's now a luxurious B&B offering both creature comforts and charm on eight acres of sylvan tranquility not far from Tanglewood. The Wermans reconfigured the interior of the house and joined it to the stable, wrapping around an idyllic courtyard terrace looking onto a duck pond. A California decorator friend furnished the place in a light and airy, uncluttered style. All is embellished by an eye-popping collection of contemporary art gathered by four artisans whom Suky, a former museum educator, represents. Guests are comfortably housed in three second-floor suites and the outlying Rock Cottage. Beds are king or queensize, dressed in Frette linens and fabric duvets. The typical sitting room has a Shaker desk with a Bose radio, telephone, a sofabed and a rocker. It opens into a bedroom with an entertainment center concealing a 27-inch flat-screen TV and DVD player. One suite has a gas fireplace and a bath with jacuzzi tub and separate shower. Other bathrooms, all full of slate, tile and marble, contain walk-in showers for two and one has a soaking tub. A stone fireplace warms an enormous living/dining room in the four-room cottage, which has a kingsize bedroom on the main floor, twin beds upstairs in an aerie called the sleeping turret and a full kitchen. The hospitable host offers wine and imported cheeses in the afternoon, by the fire in the living room or library, or outside on the courtyard terrace. A lavish breakfast is served at a table for eight in the former creamery with windows on three sides and a vaulted ceiling rising to a cupola. Tom's goat cheese omelet with sautéed mushrooms is a breakfast favorite.

(413) 637-9100. www.stonoverfarm.com. Three suites and one cottage with private baths. July-October: doubles $350, cottage $485. Rest of year: doubles $275, cottage $375.

The Inn at Stockbridge, Route 7, Box 618, Stockbridge 01262

The B&B based in this lovely pillared, Georgian-style mansion on twelve acres bordering the Massachusetts Turnpike has been enhanced and expanded by owners Alice and Len Schiller. They first upgraded the eight original bedrooms in the mansion, each with telephone and CD players and all but two with kingsize beds. The main-floor Terrace Room overlooking a reflecting pond and swimming pool features a private deck and a circular whirlpool tub in the skylit bathroom. In back is the Cottage House with four spacious rooms called junior suites. Each has a gas fireplace and TV/VCR. Two add large whirlpool tubs. Four top-of-the-line rooms occupy a new building called the Barn. Each spacious, cathedral-ceilinged room has a king bed, corner gas fireplace, double whirlpool, TV/VCR and private deck. They range from one of Shaker simplicity to the richness of the Shakespeare and Wharton rooms. Back in the main house, guests meet over complimentary wine and cheese in an expansive living room and adjacent library. A candlelight breakfast, culminating perhaps in portobello mushroom strata or vanilla french toast, is served in the dining room or in a smaller room beyond.

(413) 298-3337. www.stockbridgeinn.com. Sixteen rooms with private baths. Doubles, $165 to $345 June-October, $140 to $245 rest of year.

Applegate Bed & Breakfast, 279 West Park St., Lee 01238.

Six tranquil acres bearing apple trees, rose gardens and a swimming pool beckon sophisticates to this sparkling white Georgian Colonial with a pillared porte-cochere, built by a New York surgeon in the 1920s as a weekend retreat. Hospitable ex-New Yorkers Gloria and Len Friedman offer elegant common rooms and six guest rooms in the main house, and two luxury rooms and a two-bedroom cottage apartment in a carriage house in back. The main floor holds a large living room with a grand piano, an enclosed sun porch used for reading and TV, a dining room with breakfast tables set for four, and a screened back porch facing the pool and rose gardens. A carved staircase leads to the upstairs guest rooms. The expansive master suite lives up to its name with a kingsize poster bed, working fireplace, sitting area and a great steam shower. The premier accommodations are four beautifully appointed luxury rooms, each with kingsize bed, fireplace, double whirlpool tub, wet bar, sofa and TV/VCR. Two on the third floor open onto balconies overlooking the grounds. Two others on the ground floor of the former carriage house have private patios. The chauffeur's apartment on the second floor now has two queensize bedrooms and kitchen facilities. Godiva chocolates and decanters of brandy are in each room. The Friedmans offer wine and cheese around 5 p.m. A continental-plus breakfast is served by candlelight amid stemware and Wedgwood china.

(413) 243-4451 or (800) 691-9012. Fax (413) 243-9832. www.applegateinn.com. Ten rooms and a two-bedroom apartment with private baths. Doubles, $150 to $350 June-October, $120 to $250 rest of year.

The Taggart House, 18 Main St., Stockbridge 01262.

One of the great Berkshire Cottages with an illustrious past, this mid-19th-century mansion served as a designer showhouse before it was opened as a "luxury country manor house" B&B in 1993 by Mr. and Mrs. W. Hinckley Waitt III, who were obviously to the manor born. In 2004, new owners August and Sandra Murko refreshed what was "already a wonderful piece of artwork," adding new LCD TVs and internet access to each room. They share this most sumptuous of Gilded Age estates with guests in four bedrooms, each with ornate antique beds and imported bath appointments. The largest is the Willow Bow with a corona-fabric queen bed and a wood-burning fireplace, one of nine in the house. The public rooms furnished with stunning art and antiques and the noblesse-oblige hospitality dispensed by the hosts are the main drawing cards. Indian artifacts are showcased in the living room and a birch-bark canoe hangs from a frescoed ceiling above the table in the billiards room. Other showy rooms include a paneled library, a concert-size music room, a baronial ballroom and a sunroom. Guests are treated to gourmet treats in their rooms upon arrival, bottled water at bedside, a complimentary beverage bar and an elegant brunch by candlelight at 9:30 in the morning. The three-acre property, with gardens and a koi pond, backs up to the Housatonic River.

(413) 298-4303 or (800) 918-2680. www.taggarthouse.com. Four rooms with private baths. Doubles, $250 to $350 May-October, $175 to $250 rest of year.

Good Values

Garden Gables Inn, 135 Main St., Lenox 01240.

Prolific gardens and a 72-foot-long swimming pool are attractions at this verdant, five-acre oasis set well back from the road in the heart of Lenox. Once a homey little B&B of the old school, the accommodations have been vastly upgraded by Mario and Lynn Mekinda from Toronto. They vary widely in size and price, but each of the eleven original guest rooms now has a private bath and queensize bed, and a corner room has one of eight new fireplaces. All rooms are equipped with telephones and clock radios. More luxurious are a king bedroom with jacuzzi bath and two cathedral-ceilinged rooms above the inn's expanded dining room, each with kingsize canopy bed, sitting area in front of the corner fireplace, whirlpool bath and private balcony. Four more rooms with TV/VCR, fireplaces and queensize Eldred Wheeler canopy beds occupy a detached front cottage, which continues the gabled dormer theme of the main house. A substantial buffet breakfast is served in the dining room, which opens onto a wraparound screened porch.

(413) 637-0193. www.lenoxinn.com. Eighteen rooms with private baths. Doubles, $135 to $290 late June to late October, $95 to $210 rest of year.

The Cornell Inn, 203 Main St., Lenox 01240.

A variety of comfortable accommodations in several styles is offered by Billie and Doug McLaughlin in this, their "retirement" project after selling their Vermont inn. The couple closed the inn's restaurant and set about renovating and redecorating all 31 guest rooms in the inn's three-building complex. The thirteen rooms in the main 1888 house are done in the Victorian manner with antique appointments. Five here have fireplaces, and the premier Alexandra also has a kingsize bed, whirlpool tub and private deck. Ten deluxe rooms in the 1777 MacDonald House across the showy garden area are Colonial, all with whirlpool tubs and all but one with fireplaces and sitting areas on private porches or decks. The eight-room carriage house in the rear imparts what Billie calls a country primitive feeling. Four have whirlpool tubs and decks overlooking Kennedy Park, and four others have fireplaces. Two are loft suites with efficiency kitchens. Most beds throughout the complex are queensize. The main house offers two homey common areas, an intimate pub and a country dining room where an ample buffet breakfast includes a hot entrée of the day. The dining room opens onto a spacious deck beside a Japanese-style rock garden and koi ponds separated by a waterfall.

(413) 637-0562 or (800) 637-0562. Fax (413) 637-0927. www.cornellinn.com. Thirty-one rooms with private baths. Doubles, $120 to $350 July and August, $80 to $300 rest of year.

Birch Hill Bed & Breakfast, 254 South Undermountain Road (Route 41), Sheffield 01257.

Literally under Mount Washington along a quiet country road is this attractive 230-year-old guest house, white with black shutters and a red door. The Appalachian Trail runs through the back of the twenty-acre property. Michael and Wendy Advocate – he from New York and she from Florida – took over the old Ivanhoe Country House and renamed it. They offer seven guest rooms furnished with period antiques. Some have double beds but even the cheapest, the Sunrise, comes with a fireplace, porch and a hall bath that Wendy considers the nicest in the house. The suite-size Pineview has a king bed, a single bed, antique sofa and a table and chairs, with a kitchenette adjacent. It overlooks the manicured lawn, the lake across the road and the pool in back with the mountain as a backdrop. Wendy prepares an elaborate, multi-course breakfast that might include blueberry coffee cake with berries picked from Mount Washington and a ham and cheese breakfast soufflé.

(413) 229-2143 or (800) 359-3969. www.birchhillbb.com. Seven rooms with private baths. Doubles, $130 to $215 Memorial Day through October, $120 to $175 rest of year.

Tops for Luxury – An Italian Palace...

Wheatleigh, Hawthorne Road, Lenox 01240.

Tired of country inns? If you're feeling flush and would like to stay in an over-the-top Italian palazzo, this may be for you. And, added bonus, you can work out in its state-of-the-art fitness room, get a massage, swim in a pool hidden in a sylvan glade and walk to Tanglewood. The setting on 22 acres is grand, even palatial. But as refashioned by owners Susan and Linwood Simon and their general manager, French-trained hotelier François Thomas from Paris, the interior decoration is unexpectedly minimalist, producing what the New York Times magazine called the most European small country-house hotel in America. The imposing entrance of the honey-colored brick building framed in wrought iron leads into a soaring Great Room with modern and traditional sitting areas, parquet floors and fine art all around. To enhance the classical Renaissance architecture, the guest room style is a light contemporary look in muted beige and taupe colors with a mix of English and French antiques and European-modern furnishings. Bedrooms have French-designed bedspreads of imported silk and more comfortable seating than in the past. Bathrooms were redone in imported English limestone or Italian marble, with silver-plated fixtures from England and Bulgari toiletries from Italy. Each room now has a TV/VCR and a portable telephone for those who want to be in touch wherever they are. Nine of the best rooms have fireplaces and six have terraces or balconies. The most exotic is the Aviary Suite, an unusual two-story affair joined by an outside spiral staircase enclosed in glass. Its upstairs has a kingsize bedroom with big windows onto a garden, a dark chestnut ceiling and pale brick walls. Adjoining is an expansive "wet room" with an open shower, one of Wheatleigh's original deep soaking tubs and a separate water closet. The sitting room on the main floor is surrounded by glass and opens onto a terrace. Another recent addition is the main-floor Terrace Suite, formed by enclosing part of a portico that matches the dining portico. It has a king bed with fabric headboard and two oversize loveseats in the portico enclosed in glass, bronze and brick. A pot of hot spiced cider, served by one of the staff clad in black, warmed our arrival here on a chilly autumn afternoon.

One of the best meals of our lives unfolded that evening in Wheatleigh's main-floor restaurant. Dinner is served in an elegant dining room or the dramatic, glass-enclosed portico with lawns on three sides (lighter fare is available at peak periods in the sleek Library lounge). Executive chef J. Bryce Whittlesey heads a kitchen brigade of fifteen that prepares three prix-fixe tasting menus each evening – three-course regular and four-course vegetarian (both $88) and a six-course fish menu ($115). You might start as we did with the golden ossetra caviar and oyster "progression," the first of several that evening and yielding three choice oysters in various dress. Other starters, these from the fish tasting menu, were truly exceptional bay scallops served with apple relish and blood orange vinaigrette in large scallop shells and Maine sea urchins with Dungeness crab salad and pearl tapioca froth. Next came a whole roasted lobster with cardamom and star anise butter, followed by line-caught dover sole roasted on the bone and served with sautéed chicken oysters and poultry jus. Our other main course from the regular menu was described simply as "local young lamb with variation on butternut squash." That turned out to be two simultaneous "progressions" – lamb shoulder, confit and rack, each of the three with a different version of squash, about the only vegetables we saw all evening. Desserts were an ethereal lemon soufflé with lemoncello sauce and apple tart normande, two small apple custard tarts flanking crème fraîche and calvados-cider sorbet.

(413) 637-0610. Fax (413) 637-4507. www.wheatleigh.com. Seventeen rooms and two suites with private baths. Rates, EP. Doubles, $545 to $1,155. Suites, $1,150 to $1,550.

Prix-fixe, $88 and $115. Dinner nightly by reservation, 6 to 9 or 9:30; closed Monday-Wednesday in winter. Library, lunch daily in season, noon to 1:30; dinner, 5 to 9:30.

...And a Scottish Castle

Blantyre, 16 Blantyre Road, Lenox 01240.

Up a long, curving driveway in the midst of 85 country acres of manicured lawns and woodlands appears the castle of your dreams – one of the first Relais & Chateaux country-house hotel properties in America. In fact, the 1902 Tudor-style brick manor built as a summer cottage for a millionaire in the turpentine business as an authentic replica of the Hall of Blantyre in Scotland used to be called a castle. Faithfully restored by owner Jane Fitzpatrick of the Red Lion Inn in nearby Stockbridge, Blantyre houses guests in eight elegant rooms and suites in the mansion, twelve more contemporary quarters in a distant carriage house and four scattered about the property in small cottages. The public rooms and guest rooms are so grand in a castle kind of way as to defy description – take our word or that of those who pay up to $900 a night for the Paterson Suite with a fireplaced living room (complete with a crystal chandelier over a lace-covered table in the middle of the room), two full bathrooms and a large bedroom with a kingsize four-poster bed. A typical bathroom has a scale, a wooden valet, heated towel racks, embroidered curtains and more toiletries than one ever hopes to see. Twelve rooms in more contemporary style, several of them split-level loft suites, are located in the carriage house near the pool and tennis courts. They have been totally renovated down to the hand-painted tiles and marble floors in the bathrooms, and come with balconies or decks and wet bars. There also are four cottages – the newest the sumptuous weekend house of one's dreams, renting for $975 a night. A complimentary continental breakfast is served in Blantyre's sunny conservatory, and additional items may be ordered.

Prix-fixe dinners of three to five courses are offered to house guests and the public in Blantyre's formal dining room and two smaller rooms. British-born executive chef Christopher Brooks starts dinner here with a complimentary "surprise," perhaps foie gras or veal sweetbreads with sauternes and carrot juice. The appetizer could be glazed Maine lobster tart with tarragon sauce, loin of rabbit with carrot-ginger puree or seared foie gras with caramelized pickled pears and toasted brioche. Typical main courses are lobster and halibut with vanilla tarragon sauce, pan-roasted pheasant breast with foie gras-chestnut jus and roasted loin of antelope with huckleberry sauce. Desserts include white chocolate mousse and plum roulade with ginger-lime sauce or lemon meringue tart with blueberry compote and passion-fruit coulis. Most guests take coffee and armagnac in the Music Room, where a harpist and pianist play on weekends.

(413) 637-3556. Twelve rooms, eight suites and four cottages with private baths. Doubles $450 to $700, suites $500 to $900, cottages $750 to $1,500. Closed January to early May.

Prix-fixe, $85. Lunch in summer, Tuesday-Sunday 12:30 to 1:45. Dinner by reservation, nightly in summer and foliage season, 6 to 8:45, otherwise Tuesday-Sunday. Jackets and ties required.

High Style in the Back of Beyond

The Old Inn on the Green and Gedney Farm, Route 57, New Marlboro 01230.

Known for inspired dining, this rural stagecoach inn now attracts overnight guests with a variety of getaway options in mind. That has something to do with its quiet location out in the boondocks. But it's due more to innkeeper Bradford Wagstaff's addition of luxury accommodations in four distinctive venues: The 1760 Old Inn has four queensize guest rooms and a suite furnished with antiques and country furniture. The restored 1821 Thayer House beside the inn is a luxurious refuge of six bedrooms with fireplaces and whirlpool tubs, a common parlor, den and library, and a courtyard terrace with a swimming pool. Just down the road is Gedney Farm, a huge Normandy-style barn with a ground-level reception area and art gallery looking onto an outdoor sculpture garden. Upstairs, beneath a 30-foot-high ceiling, is a lineup of six guest rooms and six two-level suites, most with fireplaced sitting rooms and double whirlpool tubs under glass ceilings open to the roof structure. Brad's wife, Leslie Miller, decorated the rooms simply but with panache in motifs from Moroccan to French provincial. Oriental and kilim rugs are on the floors, woven or fabric coverlets top the beds, and exotic wreaths adorn the walls. Twelve more rooms and spa facilities were added lately in the 1906 Mepal Manor, a Gilded Age estate on a nearby hilltop. The operative words there are large and grand, from the fireplaced great hall and patio terrace to Victorian bedrooms decorated in rich fabrics. A generous continental breakfast at Gedney Farm is complimentary for all guests.

The inn's prix-fixe dinners ($65) are a Saturday tradition worth driving miles for. They're served totally by candlelight in as historic a setting as can be conceived. About 50 people are seated in the tavern room, a formal parlor or at the harvest table in the dining room. In each, the original wainscoting, stenciling, antiques and windows draped in velvet are shown to advantage. The unique handmade wreaths of branches and bark are fascinating, the large mural of cows grazing on the New Marlboro green is wonderful to see, and it's easy to imagine yourself transported back a couple of centuries for the evening. Chèvre and almond puff-pastry sticks accompany drinks, served in delicate stemmed glasses. From a mushroom and herb soup that is the essence of mushroom to the final cappuccino with shredded chocolate on top, things go from great to greater – all the more so since top chef Peter Platt moved here after sixteen years heading the kitchen at Wheatleigh. A recent summer meal began with a choice of mussels with julienned vegetables in orange-saffron sauce, asparagus with baby greens in a truffle vinaigrette or foie gras poached with strawberries on a black pepper brioche. The main-course options were tempura of soft-shell crabs, roasted poussin with morels or filet of beef tenderloin with red wine sauce. Dessert was bittersweet chocolate sorbet in toasted almond cups with coffee sauce, blueberry and nectarine croustade with crème fraîche, or a sampling of New England and European cheeses. A short and with-it à la carte menu is offered other nights in the tavern beside the hearth or outside on the canopied, candlelit terrace overlooking a Colonial flower and herb garden. Typical entrées range from pepper-crusted yellowfin tuna niçoise to rack of Colorado lamb provençal.

(413) 229-3131 or (800) 286-3139. Fax (413) 229-8236. www.oldinn.com. Thirty-five rooms and suites with private baths in four buildings. Doubles, $195 to $300 in inn, $205 to $325 at Gedney Farm, $200 to $350 at Mepal Manor, $325 to $365 in Thayer House.
Dinner by reservation, prix-fixe $65, Saturday 5:30 to 9:30. À la carte, $26 to $38, Sunday-Friday 5:30 to 9:30. Closed Monday and Tuesday in off-season.

┌─Retreat to Yesteryear

Historic Merrell Inn, 1565 Pleasant St. (Route 102), South Lee 01260.

History buffs particularly like this elegantly restored B&B, one of the first properties in the Berkshires to be listed in the National Register of Historic Places. Saved early in the last century by Mabel Choate of Naumkeag in Stockbridge, the 1800 brick stagecoach inn a mile east of Stockbridge now offers nine guest quarters on three floors. Most are furnished with canopy or four-poster queensize beds and antiques on wide-board floors, and four retain their original fireplaces. They have been upscaled lately with TV, telephones, Gilbert & Soames toiletries, tiled floors in the bathrooms, comfy sitting areas, fancy window treatments, and color-coordinated linens and towels. The Riverview Suite, located in a separate wing in back, has a spacious kingsize bedroom, a fireplace and a colonnaded porch overlooking the Housatonic River beneath Beartown Mountain. Guests register in the old tavern room at the birdcage bar, the only surviving circular Colonial bar still intact. It also serves as a guest parlor and sitting room. The old keeping room with a beehive oven is a beauty, with handmade Bennington pottery, well-aged woodwork and a fireplace of Count Rumford design. Guests enjoy a full breakfast here and have the run of the deep back yard, which stretches back to a screened gazebo by the river.

(413) 243-1794 or (800) 243-1794. Fax (413) 243-2669. www.merrell-inn.com. Eight rooms and one suite with private baths. Summer and fall: doubles $99 to $190, suite, $185 to $270. Rest of year: doubles $99 to $155, suite $155 to $185.

Motels

Best Western Black Swan Inn, 435 Laurel St. (Route 20), Lee 01238.

This began as a motel beside Laurel Lake, but with the addition of a twelve-room wing, it's considerably more. Half of the 52 rooms face the lake and have private decks. Nine newer rooms come with fireplaces and cast-marble hydrotubs, some have queen or king four-poster beds, and all are smartly decorated, most containing two velvet armchairs. The Lincoln Room has a log cabin quilt and a framed copy of the Gettysburg Address on the wall. In the new wing is a handsome lounge/bar with a fireplace and an old English service bar relocated from New Hampshire, as well as an exercise room and a Finnish sauna. The original motel rooms are a cut above, too.

Although there is no beach on this part of the lake, the Black Swan has a swimming pool, and pontoon and paddle boats to take out. The lakeside **Bombay Bar & Grill** dining room has large solarium windows that make you feel you're almost on the water. It offers an extensive menu of classic Indian cuisine for lunch and dinner, with entrées priced from $12 to $24 (for tandoori lobster).

(413) 243-2700 or (800) 876-7926. Fifty-two rooms with private baths. Doubles, $105 to $265 mid-June to late October, $65 to $160 rest of year.

Yankee Inn, 461 Pittsfield Road, Lenox 01240.

Long known as the Yankee Motor Lodge, this 96-room charmer is the best of the motels scattered along busy U.S. Routes 7 and 20 north of Lenox. It's solid in red brick and has been upgraded by owners Joe and Lynn Toole, who got their innkeeping start at the Chambery Inn in Lee. Rooms vary from cozy to standard to spacious to spa suites. Nicely decorated in the Colonial style, they are spread out in several buildings, back from the road and facing broad lawns. A hit in the summer is the pool, flanked by a waterfall cascading through evergreens down a mound of rocks. In other seasons, the draws are the 22 kingsize rooms with wood-burning fireplaces and the suites with Amish-crafted kingsize canopy beds, fireplaces and whirlpool tubs for two. A recent expansion produced 36 new kingsize rooms with private, rear-facing decks. The seven-acre property includes a new indoor pool and spa, an exercise room and a lounge. Breakfast is included in the rates.

(413) 499-3700 or (800) 835-2364. Fax (413) 499-3634. www.berkshireinns.com. Ninety-six rooms with private baths. Doubles, $109 to $269 July-October, $69 to $189 rest of year.

Where to Eat

Besides the aforementioned inn dining rooms, the Berkshires have their share of smart restaurants – as with lodging, you should reserve well ahead, especially on weekends. There also are casual and reasonable spots that are fun (and good), and more seem to pop up every year.

Classy Dining

Bistro Zinc, 56 Church St., Lenox.

French authenticity and nuances are everywhere evident in this chic bistro and bar opened by young Lenox native Jason Macioge in partnership with Charles Schultz. The gracefully curving bar in the rear cocktail lounge is topped with polished zinc, the restroom doors are made of lettered wood wine crates and the tables in the mirrored front dining room are as close together as any in Paris. We lunched in the bar on a lovely French onion soup gruyère, a salad of goat cheese, arugula and roasted tomato, and a special entrée of cumin-crusted lamb, fanned around couscous that never before tasted so delectable. A not-so-classic tarte tatin was nonetheless delicious, paired with vanilla ice cream drizzled with caramel sauce. The abbreviated menu sampled at lunch is similar but much expanded at night. Expect such appetizers as a charcuterie plate, mussels marinière, a lobster spring roll and crispy fried oysters with horseradish aioli. Or how about a salad of frisée with pancetta and a poached egg? Typical entrées are leek-crusted halibut with lemon beurre blanc, wood-roasted free-range chicken with tarragon jus, steak frites, and grilled lamb loin with red wine sauce. Desserts at our visit included vanilla crème brûlée, profiterole with mocha ice cream and a platter of petits fours, a lemon tart and cookies. In addition to an all-French wine list, the bar book touts single-barrel bourbons and single-malt scotches.

(413) 637-8800. www.pearlsrestaurant.com/zinc. Entrées, $22 to $28. Lunch daily, 11:30 to 3. Dinner nightly, 5:30 to 9:30.

Church Street Café, 65 Church St., Lenox
This early (1981) "American bistro" that preceded the trend seems to be everybody's favorite in Lenox. Owners Linda Forman and Clayton Hambrick specialize in fresh, light café food served inside in three small dining rooms amid showy artworks and outside on a large covered deck. Once Ethel Kennedy's chef, Clayton also worked in a creole restaurant in Washington and that background shows. Blackened redfish might be a dinner special. Louisiana shrimp and andouille filé gumbo is apt to be a dinner appetizer and a luncheon entrée. Lately, the fare has acquired Southwest and Asian overtones, as in an appetizer of smoky black bean ravioli in a red chile broth or a main dish of grilled lemongrass chicken with nuoc clam sauce. These join such traditional favorites as sautéed Maine crab cakes with dilled tartar sauce and pan roasted pork rib chop with cider jus. Our latest lunch included a super black bean tostada with three salsas and the Church Street salad, a colorful array of goat cheese, chick peas, sprouts, eggs and red pepper, with a zippy dijon vinaigrette dressing on the side and whole wheat sunflower seed rolls, so good that we accepted seconds. Clayton's chocolate mousse loaf was written up in the first issue of Chocolatier magazine, but we're partial to the apple-walnut crisp and the sensational chilled cranberry soufflé topped with whipped cream.

(413) 637-2745. www.churchstreetcafe.biz. Entrées, $22.50 to $28.50. Lunch, Monday-Saturday 11 to 2. Dinner nightly, 5:30 to 9. Sunday brunch in summer and fall. Closed Sunday and Monday in off-season.

Spigalina, 80 Main St., Lenox.
Culinary Institute of America grad Lina Aliberti transformed a house in the center of Lenox into a Mediterranean-style bistro and bar focusing on a large center fireplace with a Count Rumford oven. Forty-two diners can be seated at well-spaced tables inside, with an equal number on the front porch that is a popular gathering spot on which to sit and watch the passing parade. The menu is Mediterranean in spirit: entrées perhaps of grilled salmon niçoise, seared pancetta-wrapped pork tenderloin with marsala-lentil sauce and grilled veal loin chop with white wine veal sauce. Expect such starters as a luscious lobster and crabmeat profiterole with blood-orange vinaigrette, wild mushroom baklava, Spanish bruschetta and crispy kataifi-wrapped goat cheese on field greens. Desserts are prepared by Lisa's husband, Serge Pacaud, the Swiss baker and maitre d'hotel. They vary from poached apple and caramel mousse charlotte to a duo of coffee and caramel pots de crème.

(413) 637-4455. www.spigalina.com. Entrées, $19 to $27. Dinner nightly, 5 to 9. Closed Monday-Wednesday in off-season and in winter.

Verdura, 44 Railroad St., Great Barrington.
Ochre plaster walls and square farm-style tables with comfortable chairs convey a warm Tuscan look to this cucina rustica, one of the hottest restaurants in the Berkshires lately. Chef-owner Bill Webber became enamored with Tuscan-style trattorias while living among the vineyards of California's Napa Valley. After cooking locally at Wheatleigh in Lenox, he opened his own place in Great Barrington in 2001 and recently expanded next door with **Dué Enoteca,** a more casual "little cousin"

serving Italian and Spanish tapas in a wine-bar setting. A wood-fired stone oven in the open kitchen imparts distinctive flavors to thin-crust pizzas and roasted meat and vegetable dishes. The ever-changing bruschetta is a memorable starter, topped at a recent visit with smoked goose breast, local goat cheese and port-braised shallots. Other primi possibilities range from house tagliatelle with lobster and salsify to quail saltimbocca. Typical main courses are free-range chicken under a brick with pesto vinaigrette and braised lamb shanks with black olive-citrus jus. The signature wood-grilled tenderloin is sauced with balsamic vinegar, extra-virgin olive oil and black truffle butter. The dessert special could be wood-grilled peaches in a silken vanilla-scented sauce. The all-Italian wine list is augmented by more than twenty grappas that make a fitting ending to a meal.

(413) 528-8969. www.verdura.net. Entrées, $22 to $28. Both open for dinner nightly, 5 to 9 or 10.

Castle Street Café, 10 Castle St., Great Barrington.

Chef-owner Michael Ballon has attracted quite a following since returning to the Berkshires after several years at upscale restaurants in New York. He succeeded first with a café beside the Mahaiwe Theatre, and more recently added the Celestial Bar adjacent, featuring live music on weekends. Artworks are hung on the brick walls of the long narrow dining room with white-linened tables and windsor chairs. With appetizers like grilled shiitake mushrooms with garlic and herbs, fried shrimp dumplings, an olive sampler with focaccia, and a mesclun and goat-cheese salad and entrées like a Castle burger with straw potatoes or linguini provençal, there is something for everyone. Other main courses include broiled halibut with wasabi sauce, grilled cornish game hen, and rack of lamb with garlic and rosemary sauce. The dessert list is headed by the world's best chocolate-mousse cake, as determined by the late New York Newsday. Others include caramelized banana tart with banana ice cream and frozen lemon soufflé with raspberry sauce. A bar menu ($5 to $12) offers casual fare, from an eggplant napoleon to meatloaf with mashed potatoes.

(413) 528-5244. www.castlestreetcafe.com. Entrées, $19 to $28. Dinner nightly except Tuesday, 5 to 9:30 or 11.

Pearl's, 47 Railroad St., Great Barrington.

The high-end steakhouse launched by the owners of Bistro Zinc in Lenox is what you'd expect to find in the big city, not funky little Great Barrington. A sensuous artwork of two nudes is the focal point of a modernist, art deco dining room that's a study in wood, brick and black. Pearl's offers a straightforward but interesting menu in the steakhouse idiom, complete with the traditional side dishes. There are the usual steaks and chops, each accompanied by roesti potatoes, baby summer squash and roasted tomatoes. Seaweed salad and crispy fried calamari might garnish the seafood dishes, which range from ahi tuna and grilled salmon to lump crab cakes and lobsters. A section of the menu is devoted to "birds and game," including barbecued quail and pan-seared venison. Appetizers range from spicy tuna tartare and beef carpaccio to Peking duck rolls and oysters rockefeller. Typical desserts are molten Valrhona chocolate cake, triple coconut cream pie, strawberry shortcake and fruit sorbets. A light menu is available in the bar in an adjacent section of the building, where you're invited to "watch the evening drift by" through big windows onto Railroad Street.

(413) 528-7767. www.pearlsrestaurant.com. Entrées, $18 to $38. Dinner nightly, 5 to 10. Sunday brunch, 11 to 3.

John Andrew's, Route 23, South Egremont.

"Innovative and spectacular" are words that area chefs employ when describing this culinary star fashioned by Susan and Dan Smith and named after her grandfather, John Andrew Bianchi. The interior is romantic with sponged walls of burnt red, a green ceiling and striking chairs that came from the Copacabana and have been reupholstered and repainted in green. Metal wall sconces and a tiled fireplace add warmth, and at night the walls glow like copper. The enclosed rear porch, mod in cane and chrome, opens onto an outdoor dining deck overlooking lawn and woods. Talented chef Dan favors Northern Italian and Mediterranean cuisine. He might pair roast cod with lemon grass chile broth and coconut rice, sautéed duck breast and crisp confit with a balsamic and maple glaze, and spiced leg of lamb with a pilaf of dried cherries and sweet corn. Favorite starters include tuna and salmon tartare, crispy oysters with anchovy-mustard vinaigrette, and foie gras and sweetbreads with pear fritter, fig and thyme jam and sherry-vinegar sauce. Typical desserts are plum crisp with vanilla ice cream and caramelized apple tart with cider crème anglaise.

(413) 528-3469. www.jarestaurant.com. Entrées, $18 to $28. Dinner nightly in summer, 5 to 10. Closed Wednesday rest of year.

The Old Mill, Route 23, South Egremont.

The restaurant in this restored 18th-century gristmill has long been one of our favorites. The atmosphere is a cross between a simple Colonial tavern and a European wayside inn, warm and friendly, yet highly sophisticated. The large, L-shaped main dining room has wide-planked and stenciled floors, beamed ceilings, pewter cutlery and bottles of olive oil as centerpieces on the nicely spaced tables, and a collection of old mincing tools on the cream-colored walls. Reflections of candles sparkle in the small-paned windows. An addition to a sunken rear dining room provides large windows onto Hubbard Brook. Chef-owner Terry Moore adds a few nightly specials to supplement the ten entrées on the seasonal menu. Appetizers and smaller portions of some of the entrées turn up on the bar menu ($8.50 to $16), available in both bar and dining room except on Saturdays. The sautéed calves liver with apple-smoked bacon is a masterpiece. We've also enjoyed the broiled red snapper, baked bluefish with ginger and scallions, oven-roasted poussin with garlic and veal piccata with a lemony sauce. Save room for the mocha torte and the meringue glacé with cointreau and strawberries, both heavenly desserts.

(413) 528-1421. Entrées, $20 to $26. Dinner, Tuesday-Sunday from 5.

From Ketchup to Caviar, 150 Main St., Lee.

The quirky name derives from his wife Lynne's old catering business in Ohio, but patrons come here from all over the Berkshires. French chef Christian Urbain and his wife took over a downtown Lee restaurant, dressed up three dining rooms and a bar in soothing beige and burgundy and added two upstairs guest suites. Their short menu might open with a nouvelle treat like smoked bluefish mousse in a smoked salmon triangle with peppered fennel garnished with salmon caviar, alongside such French classics as a charcuterie plate and frog legs provençal. For entrées, Christian usually offers Maine crab cakes rémoulade, roasted Long Island duck with prunes and armagnac, and flatiron steak au poivre with cognac. The menu carries lighter items, too. You can sup on a black angus cheeseburger with the works plus ketchup – to carry out the restaurant's name, as does the salmon caviar appetizer. Or how about a classic salad niçoise for dinner? We were smitten by that, the white bean minestrone, the pot pie of escargots topped with a beehive of puff pastry and the succulent Prince Edward Island mussels, steamed in a broth of garlic and shallots that proved so addictive that we sopped up every last drop with the wonderful French bread. Almost everyone finishes with the signature profiteroles, a massive plateful of four with a choice of ice creams and a generous topping of chocolate sauce.

(413) 243-6397. www.fromketchuptocaviar.com. Entrées, $18 to $25. Dinner, Wednesday-Sunday from 5.

Trúc Orient Express, 3 Harris St., West Stockbridge.

This enchanting place beside the Williams River testifies to the successful saga of a courageous Vietnamese family reunited and starting anew after fleeing Saigon in 1975. Starting here in a little house after leaving Truc's restaurant in Hartford to her son, Trai Thi Duong greatly expanded with 110 seats on two floors of a building next door. Truc's is drop-dead elegant, with lacquered burgundy chairs at well-spaced tables set with white damask linens, polished wide-board floors with beautiful oriental rugs scattered about, and some gorgeous screens and huge black vases inlaid with mother of pearl. An open staircase leads past lovely stained-glass windows to more dining areas beneath vaulted ceilings and skylights on the second floor. Haunting Vietnamese music plays in the background, and haunting aromas based on garlic waft from the kitchen. The occasional communications gap with the Vietnamese staff is bridged by pointing to the numbers of the 65 items on the exotic menu. We cherish the Vietnamese egg rolls, the roast pork sautéed with cashews and vegetables and the crispy duck with lemon grass. The "singing chicken" and Mongolian hotpot also are great, but one of us can never order anything here but the crispy happy pancakes, the best ever.

(413) 232-4204. Entrées, $10.95 to $18.50. Dinner nightly, 5 to 9. Closed Tuesday in winter.

┌─*A Page from the Past*───────────────

Jacks Grill, Main Street, Housatonic.

The little hamlet of Housatonic, where Alice of Alice's Restaurant fame had her second restaurant, is home to this fun eatery fashioned from an old hardware store and now operated by the Fitzpatrick family as "a footloose subsidiary of the Red Lion Inn." An electric train runs around the ceiling, enlivening the prevailing expanse of wood tables and floors. The original store shelves at either end display family artifacts like old lunch boxes, cookie jars, toys, china dolls and Jack Fitzpatrick's old football helmet. Behind the stairs on the way to the loo are original fashion drawings by Jane Fitzpatrick of Country Curtains fame. The menu is a mixed bag, modestly priced and ranging widely from a hamburger (and a garden burger) to grilled swordfish with citrus butter. Other possibilities include chicken pot pie, meatloaf, pot roast like your grandmother used to make and grilled salmon with black bean and corn salsa. The only item on a recent menu over $13 was grilled ribeye steak for $21. Starters could be nachos, fried calamari and crispy popcorn shrimp. Desserts are out of the past: a root-beer float, tollhouse cookies, chocolate pudding and jell-O. And it really is Jacks Grill, as the menu says: "no confounded apostrophe in Jacks and no pretentious 'e' in Grill." That's the way the locals like it.

(413) 274-1000. www.jacksgrill.com. Entrées, $11 to $21. Dinner, Tuesday-Sunday from 5, Sunday brunch 11 to 2. Closed November-May.

Changes of Taste and Pace

For a touch of Provence, head to **Bizalion's Fine Food,** a charming new charcuterie, cheese shop and café-of-sorts at 684 South Main St., Great Barrington. Francois Bizalion and his Irish wife Helen charm regulars with their salades and assiette platters, panini, fondues, espresso and more, to enjoy at a communal table in front or to take out for a picnic in the countryside.

At the top of offbeat Railroad Street in downtown Great Barrington stands **Martin's Restaurant,** its sign proclaiming "breakfast served all day." Martin Lewis, formerly a chef at the Waldorf-Astoria, packs them in with potato omelets, corned-beef hash with poached eggs and toast and a "tower of bagel," at $9.95 by far the priciest item and loaded with smoked salmon, cream cheese, tomato and bermuda onion.

Helsinki Tea Co. Café at 284 Main St. is a colorful place hidden behind a shopping arcade. The funky ambiance is old European, the service laid-back and the combination of teas, liquors and wines unusual. But exotic treats emanate from a pint-size kitchen for lunch and dinner. They range from Asian red and black tuna and borscht to Finish meatballs and the specialty Russian latkes with gravlax. And the music from the attached **Club Helsinki** is live.

Adjacent (in a roundabout kind of way) is **Baba Louie's,** where the wood-fired oven produces organic and San Francisco sourdough pizzas with a mix of exotic ingredients, most of them wholesome organic. Toppings include figs, gorgonzola, prosciutto, roasted red potatoes, fennel and even roasted parsnips. The interior is cramped and cozy; there's a take-out counter in the arcade in back.

For an ice cream fix, head to **Bev's Homemade Ice Cream,** 5 Railroad St., or in Lenox at 38 Housatonic St. Beverly Mazursky and sons used to make the wonderful flavors in machines behind the counter, but most come now from their new factory at 955 South Main St., Great Barrington. They're known for their raspberry-chocolate chip, served in a sugar cone. You can order gelatos, frappes, smoothies, sherbet coolers and even a banana split, as well as espresso and, for lunch, their ever-popular Jamaican patties (different kinds of Caribbean breads with such fillings as beef, mixed veggies and broccoli-cheese).

Next door at 26 Housatonic in Lenox is **Betty's Pizza Shack,** the third effort of young restaurateur Jason Macioge (of Bistro Zinc and Pearl's in Great Barrington). A potted palm tree at the entry sets the stage for a "shack" like you thought you'd never see: A riot of blues, reds, purples and orange. Walls and ceiling of corrugated silver. A decor of surfboard and sharks and different colored lights. A curving counter with seats of cushion-topped garbage cans. Oh, yes. The food is a hip collection of pizzas, salads, "samiches" and "bevvies" for the hip young crowd that frequents the place.

The lately reinvented Lenox Shops along Route 7 north is home to **Chocolate Springs,** a chocolate and pastry café. Chef-owner Joshua Needleman returned to his home area after training at pastry boutiques in New York and Paris. Here he produces exotic chocolates and delectable dessert pastries, served with coffee or tea in a sleek retail showroom and salon-style dining area. One taste of his champagne-cognac bonbon and we were hooked.

FOR MORE INFORMATION: Berkshire Visitors Bureau, The Berkshire Common, Pittsfield 01201, (413) 443-9186 or (800) 237-5747. Individual chambers of commerce have information centers in Lenox, Stockbridge and Great Barrington.

Orchards Inn wraps around landscaped courtyard to create its own tranquil setting.

Williamstown/North Adams, Mass.

Arts Capital of New England

The congnoscenti knew, but how many others realized that a sedate little college enclave and an economically distressed industrial town five miles apart in the northern Berkshires would become the arts center of New England?

Until it happened. Then they certainly did.

The opening in 1999 of MASS MoCa, short for Massachusetts Museum of Contemporary Art, in a decaying mill complex cemented the area's reputation as a national player in the arts. Suddenly, people from across the country converged on North Adams to view the largest contemporary arts center in the world. The gritty factory town of 14,700 morphed into an up-and-coming cultural and entertainment hub. New inns and restaurants emerged to serve visitors in style.

Knowing visitors already were aware of the treasures of neighboring Williamstown, cited locally as "the most culture-saturated rural spot in the nation." Blessed with an uncommonly scenic setting and the riches that prestigious Williams College attracts and returns, the diminutive college town had quietly become an arts center of national significance.

Connoisseur magazine said its three leading museums make it "an unlikely but powerful little art capital." Newsweek hailed the annual Williamstown Theatre Festival as "the best of all American summer theaters." U.S. News and World Report ranked Williams College tops among the country's academic institutions.

Williams, its associates and benefactors inspired these superlatives. But they have geography and nature to thank for what some call "The Village Beautiful." Rather isolated in a verdant bowl, this Brigadoon in the Berkshires dwells at the foot of Mount Greylock, the highest peak in Massachusetts, enclosed by Vermont's Green and New York's Taconic mountains. Not only do these provide great outdoor activities (in particular, golf, hiking and skiing). They also help Williamstown retain a charmed rural flavor that seems far more village-like than its official population of 8,200 might suggest.

Williamstown is a sophisticated college town of great appeal, one that unfolds as you delve. To its traditional charms you now can add the contemporary attractions of North Adams.

Seeing and Doing

Art and history are best appreciated when viewed close up, away from the crowded settings of the huge museums. As Connoisseur magazine reported, this intimacy is "the great gift" of Williamstown.

Sterling and Francine Clark Art Institute, 225 South St., Williamstown.

The best known of the town's museums chanced upon its sylvan Williamstown location through an old family connection with Williams College and the fact that eccentric collector Sterling Clark, heir to the Singer sewing machine fortune, wanted his treasures housed far from a potential site of nuclear attack. Clark's neoclassical white marble temple opened in 1955 (he and his wife are buried under its front steps) and was subsequently expanded with two additions housing more galleries and one of the world's outstanding art reference libraries. Lately mounting major exhibitions that draw more than 100,000 visitors a summer, the Clark has particularly strong holdings of French 19th-century paintings (36 Renoirs), English silver, prints and drawings. The Clark was the single largest source for the Renoir exhibition at Boston's Museum of Fine Arts. Shown mostly in small galleries the size of the rooms in which they once hung, the highly personalized collection of Monets, Turners and Winslow Homers quietly vies for attention with sculptures, porcelain and three centuries worth of silver (Sterling Clark liked good food and the silverware to go with it). All this is amid an austere yet intimate setting of potted plants and vases of dried flowers, furniture and benches for relaxation. Outside are 140 acres of lawns, meadows, a lily pond and walking trails. Lunch and snacks are available from the Clark Café, inside or outside on the grounds.

(413) 458-2303. www.clarkart.edu. Open 10 to 5, daily in July and August, Tuesday-Sunday rest of year. Adults $10, June-October; free, rest of year.

Williams College Museum of Art, Main Street, Williamstown.

A $4.5 million extension to its original octagonal building in Lawrence Hall makes this museum a sleeper in art circles. Itself a work of art, it contains an 1846 neoclassical rotunda with "ironic" columns that are decorative rather than functional. The eight sides of the rotunda are repeated in soaring newer galleries with skylights, some of their walls hung with spectacular wall art. Once headed by Guggenheim director Thomas Krens, the museum houses fourteen galleries and a staggering 12,000 works spanning the history of art, from 3,000-year-old Assyrian stone reliefs to the last self-portrait by Andy Warhol. In an effort to complement the better-known Sterling and Francine Clark Art Institute's strengths in the 19th century, this museum stresses contemporary, 17th- and 18th-century American art and rare Asian art. Its traveling and special exhibitions rival those of many a metropolitan museum.

(413) 597-2429. www.williams.edu/WCMA. Open Tuesday-Saturday 10 to 5, Sunday 1 to 5. Free.

Nearby is the **Hopkins Observatory,** the oldest working observatory in the United States (1836), offering exhibits on the history of astronomy plus planetarium shows and viewings through college telescopes.

Chapin Library, Stetson Hall, 26 Hopkins Hall Drive, Williams College.

Nowhere else are the founding documents of the country – original printings of the Declaration of Independence, the Articles of Confederation, the Bill of Rights and drafts of the Constitution – displayed together in a simple glass case on the second floor of a college hall. Every year on July 4, actors from the Williamstown Theatre Festival are drawn to Chapin Library to read the Declaration to the community. On display with the four founding documents is the signed copy of *The Federalist* presented to George Washington by Alexander Hamilton and James Madison. This remarkable library of international stature contains more than 50,000 rare books and first editions and 40,000 manuscripts. Ask to see James Madison's copy of Thomas Paine's *Common Sense.* One floor below is the Williamsiana Collection of town and gown. The lowest level of Stetson contains the archives of band leader Paul Whiteman, with 3,500 original scores and a complete library of music of the 1920s.

(413) 597-2462. Open Monday-Friday, 10 to noon and 1 to 5. Free.

'The Future Is Here'

MASS MoCA, 87 Marshall St., North Adams.

The country's largest center for contemporary visual and performing arts occupies a thirteen-acre campus of renovated 19th-century factory buildings that make up about a third of the North Adams business district. Galleries, sculpture parks and performance arenas co-exist with e-commerce start-ups in a phenomenon locally (and hopefully) called Silicon Village. Some 27 red-brick buildings, abandoned following the 1985 closing of the once-mighty Sprague Electric Co., are linked by an elaborate system of interlocking courtyards, viaducts and elevated walkways.

If conventional museums are boxes, as its backers attest, MASS MoCA is an open platform – a rather overwhelming one that aims to foster dynamic interchange between the visual and performing arts and between those who make art and those who view it. Nineteen high-ceilinged, light-filled galleries – one as long as a football field – total more than 100,000 square feet of ever-changing exhibit space. MASS MoCA focuses on the work of artists charting new territory, works that blur the lines between visual and performing arts, and works that have never before been exhibited because of their size or materials (including a Chinese dragon boat at a recent visit). A lack of signage and edifying descriptions suggests the uninformed seek enlightenment through guided tours (offered several times a day in summer and fall and weekends year-round).

The museum opened in 1999 after being given up for dead at least four times in a dozen years of ups and downs from concept to reality. Now it is a national model of not only how to re-use old buildings but how to experience art and architecture today. "I have seen the future," wrote a Wall Street Journal reporter, "and it is MASS MoCA." Even if you don't like modern art, you'll likely be impressed, if not overwhelmed.

(413) 662-2111. Open daily 10 to 6, July and August; Wednesday-Monday 11 to 5, rest of year. Adults $10, children $4. Guided tours weekends at noon and 3.

Williamstown Theatre Festival, Adams Memorial Theater, Williams College.

Founded in 1955, this professional summer festival presents "some of the most ambitious theatre the U.S. has to offer," in the words of the Christian Science Monitor. It won the 2002 Regional Theatre Tony Award for outstanding achievement and contribution. Such luminaries as Dick Cavett, Edward Herrmann and Marsha Mason return summer after summer to the festival they call home for productions of everything from Chekhov, Shakespeare and Ibsen to Tennessee Williams, Noel Coward and Broadway tryouts. The festival presents more than 200 productions in its summer season on its 520-seat Main and adjacent 96-seat Nikos stages, outdoor Free Theatre and weekend Cabaret in Goodrich Hall.

(413) 597-3400. www.wtfestival.org. Festival performances Tuesday-Saturday, mid-June through August. Tickets prices vary, from $20 to $53.

Williams College. Besides the aforementioned highlights, the campus as a whole is worth exploring. Its buildings (more than 50 and counting), predominantly in red brick and gray granite, range through almost every period of American architecture. The lawns and plantings and sense of nature all around contribute to a pleasant walking tour.

NATURE. The prime spot – as well as the area's dominant feature – is the **Mount Greylock State Reservation,** a series of seven peaks with a 3,491-foot summit that is the highest in Massachusetts. The Mount Greylock visitor center is on Rockwell Road in Lanesboro, (413) 443-0011. The Appalachian Trail crosses Greylock, and the Appalachian Mountain Club's rustic 34-bed **Bascom Lodge** at the summit is booked by people wanting to see the famous Greylock sunrise and sunset. You can drive, hike or bike to the summit for a spectacular 100-mile view encompassing five states. Those who haven't hiked up the Hopper Trail out of Williamstown might tackle the steps up the 92-foot-high War Veterans Memorial Tower, a lighthouse destined for Boston Harbor but diverted to Greylock in 1931. Its beacon, according to a plaque at the summit, would "guide aviators in their long night-time journeys over the treacherous mountain range."

Other memorable views are obtained by driving the Taconic Trail west through Petersburg Pass and heading east on the Mohawk Trail switchbacking sharply above North Adams.

The 2,430-acre **Hopkins Memorial Forest** northwest of the Williams campus is an experimental forest operated by the Williams College Center for Environmental Studies, with fifteen miles of nature and cross-country trails, plus the Moon Barn museum showing old photographs, farm machinery, implements and tools, and the Buxton Garden, a one-acre farm garden designed to have different flowers in bloom at all seasons. Williams College also recently acquired **Mount Hope Park,** a former estate with extensive gardens and grounds.

RECREATION. Golf is the seasonal pastime at two 18-hole courses open to the public. The semi-private **Taconic Golf Club,** 19 Meacham St., (413) 458-3997, is operated by Williams College on the south edge of town from mid-April to mid-November. Rated the sixth best public course in Massachusetts by Golf Digest, it charges greens fees from $125. In the valley at South Williamstown, **Waubeeka Golf Links,** 137 New Ashford Road, (413) 458-5869, claims "quite possibly the most challenging, beautiful and memorable 6,000 yards you'll ever encounter." Greens fees are $43 weekends, $33 midweek; open April-November.

In summer, you can swim in the 74-degree thermal mineral waters of **Sand Springs Pool & Spa,** 158 Sand Springs Road, (413) 458-5205. Founded in 1813 and the oldest springs resort still in operation in the country, the family-run venture has a large swimming pool plus indoor and outdoor spa tubs, all fed by a mineral spring.

SHOPPING. Williamstown's college-community stores are generally along Spring Street, which runs south off Main Street opposite the Williams campus and between such campus appendages as museum, science center and sports complex. **Zanna** and **Jackie's** carry apparel of appeal to college women. Try the **Clarksburg Bread Co.** for chunky cheddar cheese bread or an oatmeal-cranberry scone. More than 40 varieties of coffees and 25 of loose teas are available at **Cold Spring Coffee Roasters. Library Antiques** shows dhurrie rugs, English country pine furniture, Turkish pillows, china, gifts and more, as well as Asian art at the related **LiAsia Gallery** across the street. More good art is available at **Harrison Gallery.** The **George M. Hopkins Store** offers wood furniture and collectibles.

Water Street, a parallel street that blossomed later, has distinctive shops including the **Cottage** for classy gifts and clothing, **The Mountain Goat** for outdoors equipment, the **Plum Gallery** and **Room,** for home accessories.

For foodies, the most interesting shopping of all may be at **The Store at Five Corners,** an 18th-century general store gone upscale, just south of Williamstown at the junction of Routes 7 and 43. Expect to find Epicurean spices, Mendocino pastas, interesting wines, gifts, Italian biscotti and homemade fudge along with an espresso bar, baked goods from the store's bakery, and an assortment of breakfast and lunch items from the deli. There are tables upon which to enjoy, inside or out.

Where to Stay

The Orchards, 222 Adams Road (Route 2), Williamstown 01267.

Partially hidden behind imposing gates on the busy eastern outskirts of Williamstown, this three-story hotel and restaurant meanders around a small, landscaped courtyard containing a free-form, rock-bordered pond with a fountain. Built in 1985, it has aged well and has been considerably enhanced following its rescue from foreclosure by Sayed M. Saleh, a hotel executive from Boston, who moved here with his wife and daughter. The interior layout separates the restaurant and lounge from the 48 guest accommodations. Winding corridors expand into a gracious drawing room, where afternoon tea is served amid polished antique furniture and intricate chandeliers. Coffee and breakfast pastries are served there (gratis) before the dining room opens in the morning. The Orchards' original pink and green motif (for the location's heritage as an orchard) has been muted in favor of a more sumptuous Pierre Deux look – or, as the owner put it, "tastefully decorated in the style of a graceful English country estate, with antique furniture and artwork." Twelve rooms have working fireplaces, including a third-floor suite (recently reconfigured from two large rooms) with king bed and a multi-spray shower and jacuzzi tub. A premier room we liked had a king bed with a wood and curtained canopy headboard and a fainting couch at its foot, three plush chairs plus a window seat in the bay, a corner fireplace and a writing desk. Amenities include telephones in bathrooms as well as in bedrooms and TV/VCRs secreted in armoires. Each room is different within the prevailing theme: marble bathrooms with terrycloth robes and Lord & Mayfair bath oils and soaps, separate dressing areas with a second vanity and a small refrigerator. Homemade cookies are left when the beds are turned down at night. The inn has a sauna and jacuzzi, exercise room, an antiques shop, a plush cocktail lounge with a fireplace and a small outdoor pool flanked by a sundeck.

Three meals a day are available in the elegant dining room, recently redecorated with gold brocade walls, blue carpeting and a wall mural of a Berkshires scene. Tall, curving windows on one side look out onto the attractive courtyard. Now called **Yasmin's** (for the owner's daughter), it offers a short menu of contemporary cuisine. Dinner choices at our latest visit ranged from seared Maine scallops on truffled risotto to yogurt-marinated lamb loin skewers on saffron couscous. Although the dining room strikes some as pretentious, the inn merits its ranking as the only Mobil four-star, AAA four-diamond hotel in Massachusetts west of Boston.

(413) 458-9611 or (800) 225-1517. Fax (413) 458-3273. www.orchardshotel.com. Forty-seven rooms and two suites with private baths. Memorial Day to early November: doubles $195 to $325, suites $395. Rest of year: doubles $170 to $270, suites $345. Two-night minimum weekends in season.

Entrées, $26 to $31. Lunch daily, noon to 2. Dinner, 5:30 to 9. Sunday brunch, 10 to 2.

Field of Dreams

Field Farm Guest House, 554 Sloan Road, Williamstown 01267.

How about a stay in a veritable house museum of modern art and architecture? Out in the country on a hilltop, surrounded by nature with landscaped gardens and walking trails on 316 acres of conservation land? Both treats are yours if you can book a room at this dream-like B&B. The architect-designed, 1948 American Modern house was the home of arts patron Lawrence H. Boedel, avid modern art and furniture collector, and his wife Eleanor until 1984, when it was willed to the Trustees of Reservations, who authorized its use as a B&B. Built of Western cedar and fronted by a mass of yellow creeping hydrangeas, the Bauhaus-inspired house looks much as the Bloedels left it. Modern artworks enhance the interior, which is a lived-in museum of mid-20th century furnishings, including a Noguchi coffee table, a Kagan sofa and an Eames chair in the living room. Thirteen sculptures, including works by Richard M. Miller and Herbert Ferber, grace the landscaped gardens and grounds, which are striking for their trails and views of Mount Greylock. Overnight guests have the run of a spacious living room, dining room, galley kitchen and grounds. Much of the furniture in the 5,000-square-foot house was made by Bloedel, a Williams graduate and onetime college librarian. The house has five bedrooms, all with their original baths. The huge main-floor Gallery Room, which Bloedel used as a studio, comes with a kingsize bed, a black walnut floor and a separate entrance. Upstairs are four more guest rooms, recently updated with king or queensize beds. In the North Room, tiles of butterflies flank the fireplace. It has its own balcony, a dressing table with mirrored surface and a walk-in closet with sliding drawers. The newly renovated, sleekly modern master bedroom features a kingsize platform bed with handmade mattress, designer furnishings, a fireplace with tiles of trees and birds, and an enormous private deck. Outside are the original swimming pool fed by an underground spring, a tennis court, picnic tables, woodlands, pastures for dairy cows, cornfields, a pond, and four miles of trails for wildlife-watching or cross-country skiing. Resident innkeepers serve an imaginative breakfast in the dining room, which opens onto a small porch.

(413) 458-3135. Fax (413) 458-3144. www.guesthouseatfieldfarm.org. Five rooms with private baths. Doubles, $150 to $250.

The Williamstown Bed and Breakfast, 30 Cold Spring Road, Williamstown 01267.

An attractive white Victorian house built in 1880 with room to spare, this sparkling B&B is lovingly tended by Kim Rozell and Lucinda Edmonds. They offer four spiffy and sizable guest rooms with updated baths and comfortable wing chairs on the second floor. Two rooms have queensize poster beds, a third has a double bed and one has two twins. White cotton comforters top each bed. Appointments are a blend of antique and modern, with an emphasis on oak furniture, mini-print wallpapers with vivid borders and a refreshing absence of the clutter often associated with Victoriana. As opposed to the antiques elsewhere in the house, the comfortable living room is outfitted in a crisp, almost contemporary style. Guests relax here as well as on the front porch or in Adirondack chairs and a hammock near the perennial gardens in the side yard. The convivial breakfasts are feasts, taken at a table for eight in the dining room. Start with fruit, cereals and oatmeal scones, but save room for the main course – perhaps blueberry pancakes, waffles, baked eggs or cheese blintzes. The personable hosts, who do all the work themselves, have a handle on all the area's highlights and share their enthusiasm with guests.

(413) 458-9202. www.williamstownbandb.com. Four rooms with private baths. Doubles, $130 to $150 April-October, $125 to $140 rest of year. No credit cards.

Le Jardin, 777 Cold Spring Road (Route 7), Williamstown 02167.

A babbling brook and ducks in a pond greet guests at this old inn astride a hill in the countryside south of town. The tranquil setting remains, but the interior has been totally refurbished by new owner Jae Chung, who closed the inn and restaurant for renovations in 2004. Former owner Walter Hayn stayed on as resident innkeeper and chef. The six guest quarters have been refreshed in the style of Jae's Inn in North Adams, though Walter considers Le Jardin's rooms more upscale. The furnishings are crisp and rather modern, with TV/DVDs and high-speed internet access, good Vermont artworks on the walls, and carpeting or oriental rugs on hardwood floors. Room configurations vary from snug to suites. A large suite with kingsize bedroom has a dining/living room area with a sofabed and a granite and marble bathroom. The master suite also has a kingsize bed and sofabed plus a brick fireplace in the bedroom and a whirlpool tub in the bath. Two small rooms with brick fireplaces and double beds can be joined to form another suite. A front room has a sleigh bed and brick fireplace, while a queen bedroom opens onto a rear deck. Continental breakfast is complimentary in the downstairs restaurant.

(413) 458-8032. Fax (413) 458-8792. www.lejardininn.com. Five rooms and one suite with private baths. Doubles, $145 to $245 June-October, $95 to $195 rest of year.

River Bend Farm, 643 Simonds Road (Route 7 North), Williamstown 01267.

Relax by the taproom fire and "slip back in time," urge innkeepers Judy and David Loomis. It would be hard not to. Spending a night or two in this painstakingly restored Georgian Colonial built in 1770 by one of the founders of Williamstown is to immerse oneself in history. Or, as Judy tells it, "guests say it's like staying in a museum but you can touch the stuff." The house, which exudes 18th-century authenticity, contains what authorities consider to be the best examples of period woodwork in town, as well as notable corner cupboards, paneling and iron work. Guests enter the rear taproom, where black kettles hang from the huge hearth, one of five fireplaces off a central stone chimney. All the lighting here and in the adjacent parlor comes from small bulbs in tin chandeliers and period lighting fixtures. Four bedrooms share two baths, one upstairs with a tub and the other downstairs in the old pantry and harboring an ingenious corner shower with tiles that David fashioned from roof slate. Three rooms are upstairs off a hall containing a giant spinning wheel. The front corner room has a crocheted coverlet over the four-poster double bed and plenty of room for two wing chairs in a sitting area. Each of the other rooms contains a double and a twin bed. A downstairs room with a double bed in a former parlor is lovely, decorated in blues and whites with well-worn oriental rugs. The hosts serve a healthful continental breakfast of fresh fruit, homemade granola, honey from their own beehives, muffins and breads.

(413) 458-3121. www.riverbendfarmbb.com. Four rooms with two shared baths. Doubles, $100. Closed November-March.

The Porches Inn at MASS MoCA, 231 River St., North Adams 01247.
Seven Victorian row houses across the street from MASS MoCA – built in the early 1900s as worker housing for the mills of North Adams – have been transformed into a 50-room inn at the cutting edge. The museum director persuaded Williams College graduate John Wadsworth Jr., retired chairman of Morgan Stanley/Asia, to develop the project and turn management over to the Fitzpatrick family of the Red Lion Inn in Stockbridge. The structures originally had individual porches, so two broad front porches – reminiscent of that at the Red Lion Inn – were built to link the structures. The focal point here is one building that holds the reception area, a couple of breakfast rooms and two small living rooms. The one in the front has a blazing fireplace on the side and four vivid red leather chairs around a circular coffee table in the center. The consciously clever interior design is not at all the antique look of the Red Lion Inn or that of the buildings' late 1800s period. The management calls it ''retro-edgy, industrial granny chic,'' a style that harmonizes well with the museum's combination of old-mill nostalgia and high tech. Eight to ten guest rooms are in each of six connected houses. They vary in size but generally are quite spacious, and eight on the second floor have private porches. Some quarters are loft suites on two levels, connected by spiral staircases. Dressed with Frette linens and topped with feather duvets, beds are king or queensize and in some cases there are two queens or an extra sofabed. TV/DVDs are hidden in armoires, and telephones are cordless. Many of the slate-floor bathrooms have jetted or clawfoot tubs and separate "deluge showers." Shaker-style wall pegs serve as towel and bathrobe holders. Mirrors have been ingeniously fashioned from recycled window frames. The vintage 1950s lamps in each room were purchased off eBay, as were accessories and artworks in a quirky art collection dominated by paint-by-number pictures. Carved into a wooded hillside out back is a heated swimming pool with an adjacent hot tub. A pavilion beside holds an indoor recreation room and sauna. Breakfast is continental-plus, available in a cheery breakfast room, in guest rooms or on the porch. For breakfast in bed, the meal is delivered in a retro-style, stainless-steel workman's lunchbox, with a vase of flowers on the side.

(413) 664-0400. Fax (413) 664-0401. www.porches.com. Twenty-nine rooms and 21 suites with private baths. Memorial Day to Veterans Day: doubles $160 to $295, suites $225 to $435. Rest of year: doubles $125 to $239, suites $175 to $329.

Jae's Inn, 1111 South State St. (Route 8), North Adams 01247.
Here is one of the more distinctive small, full-service country inns to appear in New England in years. Boston restaurateur Jae Chung returned to his home area to transform a modest inn two miles south of North Adams into an upscale inn, restaurant and spa with a contemporary Asian accent. He artfully renovated and

expanded the century-old building to produce eleven guest rooms with mostly queensize beds, marble baths and jacuzzi tubs, gas fireplaces and flat-screen TVs with DVD players. Much of the furniture is pine, as are the flooring and the occasional wainscoting, and the light-colored walls are dominated by colorful artworks. Each room has a desk (some of them rather old-fashioned and child-like), a rocking chair and, usually, a single armchair. Three on the walk-out lower courtyard level beneath the dining porch open onto private patios at the side. A less-compact room on the main floor harbors the inn's only kingsize bed. Sections of the main floor and lower level hold a variety of fitness and spa facilities, from treadmills and universal weight system to two massage rooms, a sauna and a beauty parlor. In back are a porch and a flagstone patio with lounge furniture and an ornamental kiva stove beside a small, angular swimming pool. Beyond the pool are a tennis court and a basketball hoop. Continental breakfast is included in the rates. Lunch and dinner are available in the main-floor restaurant and lounge (see Where to Eat).

(413) 664-0100. Fax (413) 664-0105. www.jaesinn.com. Eleven rooms with private baths. Doubles, $160 weekends, $95 to $125 midweek.

The 1896 House Country Inn & Motels, 910 Cold Spring Road (Route 7), Williamstown 01267.

All the makings for a romantic getaway await at this motel and inn complex marketed with hyperbole. Two motels, a barn with upscale suites and a restaurant are set back from the road on either side in a wooded, park-like setting south of town. The motel units in which the place got its start are a cut above. Eleven units in the Brookside section beside Hemlock Brook are furnished in maple with Waverly-Schumacher appointments. Twelve in the Pondside section beside a duck pond are furnished in lighter Cape Cod beach style. A new Sweetheart Room here has a lacy queen canopied bed and a double whirlpool tub. A three-room suite with queen bedroom, living room with sofabed, kitchen and bath with double whirlpool tub has a private deck from which, owners Denise Richer and Sue Morelle suggest, you can "observe the intrigues of waterfowl and pond life." The ultimate intrigues are reserved for the six Barnside suites in the 1896 red barn. Enter each from a wicker-filled porch. Inside is a 48-foot-deep space with a large living-dining area and gas fireplace, disappearing into a kingsize pillow-top bed area. A dressing room opens onto a bath with a double whirlpool tub. Furnishings vary from antiques to TV/DVDs, from coffeemakers to terry robes. Each has a different "period personality," from early American to Georgian to Victorian. The Empire Suite, the promotion says, "is opulent, glamorous and slightly pompous." The barn also holds the **Hunt Club** restaurant for "high spirits and gracious fare." Here in a salon-style setting of wing chairs you may order a light tavern meal beside four TVs at the round bar. Or order from a steakhouse/continental menu executed by chef-owner Bob Ayers in the paneled dining room. Know that for your "spontaneous urge to swing to the old standby tunes, there is a dance floor positioned by a mood fireplace." Outside, the duck pond with a curved stone bridge creates "a mini Shangri-La" at Pondside, Enjoy breakfast in a gazebo or at patio tables beside Hemlock Brook at Brookside. The romantics at Barnside indulge in a three-course breakfast by candlelight.

(413) 458-1896 or (888) 999-1896. www.1896house.com. Twenty-nine rooms and seven suites. Summer and foliage, doubles $120 to $169, suites $199 to $269. Rest of year, doubles $60 to $169, suites, $169 to $249.

Dinner, Wednesday-Saturday from 5:30, Sunday from 1; entrées, $19 to $28. Tavern, daily from 4; entrées, $9 to $12.

The Williams Inn, Junction of Routes 7 and 2, Williamstown 01267.

After the old Williams Inn was taken over by Williams College, the Treadway chain built a replacement (supposedly "on-the-green at Williams College," though not by standard definition). Not your typical inn, this is a full-service Colonial-modern hotel/motel, now independently owned. The 103 air-conditioned rooms on three floors come with two double beds (a few kingsize), TVs and early American furnishings. A North Wing in 2003 added 22 "premier king-bedded rooms" and a two-room suite, furnished in hotel style.

Meals are served in a large and formal dining room with high-back, leather-seat chairs beneath ten big brass chandeliers. The dinner menu pairs traditional yankee pot roast and a liver and onions tart with baked chicken wrapped in prosciutto and stuffed with gouda cheese, roast duck bigarade and veal piccata.

(413) 458-9371 or (800) 828-0133. Fax (413) 458-2767.www.williamsinn.com . One hundred twenty-five rooms and one suite with private baths. Mid-April to mid-November: doubles $165 to $275, suite $500 to $600. Rest of year: doubles $135 to $250, suite $375 to $425.

Entrées, $17.25 to $25.50. Lunch, Monday-Saturday 11:30 to 2:30. Dinner nightly, 5:30 to 9:30 or 10. Sunday, brunch 11:30 to 2:30, dinner 5 to 9.

Where to Eat

Mezze Bistro & Bar, 16 Water St., Williamstown.

Williamstown's best restaurant shares space with its most stylish nightspot in owner Nancy Thomas's sophisticated bistro and bar. After fire destroyed the original in a former craft gallery, Mezze relocated up the street to larger quarters in a former general store retailored for the purpose. Upright slabs of lumber serve as a divider in the entry foyer. To one side is a black and white dining room, where a birch tree trunk forms one of the columns beneath a skylight and white-clothed tables are spaced well apart on polished wood floors. The other side of the foyer leads to a spacious bar/lounge, mod and spare with wide-board floors and banquette seating. A tavern menu is available here, and it's *the* place to see and be seen. Executive chef James Tracey, who was invited to prepare a Berkshire holiday dinner at the James Beard House in New York in 2004, oversees the contemporary American fare. Typical starters are cabbage leaves stuffed with foie gras and shiitakes in an oxtail consommé, scallop ceviche with avocado, pickled red onions and cilantro, and variations on salad, as in frisée with a poached egg, apple slices and house-smoked bacon vinaigrette. Main courses range from roasted wild coho salmon in a porcini mushroom broth to rack of lamb with thyme. Roasted skate, roasted free-range chicken, seared duck breast and braised beef short ribs were recommended at a recent autumn visit, as was a dish called confit of pig with lentils, savoy cabbage and apple cider vinegar sauce. Desserts included chocolate-peanut tart with caramel ice cream, coconut macaroons with concord grape sorbet, and maple pot de crème with a gingersnap cookie. A Mezze plate of antipasti plus beef stroganoff and grilled hanger steak with bordelaise sauce were featured on the bar menu.

(413) 458-0123. www.mezzeinc.com. Entrées, $22 to $26. Dinner nightly, 5 to 9 or 10.

Le Jardin, 777 Cold Spring Road, Williamstown.

Under new ownership, this old-timer has a new look but the same acclaimed French cuisine. Boston restaurateur Jae Chung redecorated two dining rooms and the cocktail lounge, added a deck out front and installed a new kitchen in 2004.

German chef Walter Hayn, the former owner whose 32-year tenure is the longest in town, stayed on as innkeeper and chef. His menu remains classic French, from the French onion soup to the escargots en casserole. A new raw and steam bar adds some novelty, as does a section of the menu categorized as steaks and roasts (five steaks from tournedos bordelaise to steak frites, plus grilled pork and lamb chops and grilled chicken breast). The "chef's menu" runs the gamut from frog's legs and sole florentine to Long Island duckling, all nicely prepared and many with fine cream sauces. Another returning favorite is grilled chicken breast with artichokes and béarnaise sauce. Desserts tend to be rich, among them death by chocolate, hot fudge sundae, New York cheesecake and pecan pie. Sunday brunch is offered for $9.99. Wines from across the world have joined the previous mostly French wine list.

(413) 458-8032. Entrées, $19 to $29. Lunch, Monday-Saturday from 11:30. Dinner nightly, 4:30 to 9 or 10. Sunday brunch, 10:30 to 2:30.

Hobson's Choice, 159 Water St., Williamstown.

This country-rustic place with paneled walls and beamed ceilings is a favorite of locals, so much so that it expanded into a rear addition. Old tools hang on the walls, Tiffany-type lamps top tables and booths, and there are a few stools at the bar in back. Chef-owner Dan Campbell from Montana imparts a Western accent to the extensive steak and seafood menu. Hand-cut steaks, prime rib, five versions of chicken, cajun shrimp and grilled or blackened Norwegian salmon, scallops and fish of the day are featured for dinner. You can create your own surf and turf combo, perhaps Alaskan king crab and buffalo steak. Or you can make a meal out of pasta marinara or the salad bar, which is known for its organic produce. Start with shrimp wontons, sautéed mushrooms, tuna carpaccio or fried calamari. Finish with mud pie, grand marnier fudge parfait, apple strudel or death by chocolate.

(413) 458-9101. Entrées, $15 to $21. Dinner nightly, 5 to 9:30.

Thai Garden, 27 Spring St., Williamstown.

The Thai food is exotic and highly rated at this serene offshoot of a gourmet Thai restaurant of the same name in Keene, N.H. The menu is designated as to spiciness – up to three chiles (for drunken squid stir-fried with bell peppers, baby corn, mushrooms, string beans and basil). Seafood gra prow, seafood curry and spicy fish fillet are two-chile dishes. But the menu notes that the chiles and spices are toned down by other ingredients on the principle that "there must always be a harmony in a dish." Those preferring less incendiary tastes can opt for steamed ginger salmon, tamarind duck or a combo called "three buddies" – chicken, beef and pork loin sautéed with pineapple, corn, snow peas, mushrooms and more. Desserts include homemade Thai custard, coconut and ginger ice creams, and chilled lychees.

(413) 458-0004. Entrées, $7.95 to $15.95. Lunch daily, 11:30 to 3. Dinner nightly, 5 to 10.

Spice Root, 23 Spring St., Williamstown.

Modern Indian cuisine is served up in a modern Indian setting in this, the fifth in a series of highly rated Indian restaurants run by the Chola Group in New York and Connecticut. The decor is anything but traditional Indian. It's spare in rich reds, with a few beaded wall hangings, iridescent colored light spheres suspended from the ceiling and gleaming silver steel-backed chairs at close-together tables. The weighty copper menu reveals the usual Indian fare, from "hot! hot!" shrimp vindaloo to lamb cooked with mint and mango in a masala sauce. Tandoori specialties include various kabobs. The menu lists ten vegetarian specialties and seven "popular dishes" from Bombay. Appetizer platters include a sampling of vegetable or meat treats, including samosas. There's an $8.95 lunch buffet daily, and lunch boxes are available to go.

(413) 458-5200. www.fineindiandining.com. Entrées, $12 to $19. Lunch, Monday-Saturday 11:30 to 2:30, Sunday noon to 3. Dinner nightly, 5 to 10 or 11.

Eleven, 1111 MASS MoCA Way, North Adams.

The fine-dining restaurant in MASS MoCA's Building Eleven is not unlike the museum itself: cool and contemporary, and an artistic as well as a culinary treat. Some find the modernist look with sculpted multi-level white ceiling, cream-colored walls, mod gray upholstered chairs at bare tables and gray-tinted glass windows onto the outdoor courtyard stark to the point of being austere. But the bud vases with different flowers on each table are creative, and the recessed colored fluorescent lighting turns the space into a work of art, especially at night. "People interested in contemporary art are also interested in contemporary food," says chef-owner Nancy Thomas, who opened here shortly after fire temporarily interrupted her trendy Mezze restaurant venture in Williamstown. Lunch-goers find a short, affordable menu of soups, salads (perhaps cobb or tuna niçoise) and sandwiches, plus extras like pad thai, a Mezze cheese and Berkshire Mountain bread plate, and spicy lump crab summer rolls. The dinner menu adds starters like crispy calamari with chipotle aioli and pulled pork quesadilla. Nighttime entrées range from roasted cod with grilled corn risotto and tomato-basil relish to grilled hanger steak with shallot-mustard aioli. More basic fare might be a caramelized onion, mushroom and fontina pizza, black pepper tagliatelle with creamy walnut sauce and pecorino, and a burger with fries. Carrot cake with walnut-ginger icing is a typical dessert.

(413) 663-2004. Entrées, $15 to $19. Lunch daily, 11 to 3. Dinner, 5 to 9 or 10. Closed Monday-Wednesday in winter.

Gramercy Bistro, 24 Marshall St., North Adams.

Identical twins Ned and Sandy Smith sold their hot-shot Williamstown restaurants to join what Ned called "the up-and-coming North Adams scene." The brothers gutted a downtown diner to produce a casual bistro dispensing eclectic food at reasonable prices. Gramercy translates to "great things," according to Ned, which applies more to the food than the decor. The bistro retains elements of its diner heritage, including a linoleum-look floor and diner stools at a counter facing the bar and kitchen. Linens and candles dress the tables at night. The short but sweet menu is divided into salads, small plates and large plates, each so tempting that you're apt to have difficulty choosing. You might start with the signature mussels steamed with cilantro in a coconut-Thai broth, a goat cheese tartlet or a crab cake with wasabi vinaigrette. Main courses range from seared sesame tuna with soy-ginger vinaigrette to sautéed venison with green peppercorn sauce. Paella, red Thai curry shrimp with coconut milk and cilantro, sautéed sweetbreads with beurre noir and capers and filet mignon with mushroom duxelle and bordelaise sauce were on a recent autumn menu. Worthy endings are crème brûlée, chocolate torte or key lime pie. For a Sunday brunch pick-me-up, try the "good morning cosmo" and the kahlua-spiked Mexican french toast.

(413) 663-5300. www.gramercybistro.com. Entrées, $16 to $21. Dinner nightly except Tuesday, 5 to 9 or 10. Sunday brunch, 10 to 1.

Gideon's, 34 Holden St., North Adams.

Bill Gideon has cooked for presidents, royalty, actors and Julia Child, but claims he likes best cooking for the folks in North Adams. Barely 40 but having worked in Beverly Hills and Four Seasons hotels hither and yon, he got his own show in 2004 when he took over the dramatic storefront space where short-lived restaurants Il Tesora and Dora's Fine Dining used to be. The former musician-turned-chef continues the theatrics here, working from an open kitchen that's a stage for interaction with his customers. Upwards of 125 diners can be seated at white-clothed tables in a high-ceilinged space that's stylish in black, sage green and burgundy, with brick walls on one side and tall windows onto the street. A smaller side room holds a sophisticated bar and lounge. Expect an eclectic mix of Mediterranean, Asian and New England fare. Main courses vary from Asian-roasted, soy-glazed sea bass to herb-crusted rack of lamb with the chef's signature cheddar bread pudding. Start with barbecued duck spring rolls, crab cakes with mango salsa or a chunky lobster martini with a crisp fried olive stuffed with boursin cheese. Finish with pumpkin cheesecake, fuji apple pie or a tiramisu martini laced with frangelico and rum and served in an oversize martini glass. For that matter, martinis are huge here. The martini menu offers six zippy concoctions that could pass for liquid desserts for a cool $5.50 each. Gideon doesn't stop here, however. In 2005, he was about to open a second Gideon's at 23 Eagle St. with a lunch café and a second-floor "nightery" with lounge and dance floor.

(413) 664-9449. www.gideonsrestaaurant.com. Entrées, $15.95 to $24.95. Dinner, Tuesday-Saturday 5 to 10, Sunday 4 to 9.

Jae's Inn, 1111 South Main St., North Adams.

The Asian cuisine that captivated Boston fans has been transplanted to an unlikely outpost south of North Adams. Jae Chung returned to his home area to open a sleek Korean-Japanese-Thai fusion restaurant with a living-room-like lounge and fireplace in the front portion of his new inn and spa. Modern Asia meets traditional New England in a small dining room and a larger, more casual enclosed dining porch paneled in pine, even on the ceiling. Oriental artworks, small colored lights dangling from the ceiling, and angular blue cobalt wall sconces and glassware add color. Autumn leaves were artfully nested in the potted palms at our October visit. A couple of "lunch boxes" ($7.95 to $8.95) produced a fine midday repast of extra-good hot and sour soup with shrimp tempura in one case, the signature "tidbits" (chicken satay, grilled shrimp and a sea scallop) in the other. Each came in a box with two sauces, rice, salad, broccoli, a California roll and a couple of shrimp dumplings called shumai. At night, the kitchen turns out all kinds of decorative (and tasty) morsels, from a seafood pajon pancake and tuna tartare to ginger custard, dark chocolate mousse and lemon framboise for dessert. In between are all kinds of noodle, pad thai, rice and curry dishes. We'd gladly try the hosomaki in seaweed rolls, the hot and spicy kimchi stew, the famous Korean bibim bab (marinated chicken or beef with vegetables cooked in a hot stone pot), the ribeye bulgoki, the spicy Korean pork, the grilled tuna steak with wasabi dipping sauce – in fact, almost everything on the menu.

(413) 664-0100. Entrées, $11.95 to $16.95. Lunch daily, 11:30 to 4. Dinner nightly, 5 to 9 or 10.

FOR MORE INFORMATION: Williamstown Chamber of Commerce, Box 357, Williamstown, MA 01267, (413) 458-9077 or (800) 214-3799. www.williamstownchamber.com.

Glamorous table on porch at Straight Wharf Restaurant overlooks Nantucket harbor.

Nantucket, Mass.

Island of History and Romance

After a ferry ride nearly 30 miles into the Atlantic, arriving at Nantucket's Steamboat Wharf is a bit like stepping onto another land in another time. Everything about this elbow of sand, moors and history – the "faraway land," as the Native Americans named it – epitomizes an island at sea. Fourteen miles long and barely three miles wide, it wears the patina of age of an "island that time forgot," as a local visitor guide calls it. "Steeped in tradition, romance, legend and history, she is a refuge from modernity."

Flanked by brick sidewalks, gas lamps and towering shade trees, the town's ancient cobblestone streets lead past fine old sea captains' homes still standing from its days as the greatest whaling center in the world. The 400-plus structures from the late 1700s and early 1800s in the national historic district represent one of the greatest concentrations in America, evoking the town's description as "an architectural jewel."

So much for the island that time forgot. The island's mystique draws well-heeled visitors to a sophisticated side of Nantucket that is seriously chic and contemporary. More distant than other islands from the mainland and yet readily accessible to the affluent, Nantucket is all the more exclusive.

That's the way island preservationists and benefactors planned it when they created the Nantucket Historical Trust in 1957 and later the Nantucket Conservation Trust. Their efforts led to the preservation of 11,800 acres of open space – nearly 40 percent of the island's land total. Gentrification transformed the historic town into what magazines call "a perfect oasis – neat, tidy and relentlessly quaint – for upscale vacationers."

It's a bit precious and pricey, this year-round community of 9,000 in which whaling fortunes were amassed and which now is predicated on rest and relaxation for the elite. Tourism has been nurtured and the season extended – starting with the annual Daffodil Festival in late April and ending with the month-long Nantucket Noel celebration on New Year's Eve. The famed Christmas Stroll the first full weekend in December fills virtually every hostelry on the island.

Away from Nantucket town and Siasconset, the folks along the south beaches and the west side of the island let their hair down. The week our family roughed it, so to speak, in a friend's beach house at Surfside was far different from the fall weekends starting a decade later when we returned, as so many couples do, for getaways in Nantucket town, 'Sconset or Wauwinet.

Nantucket is perfect for an escape – away from the mainland and into a dream combining Yankee history and the *Preppy Handbook*. You don't have to wear Nantucket red trousers or carry a lightship basket, although many do. Just pick a nice place in which to stay. Eat well. Do a little touring, visit the historic sites, browse the shops. Relax and savor the good life. So what if when you leave your credit cards are maxed out?

Seeing and Doing

Nantucket's attractions run the gamut from beaches and moors to history and architecture to art and antiques to quaint wharves and rose-covered cottages. Except for the beaches and moors, almost everything the visitor needs or wants to do is right in Nantucket town.

Touring

Getting Around. Cars are discouraged, except for homeowners and those staying a long time. The heart of town is congested, streets are narrow and some are one way, parking is limited and the cobblestone streets are rough on the shock absorbers. Bicycles and mopeds are the preferred means of getting around, other than on your own two feet. For those who require wheels, there are taxis, a few rental cars and the Nantucket Regional Transit Authority Shuttle, (508) 228-7025. Its buses cover most of the island, serving Madaket, Miacomet, Siasconset and Surfside and Jetties beaches. They run daily from 7 a.m. to 11:30 p.m., June-September. Frequency and fares vary, from $1 to $2.

SIGHTSEEING TOURS. The island is big enough and the road network confusing enough that most first-time visitors need some orientation. **Barrett's Tours,** 20 Federal St., (508) 228-0174 or (800) 773-0174, offers three 90-minute bus tours daily, with stops in Siasconset. **Nantucket Island Tours,** Straight Wharf, (508) 228-0334, boards passengers on its mini-bus for an hour-long, 30-mile journey around the island.

WALKING TOURS are offered by the **Nantucket Historical Association (**see below) and by individuals. One of the more informative is the 90-minute tour led by **Dirk Gardiner Roggeveen,** (508) 221-0075, a twelfth-generation Nantucketer and island historian. He goes "where the buses don't," through hidden alleys and byways, all the while spinning tales of Nantucket lore. **Robert Pitman Grimes,** (508) 228-9382, also a Nantucket native, entertains visitors with interesting tidbits about island history on a nearly two-hour tour of the island in a suburban van. Ninety-minute van tours are offered three times daily by Gail Nickerson Johnson of **Gail's Tours,** (508) 257-6557. **Ara's Tours,** (508) 221-1951, offers 90-minute photo-op tours as well as three-hour tours that take in three lighthouses. **Great Point Natural History Tours** are offered by the Trustees of Reservations, (508) 228-6799. The three-hour guided tour over ten miles of barrier beach includes a climb to the top of Great Point Lighthouse.

BICYCLING. Bikes or mopeds are the best way to see the outskirts of Nantucket town (the cobblestone streets of downtown pose a problem there), and are a good way to get out to Surfside Beach. The ride is flat, on a path bordering the roadway. The most popular trip is out the bike path bordering the road to Siasconset, an easy, eight-mile straightaway past the airport with the wind generally from behind. The beguiling east-end village perched on a rose-dotted bluff is very different from busy Nantucket town. The sand dunes, the turquoise ocean, the golf courses and the birds a-twitter between vine-covered cottages present "a magical setting like that of Bermuda," as a Summer House manager reminded us. Instead of retracing your path, return via the winding, sometimes up-and-down loop road past Sankaty Light, Quidnet and Polpis. Here you'll see cranberry bogs and ponds, striking homes and rolling moors, and you'll get a feel for the real island. The real island is also sensed from the bike path out to Madaket and you get the same kind of ups and downs and arounds on the pleasant, paved path beside the road – rather than being in the road, as on the Polpis loop. Bikes and mopeds may be rented in the vicinity of the ferry landings from **Nantucket Bike Shop, Young's Bicycle Shop** and **Cook's Cycle Shop,** and from **Island Bike & Sport** at 25 Old South Road.

Historic Nantucket

Dating to 1659 when Thomas Macy arrived as the first settler, Nantucket town has more than 2,400 historic houses, an extraordinary total. About 800 structures predate the Civil War (including several from the late 1600s). Walk up Main Street for a look at the Three Bricks, impressive Georgian mansions built by whaling merchant Joseph Starbuck.

Twelve buildings of special significance are open to the public by the **Nantucket Historical Association,** 2 Whalers Lane, (508) 228-1894. They include two museums and five period houses of different eras. On the outskirts, don't miss the Oldest House (1686) on Sunset Hill, the Old Mill (1746) and the Old Gaol (1805). Buildings are open mid-June to Labor Day, Monday-Saturday 10 to 5 and Sunday noon to 5; reduced hours in spring and fall. Tickets may be obtained in combination with the whaling museum (adults $18, children $9) or individually or for the historic sites only (adults $6, children $3).

Public walking tours are led by NHA interpreters. They start at the Nantucket Whaling Museum and cover the development of the downtown core from a Colonial outpost into an international whaling port and today's seasonal resort. The 90-minute tours are offered Monday-Saturday at 10:15, 11:15, 1:15 and 2:15 and Sunday at 2:15, Memorial Day to Labor Day, and daily at 2:15 from Labor Day to Columbus Day. Adults $10, children $4.

Nantucket Whaling Museum, 15 Broad St., Nantucket.
The single largest attraction in town is the association's Whaling Museum, as

befits a community that was America's leading whaling port until petroleum replaced whale oil and candles as illuminants. Fortunes were made here when the whalers' cargo was sold at great profit to mainland refineries for use in lamps, street lights and industrial purposes. That heritage is detailed in the inviting red-brick building, a former candle factory just off Steamboat Wharf. The museum opened in 1930 as an outgrowth of the private collection of summer resident Edward F. Sanderson and has expanded since. The museum closed in 2004 for a year's restoration to reveal the building's original fabric, including the original beam press still poised to render whale spermaceti into wax for candles and oil. It reopened with a new "museum center" orientation and gallery building joining it to the Peter Foulger Museum next door. The Whaling Museum's extensive exhibits include a 43-foot finback whale that washed onto the north shore in 1967 and an eighteen-foot whale jaw with teeth. Rooms hold a world-renowned collection of scrimshaw, whaling equipment and objects brought home by seamen from the South Seas. Whalecraft shops – a sail loft, cooperage, shipsmith and such – are among the attractions.

(508) 228-1894. www.nha.com. Open daily 10 to 5, Memorial Day through October; weekends 11 to 3 in fall and spring. Adults $15, children $8.

Maria Mitchell Association, 4 Vestal St., Nantucket.

This complex consists of the birthplace of America's first woman astronomer, a small aquarium, a museum of natural history, an observatory and a science library. The woman who discovered the Mitchell comet was raised on Nantucket and served at age 18 as the first librarian of the Nantucket Atheneum, the island's library and cultural center. Her home remains as it was in 1818 and features the only public roofwalk on Nantucket. Next door is a memorial observatory. The museum of natural history is housed in the Hinchman House, 7 Milk St. It contains many living island reptiles as well as preserved birds and fauna. Marine life indigenous to Nantucket's salt marshes and harbors is displayed in the quaint aquarium on the harbor at 29 Washington St.

(508) 228-9198. www.mmo.org. Open Tuesday-Saturday in summer, 10 to 4. Combination tickets: adults $10, children $7.

Nantucket Life Saving Museum, 158 Polpis Road, Nantucket.

This fascinating place is said to be the only one of its kind in the world. The new museum building is a re-creation of the original Surfside Station, built by the U.S. Life Saving Service in 1874. The drama of rescue at sea is presented through photos, original boats and life saving equipment, quarterboards of vessels wrecked around Nantucket and more. Featured are items recovered from the Italian liner Andrea Doria, which sank more than 40 years ago off Nantucket's southeast coast. Also exhibited is the top of the original Great Point Light and the original 1856 Fresnel lens from the Brant Point Lighthouse.

(508) 228-1885. Open daily 9:30 to 4, mid-June to Columbus Day. Adults $5, children $2.

Nantucket Lightship Baskets. The lightships that protected boats from the treacherous shoal waters off the south and east end of the island in the mid-18th century spawned a cottage industry indigenous to Nantucket. The crews of the South Shoal Lightship turned to basket-weaving to while away their hours on duty. Their duty ended, the seamen continued to make baskets ashore – first primitive and heavy-duty types for berry gathering or carrying laundry or groceries, later more beautiful handbags appealing to visitors. The latter were inspired by the Sayle family, who continue the tradition at their shop at 112 Washington St. Today, Nantucket's famed baskets come in all shapes and sizes (including 14-karat gold miniatures) and seem to be ubiquitous in the shops and on tanned arms. The handbags have ivory carvings on top and carry hefty price tags. Special exhibits are staged each year in the **Nantucket Lightship Basket Museum** at 49 Union St., (508) 227-1177. It's open Tuesday-Saturday 10 to 4; adults, $4.

SHOPPING. Nantucket is a shopper's paradise and, were it not for the cobblestoned streets and salt air, you could as easily picture yourself in Newburyport or New Canaan, not on a "faraway" island. In a town where **The Hub** newsstand and sundry store on Main Street is a local institution, residents bemoaned the arrival of Benetton, the first mainland chain store other than the old Country Store of Concord and Crabtree & Evelyn, both of which passed muster.

Specialty stores with names like **Nobby Clothes, Beautiful People, Nantucket Panache** and **The Cashmere Shop** compete with the more traditional like **Murray's Toggery Shop** and **Mitchell's Book Corner,** all across the several square blocks of "downtown" Nantucket. We like the **Lion's Paw,** an exceptional gift shop full of cheerful pottery; check out the animal's tea party. Other standouts are **Zero Main** for suave women's clothing, **Rosa Rugosa** for painted furniture and household decorative items, and **Nantucket Looms** with beautiful, whimsical woven items and a sweater in the window for "only $1,000." **Majolica** offers colorful hand-painted Italian ceramics. **The Spectrum** is good for arts and crafts. **The Complete Kitchen** is one of the better kitchenware stores we've seen. **Claire Murray** has fabulous hand-hooked rugs, and **Lilly Pulitzer** offers her trademark apparel. **L'Ile de France** displays china, pottery, collectibles and clothing.

Water Attractions

Nantucket Harbor Cruises, Straight Wharf, (508) 228-1444. If you've already arrived by ferry, these may seem redundant, but at least you find out what you were looking at. Lobstering cruises leave at 9:30 daily June to September; shoreline sightseeing cruises are offered three times in the afternoon and a sunset cruise is offered in the evening. Finally, at the end of the day, leaving at 8:45 in July and August is a Harbor Lights cruise of 45 minutes. Costs range from $12.50 to $25 for the 1¼-hour sunset cruise.

SWIMMING. The north shore beaches facing Nantucket Sound tend to be calmer and more tranquil than those facing the open ocean. On the south shore, the waters from the Gulf Stream are warmer (up to 75 degrees in summer), the ocean bottom slopes more gently and the beaches are wider. Just north of town is **Jetties Beach,** the best all-around for calm waters and named for the jetties that jut out into the ocean from its sandy shore. Bathhouses, lifeguards and a snack bar are available. **Children's Beach,** closer to the center off Harbor View Way, reflects its name and has a playground. More secluded and harder to reach on the north shore is **Dionis**, a harbor beach sheltered by dunes and favored by snorkelers and children. On the south shore, our favorite all-around is **Surfside,** four miles south of town. It has lifeguards, a food concession, bike racks, changing areas and an impressive surf – the beach is most expansive, of course, at low tide. Less crowded and more private is **Siasconset Beach,** a pleasant strand along the east shore. Heavy surf is found at **Nobadeer, Miacomet** and **Cisco** beaches on the south shore. The beaches at **Great**

Point, Coskata and **Coatue** are popular with those who can get to them, either by boat or jeep. At the island's west end is **Madaket,** a great place for sunset-watching and isolated beaching; here the water deepens rapidly.

Wildlife Refuges. Twenty-one miles of ocean, harbor and sound shoreline are protected by the Coatue, Coskata-Coatue and Great Point-Nantucket national wildlife refuges. Mainly barrier beaches, marshes and dunes, they harbor a variety of birds, shellfish and even jackrabbits. Coatue is part of the Nantucket Conservation Foundation, which has protected more than 6,100 acres of the island. Great Point is a remote and desolate stretch, reached by jeep or foot. On the way out, you'll see clamming and oyster ponds, eagle and tern nesting grounds, and bayberry forests as you cross the dunes to the ruins of America's oldest working lighthouse, now being restored.

Where to Stay

Four by the Shore

The Wauwinet, 120 Wauwinet Road, Box 2580, Nantucket 02554.

This restored "country inn by the sea" is among the most posh yet serene getaway retreats in New England. Boston developer Stephen Karp and his wife Jill, longtime Nantucket summer homeowners, transformed a weathered old hotel into a Relais & Chateaux member property. The secluded location next to the Great Point Wildlife Sanctuary is unsurpassed – a parkland/residential area on a spit of land with the Atlantic surf beyond the dunes and an endless beach across the road in front, the waters at the head of Nantucket Harbor lapping at the lawns in back. Our room, one of 25 in the inn, was snug but nicely located on a third-floor corner facing the harbor, the better to watch spectacular sunsets at night. It had a queensize bed with lace-trimmed pillows, wicker and upholstered armchairs, and a painted armoire topped with a wooden swan and two hat boxes (one of the inn's decorating signatures). Deluxe rooms with kingsize or two queen beds include bigger sitting areas, but many did not seem to be as well located as ours. Every room holds a TV/VCR, tapes for which may be ordered from a library of 500, along with a bowl of gourmet popcorn. Courtyard cottages across the road contain five more guest accommodations. One is a four-bedroom cottage with kitchenette and fireplace, for those who want the entire family to share their getaway. The inn's main floor harbors a lovely living room and library done in floral chintz, a back veranda full of wicker that you sink into, an award-winning restaurant and a small, classy lounge. Outside, chairs are lined up on the back lawn beside the harbor, a croquet game is set up, drinks and snacks are available at a small beachside grill, and two tennis courts are tucked away in the woods. A full breakfast is included in the rate.

Toppers, the inn's restaurant, is named for the owners' dog, whose portrait is in one of the dining rooms. It's a favorite of the Nantucket gentry, who book its tables far in advance. Dining is leisurely in two elegantly appointed, side-by-side rooms with large windows. Upholstered chairs in blue and white are comfortable, tables are well spaced (or screened from their neighbors), and masses of flowers are all around. Among appetizers, we liked the grilled quail on a toasted brioche and the lobster and crab cakes with smoked corn, jalapeño olives and a divine mustard sauce. Chef Christopher Freeman's main courses include a signature Nantucket lobster stew, caramelized sea scallops with seared foie gras vinaigrette, roast duck with seared black plums and rhubarb chard, and a superior roast rack of lamb with potato-fennel brandade. The wine list, featuring more than 800 vintages and 18,000 bottles, is a consistent winner of the Wine Spectator Grand Award. After a meal like this, the homemade ice creams and sorbets appeal to us more than the richer pastries that catch many an eye. Lunch on the outdoor terrace is also a treat. An extra perk for people staying in town is boat service aboard the **Wauwinet Lady,** which shuttles diners out to Topper's for lunch or dinner.

(508) 228-0145 or (800) 426-8718. Fax (508) 325-0657. www.wauwinet.com. Thirty-three rooms and two cottage suites with private baths. Mid-June to mid-September: doubles $500 to $1,020, cottage suites $1,025 to $2,300. Off-season: doubles $200 to $850, cottages, $580 to $1,500. Four-night minimum in summer. Closed late October to early May.

Entrées, $32 to $42. Lunch, Monday-Saturday noon to 2. Dinner nightly, 6 to 9:30; jackets requested. Sunday brunch, noon to 2.

The White Elephant, 50 Easton St., Nantucket 02554.

For sheer luxury beside the harbor and close to the in-town action, The White Elephant is tough to beat – especially since its upgrade by the owners of the Wauwinet. Its waterfront location offers lush lawns, fancy walkways lined with hedges, and plantings that focus on a white elephant statue in the middle. There are two nine-hole putting greens and a pleasant pool to the side of the outdoor terrace and restaurant. The newest lodgings in the renovated hotel have kingsize beds, and many have working fireplaces. Rooms vary widely in terms of size and view. We like the corner rooms with windows onto Children's Beach, although others might find them too public and seek the privacy of the interior. Seclusion is an asset in the eleven rose-covered garden cottages scattered about the property. They offer one to three bedrooms and the living rooms of some have bay windows overlooking the water. Some have fireplaces and a few have kitchenettes. The Breakers annex, located on the White Elephant's grounds, is like a small inn. It offers 25 spacious guest rooms, many with harbor views and all with private patios or balconies. Breakfast may be enjoyed there or in the hotel's new harborside lounge. The main hotel includes a new fitness center and offers spa treatments. Breakfast is included in the rates.

The hotel's **Brant Point Grill** is billed as Nantucket's premier steak and seafood house, featuring native lobster, prime aged beef and gourmet chops. The casually elegant dining room occupies several levels, some with water views through a gently curved wall of large windows. You might start with a chilled shellfish sampler, kobe beef tartare or lime-marinated tuna atop a green wakame salad. Expect main courses like tuna steak rubbed with fennel and coriander, grilled swordfish with mushrooms and sherry beurre blanc, crisp Long Island duck with vanilla-rum glaze, veal loin chop or chargrilled filet mignon enhanced with a dried cranberry sauce. Desserts vary from a chocolate turtle cake on caramel-pecan sauce to cranberry bread pudding with citrus curd. The changing trio of sorbets is served in an edible cookie cup. A large harborfront terrace beside the pool makes the restaurant a favorite for lunch. A light menu is available day and night, and a raw bar is featured in late afternoon on the terrace.

Hotel: (508) 228-2500 or (800) 475-2637. Fax (508) 325-1195. www.whiteelephanthotel.com. Twenty-two rooms, 31 suites and eleven cottages with private baths. Late June to September: doubles $450 to $600, suites $515 to $900, cottages, $470 to $1,400. Off-season: doubles $270 to $600, cottages $400 to $1,200. Closed late October to early May.

Grill: (508) 325-1320. www.brantpointgrill.com. Entrées, $28 to $45. Lunch daily, noon to 2:30. Dinner nightly, from 6. Closed late October to early May.

Cliffside Beach Club, Jefferson Avenue, Box 449, Nantucket 02554.

You want to stay near the beach at the edge of town? You can be right beside it at the venerable Cliffside Beach Club, located in an exclusive residential section on the north shore. Here on a glorious 400-foot strand, members used to wait years to reserve one of the prime sections of the west beach, and the same umbrellas and chairs are still in the same spots, according to general manager/owner Robert F. Currie, whose grandfather founded the club. Some of the old-fashioned changing rooms have been transformed into fourteen airy, contemporary guest quarters with cathedral ceilings and modern baths. All the queensize beds, tables, vanities, doors and even the pegs for the beach towels were built by Nantucket craftsmen. The woodwork from the old bathhouses is handsomely accented by dark green colors and prints by local artists. Nine beachfront studio apartments, each with a private deck and the phones and TVs characteristic of all the rooms, and several suites are of newer vintage. Continental breakfast is served in the club's spectacular fireplaced lobby, full of smart wicker furniture and planters, and topped by quilts suspended from the beamed cathedral ceiling.

For lunch or dinner, there's no better beachfront location than **The Galley at Cliffside Beach,** a summery restaurant with a canopied, flower-lined deck right beside the ocean. Rimmed with red geraniums and hanging plants, the blue wicker chairs and white tablecloths make an enticing setting against a background of azure water and fine sand. We enjoyed a couple of the best bloody marys ever before a lunch of salade niçoise and chicken salad Hawaiian. A jazz pianist plays at night, when the place conveys a clubby air. The seafood-oriented dinner menu ranges from pan-roasted halibut with a caviar beurre blanc, served over tiny French green lentils, to roasted lobster and local shellfish with riesling-braised leeks, fire-roasted baby corn and "young" potatoes. Start with the signature New England clam chowder with smoked bacon, a lobster spring roll or shrimp tempura with Asian slaw. Finish with homemade cognac ice cream, blood orange meringue tart or chocolate-soufflé cake.

Club: (508) 228-0618. Fax (508) 325-4735. www.cliffsidebeach.com. Thirty-one rooms and suites with private baths. Mid-June to Labor Day: doubles $395 to $625, suites $755 to $1,535. Off-season: doubles $255 to $445, suites $450 to $1,115. Closed Columbus Day to Memorial Day.

Galley: (508) 228-9641. Entrées, $29 to $45. Lunch daily in summer, 11:30 to 2. Dinner nightly, 6 to 10, early June to mid-September.

The Summer House, 17 Ocean Ave., Siasconset 02564.

Romantic, rose-covered cottages and an atmospheric restaurant present an idyllic oceanfront scene worthy of Bermuda on the south side of 'Sconset, as the islanders call it. Under a canopy of trees and ivy, the cottages are sweetly decorated with colorful wallpapers, eyelet-embroidered pillows, lace curtains, English antiques and such. Interesting roof lines, painted floors and chests, stained glass, leaded windows, stenciling, and little nooks and crannies add to the charm. Contemporary as can be are the newly remodeled bathrooms, all with marble jacuzzis. The Jimmy Cagney cottage, where the actor frequently was ensconced, offers two bedrooms, one with a kingsize bed with real ivy growing over it and another smaller room with a queen bed. Cottages have one or two bedrooms, two have kitchens, one has a sitting room and another a working fireplace (that's Penrose, which we found particularly attractive with barnwood walls, arched pickled wood ceilings and a kingsize bed). Our quarters had no good place to sit except on the front patio, where we felt rather on display as customers paraded up the path to the low-slung, Southern-style main house for dinner. The property includes a heated pool halfway down the bluff across the road, beside the dunes leading to the open Atlantic, where the beach extends for miles in either direction. Guests enjoy tennis privileges at the Sconset Casino, a private club. Continental breakfast is served to overnight guests on the inn's front veranda.

Where could be a more romantic setting for dinner than at a candlelit table on that veranda yielding a view of the moon rising over the ocean at the foot of the bluff across the road? Or at a table in the summery interior dining room, where a pianist entertains amidst an arty mix of white chairs and painted floors, good 'Sconset oils and watercolors on the whitewashed walls, and fresh flowers and plants everywhere. The setting remained etched in memory longer than our dinner, which was more ordinary than the tab would have suggested (the food is reported to have improved lately). Typical appetizers might be a smoked salmon, lobster and scallop sausage with black caviar, and a spring roll of goat cheese, citrus, mint and snap peas with fennel and watercress. Assertive, complex flavors continue in such entrées as tuna nori and Szechuan seared tuna with tempura lobster tail, tangerine soy emulsion and grapefruit-braised greens; amandine roast trout and littlenecks with asparagus and truffle risotto, and grilled beef tenderloin with a jonah crab cake, marrow-crusted potato roesti and elephant garlic crème fraîche. A brandy tart with dollops of whipped cream, blueberries and slices of kiwi was a good choice for dessert. Our meal was enlivened by piano music that makes you want to linger over one of the island's largest selections of cognacs, ports and single malts. Lunch is available at the **Beach Café** on a landscaped terrace beside the pool, sequestered halfway down the bluff in the dunes above the beach.

(508) 257-4577. Fax (508) 257-4590. www.thesummerhouse.com. Seven cottage rooms and suites and three two-bedroom cottages with private baths. Cottages, $575 to $675, June to mid-September; $225 to $425 rest of season. Closed January to mid-April.

Restaurant: (508) 257-9976. www.the-summer-house.com. Entrées, $32 to $48. Lunch daily in summer, 11 to 3. Dinner nightly, 6 to 10:30. Closed Monday and Tuesday in off-season and mid-October to mid-May.

Inns and B&Bs

Union Street Inn, 7 Union St., Nantucket 02554.

This restored 1770 house, now a luxury B&B, is close to downtown, harbor and ferry docks. Its twelve spacious guest quarters come with antique furnishings, air conditioning and TV. Six have working fireplaces with their original mantelpieces. Many have canopy or four-poster queen beds, and scatter rugs dot the original wide-plank pine floors. Designer wallpapers, Frette linens and fluffy duvets convey elegance. A second-floor suite offers a sitting room with a loveseat and telephone and a bedroom with queen canopy bed, fireplace, VCR, refrigerator and wet bar. The popular main-floor Captain's Room comes with a kingsize poster bed and a fireplace. Because of its zoning, the Union Street can offer more than Nantucket's highly regulated continental breakfasts. Owners Ken and Debbie Withrow serve things like blueberry pancakes and eggs benedict. The repast is taken in a large dining room or at three handsome garden tables on the side patio beneath an ivy-covered hillside.

(508) 228-9222 or (800) 225-5116. Fax (508) 325-0848. www.union-street-inn.com. Eleven rooms and one suite with private baths. Mid-June through mid-September: doubles $275 to $410, suite $445. Spring and fall: doubles $140 to $210, suite $235. Closed December-March.

The Pineapple Inn, 10 Hussey St., Nantucket 02554.

This welcoming and stylish B&B is in an 1838 Greek Revival whaling captain's house on a side street. Taking the name from the Colonial symbol of hospitality, Caroline and Bob Taylor offer twelve air-conditioned guest rooms with white marble baths. Each has a handmade Eldred Wheeler king or queen canopy bed topped with a goose down comforter. Oriental carpets, reproduction furniture, 19th-century antiques and artworks, TVs and telephones with data ports are standard. Guests gather in front of a fireplace in the side parlor or outside beside a fountain on a brick garden courtyard. The Taylors, who were known for their breakfasts when they owned the Quaker House Inn and Restaurant here, had to scale down breakfasts to continental, but serve the best granola dishes and pastries in town. Their nectarine and blueberry clafouti is a favorite, accompanied by cappuccino or latte.

(508) 228-9992. Fax (508) 325-6051. www.pineappleinn.com. Twelve rooms with private baths. Mid-June to late September: doubles, $215 to $375. Off-season: doubles, $110 to $175. Closed late October to late April.

The Sherburne Inn, 10 Gay St., Nantucket 02554.

Contemporary amenities enhance this lodging residence fashioned from the old Atlantic Silk Factory headquarters dating to 1835. After renovating and redecorating, Dale Hamilton III and Susan Gasparich offer eight guest rooms with king or queen beds. Four are on the main floor and four on the second; a beautiful winding staircase connects the two. Interestingly, there's a parlor with working fireplace and television on each floor. The bedrooms, bright and cheery, are decorated to the Federal period. They contain canopy and poster beds, oriental rugs and fine artworks as well as TV/DVDs and high-speed internet access. We liked No. 8 upstairs in the rear with a king bed, clawfoot tub with shower and a private balcony overlooking the side and rear yards. Continental breakfast is taken in the main-floor parlor, on a deck on one side of the house or in the yard surrounded by gardens and a privet hedge.

(508) 228-4425 or (888) 557-4425. Fax (508) 228-8114. www.sherburneinn.com. Eight rooms with private baths. Doubles, $195 to $325 Memorial Day to mid-October, $115 to $295 rest of year.

Ships Inn, 13 Fair St., Nantucket 02554.

Nicely restored by chef-owner Mark Gottwald and his wife Ellie, this 1831 whaling captain's home claims some of Nantucket's most comfortable accommodations as well as a small restaurant of distinction (see Where to Eat). The ten guest rooms contain many of the original furnishings and most have queen beds, although bed configurations vary. They have been refurbished with new wallpapers and tiled baths and come with interesting window treatments, Neutrogena toiletries and mini-refrigerators in cabinets beneath the TV sets. Most have reading chairs and half have desks. All but two tiny single rooms are more spacious than most Nantucket bedrooms. Guests enjoy mid-afternoon tea with coffeecake and cookies in the large living room. A continental-plus breakfast is set out in the morning.

(508) 228-0040. www.nantucket.net/lodging.shipsinn. Ten rooms with private baths. Doubles, $210 to $235. Three-night minimum in season. Closed late October to Memorial Day.

Cliff Lodge, 9 Cliff Road, Nantucket 02554.

This hillside B&B's lofty rooftop deck is a great vantage point from which to enjoy a broad panorama of Nantucket Sound as well as the brilliant colors of sunrise and sunset. The 1771 sea captain's house in a residential neighborhood overlooking town and harbor offers twelve guest rooms, designed for comfort and decorated with a summery, beach look. Bedrooms are notable for spatter-painted floors, Laura Ashley wallpapers, frilly bedding, fresh flowers and antiques. Many have kingsize beds and fireplaces, and all have telephones and TVs nicely built into the walls or concealed in armoires. A main-floor apartment offers a kingsize bedroom, a queen sofabed in the living room, kitchen and private porch. Few B&Bs have so many neat places to sit and relax, inside or out. There are five sitting rooms on three floors, plus the rooftop deck, reading porches and a couple of brick patios beside lovely gardens. Innkeeper Sally Beck serves a buffet breakfast in one of the sitting rooms, or guests can adjourn to the side patio, where she matches the tablecloths with the flowers that are in bloom. Fresh fruit, cereal, muffins and Portuguese toasting bread are typical fare.

(508) 228-9480. Fax (508) 228-0049. www.clifflodgenantucket.com. Eleven rooms and one apartment with private baths. Doubles, $195 to $295, off-season $140 to $210. Apartment for four, $450.

Nantucket Whaler Guest House, 8 North Water St., Nantucket 02554.

Some of the town's more urbane accommodations are offered in this growing complex launched by two women from Manhattan's Upper East Side. Calliope Ligeles and Randi Ott started by renovating a former whaling captain's home. The 1850 Greek Revival structure now has four studio rooms, three one-bedroom suites and three two-bedroom suites – all considered spacious by Nantucket standards. Every suite has its own private entrance, and nearly all face a back yard landscaped with rhododendrons, antique roses and lilies. Suite 2 is the most private, with its own little white porch facing a quiet cobblestone street. Suite 4, the most romantic, has lovely views of the garden. Studio 7 occupies an entire corner of the second floor and opens onto an outdoor deck. Bedrooms are lavished with flowers, well-chosen antiques, fine linens and plush robes. The early American and English country furnishings are augmented by modern conveniences like TV/VCRs, CD players, wet bars, refrigerators, microwaves and toaster ovens. The latest addition is a second house at 4 Step Lane with a guest room and a penthouse suite with a harbor view. No breakfast is included (this is a guest house, not an inn or B&B), but you can make your own or the owners will supply the makings in a "lite bite basket" ordered beforehand.

(508) 228-6597 or (800) 462-6882. Fax (508) 228-6291. www.nantucketwhaler.com. Five rooms and seven suites with private baths. Mid-June through September: doubles $325 to $425, suites $400 to $650. Off-season: doubles $275 to $400, suites $375 to $625.

Where to Eat

21 Federal, 21 Federal St., Nantucket.

One of Nantucket's larger and higher-profile restaurants, 21 Federal is on two floors of a sand-colored house with white trim, designated by a brass plaque and elegantly decorated in the Williamsburg style. There are six dining rooms of museum-quality, Federal period decor, some with their white-linened tables rather close together. This is the icon where chef Robert Kinkead got his start before opening his widely acclaimed restaurant in Washington, D.C. Lunch in the summer is on the rear courtyard, where white-linened tables create an elegant setting. Our latest produced a smashing pasta – spaghettini with two sauces, one thyme-saffron and one smoked tomato, topped with crabmeat-stuffed shrimp – and a grilled shrimp salad with Greek olives, feta cheese, pine nuts and spinach. Chef Russell Jaehnig changes the short dinner menu weekly. Typical main courses are grilled swordfish with mole and avocado salsa, sautéed halibut with lobster risotto and foie gras butter and, from the grill, aged sirloin steak or veal loin chop with a creamy gratin of potatoes and leeks. For starters, how about tuna, crab and avocado napoleon with cilantro vinaigrette or a slow-roasted portobello mushroom with parmesan pudding? Finish with warm chocolate lava cake with kahlua caramel or one of the great homemade ice creams and sorbets. This is Nantucket dining at its best, not as pretentious or as pricey as some and more exciting than some of the others.

(508) 228-2121. www.21federal.net. Entrées, $23 to $38. Lunch, Monday-Saturday in summer, 11:30 to 2:30. Dinner, Monday-Saturday 6 to 9:30. Closed January to mid-May.

Wine and Roses

The Chanticleer, 9 New St., Siasconset.

This elegant French restaurant on two floors of a large 'Sconset cottage is renowned across the world. À la carte lunch (entrées $25 to $28) in the outdoor garden, at tables beneath trellised canopies of roses and beside impeccably trimmed hedges, is a 'Sconset tradition. So is an after-dinner drink accompanied by piano music in the beamed and nautical **Grille Room,** formerly the Chanty Bar. Amidst heavy silver and pretty floral china, dinner is served in the lovely fireplaced dining room opening onto a greenhouse, in the Grille or upstairs in a pristine peach and white room. Although you can order à la carte, prix-fixe dinners are $75 "and worth every cent," townspeople informed us. Regulars put themselves in the hands of a knowledgeable staff to steer them to the right choices on an ambitious and complex menu. For appetizers, we liked the lobster and sole sausage poached with a puree of sweet red peppers and the oysters served in a warm mussel broth topped with American sturgeon caviar. From a choice of six entrées (all of which we would happily have tried), the Nantucket-raised pheasant, stuffed with mushrooms and ricotta, and the roasted tenderloin of lamb served with a venison sauce were superb. The possibilities are limited only by chef Jean-Charles Berruet 's imagination and the sensibilities of his kitchen staff of eleven. The award-winning wine cellar contains 1,200 selections, with good values at the high end.

(508) 257-6231. www.thechanticleerinn.com. Entrées, $42 to $45. Prix-fixe, $75. Lunch in summer, Tuesday-Sunday noon to 2. Dinner, Tuesday-Sunday 6:30 to 9:30. Closed Monday, also Tuesday and Wednesday in off-season. Reservations and jackets required except in the Grille. Closed mid-October to May.

The Boarding House and The Pearl, 12 Federal St., Nantucket.

The Boarding House provided our first great meal on Nantucket during its inaugural summer of 1973. It since has moved around the corner to considerably larger quarters, and several owners and chefs have come and gone. Taken over by Seth and Angela Raynor (he a former sous chef at 21 Federal and both veterans of the famed Chanticleer in Siasconset), it's better than ever. A cathedral-ceilinged Victorian lounge with small faux-marble tables on a flagstone floor opens into a sunken dining room. The latter is romantic in cream and pink, with a curved banquette at the far end in front of a mural of Vernazzia. Villeroy & Boch china of the Florida pattern graces the nicely spaced tables, which allow for one of Nantucket's more pleasant dining situations. We were well pleased with our latest dinner here: mellow sautéed crab cakes with scallion crème fraîche and grilled quail with crisp fried onion rings and baby mixed greens, for starters. Main courses were pan-roasted salmon with Thai curried cream and crisp rice noodles and a spicy Asian seafood stew with lobster, shrimp and scallops. Coffee ice cream with chocolate sauce and a dense chocolate-kahlua terrine were worthy endings. The outdoor terrace appeals for cocktails and a bistro lunch or supper. It's also a felicitous setting for an after-dinner liqueur while watching the late-night strollers pass by.

Upstairs is **The Pearl,** a showy, aquatic-look, designer restaurant of newer vintage, specializing in high-style coastal cuisine. It's ever so cool in white and blue, with an aquarium at the entrance and a scrim curtain giving the illusion of floating at sea. Typical of starters here is an island-style seafood platter bearing Nantucket oysters, sashimi of striped bass, a martini of yellowfin tuna and steamed ginger shrimp dumplings. For a main course, Seth might dish up wok-seared lobster with Thai curry, coconut and cilantro or grilled angus tenderloin with seared foie gras and caramelized cippolini onions. Dessert could be lemon grass-infused crème brûlée. The chef's Zen-like courtyard garden tasting table provides gourmands with a multi-course culinary adventure and a bird's-eye view into the state-of-the-art kitchen.

Boarding House, (508) 228-9622. www.boardinghouse-pearl.com. Entrées, $26 to $38. Lunch in summer, Wednesday-Sunday noon to 2; dinner nightly, 6 to 10, fewer nights in winter.

The Pearl, (508) 228-9701. Entrées, $36 to $48. Dinner nightly, 6 to 9:30, late-night menu to midnight. Closed January-March.

Oran Mor, 2 South Beach St., Nantucket.

Former Wauwinet executive chef Peter Wallace took over the old Second Story restaurant space with windows toward the harbor and renamed it for a Gaelic phrase meaning "Great Song." Three small, off-white dining rooms with seafoam green trim are dressed with paintings by local artists. Peter considers it a soothing backdrop for international cuisine that is at the cutting edge. For starters, we liked his champagne risotto with sweetbreads and wild mushrooms, and his Asian fried quail with sticky rice. Expect other choices like tuna tartare with essence of celery and ossetra caviar, a Thai littleneck clam hot pot with somen noodles and a salad of soft-shell crab over field greens. Main courses vary from grilled squab paella with shrimp and spicy chorizo sausage to organic ribeye steak diane. We enjoyed the seared tuna with shallot jus and spinach, and grilled swordfish with orange and black sesame seed butter. Wife Kathleen's desserts include fresh fruit croustade in a tulipe, quenelles of chocolate mousse topped with pralines, and molten chocolate cake with a trio of ice creams.

(508) 228-8655. Entrées, $25 to $34. Dinner nightly in season, 6 to 10. Closed Sunday-Wednesday in winter.

Straight Wharf Restaurant, Straight Wharf, Nantucket.

Seafood is showcased in this summery restaurant that is the height of chic on the waterfront. The interior is a pristine palette of shiny floors and soaring, shingled walls topped by billowing banners and hung with striking paintings by an island artist. Beyond is a canopied, rib-lit deck overhanging the harbor. The "in" place is the noisy side bar and lounge, with crowds usually spilling outside onto a terrace in front. The same kitchen serves both, with a sophisticated seafood menu in the dining room and deck and more rustic, casual grill fare in the bar. Among superlative starters are the signature smoked bluefish pâté with focaccia melba toasts, a rich lobster bisque heavily laced with sherry and seared beef carpaccio with shards of parmigiano-reggiano, white truffle oil and mesclun. A sauté of halibut with lobster and morels and grilled rare tuna with white beans, escarole and roasted garlic were excellent main courses. Choices range from butter-poached Nantucket lobster with green tomato chutney to rosemary-grilled rack of lamb with olive tapenade and tabouleh. The dessert specialty is warm chocolate tart with orange cardamom gelato, but we usually go for the trio of refreshing fruit sorbets.

(508) 228-4499. Entrées, $31 to $39. Dinner by reservation, Tuesday-Sunday 6 to 10:30. Open Memorial Day to late September. Grill, $16 to $22, no reservations.

Company of the Cauldron, 7 India St., Nantucket.

In a dark red Colonial house with ivy-covered windows, this tiny restaurant is full of charm and romance. An antique wrought-iron baker's rack is laden with flowers at the entry, and copper pots, cauldrons and ship's models hang from the stucco walls. A mix of orange and purple floral cloths covers the old wood tables, which are lit only by candles. It's all very dark and intimate for a dining experience likened to being a guest at a dinner party with a private chef. Owner Allen Kovalencik, a Hungarian from New Jersey who bought the place after serving as its chef since 1987, and his wife Andrea post the night's prix-fixe, no-choice menu a week in advance. You reserve (early) for the evening's meal you want and take what's served, which is produced and served with great finesse. A harpist plays as a typical dinner evolves, bringing perhaps a trio of lobster, crab and smoked salmon cakes with individual sauces, an arugula and watercress salad, beef wellington and bourbon pecan pie with vanilla ice cream. The next night you might be served a classic pappardelle Bolognese, a mixed green salad, Atlantic sole and lobster in parchment with champagne beurre blanc, and chocolate soufflé cake with raspberry sauce. Every once in a while you might get the signature vinewood-roasted salmon, wood-grilled châteaubriand over roasted wild mushrooms or the ginger-crusted rack of lamb with sweet plum sauce.

(508) 228-4016. www.companyofthecauldron.com. Prix-fixe, $50. Dinner nightly, seatings at 7 (also at 9 on busy nights). Closed Columbus Day to mid-April.

Ships Inn, 13 Fair St., Nantucket.

The charming dining room on the lower level of an 1831 ship captain's home is the showcase for the California-French cuisine of chef-owner Mark Gottwald, who trained at Le Cirque in New York and at Spago in Los Angeles. The wainscoted dining room is atmospheric with exposed beams, a white fireplace in the center of the room and candles flickering in the many-paned windows. White-linened tables, some in intimate alcoves, are dressed with candles and fresh flowers. There also are tables for eating in the adjacent Dory Bar. Dinner might start with a cold terrine of foie gras or a smoked sirloin salad with white truffle vinaigrette. Among entrées, you might find grilled yellowtail flounder with lemon-thyme beurre blanc, grilled shrimp with Asian greens and lime-soy broth, braised local cod with kaffir lime and coconut-curry cream, roast duck with plum wine jus and steak au poivre. Or consider a pasta, perhaps rigatoni with duck confit and port-wine glace. Finish with raspberry sorbet or chocolate-soufflé cake. The chef and his wife Ellie winter with their children in Vero Beach, Fla., where they operate Ellie's, a American restaurant. They and many of their staff go back and forth between Vero Beach and Nantucket.

(508) 228-0040 or (888) 872-4052. Entrées, $22 to $34. Dinner nightly except Tuesday, 5:30 to 9:30. Closed November-April.

American Seasons, 80 Centre St., Nantucket.

Off the beaten path is this popular restaurant serving eclectic American food. Whimsical decor characterizes the simple square dining room, in which a local artist hand-painted the table tops to resemble game boards and added a stunning wall mural of a vine-covered Willamette Valley hillside in Oregon. An outdoor patio is pleasant in summer. Chef-owner Michael LaScola categorizes the menu by regions – Pacific Coast, Wild West, New England and Down South – each with two or three appetizers and entrées. You're supposed to mix and match, pairing, say, a Florida rock shrimp gumbo with andouille sausage, okra and biscuits with a lobster and corn enchilada in a blue cornmeal crêpe from the West. Those plus a lentil salad with goat cheese, a Pacific foie gras crème brûlée with quince-ginger jam and a "New England" main course of grilled leg of lamb in a candied garlic sauce contributed to a memorable meal. Dessert was fabulous raspberry-mango shortcake with raspberry coulis.

(508) 228-7111. www.americanseasons.com. Entrées, $26 to $34. Dinner nightly in summer, 6 to 10, fewer nights in off-season. Closed January to April.

The Club Car, 1 Main St., Nantucket.

The red train car at the side of this luxurious establishment with the profuse flower boxes is a lounge that's open from 11 o'clock daily and enlivened by a piano bar nightly. Beyond is an expansive dining room of white-over-red-linened tables topped by enormous wine globes, with upholstered cane-back chairs, an array of large artworks and a colorful shelf of copper pans. Here is where chef-owner Michael Shannon, a culinary icon locally, serves up some of the island's priciest food to a clubby clientele. The continental menu varies only modestly from year to year. Appetizers start at $14 for broiled sesame eel and go to $100 for beluga caviar on warm toast points with Stolichnaya vodka. Grilled quail with truffle polenta, cold Nantucket lobster with citrus and avocado and "Octopus in the Style of Bangkok" are among the possibilities. Typical main courses are calamari steak provençal, Norwegian salmon with truffle vinaigrette, veal sweetbreads grenobloise, roasted poussin stuffed with goose liver pâté and roast rack of lamb glazed with honey mustard and served with minted madeira sauce. Desserts include chocolate-mousse cake with crème anglaise and fresh berries in devonshire cream.

(508) 228-1101. Entrées, $30 to $45. www.theclubcar.com. Dinner nightly, 6 to 10. Closed Monday-Wednesday in off-season and Christmas Stroll to Memorial Day.

Fifty-Six Union, 56 Union St., Nantucket.

Light, healthful global fare is served up by chef-owner Peter Jannelle and his wife Wendy in this casually elegant eatery located in a former diner called the Elegant Dump on the outskirts of downtown. Tourists seldom find the place, which seats about 100 in a pair of dining rooms set with nicely spaced white-clothed tables flanked by black windsor chairs. Those in the know go for appetizers like Thai curried mussels over scallion and ginger rice or sweetbread strudel with walnuts, chèvre and prosciutto in a brandy-walnut demi-glace. Everyone raves about the Javanese spicy fried rice, a year-round menu fixture in which shrimp and chicken are tossed with sambal, ginger and Asian vegetables. Other main dishes range from pan-seared ahi tuna rubbed in Japanese seven-spice powder and served with sesame-garlic vinaigrette to a mixed grill combining lamb, smoked lemon-chicken sausage and pork tenderloin with creamy mascarpone polenta. For dessert, the chocolate mousse tower bears chocolate rum mousse, hazelnut praline ganache and a chocolate shortbread crust.

(508) 228-6135. Entrées, $24 to $33. Dinner nightly in summer, 6 to 10, Wednesday-Sunday 6 to 9 in off-season. Sunday brunch, 10 to 1.

Black-Eyed Susan's, 10 India St., Nantucket.

This small storefront – for years merely a breakfast diner – is lovingly tended by Susan Handy and Jeff Worster, both with long backgrounds in local restaurants. They still serve breakfast, featuring treats like sourdough french toast with orange Jack Daniels butter and pecans and a spicy Thai curry scramble with broccoli and new potatoes. Most dishes come with a choice of hash browns or black-eyed peas. Jeff, a self-taught chef, obtained many of his cross-cultural culinary ideas while cooking in Beverly Hills. From his open kitchen behind the dining counter come such dinner dishes as wild-mushroom ravioli on carrot-ginger puree with organic greens and romano cheese. Moroccan lamb stew on minted couscous, grilled halibut with salsa verde and oyster gumbo were a few of the intriguing dishes on his fall dinner menu. There's one dessert a night, perhaps a cobbler or bread pudding. As in a European café, the atmosphere is social at dinner, and singles love to eat at the long counter. Summer diners often face long waits for a table.

(508) 325-0308. Entrées, $17 to $26. Breakfast daily, 7 to 1. Dinner, Tuesday-Saturday 6 to 9. BYOB. No credit cards. Closed six weeks in winter.

Tuscan Treat, Tried and True

Sfoglia, 130 Pleasant St., Nantucket.

You have to know about this intimate and true trattoria, hidden in a former fish market across from the Stop & Shop supermarket. But ignore the disarming area and facade and enter for a meal like grandmother used to make – if that grandmother happened to be from rural Italy. A pair of young Culinary Institute of America grads who cooked in cutting-edge Boston and New York restaurants serendipitously chose Nantucket to spawn their solo venture, which would "blow away the competition were it in Boston," according to a Boston Herald reviewer. Chef Ron Suhanosky named the place for his favorite sheet of uncut pasta. He does the cooking and his wife Colleen bakes focaccia that's sold across the island and dessert pastries that are to die for. Like their grandmothers' kitchens, the enamel-topped tables are mismatched and apt to be shared, the all-Italian boutique wines are poured in squat glasses and dining is convivial by candlelight. The meal progresses through simple antipasti, handmade pastas like potato gnocchi with artichokes and fennel cream and pappardelle alla Bolognese. Secondi could be Sicilian orata baked under a soufflé of egg whites and sea salt, chicken crisped under a brick or braised veal with pickled red onions. Desserts include biscotti, panna cotta and gelati. The food is out of this world, according to our well-traveled Nantucket informants, who liked their first dinner so much they returned with friends the next night.

(508) 325-4500. www.sfogliarestaurant.com. Entrees, $18 to $24. Dinner, Monday-Saturday 6 to 9. No credit cards.

FOR MORE INFORMATION: Nantucket Island Chamber of Commerce, 48 Main St., Nantucket, MA 02554, (508) 228-1700. Visitor information center is at 25 Federal St. (508) 228-0925. www.nantucketchamber.org. or www.nantucket.net.

Guests enjoy panoramic water view from wraparound porch at Land's End Inn.

Provincetown, Mass.

Escape to Land's End

Ever since the Pilgrims made Provincetown their first landing in the New World in 1620, the storied town poised on a fragile sandbar at the very tip of Cape Cod has been a refuge for people looking for an escape. The Pilgrims were getting away from the old world. Today, people get away from the mainland – and the mainstream.

For the Pilgrims, Provincetown was too primitive. They stayed only five weeks before sailing across Cape Cod Bay to find shelter and fresh water at what became Plymouth. Provincetown eventually was settled in the mid 1700s not by Puritans from the Massachusetts Bay Colony but by Portuguese fishermen and their families. Before the tourists arrived in the 20th century, artists were drawn by the "Cape light" that is at its strongest in Provincetown. They found it "a place hard to get to and hard to get out of," as Eugene O'Neill famously described it. Free-living and free-thinking, they cast a spell over Provincetown that pulsates to this day.

The population at land's end (3,200) increases ten-fold in summer. The populated part of P-town, as it's called, three miles long and generally two blocks wide, curves cheek-by-jowl for three miles around the harbor facing sheltered Cape Cod Bay. On the north side are the towering dunes and beaches of the Cape Cod National Seashore and the open Atlantic.

The combination of edgy town, turbulent seas and shifting sands seems to release people from their past. They come here for a new beginning in an open community, free of constraints and conformity, much as in Key West, that other land's end down the East Coast. The result is a unique mix: artists and actors, a gay majority (both male and female), a fishing community, the Portuguese, townies, summer residents and tourists.

If Provincetown has a center, it's MacMillan Wharf and, around the corner, the Town Hall. Park yourself on a bench in front of Town Hall and observe the passing parade along the "downtown" section of Commercial Street – people watching seems to be even more popular than whale watching, the official No. 1 tourist attraction here. P-town's East End, relatively quiet and residential, houses many year-round residents and art galleries. The West End yields to a more leisurely flow of guest houses, restaurants and private residences, some of them quite substantial.

From the busy wharves come and go commercial fishing boats and excursion boats, plus express catamarans to and from Boston. Whale watching tours started on the East Coast here in 1975, taking advantage of the fertile feeding grounds of the Stellwagen Bank sanctuary offshore.

Away from the fray are the moors at the far West End and the National Seashore parklands along the north side. Golden dunes, nature trails, bike paths and wide-open beaches invite exploration. Even in quirky Provincetown, Mother Nature manages to upstage the human show.

Seeing and Doing

Because it is at land's end, Provincetown in most respects is less accessible than the rest of the Cape, and a car is usually necessary to get here by land. That car, however, becomes an impediment at peak season in town, where the streets are narrow (and clogged with pedestrians and bicyclists, many zigzagging every which way) and parking is hard to come by. In one respect, Provincetown has become more accessible than the rest of the Cape, thanks to two 90-minute passenger ferries direct from Boston. **Boston Harbor Cruises,** (877) 733-9425, runs a fast-ferry catamaran one to three times daily in season (adults, $38 one way, $59 round trip). Another fast-ferry catamaran and a larger three-deck excursion boat operate under auspices of **Bay State Cruise Co.,** (866) 903-3779. Its catamaran runs three times daily Memorial Day to Columbus Day (adults, $38 one way, $59 round trip). The three-hour Provincetown II excursion runs once a day Friday-Sunday, late June to Labor Day (adults, $18 one way, $29 round trip).

Once in town, a good way to get oriented is to take the **Provincetown Trolley,** (508) 487-9483, which gives 40-minute sightseeing tours around town and the National Seashore. Trolleys leave from Town Hall on Commercial Street between Ryder and Gosnold streets every half hour from 10 to 4 and hourly in the evening; adults $9, children $5. The tours are narrated and quite informative. More personalized tours are offered by horse-drawn carriages, also parked in front of Town Hall.

The best way to get around town is to walk, bicycle or take the seasonal **Breeze Shuttle,** which circles the town and beaches every twenty minutes (single ride $1, day pass $3, children free).

Town Attractions

Three strands of its heritage – the Pilgrims, the Portuguese fishermen, and the artists and free spirits – make Provincetown the melting pot it is today.

Contrary to popular perception, the Pilgrims landed first not at Plymouth but in

Provincetown. First Landing Park, a small landscaped memorial in the middle of a traffic rotary in the West End, commemorates their arrival. It stands in quiet contrast to the hoopla surrounding Plymouth Rock. The drama of the Mayflower Compact is rendered in a bas-relief at the foot of the landmark Pilgrim Monument.

The influence of the Portuguese fishermen who settled the town in the mid-1700s is evident in the names of the fishing boats along Fisherman's Wharf, the Portuguese Bakery on Commercial Street and the annual Portuguese Festival and Blessing of the Fleet in late June.

The artists who were inspired by the Cape Cod "light" and each other formed the nation's largest arts colony. You can see the dune shacks that they occupied as well as some of their works in the town's museums and galleries. Also evident are all the accoutrements of what, as one leading local inn's website proclaims, "of course is also known as the gayest place on earth." You, too, will quickly know.

Pilgrim Monument and Provincetown Museum, off Route 6 on High Pole Hill.

The tallest granite structure in the country offers a panoramic view of Cape Cod from its 252-foot-high observation deck. Its top is reached by walking up an inclined ramp and stairs as in an Italian tower. The monument was built in 1910 to honor the first landing of the Mayflower. At its base is a museum with a collection of artifacts tracing the history of the Outer Cape. Displays include dioramas, ship models, scrimshaw, a map of the Mayflower's route, whaling equipment, items salvaged from nearby shipwrecks and even preserved polar bears, part of an unusual North Pole collection in honor of native son Donald MacMillan, who explored the Arctic with Commodore Robert Peary. The Pilgrim Room contains Mayflower memorabilia as well as Colonial and Victorian china, silver and pewter.

(508) 487-1310. www.pilgrim-monument,org. Open daily, 9 to 7 in summer, 9 to 5 in spring and fall. Closed December-March. Adults $7, children $3.

Provincetown Heritage Museum, 356 Commercial St.

Located in the former Methodist church built in 1860, this was established in 1976 by the town to depict the history of Provincetown. It holds one of the world's largest indoor models of a Grand Banks fishing schooner, the 66-foot-long Rose Dorothea. Other attractions range from one of the oldest library collections in the country and paintings by local artists to antique fire equipment and exhibits of marine gear, fishing equipment and harpoons.

(508) 487-7098. Open daily 10 to 5:30, Memorial Day to Columbus Day. Adults $4.

Stellwagen Bank National Marine Sanctuary Exhibit, 115 Bradford St.

Dive onto the Stellwagen Bank sanctuary without getting wet, or even boarding a boat. The new high-tech exhibit in the center of town has an introductory video to the fertile offshore fishing grounds as well as four touch-screen computers with fascinating information and images. Thanks to videotapes filmed by underwater robot vehicles and viewed through simulated periscopes, you see marine creatures in their natural habitats. Two touch screens show information about whales.

(508) 487-6115. Open Thursday-Sunday, 10 to 7 in July and August, 11 to 6 in May-June and September-October. Free.

Expedition Whydah Sea Lab and Learning Center, 16 MacMillan Wharf.

This traces the story and displays the treasures of the pirate ship Whydah, which sank off nearby Wellfleet in 1717. "Black Sam" Bellamy's Whydah is the first pirate ship recovered from the deep. Visitors find cannons, jewelry and coins salvaged from the brig, as well as a working conservation library.

(508) 487-8899 or (800) 949-3241. www.whydah.com. Open daily 10 to 7 in summer, to 4 in spring and fall, weekends only Columbus Day to New Year's. Adults $8, children $6.

THE ARTS. The nation's oldest continuous arts colony dates to 1899, when Charles Hawthorne began teaching painting to hundreds of artists who flocked here to take advantage of the open air and changing light. Visiting artists still occupy some of the historic dune shanties each summer. Plein air artists paint on the streets and dunes. Literally dozens of galleries flourish across the town, with a concentration in the East End. On Friday evenings in season, galleries light up for the openings.

Writers and playwrights soon joined the artists here. The famous Provincetown Players originated in 1916 when Eugene O'Neill's "Bound East for Cardiff" debuted on a foggy night in an old fishhouse-turned-stage on Lewis Wharf. They wintered in Greenwich Village and after several seasons relocated to New York. A plaque at 570 Commercial St. commemorates the Players and the first O'Neill production as the birthplace of modern American theater. O'Neill, Thoreau, John Dos Passos, Tennessee Williams, Edna St. Vincent Millay and Norman Mailer all found inspiration here. The Provincetown Theater Company and the Provincetown Repertory Theatre are in residence in the $3.1 million Provincetown Theater at 238 Bradford St., (508) 487-7487.

Provincetown Art Association and Museum, 460 Commercial St.

The association was established in 1914, and by 1916 the Boston Globe ran a front-page article headlined "Biggest Art Colony in the World in Provincetown." Edward Hopper, Jackson Pollock and Robert Motherwell were among those who worked in town. The museum has a permanent collection of more than 1,500 works, shown throughout the year in four galleries. It also stages exhibitions of works by established and emerging artists.

(508) 487-1750. www.paam.org. Open daily noon to 5, Memorial Day to October, also 8 to 10 p.m. in summer and weekends in June and September; rest of year, weekends noon to 4. Adults $2, children free.

SHOPPING. For most, the people-watching takes priority over shopping along tight, congested Commercial Street, the main drag (in more ways than one). Like so much else in Provincetown, stores come and go. They also tend to cater to the offbeat, as in **Freak Street Clothes and Accessories**. Other than the art galleries, standouts for us are **Utilities,** with good home accessories; **Impulse Gallery,** lots of colorful glassware; **D. Lasser Ceramics; Frenchware,** with clothing and dry goods for the Francophile; **Undercover** for bed, bath and home, and the **Northern Lights Hammock Shop**. **Marine Specialties,** a warehouse of a place also known as the Army Navy Store, advertises demilitarized clothing, boots, boating gear and, more than anything, "good junk."

On or Near the Water

Cape Cod National Seashore.

The Cape's most expansive national treasure, the seashore was established in 1961 under the administration of President John F. Kennedy, for whom Cape Cod was his summer home. The 43,500-acre seashore protects 40 miles of ocean beaches, rolling dunes, swamps, marshes, wetlands, pine barrens, forests, wildlife and historic structures, all culminating around the tip of the Cape at Provincetown. Self-guiding nature trails, as well as biking and horseback riding trails, wend through these landscapes. Guided walks and lectures are offered April-November. The Province Lands Visitor Center, Race Point Road off Route 6, dispenses information and shows a film on Provincetown, daily 9 to 5, May to late October. From its upper-level observation deck you can look out across much of the dune and beach area. *(508) 487-1256. Open year-round. Free. Beach parking fee in summer, $10.*

SWIMMING. When the tide is out, people swim along the bay beaches from Truro into Provincetown Harbor and the West End. Out on the seashore, Herring Cove Beach is the best, according to locals. The Cape Cod Bay water is calmer and warmer than that on the ocean side. Signs at the entry warn "public nudity prohibited," although that's occasionally disregarded. Provincetown's most popular gay beach is to the left or south here. The first stretch is primarily female, beyond is primarily male. The northern stretch has a family clientele. So does the north-facing Race Point Beach, where the ocean surf rolls in and the sand is smoother. Here is where the currents of ocean and bay meet in a boiling rush known as "The Race." Both National Seashore beaches have lifeguards and bathhouses, and Herring Cove has a snack bar. To avoid the daily parking fee, those in the know buy a National Seashore season pass for $20, which gives free parking at all the beaches. Windsurfing within the National Seashore is permitted outside lifeguard-protected beaches.

For a change of pace, hike along the beach from the Herring Cove parking lot out to a smaller cove between Herring Cove and Race Point, called **Hatch's Harbor**. Once a raucous shantytown frequented by pirates and local renegades, today it is a smooth beach that fills up at high tide with warm pools in which youngsters like to paddle about.

Old Harbor Lifesaving Station, Race Point Beach. The century-old station, floated here from Chatham in 1977, houses displays of shipwrecks and heroic rescues by the U.S. Lifesaving Service at sea. Every Thursday at 6, the staff re-enacts a 1902 rescue drill. Open in summer, Friday-Wednesday 3 to 5 and Thursday 6 to 8. Donation.

HIKING AND BIKING. From the parking lot off Race Point Road in the National Seashore, hike the **Beech Forest Trail** into the heart of a picturesque beech forest. The one-mile loop skirts the shallow Beech Forest Pond and hugs dunes that are gradually engulfing parts of the forest. About eight miles of paved bicycle trails wind through the dunes. We enjoyed biking the 5.5-mile **Province Lands Trail** out to Race Point and Herring Cove beaches and returning past Pasture and Bennett ponds and beside Beech Forest. But watch out for sands shifting across the pavement. Unwary riders may find themselves suddenly upended.

In town, public landings every few blocks make the bay beach accessible to everyone. You can walk the beach along the harborfront at low tide for a boater's view of Provincetown. At high tide the gentle waves lap right up to the buildings on the south side of Commercial Street. Low tide exposes shifting sandbars or "flats," as the locals call them.

You also can hike out the rock breakwater from the West End rotary off Commercial Street to Wood End and Long Point lights. The moors to the west, nearly dry at low tide, show the wildlife and ecology of the salt marshes. The mile-and-a-half walk is tricky and at times you have to hop from rock to rock. Parts of the breakwater may be submerged at particularly high tides. **Long Point** itself is starkly beautiful – a getaway place where you really are at land's end, but with Provincetown a comforting sight back in the distance.

Foss Woods in the East End, acquired by the town in an effort to preserve conservation land, surrounds the old railroad right of way. It now makes for a good walking trail.

Active hikers enjoy treks across high dunes from a couple of access points, and dune climbers are sometimes a startling sight for first-time visitors approaching along Route 6. At Snail Road and Route 6 in the East End, a fire road cuts into the scrub pine forest and leads to the dunes. At the Pilgrim Heights parking lot in Truro, another fire road heads out to the beach, just north of Head of The Meadow.

DUNE TOURS. The towering dunes give Provincetown its unique light and scope. For an entertaining look, hitch a ride with **Art's Dune Tours,** corner of Commercial and Standish streets, (508) 487-1950 or (800) 894-1951. Art Costa started giving dune tours in 1946 in an old Ford Woody. Today you'll likely be in a four-wheel-drive GMC Suburban van as you drive around the National Seashore through grasses and along cranberry bogs, pass the remains of the Peaked Hill life-saving station that rescued shipwrecks, and get a look at the famous dune shacks where artists and writers became inspired (and still are). The first was built in 1794 as a refuge for shipwrecked sailors. Now eighteen cottages, most built between 1935 and 1950, dot the ridges and valleys between Race Point and High Head in Truro. Part of the National Register of Historic Places, four are available each summer to artists and writers as retreats. Dune tours of one to one and one-half hours, daily 10 to 5:30; fares, $12 to $15.

WHALE WATCHING. Whales, which played an important role in the Provincetown economy in the 19th century, now attract thousands of visitors who depart from Provincetown Harbor each year to observe, rather than kill, the now-endangered species in their natural habitat. The tradition began in 1975 when scientists from the Provincetown Center for Coastal Studies teamed with charter fishing boat captain Al Avellar to study the three species of whales found offshore. His **Dolphin Fleet,** (800) 826-9300, launched the guided whale watching phenomenon on the East Coast. Beyond Race Point back toward Boston and Cape Ann lies the Stellwagen Bank, a newly proclaimed National Marine Sanctuary, the only one in the Northeast. Nearly the size of Rhode Island, the 842-square-mile bank is a shallow, underwater plateau that is a rich feeding ground for whales, dolphins and seals, and Provincetown is its closest land neighbor, eight miles away. Whale watch excursions of three to four hours leave from MacMillan Wharf three times a day. More than 50 humpback, right and finback whales are often seen on a single trip. Naturalists from the Center for Coastal Studies add insights as they guide all Dolphin cruises. Three boats give morning, afternoon and sunset tours mid-April through October. Adults $24, children $20.

Three-hour naturalist-conducted tours also are offered by **Portuguese Princess Excursions,** (508) 487-2651 or (800) 442-3188. Tours depart from MacMillan Wharf daily May-October, adults $19 to $22.

Where to Stay

Except for larger motels and resorts, most lodging establishments cater to gays or lesbians and/or welcome them. As the manager of the Watermark Inn advised, "everyone who comes here should be open-minded." Her inn's clientele is "mixed," meaning a mix of straights, gays and lesbians. Others run a range of mixed (those included here) to strictly gay or lesbian. The *Out and About* testimonials reprinted in brochures and the rainbow flags flying in front of guest houses speak volumes.

Guest Houses and B&Bs

Watermark Inn, 603 Commercial St., Provincetown 02657.

With a terrific waterfront location in the primarily residential East End, this shingled, contemporary beach house is one of Provincetown's largest and most luxurious. Architect Kevin Shea and his wife, Judy Richland, transformed a former inn-turned-restaurant into a summery haunt perfect for the Cape. The rear of the weathered Cape Cod shingled structure opens up onto two levels of full-length decks, the lower one right out over the water at high tide. Six of the ten one-bedroom suites offer head-on bay views and private decks. Furnishings are contemporary, with plump sofas and chairs upholstered in grays or taupes to contrast with white walls and ceilings. Sliding glass doors, large windows, vaulted ceilings and skylights make each living area bright and airy, oriented toward the water. Bedrooms are darker and located toward the street side. Beds are king or queensize and covered with quilts. All suites have kitchenettes and one has a full kitchen. Two have working fireplaces. Telephones and small TVs are standard. Suite 7, the most expensive, offers a corner view toward Provincetown and the sunset from its two-sided deck as well as a water view from its kingsize bed. Rates are generally by the week in summer, booked far in advance, and nightly the rest of the year. There's parking for guests – a sought-after commodity in Provincetown. Most don't venture far, however, from their beachfront paradise with all the comforts of home.

(508) 487-0165. Fax (508) 487-2383. www.watermark-inn.com. Ten suites with private baths. Doubles, $190 to $400 nightly, $1,200 to $2,510 weekly in summer; $85 to $290 nightly rest of year.

The Brass Key Guesthouse, 67 Bradford St., Provincetown 02657.

Cloistered behind shrubbery and a gatehouse, this luxurious new boutique hotel elevated Provincetown accommodations to a higher level. Owner Michael MacIntyre worked for the Ritz-Carlton and it shows, as does the influence of his prototype B&B in Key West, Fla. As in Key West, a "private, gated compound" wraps around an enclosed courtyard with a pool, large spa and brick terraces harboring chaise lounges, umbrella-topped tables, flowering shrubs and colorful plantings. Accommodations are in a restored 1828 Federal whaling captain's house, a Second Empire Victorian banker's mansion and adjacent carriage house, a Greek Revival residence, three Cape cottages and the gatehouse. Turned into itself, the Brass Key brooks no quarter with the outside world, except for the panoramic view above it all from a rooftop widow's walk. Furnished with fine fabrics and New England antiques, each guest room is different with a teddy bear loft here, a wrought-iron balcony there. Half the rooms have kingsize beds and half queensize (plus one with two twins), all outfitted with 250-count linens and goose down pillows. Nine rooms have whirlpool tubs and ten have gas fireplaces. Three of those with both have a private balcony or deck. Telephones, TV/VCRs, Bose radios, mini-refrigerators and baths with massaging shower heads or wall jets, seersucker robes and heated towel racks are standard. The compound has two common living rooms, one furnished with country pine antiques in the Gatehouse. A continental breakfast is offered here or on the poolside terrace. Tea and later wine and beer are offered in the afternoon. Godiva chocolates are put out at turndown.

(508) 487-9005 or (800) 842-9858. Fax (508)487-9020. www.brasskey.com. Thirty-three rooms with private baths. Doubles, $265 to $465 July to Labor Day; $115 to $325, off-season. Closed January-March.

Crowne Pointe Historic Inn & Spa, 82 Bradford St., Provincetown 02657.

A multi-million renovation and plenty of extras helped this inn earn a four-diamond rating shortly after opening. David Sanford and Tom Walter from New Jersey purchased the former Dusty Miller Inn and adjoining Sea Drift Inn. After four months of whirlwind restoration of a sea captain's mansion and various carriage houses, they settled into a new role as innkeepers. Common rooms and some of the 40 guest quarters are graced with period antiques, moldings, wainscoting and hardwood floors. All accommodations include a queensize bed dressed in 250-thread-count cotton linens, TV/VCR, aromatherapy bath amenities, chairs with reading lamps, a coffeemaker and refrigerator, as well as access from the main house to a two-story wraparound porch. Deluxe accommodations add "an expanded amenity," such as a kingsize bed, outdoor deck, fireplace or a whirlpool tub, and a few have two. Some open onto a private porches or a spacious sundeck. Guests are welcomed with afternoon tea and desserts. An elaborate hot buffet breakfast is offered from 8 to 11 in the morning in the dining room or on the patio. The property atop a bluff in the center of town includes a nicely landscaped garden courtyard with a heated pool and a couple of ten-person whirlpool spas. A new Shui Spa, accessed via a bridge across a koi pond, offers full-service treatment rooms with licensed therapists. **The Bistro at Crowne Pointe** is open for dinner nightly in summer, Thursday-Sunday in winter. The short menu (entrées $21 to $28) ranges from steamed salmon served atop a vegetable slaw to spice-crusted grilled lamb steak with apricot-almond-mustard chutney. Spa lunches are served at the Shui Spa.

(508) 487-6767 or (877) 276-9631. Fax (508) 487-5554. www.crownepointe.com. Thirty-six rooms and four suites with private baths. Doubles, $199 to $469 in summer, $110 to $379 rest of year.

The Red Inn, 15 Commercial St., Provincetown.

Long known for its restaurant (see Where to Eat), the historic Red Inn now offers prime waterfront accommodations as well. A quartet of four men from varied backgrounds took over the establishment in 2001 and added two "residences" to the lineup of six rooms right beside the beach in a quiet West End residential section. The main, barn-red 1805 sea captain's home contains four guest rooms and two suites. Bay windows yield head-on views of the water at the far end of rooms that are decorated to the elegant hilt. The Harbor's End quasi-suite has an oversize chair for two in the front section and a pillow-top queen bed beside the water-view patio in back. Decor is formal and sumptuous, the kind that might appeal more to vacationers in the off-season than to beachgoers in summer. The three accommodations on the ground level open onto a sandy seawall, where Adirondack chairs await. Next door, an enormous deck serves guests in two cottage-style residences, both with kitchens and fireplaces. The living room of the Delft Haven, with windows onto the water on two sides, holds a baby grand piano in one corner. Continental breakfast is provided in the morning.

(508) 487-7334 or (866) 473-3466. Fax (508) 487-5115. www.theredinn.com. Four rooms, two suites and two residences with private baths. Doubles, $210 to $295. Residences, $425 and $485. Five-night minimum stay in summer.

Anchor Inn Beach House, 175 Commercial St., Provincetown 02657.

A $5 million renovation turned this aging waterfront Victorian on the bay side of Commercial Street into one of Provincetown's more luxurious B&Bs, now run by the holding company that also owns the Red Inn. Rooms feature whirlpool baths or deluxe showers and all but three have gas fireplaces. All rooms come with TV/VCR, twin-line telephone with dataport, wet bar with refrigerator, and bath amenities such as robes and hair dryers. Most deluxe are rear rooms facing Cape Cod Bay. They include four ground-floor cottage rooms with private entrances, decorated like early 19th-century cottages with wicker furniture and cozy porches. Nautical themes prevail in the first-floor "yacht cabins," furnished to the 1930 period with boat beds and wood cabin walls. Six deluxe captain's suites offer kingsize beds, double whirlpool tubs and french doors onto a balcony overlooking the harbor. These are decorated in English chintz or with handmade furniture from the West Indies. Three rooms in the tower on the east side of the house offer balconies with side water views, four-poster beds and sitting areas. Six rooms facing Commercial Street have large front balconies. Guests enjoy an expansive foyer that doubles as a living room and dining area. The staff puts out a continental breakfast of pastries, cereals and yogurt.

(508) 487-0432 or (800) 858-2657. Fax (508) 487-6280. www.anchorinnbeachhouse.com. Seventeen rooms and six suites with private baths. Doubles, $175 to $375.

The Land's End Inn, 22 Commercial St., Provincetown 02657.

A place unto itself atop Gull Hill, the highest point in Provincetown's West End, this exotic inn commands panoramic views of town, dunes and Cape Cod Bay. The views inside the weathered wood structure with a cupola-topped turret are exotic, too. Ditto for the ambiance. The main floor is a showy clutter of architectural refinements and collections. Many are original to the house, built as a summer bungalow at the turn of the last century by a Boston merchant. The stained glass, Asian wood carvings and antiques like a "grandmother's clock" are notable. If the interior looks like an art deco museum, the exterior is idyllic: wraparound porches and alcoves, studded with heavy wood and log tables and chairs, with water views that won't quit. Prolific gardens add to the setting, although since longtime owner David Adam Schoolman's death, they have been toned down and manicured and the jungle of plants removed from the interior. Now owned by Michael MacIntyre of the Brass Key guesthouses in Provincetown and Key West, the inn offers sixteen accommodations with queen or king beds. They vary widely, but each is a mini-museum of antiques and collections. Several have private decks or balconies. Three apartments with cooking facilities accommodate up to four. Rising above the house are three tower rooms and the Schoolman Suite. Two of the latter plus a kitchenette apartment are rented by the week in summer. Guests mix in the ramble of living-room areas. Continental breakfast is taken in the dining room or on the porch.

(508) 487-0706 or (800) 276-7088. www.landsendinn.com. Sixteen rooms and suites with private baths. Doubles, $245 to $445 nightly, $1,350 to $2,875 weekly. Off-season: $110 to $295. Closed November to early May.

BayShore & Chandler House, 493 Commercial St., Provincetown 02657.

Nineteen apartments are available in the waterfront BayShore and its companion North Houses across the street. Formerly known as the Hargood Guest House and long run by Ann Maguire and Harriet Gordon, it has been condominiumized but facilities are rented out daily or weekly as available. The BayShore complex has five Cape-style houses converted to two studios and fourteen one-bedroom and three two-bedroom apartments, all but one with private decks or patios and some with fireplaces. Each living room contains a sofabed and TV. Rates vary with proximity to the water. The lodgings are grouped around a green lawn with a sunken garden and a terrace with umbrellaed tables and loungers overlooking the beach. All have private entrances, modern baths and complete kitchens (with everything from dishwasher to stemware and china to a garlic press). Fully renovated in 1997 is Chandler House, four doors closer to town. It has an expansive two-bedroom Gallery apartment with a huge fireplaced living room and deck, plus a one-bedroom Beach House cottage with fireplace and deck at water's edge. In the Captain's House are four apartments with fireplaces, including the one-bedroom Penthouse with cathedral ceiling and sweeping water view.

(508) 487-9133. Fax (508) 487-0520. www.bayshorechandler.com. Twenty-four apartments and one cottage with private baths. Doubles, $1,200 to $2,300 weekly in summer, $105 to $230 nightly (two-night minimum) rest of year.

Motels

Best Western Tides Beachfront, 837 Commercial St., Provincetown 02657.

Nicely located along the shore Route 6A on the eastern outskirts of Provincetown, this is set well back from the road on six acres. It's right on Cape Cod Bay near the Provincetown border with Truro. A 600-foot-wide beach expands with the receding tide, and guests like to walk the flats amid the undulating sandbars. Taken over by Best Western, the old Tides resort was designed for self-sufficiency. A small breakfast and lunch restaurant is part of the resort. The grounds are landscaped, the lawns are lush and the outdoor pool is heated. All rooms in the main two-story motel have sliding doors opening right onto the beach or upstairs balconies. Room furnishings are pleasant, and many units include a refrigerator. At the western end of town is the 54-room **Best Western Chateau Motor Inn** at 105 Bradford St. West, with similar rates. Its landscaped hilltop location offers great views of the dunes and distant waters surrounding Provincetown.

(508) 487-1045. Fax (508) 487-3557. www.bwprovincetown.com Sixty-four rooms with private baths. Doubles, $139 to $249, off-season $79 to $199. Closed late October to early May.

Surfside Hotel & Suites, 543 Commercial St., Provincetown 02657.

New ownership has upgraded this property, which began in the early 1960s as a midrise motor inn typical of beach communities up and down the Atlantic coast but such an anomaly in Provincetown that it was dubbed "the green monster." Not much could be done to change the facades of the two buildings on either side of Commercial Street in the residential East End. But the gardens and landscaping have been enhanced, the rooms and baths refurbished, and the name changed from its earlier designations as motel and inn. Thirty-eight rooms and two suites in the four-story waterfront building face Cape Cod Bay, from ground-floor patios on the beach and shared balconies on upper floors, which are served by an elevator. Across Commercial Street is a three-story building where seventeen rooms face the street, seventeen face the parking lot and twelve look onto the pool and garden area. There are plenty of lounge chairs around the pool, which at our visit was heated to a sultry 86 degrees. Because of its setback, Surfside retains its beach even at high tide, when its neighbors lose theirs to the rising waters. All rooms in both buildings come with refrigerators and TV. Bed configurations vary from king and queen to one or two doubles. Continental breakfast is complimentary.

(508) 487-1726 or (800) 421-1726. Fax (508) 487-6556. www.surfsideinn.cc. Eighty-four rooms and two suites. Doubles, $140 to $340. Suites, $450 to $550. Closed mid-November to April.

Provincetown Inn, 1 Commercial St., Provincetown 02657.

No more secluded location is offered by any Provincetown motel than this, which occupies its own isthmus surrounded by water on three sides. It calls itself a seaside resort and conference center, but this is essentially an aging motor inn, especially its one-story U-shaped buildings facing Cape Cod Bay on the outside and a parking lot on the inside. The water views from the subdivided patios are awesome; the inside corridors off the parking lot are not. Rooms in the priciest Cape Tip cross-section of the U face south. The Harborside section faces the pool area and Provincetown, while the Breakwater section looks toward the breakwater leading to Long Point and the dunes beyond. Corner accommodations in the Cape Tip section are suites: the Honeymoon has a king bed and sitting area, while the Captain's Suite has a queen bedroom, living room, dining area and eat-in kitchen. A two-story motel section along Commercial Street looks onto a pool area and the beach, although some rooms here face the street. The place has history. It's located opposite the little Pilgrims First Landing Park at the West End traffic rotary, near where the pilgrims landed in America. Hand-painted murals depict the history of Provincetown. Cocktails and lunch are served at the Pilgrim Pool Bar & Grill around the Olympic-size pool in season. The Inn Pub offers appetizers, sandwiches and light entrées as well as Keno. When we were here at midweek in late May, the place seemed eerily quiet with only a few rooms occupied. It was advertising romantic bed and breakfast getaways in advance of the hordes of summer. A continental breakfast buffet is included in the rates.

(508) 487-9500 or (800) 942-5388. Fax (508) 487-2911. www.provincetowninn.com. One hundred rooms and two suites with private baths. Doubles, $139 to $219. Suites, $259 to $369. Waterfront units closed November to mid-April.

Where to Eat

Amid an incredible variety of options, Provincetown harbors some of the best dining establishments on the Cape.

Chester, 404 Commercial St.

Located in an 1800s Greek Revival sea captain's house in the East End, this stylish restaurant garnered rave reviews shortly after opening – one calling it the town's best and probably the hottest restaurant on the entire Cape. Others find it rather precious and pretentious, not the place for a jovial night on the town. Owners John Guerra and Jay Coburn, who know their food and wine, named it for their pet airedale terrier. The dining room with golden walls and white trim is attractive, pristine and serene. Understated, beautifully presented food is the hallmark of the chef, who procures local seafood and picks vegetables from a garden behind the restaurant. The menu is short and focused, but whatever you choose will be first-rate. One autumn menu featured seared diver scallops with apple cider glaze, pepper-crusted salmon with shallot-madeira sauce, lamb sirloin seared with pancetta and porcini mushrooms, and angus tenderloin with foie gras truffle butter and a port-red wine demi-glace. Appetizers included cod cakes with celery root rémoulade, roasted beet napoleon with arugula pesto and Vermont chèvre, and an item called "quack, quack: confit of duck with polenta and house-smoked duck breast with micro greens salad." Desserts were frozen orange blossom honey mousse with caramelized oranges and blood-orange sorbet, individual goat cheese cakes with poached figs and pistachio praline, homemade ice creams and sorbets, plus a selection of New England farmhouse cheeses. Chester's award-winning wine list features more than 160 vintages from small producers around the world, most priced between $30 and $100 and not commonly seen in the area.

(508) 487-8200. www.chesterrestaurant.com. Entrées, $28 to $39. Dinner nightly in season, from 6; fewer nights off-season. Closed January-March.

The Mews, 429 Commercial St.

Great food is offered here in a dynamite waterfront setting – a romantic downstairs dining room that looks like an extension of the beach just outside its walls of glass. The designer even took samples of sand to Boston to match with the paint on the terra cotta walls, which are hung with changing abstract art. Floodlights illuminate the beach, and from virtually every white-clothed table you have the illusion of eating outside. Owner Ron Robin and executive chef Laurence de Freitas feature American fusion cuisine. A bowl of olives and breads arrived as we were seated for dinner. Among appetizers, we liked the oysters with crabmeat béchamel and pancetta, albeit a precious little serving that we had planned to share, and a classic caesar salad. Main courses range from mirin-glazed Atlantic salmon with rhubarb and cucumber yogurt to Mediterranean spice-rubbed rack of lamb. The smoked pork tenderloin with apricot-serrano chile sauce was served with sweet potato polenta, while the shrimp curry came in a puff pastry with black mission figs. Key lime pie was a hit from the dessert tray, as was coffee ice cream drizzled with hot fudge sauce. Service was polished and the food preparation more than competent, but the romantic beachside setting – illuminated as darkness fell – is what remains etched in our memories. Next time we might opt to eat in the lively upstairs bar area called **Café Mews,** which offers an American bistro menu of appetizers, sandwiches, pastas and lighter entrées. Here you'll also find a vodka bar, billed as the largest in New England if not the country, with more than 175 brands from 27 countries.

(508) 487-1500. www.mews.com. Entrées, $22 to $32. Dinner nightly, from 6. Sunday brunch, 11 to 2:30, Easter through October.

Front Street Restaurant, 230 Commercial St.

Chef-owner Donna Aliperti has endowed this perennial local favorite with her special creative touch nurtured by Julia Child. Gourmet magazine requested her recipe for corn and crab chowder, while Bon Appétit inquired about her coffee-toffee pie. She and Kathy Cotter, sous chef and pastry chef, offer two menus: an Italian featuring authentic recipes and a continental menu that changes every Friday. Potato-crusted salmon with raspberry butter and thyme, tea-smoked duck, herb-crusted rack of lamb and grilled angus ribeye with white truffle cream sauce are perennial favorites. Good starters are tuna carpaccio, smoked-salmon chowder, grilled quail framboise and the mozzarella antipasto, made daily on the premises.

The raspberry-chocolate tiramisu, deep-dish peach-praline pie, and the pistachio and white chocolate terrine are to groan over. If they don't finish you off, the homemade ice creams and sorbets will. The dining room with brick walls in the cellar of a Victorian house is dark, intimate and very bistro-ish. Striking tables made by a local artist are topped with tiny pieces of cut-up wood under a layer of polyurethane. Wines are showcased in backlit storage shelves along one wall.

(508) 487-9715. www.frontstreetrestaurant.com. Entrées, $15 to $27. Dinner nightly, 6 to 10. Closed January-April.

The Red Inn, 15 Commercial St.

Three waterfront dining areas are strung out along the rear of this recently renovated 1805 sea captain's house that sports a polished, more contemporary look than its wide-board hardwood floors and beamed ceilings would indicate. The inn proclaims a gold medal award for "best water view dining on the Cape," and the new American cuisine is equal to the setting. One of the four owners, Phillip Mossy from Louisiana, is the head chef. Repeat diners tend to go for the raw-bar selections as preliminaries to the inn's "big 22-ounce porterhouse steak" or pepper-crusted filet mignon with Jack Daniels sauce. Others like to start with the spicy lobster corn chowder and perhaps a bacon-wrapped oyster brochette or lobster and artichoke fondue in a warm sourdough bowl. Chef Mossy imparts Louisiana accents to such main courses as shrimp and crawfish sautéed with mushrooms in a sherry-creole tomato cream sauce over pasta and creole-seasoned duck breast grilled with a passion fruit-maple glaze. His pan-roasted local cod might be served on a bed of rosemary potatoes and applewood bacon with a lemon-garlic confit.

(508) 487-7334. www.theredinn.com. Entrées, $22 to $42. Dinner nightly, 5:30 to 10, May-October; Thursday-Sunday in off-season. Brunch, Thursday-Sunday 10 to 2:30 in summer, weekends in late spring and early fall. Closed January to mid-April.

Martin House, 157 Commercial St.

A talented, long-term super-chef and an historic Cape Cod house combine to make this with-it, family-run restaurant a favorite in Provincetown. "In this house, you *know* you're on Cape Cod," host Glen Martin said of the shingled 1750 sea captain's residence snuggling up to the harbor on the Atlantic Street Landing, away from the downtown hubbub. He and his brother Gary offer six cozy dining rooms with fireplaces upstairs and down (check out "the cave" where the three chimneys meet), plus a trellised garden patio beside the harbor holding a handful of tables for two. The signature oysters Claudia on the half shell with a ponzu dipping sauce, wasabi and pickled ginger makes a fabulous starter from a menu strong on first courses and small plates. Others could be smoked sea scallops with red chile sauce and poblano cream, and the house salad with organic greens, roasted cashews and papaya-lime vinaigrette. Executive chef Alex Mazzocca favors the local catch, and often buys whole fish fresh from the back beach minutes before the restaurant opens. Typical main dishes are tasso-wrapped halibut fillet, fennel-dusted salmon fillet with saffron cream and shellfish steamed in sangria with roasted vegetables and yellow rice. We were well pleased with the sautéed lobster topped with red pepper crème fraîche and the duck breast saltimbocca with lemon-white wine sauce. Treats like roasted and stuffed green tomatoes with herbed quinoa, corn and okra in a spicy file tofu cream sauce impress vegetarians.

(508) 487-1327. www.themartinhouse.com. Entrées, $25 to $34. Dinner nightly, 6 to 10 or 11. Sunday brunch, 10 to 2. Closed Monday-Wednesday in the off-season.

Provincetown Personified

Napi's, 7 Freeman St.

For local character, you can't beat this venerable and beloved restaurant that's a favorite of local artists and musicians. That the food offered by Helen and Napi Van Dereck is so good is a bonus. On two floors of a veritable art gallery, Napi's is a showcase of local art, from cartoons by Howie Snyder to a freeform brick wall sculpted by Conrad Malicoat. The lampshades are made of scallop shells, a couple of colorful carousel horses prance atop a room divider, and the amount of antique stained glass is awesome. So is the variety on the menu: page after page of beef, chicken and seafood dishes, plus categories for shrimp and scallops, fresh catch, mussels, stir-fries, vegetarian dishes (even organic salads) and pastas. There's everything from Greek grape leaves to Chinese dumplings with hot sesame sauce, from shrimp feta to Brazilian shrimp with a banana fritter, from a Syrian falafel melt to a chock-full Portuguese bouillabaisse. Half a loaf of Helen's excellent whole-wheat bread comes with dinner. Save room for the "double fudge madness," a chocolate-glazed rum custard cake or the apricot mousse. Ice creams – how about the white russian made with vodka and kahlua? – come from Van Dereck's Ice Cream parlor around the corner. Upstairs is Charlie's Bar, named for the restaurant's late cat – a framed picture says "a better friend and cat never lived."

(508) 487-1145 or (800) 571-5274. www.napis-restaurant.com. Entrées, $15.95 to $22.95. Lunch daily from 11:30, October-April. Dinner nightly, from 5.

L'Uva Restaurant, 133 Bradford St.

The entry to this 1840 white shingled house with red trim is identified by a cluster of grapes to go with its name. L'Uva retains the aura of a private residence with its warren of small, candlelit dining rooms where white-clothed tables are set against a backdrop of pale sunset hues. Greenery strung with white lights envelops the garden terrace in season. Chef Christopher Covelli, co-owner with Peter Garza, divides the main part of his menu into French, Italian, Spanish and "haute American" categories relating to his background. His Italian heritage is reflected in such pastas as pappardelle with bacon, tomatoes and shrimp, and ravioli stuffed with crabmeat and lobster. Duck à l'orange and chicken breast provençal testify to his French training. His Spanish offering might be cod in Iberian serrano ham sauce. Pork tenderloin Rio Grande style and rack of lamb with a roasted garlic demi-glace are representative American choices. Look for starters like Portuguese chickpea soup, salmon tartare, a dim sum plate and escargots. Desserts include lavender crème brûlée, panna cotta with grilled pineapple and a pastry crisp filled with white pistachio ice cream and blueberries. Adjourn to the upstairs bar – arguably the most atmospheric in town – for an after-dinner grappa.

(508) 487-2010. www.luvarestaurant.com. Entrées, $19 to $27. Dinner nightly in summer, from 6; Thursday-Sunday in off-season.

The Lobster Pot, 321 Commercial St.

Tourists rub elbows with locals at this institution known for consistent, abundant seafood. There's the typical lobster-shack decor, but not the typical menu. Some fairly sophisticated fare comes out of the rows of kitchens opening off the long corridor leading to the rear dining rooms, one on the main floor and one upstairs, both overlooking the water. We certainly liked executive chef Tim McNulty's prize-winning clam chowder, rich and creamy, and the mussels marinara with the plumpest mollusks ever. The shrimp chantilly tossed with spinach fettuccine is a lunchtime classic. Tortilla-crusted halibut, shellfish algarve, cajun bouillabaisse, cioppino and sole rockefeller are among the seafood offerings at dinner. Lobster comes in at least seven variations, from a clambake to lobster newburg. Run for more than 30 years by the McNulty family, the Lobster Pot also has a fish market, bakery and gift shop.

(508) 487-0842. www.ptownlobsterpot.com. Entrées, $16.95 to $25.95. Lunch daily, 11:30 to 5. Dinner, 5 to 10 or 11. Closed January-March.

Jackson's at the Flagship, 463 Commercial St.

Like the highly acclaimed restaurant Chester on the other side of the street, this newcomer in the old Flagship restaurant is named for the dog of one of its founding partners. Windows on three sides yield views of the water, framing a dark and nautical interior of booths and tables. The weathered but stylish East End space is popular for its original dory bar and fireplace, as well as its international fare. The short menu might begin with shrimp and cabbage dumplings, Thai-inspired mussels and sesame-crusted tuna sashimi. Main courses are as varied as a classic bouillabaisse and a "killer" meatloaf. Typical are tropical grilled halibut, crispy seared salmon with a jalapeño-peanut sauce, osso buco and peppercorn-coated sirloin steak with a roasted garlic demi-glace.

(508) 487-2813. www.jacksonsflagship.com. Entrées, $16.95 to $29.95. Dinner nightly, from 6. Closed mid-November to April.

Ross' Grill, 237 Commercial St.

Some of the most interesting food in town is served at this urbane and hip café and raw bar. The place is right above the beach, on the second level at the far end of a shopping arcade called Whaler's Wharf. The pity is it's so small and, for the not so hip, rather uncomfortable. Beneath a high jet-black ceiling stand eight bleached-pine tables, half of them of the high bar variety flanked by bar-stool perches. Thirteen more seats for dining line the central bar. From a tiny open kitchen beside the entry, chef-owner Ken Ross prepares the likes of crispy Tuscan cod, shellfish risotto, crab cakes with spicy rémoulade sauce, steak frites, and rack of New Zealand lamb. Start with his escargots in puff pastry, chicken liver and pistachio pâté or even a basket of hand-cut french fries. Finish with a dessert from the pastry case beside the door. Cobb salad and oyster po-boys star on the lunch menu.

(508) 487-8878. Entrées, $16 to $30. Lunch, Wednesday-Monday 11:30 to 4. Dinner, Wednesday-Monday 5:30 to 9:30. Closed in February.

Fanizzi's By the Sea, 539 Commercial St.

The tired old Pucci's Harborside restaurant gave way to this worthy successor, highly recommended by East End hoteliers for good Italian-American food, value and friendly service. The old waterfront deck is long gone, in favor of a renovated and enclosed sun-porch affair with windows on three and one-half sides. Owner Paul Fanizzi's repertoire is enormous – indeed, the day's specials list is longer than many a restaurant's regular menu. But the kitchen's reach does not exceed its grasp, as attested by a recent lunch: an oversize crab cake sandwich and the specialty burger marinated in ale and herbs and served with cheddar and bacon on an English muffin. Each was accompanied by a slew of french fries and a zesty coleslaw. The portions rendered desserts redundant and the prices were easy on the pocketbook. At night, you can choose among appetizers (from nachos to a Mediterranean platter), burgers, sandwiches and entrées ranging from fish and chips and roasted garlic chicken to mustard nut-crusted cod, veal dishes and grilled ribeye steak.

(508) 487-1964. www.fanizzisrestaurant.com. Entrées, $13.95 to $20.95. Lunch daily, 11 to 4. Dinner nightly, from 4. Sunday brunch, 10 to 2.

Pepe's Wharf, 371 Commercial St.

Nils (Pepe) Berg, arguably the town's most celebrated chef, left his acclaimed Dancing Lobster Café/Trattoria in 2004. The family-owned restaurant was in transition, reverting to its original name, Pepe's Wharf (named for him), and being run by his sister Astrid. The reborn Pepe's retained the grand waterfront setting – an elegant, white-linened dining room with windows all around on the main floor, plus an open upstairs deck for lunch and bar food overhead. The new theme: "pasta and pizza with pizzazz." Seven varieties of Napolitan or "ultra-thin-crust" pizzas were featured in the highest-style pizza setting around. Otherwise, the dinner menu when we were there was limited to appetizers, salads and pastas, from spaghetti with "homemade pork meatballs" to fettuccine with grilled tuna. The only exception was New England cioppino, served in a homemade sourdough bread bowl.

(508) 487-4995. Entrées, $14 to $25. Lunch daily, 11:30 to 3. Dinner nightly, from 6. Closed Monday-Wednesday in off-season.

Devon's, 401½ Commercial St.

This succeeded the Little Fluke Café, a tiny place with a neat name that offered some neat food, too. When his co-owner left, Devon Ruesch partnered with chef Bari Hassman to reopen in 2004 with a new name and a reprise of innovative breakfasts and dinners. An open kitchen takes up much of the intimate dining area, which has a rear-view glimpse of the water. About half the three dozen seats are on a canopied sidewalk café facing the street. Bari executes a short menu featuring peasant bouillabaisse ladled over french bread and rouille, grilled wild Pacific salmon with saffron-mussel sauce and skillet-seared moulard duck breast with red wine sauce. A favorite starter is crab cakes with a spicy avocado sauce. Strawberry and mascarpone trifle with riesling syrup is a good dessert. Eggs benedict and Portuguese sweet bread french toast are among breakfast standbys.

(508) 487-4773. www.devons.org. Entrées, $20 to $28. Breakfast daily except Wednesday, 8 to 1. Dinner, Friday-Sunday from 6.

Eclectic to Go by the Sea

Clem & Ursie's Seaside Lobsters, 205 Commercial St.

Hidden at the end of the Aquarium Mall shopping arcade is this new offshoot of the popular Clem & Ursie's Restaurant & Market, an expanding venture that overlooks a commercial parking lot at 85 Shank Painter Road. Here is an unpretentious little takeout stand, dispensing many of the Silva family favorites – lobsters, chowders, pot pies and casseroles, barbecued ribs, sandwiches, grilled seafood, "daily Jamaican specialties" and who knows what all? It's all to go, obviously, and there's no more eclectic waterfront place for the partaking than the picnic tables beside a funky seaside garden and a raised deck right beside the water. The sea clam pie and "Southern iced tea" really hit the spot.

(508) 487-6722. www.clemandursies.com. Entrées, $7 to $21. Open daily in season.

FOR MORE INFORMATION: Provincetown Chamber of Commerce, 307 Commercial St., Box 1017, Provincetown, MA 02657, (508) 487-3424. www.ptownchamber.com.

Boston skyline shimmers in water in front of rotunda at Boston Harbor Hotel.

Boston, Mass.

Big-City Style, Old and New

For New Englanders, Boston is "The Hub" – the hub of New England, if not of the country, the world, the universe.

It's been that way since the Puritans settled the Massachusetts Bay Colony in 1630. More than any other city, Boston is where the nation's history began, 150 years before the republic was established. It is Boston that helps define New England's sense of place.

Boston has long been a big city, but one that is traditional and proper, in an old Puritan/Brahmin sense. In the last generation it has added style, becoming cosmopolitan like San Francisco, the West Coast counterpart with which it often is compared.

For most Boston visitors, the focus is around the downtown area, which grew up beside the harbor where the early settlers landed. The Boston of the history books lies along the waterfront, around the Boston Common and the Public Garden, up sedate Beacon Hill and into the fancy section known as Back Bay.

The other Boston – the Boston metro where most of the three million people live – spreads outward through city neighborhoods and suburbs in a fan-like swirl to the South Shore, points west and the North Shore.

Boston is a place apart with a sense of place: Boston beans, Boston scrod, even a Boston accent. It surely is the hub of all that is New England, and as such a great place for a getaway.

It's also a place for romance. A getaway destination for the arts and culture enthusiast, for the history and architecture buff, and for the gourmet. Anybody can find the tourist's Boston. Here the emphasis is on Boston style and culture, the Boston of Bostonians, proper and otherwise.

Seeing and Doing

For the Culture Enthusiast

Museums are a big attraction in Boston. Four not to miss:

Museum of Fine Arts, Boston, 465 Huntington Ave.

This monumental art museum, among the best in the world and undergoing a major expansion in 2005, contains nearly 200 galleries. It has the largest collection of Monet paintings outside Paris, extensive Egyptian art rivaled only by the collection in the Cairo Museum, and some of the world's most prized holdings of ancient Greek and Roman art. Its collection of oriental art is considered the finest under one roof in the world. The MFA's American art collection – which museum director Malcolm Rogers calls "arguably the finest" in the world – includes folk art, early silver and furniture, and more than 60 works by painter John Singleton Copley. Many of the museum's finest masterpieces by Copley, Gilbert Stuart and John Singer Sargent were given by descendents of the original owners or those in the portraits. The modern West Wing designed in 1981 by architect I.M. Pei shows contemporary art and special exhibitions. The new East Wing will house the internationally recognized Art of Americas collection and increase its gallery space by 50 percent. The MFA also is doubling the West Wing space devoted to late 20th-century and contemporary art and is enclosing the East Courtyard in a showy glass and steel "jewel box." Because the museum's encyclopedic collection of 400,000 permanent objects is so extensive that it cannot be comprehended in a single day, the museum has changed its admission policy to allow ticket purchasers a second visit within ten days. For instance, one day they can investigate the celebrated Japanese collection or the musical instruments collection, and a few days later they can return to view the 43 Monets and other French Impressionist artworks. In summer, the MFA presents an evening Concerts in the Courtyard series and opens the shaded terrace of its Bravo restaurant for al fresco dining overlooking the elegant Calderwood Courtyard, one of the most beautiful spots in Boston.

(671) 267-9300. www.mfa.org. Open daily, Monday and Tuesday 10 to 4:45, Wednesday-Friday 10 to 9:45, Saturday and Sunday 10 to 5:45. Adults $15, children $6.50.

John F. Kennedy Library and Museum, Columbia Point.

This emotionally moving museum, a starkly contemporary building designed by architect I.M. Pei on a park-like setting along the waterfront south of downtown next to the Boston campus of the University of Massachusetts, is the nation's official memorial to Boston's native son, the 35th president. Twenty-one multi-media exhibits and period settings draw on rare film and television footage, presidential documents, family keepsakes and White House treasures to recreate the world of the Kennedy presidency. Visitors watch a stirring seventeen-minute introductory movie produced for the library and then view excerpts from his televised press conferences, listen to his mother's recorded recollections of his early life and perhaps watch a film on the life of his brother Robert. The fascinating Cuban Missile Crisis exhibit includes a twenty-minute movie. Exhibits on personal and family interests capture the style not only of his presidency but also of the Kennedy years. Only the cynical fail to be inspired by his vision – portrayed well by the museum – that one person can make a difference and everyone should try.

(617) 929-4500 or (866) 535-1960. www.jfklibrary.org. Open daily, 9 to 5. Adults $8, children over 12, $4.

Art and Garden Spectacle

Isabella Stewart Gardner Museum, 280 The Fenway.

This replica of a 15th-century Venetian palace in the middle of Boston is a museum displaying the collections of Isabella Stewart, a New Yorker who married John Lowell Gardner of Boston but was never fully accepted into Boston society. For the opening of her palace on New Year's Day in 1903 she invited guests to listen to the music of Bach and Mozart, gaze at her indoor courtyard full of flowers and view one of the nation's best private art collections. Since her death in 1924, the museum has remained essentially unchanged. The building itself holds a remarkable hodgepodge of architectural details and furnishings that Mrs. Gardner purchased outright from great European palaces and churches. Three floors of galleries surround a skylit garden courtyard blooming year-round with flowers grown in the museum's greenhouses and changed every two months. The galleries are filled with paintings, sculptures, tapestries, furniture, ceramics, rare books, jewelry and decorative arts from cultures spanning 30 centuries. The Italian Renaissance is best represented, but paintings by artists as diverse as Botticelli, Rembrandt, Velázquez, Matisse, Degas and her friends James McNeil Whistler and John Singer Sargent harmonize with Venetian chairs, wrought-iron railings, medieval processional crosses and Japanese screens in this spectacular museum. It's an intimate treasure of more than 2,500 pieces, arranged as Mrs. Gardner prescribed in her will. The museum's own Gardner Chamber Orchestra and guest musicians present Sunday afternoon concerts from September to May in the stunning Tapestry Room in the longest-running museum music series in the country. An intimate café overlooks the garden, and diners spill outside in season.

(617) 566-1401. www.gardnermuseum.org. Open Tuesday-Sunday 11 to 5. Guided tours, Monday-Friday at 2:30. Adults, $10 weekdays, $11 weekends.

Institute of Contemporary Art, 955 Boylston St.

For nearly 70 years, the Institute of Contemporary Art has been introducing visitors to some of the most important contemporary artists of our time, from Pablo Picasso and Robert Rauschenberg to Andy Warhol and Cindy Sherman. Situated rather creatively in a 19th-century brownstone police station in Back Bay, it is the first non-collecting contemporary art museum in the country. It mounts rotating exhibits of art from the 20th and 21st centuries, featuring cutting-edge painting, photography, sculpture, video and performance art. The ICA was building a stunning new museum on Fan Pier along the downtown Boston waterfront. Upon opening in 2006, the cantilevered landmark will triple its current exhibit space and add a performing arts theater with glass walls facing the harbor, a gift shop and a restaurant.

(617) 266-5152. www.icaboston.org. Open Tuesday-Friday noon to 5, Thursday to 9, Saturday-Sunday 11 to 5. Adults $7, children under 12 free.

Historic **Symphony Hall,** 301 Massachusetts Ave., is home to the **Boston Symphony Orchestra** and its Boston Pops Orchestra. Now led by music director James Levine of the Metropolitan Opera, the BSO presents more than 250 concerts a year, generally here from October through April and during the summer at Tanglewood in the Berkshires. Tickets for regular-season BSO concerts on Tuesday and Thursday evenings and Friday and Sunday afternoons are priced from $27 to $95; concerts on Friday and Saturday evenings are $29 to $105. A limited number of rush tickets for subscription concerts on Tuesday and Thursday evenings and Friday afternoons are sold on the day of the performance for $8 each, one to a customer, at the box office. Open rehearsal tickets on Wednesday evenings and Thursday mornings are $16 each (general admission). Tickets may be purchased by phone at (617) 266-1200 or (888) 266-1200, in person at the Symphony Hall box office, or online at www.bso.org.

The legendary **Boston Pops,** "America's Orchestra" under the baton of Keith Lockhart, offers Evenings at Pops and the Holiday Pops series at Symphony Hall plus summer pops concerts on the Charles River Esplanade. Tickets are generally $23 to $107.

Not far from Symphony Hall are two major music schools that offer frequent concerts, the **New England Conservatory of Music** and the **Berklee College of Music.**

Boston's **Theater District** has been rejuvenated lately. The Opera House at 539 Washington St., a dramatic Beaux-Arts palace with touches of the Baroque, has been restored. It reopened in 2004 with a touring production of "The Lion King." The restored, 3,600-seat Wang Theater at the Wang Center for the Performing Arts hosts Broadway, theater, music, ballet, opera and film productions. Others are staged at the more intimate 1,600-seat Schubert Theater, the ornate Colonial Theater and Emerson College's Majestic Theater. In summer, the nearby Boston Common makes a fine open-air theater for Shakespearean plays performed by the Commonwealth Shakespeare Company in collaboration with the Wang Center.

For the History Buff

American history as we know it began in Boston with its settlement in 1630, not long after the Pilgrims landed at Plymouth Rock. Much of the city is a living-history museum, but especially the downtown/waterfront area, Beacon Hill and Back Bay.

The famed Freedom Trail connects most of the Boston National Historical Park sites of the American Revolution. Park rangers guide periodic 90-minute walking tours from the park's Visitor Center at 15 State St., (617) 242-5642. They cover the heart of the Freedom Trail from the Old South Meeting House to Old North Church.

The Freedom Trail. More than 1.5 million people walk the 2.5-mile Freedom Trail every year, some rather amazed to find so much of the Revolutionary past embedded in a modern urban environment. The trail passes sixteen of the city's most significant historic sites. Begin the walk at the information kiosk on Boston Common and follow the red brick stripe on the streets and sidewalks around downtown and the Financial District, through the North End and across the Charles River to the Bunker Hill Monument in Charlestown. Admission to sites along the trail is free except for the Paul Revere House, the Old South Meeting House and the Old State House.

Boston Common, established by Puritan settlers in 1634 as common grazing land for cattle, is America's first park – 44 acres of open space in the center of the city. Its very centrality makes it more of a presence and more widely traversed than New York's Central Park. Facing the common is the gold-domed "new" **State House,** opened in 1798 and still the seat of Massachusetts state government. It is the oldest building on Beacon Hill. Next to the 1809 **Park Street Church** is the **Granary Burying Ground,** final resting place of many a patriot. The interior of the 1754 pillared-Georgian **King's Chapel** is considered the finest example of Georgian church architecture in North America. It served the first Anglican congregation in Boston until the Revolution, when the Loyalists in the congregation retreated to England or the Canadian Maritimes. Those who stayed formed the first Unitarian congregation in America in 1787. The chapel burying ground contains the gravestone that inspired Nathaniel Hawthorne to write *The Scarlet Letter.* The trail continues past the site of the 1635 **Boston Latin School,** the oldest public school in America, and on to the 1729 **Old South Meeting House,** the largest building in Colonial Boston. Here, 5,000 angry colonists protested the tea tax and started the Revolution with the Boston Tea Party. A ring of cobblestones in the traffic island facing Filene's department store marks the site of the Boston Massacre. The **Old State House,** which served as the seat of colonial and state governments from 1713 to 1798, is now a museum of Boston history. It faces **Faneuil Hall** and Quincy Market, around which a modern marketplace emerged. Cross over the new Big Dig tunnel to the North End, Boston's oldest residential neighborhood. Here is the **Paul Revere House** (1680), the oldest building in downtown Boston. The patriot left here on his famous midnight ride in April 1775 after the sexton of nearby **Old North Church** (1723) hung two lanterns in the steeple to warn – "one if by land, two if by sea" – of the advance of British soldiers up the Charles River. Continue across the Charlestown Bridge to the **Bunker Hill Monument,** which commemorates the Revolution's first major battle, and the **USS Constitution** ("Old Ironsides"), the oldest commissioned warship in the world (1797), berthed at the Charlestown Navy Yard.

Historic houses of lesser renown include **the Nichols House Museum,** the **Harrison Gray Otis House** and the **Gibson House Museum.** All are open to the public for tours and reflect how proper Bostonians lived. They are situated north of Boston Common on **Beacon Hill,** where the Lowells spoke only to Cabots and the Cabots spoke only to God. Here is hilly Mount Vernon, the most proper of Boston streets. The charming brownstones around Louisburg Square were the 1840s model for townhouse development. At the western foot of Beacon Hill is Charles Street, where quaint antique shops and intimate restaurants hold forth.

West of the Common is **Back Bay**, which was built on a landfill over the Charles River in the 1800s when well-to-do Bostonians were running out of room in Beacon Hill. A walk along tree-lined Commonwealth Avenue, fashioned after the grand boulevards of Paris, is a study of residential architecture in Boston from the 18th to the 21st centuries. Newbury Street is a must-see destination for galleries and shopping (see below). Nearby Copley Square is a triangle of fine architecture: H.R. Richardson's Trinity Church, the Beaux Arts Copley Plaza Hotel and the McKim, Mead & White-designed Boston Public Library, the nation's oldest.

For the Shopper

Newbury Street in Back Bay is Boston's premier shopping destination. Along eight leafy blocks of Newbury west of the Common, former single-family Victorian brownstones have been converted into stores, restaurants and art galleries. Here are **Brooks Brothers, Ralph Lauren, Burberry, Armani, Versace, Kenneth Cole, Chanel, Simon Pearce** and **Louis,** Boston's own swanky clothing store.

Boylston Street, which parallels Newbury Street a short block to the south, is broader and a bit more plebian. You'll find **Lord & Taylor, Crate & Barrel, Talbots** and the local jeweler **Shreve, Crump & Low** along Boylston. At the west end are the reborn Shops at Prudential Center, a.k.a. "the city under glass," anchored by **Saks Fifth Avenue.** A block from the middle of this section of Boylston Street is tony Copley Place, home of **Neiman-Marcus, Tiffany & Co., Gucci** and **Louis Vuitton.**

A fifteen-minute walk up Boylston Street and across Boston Common takes you to Washington Street and the Downtown Crossing, Boston's tight and congested main shopping district. It's home to **Filene's**, its world-famous **Filene's Basement**, and **Macy's**, which took over the locally owned Jordan Marsh department store. Except for Filene's Basement, most of the stores here are of little visitor interest – for those, continue on via the Freedom Trail a few blocks to Faneuil Hall Marketplace, where tourists shop til they drop.

Gourmet's Digest

Parish Café, 361 Boylston St.

Between shopping forays, stop at this funky establishment for sandwiches created by some of the area's best-known chefs. Given their pedigrees, most of the sandwiches are first-rate. We liked the Lydia – lobster salad with lemon, parsley, celery leaves and balsamic mayo on Lydia Shire's peppercorn brioche. There's an impressive list of wines and ales to go with, as well as martinis created by local bartenders to precede. The prominent bar plays a major role, and a rear mural portraying laid-back diners on an outdoor patio sets the theme. The large terrace on the broad Boylston Street sidewalk is pleasant on a nice day.

(617) 247-4777. www.parishcafe.com. Entrées, $8.95 to $12.25. Open daily, 11:30 to 1 a.m., Sunday from noon.

Where to Stay

Boston accommodations are known for elegance and style. True to the proper Bostonian type, most are swanky, polished and reserved. Prices quoted are rack rates for peak periods.

Four Seasons Hotel, 200 Boylston St., Boston 02116.

Boston has no more posh, elegant hotel than this, although the Ritz-Carlton might beg to differ. Serene and grand, the top-of-the-line luxury hotel has 272 guest rooms and suites reflecting the understated style of a traditional Beacon Hill home. They have oversize beds, Henredon cherry furniture, plush fabrics, writing tables, TV in an armoire, two or three telephones, hair dryers, terrycloth robes and such, plus bay windows that open – a rare blessing for those who cherish fresh air. The 64 mini-suites add alcove seating areas. The most desirable rooms overlook the Boston Public Garden. In the hotel's luxurious eighth-floor health spa, Caribbean-style patio furniture surrounds the swimming pool and whirlpool, from which you can look out over the Public Garden and, at night, the lights of Boston. "Very romantic while relaxing in the jacuzzi," our host advised. Public rooms are quietly decorated with antiques and fine art. A five-foot crystal chandelier lights the grand stairway to the elegant, second-floor **Aujourd'hui** restaurant, one of the city's best (see Where to Eat). The airy, main-floor **Bristol Lounge** serves three meals a day, plus afternoon tea by the fireplace and weekend Viennese dessert buffets that are some of the sweetest indulgences in the city.

(617) 338-4400 or (800) 332-3442. Fax (617) 423-0154. www.fourseasons.com/boston. One hundred ninety-seven rooms and 75 suites. Doubles, $425 to $818. Suites, $1,600 to $4,250.

The Ritz-Carlton Boston, 15 Arlington St., Boston 02117.

The oldest Ritz in the United States is not just a hotel. It's an institution – *the* place where proper Bostonians put up visitors or go themselves for lunch in **The Café,** tea in **The Lounge**, or drinks and dinner in **The Bar** and **The Dining Room.** A top-to-bottom renovation in 2002 upgraded the grande-dame Ritz but retained the cachet that keeps it Boston's bastion of elegance. The elevator operators wear white gloves – yes, there still are elevator operators, to say nothing of white gloves – as they take guests up to the 275 rooms, perhaps to one of the 42 wood-burning fireplaced suites billed for romance. Romance and the Ritz are legendary: Rodgers and Hammerstein wrote many of their musical favorites here, and in the 1930s and '40s, more romantic Broadway musicals were worked on at the Ritz than at any other location in the country. Beds with feather duvets, French provincial furnishings, imported fabrics, distinctive artworks, windows that open onto a view of the Public Garden and all the amenities of a four-diamond hotel are here, even if some think they'd seen better days. The "some" included the Millennium Partners of New York, who bought the Ritz and undertook all the renovations after opening a new Ritz across the Boston Common (see below) along Tremont Street. Now there are two Ritzes, one classic and one contemporary. Cesar Ritz would be proud.

(617) 536-5700 or (800) 241-3333. Fax (617) 536-1335. Two hundred twenty-nine rooms and 44 suites. Doubles, $350 to $595. Suites, $595 to $5,000.

The Ritz-Carlton Boston Common, 10 Avery St., Boston 02111.

The slick, new Ritz that opened as part of the $500 million Millennium Place development takes the elegance of its namesake on the west side of the Public Garden and Common and gives it a contemporary twist, one that sets a benchmark for urban hotel luxury in the 21st century. And that benchmark certainly is un-Ritzlike. Traditionalists find the essence of ritz missing from the modernist gray hotel beneath a pair of crystalline towers along the east side of the common. The rooms are larger, the furnishings strikingly contemporary and the atmosphere "charged with congenial energy," according to the hotel literature. Some of the energy resides, no doubt, in the adjacent Sports Club/LA, where guests have complimentary access to the ultimate in fitness, athletic and spa options, and the nineteen-screen Loews Cineplex theaters, the largest in Boston. Public spaces are at street level, while guest rooms occupy the top four floors of the twelve-story building. Rooms are notable for kingsize or two double feather beds outfitted with Frette linens and feather duvets, large marble baths with separate showers, modern furnishings and state-of-the-art technology for the wired traveler. Teak is everywhere – in the rooms, on the doors, in the corridors and lobby, and in the hotel's dot-com styled restaurant, **Jer·ne,** pronounced journey. The lounge in the sleek, mod lobby offers afternoon tea presented tableside in the Ritz tradition. Breakfast selections include a "juice flight," an eye-opening display of five shot glasses holding fruit and vegetable juices, plus a bircher muesli cocktail and hot oatmeal with banana brûlée. Thus comes the new, high-energy Ritz style for the next generation.

(617) 574-7100 or (800) 241-3333. Fax (617) 574-7100. One hundred forty-nine rooms and 44 suites. Doubles, $495 to $595. Suites, $695 to $4,000.

Boston Harbor Hotel, 70 Rowes Wharf, Boston 02110.

A more sumptuous hotel could scarcely be imagined. Its dramatic waterside entrance is an 80-foot archway topped by a rotunda. The lobby floors are marble, the sides of the elevators are brocade, and the walls of the public spaces are hung with museum-quality fine art and antique nautical prints. Redwood furniture surrounds the 60-foot lap pool. A large lounge at the rear of the main floor has huge sofas in plums, golds and teals for relaxing as you enjoy live piano music and absorb the view of boats and airplanes around the harbor. Veteran chef Daniel Bruce's novel, wine-centric **Meritage** restaurant takes advantage of its waterfront setting, as does the more casual **Intrigue Café;** both are at the cutting edge. Luxury extends to the 230 rooms and suites on the top eight floors of a sixteen-story brick building, which looks out onto the harbor or the city skyline. Our oversize room had a kingsize bed dressed in a down comforter and 300-count sheets, a sofa and an upholstered chair with good reading lamps in a sitting area, a new custom-made work desk, lovely reproduction antiques and an enormous marble bathroom full of amenities. Breakfronts concealed the TV and a minibar. Some suites have private terraces with great harbor views. Guests enjoy the hotel's health club and spa, which besides a 60-foot lap pool has steam rooms and saunas, a hydrotherapy tub, massage treatments and an exercise room with the most up-to-date equipment available.

(617) 439-7000 or (800) 752-7077. Fax (617) 330-9450. www.bhh.com. Two hundred four rooms and 26 suites. Doubles, $375 to $565. Suites, $585 to $2,000.

Fifteen Beacon, 15 Beacon St., Boston 02108.

The intimate, dark wood lobby looks a bit like a library and the original glass-enclosed birdcage elevators seem incongruous in this newish, 61-room high-tech boutique hotel (you can see the cables rising and falling before you board and then glimpse each floor as you ascend). They reflect the historic, residential look sought by developer Paul Roiff, who transformed a ten-story Beaux Arts office building into a playground and workstation for the rich and trendy. Decorated in elegant modernist style, rooms and suites blend state-of-the-art conveniences with the intimacy of a private residence, though few residences are so overwhelmingly decked out in chocolate brown. They are stylish and decidedly masculine in shades of espresso, taupe and cream with built-in solid mahogany wall units, plump club chairs and chaise lounges, oversize writing desks and gleaming white bathroom fixtures, including a few jetted tubs and glass enclosures with plate-size overhead showers. About the only "color" is provided by fresh flowers and a bowl of tangerines or the shiny red apples in glass vases in each entry; the fruits are changed every other day to keep them edible. The four-poster queensize beds (some draped in dark canopies) are dressed in Italian 300-thread-count linens. A bedside keypad activates the TV, a surround-sound stereo system and a gas fireplace enclosed in a shimmering stainless-steel chimney surround. Most getaway-goers will ignore the room's business center with three phones, a combination fax and color printer, and direct Internet access. Instead they'll appreciate the four-inch LCD TV and heated towel racks in the bathrooms (outfitted with luxury Pevonia toiletries), imported Italian fabric robes, and in-room bars stocked with the finest liquors and half bottles of Chateau Lafite Rothschild, Opus One and Krug champagne. The hotel's eleventh floor contains a fitness room opening onto a pair of rooftop sundecks with a whirlpool tub and an outdoor bar. The main-floor **Federalist** restaurant serves three meals a day and claims Boston's finest wine cellar.

(617) 670-1500 or (877) 982-3226. www.xvbeacon.com. Fifty-seven rooms and three suites. Doubles, $495 to $650. Suites, $1,400 to 2,100.

The Fairmont Copley Plaza, 138 St. James St., Boston 02116.

Once the grande dame of Boston hotels, this was saved lately by the Fairmont chain, which poured $34 million into restoring it to its former grandeur. Built in 1912, the six-story Renaissance-revival building was designed by the architect for New York's Plaza Hotel and sports colorful red awnings and canopies around the ground floor. It faces Copley Square, with Trinity Church and the Boston Public Library on either side. Inside, the high gilded ceilings, mosaic floors and crystal chandeliers recall the days when the Copley Plaza hosted the city's debutante balls. The spacious rooms, with traditional furnishings and a residential feeling, reflect the elegance of the opulent public spaces but now come with luxury pillow-top mattresses, marble baths with granite counters, data ports and other au courant conveniences. The concierge floor includes a lounge designed to resemble a Back Bay mansion. There's a full gym. The **Oak Bar** and the **Oak Room** (named after their counterparts in New York's Plaza) are elegant, blue-blood places to enjoy a dry martini, shellfish from a raw bar and a good steak.

(617) 267-5300 or (888) 884-6060. Fax (617) 375-9648. www.fairmont.com/copleyplaza. Three hundred sixty-six rooms and seventeen suites. Doubles, $319 to $528. Suites, $849 to $2,500.

Nine Zero, 90 Tremont St., Boston 02108.

Confidently named for its address (or at least a portion thereof), this ultra-modern boutique hotel was built from the ground up in 2002 to provide 190 guest accommodations and a stylish restaurant called **Spire** (for its view of the Park Street Church spire outside). The nineteen-story hotel has roughly twelve spacious rooms on each floor with king or queensize beds (some have two queens). Frette linens and goose down comforters, striped in yellow and black, dress the beds, which are distinctive for their tall leather headboards whose curves resemble those of the two upholstered reddish wing chairs in front of windows that open. Next to an oversize work desk is what the staff dubbed "a tower of power." It's a black cylindrical entertainment center and refreshment area with rotating TV, video collection, coffeemaker with the local Karma coffee and such. Marble vanities and tubs enhance the baths, some with whirlpools, although smaller queensize rooms have glass showers in lieu of tubs. The entire top floor is given over to the Cloud Nine Suite, which claims a panoramic view of Boston.

(617) 772-5800 or (866) 646-3937. Fax (617) 772-5810. www.ninezero.com. One hundred eighty-five rooms and five suites. Doubles, $249 to $400. Suites, $600 to $3,000.

Hotel Commonwealth, 500 Commonwealth Ave., Boston 02215.

This five-story newcomer in the rejuvenated Kenmore Square area has 150 boutique hotel-style guest rooms above a retail complex, celebrity restaurant and the T-station, with a direct link to the subway below. Within grand-slam distance of Fenway Park, it quickly became popular with Boston Red Sox fans and the media types who cover them. It also is convenient for museum-goers, orchestra-goers and visitors to nearby Boston University, which partnered in building it in 2003. The elegant lobby with its dark wood furnishings, brocades and divans covered with tapestries and fringes is designed to make visitors feel as if they've stepped into a stately Back Bay residence. Guest rooms on the four floors above balance European charm with contemporary convenience, from pillow-top king or queen beds dressed with Frette linens and down comforters to marble bathrooms with L'Occitane toiletries. DVD TVs are standard. Off the lobby is **Great Bay,** a bold new seafood eatery named Esquire magazine's best new restaurant of 2003, ostensibly because of its owners, earlier award-winners Christopher Myers and Michael Schlow.

(617) 933-5000 or (866) 784-4000. Fax (617) 266-6888. www.hotelcommonwealth.com. One hundred fifty rooms. Doubles, $249 to $409.

The Lenox Hotel, 61 Exeter St., Boston 02116.

Built in 1900 as Boston's answer to the Waldorf-Astoria, this totally renovated, family-owned hotel in the heart of Back Bay is on the rise after a period of being overshadowed by the large chain hotels. High ceilings, glittering brass chandeliers, crystal lamps, armoires, marble baths, walk-in closets, windows that open and bedtime candies with nightly turndown service imbue the hotel with a charm that earned it a surprising place in Norman Simpson's old *Country Inns and Back Roads* guide. A top-to-bottom renovation, which elevated the hotel to AAA four-diamond status, shows off the 212 rooms to best advantage. The corner room in which we stayed was large and unusually quiet, and contained one of the hotel's fourteen wood-burning fireplaces. Most rooms are furnished in Drexel Colonial reproduction style, although some are done in French provincial. Rated the "best place for a romantic tryst," the hotel lures with package rates and good values. The **Azure** restaurant here ranks among the city's best.

(617) 536-5300 or (800) 225-7676. Fax (617) 267-1237. www.lenoxhotel.com. One hundred ninety-six rooms and sixteen suites. Doubles, $308. Suites, $408 to $695.

Stay in a Beacon Hill Brownstone

The Charles Street Inn, 94 Charles St., Boston 021114.

A four-story brownstone, built in 1860 as a model home to showcase Second Empire Victorian architectural styles for potential Back Bay homeowners, serves well for 21st-century visitors seeking the ultimate in residential luxury. Innkeepers Sally Deane and Louise Venden reconfigured rooms, installed deluxe spa-quality bathrooms and added an elevator to cosset guests in nine sumptuous rooms named and themed for famous Beacon Hill residents of the period. The five largest rooms with kingsize beds (one with two doubles) overlook Mount Vernon Square Park at the back of the house. Four queensize rooms in front face gas-lit Charles Street. Furnished to the Victorian hilt in fine antiques and creature comforts, each has a working marble fireplace, TV/VCR hidden in an armoire, Bose radio, Frette linens, Turkish rugs, mini-refrigerator and a lavish bath with air-jet whirlpool spa tub. Romantic reds envelop the Italian armoire, fainting couch and brass rococo chandelier in the Isabella Stewart Gardner Room in a style its namesake would have enjoyed. Antique landscape etchings and lithographs embellish the dark and masculine Frederick Law Olmsted Room. A deluxe continental breakfast is delivered to the room .

(617) 314-8900 or (877) 772-8900. Fax (617) 371-0009. www.charlesstreetinn.com. Nine rooms with private baths. Doubles, $225 to $425.

The Eliot Hotel, 370 Commonwealth Ave., Boston 02215.

Billed as one of Boston's more romantic hotels, this Back Bay relic is at a busy corner of fashionable Commonwealth Avenue, here a tight and leafy boulevard patterned after the Champs Elysée in Paris and flanked by elegant 19th-century brownstone townhouses. The neo-Georgian structure was planned by Harvard University president Charles Eliot as a residential hotel for retiring academics seeking proximity to the Harvard Club next door. Unlike hotels that have enormous public areas, the Eliot puts the emphasis on privacy and comfort. An aura of step-back-in-time luxury prevails, from the split-level marble lobby with its enormous chandelier to the pastel-hued rooms, all with king, queen or two double beds, Italian marble bath, two TVs and a CD player. The majority are one- or two-bedroom suites, some in need of updating. Part of the main floor is given over to **Clio** (see Where to Eat), one of the best restaurants in the city. The lounge includes **Uni,** a new sashimi bar.

(617) 267-1607 or (800) 443-5468. Fax (617) 536-9114. www.eliothotel.com. Sixteen rooms and 79 suites. Doubles, $255 to $415.

Where to Eat

Boston offers a roster of "hot," high-profile restaurants, whose members come and go. While they receive a lot of the media buzz, others of earlier consequence continue to appeal.

The Best of the Best

L'Espalier, 30 Gloucester St.

Ensconced upstairs in a grand Back Bay townhouse, L'Espalier raises the bar among Boston's great restaurants for contemporary French-New England cuisine, setting and style. Chef-owner Frank McClelland patrols the new-cuisine frontier, adding exotica like an unforgettable "cappuccino" of chanterelles and white truffles, a vegetarian broth with a foamy topping of essence of mushrooms and truffles steamed in the manner of cappuccino, enhanced with oysters baked with cider and cracked white-pepper glaze. His was the first mainstream restaurant in New England to offer a dégustation vegetarian menu, $75 for four remarkable courses plus dessert. The main menu is prix-fixe, $68 for three courses of multiple choices. Also available is an $85 dégustation menu chosen by the chef. We'll never forget ours that began with warm Wellfleet oysters in a champagne, leek and pumpkin nage with blinis, herb salad and caviar, followed by the "cappuccino" and an incredible dish of roasted foie gras with a savory prune, dried cherry and oatmeal crisp. Next came melt-in-the-mouth poached halibut with black truffles and crabmeat gratin, and roasted Vermont pheasant with foie gras croutons and côtes du rhône plum sauce. Desserts were a roasted banana soufflé with toasted coconut crème anglaise and "L'Espalier's study of pears." The latter was an artistic rendering of a pear stuffed with ice cream, a grilled pear and a puff-pastry tart called pithiviers. Service is friendly yet flawless in elegant, high-ceilinged rooms with marble fireplaces, carved moldings and spectacular flower arrangements in niches. Luxurious lacquered chairs flank well-spaced tables set with damask linens and flowers. The over-all dining experience is as close to culinary heaven as you're likely to find in New England.

(617) 262-3023. www.lespalier.com. Prix-fixe, $68. Dinner by reservation, Monday-Saturday 5:30 to 10.

Aujourd'hui, 200 Boylston St.

Dining at Aujourd'hui in the Four Seasons Hotel is like dining in a grand salon – although perhaps one more on a scale of a Vanderbilt mansion than a Beacon Hill brownstone. Try to book a window table for a view of the swan boats plying the pond in the Public Garden. A solicitous staff delivers modern French cuisine of the highest order. The chef's six-course tasting menu ($98) typifies the style. Ours opened with a parade of appetizers: caramelized diver scallops with calypso bean lobster ragoût, hamachi with spicy tuna tartare and oven-roasted beets, and an unforgettable, thick slice of seared foie gras with a duck confit spring roll and sour cherry compote. Fish courses were succulent baked arctic char with vegetable relish and seared ahi tuna with pickled eggplant, their multiple accompaniments creating bursts of flavors. One main course was perfectly roasted aged beef sirloin with peppercorn sauce, ragoût of chanterelles, a potato nest, leeks and pearl onions. The other was tender lamb noisettes with black olives, preserved lemon and Moroccan spices, haricots verts and baby garbanzo beans. A trio of cheeses paved the way for dessert. One was crème brûlée, fancifully decorated with spun sugar. The other was a platter of tea-scented panna cotta, lemon tart and warm chocolate cake with liquid milk chocolate truffle. A tray of "les mignardises" ended a meal that lingers in the memory as one of the best ever. The regular menu is enticing – how about poached lobster with fettuccine, truffles and sauternes? A number of selections designate reduced levels of calories, cholesterol, sodium and fat. A four-course vegetarian dinner is available for $52.

(617) 338-4400. Entrées, $32 to $46. Dinner nightly, 6 to 10. Sunday brunch, 10 to 2.

Radius, 8 High St.

A former bank at the edge of the Financial District houses this super-chic restaurant, the pace-setter in chef-owner Michael Schlow's little restaurant empire. The stark, minimalist interior of curves within curves is stylish in shades of charcoal gray and poppy red. Our long, leisurely lunch proved this to be a power-lunch destination. An appetizer of halibut tartare and fingerling potato tart with ossetra caviar and "three-minute egg sauce" was an exquisite blend of tastes and textures for a cool $16. Main courses, priced at similar levels, were a superior spice-crusted tender duck confit with tarbias bean cassoulet, carrots and red wine sauce, and a perfect loin of lamb salad with mesclun, goat cheese and baby beets. Dessert was lemon chamomile cake, served with blueberries, crème-fraîche ice cream and honey-thyme syrup. At night, serious diners join the beautiful people in partaking of an extravagant contemporary French repertoire, perhaps roasted black grouper with manila clams and saffron broth or Vermont pheasant suffused with foie gras. Or you can sample the chef's seven-course tasting menu for $105 each.

(617) 426-1234. www.radiusrestaurant.com. Entrées, $29 to $42. Lunch, Monday-Friday 11:30 to 2:30. Dinner, Monday-Saturday 5:30 to 10 or 11.

No. 9 Park, 9 Park St.

This stylish emporium occupies the ground floor of a Charles Bulfinch-designed Beacon Hill brownstone facing the Boston Common across from the gold-domed State House. It's relatively small, with a 30-seat café around the bar and two intimate dining rooms seating a total of 65. Chef-owner Barbara Lynch is known for robust yet refined country European fare. She delivered it at our autumn lunch, which began with an amusé, a demitasse cup of the day's chestnut bisque – delicate, studded with wild mushrooms and surprisingly good. One of us ordered the three-course, prix-fixe meal for $24. It yielded a perfect bibb salad, a plate of lamb ravioli with an ethereal white bean ragoût and a rich chocolate-hazelnut terrine with espresso anglaise. The other relished the chilled lobster salad – layers of lobster, mache, watercress and golden potato brunoise topped by tiny bits of red tomato that looked like caviar. After espresso, the bill came with a china box holding macaroons. The chef's signature dishes are available at night. Don't miss her crispy duck, served any number of ways but at our visit with a cider reduction, parsnips and a quince confit. Or sample her bacon-wrapped monkfish, hazelnut-crusted squab or a "duet" of beef sirloin and short rib. Dessert could be grapefruit soufflé or a lemon tasting: tarte au citron and hot and cold limoncello.

(617) 742-9991. www.no9park.com. Entrées, $29 to $43. Lunch, Monday-Friday 11:30 to 2:30. Dinner, Monday-Saturday 5:30 to 10.

Hamersley's Bistro, 553 Tremont St.

When proper Bostonians let their hair down, they're apt to do so in this, the first of the great restaurants that opened in Boston's chic South End. Gordon Hamersley and his wife Fiona, a wine connoisseur, run the fun and friendly place, a high-ceilinged, 120-seat space beside the Boston Center for the Arts, with outdoor dining on a brick patio in season. Chef Gordon and crew, bobbing around an open kitchen in Red Sox baseball caps rather than toques, show a refreshing lack of pretense as they prepare what he calls rustic, peasant food. We call it gutsy. Our dinner began with the signature grilled mushroom and garlic "sandwich" (two toasted bread slices flanking an abundance of mushrooms and watercress) and a tasty but messy whole braised artichoke stuffed with olives and mint. Among main courses, we savored a Moroccan lamb stew with couscous and the duckling with turnips, endive and apple slices – an enormous portion, including an entire leg and crisp slices grilled and blackened at the edges. The roast chicken with garlic, lemon and parsley is a menu fixture. Typical desserts are the signature souffléd lemon custard and a sticky date and toffee cake with toasted pecans and caramel. We remember fondly the trilogy of sorbets – brandied pear, green melon and concord grape – served with biscotti, a refreshing end to a terrific meal.

(617) 423-2700. www.hamersleysbistro.com. Entrées, $24 to $39. Dinner, Monday-Friday 6 to 10, Saturday 5:30 to 10:30, Sunday 5:30 to 9:30.

Excelsior, 272 Boylston St.

Higher and ever upward define the name for Boston culinary maven Lydia Shire's new shrine to haute dining. And that's what you get – both in experience and price – when you to ascend in an all-glass elevator past a wine tower holding 7,000 bottles to the romantic and urbane dining room overlooking the Boston Public Garden. Lydia teamed here with Grill 23 entrepreneur Tim Lynch to create the successor to Biba, her audacious predecessor in the space. Biba. Excelsior is men's club deluxe, tweaking "bold contemporary American cuisine" to the point where steakhouse meets cutting edge. Biba's smoky lobster pizza is back for a reprise, but now the premier attraction is a lusty char-grilled sirloin steak topped with a dollop of Berkshire blue cheese. You should still expect the unexpected: perhaps a wood oven-roasted shrimp cocktail with smoked bell pepper coulis or wild Pacific king salmon crusted with coriander and embellished with spinach-crabmeat pasta purses, wok-fried rainbow chard, curried autumn squash puree and a lime pickle. The sourdough chocolate cake with fromage blanc ice cream is a dessert masterpiece. A less expensive menu is offered in the downstairs bar.

(617) 426-7878. www.excelsior.com. Entrées, $29 to $44. Lunch, Monday-Friday 11 to 2:30. Dinner nightly, 5:30 to 10 or 11.

Clío, 370A Commonwealth Ave.

Skeptics might balk at the portions and prices, but for food-lovers, this is the hottest ticket in town. At night, the dining room in the upscaled Eliot Hotel turns into what chef-owner Kenneth Oringer likens to a Parisian supper club. Floor lamps convey the look of a living-room salon, serene in taupe and white. The former lounge is now **Uni,** a sashimi bar, where the chef works magic at the brown marble sushi counter with exotica he imports from the far corners of the world. Those not into the pricey tidbits can retreat to the dining room for Asian-accented French fare. Start with a taste of the sashimi of red shrimp with ossetra caviar, a foie gras sandwich or the cassoulet of lobster and sea urchins with yuzu and Japanese pepper. Main courses vary from caramelized swordfish au poivre to roasted muscovy duck with kumquats and chestnuts. Desserts are generally light and refreshing: frozen lemon verbena soufflé with hot chocolate mousse or mint mousse with chocolate coulant and macaroons.

(617) 536-7200. www.cliorestaurant.com. Entrées, $28 to $43. Dinner nightly, 5:30 to 10 or 10:30.

Mantra, 52 Temple Place.

Sophisticated French-Indian food fit for a sultan is served up in this sultry designer showplace. The vast Beaux-Arts interior of a former bank is a sight to behold: 30-foot-high marbleized walls, gray chain-metal "curtains" hanging as dividers, groupings of low-back upholstered chairs at well-spaced tables, and a long marble bar with a neon orange strip beneath the counter and a silvery, mirror-like wall behind. Executive chef Ernie Quinones's subtle food is Indian with a French accent. Fabulous naan bread comes with a cashew and cilantro chutney so addictive that some eat with their fingers and we attacked with a spoon. One of the more exotic starters you could ever crave is the ménage à foie: a torchon of foie gras with apple quince, pâté with black truffle and brioche toast, and seared foie gras with lobster, a morel and goat cheese dumpling and sour cherry sauce. Main courses include a succulent spice-crusted halibut sauced with ginger, clay-oven roasted monkfish and grilled lamb loin with saffron-coconut sauce. The killer dessert is the crème brûlée tasting of tropical fruits and coconut. After dinner, retire to the exotic "hookah den," a twenty-foot-high cone of polished sandalwood slats. You and up to nine of your dearest friends can spend an hour on the red banquette inside, smoking fruit-flavored tobacco in a water pipe.

(617) 542-8111. www.mantrarestaurant.com. Entrées, $28 to $38. Lunch, Monday-Saturday 11:30 to 2:30. Dinner, Monday-Saturday 5:30 to 10:30; bar menu to 1 a.m.

Icarus, 3 Appleton St.

A statue of the mythological Icarus, poised for flight, looms above tree branches lit with tiny white lights on the rear wall of this romantic restaurant where Bostonians celebrate their milestones in style. The statue oversees a sunken, split-level room full of rich dark wood and a mix of booths and round mission oak tables. The contemporary American menu, brief and blessedly unpretentious, yields fare that is the equal of any in the city. Chef-owner Chris Douglass offers such entrées as skate wing with lobster hash and pepper cress, seared duck breast and roasted leg with cider and bourbon, and farm-raised veal chop with black trumpet mushrooms and celery root. Start with the grilled shrimp with mango and jalapeño sorbet or the crab cake with lemon, cucumber and dill. Chocolate molten soufflé cake with vanilla bean ice cream and raspberry sauce is the signature dessert. A jazz pianist adds to the romance on Friday evenings.

(617) 426-1790. www.icarusrestaurant.com. Entrées, $26 to $33.50. Dinner, Monday-Friday 6 to 10, Saturday 5:30 to 10:30, Sunday 5:30 to 9:30.

┌─ *A Boston Institution Rejuvenated* ───────────

Locke-Ober Café, 3 Winter Place.

For a taste of Boston, many people will suggest Durgin-Park, Ye Olde Union Oyster House and Locke-Ober. The first two lack style but exude character, and are great fun. Locke's has character *and* style. Boston's grand dame of fine dining took on a new life when local chef Lydia Shire and managing partner Paul Licari acquired the male-based institution that dates to 1875. They polished the original walls and adorned them with tapestries, restored the gold flecking and removed seven layers of covering to expose the hand-cut marble floor around the room-length mirrored bar crafted of hand-carved mahogany. They abbreviated the extravagant continental menu to reasonable size, but retained longtime favorites such as the baked lobster savannah that one of us first tasted here as a teenager decades ago with her father. Other classics range from broiled boston scrod with hot crab and calves liver with bacon to dover sole meunière, tripe under a pastry dome, caramelized pheasant breast and confit, and steak au poivre. Don't expect cutting-edge fare here. Instead savor classics – perhaps embellished with updated touches – such as lobster and finnan haddie chowder or baked truffled egg cocotte, prepared to perfection. Traditional desserts like the warm Indian pudding, caramel pots de crème and baked alaska are without peer.

(617) 542-1340. www.locke-ober.com. Entrées, $26 to $52. Lunch, Monday-Friday 11:30 to 2:30. Dinner, Monday-Saturday 5:30 to 10 or 11.

Troquet, 140 Boylston St.

A funny thing happened to Troquet on the way from concept to reality. Planned as a wine bar, it turned into a French restaurant of note, so successfully that it lately expanded onto the second floor to better serve its dinner patrons. It now bills itself, quite rightly, as a food and wine boutique. The main-floor wine bar and lounge offers more than 40 wines by the glass, specialty cocktails and an exotic bar menu (think yellowfin tuna ceviche and English pea soup with peeky-toe crab and tarragon crème fraîche). Upstairs is a white-linened dining room overlooking Boston Common and the State House. Troquet was the brainchild of Chris Campbell, who had run a small wine café in Boston's Brighton neighborhood. He and wife Diane moved downtown to showcase wines in the heart of the Theater District. Troquet nicely fit the bill for the pre- and after-theater crowd and also found favor with foodies more interested in dinner than theater. The short menu mates food to wine, not vice-versa. The middle section of the menu lists fairly priced wines by two-ounce and four-ounce pours. On either side are matching appetizers and entrées. In the mood for assertive rieslings? Try the salmon tartare appetizer and the pan-seared wild striped bass for a main course. Feel more like cabernet? Go for the crispy duck confit with flageolet beans and black mission figs and the pan-roasted rib steak with glazed onions. Ports are recommended for the cheese plates, a choice of three or six, for those looking to keep the wine flowing. The owner personally shows the night's selections and he knows his fromage. The setting is sleek but stark in grays and blacks, with mirrors and French posters for decorative accents. Chocolate truffles and almond slices arrive with the bill.

(617) 695-9463. www.troquetboston.com. Entrées, $26 to $38; bar menu, $9 to $22. Dinner, Tuesday-Sunday 5 to midnight.

Pigalle, 75 Charles St.

The front awning bears the address "75, Rue Charles Sud" and the interior is dark and cozy in the image of an early 20th-century French jazz club, perhaps. This is the small and stylish French bistro run by chef Mark Orfaly and general manager Kerri Foley. The dominant motif of chocolate brown is leavened by a beige ceiling supported by thick pillars and white-clothed tables flanked by leather chairs or plush booths. The contemporary French menu is short and to the point. Its signature tuna martini isn't so much sipped as spooned, a cocktail with a kick of raw yellowfin tuna, seaweed salad and spicy crème fraîche. But don't overlook such appetizers as steak tartare with gaufrette potato chips and toasted brioche, a hazelnut-crusted goat cheese cake with frisée and bacon lardons, and a truffled cheese and braised leek tart with a petite herb salad. For main courses, how about spice-crusted black bass with harissa couscous, a cassoulet of braised lamb shank, slab bacon and duck confit, steak frites or a duet of sliced sirloin and oxtail-stuffed cabbage with madeira glaze? The fare is so rich and full of flavor that you may not have room for dessert. Succumb, however, to an apricot tart with basil ice cream, a selection of homemade sorbets or profiteroles with praline ice cream and bittersweet chocolate sauce.

(617) 423-4944. Entrées, $19 to $29. Dinner, Tuesday-Saturday from 5:30, Sunday from 5.

Torch, 26 Charles St.

After apprenticing in Paris and New York, chef Evan Deluty returned to his native Boston, where he and his wife Candice created a stylish French bistro at the foot of Beacon Hill. Shiny copper wainscoting, cranberry-colored walls and vivid velvet draperies lend a plush look to a setting of close-together tables dressed in white. Modern French fare with an Asian slant shows up in entrées ranging from pan-seared salmon with lemon grass and coconut nage to hanger steak with truffle vinaigrette. Balsamic-glazed native halibut served with mixed olive tapenade and fingerling potatoes illustrate the chef's style. Typical starters are salmon tartare with Japanese rice and wasabi vinaigrette, seared sea scallops with roasted beets and mache, and seared foie gras with green apples and juniper. The dessert list is short but sweet: perhaps Candice's chocolate mousse in a crispy tuile, mixed berry tart with bourbon vanilla bean ice cream, and assorted fruit sorbets.

(617) 723-5939. Entrées, $19 to $25. www.bostontorch.com. Dinner, Tuesday-Sunday 5:30 to 10:30.

Sage, 69 Prince St.

Boston's storied Italian North End – cheek-to-jowl restaurants encroaching on the home of Paul Revere – has undergone quite a transformation lately. An outbreak of cutting-edge restaurants is exemplified by this 30-seat charmer that defines the word intimate. From a closet-size kitchen young chef-owner Anthony Susi and his sous-chef dispense the North End's highest-rated cuisine. They'll stun you with such starters as salt cod brandade on saffron toast or grilled Vermont quail with chickpea blini and preserved fig marmalade. The light-as-a-feather, hand-rolled potato gnocchi in porcini cream and braised lamb ragu is one of the sensational pasta offerings. For main courses, you might find seared mahi mahi over braised white beans, cabbage and manila clams or braised rabbit leg and roasted loin with smoked tomato risotto. Given its size, Sage offers no desserts or coffees – the idea being to turn the tables since there are plenty of dessert and espresso bars in the area.

(617) 248-8814. Entrées, $20 to $29. Dinner, Monday-Saturday 5:30 to 10:30.

An Epic Labor of Love

Lala Rokh, 97 Mt. Vernon St.

Open the door to this townhouse in the heart of Beacon Hill and enter another world. Chef Azita Bina-Seibel and her brother Babak Bina offer the tastes and ambiance of their parents' native Azerbaijan in northwest Iran, recreating the home-style Persian cuisine they grew up with. They named it after the epic romance by 19th-century poet Thomas Moore about a young princess on a journey of love and discovery through the Near East. Just as the book epitomizes European fantasies about the East, so does their labor of love, the only eastern Mediterranean restaurant of its kind. The family's notable collection of early Persian memorabilia – framed photographs, antique maps and calligraphy dating to the ninth century – adorns the walls of two dining rooms cheery in mustard yellow and burgundy. It's a serene setting for food that is aromatic, heavily spiced and ever so good. The staff can steer you through a succession of mix-and-match appetizers, entrées and side dishes that make for novel taste sensations. Eggplant, a staple of the cuisine, appears in several appetizers, one of the best being kashk-e-bademjan, a warm dip of roasted eggplant, caramelized onions and goat's milk yogurt, to stand alone or to spread on the sesame-topped bread. Main courses are categorized by cooking style and yield flavorful combinations mainly of chicken, beef, lamb and veal with basmati rice. Particularly good are abgusht (lamb shank in spiced broth with string beans, chickpeas, okra and eggplant) and joojeh (a kabob of grilled chicken breast marinated in saffron, lemon and onions and served with saffron-perfumed basmati rice). For dessert, try ranghinak, squares of layered dates stuffed with walnuts and dusted with pistachio, or Persian ice cream scented with saffron and rosewater and studded with chunks of frozen cream.

(617) 720-5511. www.lalarokh.com. Entrées, $14 to $19. Lunch, Monday-Friday noon to 3. Dinner nightly, 5:30 to 10.

A Pair for Romance

Hungry I, 71 Charles St.

"Ouch," says the hand-painted exclamation on the low arch above the doorway to the subterranean quarters of this intimate charmer in a restored 1840s brownstone at the foot of Beacon Hill. Once past the head-basher, you'll find yourself in a long, narrow warren of small dining rooms that bespeak romance with the glow of candlelight, a couple of fireplaces, upholstered banquettes embellished with embroidered throw pillows, and polished copperware and paintings on exposed brick walls. It's a cozy, beguiling setting for the country French fare of Peter Ballarin, proclaimed on the restaurant's sign as "chef-proprietor since 1981." The short repertoire might offer pecan-crusted Costa Rican snapper with a citrus-wine sauce, rabbit moutarde baked in a pastry-crusted crock, and venison au poivre noir, flamed with cognac and reduced with red wine and sour cream. To start, how about lobster cannelloni, duck and sausage cassoulet or escargots and portobello mushrooms en croûte? Fitting finales include tarte tatin, walnut pie, almond-ricotta cheesecake and fig meringue with zuppa inglese. Brunch is served on an outdoor terrace in summer.

(617) 227-3524. Entrées, $21 to $34. Lunch, Thursday-Friday noon to 2. Dinner Tuesday-Sunday 5:30 to 10. Sunday brunch, 11 to 2.

B&G Oysters Ltd., 550 Tremont St.

Where fellow celebrity chef Jasper White's version of a seafood shanty became the huge Summer Shack in Cambridge, Barbara Lynch opted for diminutive. For their second act, she and partner-manager Garrett Harker turned a former crêperie into a neighborhood oyster bar for the young and hip in Boston's trendy South End. They dubbed it B&G for their initials and decked it out in marble and mosaic tiles in oceanic colors of cobalt and gray to suggest a Mediterranean cottage, which is about the size of it. There are a handful of tables, a few seats at the bar and an open kitchen inside and a gravel patio outside. It's basically a stand-up place and quite the scene as folks nosh on succulent oysters from around the world ($2 apiece, and the bill mounts fast). Other than oysters in several guises (from basic fried to oyster stew with caviar croutons), the menu is wisely limited. There are actually more lobster choices: bisque, fritters, roll and a knockout lobster BLT for a cool $18. You can get tuna salad niçoise, mussels frites with rouille, fried clams, broiled scallops, seared halibut, wild king salmon and that's about it. Finish with butterscotch pudding or banana royale, if need be. Those lucky enough to snag the lovers' nook, a table for two behind a railing amid the bedlam, can hang out and feed each other their favorite aphrodisiac.

(617) 423-0550. www.bandgoysters.com. Entrées, $17 to $21. Open daily, 11:30 to 11.

Indulge Your Sweet Tooth

Finale, 1 Columbus Ave.

In a sweet variation on the eat-dessert-first credo, this large desserterie/bistro/bakery/bar in the Theater District inspires you to eat nothing but. Just one sample of the pastry chef's creations will indicate why. You can get salads and appetizers, but they're mere "preludes" to the sweet priorities: perhaps the signature molten chocolate cake, vanilla crème brûlée garnished with orange-butter cookies and fresh fruits, an Italian "teaser" or a profiterole "party." Chocaholics find euphoria in the chocolate bliss for two ($26.95). It features espresso mousse torte, molten chocolate cake, caramel gelato in a coconut cookie cup and pear sorbet in a chocolate tuille cup, all garnished with assorted truffles. Wines, cordials, teas, espresso and international coffees also are available. All this indulgent eating and drinking takes place at lipstick-red velvet and chocolate brown banquettes and booths amid mustard yellow walls and plate-glass windows onto the street.

(617) 423-3184. www.finaledesserts.com. Desserts, $7.95 to $16.95. Lunch, Monday-Friday 11:30 to 3. Prelude and desserts, Monday-Saturday 6 to 11 or midnight, Sunday, 4 to 11.

FOR MORE INFORMATION: Greater Boston Convention & Visitors Bureau, 2 Copley Place, Suite 105, Boston, MA 02116. (617) 536-4100 or (888) 733-2678. www.bostonusa.com.

Salem harbor is backdrop for showy gardens outside House of Seven Gables.

Salem, Mass.
Beyond Witchcraft

There are witches almost everywhere in this old "Witch City:" ancient witches, live witches, wax witches, wannabe witches. The witch icon is emblazoned on the city's police cruisers, soars across the masthead of the daily newspaper, adorns T-shirts and coffee mugs, and is incorporated in the logos of far more businesses than one can shake a broom at. The city makes a month-long festival out of Halloween and attracts (real) witches and their devotees to see what all the fuss is about.

But witches and their hokey, ghoulish offshoots (wax museums, dungeons, spook houses and cemetery tours) have been a turn-off to at least as many potential visitors as they have attracted since witchery went big-time in the late 1970s with the opening of the Salem Witch Museum and the arrival of practicing witches in town.

The Witch City is starting to play down the history that has linked it to the supernatural ever since nineteen accused witches were tried and hanged on Gallows Hill in 1692. It has refocused, broadened and, yes, uplifted its appeal to engage a different kind of visitor.

The shift coincides with the $125 million expansion of the Peabody Essex Museum, the nation's oldest museum, from a sleeper of a regional destination into a world-class art and culture museum that's among the largest in New England. Trendy new restaurants have opened, and a waterfront hotel debuted in 2004.

The Peabody Essex, an amalgamation of two museums dating to 1799, is a treasure chest of exotica delivered from the farthest points of the globe by Salem sea captains and ships during the heady days of the East India and China trade. The museum opens seamlessly off the Essex Street Mall, the main street that was closed to traffic and turned into one of the first downtown pedestrian malls in New England.

One end of Essex Street extends toward Chestnut Street, the heart of the McIntire Historic District and an enclave of stately Federal-style homes producing one of the most beautiful residential streets in America. The other end of Essex Street leads to Hawthorne Boulevard, named for Nathaniel Hawthorne, the great 19th-century novelist.

A short block to the north lies the leafy Washington Square, a park transformed in 1801 from the "town swamp" (as the Salem Common was then called), flanked by the Hawthorne Hotel and a Gothic church, now the Salem Witch Museum.

A long block to the south is the waterfront. Here the Salem Maritime National Historic Site preserves Salem's seafaring heritage from the early 1800s when its merchant fleet profited mightily from the opening of trade routes to the Far East. Nearby, Pickering Wharf captures tourists with a changing array of shops and restaurants. Beyond is the nation's largest collection of 17th-century buildings open to the public, including the landmark House of Seven Gables portrayed in the Hawthorne novel of that name.

All these attractions are within walking distance of each other. It's a good thing, because streets are congested and narrow in Salem's historic center, and directions are hard to find – and follow. That helps make Salem an appealing getaway for those who like their treats close at hand.

Seeing and Doing

Salem was the capital of the Massachusetts Bay Colony from its founding in 1626, but is better known as "The Witch City," as every school child knows. During the 1692 witchcraft trials, a group of hysterical women and children caused nineteen innocent people to be sentenced to death. Elements of the witch-hunt heritage are portrayed tastefully at the National Park Service's excellent Salem Visitor Center and at the Peabody Essex Museum, and less so at more touristy attractions.

Facing Washington Square and the broad green that is Salem Common is the imposing Gothic structure built in 1845 as a Unitarian church. Now the **Salem Witch Museum,** it is considered the best single place to visit for anyone with only a passing interest in the witch story. Its 30-minute multimedia presentation nicely summarizes the events of 1692. A gallery reviews the changing perceptions of witches through the centuries. Some people emerge "so bewitched, bothered and bewildered," in the words of a guide on the Salem Trolley, that they snap photos of the stern, pilgrim-hatted statue in front of the museum. Too late do they realize it is not a witch but town founder Roger Conant

The dark brown and rather foreboding 1642 **Witch House** at 310 Essex St. is the only home still standing in Salem with direct ties to the witch trials. It was the home of trial judge Jonathan Corwin, who was believed to have done pre-trial examinations of those accused of witchcraft. Restored and furnished to the colonial period, it offers guided tours detailing the history of the house and its occupants as well as their involvement in the trials.

The **Witch Dungeon Museum** at 16 Lynde St. presents a dramatization of witch trials with mannequins, followed by a tour through a recreated dungeon. More compelling is **Cry Innocent** in the Old Town Hall at Derby Square, a live re-enactment of the witchcraft examination of Bridget Bishop, the first to hang in the witch trials. An interactive show in which the audience acts as the Puritan grand jury, it's the longest continuously running show in the state north of Boston.

Peabody Essex Museum, East India Square, Salem.

Spread across two city blocks, the oldest continuously operating museum in the country possesses some of the most important collections of art, architecture and culture from New England to Imperial China. Founded as the Salem East India Society at the peak of the China trade in 1799, the Peabody required members to collect "natural and artificial curiosities" from the far reaches of their merchant trade routes and has continued to collect aggressively ever since. The Asian-oriented Peabody and the New England-oriented Essex Institute across the street merged in 1992 to produce New England's largest treasure chest of exotica, as delivered by Salem sea captains from around the globe. Designed by noted architect Moshe Safdie, a $150 million expansion in 2003 produced 250,000 square feet of new and renovated galleries and public spaces. Included are a soaring atrium entry connecting various buildings, six art galleries, public gardens and Yin Yu Tang, a reconstructed 18th-century Qing dynasty merchant's house relocated with its original furnishings from rural China.

The expansion allows visitors to see all of the museum's permanent collections, revealing more than two million objects that had been hidden in storage for lack of space. Many are extraordinary: its Asian export art collection, which embraces everything from an ornate moon bed to a teapot depicting a Malay village to minute scenes intricately carved into ivory, is the foremost in the world. The Japanese collection of household arts and crafts surpasses anything in Japan. The Korean collection is the first of its kind in the United States, as is the gallery devoted to the contemporary art of India. The marine artworks and Native American exhibits are unparalleled. Some of the finest examples of New England architecture are on display in houses dating from 1684 to 1812.

But the star of the show is Yin Yu Tang, the 200-year-old home that housed eight generations of the Huang family. It was dismantled from its southeastern China site and rebuilt on the museum grounds to become the only example of Chinese vernacular architecture in this country. Limited numbers of timed tickets are available for a surcharge. The Peabody also has one of the finest museum gift shops we have seen.

(978) 745-9500 or (866) 745-1876. www.pem.org. Open daily, 10 to 5. Adults $13, students $9, children free. Admission to Yin Yu Tang, $4.

The House of the Seven Gables, 54 Turner St., Salem.

The house that inspired Nathaniel Hawthorne is New England's oldest surviving mansion and part of one of the earliest historic compounds opened to the public in America. Known as the Turner-Ingersoll Mansion for its early occupants, it was ambitious when it was built by wealthy sea captain John Turner in 1668, but in terms of size the handsome, dark wood structure sidling up to the Salem waterfront would probably qualify only as a McMansion today. Long before Deerfield or Sturbridge came into historic play, Salem philanthropist Caroline Emmerton assembled a complex of nine 17th-century structures – the largest of its kind in America – around the restored mansion in which the author had visited his Ingersoll cousin. The pioneering preservationist laid out a Jacobean-style seaside garden in 1909 and opened the property for tours. The proceeds fund services for her settlement house to this day.

Half-hour guided tours start in the original, low-ceilinged Turner kitchen, its enormous hearth built of some of the earliest bricks made in America. From the dining room beyond, a door opens into the hearth and a much-celebrated secret staircase winding steeply to the second floor. The agile duck to all fours to make the climb. Upstairs, the costumed guide takes apart a dollhouse-size model of the house that shows it without four gables the Ingersolls had removed during the Federal period when Hawthorne wrote the novel. You're told that the servants' bedroom in the attic represents one of the country's oldest surviving domestic quarters, and you see the high-ceilinged bedroom a later Turner added in 1675 when the cost was no object. The guided tour ends in the "parlor" below, an elegant space that doubles as a dining room, where the guide points out its original look through paint that weathered blue inside the china cabinet. The room was restored lately to its early verdigris green paint and vivid chintz wallpaper that belies the Puritan reputation for drab colors. The affluent Turners were ahead of the trends with their cutting-edge Georgian interior, it seems.

Across the colorful colonial revival garden, reflecting a changing spectrum of period plantings through the seasons, is the circa-1750 red house in which Hawthorne was born in 1804. Furnished to the period but with little connection to the family, it is open for self-guided tours. Others of the nine structures in the historic compound include the 1655 house of famed shipbuilder Retire Beckett, who designed the first American yacht. It serves today as the museum store. The Seamans Visitor Center, in which a year-long exhibition marking Hawthorne's 200th birthday was shown in 2004-2005, contains a garden café offering a modest sandwich menu. Take a picnic lunch outside to tables beneath the wisteria arbor or along the harborfront.

(978) 744-0991. www.7gables.org. Open daily 10 to 5, to 7 July-October. Adults $11, children $7.25.

Salem Maritime National Historic Site, 193 Derby St.

Twelve structures from 1670 to the early 1900s along the Derby Street waterfront are part of this nine-acre national historic site, the first in the national park system. The site documents New England's maritime history, which was centered in Salem into the early 19th century. Start at the orientation center in the restored Central Wharf Warehouse, which shows an eighteen-minute film on the pioneering development of the lucrative East Indies and China luxury trade that turned Salem into the sixth largest city – and richest per capita – in the country. Salem's merchants took great risks and reaped great rewards in sending ships on long trading voyages "To the Farthest Ports of the Rich East" – the title of the movie.

Park rangers lead tours for 25 people up to ten times daily to three buildings across Derby Street. The major one is the 1819 Custom House, whose front windows face Derby Wharf, the longest and last of more than 50 wharves that once were lined with cargo warehouses. It was here that Nathaniel Hawthorne was in charge of fifteen customs officers as surveyor for the Port of Salem for four years until his political enemies got him fired – a dismissal that, combined with his mother's death, preceded the publication of *The Scarlet Letter,* a story into which he poured all the rage and frustration of his trying summer of 1849. The introduction to the novel is set in the Custom House. Objects belonging to Hawthorne, including the desk he used, are on display in the office.

Also open during guided tours is the nearby **Derby House,** the oldest brick house in Salem, built in 1762 for shipowner Elias Haske Derby, the "king" of Salem's waterfront and America's first millionaire. Rangers also open the **Narbonne-Hale House,** built in the 17th century as a home and shop for craftsmen and tradesmen.

Tour participants can board the tall ship **Friendship** moored along Central Wharf in the harbor. The largest wooden sailing vessel to be constructed in more than a century, it's a replica of the three-masted Salem East Indiaman built in 1797 by shipwright Enos Briggs at his shipyard across from the site.

Also part of the historic site is the scale house where customs officers weighed cargo to collect duties, the 1780 Hawkes House that Derby used as a privateer prize warehouse and, dwarfed by its larger neighbors, the tiny West India Goods Store where imported cargoes were sold at retail. You can walk out to the end of Derby Wharf to see the 1871 lighthouse.

(978) 740-1660; Fax (978) 740-1665. www.nps.gov/sama. Orientation center and site open daily 9 to 5, free. Reservations advised for tours for up to 25 participants, scheduled seven to ten times daily in summer, two or three times daily October to May; adults $5, children $3

Touring Salem. The best way to get oriented to Salem's attractions is via the **Salem Trolley,** 191 Essex St., (978) 744-5469. Informative guides narrate lively tales of people and places on a leisurely, hour-long ride past all the major points of interest, from the Chestnut Street historic district past the waterfront out to the old summer colony at Salem Neck, Winter Island Maritime Park and Salem Willows Park – the last three are areas most visitors otherwise would never see. The trolley departs every half hour and boards and unloads passengers at twelve stops along the route. If you plan your itinerary right, you can hop on the trolley at will to get between sites around downtown, Chestnut Street and the waterfront. But if you board at the waterfront, there's no shortcutting back – the trolley meanders for more than half an hour through the city's east end before returning to downtown, where the sightseeing action is. The trolley runs daily 10 to 5, April-October. Tickets valid all day: adults $10, children $3.

You help with the pedaling on 45-minute guided tours with **Salem Surrey Bike Tours,** Museum Place Mall, (978) 248-2031. Its surrey bike holds up to five seated passengers and two toddlers in a basket seat. Adults $12, children $6.

Three guided walking tours are offered by **Salem Historical Tours,** 98 Central St., (978) 745-0666. Hour-long tours cover the Olde Burying Point cemetery and the Witch Trials Memorial, Wednesday-Monday at 2, and Salem history and architecture, Wednesday-Monday at 4; adults $5, children $3. A 90-minute Haunted Footsteps Ghost Tour is offered May-October nightly at 8; adults $12.50, children $8.

Two of Salem's leading lights are subjects of self-guided walking tours. **Nathaniel Hawthorne's Salem,** an excellent publication of the National Park Service, outlines three walking tours exploring the people, places and events familiar to Hawthorne during his years in the city. Well connected locally, he was born here in 1804 and occupied various houses off and on until 1850, when he left and rarely returned. He moved to Lenox after his firing from the Custom House position and later to Wayside in Concord, his home at his death in 1864.

Bowditch's Salem, a walking tour of the Great Age of Sail, links maritime and other sites associated with mathematician/astronomer Nathaniel Bowditch, the Salem native who produced in 1802 *The New American Practical Navigator,* one of the more remarkable books published in early America. Naval ships still carry a "Bowditch," a manual for the ordinary sailor. Bowditch made other significant scientific contributions, later headed insurance companies in Salem and Boston, and redirected New England's seafaring economy into manufacturing, building some of the early mills of the Industrial Revolution.

A Treasure That's Free

Stephen Phillips Memorial Trust House, 34 Chestnut St.

Salem's most informative, personalized house tour is offered free, of all things. That's because a descendant left an endowment for the house as well as for student scholarships. The only Federal mansion on famed Chestnut Street that is open to the public, the house dates to 1800 when it was built in nearby Danvers by the daughter of Elias Derby, a self-made millionaire from the Salem sea trade. The daughter's divorced husband, wealthy shipping merchant Nathaniel West, had the house dragged in two sections by a team of oxen into Salem, where the two parts were rebuilt with a wide interior hall between them and a third floor and a back ell were added. The house was purchased nearly a century later by Stephen Phillips, descendant of a Salem merchant sea captain, who moved in with his wife and five generations of family furnishings. He lived in the house until his death in 1955 and the house remains as it was then – an understated display of eclectic collections representing the illustrious Salem family's world travels. The hour-long tour starts in the rear kitchen, where you find preparations under way for a dinner party. The guide shows the hand-written menu, the plate warmers, the copper sink for washing the prized Limoges china and the elegant dining-room table set for six. The men gathered in the front library with its wall shelf of first editions for a history lecture, and the women were invited to the upstairs sitting room where Anna Phillips might sing an aria. "So you earned your dinner," visitors are told. Son Stevie's front bedroom with a canopy bed is more formal than his parents' master bedroom in the rear. The personal tales of how a wealthy family and servants lived early in the 20th century impress more than the collections in a house furnished in what the guide called mix-and-match styles and eras. Little beyond Fiji paddles, African wood carvings and China porcelain stands out, except for vehicles in the rear carriage house. There you get up close to the family's 1936 Pierce-Arrow limousine, a 1924 Pierce-Arrow touring car, a 1929 Ford Model A, a ladies' wicker phaeton with a rumble seat for the stable boy, a one-horse open sleigh and even a canoe.

(978) 744-0440; Fax (978) 740-1086. www.phillipsmuseum.org. Open Memorial Day through October, Monday-Saturday 10 to 4:30. Free.

The McIntire Historic District. A self-guided walking tour encompasses a five-block area with more than 300 historic structures, including several of local architect Samuel McIntire's significant houses. The centerpiece is Chestnut Street, where three-story Federal mansions built between 1800 and 1830 line up in perfect formality with equal setbacks from the street. The walking tour, developed by a local group and the National Park Service, covers a little over a mile and takes about 45 minutes. A glossy twelve-page guide points out salient features of the houses and their occupants, many of whom were notable in fascinating ways. The route is detailed in a glossy twelve-page guide and marked on posts and sidewalk plaques by a sheaf of wheat, designed by McIntire to symbolize Salem's prosperity.

The district contains one of the largest concentrations of significant 18th- and 19th-century buildings in the United States. The route passes fine examples of Georgian, Greek Revival and Colonial Revival architecture, but is best known for its Federal-era homes designed by McIntire, Salem's self-taught architect of the airy, four-square Federal style. The wealth generated during the apex of the city's East India and China trade led to the construction of many buildings in the district today.

Highlights include the Gothic Revival First Church of Salem, housing the oldest continuous Protestant congregation in America, and the Pickering House, said to be the only house in America to be occupied by eleven generations of one family since 1651. The Alexander Hamilton Hall remains a social gathering place that hosted a reception for the Marquis de Lafayette in 1824 and annual Salem Assembly balls for debutantes from 1807 to 1980.

BOAT CRUISES. You can sail on the waters where pirates, East Indiamen and men of war made history for hundreds of years. A full-scale reproduction of the privateer **Schooner Fame,** which sailed out of Salem Harbor during the War of 1812, offers nearly two-hour cruises from Pickering Wharf Marina. Cruises leave at noon, 2, 4 and 6 in summer and on spring and fall weekends; adults $25, children $15.

A 90-minute harbor tour aboard the 90-foot yacht **Privateer** is offered by Seven Seas Salem Tours & Charters, Pickering Wharf, (978) 741-0434 or (800) 745-9594. The tour views lighthouses and islands, hauls a lobster trap and fires a cannon salute daily at 1:30, 3:30 and 6:30; adults $20, children $10.

Whale watch excursions are available through the **East India Cruise Co.,** 57 Wharf St., (508) 741-0434 or (800) 745-9594. Trips depart daily at 9 and 2 in summer; adults $27, children $18.

Where to Stay

Hawthorne Hotel, On the Common, 18 Washington Square West, Salem 01970.

In an era when local hotels are few and far between, this six-story brick Federal structure at the eastern edge of downtown stands out. Named for the Salem author, it opened in 1925 after citizens of Salem established an unusual public subscription drive to build "Salem's own hotel to meet the needs of Salem, its guests and visitors." It has been updated over the years and offers comfortable accommodations plus fine dining. The lobby with fluted columns, oriental rugs and potted palms was a beehive of activity the late Friday afternoon we stopped by – the hotel and its lounges and function rooms are still a local gathering place as well as a refuge for overnight visitors, as envisioned more than 80 years ago. Rooms and suites on the upper floors are appointed with 18th-century reproduction furnishings to reflect a New England character. Morning coffee is complimentary in the lobby. Salem gourmands sing the praises of **Nathaniel's,** the hotel's elegantly restored dining room, serving lunch and dinner daily. An extensive menu of lighter fare is offered in the fireside tavern.

(978) 744-4080 or (800) 729-7829. www.hawthornehotel.com. Eighty-nine rooms and six suites. Doubles, $125 to $189. Suites, $204 to $319.

The Salem Inn, 7 Summer St., Salem 01970.

At the western edge of downtown in the McIntire Historic District, this began in a handsome, four-story brick Federal structure consisting of three attached townhouses built in 1834 by sea captain Nathaniel West. It has expanded into two other historic buildings over the years. Owners Richard and Diane Pabich offer a comfortable common living room with a fireplace and 23 accommodations in a range of sizes and styles in the West House. Most beds are king or queensize, but quarters vary, from spacious rooms with fireplaces (some with jacuzzi tubs) to top-floor family suites (no elevator) with kitchenettes to small rooms with private hall baths. Furnishings are antique or reproductions, and televisions and telephones are standard. Around the corner is the Curwen House, a wood-frame, three-story Italianate Revival building dating to 1854. Among its eleven romantic rooms with queen beds are three honeymoon suites with canopy beds, working fireplaces and double whirlpool tubs. Two rooms and four family and two luxury suites with fireplaces and whirlpool tubs are available in the Peabody House, a three-story Colonial structure built in 1874. A complimentary light breakfast is offered in the brick breakfast room on the lower level of the main West House or outside on a brick patio.

(978) 741-0680 or (800) 446-2995. Fax (978) 744-8924. www.saleminnma.com. Twenty-six rooms and sixteen suites with private bath. Mid-April to October: doubles $129 to $189, suites $189 to $229. Rest of year: doubles $119 to $149, suites $169 to $189.

Morning Glory Bed & Breakfast, 22 Hardy St., Salem 01970.

A pair of decks yield glimpses of the harbor from this barn-red Georgian Federal residence built around 1808 across the street from the historic House of Seven Gables compound. Owner Bob Shea offers inviting common areas and four guest accommodations with queen beds in what until 1995 had been a two-family house. Decor is crisp and uncluttered as befits the period. The spacious Jackie O offers a fireplace, while the Angel Room opens onto a second-floor deck. In back is the Canopy Room, so named for its fishnet canopy bed. The third floor with its original beams is a suite with a poster bed in one room, a sitting room with TV and refrigerator in another and a skylit bathroom in the middle. Here also is a common rooftop deck with lounge chairs for taking in the harbor view. Bob's mother bakes Irish breads and other pastries for the deluxe continental breakfast served at a table for eight in the dining room.

(978) 741-1703. www.morningglorybb.com. Three rooms and one suite with private baths. Doubles, $115 to $160.

The Coach House Inn, 284 Lafayette St. (Route 114), Salem 01970.

Built by a sea captain in 1879, this late Victorian mansion is situated about a mile south of downtown on the road to Marblehead. The one-time boarding house was converted into a B&B in 1980 by Pat Kessler, who tends to guests from her residence in the carriage house out back. She offers ten rooms and a two-bedroom suite, furnished in "eclectic style" with poster beds, colorful wallpaper and antiques. Each room has TV and a coffeemaker. Continental breakfast is delivered to the room in a basket left outside the door.

(978) 744-4092 or (800) 688-8689. Fax (978) 745-8031. www.coachhousesalem.com. Ten rooms and one suite with private baths. Doubles, $110 to $180. Suite, $220 for four.

Henry Derby House, 47 Summer St., Salem 01970.

Owner Peg Camarda is a gardener, a florist and a shopkeeper as well as an innkeeper. That accounts for the Victorian gardens beside and in back of the 1835 Greek Revival house, as well as the award-winning window boxes, the potted flowers lined up on the sidewalk in front and the clutter of plants, floral crafts, primitives, gift items and what-not on the main floor of the interior, which it turns out is also the Derby House Boutique. Peg has lived in the house since 1976, but only started adding B&B guests to the equation in 2000. Those guests are nicely cosseted on the second floor in a pink room with a queen bed, a yellow room with twin beds and a two-room suite with a king bed and a twin. All contain the original, non-working fireplaces. The queen room we saw at the back of the house looked comfortable and uncluttered, though everything in it – as well as in the rest of the house – is available for sale. Everything, that is, except "my family and my kitties Bogeyman and Chill," who reside on the third floor. Peg prepares a continental breakfast of fruits and homemade breads and pastries. It is taken beside an Italian marble fireplace in the dining room or outside in the courtyard garden.

(978) 745-1080. www.henryderbyhouse.com. Two rooms and one suite with private baths. Doubles, $125.

Amelia Payson House, 16 Winter St., Salem 01970.

Built in 1845, this blue house with white columns is one of Salem's best examples of Greek Revival architecture. Ada and Don Roberts have welcomed guests since 1985 with a personal touch that is missing in many of Salem's lodging establishments. Although they lack the larger beds and extras like jacuzzis that some others offer, they have added TVs and hair dryers lately. The bright and airy rooms here are fancily decorated in white and shades of mauve and pink. Antique brass and canopy beds, period furnishings and homey touches are standard. Guests enjoy a parlor with a grand piano as well as an upstairs reading room. A continental breakfast of muffins and scones is served in the dining room.

(978) 744-8304. www.ameliapaysonhouse.com. Four rooms with private baths. Doubles, $115 to $145 July-September, $95 to $125 off-season. Closed November-March.

Salem Waterfront Hotel & Suites, 225 Derby St., Salem 01970.

This newly built Best Western hotel opened in 2004 perpendicular to Salem's historic waterfront. Its central location and free parking lot in front guaranteed a high occupancy rate. The 86 accommodations in the five-story structure topped by a cupola are standard-issue hotel. Six one-bedroom suites and sixteen mini-suites help it live up to its name. The main floor includes an indoor swimming pool and fitness center. The **Regatta Café and Pub** had not yet opened at our visit, and the smallish lobby looked rather sterile as if it had not been finished. Continental breakfast is included in the rates.

(978) 740-8788 or (888) 337-2536. Fax (978) 740-8722. www.bwsalem.com. Eighty rooms and six suites. Doubles, $139 to $209. Suites, $299.

Harbor Light Inn, 58 Washington St., Marblehead 01945.

Some of the area's nicest accommodations are offered at this large B&B housed in two adjacent Federal mansions in historic Marblehead, Salem's neighbor to the east, a town that is well worth exploring. Owners Peter and Suzanne Conway offer 21 rooms handsomely furnished to the period. They are generally spacious and outfitted with TVs and telephones, fine antiques and oriental rugs. Five bedrooms have whirlpool tubs, eleven have working fireplaces, most have sitting areas and several have private balconies and decks. A big (for Marblehead) back yard contains lounge chairs and a heated swimming pool. An elaborate continental breakfast spread is put out in the formal dining room, or the meal can be taken on trays to one of the two elegant front parlors or to tables beside the pool. The fare when we were there included melon, lemon bread and especially good blueberry and cranberry-walnut muffins. Tea is offered in the afternoon.

(781) 631-2186. Fax (781) 631-2216. www.harborlightinn.com. Nineteen rooms and two suites with private baths. Doubles, $125 to $195. Suites, $195 to $295.

Where to Eat

The Grapevine, 26 Congress St.

Salem's most exciting culinary action emanates from this restaurant in a former garage across from Pickering Wharf. Walk past the sleek bar, where there are a few tables and an espresso machine, to the rear dining room with a soaring ceiling, striking rows of bare light bulbs on the beams and sturdy wood chairs at tables dressed in paisley prints. Beyond is a lovely garden courtyard for outdoor dining. For starters, consider the half avocado stuffed with shrimp and goat cheese, the grilled calamari with arugula, olives and feta cheese or the crispy beef and Thai basil spring rolls with pickled ginger dipping sauce. There are some heavenly light pastas, perhaps the penne with smoked salmon, radicchio and vodka cream sauce or the capellini with rock shrimp, sweet tomatoes and arugula that we so enjoyed at an early visit. But chef-owner Kate Hammond's specialties are such gutsy dinner entrées as pan-roasted cod loin with littlenecks, bacon and escarole; rabbit simmered with peppers, onions, olives and tomatoes; and veal scaloppine with melted taleggio, prosciutto and spinach. Typical desserts are chocolate truffle cake, crème caramel and poppyseed cake.

(978) 745-9335. www.grapevinesalem.com. Entrées, $21 to $27. Dinner nightly, 5:30 to 10.

Capt.'s Waterfront Grill & Club, 94 Wharf St.

The latest addition to Pickering Wharf is this two-story beauty with great views of the harbor through soaring windows and a second-floor deck. The former home of the Rockmore Drydock Restaurant (parent of the Rockmore's floating barge restaurant in Salem Harbor), this has been extensively renovated by owners Dirk and Diana Isbrandtsen. They liken the ambiance of the wraparound upstairs dining room and the downstairs lounge to that of "a simple, elegant yacht." As we overlooked the moored schooner Friendship, we almost felt asail on the canopied second-floor deck during a lunch shared with impertinent pigeons on a warm October day. The day's hearty tomato and fennel soup was first-rate in tandem with a grilled crab melt panini with avocado and fries. The star of the meal was a succulent grilled swordfish steak with a tangy fruit salsa. It's a fixture on the dinner menu that ranges from the specialty charcoal grilled lobster through a variety of grilled seafood to grilled chicken and steaks. A dessert of sticky toffee pudding with figs and vanilla ice cream was upstaged by the spectacular "banana three ways," caramelized bananas in a five-spice wonton with banana ice cream and banana chantilly. Upstairs or down, you also can make a meal out of interesting small plates or contemporary salads with grilled fish or meats.

(978) 741-0555. www.capts.us. Entrées, $15.95 to $28.95. Lunch daily, noon to 5. Dinner nightly, 5 to 9:30 or 10.

Lyceum Bar & Grill, 43 Church St.

Founded in 1830, the Salem Lyceum hosted some formidable Americans, and history was made here in 1877 when Alexander Graham Bell demonstrated the first telephone, talking to Thomas Watson, eighteen miles away in Boston. Former Marblehead restaurateur George Harrington took over Salem's first fine-dining restaurant in 1989. He restored the original windows and upscaled the decor to create a soft, warm dining room, a bar with a library look and a rear enclosed patio with brick walls, large windows and skylights. His chef creates global fare, from crab cakes with ginger cream, hoisin sauce and two salsas for an appetizer to whole crispy red snapper with ginger, jade rice and a cucumber relish for the lead-off entrée. But the appetizer of choice remains the grilled portobello mushrooms with George's famous marinade. Main courses include the legendary baked stuffed lobster as well as crispy free-range chicken with riesling wine sauce, plus what George calls "my semi-famous flank steak," served on Portuguese bread, and grilled filet mignon with his favorite grilled portobello mushrooms. The mushrooms have been known to make up an open-face sandwich or be paired with chicken on penne pasta on the lunch menu. Among desserts are chocolate decadence cake with raspberry sauce, and a trio of sorbets.

(978) 745-7665. www.lyceumsalem.com. Entrées, $17.50 to $28. Lunch, Monday-Friday 11:30 to 3. Dinner nightly, 5:30 to 10. Sunday brunch, 11 to 3.

Finz, 76 Wharf St.

Almost as hip as its subtitle, "oh-so-hip-seafood," is this seafood grill on Pickering Wharf, Salem's paean to shopping and dining along the restored waterfront. The old Chase House restaurant building has been opened up into a large and airy expanse of glass brick and windows, with no "decor" to speak of. Windows on three sides overlook a marina and a large waterside deck is open in season. The place is crisp and contemporary and, well, hip, so much so that the young informant at the Salem Visitor Center advised it's "the place to go to see and be seen." We'd go for the oysters from the well-stocked raw bar – perhaps six on the half shell topped with wasabi caviar and a splash of raspberry Stoli, or a flight of eight assorted. Or we'd start with the smoked-salmon quesadilla, splashed with a caviar crème fraîche vodka sauce, or the seared rare ahi tuna, drizzled with wasabi and pickled ginger and served over green papaya and daikon radish slaw. We'd move on to jerk-rubbed Caribbean salmon with mango and pineapple salsa, spicy pecan-crusted catfish with lobster-brandy sauce, lobster ravioli, bouillabaisse or perhaps the crabmeat-enriched swordfish oscar, resting atop a mushroom-potato hash and drizzled with porcini mushroom broth. The only non-seafood options are espresso-rubbed filet mignon, ricotta-stuffed chicken breast and a vegetarian dish that changes daily. Four-berry shortcake and blood-orange tart are refreshing desserts.

(978) 744-8485. www.hipfinz.com. Entrées, $17.95 to $24.95. Lunch daily, 11:30 to 5. Dinner, 5 to 10 or 11.

Cilantro, 282 Derby St.

Mexican food is elevated to new heights at this sparkling eatery along bustling Derby Street near the harbor. The two owners, including chef Esther Marin, are from central Mexico and have won a loyal following. Yes, you can order the Mexican standbys, here called Cilantro "classics" – quesadilla, tamales, fajitas and such. All are enhanced by a chef who knows what they're really about and isn't shy about tempting adventurous palates with the likes of jalapeños rellenos or a spicy beefsteak topped with the works. True believers savor the Cilantro "specialties," eight authentic Mexican dishes including whole red snapper sautéed in olive oil and topped with chopped garlic and herbs, and broiled filet mignon topped with chorizo sausage and melted chihuahua cheese. The namesake cilantro enhances almost every dish. Desserts include the traditional flan and homemade rice pudding. Mexican artworks are the only sign of Mexican decor. Otherwise you might think you were walking into a typical, brick-walled storefront bistro with close-together tables and a convivial bar where high tables are perched for dining alongside.

(978) 745-9436. www.cilantrocilantro.com. Entrées, $18 to $23.50. Lunch, Tuesday-Saturday 11:30 to 2. Dinner nightly, 5:30 to 10 or 11, Sunday to 9.

Strega Restaurant and Lounge, 94 Lafayette St.

This stylish new Italian eatery and nightspot caters to its host city in name – ''Strega" is Italian for witch – and in drinks like the strawberry witch cocktail or the wicked witch martini. It dares to be "dramatically different," but the accent remains on the food, as in the signature seafood "cauldron" of scallops, mussels, clams and monkfish in a garlicky tomato broth. You might also find grilled Maine sea scallops with tomato pan stew or braised lamb shank with creamy goat cheese polenta and a tomato and olive gremolata. Start with a duck confit calzone, the shrimp risotto with parmesan and peas or the fried olives stuffed with gorgonzola.

(978) 741-0004. www.stregasalem.com. Entrées, $16 to $27. Dinner, Tuesday-Sunday, 4 to 12:30.

Victoria Station, 86 Wharf St.

Part of the chain, always quite amusingly decorated with British Railways memorabilia, this particular one enjoys one of the best locations in Salem, right on the harbor at the edge of Pickering Wharf. In season, you can eat outdoors on a couple of spacious decks if you can snag a table. In its 30 years here, Victoria Station has made its mark with prime rib and steaks, although there are seafood and chicken dishes as well, plus an all-you-can-eat soup and salad bar ($9.95). For lunch, you can order burgers, the specialty roast prime rib sandwich and baked haddock or fried scallops. The dinner menu broadens to include entrées like baked stuffed shrimp, pan-seared halibut, "smothered" chicken breasts, four cuts of prime rib and bourbon ribeye steak. The portions are abundant and the food straightforward. There's a lot to look at, including a red telephone booth from London and a plant-laden rowboat, suspended from the ceiling near the huge black fireplace in the tree-filled lounge. Try the specialty Revolutionary War drinks, the Wharf Rat and the Rat in the Hat, if you dare.

(978) 745-3400. www.victoriastationinc.com. Entrées, $14.95 to $27.95. Lunch daily, 11:30 to 4. Dinner, 4 to 10 or 11.

FOR MORE INFORMATION: Salem Office of Tourism and Cultural Affairs, 63 Wharf St., Salem, MA 01970, (978) 744-3663 or (877) 725-3662. www.salem.org.

Pristine white facade of Equinox resort hotel is symbolic of Manchester Village.

Manchester, Vt.

Vintage Charm

The destination region is known as Manchester and the Mountains, but its focus is Manchester, a year-round resort area in the shadow of Mount Equinox.

Among the elite, Manchester is as favored for sporting sojourns today as it was for golf, fly-fishing and escapes from urban life in the old days. Mrs. Abraham Lincoln and her sons spent summers at the early Equinox Hotel prior to the family's adopting Manchester Village as their summer home.

The famous Manchester everyone knows and loves is actually Manchester Village, a mile-long stretch along Historic Route 7A that is vintage New England: a stately lineup of elegant, mostly white, black-shuttered clapboard homes centered on the restored Equinox, for more than 200 years the area's premier resort hotel.

These days, Manchester's Norman Rockwell charm as exemplified by the village co-exists with designer-outlet chic in the other Manchesters – Manchester Depot and Manchester Center, home to increasing numbers of trendy outlet stores as handsome and affluent as many of the customers they serve.

The various Manchesters and those who live or visit there all converge at the intersections of Route 7 and 11/30, where a four-way yellow flashing light serves as gatekeeper. It's a no-man's land that the locals shun as "Malfunction Junction" but that others find works, at least during off-peak periods.

The busiest stores and restaurants are found along Route 7 near the junction in the heart of Manchester Center and along Route 11/30 in Manchester Depot and beyond, up toward Bromley Mountain. Take the slow road south toward Manchester Village and Mount Equinox and you'll get away from the congestion. You will find fine inns and resorts, unusual recreational opportunities and attractions like the impressive Southern Vermont Arts Center and magnificent Hildene, the fascinating home of President Lincoln's descendants. Walk the marble sidewalks and enjoy an expanse of green in summer or pristine white in winter, plus considerable tranquility and charm year-round.

Seeing and Doing

Manchester and its namesake appendages are nestled in a valley between Mount Equinox and Mother Myrick Mountain on the West and the Green Mountains on the East. The mountains provide plenty to see, and the villages much to do.

Mount Equinox, Route 7A.
Not your usual "mountain," this is really a very high ridge rising to 3,848 feet – the highest in the Taconic Range. It guards Manchester on its western flank and is the dominant presence in the area. You can access the top of the mountain by car on the Skyline Drive or by foot on several hiking trails from Manchester Village, but you're probably not aware of "the man behind it all." Most of the mountain was owned by scientist-inventor Joseph G. Davidson, who vacationed there and built the road that became the Skyline Drive to serve the large ranch-style house he built near the summit. The pioneering Union Carbide chemical executive was instrumental in development of the atomic bomb and, as if in expiation, he founded the first Carthusian monastery in the United States on the mountain. The secluded site suited the 900-year-old Roman Catholic monastic order devoted to silence and solitude. Davidson built a massive granite charterhouse for the monks. Shortly before his death in 1969, he deeded 7,000 acres to the monks and charged them with managing the mountain. His hydro-electric power stations and the subsequent Mount Equinox Wind Farm remain visible today, as does the monastery – although it is not open to the public because the monks want total seclusion.

The **Equinox Preserve** consists of 850 acres on the slopes of Mount Equinox closest to Manchester. The Equinox resort owns the land, which is open year-round for non-motorized recreation. The rich northern hardwood forest on the fertile slopes is considered the largest and best of its type in New England, and one trail is named for the trillium that grows alongside in spring. A trail guide offers four suggestions for hikes, from one hour (around Equinox Pond) to all day (the Blue Summit Trail to the top of the mountain). A three-hour trip via two trails goes to the Southern Vermont Arts Center.

The Skyline Drive, Route 7A.
Starting from the Toll House on Historic Route 7A in Sunderland south of Manchester Village, the 5-2-mile Skyline Drive climbs upward from 600 to 3,848 feet. The road winds and twists around hairpin turns, offering occasional turnouts for scenic views. Guard rails along almost the entire length of the drive help to make it one of the safest and reputedly one of the best engineered mountain roads in this country. It's also the longest privately owned paved toll road in the country – owned by the Carthusian monastery, which you can see from the top. Along the way there are six picnic areas – some of the tables are made from marble quarried on neighboring Dorset Mountain.

(802) 362-1115. Open daily, 9 a.m. to dusk, May-October. Toll: $7 car and driver, $2 each passenger over age 12.

Hildene, 1005 Hildene Road, Manchester Village.

Abraham Lincoln's descendants lived until 1975 in this 24-room Georgian Revival mansion on a promontory surrounded by mountains and overlooking the Battenkill Valley. Named to convey "hill" and "valley," Hildene was built in 1905 by Robert Todd Lincoln, the only one of the president's four sons to live into adulthood. While a student at Harvard he had summered with his mother at the Equinox Hotel in 1863 and 1864 and 40 years later was lured back to Manchester by Edward Isham, his Chicago law partner, who had a summer home named for local Revolutionary War hero Gideon Ormsby in front of the 412 acres that Lincoln decided to purchase. Robert Lincoln summered here for 21 years, and the house was the only one in America in which all of President Lincoln's descendants would eventually reside.

Ninety-minute guided tours begin with a wagon ride to the Carriage Barn visitor center for an orientation slide show. Most visitors pause to view daughter Jessie's 1928 Franklin roadster on display in a garage nearby. The house contains family memorabilia and original furnishings, including the 1,000-pipe Aeolian organ from 1908, believed to be the oldest residential pipe organ with a player attachment still in its original location and in working order. A tune from one of its 242 rolls is played on every tour. Among Hildene's treasures are one of the president's last three surviving stovepipe hats, a mirror from the White House dressing room where the president is believed to have last glanced at himself before heading out to Ford's Theater the night he was assassinated, and a number of volumes from the president's library. Near the house is an observatory, where visitors can view Robert Lincoln's telescope.

The formal gardens are magnificent, especially the riot of peonies that bloom each June. Designed by Robert's daughter in 1907 to resemble a cathedral window, the main garden changes weekly from early spring to late fall as varieties of roses, lilies and the like transform the colors of the "stained-glass panels." The garden promontory overlooking the Battenkill Valley yields spectacular views of the mountains on either side and of Hildene's farm and the British School of Falconry in the meadowlands 300 feet below. The cutting and kitchen gardens have been restored lately, and the original potting shed now houses exhibits and provides space for the volunteers who maintain the gardens. The estate hosts a variety of special programs and events, from craft festivals to polo matches. Twenty-one groomed trails are available for cross-country skiing in winter.

(802) 362-1788. www.hildene.org. Guided tours on the half-hour, daily 9:30 to 3, mid-May through October, also Saturday-Sunday 11 to 4, Thanksgiving weekend through December. Adults $10, children $4. Grounds only, adults $5, children $2.

Southern Vermont Arts Center, West Road, Manchester Village.

Its mountainside setting high up the slope of Mount Equinox makes this art museum and performing arts center unique and so popular it now operates year-round. Hatched by five men who would come to be known as the Dorset Painters, the oldest cultural institution in Vermont offers a variety of art exhibitions and related activities throughout the year. Inside a 28-room Georgian Colonial mansion known as Yester House are ten galleries with changing art exhibits. Behind it is the new Elizabeth deC. Wilson Museum, a stunning contemporary facility with soaring, skylit spaces in which to display the center's 800-piece permanent collection of 19th- and 20th-century works as well as periodic traveling exhibitions. The center's performance space, the 400-seat Arkell Pavilion, hosts frequent concerts and theater productions. The expansive lower meadow and rolling lawns provide a dramatic showplace for internationally known sculptors whose works come and go in the mobile Sculpture Garden. The sprawling 400-plus-acre "campus" includes the Boswell Botany Trail, a three-quarter-mile walk past hundreds of wildflowers and 67 varieties of Vermont ferns, all identified by Manchester Garden Club members who maintain it. The Garden Café is a fine place for lunch or brunch (see Where to Eat).

(802) 362-1405. www.svac.org. Open Tuesday-Saturday 10 to 5, Sunday noon to 5. Adults $6, students $3.

The American Museum of Fly Fishing, 4070 Main St., Manchester.

This one-of-a-kind institution holds the largest collection of fly-fishing paraphernalia, art and artifacts in the world. The oldest documented flies are among the 20,000 flies in the Mary Orvis Marbury collection at the museum, which moved in 2004 from its location near the Equinox resort to larger quarters just south of the Orvis flagship store. On display are more than 1,000 rods and reels owned by such luminaries as Ernest Hemingway, Bing Crosby, Babe Ruth and Dwight Eisenhower.

(802) 362-3300. www.amff.com. Open daily, 10 to 4. Adults $5, children $3.

Fishing and Floating on the Battenkill

The legendary Battenkill River starts in Dorset, flows past the Orvis Company headquarters in Manchester and widens as it veers west out of Arlington and passes under four covered bridges on its way to the Hudson River in New York State. Sometimes spelled Batten Kill and locally known as the 'Kill, it is generally recognized as Vermont's best wild trout stream. That's why the Orvis Company began manufacturing bamboo rods in Manchester Village near the spot where they still are produced. Cold crystal-clear water, scenic mountains and the fussy wild browns and brook trout draw anglers year-round to a pastoral setting seemingly re-created from Isaac Walton's 1653 *Compleat Angler.*

The Battenkill is nothing less than "the perfect all-around river," says Jim Walker at **BattenKill Canoe Ltd.,** 6348 Historic Route 7A, Arlington, (802) 262-2800 or (800) 421-5268. When not leading canoe trips to Belize or France, he and his staff rent canoes and kayaks and lead inn-to-inn canoe trips. Kayak rentals are $30 to $35 a day, and canoes rent for $48 to $60. **Battenkill Riversports** arranges canoeing, kayaking and tubing trips on a stretch of the river along Route 313 outside Arlington, (518) 677-8868 or (800) 676-8768.

The Sporting Life

You know that you can golf and ski around Manchester. Outdoor sportsmen also come here for not only fly-fishing but the ancient sport of falconry, archery and even off-road driving. The last are coordinated by Country Pursuits at the Equinox, 69 Union St., Manchester Village, (802) 362-7873.

Learn how to handle and fly a hawk at the much-celebrated **British School of Falconry** in the Hildene meadowlands at the Equinox. Falconry, for those not in the know, is reputed to be oldest sport in world, originating in the Far East about 2000 B.C. Originally devised as a way of obtaining game for the table, it became the "sport of kings" in Britain. This is the only falconry school in America where you get to handle the birds yourself. They say the moment when the hawk first lands on your gloved fist is one that you will never forget. The experience costs $85, the price of a 45-minute introductory lesson. Repeat the thrill as you partner with your hawk and perhaps a hunting dog on a hawk walk for another $145 an hour.

Also based in the Hildene meadowlands is the **Archery School,** where instructors teach people how to mount and draw a recurve bow or crossbow to zap arrows at a target.

For more of an adrenalin rush, **Off Road at the Equinox** teaches off-road driving techniques for all seasons and driving conditions. Take the wheel of a luxury Land Rover or Hummer and experience numerous challenges on an 80-acre course built for the purpose and beyond on an extensive trail system. Why you can even enroll your children in the Junior Off Road School. The brochure entices: "Imagine the expression on the face of your child as it successfully pilots a replica Land Rover over a course of off-road obstacles." Can you stand it?

The Gleneagles Golf Course at the Equinox, Union Street, Manchester Village.
Originally built in 1927 by Walter J. Travis, this eighteen-hole championship course was restored by architect Rees Jones in 1992 in a $3.5-million upgrade to modern standards within the confines of the original routing and rustic Scottish flavor. The 6,423-yard course, named after its famous sister course in Scotland, is rated one of the top 75 courses in the country by Golf Digest. It's open to the public, who also can enjoy lunch daily plus dinner on weekends in the Dormy Grill on the deck of the clubhouse.
(802) 362-3223. Greens fees, including cart: $125 weekends, $110 midweek.

Bromley, Route 11, Manchester Center.
Six miles east of Manchester Center, Bromley was the area's first ski resort, and is cherished for its sunny, south-facing trails that make for pleasant skiing on cold days. It is also known for wide, easy skiing on manicured slopes – not for nothing is one of our old favorites called Boulevard. The newer East Face has some challenging runs, for example Havoc, which our then-teenagers liked for its moguls, and Pabst Peril, for its steep cruising. The area is proud of its firsts: first slopeside nursery, first major snowmaking installation – and its awards for family programs, trail grooming and value. Ten lifts take skiers and snowboarders up the 1,334-foot vertical rise. Winter is not its only gig. The Bromley Thrill Zone bills itself as Vermont's largest summer fun park, with an alpine slide, a water slide, space bikes, go-karts, a 24-foot climbing wall ride and, oh yes, scenic chairlift rides.
(802) 824-5522. www.bromley.com. Open 10 to 5 daily, mid-June to Labor Day; weekends in June and September to mid-October. Winter, open daily 9 to 4, from 8:30 on weekends. Lift tickets: adults, $57 weekends, $49 midweek; juniors, $37 weekends, $34 midweek.

SHOPPING. It's a stretch to call this "Fifth Avenue in the Mountains," as some do. But shopping certainly is big business, more than in similar resort areas, as evident from all the designer outlets that have moved into the area in the last two decades. The outlets – more than 120 and counting – are spread along Main Street and Depot Street (the principal Routes 7 and 11/30 respectively) in Manchester Center. They're housed in new clapboard buildings and old, individually or collectively, with convenient parking but good pedestrian access between them. Over-all, the combination is more inviting than, say, North Conway or Kittery. The most distinctive are high-end: **Giorgio Armani, Brooks Brothers, Burberry, Baccarat, Coach, Escada, Anichini, Peruvian Connection** and such.

Some of our favorites are longer established. The **Frog Hollow Vermont State Craft Center** is a big draw among the Equinox Village Shops across from the Equinox resort in Manchester Village. **Gallery North Star** is one of Vermont's better art galleries.

The large and rambling **Orvis Flagship Store** is part fishing museum, part natural history center and a total shopping experience, from the predictable fishing gear to clothing, home furnishings, gifts, kitchenware and specialty foods. It has an indoor trout pond and a private gun room, but for some the attraction is the store's centerpiece stained-glass window, a sixteen-by-twelve-foot beauty called "The Lure of the Fly." It took a local craftsman three months and 1,100 pieces of glass to create.

The **Jelly Mill & Friends Marketplace** is a fun, four-story collection of shops in a century-old dairy barn. It typifies more traditional Vermont merchandising, from toys to apparel to gifts to crafts, plus a good little restaurant called The Buttery.

Where to Stay

Lodging and Dining

The Equinox Resort & Spa, 3567 Main St. (Route 7A), Manchester Village 05254.

In a class by itself is the grand old Equinox, a landmark dating to 1769 and renovated twice in the last two decades to the tune of more than $32 million. A partnership whose majority owner is Guinness, the beer company that owns the noted Gleneagles Hotel in Scotland, applied the finishing touches: renovations to the hotel's 141 guest rooms and eleven suites, a dramatic new lobby, a vastly expanded Marsh Tavern and the formal Colonnade dining room. Now a Rockresort, the classic, columned white facade embraces a world of lush comfort. All bedrooms have been equipped with modern baths, TVs and telephones, and dressed in light pine furniture, new carpeting, and coordinated bedspreads and draperies. Rooms come in five sizes (standard, superior, deluxe, premium and suite), and anything smaller than deluxe could be a letdown. If you really want to splurge, settle into one of the suites in the Equinox's nearby **Charles Orvis Inn,** the famed fisherman-innkeeper's former home and inn renovated for $2.8 million. From the fly-fishing gear framed in the "lift" to the game room with not one but two billiards tables next to the cozy Tying Room Bar, it raises club-like luxury to new heights. The three sumptuous one-bedroom and six two-bedroom suites come with king or queen beds, stereos and TVs in armoires in both bedroom and living room, gas fireplaces, marble bathrooms with whirlpool tubs, full cherry-paneled kitchens, and rich colors and furnishings in the English manor style. Charles Orvis "would have approved," according to its elaborate brochure. The resort's challenging Gleneagles Golf Course is a major attraction for guests. So is the state-of-the-art Avanyu Spa with an exotic indoor pool flanked by sculpture and topiary, sauna and steam rooms, an exercise room with Nautilus equipment, massage and spa therapy, aerobics programs, the works. You can learn to handle and free-fly a hawk under auspices of The British School of Falconry, or learn off-road driving techniques at the Land Rover Driving School and Shop.

Everyday dining is in the 1769 **Marsh Tavern,** fashioned from the old lobby and quite sumptuous in deep tones of green, red and black. The tavern is four times as big as before with a handsome bar and well-spaced tables flanked by windsor and wing chairs and loveseats. We found it too bright one winter's night with lights right over our heads, although the hostess said that was a new one on her – most folks thought the place too dark. We enjoyed an elegant and rather pricey "supper" from the tavern menu. The fare and prices were elevated after the tavern became the resort's main dinner venue. Nowadays, expect straightforward contemporary American entrées ranging from charbroiled Atlantic salmon with arugula pesto to pan-seared New York strip loin with red wine demi-glace. Appetizers might be a tad more innovative, as in lobster cakes with corn custard and baby greens or pan-seared buffalo skewers with mango relish. Desserts include a fine cranberry-walnut torte, warm chocolate truffle cake or chocolate espresso mousse. A trio plays here most nights after 9:30. The barrel-vaulted ceiling in the enormous **Colonnade** dining room was stenciled by hand by a latter-day Michelangelo who lay on his back on scaffolding for days on end. The Colonnade is suitably formal for holiday dinner buffets and Sunday brunch. There's no better setting for a summer lunch than the seasonal **Dormy Grill** on the veranda at the golf-course clubhouse, where the evening lobster fest and cookout also is a draw weekends in summer.

(802) 362-4700 or (800) 362-4747. Fax (802) 362-4861. www.equinoxresort.com. One hundred seventy rooms and townhouses and thirteen suites. Rates, EP. Doubles, $239 to $459. Suites and townhouses, $399 to $1,209. Orvis suites, $609 to $899.

Marsh Tavern: (802) 362-7833. Entrées, $21 to $29. Lunch, Monday-Saturday noon to 2:30; dinner nightly, 6 to 9. Dormy Grill, lunch daily, 11:30 to 4, late May to mid-October; lobster fest dinner on summer weekends, 5:30 to 8. Colonnade, Sunday brunch noon to 2:30.

The Reluctant Panther Inn & Restaurant, 39 West Road, Box 678, Manchester Village 05254.

This inn is distinctively decorated from the facade – deep lavender with yellow shutters – to the splashy florals and stripes in sixteen comfortable guest rooms in two buildings. Owners Robert and Maye Bachofen, he a Swiss hotelier and she a personable Peruvian, offer first-class dining as well as some of the most sumptuous accommodations in town. Creature comforts they provide aplenty in twelve rooms in the main inn and in four suites in the Mary Porter House next door. All rooms have king or queen beds, TVs and telephones. Twelve come with fireplaces and five have porches or decks. Goose down duvets cover the beds and guests find a half bottle of wine awaiting their arrival. During our tenure in the Seminary Suite we were enveloped in comfort, although the deluxe bathroom paled next to the one we'd observed earlier in the Mark Skinner Suite downstairs. That has a double whirlpool tub in the center of one of the largest bathrooms in Vermont, with a fireplace opposite, two pedestal sinks and a separate shower. "If you ever find another room like this, you tell me," Maye said proudly. She found one herself, creating an even larger Pond View Suite lately in a third building. A wide deck with three sets of french doors opening onto it, a living room with a huge fireplace also open to the kingsize bedroom, and a marble bathroom with another fireplace and a double jacuzzi are fit for the most self-indulgent. A full breakfast, served at round marble tables topped with floral mats in a fireplaced breakfast room, is included in the rates..

The attractive dining room, crisply dressed in white linens and fine china, harbors a plant-filled solarium at one end. Robert does the cooking and changes the menu seasonally. An amuse-gueule – lobster salad in a hollowed-out cucumber slice – preceded our appetizers, an excellent terrine of pheasant with sundried-cherry chutney and an assertive caesar salad topped with three grilled shrimp. Main courses range widely from yellowfin tuna with a red pepper and sweet basil coulis to coq au vin and steak frites. House specialties are Swiss veal Zurich, wiener schnitzel and pot-au-feu. We enjoyed the medallions of New Zealand venison with green peppercorns and Beefeater gin and, one of Robert's favorites, the fricassee of Vermont rabbit with local chanterelles and pearl onions – good but rather rich and more than we could eat. Among the delectable desserts were a fan of berries in sparkling wine around apricot sherbet and plums baked in a light cointreau custard. For a change of pace, visit the Panther's new **Swiss Fondue Stübli,** offering cheese, meat and chocolate fondues by the fireplace in the original 1850s walkout marble cellar, Thursday-Saturday 6 to 8:30.

(802) 362-2568 or (800) 822-2331. Fax (802) 362-2586. www.reluctantpanther.com. Twenty-one rooms and suites with private baths. Doubles, $149 to $349. Suites, $399 to $459.

Entrées, $25 to $32. Dinner, Monday-Saturday 6 to 8:30 or 9, June-October; weekends only, rest of year.

The Wilburton Inn, River Road, Manchester Village 05254.

A winding drive past stone walls leads up a hillside to the imposing porte cochere of a baronial, red-brick Tudor mansion, billed as a "grand country estate – 1902." Away from the hubbub, the twenty-acre setting overlooking the Battenkill Valley could not be more serene, and under the auspices of Albert and Georgette Levis – he a Greek-born psychiatrist and she the sister of playwright Wendy Wasserstein – the inn has become a year-round resort. The site lends itself to weddings, which the Levises host frequently and with flair. Guests who book at times when weddings and functions aren't dominating find a special place as well – with an aura of mystery cast by Dr. Levis's evolution of the inn as a forum on his findings about the nature of the creative process, which helps explain all the art exhibits, the sculpture walk and his "Museum of the Creative Process." The mansion's rich, dark interior of carved mahogany paneling, moldings, beamed ceilings, fancy brass doorknobs and leaded windows is enhanced by oriental rugs and the owners' art collection. Some of its eleven rooms and suites are spacious and of the old school with enormous bathrooms and walk-in closets. Nineteen more rooms and suites are available in outlying buildings called villas, spread across grounds dotted with sculpture. Four suites in the Twenties Villa come with fireplaces and mountain-view decks. The Thirties Villa contains eight of the largest rooms with kingsize or two queen beds. Six accommodations come with fireplaces and four with jacuzzi tubs. Rooms are generally outfitted with chaise lounges and down comforters, and all except the smallest on the third floor of the mansion have TVs. Some have seen better days, a factor due in part to Dr. Levis's latest thrust. He purchased a nearby house that had been built by the original owner as a wedding gift for his daughter and later was known as the Olde English Inn. After two years of restoration, it was scheduled to reopen in 2005 as **Teleion Holon** (Greek for "the perfect universe"), a holistic wellness retreat with ten guest rooms and a vegetarian dining room. Meanwhile, back at the inn, breakfast is served at wrought-iron tables in the summery Terrace Room overlooking a stone terrace and the valley beyond. The grounds include hiking trails, three tennis courts and a swimming pool, plus a sculpture walk leading to Teleion Holon.

Reports on dinner at the Wilburton are mixed. The seasonal New American menu ranges from wild king salmon in a polenta crust with sesame-sherry vinegar sauce to seared venison tenderloin with blueberry sauce. Our house-smoked duckling breast served with maple-glazed apple slices tasted amazingly like ham and was delicious, as was the rack of lamb with a mint pesto sauce. Good starters were the beef carpaccio drizzled with white truffle oil and the escargots with sambucca and garlic on a bed of spinach. The kitchen has a way with desserts, including a wonderful apple crisp with ginger ice cream, Swiss profiteroles and melon or raspberry sorbet. Dining generally takes place in the clubby Billiard Room amid dark paneling, crisp white linens, heavy leather chairs and a tiled fireplace.

(802) 362-2500 or (800) 648-4944. Fax (802) 362-1107. www.wilburtoninn.com. Twenty-six rooms, four suites and three guest houses. Doubles, $155 to $300; $115 to $190 off-season.

Entrées, $25 to $34. Dinner nightly except Tuesday, 6 to 9, Memorial Day-October; weekends and holidays, rest of year.

Lodging

The Inn at Ormsby Hill, 1842 Main St. (Route 7A), Manchester Village 05254.

Chris and Ted Sprague, who turned the dining room at their Maine inn into a destination for gourmands, now lend their considerable innkeeping talents to this expanded B&B in a 1764 manor house backing up to Robert Todd Lincoln's Hildene estate. They upgraded the accommodations, especially in five luxury rooms they added in an unfinished wing of the sprawling house, long owned by Edward Isham, senior partner in a Chicago law firm with Abraham Lincoln's son, whom he entertained here. Each has a gas fireplace, whirlpool tub and handsome decor. Rooms come with interesting angles and novel touches, a see-through fireplace between the bedroom and corner jacuzzi in one, a jacuzzi accessed through cupboard doors in another, and shuttered doors that open to reveal fireplaces in a couple more. The main part of the house offers five comfortable guest rooms, all with fireplaces and two-person whirlpool baths and separate showers. All contain king or queen canopy or four-poster beds, plush armchairs, antique chests, artworks and oriental rugs. We stayed in the main-floor library room, beamed and dark with well-stocked bookshelves and a wood-burning fireplace. Some are partial to the Spragues' Tower suite, a three-level affair located in the tower section of the inn. There's a writing desk in the foyer, which leads to a raised bedroom with fireplace, sitting area and a tiger maple queensize canopy bed. The top level has a tiled bathroom with an oversize whirlpool tub in the corner and an oversize shower that doubles as a steam shower for two. The common rooms and the culinary treats are laudable. The main foyer leads to a front parlor furnished with antiques. From here one looks to the rear through a spacious library with a fireplace into a conservatory dining room extending 40 feet back. At first glance, the total depth, in what is a strikingly wide house, is breathtaking. So is the view across the terrace, back yard, gardens and Hildene property to mountains through the many-paned windows. Cookbook author Chris creates a lavish breakfast buffet, taken in the conservatory or on the outdoor terrace. The main dish could be bacon and egg risotto, blueberry bread pudding, leek-bacon-gorgonzola polenta or ricotta cheese pie.

(802) 362-1163 or (800) 670-2841. Fax (802) 362-5176. www.ormsbyhill.com. Ten rooms and suites with private baths. Doubles, $265 to $330 weekends, $205 to $270 midweek. Foliage, $320 to $385.

1811 House, Route 7A, Box 39, Manchester Village 05254.

Bowls of popcorn and no fewer than 65 single-malt scotches – the biggest selection in Vermont, owners Marnie and Bruce Duff say – are available in the intimate pub of this elegant B&B full of antiques, oriental rugs and charm. Although it's supposed to be a reproduction of an early American tavern, to us it looks like a

Scottish pub with its Duff family tartan seats and horse brasses, and a Duff coat of arms above the polished wood bar. Pewter mugs hang from the beamed ceiling. A warming fireplace, a regulation dart board and Waterford glasses add to the charm. Nearby are an elegant yet comfortable parlor and library. Each has a fireplace, dark wood paneling, fine paintings and porcelains, and stenciled flowers of the British Isles (the thistle, shamrock, rose and daffodil). The ten guest quarters in the nationally registered Federal house are air-conditioned and, except for one with a double bed, are quite spacious. One has a private porch and four have fireplaces, including a corner main-floor suite with a sitting room and a kingsize canopy bed. The bedroom of Mary Lincoln Isham (Abraham Lincoln's granddaughter, who lived here for a short time) contains a marble enclosure for the bathtub that she had put in. The Robinson Room with kingsize canopy bed offers a private porch overlooking the grounds, pond and mountains. An addition in a rear cottage contains three deluxe rooms with kingsize beds, fireplaces and LCD flat-screen TVs (the last are featured in the inn's two suites as well). A hearty English breakfast is served in the dining room or pub amid Villeroy & Boch china and the family sterling.

(802) 362-1811 or (800) 432-1811. www.1811house.com. Eleven rooms and two suites with private baths. Doubles, $140 to $270. Suites, $280.

The Inn at Manchester, Route 7A, Manchester Village 05254.

Hanging baskets and pots of flowers brighten the wicker-filled front porch of this restored Victorian residence-turned-B&B, nicely situated on four acres of lawns and gardens, with a swimming pool and even a meandering brook for added refreshment. Both the main structure and the rear carriage house are on the National Register of Historic Places. Rooms are named after wildflowers and herbs, and are attractively furnished with handmade quilts, interesting posters and prints, and comfortable chairs and lights for reading. Most rooms have queen or king beds, but three on the third floor have double beds, two of them with an extra twin bed. Three second-floor suites have fireplaces, and the other has the only in-room TV. The prime accommodation is the airy new Sage Suite on the third floor with a queen bed beneath a vaulted ceiling, a fireplace, balcony and the only whirlpool tub. Four spacious queensize rooms are nicely situated in the rear carriage house. Innkeepers Frank and Julie Hanes mingle with guests in their new pub. Breakfast is a three-course feast, including homemade granola and featuring perhaps apple pancakes or belgian waffles.

(802) 362-1793 or (800) 273-1793. Fax (802) 362-3218. www.innatmanchester.com. Thirteen rooms and five suites with private baths. Doubles, $155 to $185 weekends, $135 to $155 midweek. Suites, $215 to $255 weekends, $185 to $205 midweek.

The Ira Allen House, Historic Route 7A, Box 251, Manchester Village 05254.

A state historic marker beside the driveway five miles south of the village identifies this old farmhouse, built by Ira Allen in 1779 and home to Ethan Allen of Green Mountain Boys fame. The hand-hewn beams, hand-blown panes of glass and wide-board floors convey a certain patina of age. Innkeepers Ed and Maria Jones offer five suites that are the antithesis of their peers today: simple but comfortable period furnishings, beds covered with quilts, hooked rugs on the floors and hand stenciling on the walls. You get a lot of room for the rate in these rambling suites, each with bath and TV. Consider the Remember Baker Suite with a wood-burning fireplace in the bedroom, a day bed and chair in the sitting room and a private back porch. Even the smallest Ethan Allen Suite has a queen sleigh bed, a small corner stove and a sitting room with a twin bed. The Ira Allen Suite has two bedrooms with king/twin beds and a living room with fireplace. The premier two-bedroom Green Mountain Suite occupies the entire third floor, which was once a ballroom. The Joneses serve a full country breakfast. Adirondack chairs on the banks of the Battenkill invite relaxation and the river is good for fishing, canoeing and a cooling dip in a ten-foot-deep swimming hole.

(802) 362-2284 or (877) 362-2284. www.iraallenhouse.com. Five suites with private baths. Suites, $125 to $275.

High-Style Motel Rooms, Mountain Views

The Manchester View, Route 7A, Box 1268, Manchester Center 05255.

"A view from every room" is offered by this inn-style motel that crowns a rural ridge off Route 7 north of town. Some of the area's most unusual and sumptuous accommodations are offered in five dark brown buildings with white trim. Among the twenty-one motel-type rooms are six deluxe, nicely decorated rooms with fireplaces and one kingsize or two queensize beds. Even the eight standard rooms have queen beds. All have TV/VCR, refrigerators, hair dryers, and decks or balconies with views of the mountains. Most in demand are the "specialty rooms" and suites, three with two bedrooms and all with fireplaces. The enormous, cathedral-ceilinged Calvin Coolidge Room has a kingsize bed plus sofabed, whirlpool tub and photos of one of Vermont's favorite sons. Even bigger is the Ethan Allen Room with a queen canopy bed, whirlpool tub and a Colonial setting in a converted barn. The Norman Rockwell Suite contains a sitting room with a sofabed, kingsize bedroom, double whirlpool tub and a large private deck. The Grand Suite – billed as among the most luxurious in southern Vermont – comes with a large living room with fireplace, powder room, kingsize bedroom and a two-room bath with double whirlpool tub and a walk-in shower. All suites have two or three TVs and a DVD. A pleasant heated outdoor pool is surrounded by a large sundeck. A continental-plus breakfast is offered in the morning. Owners Pat and Tom Barnett are responsible for all the upgrades to this grand complex over the last 25 years. Mother Nature provided the exceptional setting.

(802) 362-2739 or (800) 548-4141. www.manchesterview.com. Twenty-seven rooms and six suites with private baths. May-November: doubles $105 to $210, suites $200 to $275. Rest of year: doubles $85 to $230, suites $185 to $275.

The Battenkill Inn, Historic Route 7A, Box 31, Manchester Village 05254.

On seven acres across from the entrance to the Mount Equinox Skyline Drive, this classic square 1840 farmhouse backs onto meadows stretching down to the Battenkill River. There's plenty of room for guests to spread out in two high-ceilinged sitting rooms with fireplaces, two dining rooms and porches looking onto the rural scene. Guest rooms furnished to the period are at the rear of the main floor and on the second floor. Some of the most appealing open onto porches. Six rooms (three with fireplaces) have queen beds and three have king beds. The bi-level Adams suite comes with a wood-burning fireplace in the sitting room and a kingsize poster bed in the bedroom, while the cozy Ladybird Suite has the only in-room TV. New innkeepers Tom Mosher and Sam Sassano provide a country breakfast. They also invite guests to bring their fishing gear to try their luck along the banks of the Battenkill.

(802) 362-4213 or (800) 441-1628. Fax (802) 362-0975. www.battenkillinn.com. Nine rooms and two suites with private baths. Doubles, $145 to $165. Suites, $165 to $195.

Aspen Motel, 5669 Main St., Box 548, Manchester Center 05255.

The nicely landscaped country setting of this one-story motel set back from the road in a quiet area is special, and the rates represent good value. On a nine-acre property, the motel occupies two buildings behind an attractive swimming pool and area for lawn games, including shuffleboard, badminton and horseshoes. Homey rooms come in a variety of configurations, with at least a double bed plus a twin bed, and most with queen, king or two double beds. Two rooms join to form a suite. Also available is the Birches, a two-bedroom efficiency cottage with a fireplace. The Welsh family who own the motel offer guests golf and tennis privileges at the Manchester Country Club nearby.

(802) 362-2450. Fax (802) 362-1348. Twenty-four rooms and one efficiency suite. Doubles, $75 to $115.

Barnstead Innstead, 30 Bonnet St. (Route 30), Box 988, Manchester Center 05255.

A New England hay barn built in the 1830s has been converted into one of the area's coziest places in which to stay. Fourteen rooms with queen, king or two double beds look like typical inn rooms with weathered beams and colorful quilts. All have rough pine furniture, carpeting, TVs and coffeemakers. The lamps are in brown crocks and calico wall hangings adorn the walls. We liked our room paneled in barnwood with a kingsize bed, a comfy chair and two old school desks that doubled as chairs and nightstands. A light breakfast is served in the Stone Wall Tavern, with stone floors as well as walls. It's a place for BYOB in the evenings. The swimming pool is popular in summer.

(802) 352-1610 or (800) 331-1619. www.barnsteadinn.com. Fourteen rooms with private baths. Doubles, $99 to $170. Suites, $140 to $210.

Where to Eat

Mistral's at Toll Gate, 10 Tollgate Road, Manchester Center.

This is a French restaurant with a difference. Gone is the haute demeanor of the old Toll Gate, one of Vermont's original Travel-Holiday award winners with a tuxedoed staff and sky-high prices. In its place is a less intimidating dining room, a simpler menu and the hospitality of chef-owners Dana and Cheryl Markey. Both local, they met as teenagers at the Sirloin Saloon, worked their way through area restaurants and ended up here, living upstairs in the rustic structure that looks like Grandmother's cottage in the woods. Although the two dining rooms seating 80 are country pretty with dark wood, lace curtains, blue and white linens, and gold-edged white china, it is the views through picture windows looking onto the trickling flume of Bromley Brook that are compelling. After dark, when the brook and woods, accented in summer by purple petunias and brilliant impatiens, are illuminated, the setting is magical. The menu offers a choice of about ten starters and a dozen entrées, most classic French with some nouvelle and northern Italian touches. Tempting starters include french onion soup gratinée, crab cakes grenobloise, smoked salmon blinis and escargots bourguignonne en croûte. Main courses range from breast of chicken provençal to grilled filet mignon with roquefort ravioli. The options could be roulade of sole with lobster and asparagus, prosciutto-wrapped monkfish with buttery lemon-caper sauce, crispy sweetbreads dijonnaise, and medallions of venison with black truffle-cabernet sauce. The specialty châteaubriand béarnaise and rack of lamb rosemary are offered for two. The signature dessert is coupe mistral (coffee ice cream rolled in hazelnuts with hot fudge sauce and frangelico). *(802) 362-1779 or (800) 279-1779. Entrées, $24 to $34. Dinner nightly except Wednesday, from 6. Closed in April.*

Bistro Henry, 1942 Routes 11 & 30, Manchester Center.

Some of the area's most exciting food is offered by Henry and Dina Bronson, who met in the kitchens of top Manhattan restaurants and moved to Vermont to pursue their dream. They first opened Dina's, a contemporary American dining room in an inn north of town, and then resurfaced in a motel dining room they called Bistro Henry. In 2003, they moved up the road to a green farmhouse they could call their own. With seating for about 100, it's the perfect spot for what Henry calls "a restaurant for today," as well as a home for Dina's growing Vermont Baking Co. business. Henry executes a Mediterranean bistro menu, based on the food they enjoyed while living and working in France. He has adapted the classics to 21st-century tastes, and his food sparkles with authenticity. Recent examples were grilled rare tuna with wasabi and pickled ginger, Moroccan grilled chicken with couscous, merlot-braised lamb shank, steak frites and grilled veal chop with mushroom sauce. As always, the menu was supplemented by tempting specials, among them soft-shell crab sauté, red snapper with orange-basil butter, organic Pacific salmon with pinot noir sauce and beef wellington with truffle sauce. Start with a classic onion soup gratinée or the more innovative sweetbread éclair with madeira cream. Finish with one of Dina's great desserts, perhaps her ever-famous fruit crisp, grand marnier crème brûlée, bananas foster cheesecake or lemon sorbet. She sells them retail and wholesale from her bakery. *(802) 362-4982. Entrées, $21 to $36. Dinner, Tuesday-Sunday from 5.*

The Black Swan, 4384 Main St., Manchester Village.

This 1834 brick Colonial house, originally part of the Munson dairy farm along with the Jelly Mill complex next door, has served since 1985 as the culinary stage for ex-San Francisco chef Richard Whisenhunt, formerly of Le Cirque in New York, and his wife Kathy, who manages the front of the house. Fireplaces and fresh flowers enhance the white-tableclothed dining rooms. The eclectic menu might start with broiled soft-shell crab with avocado-mango salsa, Maine crab cake with cajun mayonnaise or homemade duck sausage with cranberry relish. Entrées range from macadamia nut-crusted tilapia with orange compound butter and grilled ahi tuna with pickled ginger and soy sauce to rack of lamb with lingonberry-mint sauce or steak diane. Spicy jambalaya, coq au vin and osso buco were on a recent winter menu. The select wine list is affordably priced. *(802) 362-3807. www.blackswanrestaurant.com. Entrées, $16.50 to $32. Dinner nightly except Wednesday, from 5:30.*

Chantecleer, Route 7A, East Dorset.

The food is consistently good and the atmosphere rustically elegant in what some consider the area's finest restaurant. Swiss chef Michel Baumann acquired the contemporary-style restaurant fashioned from an old dairy barn in 1981. His menu features Swiss and French provincial cuisine, from whole dover sole filleted tableside to crispy Peking-style roast duck breast and leg with sour cherry sauce. Our party of four sampled a number of offerings, starting with a classic baked onion soup, penne with smoked salmon, potato pancakes with sautéed crabmeat and a heavenly lime butter sauce, and bundnerfleisch fanned out in little coronets with pearl onions, cornichons and melba rounds. For main courses, we savored the rack of lamb, veal sweetbreads morel, sautéed quail stuffed with mushrooms duxelle and the night's special of boneless pheasant from a local farm, served with smoked bacon and grapes, among other things. Fabulous roesti potatoes upstaged the other accompaniments, puree of winter squash, snow peas and strands of celery. Bananas foster, grand-marnier layer cake, crème brûlée and trifle were worthy endings for a rich, expensive meal. A number of Swiss wines are included on the reasonably priced wine list, and Swiss yodeling music may be heard on tape in the background.

(802) 362-1616. Entrées, $28 to $36. Dinner by reservation, nightly except Tuesday from 6.

The Perfect Wife, 2594 Depot St., Manchester Center.

Chef-owner Amy Chamberlain always imagined herself as the perfect wife, but she's seldom home. Instead she's at her innovative restaurant and lively tavern, dishing up flavorful freestyle cuisine and arranging live entertainment on weekends. Hers is a place for all people and all tastes – whether you're in the mood for an exciting four-course meal or a game of darts and some dancing. Gourmet dining takes place in the rustic cobblestone-walled restaurant or an airy greenhouse garden room. The menu offers an eclectic mix, perhaps wild king salmon glazed with maple syrup, pecan-crusted pork tenderloin with apricot-rum butter, grilled loin of New England venison with a caramelized shallot and sundried cranberry demi-glace and even turkey schnitzel. You could begin with sautéed crab cakes rémoulade or the signature Peking duck rolled in a sesame pancake. Desserts sound simple but that's deceptive. Witness the mixed berry pie with an orange marmalade lattice crust topped with crème anglaise. Some mighty interesting comfort food is offered in the tavern.

(802) 362-2817. www.perfectwife.com. Entrees, $16 to $28. Tavern, $7.95 to $16.95. Dinner, Monday-Saturday 5 to 10, tavern from 4.

Garden Café, Southern Vermont Arts Center, West Road, Manchester Village.

Halfway up Mount Equinox, this seasonal café at the Southern Vermont Arts Center is a terrific place for lunch with a view of the sculpture garden as well as the sweeping lawns, birch trees, hills and valleys. Dine inside or on the outdoor terrace at tables covered with brightly colored linens and flanked by ice-cream-parlor chairs. The changing menu depends on the season's concessionaire, lately Richard and Kathy Whisenhunt of Manchester's Black Swan Restaurant. At one visit, the fare included choices like crab and asparagus melt over a toasted English muffin, warm ham and cheese croissant, a chicken caesar salad, poached salmon and vermicelli, and a burger topped with Vermont cheddar. We remember a fantastic tomato-orange soup and a good chicken salad with snow peas. Dessert could be a crispy apple tart or melon with berries. Dinner is available on performance evenings.

(802) 366-8298. Entrées, $8 to $10.50. Lunch, Tuesday-Saturday 11:30 to 2, June to early October. Sunday brunch in summer, noon to 2.

Light Fare

The Little Rooster Café, Route 7A south of Manchester Center, started as an offshoot of the Chantecleer restaurant, and the chef continues the tradition. For breakfast, the Rooster tops an English muffin with poached eggs, Canadian bacon, creamed spinach and smoked salmon in a light mustard sauce. The french toast triple-decker, layered with smoked ham and pineapple, is served with raspberry butter. For lunch ($6.50 to $9.95), we've enjoyed the crab cake baguette, the leg of lamb sandwich and the grilled tuna niçoise salad. There's a wine list, plus the usual coffees. Open daily except Wednesday, 7:30 to 3.

Across the street is **The Buttery at the Jelly Mill,** on the second floor of a fun, four-story collection of shops selling gourmet foods and kitchenware, among other things. It purveys many sandwiches, including smoked salmon on a toasted croissant with capers. The Buttery special is ham, cheese, artichoke hearts and hollandaise on toasted rye. Snacks like nachos, soups, salads and specials such as a tomato, bacon and cheddar quiche are offered, and you can end with neapolitan mousse torte or amaretto bread pudding. Open daily, 9 to 4; weekend brunch, 10 to 1.

More exotic sandwiches and salads are available at **The Village Fare Café & Bakery,** Union Street, Manchester Village. Guests at the nearby Equinox resort take a break from high living to lunch on a tuna rollup, a roast beef and boursin sandwich, or quiche of the day in the $6 to $9 range. You can get soup and half a sandwich or a choice of four deli salads with a side of bread. The pastries change daily, but they always include the biggest muffins you ever saw. Stop in the morning for espresso and the pita eggwich (scrambled eggs, peppers, onions and diced tomatoes with provolone). Or come in the afternoon for coffee and a fancy dessert. Open Tuesday-Saturday 6:30 to 4, Sunday 7:30 to 4.

Up for Breakfast, Main Street, Manchester Center, is just what its name says: upstairs above a storefront, and open for breakfast only. Although reports on the food lately have been mixed, you'll find pain perdu, cajun frittata, huevos rancheros and belgian waffles in the $5 to $7.25 range. We chose "one of each" – one eggs benedict and one eggs argyle (with smoked salmon). These proved hearty, as did the heavy Irish scone, both dishes garnished with chunks of pineapple and watermelon. Only after we'd eaten did we see the blackboard menu around the side, listing some rather exotic specials like rainbow trout with eggs and mango-cranberry-nutmeg pancakes. Open weekdays 7 to noon, weekends 7 to 1.

⸺ *Gourmet Sweets* ⸺

Mother Myrick's Confectionery & Ice Cream Parlor, Route 7A, Manchester Center.

Few can resist stopping at Mother Myrick's, the ultimate ice-cream parlor and confectionery shop. One of the things that lures us is the fudge sauce – so good that a friend to whom we give it hides her jar in a cupboard and eats it with a spoon. Here you can buy the most extraordinary homemade chocolates, get a croissant and cappuccino in the morning, tea and a slice of Vermont maple cheesecake in the afternoon, or a piece of grand marnier truffle cake and espresso at night. Ice-cream sodas, milkshakes, floats, sundaes and pastries are served in a fantastic art-deco café setting or outside on a front deck.

(802) 362-1560 or (888) 669-7425. www.mothermyricks.com. Open daily 10 to 6, summer and peak periods, 10 to 10.

FOR MORE INFORMATION: Manchester & The Mountains Chamber of Commerce, 5046 Main St., Suite 1, Manchester Center, VT 05255, (802) 362-2100 or (800) 362-4144. www.manchestervermont.net.

Green Mountains are backdrop for Middlebury College campus and town.

Middlebury/Champlain Valley, Vt.

Robert Frost Country

The poet Robert Frost spent the last 23 summers of his life in the mountains outside the college town of Middlebury. Little wonder. The rather rugged area enveloping a lively academic community is mountain country, Frost counttry, an area of rambling white houses, red barns, and green fields and hills – the essence of Vermont, if you will.

The poet who adopted New England and made it his own also adopted the Middlebury area. The small cabin where he slept is not open to the public, but an interpretive nature trail nearby gives you a taste of his enduring poetry and the sights that inspired him. The Middlebury College library houses many of his first editions. The founder of the town's Vermont Book Shop knew the poet well and the store stocks many of his works. And the college's Bread Loaf mountain campus carries on his tradition with its annual summer writers' conference.

Middlebury is, for us, the quintessential New England college town, settled in the late 1700s around a wide waterfall of Vermont's longest river – Otter Creek – that powered the early mills and marble works. Soon to develop was Middlebury College, whose sprawling hillside campus on the town's west side is stunningly picturesque, with abundant green space between signature gray limestone buildings dating to the college's founding in 1800. One of us first came upon this scene on a snowy April day and decided then and there that this was to be the college for him.

The college gives the town its solid heritage and vibrant character. ("The strength of the hills is His also" are the words etched above the portals of the landmark college chapel in which Robert Frost lectured to turn-away student audiences every few years.) And a returning alumnus is struck by a new dynamic – an array of entrepreneurial enterprises, restaurants and shops that is remarkable for a town its size (8,000).

Rural tranquility spreads out on all sides from Middlebury and its under-named Otter "Creek." To the east are the Green Mountains and East Middlebury and Ripton, quiet mountain hamlets, Middlebury's bucolic Bread Loaf campus and the college's impressive Snow Bowl ski area. To the north is Vergennes, which claims to be one of the nation's oldest and smallest cities, a mere speck on the rolling landscape but a rejuvenated one these days. To the west lies the Champlain Valley, a surprisingly vast and undeveloped expanse sidling up to Lake Champlain. Here mountains and lake meld in a wondrous panorama – the Green Mountains on the east, New York's Adirondacks to the west and the Northeast's longest lake shimmering in the middle.

This is an area of charming contrasts, one where lake and mountains, simplicity and sophistication, co-exist to near perfection. You can be as active as you like or simply relax in restful contemplation of the wonders of nature.

Seeing and Doing

Middlebury, the shire town of Addison County and the lower Champlain Valley, spreads out from the Otter Creek falls around which the early settlement developed. The historic downtown is split into two sections by the broad Otter Creek, traversed by a scenic footbridge below and a narrow Main Street bridge above a wide waterfall that powered the town's early mills and marble works. The northern side of downtown is crowned by Court Square and the sloping town green, where a pair of inns and a white-spired Congregational church stand sentinel. Brick stores and offices from the 18th and 19th centuries line Merchants Row and Main Street past Otter Creek. The southern side of downtown harbors the triangular Cannon Green descending to the mill buildings of Frog Hollow. A diminutive traffic rotary points the way to Middlebury College, which takes up much of the southwestern portion of town.

Frog Hollow Vermont State Craft Center, 1 Mill St., Middlebury.

With windows onto the Otter Creek falls in the heart of Middlebury, this exceptional craft center just off Main Street is picturesque as well as one of our favorite crafty places anywhere. Inside the renovated mill is a 3,000-square-foot treasure trove of traditional and contemporary pottery, sculpture, stained glass, pewter, quilts, pillows, wall hangings, jewelry, and stuffed and wooden toys, all by more than 250 juried Vermont artisans. We managed to resist some great sculptures of dogs and bunnies ($450 to $675). We could not resist a woodcut print by leading Vermont artist Sabra Field, a Middlebury grad with a wonderful sense of design. Her "Apple Tree Winter" with chickadee perched on a branch was the forerunner of a small collection of Field prints that kindles Vermont memories throughout our house. The nation's first state craft center has expanded to locations in Burlington and Manchester.

(802) 388-3177. www.froghollow.org. Open Monday-Saturday 9:30 to 5, also Sundays 11 to 4, spring through fall. Free.

SHOPPING. The compact center of Middlebury is still a downtown, claiming an old-line Ben Franklin variety store, a movie theater, museums and public buildings. The biggest store in town is the **Alpine Shop,** corner of Main and Merchants Row. Inside in a ramble of rooms on two floors you'll find summer and winter clothes,

Austrian boiled wool jackets, cuddly nightgowns, boots for all reasons, jewelry, gifts and skiwear. It even carries Lederhosen. The shop's predecessor was the first and biggest single customer of Geiger of Austria, a partnership that prompted the location of the Geiger factory off Route 7 on Exchange Street just north of town (it sells overstock at its **Geiger Collections** store at 38 Pond Lane). The neatly jumbled **Vermont Book Store,** whose founder knew Robert Frost, has one of the country's largest collections of Robert Frost works, including out-of-print collector's items. Also along Main Street you'll find funky women's clothes at **Wild Mountain Thyme,** antique jewelry and vintage apparel at **Bejewelled,** and kitchenware and housewares at **dada. Greenfields Mercantile** is a showcase for the eco-friendly clothing, bags and accessories of American designers working in hemp and other sustainable and recycled fibers. **Sweet Cecily,** billed as "a country store for today," stocks great cow pottery, cow placemats and painted cabinets among its folk art and fine crafts. **Forth 'n Goal** is a sporting goods store that features the Middlebury Collection of college clothing and accessories.

Other shops are found in restored mill buildings around Frog Hollow Fun gifts and accessories are among the eclectic stock at **4 Dogs & a Wish,** "a store for eccentric people and their pets." Robert Crystal shows his functional and decorative pottery along with works of other artisans in the **Otter Creek Craft Gallery** located in the old Star Mill. **Middlebury Mountaineer** carries outdoor sporting gear and apparel. Up a staircase beside the Otter Creek falls, **Great Falls Collection** has unusual jewelry, home accessories and nature and garden items. From Frog Hollow a 276-foot pedestrian bridge across Otter Creek yields a view of the falls and connects with the historic **Marble Works** complex, a collection of businesses, offices and specialty stores in restored white marble factory buildings. Local producers back up their trucks and tailgates to the parking lot for the small farmer's market (where we bought some delicious bread, corn and salsa) beside the falls on Wednesday and Saturday mornings. Here also is the showroom for **Danforth Pewterers,** where you can watch handcrafted pewter jewelry and tableware being made, either spun on a lathe or cast in a bronze mold. A pewter dolphin on a corded necklace for $12 caught our eye. Sweaters, dresses and other knitwear is fashioned by Dia Jenks and artisans at **dia,** a design company with a retail showroom. The new **American Flatbread Restaurant** sells gourmet pizzas to go and is open for dinner Friday and Saturday evenings. Restaurant seating is in the oven room, where diners can see the fire as bakers and cooks prepare each flatbread to order.

Where the Cows Come Home

Woody Jackson's Holy Cow Store, 44 Main St., Middlebury.

The Champlain Valley landscape is his inspiration, and the cows and colors of Vermont his product. All are on display in this whimsical shop showcasing the work of local artist/author Woody Jackson, creator of the cows that became famous worldwide as ambassadors for Ben & Jerry's ice cream. The Middlebury graduate's trademark cows are the motif on everything from golf balls to light switch plates, pocket knives to tablecloths. Here are many of the items available on his clever "cowtalogue" website and then some. The gift shop relocated into the center of town from the main floor of his production facility at 52 Seymour St.

(802) 388-6739. www.woodyjacksoncows.com. Open Monday-Saturday 9 to 5, Sunday noon to 5.

Heaven for bow-tie wearers is **Beau Ties Ltd.,** 69 Industrial Ave., off Route 7 north of town. Here you can tour the facility and watch handcrafters making the catalog company's ties and, of course, buy a few along with ascots, cummerbunds, cravats and pocket squares in the retail store, open weekdays 10 to 4. Watch master soapmakers create some of the mildest soaps in the world at **Vermont Soapworks,** 616 Exchange St. Billed as the largest producer of natural handmade soap in America (more than 7,500 bars a day), it has a soap museum and discount factory outlet where seconds are available.

Stop for a beer at the **Otter Creek Brewery,** 85 Exchange St., where tours are given daily at 1, 3 and 5 and you can sip free samples and browse through the brewhouse gift store. Open Monday-Saturday 10 to 6, Sunday 10 to 4.

Henry Sheldon Museum of Vermont History, 1 Park St., Middlebury.

Bachelor Henry Sheldon bought the brick 1829 Judd-Harris House opposite Cannon Park and opened it in 1884 as the first village museum in the country, drawing visitors with a twenty-foot sign that read "Sheldon's Art and Archeological Museum." His vast and idiosyncratic collection includes furniture, portraits, clothing, textiles, tools and household objects. The place is filled with all sorts of odd but interesting items like a mousetrap that kills a rodent by drowning it in a cylinder of water, a pair of shoes worn by Calvin Coolidge as a child and a collection of old dentist's tools, including a primitive ether bottle. There's even a stuffed cat – it seems that Sheldon, the town clerk, saved everything. The highlights of one of the most exemplary museum collections in Vermont are exhibited in ten rooms in the elegant Federal house built by the owners of a quarry and marble works near the falls of Otter Creek. The marble columns and window lintels and six fireplaces of rare black marble testify to their expertise. Middlebury's garden clubs have created an early Victorian garden next door. Changing history and art exhibits are shown in the Walter Cerf Gallery.

(802) 388-2117. www.henrysheldonmuseum.org. Open Monday-Saturday 10 to 5, late May to mid-October, Tuesday-Saturday rest of year. Adults $5, children $3.

Vermont Folklife Center, 3 Court St., Middlebury.

Founded in 1984 to display the folk art and traditions of Vermont, this small but rewarding educational venture occupies the restored 1823 Masonic Hall facing Court Square. Of particular appeal to specialists, video shows and changing exhibits portray the people and places that make Vermont's folk art and rural traditions distinctive. The works of Franco-American wood carvers were displayed front and center at one visit and 200 years of handweaving at another. The Heritage Shop features the works of 25 contemporary folk artists and artisans, from whirligigs to beeswax candles, from hooked rugs to carved wooden utensils.

(802) 388-4964. www.vermontfolklifecenter.org. Gallery and shop open Tuesday-Saturday 11 to 4. Free.

University of Vermont Morgan Horse Farm, 74 Battell Drive, Weybridge.

Col. Joseph Battell of Middlebury, whose name graces three college dormitories, began breeding Vermont's famously versatile Morgans in the 1870s at his farm, just northwest of Middlebury past a landmark covered bridge across Otter Creek. The Morgan, America's first breed of horse, is Vermont's state animal. Most of the Morgan horses alive today can be traced to this site, where they are bred, trained and sold. You can tour the stables on the hour, watch a twenty-minute video show and observe the 60 to 80 registered stallions, mares and foals as they are trained. At the right times, you can even hear the horses neighing and see them waiting for their hay, which slides down a trough into their stalls three times a day. The lush lawns include a picnic area and a life-size statue of the first Morgan, named Figure. The 1878 main barn is on the National Register of Historic Places. The farm's gift shop offers hundreds of equine-related items.

(802) 388-2011. Tours daily on the hour, 9 to 4, May-October. Adults $5, children $2.

Middlebury College, Route 125, occupies a 1,200-acre campus on the southwestern side of Middlebury. It is notable for the consistent use of gray limestone in its buildings as well as for its summer foreign language schools. Founded in 1800, the college has evolved from the lower Old Chapel-Painter Hall row to the skyscraping Bicentennial Hall straddling a hill looking east and west. Now more than 2,200 undergraduates are enrolled at one of the top-ranked liberal-arts colleges in the country. Hundreds of graduate students flock to the nine Summer Language Schools and the Bread Loaf School of English, where 250 writers attend the annual Bread Loaf Writers Conference, the oldest and largest in the country (Robert Frost is remembered as "the godfather of Bread Loaf.") The spanking new college library has excellent collections in its Robert Frost Room. Middlebury's $16 million Center for the Arts is a state-of-the-art showplace for the performing arts, five galleries housing the Middlebury College Museum of Art, the college's top-flight concert series and even a café called Rehearsals.

HIKING AND BIKING. The Green Mountains and the rolling Champlain Valley are a paradise for hikers and cyclists, who turn out in droves here in summer and fall. The Middlebury Area Land Trust's emerging "Trail Around Middlebury," a fourteen-mile footpath linking town lands and local landmarks, is accessible from downtown and crosses a suspension footbridge over Otter Creek south of town. The Green Mountain National Forest offers more challenging hikes crisscrossing Mount Abraham, Bread Loaf Mountain and Romance Mountain. You'll find countless signs identifying hiking trails, including the Long Trail, along Route 125 from Hancock through Ripton and East Middlebury. Bicycling trails outlined by the Lake Champlain Bikeways organization include Rebel's Retreat, an easy loop along Lake Champlain, and Otter Creek Wandering, a more strenuous loop along Vermont's longest river.

Mountain Tours. A favorite mountain loop starts in East Middlebury and follows Route 116 to Bristol, a town perched on a shelf and notable for its Lord's Prayer Rock (the prayer is chiseled on the rock along the New Haven River just east of town). Head east on Route 17 past the entry to the Lincoln Gap (itself worth a detour) onto what's locally called the McCullogh Turnpike to the top of the Appalachian Gap. Continue down the east slope past Mad River Glen and Mount Ellen/Sugarbush North ski areas to Route 100 in Waitsfield. Head south through Warren to Hancock, where you turn west on Route 125 past Texas Falls, a beautiful little series of cascades in a chasm where Middlebury students cooled off in the days before guard rails were added and swimming was prohibited. At the top of the Hancock Gap is the Middlebury College Snow Bowl and, starting down the west slope, the college's Bread Loaf mountain campus with its old yellow wood dormitories and green Adirondack chairs scattered about the lawns. The Middlebury River along

Route 125 below Ripton is another favorite cooling-off or picnicking spot in season. For a more spectacular option (in terms of mountain panoramas) from Route 100 on the east side of the Green Mountains, head west through the Brandon Gap (Route 73).

The Middlebury College Snow Bowl, Route 125, offers uncrowded skiing in winter on a fifteen slopes and trails served by a triple chairlift and two double chairs. One of us used to ski here nearly every winter afternoon on a $25 student season pass good for the original single pomalift. Now, students ski for $28 a day on weekends, $23 midweek, and adults pay $35 and $28, still below the going rates. The Snow Bowl is open daily 9 to 4, weekends and holidays 8:30 to 4. There's cross-country skiing nearby on 42 acres of groomed trails at the college's Rikert Ski Touring Center in Ripton, as well as on the Ralph Myhre Golf Course at Middlebury College. Ice skating is available in the college's Nelson Arena.

─ *The Road Less Traveled* ────────

Robert Frost Interpretive Trail, off Route 125 between Ripton and Middlebury's Bread Loaf campus.

"Please take your time and leave nothing but your footprints," urges the sign at the start of this easy-to-walk, three-quarter-mile trail blazed in 1976 by the U.S. Youth Conservation Corps. Several benches are strategically placed for creative contemplation. This is a delightful way to spend an hour or two, reading some of Frost's poems mounted on plaques en route. Meadows, woods, groves of birches and streams are traversed and identified. Frost lived and worked within a mile of here; the fields and forests were the inspiration for his poems and mentioned in many. Nearby is the Robert Frost Wayside Area with picnic tables and grills in a grove of red pines that Frost pruned himself. Up a dirt road is the Homer Noble Farm, site of the log cabin where Frost spent his last 23 summers.

Covered Bridges. Addison County possesses four of Vermont's most treasured landmarks, which are some of the best preserved in the nation. Closest to Middlebury is the Pulp Mill Covered Bridge, the oldest in the state, which spans the town lines of Middlebury and Weybridge off Route 23 and the Morgan Horse Farm road. It is a two-lane bridge of three spans, one of only six remaining in the United States. Just northeast of Middlebury is the Halpin Road Covered Bridge above a waterfall, the highest bridge over a stream bed in Vermont. Other covered bridges are in Shoreham and Cornwall.

Lakeshore Tours. Southeast of Middlebury is Lake Dunmore, a small lake favored by summer cottagers and Middlebury College sailors. A favorite destination is **Branbury State Park** where you can swim in Dunmore, hike to Silver Lake or the Falls of Llana, and climb the Rattlesnake Cliffs Trail to Rattlesnake Point, a large rock outcrop at the southern end of Mount Moosalamoo.

For glimpses of the lower stretches of Lake Champlain to the north and west of Middlebury, head southwest to Orwell and then follow the rural lakeshore road, variously called Lake Road and Lake Street from Shoreham north through Bridport, Addison and Panton to Basin Harbor. You'll be surprised to discover how undeveloped the shoreline along such a large lake can be. About the only commercial enterprises we encountered were the Bridge Family Restaurant near Chimney Point, the Yankee Kingdom Farm Stand and Vermont's Own Products. A couple of waterfowl areas, the DAR and Button Bay state parks, and a couple of state historic sites are worthwhile stops along the way. The M/V Carillon, (802) 897-5331, gives 90-minute cruises in summer and fall on Lake Champlain from Larrabee's Point in Shoreham, stressing the military significance of the area around Mount Independence and Fort Ticonderoga. Also at Larrabee's Point, a ferry established in 1759 runs across Lake Champlain from May-October.

—Revolutionary Remains—

Mount Independence State Historic Site, off Route 73, Orwell.

On this Gibraltar-like promontory jutting into Lake Champlain opposite New York's famed Fort Ticonderoga, the colonists held off the British attacking from Canada for a year in a confrontation that altered the course of the Revolutionary War. The significance of the war's most intact surviving site is commemorated in a 400-acre park, a National Historic Landmark that opened in 1996 and won an award as the finest museum in Vermont. The odd-looking visitor center is shaped like the upside-down shell of a boat. The inside is fascinating, especially the fiberglass "talking heads" custom-designed in Montreal – one British, one American – whose lips appear to move ever-so-realistically as they tell opposing versions of the story. Exhibits detail the military life of the period and include an 18th-century cannon recovered from the bottom of the lake and artifacts found in a continuing archaeological dig – more than 700 items in one summer alone. Several miles of hiking trails wind past the star fort, blockhouses, hospital, barracks and other well-preserved remains of the once-bustling military complex that was among the largest communities of the time in North America.

(802) 759-2412. www.historicvermont.com. Open late May to mid-October, daily 9:30 to 5. Adults $5, children free.

Farther north at Chimney Point is a Vermont Route 17 highway bridge crossing to Crown Point, N.Y. The **Chimney Point State Historic Site,** a late 1700s tavern on a strategic bluff overlooking the lake in Addison, offers exhibits and programs on Vermont's native Abenaki tribe as well as the early French settlers who torched the site at the end of the French and Indian War, leaving only the charred chimneys that inspired the point's name.

A mile north of the Crown Point Bridge is the **DAR John Strong Mansion Museum,** 6656 State Route 17, Addison, (802) 759-2309. The stately brick home was built about 1790 by Revolutionary War General John Strong, one of the early settlers in Addison after the French left Chimney Point. Operated by the Vermont State Society, Daughters of the American Revolution, it contains fine period furnishings and exhibits portraying early life in the colonies. It's open Saturday and Sunday 10 to 5, Memorial Day through Labor Day; adults $3, students $1, family rate $5.

Lake Champlain Maritime Museum, 4472 Basin Harbor Road, Vergennes.

This expanding museum is located in a complex of a dozen buildings near the entrance to the Basin Harbor Club. Dozens of small boats built around the lake over a period of 150 years, regional watercraft memorabilia, a working blacksmith forge and an operational boat-building shop are featured. Exhibits inform about the largest collection of wooden shipwrecks in North America, buried on the lake bottom. Visitors get to board a 54-foot-long replica of Benedict Arnold's sunken

Revolutionary War gunboat *Philadelphia II,* built at the museum and rigged, armed and afloat in the harbor. A good collection of Champlain Valley artifacts from Indian through modern times is shown in the restored 19th-century limestone schoolhouse in which the growing museum started. The museum has expanded to the downtown Burlington waterfront with the Burlington Shipyard, where the replica schooner Lois McClure was rebuilt and launched in 2004.

(802) 475-2022. www.lcmm.org. Open May to mid-October, daily 10 to 5. Adults $9, children $5.

Vergennes. Lately a tad rejuvenated, this "city" in the northwest corner of Addison County claims to be one of America's oldest (incorporated in 1778) and one of its smallest (one square mile, population 2,741). It even built a statehouse in 1798 in hopes of becoming the state capital. Vergennes (pronounced Ver-JENS) is off the beaten path, having been bypassed by U.S. Route 7, and not really on the way to much of anywhere but the shores of Lake Champlain. The restored 1897 Vergennes Opera House on the second floor of City Hall at 120 Main St. offers concerts and silent "Friday Flicks" and is open weekdays for self-guided tours. A small upstairs museum in the Bixby Memorial Library displays a collection of Abenaki Indian artifacts, fossils, mementoes from one of Benedict Arnold's ships and a letter written in 1774 from the Count of Vergennes, France's foreign minister for whom the city is named, who aided Ethan Allen's upstart Vermonters in their fight for independence. Below downtown beside the Otter Creek's three waterfalls plunging 37 feet is MacDonough Park, a modest patch of green on the site of a former shipyard where Commodore Thomas MacDonough commanded the building of a naval fleet to defend Lake Champlain against British invasion. The park is now a picnic spot and recreation area for fishing, kayaking and canoeing.

A few restaurants have popped up along Main Street and around the green, including the celebrated **Christophe's on the Green** (see Where to Eat), the down-to-earth **Black Sheep Bistro,** 253 Main St., and a European-style deli-café, **Eat Good Food,** 221 Main St. At the **Kennedy Brothers Factory Marketplace** at 11 Main St., Vermont products are displayed in shops and booths of what was once the Kennedy Brothers woodenware factory. Craftsmen offer their wares direct to the customer on the first floor, and antiques shops are scattered about upstairs. You can watch fudge and organic cheese being made in the country store.

The Best View of All

Mount Philo State Park, 5425 Mount Philo Road, off Route 7, Charlotte.

This knob of a mountain (elevation, 968 feet) rising from the plateau above Lake Champlain north of Vergennes offers awesome vistas of the lake and Champlain Valley to the south. Drive up a winding, narrow road through the woods to the top, where you pay a day-use fee for the 168-acre park, Vermont's oldest. A short walk leads to scattered picnic tables perched at mountain top's edge, great spots for a snack on a summer day. A telescope atop a rocky outcropping brings distant panoramas up close. Ten tent campsites and three lean-tos are hidden in the woods for those who want to spend the night away from it all.

(802) 425-2390. Open daily, May 20 to Oct. 15. Adults $2.50, children $2.

Where to Stay

Swift House Inn, 25 Stewart Lane, Middlebury 05753.

A rambling white clapboard manse, built in 1814 and once the home of a Vermont governor, is the focal point of this attractive and relaxing inn acquired in 2004 by Dan and Michele Brown, formerly of the Pilgrim's Inn in Maine. They were updating some of the ten rooms in the main house, which vary in size and amenities from a pair of small rooms with queen or twin beds but no TVs to two extra-spacious rooms with kingsize beds, TVs and whirlpool tubs. Rooms are handsomely outfitted with poster beds and handmade quilts, and some of the bathrooms are knockouts. The modest Victorian Gatehouse at the foot of the property offers five smaller rooms of considerable value, given that each has a king or queen bed, TV, telephone and coffeemaker and three have whirlpool tubs. The prime accommodations are in the restored 1886 carriage house at the top of the hillside property: six deluxe rooms with kingsize beds, fireplaces and whirlpool tubs. The prized Mansfield room on the lower level of the carriage house is large, light and airy in bleached pine with an abundance of windows screened by Indian shutters. We enjoyed cocktails on our own patio beside a rose garden, watched the TV news from a sofa and wing chair (each flanked by good reading lamps) in the ample sitting area, and slept in a step-up poster bed. The front foyer had a closet with an ironing board, the dressing area was equipped with a coffeemaker, and the lavish bathroom with double jacuzzi positively shone with solid brass fixtures. Public rooms in the inn include a wide hall used as a parlor with one of the inn's many fireplaces and a comfortable little cocktail lounge with five seats at the bar. A steam room and sauna are available in the carriage house. The expansive grounds are dotted with Adirondack chairs and private hideaways for two. Dinner is available for guests and the public in the inn's gracious dining rooms (see Where to Eat). After breakfast (included in the rates), settle on the front porch for a look down the wide lawns toward the Adirondack mountains in the distance.

(802) 388-9925. Fax (802) 388-9927. www.swifthouseinn.com. Twenty-one rooms with private baths. Doubles, $100 to $185. Carriage house, $235 to $255.

Middlebury Inn, Court House Square, Middlebury 05753.

Since 1827, this mellow red-brick Georgian inn has overlooked the village green, with the obligatory rocking chairs lined up on the marble floor of the side porch near the entry. The 45 rooms in the rambling building have been renovated and redecorated but remain more like those in a period hotel than in a country inn. Ten more rooms are available in the adjacent 1816 Porter House Mansion. Varying in shape and size, all have high ceilings, brass fixtures and intricate moldings as well as TV and two telephones. Four have whirlpool tubs and five are two-bedroom suites. Middlebury alumni of a certain age prefer the twenty large and modern rooms in a rear motel annex. Each contains two double beds or a double and twin bed plus a queensize sofabed. The inn's spacious lobby, where complimentary afternoon tea is served, has nooks for reading or playing checkers. The Country Peddler gift shop offers everything from books to maple syrup.

Cocktails and sandwiches are served on the screened porch in summer, and lunch and dinner entrées are available in the **Open Book Café.** Traditional New England cuisine takes on contemporary accents in a dinner menu ranging from potato-crusted salmon fillet to venison with bourbon-chutney glaze. Light fare and desserts like baked Vermont apple crisp and maple-marble cheesecake are among the evening offerings in the pleasant **Morgan Tavern.** Continental breakfast is included in the rates.

(802) 388-4961 or (800) 842-4666. Fax (802) 388-4563. www.middleburyinn.com. Seventy-five rooms and suites with private baths. Doubles, $98 to $270. Suites, $145 to $375. Entrées, $16.75 to $24.95. Lunch, 11:30 to 2. Dinner, 5:30 to 8:30.

Whitford House, 912 Grandey Road, Addison 05491.

If you really want to get away, seek out this restored 1790s house located along a gravel road on 37 acres in the back of beyond, with a panoramic view of the Adirondack Mountains across nearby Lake Champlain. Book a stay in the rear guest cottage where we spent a night and would happily have stayed the summer. It harbors a comfortable sitting room, a large bedroom with a kingsize bed, a full bath with a radiant-heated floor, a kitchenette and big windows all around to take in the views. Your only "company" may be geese from a nearby wild bird preserve and a few sheep who share the back yard with a stunning sculpture of a horse made of vines and sticks. Plus, of course, genial hosts Barbara and Bruce Carson, who fell in love with the area when their daughter attended Middlebury College and decided to "retire" here to run a B&B of great appeal. They share their spacious house with guests in three bedrooms, one on the main floor with a four-poster double bed and two upstairs with king/twin beds. The entire place is stylishly furnished with family heirlooms, antiques and unexpected finds, including an old milk chest from a dairy barn that was converted into a corner china cabinet in the dining room. The room is lit entirely by candles for breakfast, a hearty affair that yielded at our visit homemade granola with yogurt and rhubarb sauce, spiced apples (from the yard) and poached eggs on toast with roasted tomatoes (from the garden). The Carsons offer wine, beer and hors d'oeuvres in the afternoon in their stunning great room with fieldstone fireplace, baby grand piano and tall windows onto the mountains. They also offer candlelight dinners to guests by reservation. That's fortuitous, because you'll likely find their welcome so warm and the surroundings so relaxing that you won't want to leave the property.

(802) 758-2704 or (800) 746-2704. Fax (802) 758-2089. www.whitfordhouseinn.com. Three rooms and one cottage with private baths. Doubles, $110 to $150. Cottage, $225 to $250.

The Inn on the Green, 19 South Pleasant St., Middlebury 05753.

The Middlebury green gained a second hostelry with the opening of this 1803 Federal-style landmark listed on the National Register. Steve and Micki Paddock restored the stately house, painted gray-blue with white trim, with great care and with guests' privacy in mind. The main floor holds a small common room that doubles as a reception area/office, and two queensize suites with sitting rooms, one with two bedrooms. The walls here and throughout the house are painted interesting colors (one sitting room dark blue, the bedroom pale yellow) and are decorated with quilts, plates and paintings for sale. Other guest rooms, all with queen beds and TVs, are located upstairs in the house and on two floors of a carriage house to the side and rear, next to a Baptist church. Those on the upper level of the carriage house are cozy with slanted ceilings. There being limited common areas, the staff delivers continental "breakfast in bed" to the guest rooms.

(802) 388-7512 or (888) 244-7512. www.innonthegreen.com. Nine rooms and two suites with private baths. July-October: doubles $139 to $159, suites $219 to $259. Rest of year: doubles $99 to $139, suites $149 to $219.

Cornwall Orchards Bed & Breakfast, 1364 Route 30, Cornwall 05753.

Sturdy Adirondack-style chairs on the idyllic rear deck here overlook what remains of Cornwall Orchards, once the town's biggest employer, and the distant Adirondacks. Some of the apple trees still dot the property, but the original 1783 farmhouse on fourteen rural acres two miles south of Middlebury has been turned into a stylish B&B by Robert and Juliet Gerlin, Connecticut transplants who got to love the area when their children went to Middlebury. The rambling, pale yellow structure lent itself to becoming a B&B, what with a comfortable living room with fireplace, a dining room and a substantial country kitchen opening onto that great rear deck. Three guest rooms with full baths occupy wings on the ends of the main floor. The largest is typical with a down duvet on the queensize bed, shiny hardwood floors and white walls. Decor is crisp yet simple here and in two upstairs rooms, one with queen bed and the other with twins. Ingredients from nearby farms go into Juliet's breakfasts, perhaps scrambled eggs or organic blueberry pancakes.

(802) 462-2272. www.cornwallorchards.com. Five rooms with private baths. Doubles, $100 to $125. No credit cards.

Courtyard by Marriott, 309 Court St. (U.S. Route 7 south), Middlebury 05753.

Whoa, what's this – a chain hotel popping up in 2004 in a meadow south of quaint old Middlebury? The three-story hotel looks rather like an old Vermont farmhouse (white with green shutters and a wraparound porch). And it does fill a niche in an area where accommodations can be hard to come by at peak periods. The interior is typical of the Courtyard genre. There are 89 modern guest rooms and suites, with kingsize or two queen beds. Seven suites have gas fireplaces and whirlpool tubs and two have fireplaces. The usual hotel and business amenities abound. Guests enjoy an indoor pool, whirlpool and exercise room. A full breakfast buffet is available in the Courtyard Café for $9.95.

(802) 388-7600 or (800) 388-7775. Fax (803) 388-7602. www.middleburycourtyard.com. Seventy eight rooms and eleven suites. Doubles, $129 to $349 weekends, $119 to $269 midweek.

Waybury Inn, 457 East Main St. (Route 125), Box 27, East Middlebury 05740.

This charming inn has been attracting travelers since 1810, and it drew one of us in our Middlebury College days for dinner (always london broil with the best mushroom sauce ever) in the rear tavern. Many thousands of meals and inns later, it is not quite as enticing as in our memories, although having been pictured as the fictional New England inn on the Bob Newhart show has kept it reasonably thriving. Lately under the auspices of Joe Sutton, a Burlington hotelier, and his wife Tracey, the Waybury is away from the mainstream, quiet and peaceful, with a wide, shaded front porch and a side deck upon which to while away the hours. You can swim in a river gorge almost across the street, or stroll up the road into the mountains. The fourteen guest rooms, many with king poster and queen sleigh beds, are simply furnished in homey Vermont style. Top of the line are the Breadloaf, a roomy space with king bed and sitting area, and the refurbished Robert Frost, the "honeymoon suite" with a kingsize poster bed and an antique desk in which couples leave notes in a secret drawer. The recently spiffed-up parlor and reception area on the main floor harbors books, games and a small TV. A full country breakfast is included in the rates.

(802) 388-4015 or (800) 348-1810. www.wayburyinn.com. Fourteen rooms with private baths. Doubles, $110 to $225 in summer and fall, $95 to $165 in winter and spring.

┌─A Mountain Retreat─

The Chipman Inn, Route 125, Ripton 05766.

In a real mountain hamlet in the heart of Robert Frost country, this small, informal inn dates from 1828. Innkeepers from way back, Bill Pierce and his wife Joyce Henderson offer lots of space to spread out in what looks to be someone's handsome home – in the comfy parlor with a big fireplace by the little bar, in a lounge full of hooked rugs, in a sitting area with magazines in the upstairs hall, and in the stenciled dining room where prix-fixe dinners are served occasionally by reservation at 7:30 for $25. All eight homey guest rooms are pleasantly furnished with antiques. One of the smallest has a sitting room and another a skylight. They generally have a double or queen bed and a twin bed, or combination thereof. Two have a double bed and one has a double and two twins. There's no television except in the lounge, Joyce is quick to point out, but there are plenty of books for amusement. And there's no pool, "but mountain lakes and streams abound." Bill makes granola for the hearty breakfast, which includes a choice of egg dishes.

(802) 388-2390 or (800) 890-2390. www.chipmaninn.com. Seven rooms and one suite with private baths. Doubles, $95 to $135; foliage, $115 to $150. Children over 12.

Strong House Inn, 94 West Main St., Vergennes 05491.

This 1834 Federal-style B&B, listed on the National Register of Historic Places, is situated on six acres on the crest of a hill at the western edge of Vergennes. The main house, built by the local bank president for whom it is named, offers six rooms and a simple Victorian suite with queen poster bed up against the wall and a sitting room with a sloping ceiling and a tapestry sofabed. Rooms vary widely in size and style, from the queen-canopied Empire Room with two leather chairs facing a fireplace to the new Vermont Room, a hideaway with beamed ceiling, sturdy queen country pine bed and french doors opening onto a small balcony. The recently built Rabbit Ridge Annex adds six more deluxe rooms. Two on the second floor with beamed cathedral ceilings offer kingsize poster beds, fireplaces and french doors onto private balconies. The ultimate is the Adirondack Room, done in the style of the great Adirondack camps with a twig-canopied kingsize bed, a floor-to-ceiling stone fireplace, wet bar, double jacuzzi tub and private deck. Mary Bargiel, innkeeper with her husband Hugh, stenciled the ivy in one room, made the bed quilts and offers quilting seminars. She also offers afternoon snacks and a breakfast to remember in the large and fancy dining room. The fare at our visit was fruit crêpes with strawberry topping. On summer evenings, guests can enjoy a bottle of wine taken from the inn's little tavern to the back-yard gazebo as the sun sets over the Adirondacks. The grounds also contain a goldfish pond, skating pond, snowshoeing and walking trails, and two sled runs.

(802) 877-3337. Fax (802) 877-2599. www.stronghouseinn.com. Thirteen rooms and one suite with private baths. Doubles, $90 to $280. Suite, $140. Add $30 for foliage and special-event weekends.

An All-Around Resort by the Lake

The Basin Harbor Club, 4800 Basin Harbor Road, Vergennes 05491.

Spread out on 700 acres beside Lake Champlain, this charming and secluded resort has something for everyone. Basic rooms are in the inn, the Champlain

House and the Harbor Homestead. The 77 most prized accommodations are in wood-paneled cottages, some with super screened porches overlooking the water and others with decks onto the golf course. Cottages vary from one to three bedrooms, and one-third of them have stone fireplaces. Rooms have phones but no TV. All have been redecorated lately. Guests relax in brightly colored Adirondack chairs, play golf on the eighteen-hole, 6,5011-yard course or tennis on five courts, and swim in a large heated pool or at the waterfront. Four generations of the Beach family have run Basin Harbor since Ardelia Beach started taking in guests in her farmhouse in 1886, and they do it very well indeed.

If you can't stay here, at least drop in for the lavish luncheon buffet in the summery Ranger Room with a view of the pool, or book a table for dinner. One of the Basin Harbor's enduring traditions is that "gentlemen over the age of 12" are required to wear coats and ties for dinner in the main dining room in July and August. Grilled shrimp with thyme beurre blanc and rack of lamb dijonnaise are signature dishes. The Sunday jazz brunches are legendary, and seafood buffets and cookouts are perennial favorites. The casual **Red Mill** beside the club's air strip features lighter fare of burgers, salads, vegetarian items and seafood.

(802) 475-2311 or (800) 622-4000. Fax (802) 475-6545. www.basinharbor.com. Thirty-eight rooms and 77 cottages. Rates, AP. Mid-June to Labor Day: doubles, $262 to $336. Cottages, $383 to $504, slightly lower in spring and fall. B&B and MAP rates also available in spring and fall. Closed mid-October to mid-May.

Lunch buffet $18.50, Monday-Saturday 12:30 to 2:30. Dinner nightly, 6 to 8:30, prix-fixe $39. Red Mill, open daily 11:30 to 10.

Where to Eat

The Storm Café, 3 Mill St., Middlebury.

The setting for dinner in the Frog Hollow Mill is perfect, intimate in the lower level of an 1840 mill building or outside on a deck overlooking the churning Middlebury Falls of Otter Creek. Chef-owners Karen and John Goettelmann, both Culinary Institute of America graduates, share cooking duties to implement an eclectic menu. At a recent winter visit, you could make a meal of paneer masala or "stormy gumbo," a warming and moderately spicy creole stew of shrimp, scallops, chicken, chorizo sausage, tomatoes, vegetables and okra. Or you could opt for grilled salmon fillet over wilted greens tossed with shiitake mushrooms, sundried tomatoes, bacon and red onions; paella "with a stormy twist" (apparently the variety of toppings), and peppered New York strip steak topped with brie and a rich port wine demi-glace. Appetizers include the signature roasted garlic and potato soup, a smoked salmon napoleon and sautéed shrimp tossed with a zesty concoction of bloody mary ingredients (including vodka). Dessert could be warm apple crêpes, espresso profiteroles or frozen apricot soufflé.

(802) 388-1063. www.stormcafe.com. Entrées, $15.95 to $21.95. Lunch, Tuesday-Saturday 11:30 to 2:30. Dinner, Tuesday-Saturday 5 to 9.

Tully & Marie's, 5 Bakery Lane, Middlebury.

This is the worthy successor to the long-running Woody's, a California-style eatery lovingly tended by Woody Danforth, who retired far too early. New chef-owner Laurie Tully Reed and his wife, Carolyn Dundon, changed the name to incorporate each of their middle names but kept things much the same. The contemporary, four-level restaurant with enormous windows overlooking Otter Creek looks like a cross between a sleek diner and an ocean liner. Eating outside on the curved wraparound deck, right above the creek, is like being on a ship – an illusion heightened by mirrors in the interior dining areas. New American fusion cuisine with Asian, Italian and Mexican accents is featured. At an autumn lunch we sampled a fiery sweet potato and jalapeño soup, an ample Thai chicken salad and a hefty avocado, tomato and bacon melt on focaccia with sweet potato fries, all delicious. At dinner, entrées range from organic Scottish salmon with wasabi aioli to chicken tostadas mole, pecan-chipotle pork tenderloin and filet mignon au poivre. Among the better desserts are pear-mascarpone trifle, midnight espresso mousse and crème caramel.

(802) 388-4182. www.tullyandmaries.com. Entrées, $15.95 to $19.95. Lunch, Monday-Saturday 11:30 to 3. Dinner nightly, 5 to 9 or 10. Sunday brunch, 10:30 to 3.

Swift House Inn, 25 Stewart Lane, Middlebury.

One of the legacies of the inn's beloved co-founder and chef, the late Andrea Nelson, is the restaurant that was her pride and joy. New owners Michelle and Dan Brown continued dinner service that had resumed after a three-year hiatus, but made the experience more casual and affordable (all small plates $9, all entrées $16). Dining is by candlelight in three small and serene dining rooms – one a library – appointed in hunter green. Chef Carrie Mooney's contemporary American menu features a variety ranging from pan-seared Scottish salmon with black trumpet mushroom sauce to grilled New York strip steak served with buttermilk-mashed potatoes, braised kale and rainbow chard. A complimentary amuse-bouche – goat cheese and mango salsa on crostini, garnished with an edible flower – and superior crusty sliced breads got our dinner off to a good start. One of us enjoyed an appetizer of foraged mushrooms cassoulet and a sensational duck confit napoleon with local chèvre and field greens. The other liked the roasted butternut squash soup with whipped truffle crème fraîche and fried sage leaves and the roasted duck breast with caramelized crimini mushrooms and creamy garlic polenta. Dessert was a house specialty, Andy Nelson's original coffee-toffee pecan torte, a dessert that any chocoholic would love.

(802) 388-9925. Entrées, $16. Dinner Thursday-Monday, 6 to 9.

Fire & Ice, 26 Seymour St., Middlebury.

Opened by Middlebury graduates in 1974 and greatly expanded over the years, this is a sight to behold: a ramble of rooms highlighted by Tiffany or fringed lamps, brass chandeliers, and boating and sport fishing memorabilia. One room has a copper-dome ceiling and there's an upside-down canoe on the ceiling of the lounge. Co-owner Dale Goddard's restored 22-foot Philippine mahogany runabout is moored majestically in a lobby surrounded by salad bars. "I had fun with this," says Dale, who bills it as Middlebury's "museum dinnerhouse." More than 200 people can be seated at booths and tables, in nooks and crannies – some off by themselves in lofts for two and others in the midst of the action around the massive copper bar. The stir-fries are famous, as is the shrimp bar, which includes all the shrimp you can eat. The Sunday salad bar adds soup and crab legs, and the event is billed as "just like Sunday dinner at grandma's." Prime rib and steaks are featured, anything from blackened rib to châteaubriand and steak au poivre. Roast duckling, chicken boursin and cashew chicken stir-fry are specialties. A light fare menu also includes the 55-item salad and bread bars. The restaurant's name comes from the title of a Robert

Frost poem. The fire reflects the cooking and the ice the drink mixing that goes on here.

(802) 388-7166 or (800) 367-7166. www.fireandicerestaurant.com. Entrées, $15.95 to $24.95. Lunch, Friday-Saturday noon to 5. Dinner nightly from 5, Sunday from 1.

The Dog Team Tavern, 1338 Dog Team Road, Middlebury.

Trendy restaurants come and go, but the Dog Team goes on forever, serving enormous, Sunday-dinner-type meals to generations of hungry Middlebury College students and visitors from afar. Built in the early 1920s by Sir Wilfred and Lady Grenfell, it was operated by the Grenfell Mission as an outlet for handicrafts from Labrador until it became a restaurant of note. You order from the traditional blackboard menu as you enter and wait for your table, either in the delightfully old-fashioned living room filled with nostalgia like a collection of old campaign buttons, or in the large and airy lounge, where chips and dips are served with drinks. Off the bar is a pleasant, two-level deck overlooking Otter Creek. When you're called into the charming dining room with a view of the birches and the rippling stream, you eat (and eat and eat). We've been doing so here for years, and are always amazed how they can still serve such huge amounts of food for the price, from the poor man's ham or fried chicken with fritters to the big spender's prime rib or boneless sirloin. The price of the entrée includes soup, an assortment of goodies from brass buckets on the spinning relish wheel that's rolled to your table, salad, bread sticks, the Dog Team's famous sweet sticky buns, and a multitude of vegetables like your mother used to make, served family style. For dessert, if you can face it, there might be homemade maple-oatmeal pie, chocolate delight or a Bartlett pear with crème de menthe. One of us feels that far too much food is served, but the other generally is up to the challenge.

(802) 388-7651 or (800) 472-7651. www.dogteamtavern.com. Entrées, $12.95 to $25.95. Dinner nightly, Monday-Saturday 5 to 9, Sunday noon to 9.

Waybury Inn, Route 125, East Middlebury.

This rural inn dating to 1810 was the favorite place for special-occasion dining in our college days, when the Waybury and the Dog Team had a monopoly on the fine-food business hereabouts. We're partial to the dark and cozy taproom out back. It's the prototype of an old New England pub (the outside of this inn was, after all, the backdrop for the Bob Newhart show), where the dinner menu has given way to a pub menu of late. The trademark london broil – a house signature from yore – has been missing from the menu lately, and dinners and Sunday brunch are served now in the cranberry and white Coach Room or on the enclosed side porch. Dinners begin, as they have for years, with a kidney-bean relish for which so many people requested the recipe that it has been printed on a postcard. Typical appetizers are mushrooms and goat cheese in puff pastry, wild boar sausage and pecan-fried calamari with a ginger-soy sauce. The extensive menu focuses on such entrées as the new specialty scallops (a different presentation every night), shrimp yucatan in a crispy tortilla shell, and black and tan roast duck with orange-sesame sauce. Kentucky bourbon steak and rack of lamb with rosemary brown sauce are entrée fixtures. Chocolate bombe, frangelico crunch cake and crème brûlée are popular desserts.

(802) 388-4015. Entrées, $18.50 to $29.50. Pub, $8.95 to $12.50. Dinner nightly, 5 to 9. Sunday brunch, 11 to 2.

— A Touch of Paris in Vermont —————————————————————

Christophe's on the Green, 5 North Green St., Vergennes.

For a taste of Paris, those in the know seek out French chef Christophe Lissarrague's exciting 35-seat restaurant in a corner of a former hotel facing the Vergennes village green. Tables are on two levels in a sleek, pale yellow room with dark brown trim. The with-it, contemporary menu changes weekly and is available à la carte (with all choices for each course the same price) or prix-fixe, $38 for three courses. The chef's wife Alice, the hostess and former actress who grew up in nearby Shelburne, might suggest starting with such exotica as chicken consommé with red pepper puree and foie gras raviolis, boursiche of sweetbreads and snails with tarragon sauce and baby greens, or a salad of frisée and leg of rabbit with smoked hazelnuts and carrot vinaigrette. The half-dozen main courses might range from pan-seared grouper with clams, squid ink vermicelli, black capers and baby bok choy to roasted piglet with fried prosciutto and bacon sauce. A selection of rare French cheeses is offered following the entrée. Masterful desserts include cocoa soufflé with frozen hazelnut ganache, coconut and rum savarin with caramelized pineapple and a trio of sorbets (banana, blood orange and muscat wine) or ice creams (thyme, pistachio and cappuccino), served with petits fours. If this kind of fare intrigues, try the tasting menu, $190 a couple with wine for a sampling of the finest in contemporary French cuisine.

(802) 877-3413. www.christophesonthegreen,com. Prix-fixe, $41; entrées, $25.50. Dinner, Tuesday-Saturday 5:30 to 9:30, May-October; Thursday-Saturday in December and February-April. Closed in November and January.

The Otter Creek Bakery, 14 College St., Middlebury.

Ben and Sarah Wood patterned their original café and bakery in Frog Hollow Mill on the models they know in San Francisco. Problem was that Sarah's bakery became the tail that wagged the dog and Ben closed the cafe (the space since taken over by the Storm Café) to concentrate on the growing bakery business up the street. Here the baked goods are sensational as ever, and the Woods have garnered quite a following for their mail-order cookies and dough (chunky peanut butter, maple-oatmeal-raisin and lemon-pecan among them). Not to mention their delectable raspberry almond crunch cheesecake, praline almond tort and other sweets that defy categorization. Now they're doing a land-office takeout business with sandwiches (we liked the Otter Creek pâté and the Norwegian smoked salmon) in the $4.50 to $4.95 range. They also have soups, salads and pizzettes to go. Plus, of course, the requisite fancy coffees.

(802) 388-3371. Open Monday-Saturday 7 to 6 (to 8 in summer), Sunday 7 to 3.

Two Brothers Tavern, 86 Main St., Middlebury.

Brothers Holmes and Beal Jacobs run this newish storefront restaurant and tavern facing Bakery Lane. The food runs from casual to elegant, including pastas, seafood, steaks, vegetarian and nightly kabob specials. There's a full bar, and fifteen microbrews are on tap. The place serves late-night food into the wee hours.

(802) 388-0002. www.twobrotherstavern.com. Entrées, $9.50 to $16. Lunch daily, 11:30 to 5. Dinner, 5 to 10. Late night menu 10 to 1 a.m.

FOR MORE INFORMATION: Addison County Chamber of Commerce, 2 Court St., Middlebury, VT 05753. (802) 388-7951 or (800) 233-8376. www.midvermont.com.

Shops, restaurants and sidewalk cafés lure crowds to Church Street Marketplace.

Burlington, Vt.

Dream City

"The most beautiful place in the world," William Dean Howells called it. The 19th-century novelist was referring to the lake country around Burlington, the Queen City by the lake, cradled beneath the Green Mountains against a stunning backdrop of Adirondack Mountains rising across Lake Champlain.

Many agree. Beauty unfolds all along Lake Champlain, the 120-mile-long waterway that stretches into Quebec province, and Burlingtonians make the most of it. The nation's mayors voted Burlington America's most livable city. Outdoor magazines rank it the "top American dream city."

The accolades are on-going for the state's largest city (population, 39,000), which has blossomed into Vermont's downtown – "as downtown as Vermont gets," in the laconic words of Vermont Life magazine. Here is one downtown that works, as the Church Street Marketplace and the revitalized lakefront draw throngs to the heart of the city day and night.

Church Street, the old main street, is now a wide pedestrian mall lined with specialty stores, restaurants, coffeehouses and outdoor cafés, plus a growing number of high-end national chain stores that inevitably go where the crowds are.

After years of neglect, the diamond-in-the-rough lakefront is beginning to shine. Appealing people places are the nine-acre Waterfront Park with its flower gardens and swinging park benches, and a floating Community Boathouse that spawns all kinds of water sports. A new science center and aquarium with a mouthful of a name is in its infancy. Two new excursion boats give scenic lake cruises, and an auto ferry crosses the lake hourly to and from New York State. The free College Street shuttle bus connects the waterfront to downtown shopping and the University of Vermont campus up the hill.

Just south of Burlington lies Shelburne, with its famed Shelburne Museum, the Camelot-like Shelburne Farms and a rolling, pastoral landscape that gives new definition to suburbia, Vermont style.

The area's cultural heritage is enhanced by the Flynn Theater, the Vermont Mozart Festival, outdoor Vermont Symphony pops concerts and chamber music at Shelburne Farms. A book took notice, ranking Burlington among the most hip small art towns in America.

Don't think Burlington is all culture and gleam, however. Vermont author Ralph Nading Hill summed up his native city: "Add to Burlington's natural endowments – Lake Champlain at its doorstep and the Green Mountains in its backyard – its Vermont birthright as a sensibly small but vital metropolis that has never overgrown its cultural and architectural heritage, and you have a northcountry mecca with one of New England's, and the country's, choicest futures."

Dream City is not just a good place in which to live. It's a great place to visit, too.

Seeing and Doing

Nowhere this side of Washington's Puget Sound are the vistas of lake and mountains quite so stunning, thanks to the Green Mountains on the east and the Adirondacks to the west. Little wonder they call the Burlington area "the West Coast of New England." And the best of it is around Burlington.

Explore the Lakefront

The downtown **Waterfront Park** focuses on a floating freighter known as the **Burlington Community Boathouse.** Operated under auspices of the city recreation department as a center for water sports, it rents sailboats and kayaks and offers scuba classes. There are picnic tables along the entry path, and **Splash at the Boathouse** serves casual food and drink on a floating dock beside the water. Stretching north along the lakeshore is a boardwalk promenade, where you can relax on solid wooden glider swings and enjoy Lake Champlain.

TOURING. An 8.2-mile-long **bicycle path** stretching from Oakledge Park on the south along the downtown waterfront to the Flynn Estate at the mouth of the Winooski River gets closer to the lake than any other shore route. A bike ferry, operated by the non-profit group Local Motion, transports bikers and walkers across the river, daily in summer and weekends in spring and fall (fare, $1). Across the Winooski River, the Island Line Rail Trail bikeway continues through Colchester and across a spectacular stretch of lake causeway and railbed with water on both sides. After a 200-foot turnstile bridge was dismantled, one gap remained to connect to South Hero and the Champlain Islands, where there is another series of bike routes. Access to the path is via Oakledge and Leddy parks, North Beach, Perkins Pier and the Waterfront Park. The ribbon of tarmac winds around historic sites and through verdant corridors as it offers scenic water views.

Motorists as well as cyclists can travel Pine Street south from downtown and North Avenue toward Colchester for interesting diversions. Pine Street ends near **Red Rocks Park,** a heavily wooded picnic grove with a small beach for swimming.

At the foot of Flynn Avenue, **Oakledge Park** offers picnicking, four tennis courts near the water and a rocky shoreline with good views back toward the city skyline. **Battery Park,** downtown at the foot of Pearl Street on a crest near the lake, harbors guns that repulsed British ships in the War of 1812 and telescopes for viewing 75 peaks in the Adirondacks. Out North Avenue is the **Municipal Beach,** locally known as North Beach, with the city's best swimming, campsites, picnic tables and grills, playground and a view of the ferry. Nearby **Leddy Park** also offers nicely wooded picnic sites near the shore. Up a winding road off Ethan Allen Parkway through **Ethan Allen Park** is a hilltop with a tower and the city's best all-around view: the Adirondacks to the west and the Green Mountains to the east. Continue out North Avenue and follow Route 127 to Colchester. Marble Island Road and Barney Point from Colchester Point Road give vistas of what the natives call "the Broad Lake," and Lakeshore Drive hugs the shore along Malletts Bay.

ECHO at the Leahy Center for Lake Champlain, 1 College St., Burlington.

Formerly the Lake Champlain Basin Science Center, this aquarium and science center with a mission has been renamed as well as rebuilt. The letters of its name reflect its mission – to explore the Ecology, Culture, History and Opportunity for stewardship of the Lake Champlain Basin – and recognizes Sen. Patrick Leahy for his dedication to the lake. Little-known outside Vermont, the striking, contemporary building holds more than 60 species of fish, amphibians and reptiles in its aquarium section. Its science center has a hundred hands-on interactive exhibits. The multi-sensory Awesome Forces Theater compresses 800 million years into six minutes of larger-than-life geologic forces that shaped the landscape in the Champlain basin. A twenty-foot waterfall cascades down a Vermont limestone wall as visitors ascend to a landing where they come face to face with fish, frogs and turtles in a 2,750-gallon tank. There are water-play spaces where children can build dams and float boats, and an Atlantic tide pool touch tank with periwinkle snails, horseshoe crabs, sea stars, anemones and urchins. Youngsters may work a miniature lighthouse or pop in on a painted turtle in Discovery Place. Others may control a high-tech underwater adventure as they get a glimpse of the replica historic General Butler shipwreck. Touring exhibits are showcased in the changing exhibit gallery three times a year. The museum has a gift shop and a seasonal café. A second-story balcony affords great views of the lake.

(802) 864-1848. www.echovermont.org. Open daily, 10 to 5, Thursday to 8. Adults $9, children $6.

Spirit of Ethan Allen III, Burlington Community Boathouse, Burlington.

The 500-passenger, triple-deck Spirit of Ethan Allen III is the largest excursion boat on Lake Champlain. It leaves from the Community Boathouse at the foot of College Street for 90-minute narrated cruises four times a day. Be on the lookout for Champ, the legendary lake serpent; 70 passengers aboard the original paddlewheeler tour boat in 1984 became believers in the largest mass sighting ever. We took the 2 p.m. cruise and found it quite interesting, if slow. The boat went north to Apple Tree Bay, then south to Shelburne Point and back, and much of the narration was about the height of the various Green Mountains. The noon trip includes a buffet lunch or brunch, and there is a dinner/entertainment cruise every evening at 6:30.

(802) 862-8300. www.soea.com. Trips daily at 10, noon, 2 and 4, Memorial day to mid-October. Adults $11.99, children $5.99.

Lake Champlain Ferries, King Street Dock, Burlington.

The working Burlington Ferry leaves for a scenic one-hour trip across Lake Champlain to Port Kent, N.Y., roughly every hour during the summer, from 7:30 a.m. to 7:35 p.m. You get to see more of the lake than on the Spirit, although without the benefit of narration. Walk-on passengers and bicyclists are welcomed. The Lake Champlain Transportation Co. is the oldest steamship operator in the country and one of its boats, the Adirondack (1913), is the oldest double-ended ferry still in operation. Cheaper and more frequent ferry rides are offered from Grand Isle in the Champlain Islands to Plattsburgh (crossing time twelve minutes) and from Charlotte to Essex (twenty minutes).

(802) 864-9804.www.ferries.com. Car and driver, $25 round trip, adult passengers $6.75, children $2.75; maximum car fare, $45.25.

The ferry company has outfitted a **Northern Lights Cruise Boat,** (802) 864-9669, for scenic lake cruises from the King Street Dock. The M/V Northern Lights, a 115-foot-long double-decker built in 2002 to resemble an early lake steamboat, is named for the displays of Aurora Borealis that shimmer over Lake Champlain in the night skies in late summer. Ninety-minute sightseeing cruises are offered Sunday-Friday at 2 and 4; adults $8.95, children $3.95. Lunch cruises leave Monday-Friday at noon; adults $12.95, children $7.95. Weekend brunch cruises at noon cost $18.95 for adults, $10.95 for children.

Sailing cruises and sailboat rentals are offered by **Winds of Ireland,** (802) 863-4090 or (800) 458-9301, based at the Burlington Community Boathouse. Two-hour sails take place from mid-May to Mid-October for $25 a person.

The **Whistling Man Schooner Co.,** (802) 598-6504, carries up to seventeen passengers on its classic sloop Friend Ship three or four times a day from its dock next to the Burlington Community Boathouse; adults $30, children $15.

Ride the Rails

Green Mountain Railroad, Burlington Waterfront Park, Burlington.

The mountain and lake views between Burlington and Shelburne are memorable from the **Champlain Valley Flyer** as it wends along the Burlington waterfront and Shelburne Bay, with a brief stop in Shelburne. The diesel-powered train with a couple of restored vintage passenger cars loads and unloads passengers at a covered platform beside the Burlington Waterfront Park. Narration outlines the history, folklore and attractions along the way. The round trip takes one hour.

(802) 463-3069 or (800) 707-3530. www.rails-vt.com. Train leaves Saturday and Sunday at 10, noon, 2 and 4, late June through August. Adults $10, children $7.

Enjoy Downtown

The word "enjoy" is used advisedly, for Burlington's downtown is one that's truly enjoyable. It's a prospering, people place by day and night as well as on weekends. Indeed, the Church Street Marketplace is said to be the fifth most popular tourist attraction in Vermont.

Stroll along the boardwalk in the nine-acre Waterfront Park, go up to Battery Park and through the Burlington Town Center's lawns and enclosed shopping mall to the Church Street Marketplace, an exceptionally nice, landscaped pedestrian mall transformed from the city's main street, headed by the historic Unitarian Church. The pedestrian mall is alive with shopping carts, sidewalk cafés, restaurants and stores, both local and of the variety normally associated with upscale shopping malls.

Not for nothing is Church Street so named. Close by are the spectacular Episcopal Cathedral Church of St. Paul, rebuilt after a 1971 fire and well worth a visit; the striking Catholic Cathedral of the Immaculate Conception, and the Congregational and Baptist churches with their soaring spires. A number of buildings around City Hall Park, College Street and the Battery Street waterfront are of architectural merit.

SHOPPING. Thriving Church Street has lost most of its old-line stores, and increasingly is becoming a stage set of chains, not unlike the trendy outdoor lifestyle centers. Here you'll find the **Peace & Justice Store** side by side with **Laura Ashley.** Local merchants compete head-to-head against such national retailers as **The Nature Company, Pier 1 Imports, Borders Books & Music, Banana Republic, Eddie Bauer,** the **Discovery Channel Store** and **Pompanoosuc Mills.** Among the treats for shoppers are **Michael Kehoe Ltd.** and **Champlain Clothing Co.** for apparel, **Kiss the Cook** kitchen shop, **Apple Mountain** for Vermont souvenirs and specialty foods, **Urban Outfitters, Danforth Pewterers** and the contemporary **Phoenix Gallery. Frog Hollow at the Marketplace** is a branch of the Frog Hollow Vermont State Craft Center in Middlebury.

Check out the hometown store at 87 Church St. of artist-author **April Cornell,** the reigning queen of home textiles, Canada's answer to Martha Stewart. April and Chris Cornell, who began in Montreal and now live with their family in Burlington, and their design team turn cotton prints, silk and knits into clothing, home furnishings and accessories sold in boutiques and her retail stores across North America.

Stop at **Bennington Potters North,** 127 College St., as much to see how an old brick warehouse can be restored with taste as to view the myriad items for sale: everything from aprons to egg cups to clay bird feeders to rugs and furnishings (and, of course, that good-looking pottery).

The Shelburne area has many interesting shops. The first **Talbots** store in Vermont anchors Shelburne Square, an upscale strip plaza. The **Shelburne Country Store** has been in continuous operation since 1859, but never with more flair than lately. There are still penny candy and homemade fudge, as well as room after room full of fine crafts, toys, candles, folk art notes, lamp shades, kitchenware, specialty foods and more. Sample a taste of smoked ham and you'll probably buy some at **Harrington's,** which specializes in cob-smoked meats, pheasants, turkeys and hams, and offers "the world's best ham sandwich."

More interesting shopping is found at the **Champlain Mill,** three floors of shops and restaurants fashioned from a 1909 textile mill beside the river in Winooski, Burlington's neighbor to the north. A major expansion was under way in 2005.

Shelburne Treats

Shelburne Museum, U.S. Route 7, Shelburne.

A destination in itself, this incredible 150,000-item "collection of collections" – the legacy of Electra Havemeyer Webb, wife of a Vanderbilt heir – unfolds in 39 exhibit buildings spread across 45 acres, all beautifully landscaped with wild roses twining over rustic fences, fruit trees and flowering shrubs. The almost overwhelming display of Americana, unrivaled in New England, spans three centuries and a multitude of interests.

A free jitney tram takes visitors from the visitor center near the entrance to the far ends of the grounds every fifteen minutes.

The sidewheeler Ticonderoga excursion boat that cruised Lake Champlain for 47 years is what many visitors tour first. It is especially interesting to view the staterooms – some elegant and some holes in the wall – with their corner washstands; the dining-room tables are set with Syracuse china. Among the historic structures worth visiting are a one-room schoolhouse from Vergennes, an 1840 general store, an 1871 lighthouse from the lake, a 1733 saltbox from Massachusetts, a Shaker barn filled with a fantastic collection of carriages and the last remaining two-lane covered bridge with footpath in the United States. Don't miss the Weed House, which has remarkable collections of dolls, toys, pewter and glass, and the Stencil House, with its original and very handsome stenciled walls from 1790. Our favorite is the Electra Havemeyer Webb Memorial Building, a Greek Revival mansion housing a six-room apartment taken from the Park Avenue residence of the museum founders; it is totally charming and filled with priceless paintings. The Shelburne Depot from 1890 and the private railroad car parked beside it are worth a look. The collection of wildfowl decoys here is considered the most important in the world. Altogether there are more than 80,000 pieces of Americana in this national treasure described by the New York Times as "Vermont's Smithsonian."

(802) 985-3346. www.shelburnemuseum.org. Open May-October, daily 10 to 5. Adults $18, children $9.

Shelburne Farms, 102 Harbor Road, Shelburne.

The 1,400-acre agricultural estate of Dr. William Seward Webb and his wife, the former Lila Vanderbilt, is open to the public as a working farm. Blessed with one of the more spectacular lakeside/mountain settings in the Northeast, Shelburne Farms combines an active dairy and cheese-making operation, a children's farmyard, walking trails, a bakery, a market garden, furniture-making and other leased enterprises in a working-farm setting that has a delightful, Camelot-like quality. Ninety-minute guided tours aboard an open-air wagon reveal the landscape as created by Frederick Law Olmsted, designer of New York's Central Park. Tours show the enormous Farm Barn, the Dairy Barn, the formal gardens and the Shelburne House, where they stop to view a few of the public rooms. You may see grazing along the way the choice herd of Brown Swiss cows, descended from stock raised for cheese making in Switzerland. Their Shelburne Farms farmhouse cheddar, some of the best we have ever tasted, is sold in the fine visitor center and farm store. A walking trail from the visitor center winds through woods and fields for about a mile to the top of Lone Tree Hill, which yields a superb view of Lake Champlain and the mountains.

(802) 985-8686. www.shelburnefarms.org. Open daily 8:30 to 5:30. Guided tours, mid-May to mid-October, daily at 9, 11, 1 and 3; adults $6, children $4. Day pass, adults $6, children $4.

Vermont Teddy Bear Co., 6655 Shelburne Road (Route 7), Shelburne.

Hundreds of thousands of bears are produced annually in this rapidly expanding company's playful, crayon-colored barn of a factory south of the Shelburne Museum. Who would guess that the now-national phenomenon started from a pushcart on Burlington's Church Street Marketplace? Its main 62,000-square-foot facility is one of Vermont's top tourist attractions. Guided tours offer a glimpse of the innards of the workshops where the bears are created. Costumed "bear ambassadors" lead visitors through the production line, interspersing campy comedy routines with doses of company history and a play-by-play on how teddy bears are made. After the tour, visitors can create and dress their own bears for an additional fee. The bears in the retail showroom were more expensive than we would have thought, with tiny pooh-bears going for $49.95, and rising well above $100. They take on varying human roles simply by a change of costume, of which there are more than 155. The mobs of visitors, young and old, obviously love them.

(802) 985-3001 or (800) 829-2327. Open Monday-Saturday 9 to 6, Sunday 10 to 5. Guided tours, adults $1, children free.

Other Attractions

Robert Hull Fleming Museum, 61 Colchester Ave., Burlington.

This expanded museum is a high point of the large and fairly nondescript University of Vermont campus east of downtown. More than 20,000 works of fine, decorative and ethnographic arts from early Mesopotamia to contemporary America are shown in several galleries in the museum, designed by McKim, Mead and White in 1931. A selection of Burlington artist Fleming's finest paintings and sculptures is on display in the permanent galleries. Other highlights are Northern Plains Indian Art, early 20th-century American drawings and unusual examples of Rookwood pottery. Interesting pictures and displays depict Burlington during the Victorian era and before.

(802) 656-0750. www.flemingmuseum.org. Open Tuesday-Friday 9 to 4 (noon to 4, May-August), Saturday and Sunday 1 to 5. Adults $5, students $3.

Ethan Allen Homestead, Off Route 127, Burlington.

Guided tours show the restored 1787 farmhouse of Ethan Allen, Vermont founder and Revolutionary War hero. It's hard to believe this was the rustic frontier house in which he and his wife raised six children and put up farmhands. Exhibits trace his life and times in the orientation center, where a "tavern theater" presents a multi-media show. The property consists of the timber frame house, working gardens, a museum shop and several acres with hiking trails, picnic areas and access to the Winooski River.

(802) 865-4556. Open Monday-Saturday 10 to 5, Sunday 1 to 5, mid-May to mid-October; Saturday 10 to 4, rest of year. Adults $5, children $3.

Where to Stay

The Burlington area is full of chain hotels and motels, plus a handful of inns and fifteen or so small B&Bs, many of which seem to operate only on weekends or whim.

Larger Hotels and Motels

Wyndham Burlington, 60 Battery St., Burlington 05401.

Built in the late 1970s as part of the Burlington Square retail/office complex at the edge of downtown, with a sweeping view of Lake Champlain across the street, the eight-story Wyndham is for those who want a central location and the amenities of a modern hotel. A recent $3 million refurbishment enhanced the rooms and public spaces following the Wyndham's takeover of what had been a Radisson hotel. Guest rooms are spacious and nicely decorated. The ones on the lake side and particularly those on the corners are most requested. There also are suites and cabanas beside the indoor pool. The pool has a great jacuzzi on one side, a boon for aching muscles after sightseeing, and an adjacent bar and sidewalk café. There's also a health facility. The **Oak Street Café** is for breakfast, lunch and dinner at moderate prices. Cocktails and light fare are served in the Lobby Bar.

(802) 658-6500. Fax (802 658-4659. www.wyndhamburlington.com. Two hundred forty-seven rooms and nine suites. Doubles, $159 to $289 May-October, $139 to $219 rest of year.

Sheraton-Burlington Hotel & Conference Center, 870 Williston Road, South Burlington 05403.

What started out looking like a picturesque barn on a rise near an I-89 exit is the Sheraton, which actually was built around a 150-year-old barn. It expanded like topsy in the late 1980s – to the point where you need a map to find your room and to get around the campus-like complex. Enclosed pedestrian bridges and directional signs help. Some of the 309 rooms ring an interior courtyard open to the sky. Others face the indoor atrium, some of those with sliding doors onto a garden-style restaurant with an L-shaped indoor pool and fitness center beyond. Those would be fine in winter, we suppose, but in Vermont we want a breath of fresh air; those who agree should ask for an outside room. The rooms we saw were stylish, with comfortable armchairs, work desks and TVs tucked away in cabinets. Meals are served in the four-story-high "summerhouse" atrium at **G's,** the aforementioned garden restaurant where diners could feel on public display. Drinks and light meals are available nearby in **Tuckaway's,** a lounge with a sun deck on the roof for swimmers who want some sun along with a splash in the indoor pool.

(802) 862-6600 or (800) 677-6576. Fax (802) 865-6670. www.sheratonburlington.com. Three hundred nine rooms. Doubles, $199 to $259, off-season $129 to $159.

The Inn at Essex, 70 Essex Way, Essex Junction 05452.

It's a surprise to find a country hotel and resort of this elegance in the midst of what long was a large field, seemingly in the middle of nowhere. But this is near an interchange of a new circumferential highway skirting Burlington, with a designer outlet center and cinema complex across the interchange and suburban expansion on the move. The white, three-story main structure is one of several built around what the developers liken to a New England village green and now promote as "Vermont's culinary resort." Furnishings and wallpapers in each room are different, and decor varies from Shaker to Queen Anne, from canopy to pencil-post to brass beds. Local artist Susan Sargent recently redecorated some of the rooms in vibrant colors with Scandinavian flair. Each room has a sitting area with comfortable upholstered chairs, a TV hidden in the armoire and a modern bath. Thirty have working fireplaces. An attractive outdoor swimming pool is located off the rear courtyard, and there are six new tennis courts. Guests have access to the Links at Lang Farm, an eighteen-hole executive golf course next to the inn, and the new Jack Nicklaus-designed Vermont National Country Club course nearby. Faculty and students of the New England Culinary Institute operate the inn's two restaurants: the formal, 50-seat **Butler's,** a picture of Georgian elegance, and the casual **Tavern** with a Vermont country setting. We've enjoyed superior meals in both venues.

(802) 878-1100 or (800) 727-4295. Fax (802) 878-0063. www.innatessex.com. Ninety-seven rooms and 20 suites with private baths. Doubles, $189 to $249. Suites, $229 to $499.

Hampton Inn Hotel & Conference Center, 42 Lower Mountain View Drive, Colchester 05446.

Erected at a rural location just north of the Winooski exit off I-89, this is one classy Hampton Inn that calls itself a hotel and conference center. The budget chain goes upscale here with a spacious lobby, full of comfortable seating and tables with window views onto Mount Mansfield and the Worcester Range. The 188 units on three floors are outfitted in rich greens and burgundies; those ensconced on the third floor with dormer windows present interesting angles. Rooms facing east enjoy views of the distant mountains beyond a garden patio complete with gazebo. Even the complimentary continental breakfast here is a cut above, with bagels and jars of cereals to supplement the usual. The former Lighthouse Restaurant next door, with a replica of the Colchester Reef lighthouse atop its roof, reopened as the **Kansas City Steakhouse** under separate ownership in 2005.

(802) 655-6177. Fax (802) 655-4962. One hundred eighty-six rooms and two suites. Doubles, $129 to $179, off-season $99 to $109. Suites, $179 to $209.

Inns and B&Bs

The Inn at Shelburne Farms, 1611 Harbor Road, Shelburne 05489.

On their 1,400-acre agricultural estate beside Lake Champlain, the 100-room summer home of Dr. William Seward Webb and Lila Vanderbilt Webb now serves as a grand inn of the old school. The rambling Queen Anne-style mansion offers 24 bedrooms and suites in interesting configurations. Most have twin beds and their original furnishings from the late 19th century, and seventeen have private baths. Rooms on the second and third floors vary widely from deluxe corner rooms with armoires and chaise lounges and lake views to a third-floor hideaway in the front of the house (no view) where the bedroom is dwarfed in size by the bathroom. Each is done in its own style, but four-poster beds, armoires, settees, lavishly carved chairs, writing tables and such barely begin to fill the space of the largest. The inn also rents accommodations in two outlying cottages and a guest house. The main-floor public rooms are a living museum: several sitting rooms (one for afternoon tea), a library with 6,000 volumes, porches full of wicker, a game room, and a formal dining room in which breakfast and dinner are available for house guests and the public (see Where to Eat). Between meals, guests walk the grounds designed by Frederick Law Olmsted, swim at a small beach, enjoy the gardens, play croquet, shoot billiards in a game room to end all game rooms, and thoroughly savor a choice piece of property with a delightful aura of yesteryear.

(802) 985-8498. www.shelburnefarms.org. Seventeen rooms with private baths and seven with shared baths, plus three cottages. Rates, EP. Doubles, $225 to $380 with private bath, $105 to $190 shared. Cottages, $225 to $300. Open mid-May to mid-October.

The Willard Street Inn, 349 South Willard St., Burlington 05401.

Enter the handsome cherry-paneled foyer of this 1881 brick mansion in the city's Hill Section to reach Burlington's first urbane B&B. Beverly Watson, the restaurateur who until 2001 ran Isabel's on the Waterfront, and husband Gordon bought the property that had been a retirement home in 1996 and became resident innkeepers. Fourteen guest rooms on three floors are furnished in traditional style with period antiques and reproductions, plus TVs and phones. Rooms vary widely, from a large first-floor bedroom with kingsize bed, armoire and floral wallpaper to second-floor corner bedrooms with handsome ornamental fireplaces and third-floor rooms that are small and plain. An exception is the Tower Room, whose wicker sitting area in the turret commands a smashing view of Lake Champlain in the distance. Guests share a high-ceilinged living room, a formal dining room and a large, plant-filled rear solarium furnished with six tables, as well as a plush sitting area. The solarium is the setting for afternoon tea, plus an elaborate breakfast. One day's choice was between homemade corned beef hash with poached eggs and hollandaise sauce and whole wheat pancakes with spiced peaches.

(802) 651-8710 or (800) 577-8712. Fax (802) 651-8714. www.willardstreetinn.com. Fourteen rooms with private baths. Doubles, $125 to $225.

Lang House, 360 Main St., Burlington 05401.

A restored 1881 Eastlake mansion just above downtown became another urbane B&B in 2000, thanks to Beverly Watson of the Willard Street Inn and Bobbe Maynes, Vermont's former director of tourism and until recently owner of the Heart of the Village B&B in nearby Shelburne. They joined forces here to bathe guests in Victorian grandeur and contemporary amenities. Blessed with a corner turret, the three-story white clapboard house with white shutters holds nine guest rooms, one on the lower level claiming a double whirlpool tub. A rear carriage barn adds two more rooms and quarters for resident innkeepers. All rooms have queen or kingsize beds flounced with pillows, wing chairs, oriental rugs, armoires (the original closets were converted into bathrooms), TVs and telephones. Front rooms are spacious; some others are smaller with only one chair and the bathroom vanity in the room. Decor is elegant and unfussy. The front-corner Lyon Room has a sitting area in the turret, a kingsize bed with prim canopy and a colorfully wallpapered bathroom. Its turret yields a partial view of the lake in the distance. The turret in the third-floor Van Ness Room gets a full lake view. On each dresser is a gaily decorated container marked "noise abatement program." Inside are ear plugs. The house adjoins the University of Vermont's Fraternity Row, and weekend nights can get rowdy. Breakfast is served at individual tables in the dining room or sunroom. The fare at our visit included a choice of scrambled eggs with prosciutto and asparagus in a popover or orange-macadamia nut pancakes.

(802 652-2500 or (877) 919-9799. Fax (802) 651-8717. www.langhouse.com. Eleven rooms with private baths. Doubles, $145 to $215 May to mid-September, $135 to $195 rest of year.

Heart of the Village Inn, 5347 Shelburne Road, Box 953, Shelburne 05482.

An understated Queen Anne Victorian, built by a local merchant in 1886, is now the centerpiece of a thriving B&B. Shelburne resident Bobbe Maynes, formerly Vermont's commissioner of tourism, knew what the market wanted when she and two partners opened the B&B in 1997, and new owner Pat Button is continuing their tradition. What had been a private home was converted into a five-room B&B, with plenty of main-floor common space. A rear carriage barn produced four more spacious, quieter accommodations away from the road. Bedrooms in the main house range in size from the front Van Vliet master bedroom with king bed, armoire, bath in a former closet and sink in the room to a small rear room with a double bed and the largest bath. The king-bedded Bostwick in the carriage house is housed in an old horse stall in which you can see where the horses chewed around the windows, as well as admire its original dark bead board barn walls. Upstairs is the spacious Webb suite, with queen bed and a two-person whirlpool tub. The main house has two living rooms, a wraparound porch and a large dining room where four tables are set for breakfast. The main dish might be baked puff pancakes with Vermont maple syrup.

(802) 985-2800 or (877) 808-1834. Fax (802) 985-2870. www.heartofthevillage.com. Eight rooms and one suite with private baths. Doubles, $130 to $225, foliage $150 to $245.

┌─ *Small and Tranquil* ──────────────────────────────────────

Countryside Motel, 6475 Shelburne Road, Shelburne 05482.

You want to get away from the fray? Then consider this family-run old-timer, situated as its name implies out in the countryside south of the Shelburne Museum. One of a dying breed of owner-operated motels, it has twelve traditional, well-maintained motel rooms on two levels. Beds are queensize or double. TVs, telephones refrigerators and coffeemakers are standard. The best part is the sloping, two-acre back yard with a swimming pool. Settle into the Adirondack chairs and loungers or snack at a picnic table and enjoy the rural landscape. Continental breakfast is complimentary in season.

(802) 985-2839. Fax (802) 985-8526. www.countrysidevt.com. Twelve rooms. Doubles, $102 in summer, $92 off-season.

──

Where to Eat

In summer, Burlington appears to be one big sidewalk café, especially along the downtown Church Street Marketplace. Outlying South Burlington and Shelburne claim good restaurants as well.

Downtown Choices

Smokejacks, 156 Church St., Burlington.

"Bold American food" is the billing for this innovative restaurant by chef-owner Leslie Meyers. She and executive chef Maura O'Sullivan share a fondness for smoked foods, robust tastes, a martini bar and an extensive cheese tasting menu. The pair smoke their own salmon, duck, turkey, mushrooms and more in the restaurant's smoker in the basement. Their fare lives up to its billing for boldness, starting with the focaccia and sourdough breads served with sweet butter at lunch. The maple-cured smoked salmon with pickled red onions and horseradish cream made a fine appetizer. A crispy gruyère cheese risotto square, served with sautéed spinach, was an assertive main course. The star of the show was a grilled wild mushroom bruschetta, emboldened with roasted garlic and served on sautéed greens. A lemon curd upside-down cake with strawberries and whipped cream and white-chocolate bread pudding with a rhubarb and sour cream compote and toasted almonds were memorable desserts. The dinner menu is categorized by small plates (incorporating many of the lunch dishes) and main courses. Typical of the latter are smoky grilled Atlantic salmon with roasted yellow pepper sauce, smoked Long Island duck breast and braised leg with sour cherry and blueberry compote, and grilled hanger steak with zinfandel sauce. All these bold tastes are served up in a long, narrow storefront room painted silver gray, from floors to pressed-tin ceiling. Exposed ducts, candle chandeliers over the mahogany bar, tiny cobalt blue hanging lights and splashy artworks provide accents. The sidewalk café is popular in season.

(802) 658-1119. www.smokejacks.com. Entrées, $19.95 to $22.95. Lunch, Monday-Saturday 11:30 to 3. Dinner, Monday-Saturday 5 to 9:30 or 10:30. Sunday, brunch 10:30 to 3:30, dinner, 5 to 9.

Opaline, One Lawson Lane, Burlington.

This tasty little secret originated as an elegant Victorian bar hidden at the rear of an office building. Steven Perei Jr. turned it into a bistro and wine bar like those he cherished in the south of France. This resembles an elegant, intimate club, in feeling as well as in decor. The handsome bar facing the kitchen is flanked by a handful of formal, white-clothed tables on three sides amid much dark wood paneling and etched-glass windows. Chef Denis Chauvin specializes in the fare of his native France. The short menu lists such starters as escargots in puff pastry and rosettes of marinated salmon. Typical main courses are poached fillet of redfish with ginger-garlic sauce, grilled chicken in maple-mustard sauce and rack of lamb with brown garlic sauce. The cassoulet and the roasted duck Opaline (crisp leg and sliced breast, with a red wine sauce) come highly recommended. Dessert could be sorbet, crème caramel, chocolate mousse or soufflé glacé. Linger over an after-dinner drink and you'll know why this place has such a loyal and protective following. They want to keep it for themselves.

(802) 660-8875. Entrées, $16 to $28. Dinner by reservation, Tuesday-Saturday 6 to 9.

The Iron Wolf Café, 86 St. Paul St., Burlington.

A small iron wolf over the entry identifies this European-style restaurant, which turned over its tiny Lawson Lane hideaway to Opaline and relocated into much larger quarters. German chef Claus Bockwoldt and his Lithuanian wife Danny, the hostess, renovated an old bank to produce a sleek room in black and gray, with a semi-open kitchen in the rear and glass shelves along one side holding fine vintages from their adjacent wine shop. Claus, who cooked all across Europe, prepares every dish from scratch. He calls his fare "basically classic French," with an emphasis on sauces. Look for such entrées as monkfish with tomato coulis infused with salmon and shrimp, scaloppine of ostrich with mango and onion confit, and filet of beef marchand de vin. Among appetizers are carpaccio, scallops in puff pastry, roasted red peppers marinated with goat cheese and caramelized garlic, and a watercress and endive salad with roquefort and caramelized walnuts. Dessert could be profiteroles, soufflé glacé au mocha or assorted sorbets.

(802) 865-4462. Entrées, $21 to $28. Dinner, Tuesday-Saturday from 5:30.

Leunig's Bistro, 115 Church St., Burlington.

The garage doors go up in the summer to open this European-style bistro and café to the sidewalk. The high-ceilinged interior is pretty in peach with black trim. In season, much of the action spills onto the sidewalks along the front and side. People pack the tables day and night, sipping drinks and espresso and savoring the appetizers and desserts, but increasingly they also come for full meals. New owner Robert Fuller, who also owns Pauline's Café & Restaurant in Shelburne, kept the Parisian look and ambiance to give credence to Leunig's slogan as "the soul of Europe in the heart of Burlington." The fare is international with a French accent, as in soup au pistou, duck cassoulet salad and grilled quail salad. Other possibilities range from grilled chive polenta, fried calamari with spicy chipotle aioli and grilled asparagus topped with Vermont chèvre to mussels Tuscan style, Portuguese chicken and pasta dishes. Dinner entrées such as sesame-crusted salmon fillet, sliced duck with ginger chutney and steak au poivre are highly rated by serious eaters. Homemade desserts include French tarts, fruit crisps and crème brûlée.

(802) 863-3759. Entrées, $14.50 to $18.50. Breakfast, Monday-Friday 7 to 11. Lunch, 11:30 to 3. Dinner, 5 to 10. Weekend brunch, 9 to 3.

Five Spice Café, 175 Church St., Burlington.

This little prize on two floors of a former counter-culture restaurant produced one of our more memorable lunches ever. A spicy bloody mary preceded a bowl of hot and sour soup that was extra hot and a house sampler of appetizers, among them smoked shrimp, Siu Mai dumplings, Hunan noodles and Szechwan escargots and spicy cucumbers. A vegetarian special of mock duck stir-fry in peanut sauce really did taste like duck, just as, we were assured, the mock abalone really tastes like abalone. Sated as we were, we had to share the ginger-tangerine cheesecake, which proved denser and more subtly flavored than expected. Chef Jerry Weinberg has a loyal following for his pan-Asian fare. The wide-ranging dinner menu boasts, quite endearingly, that some of the items and spices have been imitated locally but never matched. Start with Indonesian chicken wings, Thai crabby pork rolls or Vietnamese calamari. Main courses range from Thai red snapper to Southeast Asian chicken curry. Ginger-tangerine cheesecake and a blackout cake drenched with triple sec are among desserts. Flowers in pressed-glass vases and a different bottle of wine atop each table comprise the decor. Above the serving sideboard is a collection of Five Spice T-shirts emblazoned with fire-breathing dragons and the saying, "Some Like It Hot." Yes, indeed.

(802) 864-4045. www.fivespicecafe.com. Entrées, $14.99 to $18.99. Lunch daily, 11:30 to 3. Dinner nightly, from 5. Dim Sum brunch, Sunday 11 to 2:30.

Trattoria Delia, 152 St. Paul St., Burlington.

Something of an old-world ambiance and an updated menu characterize this authentic Italian trattoria run by Tom and Lori Delia, who travel to Italy each year to keep up with the latest food techniques and recipes. The beamed and timbered room is comfortable and good-looking in deep red and green, with a long bar along one side. Antipasti include bruschetta, deep-fried calamari, carpaccio and the traditional sampling of imported Italian meats, cheeses and roasted vegetables. Homemade pastas are featured as primi courses. Tagliatelle with porcini mushrooms, spaghetti with gulf shrimp and pappardelle with sea scallops are typical. Among secondi are wood-grilled fish of the day with a garlic-pepper sauce, salt cod simmered with raisins in a sweet tomato sauce, wild boar shoulder braised in red wine and served over soft polenta, veal saltimbocca and osso buco. A mixed grill might yield a handmade sausage, lamb chop and loin of rabbit, served with creamy polenta. A house favorite is filet mignon sautéed in barolo wine and perfumed with white truffle butter from Alba. Among desserts are profiteroles filled with gelati and homemade panna cotta with golden raisins and vin santo. Digestives at the end of the dinner menu include Italian dessert wines. Also offered are cappuccino and latte.

(802) 864-5253. www.trattoriadelia.com. Entrées, $17 to $26.50. Dinner nightly, 5 to 10.

Ice House Restaurant, 171 Battery St., Burlington.

Even if you don't eat here, drive by to see the charming Brueghel-like sign in front depicting ice skaters on the lake. The inside of this massive, restored stone waterfront building (it was an ice house early in the last century) is charming as well, with a few sofas to sink into in the large upstairs lounge with its huge and rough original beams. Our relatives from Montreal sometimes come here for lunch and think the deli sandwiches and snack fare are the greatest. For dinner downstairs in the main restaurant, you might start with the shrimp and crab spring rolls with Thai dipping sauce or the sautéed crab cakes served with a spicy rémoulade. Entrées could be miso-glazed Atlantic salmon, seared duck breast with ruby port and ginger sauce, and bacon-wrapped filet mignon with cabernet sauce. In nice weather, eat outside both upstairs and down on covered decks with glimpses of the lake.

(802) 864-1800. Entrées, $15.99 to $26.99. Open daily, 11:30 to 10.

Sweetwaters, 120 Church St., Burlington.

An old brick bank, built in 1925, houses one of Burlington's more popular and long-lasting restaurants, part of Tony Perry's restaurant group. Dining is on several levels around an atrium bearing an enormous mural depicting life on Church Street in the 1980s (including faces of local residents as well as dignitaries), and outside on a large, canopy-covered sidewalk café that's always crowded in summer. An all-day bistro menu offers snacks like sweet potato fries, polenta crisps, chicken wings, quesadillas and flatbread pizzas. Interesting salads and Perry Farm bison burgers, from a herd raised on the Perry restaurant chain's farm in Charlotte, are featured at lunch. Pastas and fajitas are available all day. At night, more substantial entrées include shrimp and scallop scampi, grilled cider-glazed pork chops, grilled shrimp with gazpacho sauce and couscous, grilled teriyaki steak and grilled bison strip sirloin. Warm molten chocolate cake is the signature dessert.

(802) 864-9800. www.sweetwatersbistro.com. Entrees, $10.95 to $15.95. Open daily, 11:30 to midnight or later.

NECI Commons, 25 Church St., Burlington.

Plenty of good, creative food is available at affordable prices in the New England Culinary Institute's large culinary center opening onto the Church Street Marketplace. Come here for a smoked salmon club sandwich or a turkey BLT, grilled free-range Quebec chicken or coq au vin. You can order light (a sampling of soups – perhaps carrot and ginger, Asian vegetable, and tomato and fennel – and a mini-pizza). Or you can be more ambitious with, say, an appetizer of crab cakes with black bean-corn relish and red pepper coulis, and a main dish of blackened sea bass over wilted spinach. Specials change daily, from bouillabaisse to duck à l'orange. Finish with the chef's dessert sampler for two: perhaps mocha mousse torte, vanilla bean crème brûlée and a trio of sorbets. There's a lot going on here, from the sidewalk café out front to the deli cases full of exotic food inside and, in back, dining areas and kitchens staffed by professionals and students.

(802) 862-6324. Entrées, $15.95 to $24.95. Lunch, 11:30 to 2. Dinner, 5:30 to 9:30.

On the Outskirts of Town

Pauline's Café & Restaurant, 1834 Shelburne Road, South Burlington.

One of the earliest of the Burlington area's fine restaurants (née Pauline's Kitchen in the 1970s), this unlikely-looking place with twinkling white lights framing the front windows year-round has been expanded under the ownership of local restaurant impresario Robert Fuller. The original downstairs dining room is now an exceptionally attractive cafe paneled in cherry and oak. The upstairs lounge has been transformed into a ramble of small, elegant dining rooms serene in sponged yellows and reds. Off the second floor is a hidden brick patio enveloped in evergreens and a latticed pergola decked out with small international flags and tiny white lights. Both the cafe and dinner menus are offered in the café and on the patio, which makes for unusual range and variety. With the café menu you can concoct a mighty good meal of appetizers and such entrées as fettuccine with smoked salmon, seafood mixed grill with a tangy Thai vinaigrette, maple mustard pork medallions and grilled flank steak. Our spring dinner began with remarkably good appetizers of morels and local fiddleheads in a rich madeira sauce and a sprightly dish of shrimp and scallops in ginger, garnished with snow peas and cherry tomatoes. Steaming popovers and zippy salads accompanied. The entrées were superior: three strips of lamb wrapped around goat cheese, and a thick filet mignon, served with spring vegetables and boiled new potatoes. A honey-chocolate mousse and framboise au chocolat from Pauline's acclaimed assortment of desserts ended a fine meal.

(802) 862-1081. Entrées, $15.95 to $24.95; cafe, $9.95 to $14.95. Lunch, Monday-Saturday 11:30 to 2. Dinner nightly, 5 to 9:30 or 10. Sunday brunch, 11 to 2:30.

Café Shelburne, 5573 Shelburne Road (Route 7), Shelburne.

Across from the Shelburne Museum, this small and revered provincial French restaurant is lovingly tended by chef-owner Patrick Grangien, a Frenchman who trained with Paul Bocuse. He and his wife Christine moved in upstairs and run a personal restaurant like those in the countryside of France. Patrick calls his cuisine "more bistro style than nouvelle," which is appropriate for the French bistro decor – a copper bar on one side, an elegant dining room of white-linened tables and black lacquered chairs on the other, plus a latticed rear patio decked out in grapevines. Seafood is his forte (he won the National Seafood Challenge in 1988, was elected seafood chef of the year and later won the Taste of Vermont grand award two years in a row). Try his prize-winning steamed fillet of lotte on a bed of spinach and mushrooms with a shrimp sauce or the panache of assorted steamed seafood with champagne-chervil sauce. Other entrées might be duck breast served with a duck risotto and a white wine sauce, filet mignon with green peppercorns and a creamy port wine sauce and, a staple on the menu here, steak tartare, seasoned at tableside. Start with one of the fabulous soups, a baked tomato filled with garlicky mussels and vegetables, or escargots with prosciutto, mushrooms, almonds and croutons. The delectable dessert repertoire includes warm chocolate cake soufflé, tarte au citron and assorted fruit sorbets.

(802) 985-3939. www.cafeshelburne.com. Entrées, $19 to $24. Dinner, Tuesday-Saturday 5:30 to 9.

⸻ *Farm Dining/Shelburne Style* ⸻

The Inn at Shelburne Farms, 1611 Harbor Road, Shelburne.

The main floor of this landmark inn beside Lake Champlain harbors one of the area's more acclaimed restaurants. Dining is an event in the serene Marble Room, quite stunning with formally set tables, red fabric-covered walls and tiled floors in black and white, or outside at white-clothed tables on a veranda overlooking the lake with the Adirondacks rising beyond. Head chef Geoff Mockbee incorporates produce from the farm's organic gardens and uses local purveyors in keeping with the Shelburne Farms mission of sustaining local agriculture. Dinner begins with complimentary canapés. Then there could be a choice of vichyssoise with chives and cheddar croutons, peeky toe crab ravioli with mussel sauce, or beef tartare with Shelburne Farms smoked cheddar. Main courses might be poached wild king salmon in a fennel vinaigrette, roasted Vermont quail and squab with zinfandel sauce, and roasted rack of lamb with a caramelized garlic demi-glace. Desserts vary from seasonal fruit cobblers to a chocolate mousse torte with hazelnut ganache, cherry amaretto, white peach brandy and raspberry sauces.

(802) 985-8498. www.shelburnefarms.org. Entrées, $23 to $29.50. Dinner nightly by reservation, 5:30 to 9:30. Sunday brunch, 8 to 1. Closed mid-October to mid-May.

FOR MORE INFORMATION: Lake Champlain Regional Chamber of Commerce, 60 MainSt., Burlington, VT 05401, (802) 863-3489 or (877) 686-5253. www.vermont.org.

Stowe Community Church spire soars above village, with Mount Mansfield in background.

Stowe, Vt.

Storybook Resort for All Seasons

Stowe is a storybook New England mountain resort village that claims the title, Ski Capital of the East. The requisite white spire of the landmark Stowe Community Church soars skyward against a backdrop of mountains. The Little River flows beneath a covered bridge at the blinker-light crossroads in the center of a town that looks smaller than its population of 4,300 would suggest. Nary a chain store or a fast-food restaurant is in sight, and the "downtown" appears not much changed from 50 years ago.

What has changed is the meandering Mountain Road (Route 108) that leads from the village past countless lodging facilities, restaurants and shopping complexes up to Mount Mansfield and the Stowe Mountain Resort, the ski area's official name. The ski area on the northeastern face of Vermont's highest peak looks back toward a town that is a curious blend of European flair and New England charm.

The Mountain Road links the village and ski area in a symbiotic relationship unmatched by any other ski town in the East – if not the country, although Aspen might dispute the claim. One of the oldest ski resorts in the United States, Stowe is authentic rather than plastic, understated rather than glitzy. Its distinctly alpine flavor was cast first by Sepp Ruschp, who left Austria in 1936 to be ski instructor for the fledgling Mount Mansfield Ski Club and led the development of Mount Mansfield. It was enhanced by Baroness Maria von Trapp and family, whose story was immortalized by "The Sound of Music" after they founded the Trapp Family Lodge here.

The village lies in the rolling valley between broad Mount Mansfield on the west and the Worcester Mountains on the east. Here recreation and cultural endeavors thrive throughout the year. Cross-country skiing complements downhill in winter.

Other seasons bring golf, tennis, polo, horseback riding, hiking, performing arts, art exhibits and enough sights to see and things to do to make credible the area's claim to being a world-class resort.

Seeing and Doing

Stowe offers the visitor – skier and non-skier alike – the best of possible worlds: exhilarating skiing in winter on Vermont's highest peak, and a cosmopolitan mountain village offering a host of activities year-round. An annual Bavarian-style Oktoberfest is held the last weekend in September. The year's highlight is the Stowe Winter Carnival, ten days of exuberant activity in late January.

Stowe Mountain Resort/Mount Mansfield, Mountain Road (Route 108), Stowe.
Skiing is what made Stowe famous, legions of skiers having been attracted to New England's most storied mountain since the first trail was cut in 1936 and the East's first chairlift was installed in 1940. Today, Mount Mansfield has sleek eight-passenger gondola cars among its eleven lifts, vastly expanded snowmaking and even night skiing. With a summit elevation of 4,393 feet and a 2,360-foot vertical drop, Stowe offers the longest ski runs in Vermont. Nearly one-third of its 46 slopes and trails are for expert skiers, including the awesome "Front Four" – the precipitous Liftline, Goat, National and Starr trails, so steep that on the Starr you cannot see the bottom from the ledge on top. They almost make the fabled Nosedive seem tame. There's easier terrain, including the 4.5-mile-long Toll Road, and the related Spruce Peak area across the way is an entire mountain with gentle trails, a sunny southeast exposure and a special section for new skiers. Combined with accommodations and nightlife, the total skiing experience ranks Stowe among the top ten ski resorts in the country. And it's getting even better. Stowe Mountain Resort's $250-million-plus expansion plan through 2010 calls for more lifts and snowmaking, a 35-acre ski village at the base of Spruce Peak, a 200-room slopeside hotel, 335 condos, a 60-unit private lodging facility and an eighteen-hole golf course.
(802) 253-3000 or (800) 253-4754. Snow phone (802) 253-3600. www.stowe.com. Open daily in winter, 9 to 4, Thursday-Saturday 5 to 9. Lift tickets, adults $65; juniors $45; night, adults $24, juniors $18.

Unlike most other New England ski areas, however, Stowe is not a one-horse town, so to speak. It's a winter wonderland known for cross-country skiing, snowshoeing, horse-drawn sleigh rides, tobogganing, dog sledding, ice skating and more.
Cross-Country skiing. Four interconnected ski touring centers create one of the largest, most varied trail systems in the country. Nearly 100 miles of groomed and 70 miles of back-country trails criss-cross the landscape. Favorite easy trails are along the 5.3-mile Stowe Recreation Path, but you can climb from here to Mount Mansfield's rugged ridgeline and join the 285-mile-long Catamount Trail, the longest in the country, stretching from Massachusetts to Quebec. The largest operation is run by the Trapp Family Lodge, North America's first touring center.
Snowshoeing. With some of the most extensive and diverse trails in the East, Stowe is a popular destination for what some say is winter's fastest-growing sport. A great place to start is on the flat, 5.3-mile Recreation Path, which winds its way through forests and meadows along the Mountain Road. Beginners can get used to

wearing snowshoes and more experienced snowshoers can enjoy a leisurely walk or warm up before heading to more difficult terrain.

Sleigh Rides. What's more romantic than a horse-drawn sleigh ride for two through snow-filled meadows and woodlands – especially under the light of a full moon? The Stowehof Inn & Resort is famous for its "private" sleigh rides for two to four, $25 per person, daily from 4 to 9 and weekends, 2 to 9. Edson Hill Manor and Stoweflake Resort also give intimate sleigh rides. Larger group sleighs filled with hay bales as seats are available through places like the Trapp Family Lodge, $5 per person, daily 10 to 4. Horse-drawn carriage rides are offered in summer.

All these activities and more culminate in late January in the annual **Stowe Winter Carnival,** the oldest and biggest – and some would say best – winter carnival in the United States. Stowe's first Winter Carnival was held in 1921 and featured ski jumping and tobogganing on a hill behind the public school. It continued to grow, and by 1935 included highly competitive races in both alpine and cross-country skiing. Activities include a nationally sanctioned ice carving competition, snow golf and snow volleyball events, turkey bowling, a snowshoe race, Stowe Super-G Schuss, Wintermeister Triathlon, the World's Coldest Parade, a Village Night block party and a traditional Vermont chicken pie church supper.

The fledgling **Vermont Ski Museum** at 1 South Main St. in the restored 1816 Old Town Hall in the center of Stowe traces the evolution of skiing, ski facilities and ski equipment in Vermont. You will see the lifts that took the first skiers up Vermont mountains and the skis that brought them down. You'll learn how the ski resorts developed and discover the more than 85 Vermont ski areas that disappeared along the way. Open daily except Tuesday, noon to 5, donation.

Summer at Mount Mansfield. The **Stowe Gondola** takes visitors 7,700 feet up to the Cliff House, just below Vermont's highest summit (round trip, adults $14, children $8, daily 10 to 5, Memorial Day to late October). Cars can zig-zag their way up the 4.5-mile **Stowe Auto Road,** known to skiers who ease down it in winter as the Toll Road (cars $17, daily 9 to 4, late May to mid-October). The 2,600-foot **Alpine Slide at Spruce Peak** appeals especially to children; you take a chairlift up and slide down (single rides, adults $12, children $9; daily in summer, weekends in late spring and early fall).

Smugglers' Notch. Up the Mountain Road past the ski area you enter Mount Mansfield State Park, passing picnic areas and the Long Trail. A couple of hairpin turns take you into Smugglers' Notch, a narrow pass with rock outcroppings jutting into the road in places and 1,000-foot cliffs looming on either side. The 4,000-acre natural area between Mount Mansfield and Sterling Peak is a quiet, awe-inspiring place to pause and gawk at such rock formations as Elephant's Head, Singing Bird, King Rock and the Hunter and His Dog. Stop at Smugglers' Cave and, farther on, hike into Bingham Falls. The road is not for the faint-hearted (it's closed in winter, for good reason, although snowshoers and cross-country skiers can get through). We drove back from Jeffersonville on the other side of the notch after a summer thunderstorm and found waterfalls that had been trickles on the way over suddenly gushing down the rocks beside the lonely road.

The **Stowe Recreation Path** is the pride of the community. Opened in 1984 with an extension in 1989, the much-used, nationally recognized 5.3-mile walking, rollerblading and biking greenway starts in the village behind the Stowe Community Church and roughly parallels the Mountain Road up to Brook Road. It meanders through meadows and glades, crisscrossing the West Branch River eleven times over arched wooden bridges.

HIKING. For those who want more challenge than the Recreation Path, a trail from the end of Sunset Street in the village provides a short but fairly steep climb to **Sunset Rock,** overlooking the village just above Main Street. The **Pinnacle Trail** is a longer hike east of town. From the trailhead in Stowe Hollow it's a gradual, 1.4-mile hike up the west side of the Pinnacle to the rocky summit, a 2,650-foot peak in the Worcester Range that forms the eastern border of Stowe. At the summit you'll be rewarded with a fine view of the town below and Mount Mansfield to the west. The trail is popular, so don't expect solitude. Across town lies the **Long Trail,** a 265-mile trail system running throughout Vermont, which crosses Mansfield and Spruce Peak in Stowe. The easiest access is from trailheads in Smugglers' Notch. Heading north, the Long Trail leaves from the picnic area near the bottom of the notch and climbs steadily over Elephant Head to Sterling Pond in 3.5 miles. A shorter and easier route to the scenic pond leaves from the parking area at the top of the notch. The trail is steep and rocky for the first half mile, then flattens as it traverses Spruce Peak. It is another half-mile to Sterling Pond and a round trip total of 2 miles. Seasoned climbers can head south from the notch and climb nearly 3,000 vertical feet to the top of Mount Mansfield in 2.3 miles. From the summit on a clear day you can see east as far as Mount Washington in eastern New Hampshire and west across Lake Champlain to New York's Adirondacks.

GOLF. The public can play at the **Stowe Country Club,** 744 Cape Cod Road, (802) 253-4893 or (800) 253-3754. Warm up on a 40-acre practice facility before tackling the 6,213-yard, 18-hole championship layout. Greens fees are $75 peak, $55 off-peak; open daily, May-October. Next to the golf club, the Stoweflake Resort offers a 7,000-square-foot putting green, driving range, and chip and pitch course. Across the street is the new **Stowe Golf Park,** a landscaped 18-hole putting course at 1613 Mountain Road. A miniature golf course simulating a real golf environment, it's open daily 10 to 9:30, May-October.

Horseback riding is popular in the area. Guided trail rides are offered by Edson Hill Manor Stables and Peterson Brook Farm, both along Edson Hill Road.

Sports equipment and rentals are available along the Mountain Road from **Action Outfitters, A.J.'s Life Sports, Boots 'n Boards, Mountain Sports & Bike Shop, Pinnacle Ski & Sports** and the Top Notch Resort's **Nordic Barn** as well as from **Umiak Outdoor Outfitters** along Route 100 in the Lower Village.

THE ARTS. The hills are alive with the sound of music as the **Stowe Performing Arts** series offers Sunday evening Music in the Meadow concerts in summer in the Concert Meadow at the Trapp Family Lodge. The Vermont Mozart Festival also presents concerts there. More concerts are staged at the Stowe Mountain Performing Arts Center, a 12,000-seat amphitheater at the base of Spruce Peak. The **Stowe Theatre Guild** presents its summer season at the Town Hall Theater on Main Street. The **Helen Day Art Center** hosts rotating exhibits in a restored 1863 Greek Revival structure that once was the high school on School Street.

SHOPPING. Shops and galleries are concentrated along Main Street in Stowe and scattered in ever-increasing numbers along Route 100 South and up the Mountain Road. Along Main Street in the village, **Shaw's General Store** considers itself 110 years young and carries almost everything, especially sporting goods, sportswear, footwear, gifts and oddities. Nearby are the **Old Depot Shops,** an open, meandering mall of a place containing **Vermont Furniture Works, Stowe Mercantile** and **Bear Pond Books.** Tread the creaky floorboards of **Val's Country Store** for T-shirts, maple syrup, candy and such. Look for nature items at the **Wild Life Gift Shop. Gracie's Gourmutt Sho**p features dog-emblazoned clothes and gifts as well as specialty foods from Gracie's restaurant.

Up the Mountain Road at the Straw Corner Shops are **Straw Corner Mercantile** for folk art and Americana gifts, the **Stowe Craft Gallery** and the **Stowe Coffee House.** Check out the **West Branch Gallery and Sculpture Park** behind the landmark après-ski bar, the Rusty Nail. Farther along at 108 West are **Stowe Kitchen, Bath & Linens,** with everything for the home, and the **Little River Goldsmith** for handcrafted jewelry. The gourmet-to-go **Harvest Market** is the place for specialty foods, wine and espresso. **Wendy's Closet** at the Gale Farm Center carries women's clothing and accessories. Local artists are among those showing at the **Robert Paul Galleries** in the Baggy Knees Shopping Center. At the Red Barn Shops, **Mountain Cheese and Wine** carries an impressive selection, **Samara** features works of Vermont craftsmen and **The Yellow Turtle** offers "classy clothes for classy kids."

In Stowe's Lower Village at 166 South Main St. is **Deerfield Village Furniture,** showing fine furniture handcrafted in northern Vermont. Farther south off Route 100, watch glass blowers create colorful works of art at **Little River Hotglass Studio,** 593 Moscow Road.

The **Cold Hollow Cider Mill,** south of town along Route 100, consists of a pair of large and intriguing red barns where you can see cider being made (and drink the delicious free samples). For more than 25 years the Chittenden family also have sold tart cider jelly, cider donuts and other apple products as well as cookbooks, wooden toys, gourmet foods and about every kind of Vermont jam, jelly or preserve imaginable.

Nearby along Route 100 in Waterbury, all kinds of cheeses and dips may be sampled (and purchased) at the large **Cabot Annex Store.** Also part of the Cabot complex are branches of Burlington's **Lake Champlain Chocolates,** which caters to Stowe's sweet tooth, **Vermont Teddy Bear Company** and **Snow Farm Vineyard.**

─*A Sweet Treat*─

Ben & Jerry's Ice Cream Factory, Route 100, Waterbury.

Just south of Stowe, this factory producing 130,000 pints daily of the ice cream that transplanted Vermont characters Ben Cohen and Jerry Greenfield made famous is one of Vermont's busiest tourist attractions. And with good reason. During half-hour guided tours, you see a humorous multimedia show, watch ice cream being made, learn some of the history of this intriguing outfit that donates one percent of its profits to peace efforts and, of course, savor a tiny sample, obtained by lowering a bucket on a rope to the production area below. At busy times, the place is a madhouse – with live music outside, lineups of people waiting to buy cones, a gift shop filled with Vermont cow-related items, and every bit of publicity Ben and Jerry ever got decorating the walls. If you can't get inside, at least buy a dish or cone of ice cream from the outdoor windows.

(802) 244-8687 or (866) 258-6877. Tours daily 9 to 8 in summer, to 6 in fall, 10 to 5 rest of year. Adults $3, under 12 free.

Where to Stay

Lodging and Dining

One of the assets of Stowe is its diverse lodging facilities, especially geared to those who seek more than just to ski all day and to crash at night.

Until its expansion plan progresses, the only slopeside lodging is the Stowe Mountain Resort's 33-room Inn at the Mountain (the undistinguished successor to the fabled Lodge at Smuggler's Notch) and a relative handful of townhouses at the base of the Toll House chairlift. This is not the place to find ski dorms, condominiums or high-rise hotels. The Stowe area offers better.

Edson Hill Manor, 1500 Edson Hill Road, Stowe 05672.

If you really want to get away from it all, drive up the mile-long country lane leading to this French Provincial-style manor with old English charm, a true country inn with a blueblood pedigree. Set high apart on 225 secluded acres not far from the ski resort, the manor has pleasant common rooms and a restaurant, a spectacular terrace beside a spring-fed, kidney-shaped swimming pool, a pond stocked for trout fishing, a cross-country ski center and stables for horseback riding. Owners Billy and Juliet O'Neil offer nine guest rooms in the manor house. For maximum privacy, choose one of the sixteen modern accommodations in four newer carriage houses. Each carriage house has four spacious guest rooms done in the decor of the original manor with beamed ceilings, pine-paneled walls and brick fireplaces. Billed as the inn's luxury units with one kingsize or two queen beds, they accommodate two to four people. For breakfast, the buffet table contains several hot entrées – on one winter morning, scrambled eggs with spinach and goat cheese, blackberry waffles and polenta.

Regional American cuisine with international accents is served in the inn's pleasant dining room, a destination for the public. The dinner menu might start with house-cured gravlax with a brie turnover and vodka rémoulade, cajun paella and corn-fried shrimp and scallops with mango salsa and chipotle vinaigrette. Main courses vary from seared rare tuna loin with panang-mussel sauce and nishaki rice to rack of lamb with madeira sauce. Desserts could be sour cream apple pie with coconut-raisin sauce or sweet port crème brûlée with ginger-blueberry sauce.

(802) 253-7371 or (800) 621-0284. Fax (802) 253-4036. www.stowevt.com. Twenty-five rooms and suites with private baths. Doubles, $159 to $219; May and November $99 to $139. Entrées, $17.50 to $23.50. Dinner nightly, 6 to 9.

Stoweflake Mountain Resort & Spa, 1746 Mountain Road, Stowe 05672.

Located on 60 acres of manicured lawns and gardens, this busy establishment has grown from a small ski lodge opened by the Baraw family in the 1960s into Stowe's fanciest resort and spa. The newly built Spa at Stoweflake is the largest and most complete in Vermont. The 40,000-square-foot spa building along the west side of the complex essentially completes a large square linking a series of wings – a couple of which began as separate motels – that now wrap around a central courtyard with a fountain and gardens. The spa building and renovated West Wing contain 40 of the resort's premier accommodations with kingsize or two queen beds and upscale hotel-style furnishings. Many have gas fireplaces and whirlpool baths. Other accommodations include 40 deluxe rooms and suites in the renovated East

Wing, motel-style rooms in a garden wing and 36 units in outlying townhouses. Common areas include a large lobby/living room and a library with fireplaces. Cookies and hot beverages are put out here in the afternoon. The complex includes indoor and outdoor pools, tennis courts and other recreation facilities in a dedicated Sports Club. The Stowe Country Club's golf course adjoins the property.

Modern American cuisine and an award-winning wine list are featured in **Winfield's Bistro,** the resort's dining room. Executive chef Joseph Santagini redesigned the menu to feature spa cuisine such as seared Atlantic cod stuffed with spinach leaves and topped with sautéed lobster medallions, pan-seared five-spice chicken breast and rack of Colorado lamb crusted in basil and mustard. A sushi roll of smoked salmon and trout, grilled portobello bruschetta and seared foie gras on toasted brioche are among appetizers. Casual fare is served amid the Baraw family's ski memorabilia in **Charlie B's Pub & Restaurant,** named for resort president Chuck Baraw.

(802) 253-7355 or (800) 253-2232. Fax (802) 253-6858. www.stoweflake.com. One hundred eight rooms and ten suites. Doubles, $170 to $300. Suites, $320 to $450.

Entrées, $18 to $29. Dinner nightly, 6 to 9:30, Wednesday-Sunday in off-season. Pub, daily noon to 1 a.m.

Stowehof Inn & Resort, 434 Edson Hill Road, Box 1139, Stowe 05672.

Romantics are lured here in winter for moonlit sleigh rides, but the Stowehof is an unusual and thoroughly charming place to stay as well. At the front entrance, the trunks of two maple trees support the enormous porte cochere above the door. More tree trunks are inside the huge living room, nicely broken up into intimate nooks and crannies, the two-level dining room, the downstairs game room and the Tyrolean Tap Room. The bell tower, the sod roof laced with field flowers and the architecture are reminiscent of the Tyrolean Alps. The upstairs library and game room is a replica of the interior of an old Vermont covered bridge. Little white lights twinkle all around. Owners Chris and Susan Grimes offer 46 refurbished guest rooms, some of them unusually large and sumptuous. All rooms have balconies or patios with views in summer of lovely clumps of birches, a swimming pool, a hot tub, a trout pond, lawns and the mountains. Terrycloth robes, duvet covers and Godiva chocolates are among the amenities. The Grimeses have opened an indoor pool called Poolhof with a sauna, hot tub and workout room, and added massage therapy and concierge services.

The well-appointed **Emily's** dining room comes with a beamed ceiling, fireplaces and windows looking onto outdoor pool and mountains. There's also dining in summer on the terrace. The regional American dinner menu changes several times weekly. The traditional specialties of wiener schnitzel and beef wellington have been augmented by the likes of prosciutto-wrapped swordfish, grilled rack of boar, pan-seared duck breast and house-smoked confit with a wild berry demi-glace, and steak diane. Lighter fare is available in **Coslin's Pub & Cigar Bar,** which opens onto the poolside patio.

(802) 253-9722 or (800) 932-7136. Fax (802) 253-7513. www.stowehofinn.com. Forty-six rooms with private baths. Summer and winter: doubles $113 to $248. Foliage: $150 to $305. Spring and late fall: $83 to $180.

Entrées, $22 to $30. Dinner nightly, 5:30 to 9, pub from 4.

Top Notch at Stowe Resort & Spa, 4000 Mountain Road, Stowe 05672.

This award-winning resort and spa occupies a 120-acre estate looking up at

Mount Mansfield not far from the mountain's base. A member of Preferred Hotels and Resorts Worldwide, it has been rated a top ski lodge, tennis resort and spa in national surveys, although some locally feel it is overrated. The resort offers comfortable rooms and suites – small with queen beds in the older west wing, and large and luxurious with kingsize or two queen beds in the newer North Wing. Some have fireplaces and whirlpool tubs. There are also townhouse units of one to three bedrooms. The recently expanded health and fitness spa offers a range of facilities including a 60-foot indoor pool with a waterfall, a sauna and 30 treatment rooms.

"New Vermont Cuisine" is featured in **Maxwell's,** the resort's stylish, glass-sided dining room with spectacular mountain views. Dinner might feature grilled or steamed Atlantic salmon with red wine-thyme butter sauce, seared halibut with a tomato-ginger vinaigrette, loin of venison with pear-gorgonzola cobbler and grilled veal chop with porcini mushrooms. The **Buttertub Bistro** serves lighter fare for lunch and dinner in a casual setting. Lunch is available seasonally in the gazebo next to an outdoor pool surrounded by contemporary sculpture.

(802) 253-8585 or (800) 451-8686. Fax (802) 253-9263. www.topnotchresort.com. Seventy-seven rooms, thirteen suites and 35 townhouse units. Doubles, $240 to $360. Suites, $325 to $860. Off-season: doubles $180 to $310, suites $320 to $700.
Entrées, $22 to $39. Dinner nightly, 6 to 10.

Green Mountain Inn, Main Street, Box 60, Stowe 05672.
Its deep red facade a landmark in the center of the village since 1833, this inn has been carefully upgraded and expanded in recent years to produce an unusual variety of accommodations. Most of the guest quarters are behind the main inn in a motel-type configuration, albeit with an antique look conveyed by twin or queensize canopy beds, period wallpapers and stenciling, and reproduction furniture manufactured specially for the inn. Eight luxury suites are in the new Mill House, adjacent to the clubhouse building on the site of a former lumber mill. Each has a queen canopy bed, fireplace, sitting area, VCR and a large bathroom with oversize jacuzzi opening into the bedroom. The new Mansfield House behind the inn offers the 22 most luxurious accommodations. Among them are twelve suites and two "grand rooms" with down duvet-covered king or queen canopy beds, handsome living rooms with marble fireplaces, fireside jacuzzis, marble bathrooms, mini-bars and coffeemakers, DVD/CD players and surround-sound stereo, handcrafted furnishings and original artworks. Guests here enjoy afternoon tea and cookies in the living room and a "petite breakfast" delivered with the morning newspaper to bedroom or living room. Lately the inn has opened six Depot Street townhouses of two or three bedrooms. The health center in the inn's clubhouse offers a spa program.

The complex includes the formal Main Street Dining Room for breakfast and the legendary **Whip Bar & Grill** downstairs. The latter is where the action is, in the cozy bar decorated with antique buggy whips as well as in the cafeteria-style grill and seasonally on the outdoor deck by the pool. The day's specials are chalked on blackboards above cases where the food is displayed. Some of the dishes are calorie-counted for those who are there for the inn's spa facilities. Country pâté with cornichons on toast points, smoked salmon with capers, Mexican vegetable soup, salads with dressings devised by the Canyon Ranch in Arizona, crabmeat on a croissant with melted cheddar, open-face veggie melt, flatbread pizzas – this is perfect grazing fare. Main dishes like herb-crusted halibut with orange-rosemary sauce, roast Quebec duckling with blackberry gastrique, maple-marinated pork chops and ribeye steak with English stilton in a port wine sauce are posted at night. Coffee-almond crunch tart, raspberry bash, lemon-cream carrot cake and a sac de bon bon for two are some of the ever-changing desserts.

(802) 253-7301 or (800) 253-7302. Fax (802) 253-5096. www.greenmountaininn.com. Eighty-one rooms and 24 suites with private baths. Rates, EP. Summer and winter: doubles $129 to $339, suites $219 to $409. Off-season: doubles $119 to $189, suites $189 to $259.

www.thewhip.com. Entrées, $14.50 to $21.95. Lunch daily, 11:30 to 5:30. Dinner, 5:30 to 9:30 or 10. Sunday brunch, 11 to 2:30.

Trapp Family Lodge, 700 Trapp Hill Road, Box 1428, Stowe 05672.

The Trapp family whose saga inspired "The Sound of Music" bought this sprawling property overlooking the Worcester Mountain Range four years after fleeing the Nazi takeover of Austria. They started taking in guests in a rustic 27-room lodge in 1950. After the original was destroyed by fire, an exotic 96-room resort replicated some of the original's charm in a Disneyesque kind of way. Now it's an expanding, 2,700-acre resort with panoramic mountain views, tennis courts, indoor and outdoor pools, a major cross-country ski center and a multitude of family activities, all overseen by Johannes von Trapp, who lives nearby and whose recorded voice welcomes telephone callers. Hand-carved balustrades, steeply pitched gables and a cedar shake roof with an Austrian bell tower accent the Tyrolean architecture of the main lodge, where guest rooms come with kingsize or two queen beds. They are appointed with European-style furnishings, telephones and TVs. Most have flower-bedecked balconies or patios for taking in the views. A favorite accommodation is the kingsize von Trapp Suite, once the residence of Baroness Maria von Trapp. A recent lodge addition produced 23 luxury rooms, including nine junior suites with whirlpool tubs and three executive suites with fireplaces, double whirlpool tubs and wet bars.

Traditional and modern European cuisine is served in the lodge's dining room, its lounge and in the famed Austrian Tea Room (see Where to Eat) across the road. In the lodge, executive chef Juergen Spagolla from Austria features wiener schnitzel among entrées that range from pan-seared shrimp and scallops with lemon grass-ginger sauce to Moroccan-style lamb chops with rosemary sauce. The night's game platter might yield wild boar sausage, venison chop and buffalo strip loin. Classical harp music accompanies dinner by candlelight. Casual fare is available in the lounge.

(802) 253-8511 or (800) 826-7000. Fax (802) 253-5740. www.trappfamily.com. Eighty-seven rooms and nine suites. Rates, EP. Doubles $280 to $340, suites $365 to $625. Off-peak: doubles $198 to $228, suites $275 to $525.

Entrées, $18 to $33. Dinner nightly in lodge, 5:30 to 9.

Ye Olde England Inn, 433 Mountain Road, Stowe 05672.

This restored and expanded inn is British all the way from the bright red phone booth out front to the menu in the pub and the "Anglo" and "Saxon" on the license plates of the owners' cars. Transplanted Brits Chris and Lyn Francis have developed some of the area's most luxurious accommodations. Seven of the inn's seventeen original guest rooms sport jacuzzis and are decorated in Laura Ashley style. Three luxury two-bedroom English "cottages" in a building out back beside the swimming pool each contain a fireplace, jacuzzi, cable TV, lounge-dining area and kitchen facilities. The newest are ten "super-luxurious suites" in the Bluff House, perched atop a granite bluff with spectacular views of the Worcester Mountain range. Each has a queensize four-poster in the bedroom, a bath with jacuzzi and separate shower, a private deck and a "lounge" with fireplace, sofabed, wet bar, refrigerator and microwave. English-style tea is offered in the afternoon, and an English breakfast in the morning.

Dinner is served and a pub-type menu is available all day in **Mr. Pickwick's Pub & Restaurant** with a hearthstone fireplace or outside on canopied decks, lined with umbrellas advertising British ale and presenting a scene straight from the English countryside. The extensive menu offers quite a range from fish and chips, bangers and mash, and ploughman's platter to ostrich tenderloin, venison pie, five-spice hanger steak with a ginger-plum sauce and classic beef wellington. We enjoyed a lunch of spinach salad in a tostada shell and a good steak and kidney pie served inexplicably with a side bowl of gravy (could it have been for dipping the french fries in?), all washed down with pints of Whitbread and Watneys ales, presented in proper pub glasses. The list of more than 150 foreign beers and ales is extraordinary, and one can even get ale by the yard. In the evening, live entertainment is enjoyed by the laid-back crowd.

(802) 253-7558 or (800) 477-3771. Fax (802) 253-8944. www.englandinn.com. Seventeen rooms, ten suites and three cottages, all with private baths. Rates, B&B. Doubles, $139 to $199. Cottages, $219 to $309. Suites, $159 to $359.

Dining (802) 253-7064. www.mrpickwicks.com. Entrées, $17.95 to $25.95. Lunch daily, 11:30 to 4. Dinner, 4 to 10.

— A Reborn Inn for the Thrifty —

The Stowe Inn, 123 Mountain Road, Stowe 05672.

This classic white clapboard and brick New England inn – one of the few in Stowe that look the part — was reborn in 2004 from the 1820s farmhouse that formerly housed the Inn at Little River and before that the Yodler. Jed Lipsky, who owns a contract logging company, and his wife Annika moved from the Berkshires to give the closed inn a much-needed makeover. They redecorated the fireplaced common rooms with stylish furnishings, put oriental rugs on the hardwood floors and hung the walls with their collection of original art. The inn's sixteen guest rooms were similarly updated in pastel colors, each with sleigh or four-poster beds covered with white cotton duvets and equipped with TV and telephone. The side carriage house has twenty simple, motel-style rooms that appeal to thrifty travelers. Guests in both buildings enjoy a game room with billiards, a jacuzzi tub and a small swimming pool. Breakfast is complimentary. A wraparound porch and side terrace overlook the Little River, and out front is a covered bridge that leads pedestrians into downtown.

Local restaurateur Kathy Neale came out of retirement and with son Andrew oversees **Harrison's,** the inn's candlelit restaurant and bar with tiered seating and an inviting outdoor terrace looking onto the river. The traditional American/ continental menu ranges from grilled organic Scottish salmon fillet with thyme-maple glaze to pork tenderloin with a wild mushroom-merlot ragoût and sirloin steak with bourbon sauce. Portions are so generous you may not have room for desserts like cognac-pumpkin cheesecake or white chocolate mousse in a milk chocolate cup for two. A bar menu ($8 to $17.50) is available in the tavern.

(802) 253-4030 or (800) 546-4030. Fax (802) 253-4030. www.stoweinn.com. Thirty-seven rooms with private baths. Doubles in inn, $119 to $189; in motel, $99 to $129.

Harrison's, (802) 253-7773. Entrées, $15.95 to $23.95. Dinner nightly in season, 5:30 to 9:30.

Lodging

Stone Hill Inn, 89 Houston Farm Road, Stowe 05672.

An upscale place for couples seeking romantic getaways with all the comforts of home. That's what Hap and Amy Jordan produced when they bought one of the last remaining lots along the Mountain Road approach to the ski area and designed a contemporary B&B that ranks among the best in the East. Their sprawling, nine-bedroom hilltop structure looks like a house and provides the amenities of a small hotel. Building from scratch, they provided common areas in the center and luxurious guest quarters in wings on either side. Each spacious room has a kingsize bed, plush seating, TV/VCR and french doors opening to rear lawns and gardens. Each also has a large, see-through gas fireplace open to bedroom and bath, a gleaming space with a whirlpool tub for two, thick terry bath sheets, double vanities and separate shower. The open common room has a massive stone fireplace in the center, separating a game room with a billiards table on one side from a sumptuous sitting area on the other. Tall windows look out onto showy gardens, stone walls and a man-made waterfall. A second sitting room for reading also has a fireplace. The Jordans welcome guests with substantial hors d'oeuvres – perhaps shrimp rémoulade or pan-seared duck with port wine demi-glace. An elaborate breakfast with a choice among three entrées is provided at tables for two in a sunny, high-ceilinged breakfast wing with windows on three sides. The choice might involve an apple and brie omelet, a Canadian bacon and leek quiche, and gingerbread pancakes. Romantics enjoy an outdoor hot tub, relaxing hammocks and wooded walking trails meandering down to a pond.

(802) 253-6282. Fax (802) 253-7415. www.stonehillinn.com. Nine rooms with private baths. Doubles, $315 to $390, off-season $265 to $315. Closed in April and three weeks in late November.

The Gables Inn, 1457 Mountain Road, Stowe 05672.

What some consider to be the best breakfast in Stowe is served at the Gables, either under yellow umbrellas on the front lawn (facing a spectacular view of Mount Mansfield), on the front porch or on tables inside. Breakfast service is the public front for a versatile inn offering a variety of accommodations. Owners Annette Monachelli and Randy Stern offer thirteen cozy guest rooms with country furniture and antiques in the main inn. Much in demand are four spacious rooms in the side Carriage House. These come with cathedral ceilings, wood-burning fireplaces, jacuzzi tubs, queensize canopy beds and television. Top of the line are two Riverview Suites converted from a neighboring homestead. Each has a kingsize bed made of cedar fence posts with a split-rail fence for a headboard, a dual wood-burning fireplace shared by bedroom and living room, a convenience center with refrigerator and microwave, and a double jacuzzi tub. A swimming pool and hot tub, and a large, comfortably furnished den and living room with TV are other attractions in this homey place. In winter the downstairs den becomes a cozy après-ski bar with a selection of beers and wines. Complimentary hot hors d'oeuvres accompany the beverages.

About that breakfast: it's open to the public, and some days the kitchen serves as many as 300. Aside from the old standbys, one can feast on eggs benedict served over portobello mushrooms, kippers or chicken livers with onions and scrambled eggs, matzoh brei, or "Two on a Raft," poached eggs on an English muffin garnished with tomato and herbs served beneath a blanket of molten Vermont cheddar. In the summer a chef grills chicken and burgers on the front lawn for a garden barbecue lunch – a popular break for strollers and cyclists on the Stowe Recreation Path across the street.

(802) 253-7730 or (800) 422-5371. Fax (802) 253-8989. www.gablesinn.com. Fifteen rooms and three suites with private baths. Summer and winter: doubles $83 to $190, suites $158 to $235. Off-season: doubles $78 to $115, suites $150 to $165.
Breakfast daily, 8 to 10:30, weekends to 12:30. Lunch, noon to 2, June-September.

Ten Acres Lodge, 14 Barrows Road, Stowe 05672.

Built as a farmhouse in 1826 with several later additions, this rambling and picturesque red frame house with white trim on a quiet hillside was long known for its restaurant. New owners Robin and Frank Wilson quit corporate life in Asia in 2004 to take over an inn that had fallen on hard times. They moved into a cottage on the property to become hands-on innkeepers and set about running a first-class B&B before thinking of reopening the restaurant. The Wilsons added accents from their Asian travels to the common rooms and a charming, slate-floored tavern/wine bar. There are striking wing chairs and couches piled with pillows in the plush parlor and front library, and large bay windows look out onto ever-changing vistas of valley and mountains. Seven guest rooms on two floors of the main lodge are quite spacious, furnished with king or queensize beds and decorated with a mix of country furniture and antiques. Worth the extra tab are eight deluxe rooms with wood-burning fireplaces in the newer Hill House in back. Each has a large sitting area, private deck, TV, internet access and phone. Guests here share an outdoor hot tub open to the stars. Good for couples traveling together is a renovated cottage with two bedrooms, a kitchen, fireplace and terrace with great views in every direction. The Wilsons offer afternoon beverages and hors d'oeuvres and prepare an ample buffet breakfast, which includes a lavish fruit platter, creamy scrambled eggs, smoked bacon, beignets from New Orleans and sautéed mushrooms in the British style. Frank, an avid movie fan, converted part of the lower level of the Hill House into a ten-seat cinema with a nine-foot screen and surround sound. Guests especially enjoy his James Bond films, among a repertoire of hundreds. The grounds contain a small pool, tennis court, and flower and herb gardens that beckon white rabbits. Beyond, cows graze on neighboring farmlands. Who could ask for a more tranquil setting?

(802) 253-7638 or (800) 327-7357. Fax (802) 253-6589. www.tenacreslodge.com. Sixteen rooms and one two-bedroom cottage with private baths. Doubles, $139 to $179, foliage and holidays $195 to $225, off-season $99 to $120. Cottage for four, $350, foliage $450.

Brass Lantern Inn, 717 Maple St. (Route 100), Stowe 05672.

It took a home builder's eye to see the potential in the formerly rundown 1800 farmhouse and carriage barn that housed the old Charda restaurant north of town. Andy Aldrich and his son undertook a total restoration to produce a comfortable B&B with a pleasant mix of old and new and an award from the Vermont Builders Association for restoration. The walls are stenciled and baskets hang from the beamed ceiling in the dining room. Modern baths, six with whirlpool tubs, adjoin the nine soundproofed bedrooms. Six have fireplaces and queensize beds. Each has stenciled walls, wide-planked floors, exposed beams, brass or canopy beds with handmade quilts, and two wing chairs. The honeymoon room has a heart-shaped headboard and footboard on the queensize iron bed and a couple of "frolic pillows" on the floor near the fireplace. Guests gather around the fireplace in the L-shaped living room or on a back porch and terrace overlooking the mountains. Andy features Vermont products on his breakfast menu, which changes daily. The guest book is full of raves about the apple crêpes, and his breakfasts won three consecutive awards annually from the Gourmet Dining Society of North America. His sourdough french toast and broccoli-mushroom quiche are first-rate.

(802) 253-2229 or (800) 729-2980. Fax (802) 253-7425. www.brasslanterinn.com. Nine rooms with private baths. Doubles, $95 to $165, foliage and Christmas week $115 to $225.

Where to Eat

Blue Moon Café, 35 School St., Stowe.

Well-known local chef Jack Pickett is the man behind this fine restaurant hidden along a side street in Stowe. It's amazingly small, a main room with a dining bar and five tables plus two enclosed front porches, each with three tables for two. A side patio nearly doubles the size in summer. Jack sold lately to his longtime manager, Jim Barton, and his wife Donna, but continued in the kitchen, which offers exciting food in a simple bistro atmosphere. The menu changes weekly, but dinner could begin with creamy carrot-ginger soup with cilantro, tequila-cured salmon with blue corn cake or smoked trout with lentil salad on frisée. For the main course, how about sea scallops with shaved fennel, grapefruit and avocado or grilled yellowfin tuna with tomatillo salsa fresca and smoked yellow pepper coulis? Meat-eaters go for the Asian-barbecued pork tenderloin with crispy gyoza, sweet and sour braised local rabbit and the New York strip steak with shiitake duxelle. Among desserts are an acclaimed crème brûlée, white chocolate mousse with caramelized banana, and a chocolate terrine with crème anglaise.

(802) 253-7006. www.bluemoonstowe.com. Entrées, $18.50 to $26. Dinner nightly, 6 to 9:30.

The Old Vienna Tea Room & Restaurant, 2038 Mountain Road, Stowe.

Small, charming and personal is this restored farmhouse-turned-store that started serving breakfast and now serves lunch, afternoon tea and dinner to a growing clientele that consider it among the top dining experiences in Stowe. Owner André Noel oversees and staffs the small restaurant at the side of his wife Romy's fashionable clothing and furniture store, Romy's Alpenhaus. Young chef Roland Schupfer offers a changing panoply of Austrian and domestic treats: one night a couple of exceptional wiener schnitzel dishes, chicken cordon bleu, Viennese veal goulash with homemade spaëtzle, pan-seared arctic char with tarragon crème fraîche, roasted trout with citrus beurre blanc and rack of lamb with roasted garlic-mustard sauce. You might start with one of the Austrian soups or the signature potato blinis topped with sour cream and sturgeon and salmon caviars. Finish with a trio of ice creams or a selection of Viennese cakes and pastries from the pastry shop. Dining is by candlelight at cushioned curved banquettes in the open main room behind the pastry shop and in more intimate alcoves in a side room. A small bar occupies a portion of the clothing shop.

(802) 253-9500. Entrées, $18.50 to $28.50. Lunch daily, 11:30 to 3. Tea, 3 to 5. Dinner by reservation, Tuesday-Saturday 6 to 9.

Michael's On the Hill, 4182 Waterbury-Stowe Road, Waterbury Center.

Swiss chef-owner Michael Kloeti, a veteran of New York restaurants, took over the 1820 farmhouse that used to be Villa Tragara – a culinary landmark on the road into Stowe – and wowed the Stowe crowd with his innovative European cuisine. He and his wife Laura, a Culinary Institute of America-schooled chef and manager, seat 80 diners in the enclosed wraparound porch, where every table gets a view of the mountains and countryside, and in a renovated barn room. A pianist entertains on weekends in the lounge. Expect such entrées as pan-seared rainbow trout meunière, roasted monkfish with shellfish stew, pork tenderloin with pancetta, veal chop with chanterelles and roasted garlic, and herb-crusted rack of lamb. Typical starters are grilled shrimp with a beet and pear salad with kaffir-lime vinaigrette, Maine crab salad with avocado, and seared foie gras with cherries and homemade brioche. Laura is known for her desserts, perhaps chocolate truffle torte with passion fruit sauce, maple crème brûlée and chilled peach soup with homemade raspberry sorbet.

(802) 244-7476. www.michaelsonthehill.com. Entrées, $15.95 to $29.95. Dinner nightly except Tuesday, 5:30 to 9.

Mes Amis Restaurant-Bistrot, 311 Mountain Road, Stowe.
A classically trained French chef presents affordable French and continental fare at this restaurant in a converted house perched on a hilltop. Chef-owner Carole Fisher and her husband Peter seat 55 diners in several rooms, one lit by twined lights overhead and another with a display of antique glass on high shelves. There are a timbered pub, and a patio for outdoor dining in season. The short menu would be at home in Provence. Look for starters like a classic onion soup au gratin, oysters bourguignonne, baked stuffed clams angelique, escargots en phyllo and polenta provençale with a white wine-tomato-garlic sauce. Typical entrées are sweet potato-crusted salmon with a maple-balsamic glaze, panko-crusted swordfish with the house peppercorn-brandy cream sauce, roasted duck with a "Lavina hot and sweet sauce," chicken marsala, beef stroganoff and filet mignon. Dessert could be profiteroles, meringue glacée or bananas royale flambé.

(802) 253-8669. Entrées, $16.95 to $21.95. Dinner, Tuesday-Sunday 5:30 to 10.

The Shed, Mountain Road, Stowe.
An institution among skiers for years, the Shed has grown from its original shed to include an expansive, beamed-ceilinged dining room with a stone fireplace in the center and a wraparound solarium filled with Caribbean-style furnishings, trees and plants. A microbrewery and Brewery Pub feature European-style ales brewed on the premises. Also popular is the outdoor deck brightened by planters full of petunias in summer. The with-it menu offers something for everyone, from nachos to bruschetta to onion blossoms to chalupa taco salad to Asian stir-fry noodles. You can get shrimp mediterraneo, herb-crusted tuna with roasted fennel cream sauce, chicken marsala, cranberry-glazed pork chops, filet mignon, prime rib and goodness knows what else from the extensive menu. Desserts run to cheesecake, apple pie and brownie à la mode. Sundays at the Shed now feature eggs benedict for $9.95.

(802) 253-4364. Entrées, $14.95 to $19.95. Lunch daily, 11:30 to 4:30. Dinner, 5 to 10, late menu to midnight. Sunday brunch, 10 to 2.

Olives Bistro, Mountain Road, Stowe.
Creative Mediterranean cuisine is featured in this, the latest incarnation of a series of restaurants in the Stowe Center Shops. Hand-painted murals impart the look of a walled, wisteria-laden courtyard in the mountains of Italy, and there's a flower-bedecked patio for dining in summer. Chef-owner Jeff Brynn from Shelburne and his wife Charlotte from New Zealand moved here after running a pastry shop

Down Under. The restaurant had been known for its Mediterranean flavor, including such dishes as Greek lasagna, shrimp Mediterranée and chicken Portuguese. Jeff kept those on the menu and added his own dishes, among them a dynamite steak with whisky demi-glace, pan-seared pork tenderloin with an artichoke-tomato-red wine sauce, and arctic char. Sangria mussels, Maine crab cakes with dill-dijon mustard and calamari fra diavolo are typical appetizers. To finish, look for espresso cheesecake, apple crisp and banana-chocolate torte.

(802) 253-2033. Entrées, $14.95 to $18.50. Dinner, Monday-Saturday from 5.

Austrian Tea Room, Trapp Family Lodge, Luce Hill Road, Stowe.

In summer or foliage season, there's no more charming place for lunch or a snack than the rear deck of the Austrian Tea Room, with planters of geraniums and petunias enhancing the view across the countryside and horses grazing nearby. Surely you can feel the spirit of the late Maria von Trapp (who lived at the lodge until her death in 1987) and the Trapp Family Singers. It's a majestic setting where you feel on top of the world. The broccoli, ham and swiss quiche and the grilled shrimp caesar salad are recommended, as is the curried chicken and rice salad in a pineapple shell. We opted for a bratwurst with German potato salad and sauerkraut (the latter two surprisingly mild – better for tourist tastes?) and the cold pineapple-walnut soup with a smoked salmon plate. There are open-face sandwiches, fancy drinks, cafe Viennoise and Austrian wines by the glass or liter. Those wonderful Austrian desserts – sacher torte, linzer torte, apple strudel and the like – as well as Bavarian chocolate torte, peach torte and Vermont maple cream pie are in the $4 range. With a cup of cafe mocha, they make a delightful afternoon pick-me-up.

(802) 253-8511. Entrées, $5.50 to $10.50. Open daily, 10:30 to 5:30.

Over-the-Top Dining

The Cliff House Restaurant, Atop Mount Mansfield, Stowe.

Hop aboard the Stowe gondola and glide up to the Cliff House for an unusual lunch experience. Atop Vermont's highest peak you'll enjoy a breathtaking view as well as some outstanding food – outstanding, at least, given its difficult location. The menu might be easy to execute down below, but at 3,625 feet above sea level you don't expect to get much more than burgers, cold sandwiches and perhaps chili – the typical skier's fare. Here you'll find interesting soups and salads, house-cured gravlax and steamed mussels. There are sandwiches like pineapple-pesto chicken in a grilled flatbread wrap, a spicy lobster and shrimp roll on a toasted baguette, crêpe of the day, even petite filet of beef. Yes, you also can get a burger – grilled angus or veggie – on a sourdough roll. French toast bread pudding and chocolate-hazelnut tart are typical desserts.

Executive chef Claudine Myer also oversees an innovative series of "Alpine Epicurean Adventure" summit gourmet dinners during ski season. The weekly event includes a gondola ride with hot beverages, a champagne reception at the top, a five-course themed dinner by candlelight and memories to last a lifetime – or at least until the next week.

(802) 253-3500. www.stowe.com. Summer lunch, $6.95 to $16.95, daily 11 to 3. Winter dinner, Friday 6:30 to 9:30, mid-January to mid-March, $69 per person.

FOR MORE INFORMATION: Stowe Area Association, 51 Main St., Stowe, VT 05672, (802) 253-7321 or (877) 407-8693. www.gostowe.com.

Mad River Valley, Vt.
Year-Round Sporting Mecca

With some of Vermont's tallest peaks rising on all sides, the Mad River slices through a verdant valley, rampant in spring when it lives up to its name and relatively quiet the rest of the year. From its start high in the Granville Gulf in the Green Mountains, the river plunges over the Warren Falls, creating a swimming hole in the heart of the wooded village of Warren (population 1,237), the beginning of the Mad River Valley. The river meanders a few miles north through meadows and farmlands to and through Waitsfield, a bit larger village that's more spread out. Their covered bridges and classic rural New England architecture helped place both villages on the National Register of Historic Sites.

On their western flank rises the Green Mountain National Forest, home of two storied ski areas that cast a spell over the entire Mad River Valley. One is the venerable Mad River Glen, a spartan area for hardy, serious skiers, hidden well up in the mountains away from the crowds. The other is tony Sugarbush, a bigger and more visible presence spawned by and for the jet set. Both are very much "in" with skiers, for vastly differing reasons.

The valley below the ski areas reflects a striking dichotomy: the down-home rusticity of Mad River Glen vs. the glamour and glitz of Sugarbush. There's "extreme" skiing, as in foolhardy, and extremely difficult skiing. There are luxurious lodging accommodations and some that are anything but. Some of Vermont's finest dining options are here, and others are more basic. The range of arts, culture, entertainment and nightlife reflects similar extremes.

So do the other sports and recreational opportunities that make the Mad River Valley popular, yet idiosyncratic – and a destination area year-round. After the ski season, there are the conventional athletic pursuits associated with other ski resort areas, such as golf and tennis, hiking and kayaking. There also are the more unusual: mountaineering, polo, cricket, Icelandic horse trekking, mountain biking, backpacking and soaring.

The two aspects – rustic and rich – co-exist nicely in the Mad River Valley. They make an engaging blend for a distinctive getaway.

Seeing and Doing

Downhill skiing reigns supreme and shapes the valley's character. Off-mountain, activity centers along Route 100, which links the villages of Waitsfield and Warren. Curiously, Waitsfield (the home of Mad River Glen) is busier and more hip in the Sugarbush style. Warren (the address for Sugarbush) is in the Mad River Glen tradition, more rural and seemingly bypassed by the times.

Skiing

Mad River Glen, Route 17, Waitsfield. Billed as a serious place for serious skiers, Mad River has been challenging hardy types since 1948 ("ski it if you can," is its motto). Here is a "true" Vermont place where skiing is still a sport, not an industry. There are no frills: little snowmaking, a few lifts including the original, diesel-powered single chairlift (the nation's last surviving single chairlift, with blanket wraps

Photo by James Plumpton

Artist paints floral scene in mountains of Mad River Valley.

provided to ward off the chill) to the summit, hair-raising trails like Paradise and the Fall Line, plenty of moguls and not much grooming, and a "Practice Slope" steep enough to scare the daylights out of beginners (the Birdland area is fine for intermediates). And, blessedly for skiers, snowboards are banned here. There's a Mad River mystique (blue jeans and milk runs) that you sense immediately and attracts you back. Former owner Betsey Pratt, who bought the area in 1972 with her late husband, still skis it, but the place is now owned by a cooperative of loyal skiers who banded together to buy it – the only such skier-owned mountain in the country.

(802) 496-3551 or (800) 850-6742. www.madriverglen.com. Open Monday-Friday 9 to 4, Saturday and Sunday 8:30 to 4. Adult lift tickets $50, juniors $37.

Sugarbush Resort, 2405 Sugarbush Access Road, Warren.

Founded in 1958 and among the first of Vermont's destination ski resorts, Sugarbush with its own "village" at its base appealed immediately to the jet set and fashion models and became known as "Mascara Mountain." From its original gondola lift to its expert Castlerock area, from its clusters of condos and boutiques to its indoor Sports Center, Sugarbush draws those who appreciate their creature comforts – and good skiing as well (the Glades offers some of the best glade skiing in the East). The resort has seven quadruple chairlifts among its sixteen lifts, serving 104 slopes and trails with 54 miles of skiing. Recently called the fastest-growing destination ski resort in New England, Sugarbush was acquired by Summit Ventures, three local skier/investors led by Winthrop Smith, owner of the Pitcher Inn. The home of famed extreme skiing brothers John and Dan Egan, Sugarbush offers the first guided backcountry skiing in the East. The Slide Brook Express – the longest and fastest high-speed quad in the world – connects Sugarbush's main 3,975-foot Lincoln Peak and neighboring Mount Ellen/Sugarbush North. The latter has the valley's greatest vertical drop, 2,600 feet, from its 4,085-foot summit.

802-583-6300 or 800-537-8427. www.sugarbush.com. Open Monday-Friday 9 to 4, Saturday and Sunday 8 to 4. Adults, $45 to $65, juniors $40 to $59.

CROSS-COUNTRY SKIING. The valley's ski touring centers offer an extensive network of trails for all abilities. Trails of the Mad River Path system are open for cross-country skiing, with those along the Mad River providing easy going and good views. The biggest touring center is **Ole's Cross Country Center** off Airport Road at the Sugarbush-Warren Airport in Warren, (802) 496-3430 or (877) 863-3001. It offers 30 miles of moderately rolling trails groomed for classic skiing and ski skating. Nearly ten miles of trails are left untouched for a backcountry experience and six miles are for snowshoers only. Day passes are $15 for adults, $12 for juniors. **Blueberry Lake Cross Country Ski Center,** 424 Robinson Road, Warren, (802) 496-6687, has twenty miles of groomed trails, including one mile lighted for night skiing and a trail designated for skiing with a dog. More Nordic skiing is available at the **Round Barn Touring Center,** (802) 496-6687, with twenty miles of trails, and **Sugarbush Resort,** (802) 583-2605, sixteen miles of trails.

Other Sports

This is a four-season sports area with a difference. Yes, there is golf, at the Robert Trent Jones-designed **Sugarbush Golf Club,** Golf Course Road, Warren, (802) 583-6725. It's a par-72 course with water hazards (pond or brook) affecting eight consecutive holes; daily greens fees, $58 weekends, $48 midweek. Yes, the **Sugarbush Health & Racquet Club,** 148 Sports Center Drive, Warren, (802) 583-6700, offers three indoor and six outdoor tennis courts, racquetball and squash courts, indoor and outdoor pools and hot tubs, steam room, sauna and an exercise facility. It also has the Valley Rock Gym, an indoor rock-climbing facility.

But there's much more: this is something of an equestrian center with a number of stables offering trail rides. Among them are the **Vermont Icelandic Horse Farm,** North Fayston Road, Waitsfield, (802) 498-7141. It specializes in horse trekking on one of the oldest and purest breeds in the world – anything from one-hour and half-day rides to four-day inn-to-inn rides to six-day mountain expeditions. The **Sugarbush Polo Club,** (802) 496-8938, the oldest in New England, was started in 1962 by skiers using ski poles and a volleyball. It now has three polo fields locally for games and tournaments, staged Thursday, Saturday and Sunday afternoons June through September.

Soaring via gliders and sailplanes is at its best from the Warren-Sugarbush Airport, where instruction and rentals are available from **Sugarbush Soaring,** (802) 496-2290. Biplane rides for one or two persons also go from the airport.

The Mad River and Blueberry Lake are good for swimming, canoeing, kayaking and fishing. The Mad River rugby team plays throughout the summer and fall at the Waitsfield Recreation Field. The Mad River Valley Cricket Club stages charity events. Finally, a round-robin English croquet tournament is staged in mid-summer.

HIKING AND BIKING. Year-round paths throughout the valley for walking, hiking, running, biking and cross-country skiing are maintained by the **Mad River Path Association,** based in the General Wait House at 44061 Main St., Waitsfield, (802)

496-7877. It offers trail maps to the Mad River Greenway along the river in Waitsfield, the Mill Brook Trail near the Mad River Glen access road (Route 17) in Waitsfield and Fayston, and the new Kingsbury Bridge Greenway in Warren. For more strenuous adventures, the **Long Trail** is just overhead. Hikers and backpackers can climb to the summits of three 4,000-foot peaks

Bicyclists enjoy miles of two-lane paved roads and an extensive network of mountain biking trails. Sugarbush Resort has a mountain biking center at Lincoln Peak, where you can rent a snow bike in the winter. Chairlifts provide mountain bike access to ski trails for downhill rides. Bicycles can be rented at Inverness Sports, Stark Mountain Bike Works and Clearwater Sports, all along Route 100 in Waitsfield.

Clearwater Sports, (802) 496-2708, also offers canoes and kayaks, and leads day trips for canoeing, biking and hiking.

More Activities

Scenic drives. The Lincoln Gap Road, the McCullogh Turnpike (Route 17) beyond Mad River Glen and the steep Roxbury Gap Road each have their rewards. Along the latter, stop at **Three Shepherds Farm,** 42 Roxbury Mountain Road, (802) 496-4559. Learn how to turn milk from local Jersey cows into delicious cheeses with Jackie Faillace, who calls herself America's youngest cheesemaker.

For the most open vistas and overall feeling for the area, traverse Brook Road and Waitsfield Common Road out of Warren, past the landmark Joslin Round Barn, Blueberry Lake and Sugarloaf Airport and return the back way into Waitsfield.

A longer drive south heads into Granville Gulf State Park, which covers 1,200 acres between Warren and Granville along the eastern boundary of the Green Mountain National Forest. The Mad River starts here and cuts through the park, creating scenic Moss Glen Falls along Route 100. The park offers a six-mile scenic drive. An interesting stop is at the **Granville Bowl Mill** store, (802) 767-4711, which offers Vermont gifts and antiques along with wooden salad and decorative bowls produced at the Hemenway Bowl Mill since 1857.

Nightlife. As at most ski areas, there's plenty of après-ski action in the bars and restaurants across the valley. For a different experience, check out the **Eclipse Theater,** Route 100, just north of the shopping centers in Waitsfield (802) 496-7787 or (888) 212-1142. It shows independent and mainstream films in a coffeehouse environment. Its Saturday concert series features renowned performing artists. The Eclipse also includes the Starlight Lounge with live music Thursday-Sunday.

Home-Grown Greenery

von Trapp Greenhouse, 208 Common Road, Waitsfield.

For spectacular gardens and perfect plants, find your way on the dirt road east of Waitsfield Common to the garden center run by Maria von Trapp's grandson Tobi, who grew up on a dairy farm across the road, and his wife Sally. Unlike most garden centers that purchase their stock from suppliers, this enterprise grows all its own plants from seeds, cuttings or divisions. Beautiful display gardens surround the family's alpine-style house. In season, the plants are sold at a retail shop in front of one of the six von Trapp greenhouses, which furnish lavish floral arrangements and produce for the valley's inns and restaurants.

(802) 496-4385. www.vontrappgreenhouse.com. Open Monday-Saturday 9 to 6 and Sunday 10 to 4, May-July, and Tuesday-Sunday in August and September.

Critters with Character

All Things Bright and Beautiful, 27 Bridge St., Waitsfield.

In two houses next to the second oldest covered bridge in Vermont is the ultimate collection of stuffed animals – mainly bears, outfitted in everything from a London bobby's uniform or a wedding dress to ski vests that proclaim "Save the Bear." Twin sisters Bonnie and Gaelic McTigue moved from Chicago in 1968 to preside over an enterprise that "started with Christmas and teddies" and just keeps expanding. A cheery "hello" emanated from Gael hidden behind a Christmas tree at a desk painting Christmas ornaments one summer day when we entered the **Tree Top Christmas Shop.** In the **Teddy Bear Shop** in the other house, Bonnie was assisted by Bridget the cat atop the cash register and Megan the dog on a wicker loveseat in front of one of twelve rooms chock full of character. We picked up a few of Gael's remarkable hand-painted birds for Christmas presents. It's a bit overwhelming, but the twins are both characters and their shops are not to be missed.

(802) 496-3997. www.allthingsbright.com. Open daily, 9 to 6.

SHOPPING. The Mad River Valley offers the best, most diverse shopping opportunities of any New England ski resort area. Waitsfield has three shopping complexes, each worthy of exploration: the Mad River Green and the Village Square along Route 100 and the Bridge Street Marketplace beside Vermont's second oldest covered bridge, newly revitalized following a disastrous flood. Check out the fine **Artisans' Gallery,** other art and craft galleries, antiques shops, the **Feathered Nest** gift shop and the **Bridge Street Bakery.** It offers great Portuguese breads, baked goods and snacks (cranberry buns with orange cream, gorgeous fresh fruit Danish pastries, ham and Vermont cheddar croissants, and maybe even a hearty sausage stew with French bread).

A must-stop is **The Store** in the red 1834 Methodist Meeting House along Route 100. Owner Jackie Rose, dean of the area's merchants (hers was the first store at Sugarbush Village), has an exceptional and vast array of Vermont foods, books, accessories, gifts, Christmas things, and a lovely collection of handmade quilts and pillows. A rear children's room resembles a giant toy box, while the second floor is stocked with antique furniture.

The well-known Green Mountain Coffee Roasters was founded in the Mad River Green, and the **Three Mountain Café** here continues to feature its coffees. **The Collection,** "three stores in one," offers high-quality American arts and crafts, antiques and accessories as well as gifts and toys. **A Schoolhouse Garden** shows dried floral designs, Vermont-made furniture and accents for home and garden. A farmers' market with produce and crafts is a highlight Saturday mornings from May into October.

In Village Square, the **Blue Toad** flower shop also offers particularly nice, inexpensive baskets from twenty countries and good greeting cards, as well as English tin boxes and jelly beans. **Tulip Tree** shows Vermont crafts and art, including lots of cows and many of the prints by Sabra Field, our favorite Vermont artist. **Labyrinth** features Vermont-made wooden toys and children's clothing along with gifts, pottery and handcrafted jewelry. **Ya·'lee** has spirited clothing in natural fibers for women. **Equus** carries everything for the horse and rider.

Along Route 100 are **Luminosity** stained glass and **Cabin Fever Quilts,** stocking a wondrous array of handmade quilts in the Old Church. **Waitsfield Pottery** sells nice lamps and vases and functional stoneware, mostly in greens and blues, produced in the basement of an 1845 house. You can watch glass blowers David and Melanie Leppia in action at **Mad River Glass,** a studio and spectacular gallery.

In tiny Warren, everything you need and a lot you don't expect is found at the **Warren Store,** a lively general store housed in a former stagecoach inn. It offers provisions, fine wines and a deli, plus upstairs, the **More Store** for contemporary interests, including clothing, gifts and decorative accessories nicely displayed in a museum-like setting. Up the street, blue and white stoneware made on the premises is displayed on the lawn in front of the **Warren Village Pottery. The Bradley House** shows whimsical crafts and furnishings among its sophisticated stock. We were struck by the unusual candles, bowls painted with Vermont scenes, and "Memories of Skiing," a box of old skis for a cool $500. Next door, **Parade Gallery** offers fine art and photography. Down the street is **Barn-It-All!** for antiques and collectibles.

Where to Stay

The Pitcher Inn, 275 Main St., Box 347, Warren 05674.

Spectacular, deluxe, whimsical, sumptuous. Superlatives such as these accorded the Pitcher Inn hardly do it justice, as reborn in 1997 after the original burned to the ground. A better guidepost may be its quick elevation into the lofty Relais & Chateaux realm. Sugarbush devotee Winthrop Smith of the founding Merrill Lynch family bought the property and had it rebuilt. The three-story, pristine white building is a beauty with upstairs balconies overlooking the tranquil village and rear porches looking onto the rushing Mad River. The eleven stunning guest accommodations, all but two with wood-burning fireplaces, contain all the creature comforts and then some in dazzling, dramatic decor. Whirlpool tubs, stereo systems, computer-fax hookups and hidden TV/VCRs are standard. Each room was designed by a different architect to incorporate a Vermont theme in its decor and furnishings. The Mallard – with a domed ceiling giving the illusion of a duck blind – has a bed shaped like a duck, a sofabed, antique duck decoys and antique guns in a display case. In the much-photographed Trout room, the TV pops out by remote control from beneath a flying trout sculpture separating the sitting area from the plump kingsize bed. Bedposts and columns are cut trees, looking as if they're growing out of the floor. In the bathroom, fish are painted around the jacuzzi tub, the vanity drawers are fronted by logs and birch bark surrounds the mirrors. Old skis and bamboo poles are everywhere in the lavishly rustic Ski Room, where the campy kitchenette has a picnic table, three upright toboggans form part of the kingsize headboard between two birch trees and the colorful patchwork quilt is made of discarded ski jackets. The king bed in the Mountain is in an open cabin enclosure with a ribbed tin roof. The adjacent barn holds a pair of two-bedroom suites, each with a fireplaced living room.

Two large common rooms in the main inn offer comfy seating around the fireplaces. The inn's elegant and airy dining room is open to the public for dinner and breakfast (see Where to Eat). Overnight guests have their choice of the full breakfast menu. Afternoon tea also is included. Two large common rooms in the main inn offer comfy seating around the fireplaces. There also are a library and a downstairs billiards/game room, which opens onto a porch, terrace and a colorful garden retreat beside the river. In the Tracks lounge, you'll find the tracks of moose, bear, deer and other animal footprints in the colorcast cement floor, all identified by artworks on the walls. Across the street, the inn's new Alta Day Spa offers a variety of treatments.

(802) 496-6350 or (888) 867-4824. Fax (802) 496-6354. www.pitcherinn.com. Nine rooms and two suites with private baths. Doubles, $330 to $600. Suites, $660.

The Inn at the Round Barn Farm, 1661 East Warren Road, Waitsfield 05673.

The Joslin Round Barn – a National Historic Landmark and one of the last remaining of its kind in Vermont – is a focal point of this deluxe B&B. Its three vast floors have been renovated into a cultural center, a theater, a space for weddings and cooking classes, and the headquarters of the Round Barn Farm Cross-Country Ski Center. There's even a 60-foot-long lap pool on the lower level. The inn is not in the Round Barn, but rather occupies a gracious farmhouse and connecting carriage house next door. It has extravagant guest accommodations, luxurious common rooms and a terraced, 85-acre back yard that rolls down a hill to a couple of ponds before meandering uphill past cows grazing in the distance. Tops in the main house is the Joslin Room, with kingsize canopy bed, fireplace and a huge bathroom complete with wing chair, oriental rug, steam shower and corner jacuzzi tub for two. Four mini-suites in the rear loft area of the original carriage house come with queen or kingsize beds, steam showers, gas fireplaces and separate sitting areas beneath twenty-foot beamed ceilings. The top-of-the-line Richardson with a marble fireplace contains a sunken bathroom with an oversize jacuzzi, separate shower, and his and her vanities. The newer Abbott is a true suite, with a kingsize bedroom and an adjoining living room with gas fireplace and oversize whirlpool tub in the corner. The separate bath has a double vanity and glass-enclosed steam shower. Relaxing amid pots of flowering hibiscus on the back terraces is a treat, what with flowers sprouting from piles of rocks beneath a giant apple tree and whimsical touches like a cow made out of iron and a pet pig in a pen. Animals graze and a few barns are scattered up the hill beyond an undulating, fourteen-foot-deep spring-fed pond for swimming, canoeing and fishing. Innkeeper AnneMarie DeFreest prepares interesting canapés for cocktail time. Breakfast might yield cinnamon-raisin belgian waffles with maple cream or, our favorite, an omelet blending bacon, cottage cheese, onions, red peppers and basil from the garden.

(802) 496-2276. Fax (802) 496-8832. www.innattheroundbarn.com. Eleven rooms and one suite with private baths. Doubles, $160 to $260, $190 to $285 foliage and holidays. Suite, $280, $315 foliage and holidays.

West Hill House, 1496 West Hill Road, Warren 05674.

A wonderfully secluded setting on nine peaceful acres next to the Sugarbush Golf Course and Ski Touring Center, a quaint Vermont farmhouse dating to 1862 and welcoming hosts commend this seven-room B&B. Innkeeper Dotty Kyle's artistry is everywhere evident, from the beautiful floral borders she painted to enhance the living room and bedrooms to the gourmet breakfasts she turns out each morning. Her husband, construction manager Eric Brattstrom, added a huge great room with stone fireplace and a sunroom with vaulted ceiling opening onto a side deck overlooking ponds and gardens. All guest quarters have king or queen beds, fireplaces and TV/VCRs as well as a steam bath and/or whirlpool tub and shower. We enjoyed the main-floor Stetson Suite with a TV/sitting room, whirlpool tub and two-person steam bath/shower. Tops now is the beamed Four Poster Suite, up its own spiral staircase above the great room with a queen featherbed, sitting room, deck, double jacuzzi and two fireplaces. Guests relax on the wicker-filled front porch or the large side deck facing bird feeders, tiny red squirrels, a gazebo, the ponds and prolific gardens. Another haunt is the cozy barnwood-paneled living room with its treasury of books, vaulted ceiling, wide-board floors and a large recessed fireplace at one end. Best of all is the rear great room which, Dotty thinks, sounds pretentious "but everybody says 'what a great room!'" A pantry holds a refrigerator and wet bar, where guests help themselves to cookies and beverages. Breakfast in the beamed English antique dining room might include bananas West Hill (like bananas foster, spiked with rum), scones and an herbed cheese omelet. On Saturday nights or by reservation, Dotty prepares optional candlelight dinners for guests.

(802) 496-7162 or (800) 898-1427. Fax (802) 496-6443. www.westhillhouse.com. Six rooms and two suites with private baths. Doubles, $145 to $190 weekends, $135 to $180 midweek. Add $10 for foliage and holidays.

Beaver Pond Farm Bed & Breakfast, 1225 Golf Course Road, Warren 05674.
A farmhouse this may be, but an elegant one it is indeed. Located off a quiet country road, the light green house with green roof overlooks a beaver pond, the Sugarbush Golf Club and rolling hillsides. Nancy and Bob Baron share their gorgeous property and home with guests, who enjoy a stylish living room with fireplace, a beamed dining room with a long harvest table on an oriental rug and a small library. A small bar allows guests to help themselves to complimentary coffees and teas, as well as soft drinks, or beer and wine for an additional charge. Best of all, perhaps, is a fabulous rear deck that runs the length of the house, where guests like to watch the beavers in the pond. Upstairs, reached by two separate staircases, are four guest rooms with king or queen beds dressed with fine linens and down comforters and furnished with period antiques, reproduction furniture and oriental rugs. A fifth room with queensize bed, adjoining the rear deck on the main floor, was being readied for occupancy in 2005. All come with comfy spa robes (for use in the hot tub on the outdoor deck), hair dryers and clock radio/CD players, TV and DVD players, and each is equipped for high-speed internet access. The Barons welcome guests in the afternoon with homemade cookies, Vermont cheese and crackers, finger sandwiches or hot chili and a specially prepared beverage. Breakfast is a highlight of the stay, culminating in quiche, a goat cheese and prosciutto frittata or upside-down apricot french toast with apple-maple syrup.

(802) 583-2861 or (800) 685-8285. Fax (802) 583-2860. www.beaverpondfarminn.com. Five rooms with private baths. Doubles, $139 to $159. Add $10 for foliage and holidays.

The Lareau Farm Country Inn, 46 Lareau Road, Box 563, Waitsfield 05673.
Situated in a meadow beside the Mad River, this really is a farm with gardens, two dogs, four cats, seven horses and occasionally chickens and pigs, the whole menagerie dubbed the Lareau Zoo and the name delightfully emblazoned on sweatshirts, aprons, T-shirts and the like. The 1832 Greek Revival farmhouse with a barn, woodshed and 67-acre country setting along Route 100 flatlands that were farmed until a few years ago by the Lareau family was converted into a B&B in 1984 by Pennsylvanian Sue Easley, who has been expanding and upgrading ever since. Since she pieced together the squares for ten bed quilts in her first summer, she has added bathrooms and expanded to thirteen guest rooms. In the former woodshed, the dirt floors have given way to carpeting, but the four rooms retain some of the original posts and beams amid such modern conveniences as private baths. Brass bedsteads and rockers are mixed with a profusion of hanging plants. An addition to the rear of the main house holds four guest rooms, all with full baths and queensize

beds, a much-enlarged dining room and a sitting room around the fireplace in the former kitchen. A new jacuzzi suite is among five rooms in the oldest part of the house, built in the 1700s. For breakfast, Sue whips up muffins and perhaps an egg soufflé casserole and blueberry or banana-oat bran pancakes. Guests like to laze on the assortment of porches that wrap all the way around the house, as well as the huge rear dining room with four big tables, oriental rugs and windows on three sides. They also enjoy the ten-foot-deep swimming hole flanked by rocks on the Mad River out front. Actually, there are three swimming holes: one for the public and families, one for house guests and one for skinny-dipping ("we send one couple at a time," advises Sue). The flora and fauna on the property are so interesting that Sue has published a detailed walking trail guide for guests.

(802) 496-4949 or (800) 833-0766. Fax (802) 496-7979. www.lareaufarminn.com. Eleven rooms with private baths and two with shared bath. Doubles, $80 to $135 weekends, $70 to $110 midweek, $80 to $160 foliage and holidays.

The Featherbed Inn, 5864 Main St. (Route 100), Waitsfield 05673.

There are plump featherbeds on the beds, naturally, and featherbed eggs are the breakfast specialty at this historic and stylish B&B opened by Clive and Tracey Coutts. After three years of painstaking renovations, the place bears faint resemblance to its background as the area's first B&B/ski lodge in the 1950s. Clive handled the construction, even putting 3,000 of the original bricks into the foundation and the living-room fireplace. Tracey did the decorating, window treatments and some spectacular stenciling. Two pleasant guest rooms are at one end of the main floor and share a den with television. Upstairs are three more bedrooms and two suites. A rear cottage offers two garden-level rooms and an upstairs bedroom with the original beams. All have queensize featherbeds and country furnishings. Tracey's stenciling, evident in most rooms, reaches its zenith in the informal, main-floor lodge room. Here, beneath a beamed ceiling, stenciled geese and ducks fly up and around the windows and french doors in random procession. The room is sunny in wicker, the doors open onto an outdoor deck and an open fireplace is ablaze in winter. Guests also enjoy a handsome living room, where Clive may play for singalongs around the grand piano. If not the signature featherbed eggs in individual ramekins, breakfast might be German pancakes stuffed with peaches or stuffed french toast.

(802) 496-7151. Fax (802) 496-7933. www.featherbedinn.com. Seven rooms and three suites with private baths. Doubles, $99 to $149. Suites, $140 to $169. Add $15 for foliage and holidays.

1824 House Inn, 2150 Main St. (Route 100), Waitsfield 05673.

A rural setting beside the Mad River and good food are draws at this small and personal inn in a rambling, ten-gabled farmhouse dating to 1824 and listed on the National Register of Historic Places. Innkeepers John Lumbra and Karl Klein offer four large kingsize rooms and four smaller queensize rooms on two floors, all with down featherbeds. The second-floor Bennington, off a stairwell from the dining room, has a king bed and a sitting area filled with antiques. It's considered the most romantic room, while the recently renovated main-floor Franklin Room with queen bed at the rear of the inn is the most private. By reservation, chef John offers four-course dinners for inn guests as well as outsiders who manage to book a table in the 24-seat dining area, Tuesday-Saturday 5:30 to 8. The meal is prix-fixe ($40), with several choices for each course. In the morning, an extravagant three-course breakfasts might feature a vegetable frittata or an herbed egg tart with gruyère cheese. The tranquil, fifteen-acre property includes gardens and a swimming hole in the Mad River. It enjoys direct access to the Mad River Trail for miles of walking and cross-country skiing.

(802) 496-7555 or (800) 426-3986. Fax (802) 496-7559. www.1824house.com. Eight rooms with private baths. Doubles, $143 to $153 weekends, $125 to $135 midweek.

Where to Eat

The Common Man, 3209 German Flats Road, Warren.

Here is the ultimate incongruity: a soaring, century-old timbered barn with floral carpets on the walls to cut down the noise and keep out wintry drafts. Crystal chandeliers hang from beamed ceilings over bare wood tables set simply with red napkins and pewter candlesticks. A table headed by a regal Henry VIII chair occupies a prime position in front of a massive, open fieldstone fireplace. The whole mix works, and thrivingly so since its establishment in 1972 in the site we first knew as Orsini's. Destroyed by fire in 1987, it was replaced by a barn dismantled in Moretown and rebuilt here by longtime English proprietor Mike Ware. New owners Keith and Julia Paxman continue to operate the endearing place that has an air of elegance but is without pretension. The baked escargots "served with our famous (and secret) garlic butter sauce" leads off the New American menu. Other appetizers include balsamic-glazed confit of duck and rabbit livers in puff pastry. We can vouch for the Vietnamese shrimp with chilled oriental noodles and a peanut-sesame sauce, and a classic caesar salad. Main courses like monkfish grenobloise, Caribbean spiced chicken and sautéed Vermont veal with a leek-cream sauce represent uncommon fare – not to mention value – for common folk. At one visit, the Vermont rabbit braised with marjoram and rosemary was distinctive, and the Vermont sweetbreads normande with apples and apple brandy were some of the best we've tasted. Our latest dinner produced a stellar special of penne with smoked chicken and asparagus and a plump cornish game hen glazed with mustard and honey. The mandarin-orange sherbet bearing slivers of rind and a kirsch parfait were refreshing endings to an uncommonly good meal.

(802) 583-2800. www.commonmanrestaurant.com. Entrées, $16.75 to $26.50. Dinner nightly from 6 or 6:30 (from 5:30 or 6 in winter). Closed Monday, mid-April to mid-December.

The Pitcher Inn, 275 Main St., Warren.

The luxurious Pitcher Inn, elevated by the present owners to Relais & Chateaux status after the original burned to the ground, draws gourmands from miles around. The 40-seat restaurant at the river end of the main floor is quite traditional with well-spaced, white-linened tables flanked by windsor chairs, white tapers in silver candlesticks, a large raised fireplace and accents of greenery. The Brook Room overlooking the Mad River to the side is used for overflow, and a table for two in the corner, with windows onto the flood-lit stream, is the best in the house. Chef Susan Schickler's fare is contemporary American and ever-changing. A recent dinner opened with such exotica as twice-baked cheese soufflé with parmesan cream and roasted pepper salad, escalope of veal over a smoky bacon-flageolet ragoût, and seared foie gras with glazed baby carrots, balsamic-roasted onions, salsify and clementine jus. Main courses included grilled wahoo with lemon risotto, fennel-crusted snapper with Jamaican curry butter sauce, roast duck breast with red curry jus, beef tenderloin au poivre and grilled lamb chops with roasted pepper-olive relish. Typical dessert choices are chocolate mousse torte with a walnut crust and a trio of sauces, apple-frangipane tart with maple cream sauce and crème caramel with gingersnaps. The inn's "ice cream sandwich" combines grand marnier frozen crème brûlée with chocolate wafers, citrus crème anglaise and chocolate sauce. Light fare is available in the inn's Tracks lounge. There's a table for six for tasting dinners in the 6,500-bottle basement Wine Cellar, honored by Wine Spectator with its Best of Award of Excellence. The $100 per-person tab yields a five-course dinner with wines tailored to your wishes.

(802) 496-6350 or (888) 867-4824. www.pitcherinn.com. Entrées, $24 to $34. Dinner nightly except Tuesday, 6 to 9.

The Spotted Cow, Bridge Street Marketplace, Waitsfield.

Courtly ex-Bermudan Jay Young sold his old Jay's luncheonette to open a fine-dining restaurant a week before the Mad River lived up to its name and flooded downtown Waitsfield. Although he arrived on the scene to find a refrigerator afloat in his dining room, he and his wife, Renate, decided to repair the damage to their 1850 building and open his now-acclaimed eatery. Their 30-seat restaurant is a charmer, enhanced by a changing display of potted flowers, fine artworks and a wall of windows onto an alleyway that cuts through the center of the arty marketplace beside the covered bridge. Chef Eric Bauer, who joined the Youngs from Chez Henri, cooks "classical French with regional overtones." That translates to such dinner entrées as pan-fried coho salmon finished with smoked salmon-dill butter and two caviars, hoisin-glazed free-range breast of duck with sake-ginger sauce and grilled venison loin glazed with Vermont chèvre. Be sure to try the specialty Bermuda fish chowder, a family recipe that Jay brought from his father's restaurant in Bermuda. Two "secret" ingredients – a dollop of sherry infused with peppers and a hefty splash of Gosling's black rum – are added at the table. Bermuda fish fillet and Bermuda codfish cakes are other specialties. The restaurant is a labor of love for Jay, who greets guests, tends bar and washes all the glasses and silverware by hand because he doesn't want detergent to spoil the taste of his food or wine. That's part of why he chose the name for his restaurant. Like the spotted owl, the spotted cow and the Vermont dairy farm are an endangered species. So, he feels, is the art of fine dining. He's doing his part to preserve it.

(802) 496-5151. Entrées, $19.95 to $25.95. Lunch in summer and fall, Tuesday-Sunday 11 to 3. Dinner, Tuesday-Sunday from 5:30.

Chez Henri, Sugarbush Village, Warren.

The longest-running of the valley's long runners, Chez Henri is into its fifth decade as a French bistro and an after-dinner disco. It's tiny, intimate and very French, as you might expect from a former food executive for Air France. Henri Borel offers lunch, brunch, après-ski, early dinner, dinner and dancing – inside in winter by a warming stone fireplace and a marble bar and outside in summer on a small terrace bordered by a babbling brook. The dinner menu, served from 4 p.m., starts with changing soups and pâtés "as made in a French country kitchen," a classic French onion soup or fish broth, and perhaps mussels marinière, a trio of smoked seafood with greens or steak tartare "knived to order." Entrées, served with good French bread and seasonal vegetables, often include bouillabaisse, coq au vin, roasted duck with fruit or green peppercorn sauce, veal normande, filet au poivre and rack of lamb. Some come in petite portions, and a shorter bistro menu is available as well at peak periods. Crème caramel, coupe marron and chocolate mousse are among the dessert standbys. The wines are all French.

(802) 583-2600. Entrées, $17 to $27. Open daily from 11:30 in ski season, from 5:30 July-November; hours vary. Closed May to late June.

┌─ *Fine Food, Great Value* ─

Millbrook Inn & Restaurant, Route 17, Waitsfield.

This small inn with an unexpected emphasis on fine Indian cooking is a sleeper among the better-known establishments in the Mad River Valley. It's been lovingly run since 1979 by chef Thom Gorman, innkeeper with his wife Joan. They seat 30 diners at candlelit tables covered with paisley cloths in a country-charming dining room with oriental rugs on the dark wood floor. Anadama bread, Joan's specialty, is made in house, as are pastas and acclaimed desserts. Start with mushrooms à la Millbrook, stuffed with a secret blend of ground veal and herbs. Entrées include a daily roast of Vermont lamb, pork or venison, shrimp scampi, five-peppercorn beef, vegetable pasta roulade and three-cheese fettuccine tossed with Cabot cheddar, parmesan, Vermont mascarpone and sundried tomatoes. There are also four dishes from the Bombay region, where Thom lived for two years while in the Peace Corps. The badami rogan josh, local lamb simmered in all kinds of spices and yogurt and served with homemade tomato chutney, is a longtime favorite. Another is the seafood mélange of mussels, scallops and shrimp spiced with Thai-style green curry and served over rice. Millbrook has a wine and beer license, with well-chosen selections tailored to go with assertive Indian food. As for those famous desserts, ice creams like chocolate chip and brickle candy are made here – "we're the only place in Vermont that doesn't serve Ben & Jerry's," says Thom. Look also for the signature apple brown betty and perhaps white chocolate mousse pie with a chocolate cookie crumb crust.

Upstairs are seven simple guest rooms with private baths, decorated with stenciling and interesting handmade quilts and comforters. A full breakfast with choice of menu is served. Doubles are unusually good value at $130 to $150, MAP.

(802) 496-2405 or (800) 477-2809. www.millbrookinn.com. Entrées, $12.50 to $18.95, Dinner nightly, 6 to 9. Closed Tuesday in summer, April to mid-June and mid-October to mid-December.

The Warren House Restaurant & Rupert's Bar, 2585 Sugarbush Access Road, Warren.

Skiers heading for Sugarbush once stopped at the Sugarbush Sugarhouse for pancakes and homemade syrup. Today, they stop at a vastly expanded dining establishment with a smashing greenhouse room for good food offered by owner Chris Jones, who reopened the highly rated Sam Rupert's restaurant after it closed. He offers a comfortable, welcoming bar and casual fine dining in the atmosphere of an old Vermont sugarhouse. The menu features modern American cuisine by a Culinary Institute of America-trained chef, Kurt Hekeler. Expect to start with the likes of steamed mussels in lemon-curry cream, baked escargots, slow-roasted St. Louis pork ribs with house-made whiskey barbecue sauce or a salad of greens with warm goat cheese and toasted walnuts. Typical entrées are pan-roasted arctic char with key lime-cilantro vinaigrette, bouillabaisse, grilled swordfish with red curry sauce, merlot-braised duckling with andouille sausage and spinach, balsamic braised lamb shank, and grilled New York strip steak with gorgonzola-roasted garlic butter.

Chocolate pot de crème, bittersweet chocolate torte and key lime squares typify the dessert list.

(802) 583-2421 or (800) 817-2055. www.thewarrenhouse.com. Entrées, $12.95 to $20.95. Dinner nightly, from 5:30.

John Egan's Big World Pub & Grill, Junction Routes 100 & 17, Warren.

Okay, sports fans, this one's for you. Recently relocated to a more noticeable location, it's a casual place with a skier's spirit and a mouthful of a name. Chef Jerry Nooney and maître-d' Bernie Isabelle named it for John Egan, a world-renowned "extreme team" skier from Sugarbush, who is a local contractor (he built Jerry's house) when he's not jumping off cliffs for moviemaker Warren Miller. The "big world" refers to Egan's worldwide connections and the restaurant carries out the theme. Jerry mans a wood grill in the kitchen. The menu is simple but with-it. The corn and crab stew comes in a mug. Appetizers include big world nachos, Canadian snow crab cakes with chipotle sauce, duck and scallion wontons, and "dog bones," Polish sausage in puff pastry with kraut and mustard on the side. There are burgers and sandwiches, salads (one of fancy greens with lots of roasted garlic cloves, grated asiago cheese and croutons) and pastas. Among entrées are Chinese shrimp, sea scallops with sundried tomato pesto, Hungarian goulash, wood-grilled leg of lamb and New York sirloin, grilled over a hardwood fire with cracked peppercorns and red wine butter. The signature is Big World grilled chicken glazed with cider, ginger and lime. Maple crème brûlée is a dessert specialty.

(802) 496-3033 or (866) 496-3033. www.bigworldvermont.com. Entrées, $12.95 to $17.95. Dinner nightly, from 5.

American Flatbread Restaurant, 46 Lareau Road, Waitsfield.

American Flatbread pizzas are produced for the gourmet trade in the old slaughterhouse at Lareau Farm Country Inn. Working with an 800-degree wood-fired earthen oven with a clay dome, founder George Schenk and staff create the remarkable pizzas that are frozen and sold at the rate of more than 2,000 a week to grocery stores as far south as Florida. When not freezing pizzas, they operate a wildly popular weekend restaurant, serving pizzas, great little salads dressed with homemade ginger-tamari vinaigrette, and wine and beer at tables set up around the production facility's oven room and kitchens and outside on the inn's west lawn. The delicious flatbreads with asiago and mozzarella cheeses and sundried tomatoes have made many a convert of pizza skeptics. How could they not, when the night's flatbread specials might pair roasted chicken with white beans, sage, braised kale and organic red onions, or shrimp with roasted red and yellow tomatoes, organic arugula and hand-dipped herbed ricotta? The bakers use organically grown flour with restored wheat germ, "good Vermont mountain water" and as many Vermont products as they can. Lately, George expanded the dining room and renovated part of the horse barn into a waiting room and "museum" and opened a second American Flatbread Restaurant over the mountain in Middlebury. Each night's dinner is dedicated to an employee, a friend or maybe the people of Iraq. George's heart-felt "dedications," posted around the facility, make for mighty interesting reading.

(802) 496-8856. www.americanflatbread.com. Flatbreads for two, $11.50 to $19.75. Dinner, Friday and Saturday 5:30 to 9:30.

FOR MORE INFORMATION: Sugarbush Chamber of Commerce, 4061 Main St., Waitsfield, VT 05673, (802) 496-3409 or (800) 828-4748. www.madrivervalley.com.

Horse-drawn carriage and sleigh rides pass Kedron Valley Inn in South Woodstock.

Woodstock/Quechee, Vt.

Vermont Cachet

If ever a Vermont town were to be called chic, it would be Woodstock.

Its early stature as the cradle of winter sports prompted it to be called, in a bit of hyperbole, "the St. Moritz of the East – without the Ritz." More recently, National Geographic magazine termed it, more believably, "one of the most beautiful villages in America." The Ladies Home Journal went farther, calling it "the prettiest small town in America."

These days, there's no way Woodstock could be considered St. Moritz without the Ritz. It *has* the ritz. But St. Moritz? Hardly. The postcard-perfect village of 3,500 obviously prosperous souls spreads out in serpentine valleys formed by gently meandering rivers against a backdrop of mellow mountain greenery. Much of the village is designated an historic district, which focuses on a long New England green surrounded by stately residences and public buildings of the late 18th and 19th centuries. There are three covered bridges and five Paul Revere bells. Nary a traffic light, a billboard, a utility pole, a fast-food chain or a ramshackle building mars its pristine excellence.

Woodstock's prosperity owes to its early designation as the shire town of Windsor County. As the county seat and the early legal center of the state, it was settled not by farmers and factory workers but by lawyers, bankers, doctors and tradesmen. Among them were George Perkins Marsh, the 19th-century conservationist and Congressman credited with founding the Smithsonian Institute, and railroad magnate Frederick Billings, who purchased the Marsh homestead and established a progressive dairy farm and managed forest on the Marsh farm. As a stagecoach crossroads and later a railroad link, Woodstock attracted "rusticators" seeking the tonic of mountain air. Woodstock's dual status as residential and resort community was forever joined.

Vermont's first golf course was established south of town around the turn of the last century and the nation's first ski tow was installed on a cow pasture north of town in 1934. That was the year when Laurance S. Rockefeller, grandson of John D., married Mary Billings French, granddaughter of Frederick Billings. The Rockefellers buried the utility wires underground, acquired and redesigned the golf course, bought and upgraded the Suicide Six ski area, bought and rebuilt the Woodstock Inn, built a multi-million-dollar indoor sports and fitness center, and opened the Billings Farm & Museum. The Rockefeller home and 550 acres of surrounding gardens and woodlands now form the Marsh-Billings-Rockefeller National Historic Park, Vermont's first and the first anywhere to focus on conservation history.

The nearby hamlet of Quechee adds another dimension. Sightseers by the busload gape into Quechee Gorge, which its promoters tout as "Vermont's Little Grand Canyon" in the area's only venture verging on the honky-tonk. Among modern-day sophisticates, Quechee is better known as the home of the diverse Simon Pearce glass, pottery and restaurant enterprises.

But it is Woodstock to which more people are drawn. As Sen. Jacob Collamer, confidant of President Lincoln, said back in the 19th century: "The good people of Woodstock have less incentive than others to yearn for heaven." They found their portion of paradise. The visitor gets to share it, too.

Seeing and Doing

The Woodstock area is a place where you can be as active or as sedentary as you like. You can ski at Suicide Six, not far from Gilbert's farm where Woodstockers installed the nation's first rope tow, or you can ski at nearby Killington, the East's largest ski area. You can golf at the historic Woodstock Country Club, site of Vermont's first golf course and home also of the fine Woodstock Ski Touring Center, or at a newer golf course in Quechee. You can hike through the Quechee Gorge area or the hundreds of acres of forests maintained by the Woodstock Inn. You can climb a switchback trail up Mount Tom for a bird's-eye view of the area. You can walk around the village green and center, marveling in the architectural variety. You can browse through a couple of museums and the national historic park. And you can shop. In the charming downtown area in summer, colorful flowers cascade from boxes once used for gathering maple syrup; in winter, large white Christmas lights bedeck the old-fashioned store facades. Indeed, it is arts and crafts galleries and stores that make Woodstock so appealing for many.

ARTS AND CRAFTS. A sculpture of a man walking five dogs, taken out to the sidewalk every morning, attracts visitors into the spectacular **Stephen Huneck Gallery** at 49 Central St., where the sign says "dogs welcome" on the door. Animals (especially dogs and cats) are the theme of Vermont resident Huneck, one of America's hottest artists, who's known for playful hand-carved furniture, jewelry and sculpture. The smallest pins start at $10 but you could spend up to $30,000. You'll come out of here chuckling, feeling that the world isn't a bad place, after all.

The Vermont Workshop, 73 Central St., is said to be the oldest gallery in Woodstock, having evolved from a summer workshop established in 1949.

Everything from woven mats and interesting lampshades to wall hangings and cookware is for sale in room after room of great appeal. **Gallery on the Green** shows the works of more than 40 New England artists in six galleries. Original oils and watercolors by Robert O. Caulfield are displayed at the **Caulfield Art Gallery.** Paintings, sculptures, pottery and handcrafted furniture are shown at **Polonaise Art Gallery. Southwest Accents** specializes in fine art and jewelry from Mexico and the American Southwest. **Russian Renaissance** claims one of the most extensive collections of Russian art and artifacts in this country. Handcrafted jewelry and pottery are the specialties of **Woodstock Artisans.**

SHOPPING. Check out the pottery depicting fish by Giovanni DeSimone, a student of Picasso, at **Aubergine,** a kitchenware shop, where you might find a thermos full of chocolate-raspberry coffee to sample and some dips to spread on crackers. **Unicorn** stocks handicrafts and jewelry by New England artisans and some clever games and toys. The children dressed in flannel shirts sitting outside **The Vermont Flannel Co.** looked so real that we almost spoke to them. You can barely get through the aisles at **Primrose Garden,** there are so many silk flowers spilling from the shelves. One of us admired the jewelry and the mini-birch-bark canoes at **Arjuna,** an international store "bearing antiques and adornments from as far away as Sumatra and as near as the Adirondacks." **Morgan-Ballou** offers classic apparel for the well-dressed Woodstock woman. **Who Is Sylvia** stocks vintage and antique clothing. **Howe Casual** sells unusual clothing and accessories for men and women.

F.H. Gillingham & Co. at 16 Elm St. is the most versatile store of all. Run by the Billings family for more than 100 years, it's a general store, but a highly sophisticated one – offering everything from specialty foods and wines to Quimper pottery and hardware – and so popular that it does a land-office mail-order business. Here you'll probably find every Vermont-made dressing, candy, condiment and more. Owner Jireh Swift Billings's young son represents the ninth generation of the Swift family, dating to the 1600s.

For simple – or not-so-simple – deli items, try either **The Village Butcher,** on Elm Street or Central Street's natural foods market **18 Carrots,** offering veggie burritos, sandwiches, and softball-sized muffins. Deli sandwiches and prepared foods also star at the indoor **Woodstock Farmers' Market,** self-styled as a funky, fresh-foods market at 468 Woodstock Road in West Woodstock.

The **Taftsville Country Store,** 165 years old, is an institution in tiny Taftsville, a blip in the road between Woodstock and Quechee. The things most people expect to find in a general store are in back. Up front are all kinds of upscale Vermont foodstuffs, from chutneys to cheddars.

Shops come and go on the three levels of **Waterman Place,** a 100-year-old restored house with a glass atrium and elevator above Quechee village off Route 4.

Stores of the variety that appeal to souvenir-hunting tourists are concentrated at **Quechee Gorge Village,** Route 4, next to the Quechee Gorge. Tour buses disgorge their prey for a quick look at the gorge before they descend on the Antique Center (more than 450 dealers), the Arts & Crafts Center (220 artisans), the Country Store, the Christmas Loft, even a 1946 "Yankee Dinah." For those so inclined, the village may well be "the best of Vermont in one stop." More to other tastes along Route 4 are the **Fat Hat Factory, Etc.,** a barn full of spirited hats and carefree clothing "for whatever shape your head's in," and the Scottish imports at **Scotland by the Yard.**

┌─ *Entrepreneurial Energy* ──────────────────────────────

Simon Pearce, The Mill , Quechee.

Every time we're in the area, we stop at Simon Pearce's magnificent mill, partly because it's all so fascinating and partly because there's always something new. Simon Pearce is the glass blower who left Ireland in 1981 to set up business in the abandoned flannel mill beside the Ottauquechee River. The site is inspiring: thundering waterfalls, covered bridge, beautifully restored mill and classic white Vermont houses all around. The interior has a fine restaurant (see Where to Eat) and a handsome shop offering glass, pottery and Irish woolens, all beautifully displayed, plus a second floor with seconds at 30 to 40 percent off, although even then, everything is expensive. Downstairs is a glass-blowing area, a working pottery, the hydro station with enormous pipes from the river and a steam turbine that provides enough power to light the town of Quechee as well as serve the mill's energy needs (melting sand into glass, firing clay into porcelain and stoneware). "The whole idea was to become self-sufficient and provide an economic model for small business in Vermont," says Simon. The mill is zoned utility in the sub-basement, manufacturing in the basement, retail in the restaurant and shop, office-retail on the second floor and residential on the third, where Simon once lived with his family. The enterprise is growing all the time, opening retail shops around the Northeast and expanding its production capability with a custom-designed glass facility and a pottery in nearby Windsor. We defy anyone not to enjoy, learn – and probably buy.

(802) 295-2711. Open daily, 9 a.m. to 9 p.m.

──

Attractions

Billings Farm & Museum, Route 12 and River Road, Woodstock.

This ritz of a working dairy farm and living agricultural museum on the northern edge of Woodstock portrays the Vermont farm of yesteryear. It operates in partnership with the new Marsh-Billings-Rockefeller National Historic Park across the street. The farm dates to 1871, when Frederick Billings, builder of the Northern Pacific Railroad, began importing cows from the Isle of Jersey to make a model dairy operation. Artfully presented, life-like exhibits in 19th-century barns on the farm depict the seasonal activities like maple sugaring and ice-cutting that shaped the lives and culture of rural Vermonters. The rather opulent 1890 farmhouse – hub of the farm and forestry operation more than a century ago – shows the pace-setting creamery where 5,000 pounds of butter a year were produced, the farm office, the farm manager's family living quarters and an adjoining ice house. The multi-purpose farmhouse was a model of its era – "from cellar to ridgepole it is just about perfect, and is not surpassed, if indeed it is anywhere near equaled by any other establishment of the kind in Vermont," the local Vermont Standard wrote at the time. Visitors wander through the kitchen garden, where heirloom vegetables and herb varieties grow. Down a path the modern farm is evident. Visitors can see the Jersey herd, calves, sheep, oxen and teams of Belgian horses, and the milking barn is open. "A Place in the Land," a 30-minute documentary film, is shown hourly in the visitor center's theater. It traces the history of conservation stewardship in America as it is reflected on the property through the work of George Perkins Marsh, Frederick Billings and the Rockefellers, successive residents of the estate.

(802) 457-2355. www.billingsfarm.org. Open daily 10 to 5, May-October; also weekends at Thanksgiving, in December and winter holidays, 10 to 3. Adults $9.50, children $5.

Marsh-Billings-Rockefeller National Historical Park, 54 Elm St., Woodstock. Opened in 1998, Vermont's first national park is the only one to focus on conservation history and the evolving nature of land stewardship in America. The park is named for George Perkins Marsh, father of the American conservation movement, who grew up on the property, and for Frederick Billings, an early conservationist who set up a model dairy farm there and reforested Mount Tom and Mount Peg nearby. The house was occupied until lately by Billings's granddaughter, Mary French Rockefeller, and her husband, conservationist Laurance S. Rockefeller. They established the Billings Farm & Museum to continue the farm's working dairy and left the estate's residential and forest lands to the people. A variety of ranger-led walks and talks trace the history of conservation in the surrounding 550-acre forest, which harbors twenty miles of carriage roads and trails crisscrossing Mount Tom. Ninety-minute guided tours show rooms on the first and second floors of the 1805 mansion and formal grounds. The house is simple and elegant, not opulent, and looks as if the Rockefellers had just stepped out for morning coffee and were due back any minute. The extensive collection of American landscape paintings is the most remarkable feature.

(802) 457-3368. Guided tours daily, Memorial Day through October, daily 10 to 4, reservations recommended, adults $6, children $3. Forest and trails open daily, free.

VINS Nature Center, Route 4 West, Quechee.
Visitors can get eye-to-eye with bald eagles, red-tailed hawks, snowy owls and peregrine falcons at this, the only museum devoted to living birds of prey in the Northeast. Seventeen state-of-the-art raptor exhibits are highlights of the new Vermont Institute of Natural Science nature center on 47 acres of rolling forestland just west of the famed Quechee Gorge. Having been injured in accidents, raptors undergo rehabilitation in a series of huge outdoor flight enclosures. Among the more than 40 birds we saw was Vermont's tiniest avian predator, the three-ounce saw-whet owl. From May to October raptors demonstrate their flying and hunting skills in daily programs at 11, 1 and 3:30. In the off-season, naturalists lead tours of the raptor enclosures daily at 2 and weekends at 11 and 2. Naturalists also guide tours into the Quechee Gorge on weekends at noon, weather permitting. The center, which relocated here in 2004 from a site in southwestern Woodstock, includes outdoor interpretive exhibits, nature trails and a nature shop. It represents the first phase of what is planned as a world-class center for environmental learning and conservation efforts.

(802) 457-2779. www.vinsweb.org. Open daily, 9 to 5:30 May-October, 10 to 4 rest of year. Adults $8, children $6.50.

Dana House Museum, 26 Elm St., Woodstock.
This rambling 1807 Federal-style house, its back yard yielding a prospect of meadows and Mount Tom, is the home of the **Woodstock Historical Society.** Built by Charles Dana, a prosperous dry-goods merchant, it was home to several Danas who achieved national prominence. On display in eight exhibit rooms are paintings, furnishings, decorative arts, photographs, dolls, toys, tools, costumes and other artifacts that bring to life the 200-year history of Woodstock. Guided tours are available on the hour. The museum shop in the rear is full of gift ideas and country memorabilia.

(802) 457-1822. www.woodstockhistsoc.org. Open Memorial Day to late October, Monday-Saturday 10 to 4, Sunday noon to 4. Adults, $5.

Outdoor Recreation

Thanks to the early environmental cause and Rockefeller funding, many of the area's natural resources have been preserved and are accessible to the public.

Guided **walking tours** of the village are scheduled three times weekly in season. Tours leave the information booth on the village green at 10:30 a.m. Monday, Wednesday and Saturday; cost, $2.50. Guided **hiking tours** up Mount Tom, called "A Walk on the Wild Side," are led by the Woodstock Inn forester Tuesday mornings in season. Hikers leave at 9 a.m. from the inn's lobby; cost, $8.

Walking, Jogging and Hiking. Woodstock is blessed with a public trail system close to the village center, part of it on the hundreds of acres of Woodstock Inn & Resort forest lands. From the northwest edge of the village, footpaths ascend 550 feet to the top of **Mount Tom,** where the hardy are rewarded with a bird's-eye view of Woodstock. The easier, 1.6-mile-long trail leaves from Faulkner Park on Mountain Avenue. The steeper Precipice Trail, whose upper sections cling to rocky catwalks, extends nearly a mile from the bridle trail beside River Street Cemetery. A 2.5-mile North Peak loop trail goes off the Precipice Trail. On the south side of the village, a narrow footpath loops its way from Golf Avenue 380 feet up to the summit of **Mount Peg,** an open knoll overlooking the Ottauquechee River Valley, a one-mile hike. A longer trail to the Mount Peg summit covers 3.3 miles from the Woodstock Inn Sports Center. The **Appalachian and Long Trails** pass nearby.

Quechee Gorge State Park, Route 4, Quechee. Besides the 150-foot-deep gorge that some call Vermont's "little Grand Canyon," the park offers hiking trails.

SPORTS. You can golf at the eighteen-hole, 6,000-yard **Woodstock Country Club,** designed by Robert Trent Jones Sr. on the site of Vermont's first golf course (greens fees, $85 weekends, $67 midweek), or at the newer Quechee Club's two eighteen-hole Highland and Lakeland golf courses in Quechee. The public also may use the facilities of the Woodstock Inn's **Health & Fitness Center,** where a 30-by-60-foot indoor lap pool, two indoor and ten outdoor tennis courts, squash, racquetball, croquet, aerobics, whirlpool, steam room and sauna and Nautilus equipment are available.

Downhill skiing is offered at the inn-owned **Suicide Six,** on the back side of the farm pasture where Woodstockers installed the nation's first rope tow in 1934. Today, two chairlifts and a J-bar serve 23 slopes and trails; lift tickets, adults $50 weekends, $29 midweek; children $34 and $23. Two of the East's premier ski resorts, **Killington** and **Okemo**, are each less than fifteen miles away. Some of the East's best cross-country skiing is available at the 60-kilometer **Woodstock Ski Touring Center,** the seasonal adjunct of the Woodstock Country Club. The center maintains two trail systems for a total of 60 kilometers of trails along the snow-covered golf course and along the carriage roads on Mount Tom, where a wood fire-warmed log shelter yields vistas of the village below. **Wilderness Trails,** based in a barn at the Quechee Inn, opens eighteen kilometers of cross-country trails in the Quechee Gorge and Quechee State Park area. In summer, Wilderness Trails offers canoeing, kayaking and mountain biking.

Horseback Rides. South Woodstock, home of the original 100-mile trail ride and center of the Green Mountain Horse Association, (802) 457-1509, has many riding trails. The Kedron Valley Stables, Route 106, (802) 457-1480 or (800) 225-6301, offers horse rentals, lessons and horse-drawn carriage and sleigh rides.

Woodstock Llama Treks, Route 4, (802) 457-5117. For a change of pace, explore the hills of Woodstock in the company of the highly intelligent and social llama. Brian M. Powell, based next to the Red Cupboard Gift Shop two miles west of Woodstock, offers a variety of llama treks – early morning, early evening, family, half day and romantic (music, flowers and bring your own wine and cheese for two) – from mid-May through October. Rates vary from $15 per person to $80 a couple.

Where to Stay

Inns and Resorts

Woodstock Inn & Resort, 14 The Green, Woodstock 05091.

The biggest institution in town, this is a full-service resort for those who want everything from sumptuous accommodations to the best recreational facilities. The inn faces the village green, a covered bridge and mountains, and the back looks across a pool and putting green and down the valley toward the resort's golf course and ski touring center. Other leisure facilities include the Suicide Six ski area, ten tennis courts, two lighted paddle tennis courts, and an indoor sports and fitness center. Built by Rockresorts in 1969 after Laurance Rockefeller found the original Woodstock Inn beyond salvation, the interior contains a lobby warmed by a ten-foot-high stone fireplace around which people always seem to be gathered, a comfy library paneled in barnwood, and a wicker sunroom and lounge where afternoon tea is served. The 144 guest accommodations are among the more comfortable in which we've stayed: spacious rooms with handmade quilts on the beds, upholstered chairs, three-way reading lights, television, and large bathrooms and closets. The most luxurious rooms are 34 in the newer rear brick tavern wing, 23 with fireplaces and three with sitting-room porches overlooking the putting green. They are notable for graceful reading alcoves, TVs on wheels hidden in cupboards, mini-refrigerators and double marble vanities in the bathrooms.

The long, semi-circular main dining room, lately doubled in size, has large windows onto a spacious outdoor terrace overlooking the pool, putting green and gardens. Dinner is served nightly, the contemporary fare ranging from grilled ahi tuna steak with black trumpet mushrooms to port-glazed duck breast with summer truffles and pistachio-crusted lamb loin with roasted garlic pan jus. The elaborate Sunday buffet brunch is enormously popular. The stylish **Eagle Café** offers a more casual lunch or dinner. We've enjoyed interesting salads and, most recently, smoked chicken and green onion quesadillas and a grilled chicken sandwich with melted jack, roasted peppers and herbed mayonnaise on toasted focaccia. Stop for a drink or light fare in the sophisticated **Richardson's Tavern,** as urbane a nightspot as you'll find in Vermont.

(802) 457-1100 or (800) 448-7900. Fax (802) 457-6699. www.woodstockinn.com. One hundred thirty-three rooms and nine suites with private baths. Rates, EP. Doubles $215 to $409. Suites $529 to $629. March-April and November to mid-December: doubles $139 to $278, suites $360 to $460.

Entrées, $21.95 to $31.95. Lunch, 11:30 to 2. Dinner, 6 to 9. Sunday brunch, 10 to 1.

The Jackson House Inn, 114-3 Senior Lane, Woodstock 05091.

Deluxe accommodations and a good restaurant are available in this recently expanded, three-story Victorian house on four acres of beautiful grounds west of the village. Luxury starts in the main house, where the third floor has been converted into two large one-room "suites" with queensize cherry sleigh beds, Italian marble baths and french doors onto a rear deck overlooking a spectacular English garden. These and the nine second-floor guest rooms are eclectically furnished with such things as antique brass lamps on either side of the bathroom mirror, bamboo and cane furniture, a marble-topped bedside table, an 1860 sleigh bed, Chinese carved rugs and handmade afghans coordinated to each room's colors. The latest in creature comforts are evident in four large one-room suites in a wing added off the east side of the inn. These have sitting areas, gas fireplaces and contemporary bathrooms with cherry floors, whirlpool or massage therapy jetted tubs, separate showers and towel warmers. During our latest stay in Clara's Corner, the queensize Sheraton poster bed was topped with red and gold Anichini fabrics and a sheeted duvet. Antique pots and vases graced the shelves, and an array of antique pillboxes topped a lace doily on a side table. There were fresh flowers, assorted fruits for nibbling and replacement towels at turndown. Guests gather in the elegant parlor and intimate library for champagne and wine and an elaborate buffet of hors d'oeuvres before dinner. A gourmet breakfast is served in the morning.

The pride of the expanded Jackson House is its restaurant, housed in a stunning rear addition with a cathedral-ceilinged dining room harboring big windows onto four acres of colorful gardens. The focal point is a soaring, see-through open-hearth fireplace of Pennsylvania granite. The chefs, who seem to move on with increasing frequency, prepare exotic new American cuisine. Typical entrées ranges from pan-roasted Georges Banks cod with bacon and corn to pancetta-wrapped veal loin with a pinot noir demi-glace. Our tasting dinner in the candlelit dining room included appetizers of pan-seared diver scallops with house-cured bacon vinaigrette and a pheasant confit and wild mushroom crepinette with a young field green salad. Main courses were juniper-rubbed moulard duck with cherry coulis and slow-braised short ribs of beef with an oxtail croquette. These riches were topped off by a warm liquid-center chocolate cake with white chocolate ice cream and cardamom-ginger crème brûlée.

(802) 457-2065 or (800) 448-1890. Fax (802) 457-9290. www.jacksonhouse.com. Nine rooms and six suites with private baths. Doubles, $195 to $260. Suites, $290 to $380. Prix-fixe, $55. Dinner by reservation, Wednesday-Sunday 6 to 9.

Kedron Valley Inn, Route 106, South Woodstock 05071.

This historic inn in the hamlet of South Woodstock, the heart of Vermont's horse country, has long been a favorite of the equestrian set as well as others seeking a rural getaway. New innkeepers Jack and Nicole Maiden redecorated the public rooms, installed a long bar in the tavern to make it more of a pub and started updating the guest rooms. Accommodations include thirteen rooms in the three-story inn dating to the 1830s, seven in the old tavern building, and six out back in the motel-style log lodge rechristened the Country Cottages. Most rooms have canopy beds covered with antique quilts or down duvets. Twenty have fireplaces or wood stoves, and five have whirlpool tubs. All have TV/VCRs and Bose radios. The largest rooms and suites generally are in the tavern building, where day beds or pullout sofas can accommodate the families who flock to the place. A full country breakfast, from omelets to blueberry pancakes, is served in the sunny terrace room. Above the inn is a spring-fed pond for swimming. Lawn chairs are scattered about to take in the view of cows grazing on the hillside. Equestrians can rent horses in nearby stables, and the inn can arrange horse and buggy rides or horse-drawn sleigh rides.

The new owners redecorated the main dining room in Polo/Ralph Lauren equestrian decor and created an inviting tavern/pub with a tavern menu. Guests relax on plush sofas and chairs beside a fireplace in the tavern before or after dinner, which is served at white-clothed tables lit by candles in hurricane lamps in the beamed dining room and outside on a porch in season. Chef Mark McInnis oversees a changing menu that ranges from sautéed shrimp and mushrooms tossed with fettuccine and reggiano-parmigiano to grilled filet mignon with a roasted garlic-wine demi-glace. The inn's signature salmon stuffed with an herbed seafood mousse and wrapped in puff pastry is superb. We also were impressed with a special of baked pheasant stuffed with local chèvre and topped with roasted macadamia nut butter. The tavern menu offers five kinds of burgers and a handful of entrées for lighter dining.

(802) 457-1473 or (800) 836-1193. Fax (802) 457-4469. www.kedronvalleyinn.com. Twenty-one rooms, six suites and one cottage with private baths. Doubles, $133 to $223; suites, $250 to $299. Foliage and holidays: doubles $201 to $291, suites $317 to $365.

Entrées, $22 to $29. Dinner, Thursday-Monday 6 to 9, nightly August-October. Tavern from 5, entrées $8.50 to $15.95.

The Quechee Inn at Marshland Farm, 1119 Quechee Main St., Quechee 05059.
This rambling white Vermont farmhouse is handsomely situated against a backdrop of red barns across a quiet road from the Ottauquechee River as it heads into Quechee Gorge. Built in 1793 as the home of Vermont's first lieutenant governor, it lately has served as an inn with a welcoming beamed and barnwood living room, a stenciled restaurant and 25 comfortable guest rooms and suites. Fifteen rooms are in the original farmhouse and ten more are on the second floor of a wing that houses the recently expanded common rooms and restaurant. All come with Queen Anne-style furnishings, brass and four-poster canopy beds, wing chairs, and braided and Chinese rugs on wide-plank floors. TVs and telephones are the only concessions to the modernity, most guests preferring to take advantage of the outdoor activities. The Wilderness Trails Nordic Ski School and the Vermont Fly Fishing School are based here, and guests have golf, tennis, swimming and skiing privileges at the private Quechee Club. A full breakfast buffet – from fruits and yogurts to scrambled eggs and sausages – is complimentary in the main dining room.

Most people enjoy drinks by the fire in the living room/lounge before adjourning for dinner in the antiques-filled dining room. Beamed ceilings, wide-plank floors and lovely pink and blue stenciled borders on the walls provide the setting for some interesting cuisine. Dinner might start with grilled shrimp and scallop "lollipops" or Vermont chèvre and foie gras in puff pastry. Typical main courses are Mediterranean bouillabaisse, grilled pork tenderloin with mango barbecue sauce and beef tenderloin sauced with chanterelle mushrooms. Desserts include maple-ginger crème brûlée and chocolate bread pudding with espresso crème anglaise. An appealing light supper menu is available as well.

(802) 295-3133 or (800) 235-3133. Fax (802) 295-6587. www.quecheeinn.com. Twenty-three rooms and two suites with private baths. July to mid-October: doubles $140 to $215, suites $205 to $245. Rest of year: doubles $90 to $145, suites $135 to $175.

Entrées, $19.50 to $29. Light menu, $13 to $17. Dinner nightly, 6 to 9.

Twin Peaks

Twin Farms, Barnard 05031.

For the ultimate in food and lodging, indulge at this small, luxury country resort that coddles the rich and famous. Jet-setters from across the world converge on the secluded farm once owned by writers Sinclair Lewis and Dorothy Thompson, which was converted into the East's most sumptuous resort in 1993. One of a kind, it offers six suites and nine cottages, superb dining and a staff of 50 to pamper up to 30 guests in style. The tab – if you have to ask, you can't afford it – includes meals, drinks and all kinds of recreational activities, from a private ski area and a creekside pub to a fitness center with spa treatment rooms and separate Japanese furo soaking tubs. In the main house, three living rooms, each bigger than the last, unfold as resident innkeeper Michael Beardsley welcomes guests for the owners, the Twigg-Smith family of Honolulu and Barnard. Upstairs are four bedrooms bearing some of the Twin Farms trademarks: plump kingsize feather beds, tiled fireplaces, comfortable sitting areas, fabulous folk art and contemporary paintings, satellite TV/VCR/stereos, tea trays with a coffee press and Kona coffees from the family-owned corporation, twin sinks in the bathrooms, baskets of all-natural toiletries, terrycloth robes, and unbleached and undyed cotton towels. They impart a feeling of elegant rusticity, but come with every convenience of the ultimate home away from home. Less antiquity and even more convenience are found in the stone and wood guest cottages, each with at least one fireplace, a screened porch or terrace, an incredible twig-sided carport and its own private place in the landscape. The Perch, for instance, is situated above a small stream and beaver pond. It harbors luxuriant seating around the fireplace, a dining area, a bed recessed in an alcove and shielded by a hand-carved arch of wooden roping and a wicker-filled porch where a wood sculpture of a shark hangs overhead. Its bathroom has alcoves harboring a copper tub the size of a small pool and a separate shower. The soaring Treehouse is furnished in Adirondack twig, while a Moroccan theme turns the Meadow Cottage into a desert king's traveling palace. The ultimate is the 3,000-square-foot Chalet, which has a two-story-high living room with birch-tree rafters, floor-to-ceiling stone fireplace and windows, bedroom with fireplace, and his and her bathrooms, one with a circular mosaic deluge shower and the other with a skirted soaking tub beside the window. An enclosed porch adds a hot tub.

Good food and drink (from help-yourself bars) are among Twin Farms assets. Guests meet at 7 o'clock for cocktails in a changing venue. A set, four-course dinner is served at 8 at tables for two in a baronial dining hall with chandeliers hanging from the vaulted ceiling and fieldstone fireplaces at either end. Executive chef Neil Wigglesworth's dinner might open with medallions of lobster with avocado relish and angel-hair pasta, followed by warm red-cabbage salad with slices of smoked chicken. The main course could be veal mignon with timbales of wild rice and xeres sauce or five-spiced duck with nut-brown cabbage and golden beets. Fresh figs with French ice cream and peach-caramel sauce might be dessert. In summer, guests often round out the evening with armagnac and s'mores around a campfire before they toddle back to their cottage for the night.

(802) 234-9999 or (800) 894-6327. Fax (802) 234-9990. www.twinfarms.com. Six suites and nine cottages with private baths. Suites, $1,050 and $1,200. Cottages, $1,650 and $1,850. Studio, $2,100. Chalet, $2,700. All-inclusive, except for 15 percent service charge and 9 percent state tax. Closed in April.

Bed and Breakfasts

The Maple Leaf Inn, Route 12, Box 273, Barnard 05031.

If you want to escape the "crowds" of Woodstock and environs, consider this B&B set well back from the road on sixteen wooded acres in rural Barnard. When they could not find the perfect New England inn to buy, Texans Gary and Janet Robison took the unusual step of building a Victorian-style inn from the ground up. An architectural engineer by profession, Gary designed the inn on a computer, and Janet scouted out antiques and reproduction Victorian pieces to fill it. She also did the remarkable hand stenciling that embellishes each of the seven guest rooms, five of them equipped with wood-burning fireplaces. Most are positioned so as to have windows on three sides. Quite large and luxurious, all have kingsize beds, bedside radio-tape deck combinations, televisions in armoires, comfortable chairs and, in all but one of the bathrooms, large whirlpool or soaking tubs. Guests enjoy a fireplaced living room, a small library full of travel books and artifacts from the couple's travels, a wraparound veranda with a corner gazebo and a bright and cheery dining room where breakfast is served by candlelight at tables for two. Ours included buttermilk scones, a fruit course of sautéed bananas with Ben & Jerry's ice cream and stuffed french toast with peach preserves and cream cheese, garnished with nasturtiums.

(802) 234-5342 or (800) 516-2753. Fax (802) 234-6456. www.mapleleafinn.com. Seven rooms with private baths. Doubles, $160 to $230, foliage and holidays $190 to $260. Deduct $30 midweek most of the year and weekends March-May.

The Charleston House, 21 Pleasant St., Woodstock 05091.

The most comfortable B&B accommodations in town are found in this red brick 1835 Greek Revival house named for the hometown of the original innkeeper. Listed in the National Register of Historic Places, it is furnished with period antiques and an extensive selection of art and oriental rugs. Four guest rooms upstairs in the main house have queen beds and one has twins. A substantial addition – nicely secluded in back – contains three deluxe guest rooms with queen beds, jetted tubs, fireplaces, TVs and porches that look onto a wooded area. Another favorite room is the Summer Kitchen, downstairs between the original house and the addition. It is cozy and romantic with a four-poster queen bed, TV and two wing chairs angled beside the fireplace. Innkeepers Willa and Dixi Nohl serve breakfast by candlelight in the elegant dining room.

(802) 457-3843 or (888) 475-3800. Fax (802) 457-3154. www.charlestonhouse.com. Nine rooms with private baths. Doubles, $115 to $220; foliage, $125 to $235. Two-night minimum weekends and during foliage.

Ardmore Inn, 23 Pleasant St., Woodstock 05091.

The restored white Georgian Greek Revival house that for years was the home of the well-known F.H. Gillingham family was converted into a B&B by an Irish priest who named it Ardmore, which means "Great House" in the Irish tradition. Charlotte and Cary Hollingsworth from Southern California, who took over the vintage 1850 inn virtually sight unseen, liked what they found: an impressive house with distinguished palladian windows, etched glass in the solid mahogany front door, circular moldings around the original light fixtures on the ceilings, recessed pocket windows screened with Irish lace curtains in the fireplaced living room, and baths with marble floors. The five guest rooms are painted in light pastel colors, furnished with antiques and oriental rugs, and outfitted with Waverly fabrics. A couple have fireplaces and the main-floor Sheridan has a jacuzzi and a walk-in marble shower. The biggest is Tarma, Irish for sanctuary, which has a kingsize bed, a loveseat facing a marble coffee table and guardian angels as night lights. Breakfast, served at an English mahogany banquet table inlaid with rosewood, might feature ham and cheese frittata or stuffed french toast. Afternoon refreshments are offered on the rear screened veranda in summer.

(802) 457-3887 or (800) 497-9652. Fax (802) 457-9006. www.ardmoreinn.com. Five rooms with private baths. Doubles, $135 to $195, foliage $155 to $215.

The Carriage House of Woodstock, 455 Woodstock Road (U.S. Route 4 West), Woodstock 05091.

They knew they wanted to be innkeepers ever since they became engaged on a trip to Woodstock. The opportunity for Debbie and Mark Stanglin arose a decade later when they took over this turreted Victorian with a wraparound veranda. The couple offer seven queensize bedrooms on three floors of the main house, all named after covered bridges in Vermont. One on the third floor has a TV/VCR and an extra twin bed and another adds a whirlpool tub. Two other premium rooms are in the walkout basement beneath the rear carriage house. Each comes with a whirlpool tub, TV and french doors to the outside. The largest, the Stowe Hollow Room, has a kingsize bed and a fireplace. Victorian antique display items and family mementos are housed in custom-made glass cases separating the newly fireplaced living room and the dining room in the main structure. From the spectacular cathedral-ceilinged kitchen come breakfasts of strawberry-oatmeal Belgian waffles, orange-coconut pancakes or breakfast burritos with sweet roasted jalapeño salsa.

(802) 457-4322 or (800) 791-8045. www.carriagehousewoodstock.com. Nine rooms with private baths. Doubles, $100 to $155 June to late September, $125 to $190 in foliage, $95 to $150 rest of year.

Motel Rooms, Inn Style

The Shire, 46 Pleasant St., Woodstock 05091

Here is a riverside retreat in the midst of the village, a refurbished motel that acts like an inn. Owners Dorothy and Vince DiCarlo consider their river-view rooms the nicest in town. Each different in size and decor, accommodations on the new second floor look like inn rooms with four-poster kingsize beds, wing chairs and reproduction furniture, plus mini-refrigerators and double vanities. Ten rooms have fireplaces and three have whirlpool tubs. One is a large suite with vaulted ceiling and a full kitchen. The white rockers on the common balcony facing the street in front of each upstairs unit appeal, but the deal is sealed by the views out back onto the Ottauquechee River and across a meadow toward the mountains. The older rooms downstairs have french doors onto rear porches or decks for taking in the scene. The best view of all is from the reading deck at the far end of the upstairs balcony, overlooking a curve in the river. Coffee is served here in the morning.

(802) 457-2211. www.shiremotel.com. Forty-one rooms and one suite. Mid-June to mid-September: doubles $128 to $218, suite $300. Foliage and holidays: doubles $158 to $218, suite $318. Rest of year: doubles $78 to $178, suite $200.

Where to Eat

Among the choices are the dining rooms at the inns detailed above. The dining experience at each is well regarded, but there are other good options, too.

Fine Dining

The Prince and the Pauper, 24 Elm St., Woodstock.

A cocktail lounge with the shiniest wood bar you ever saw is at the entry of what many consider to be Woodstock's best restaurant. Tables in the intimate, L-shaped dining room (many flanked by dark wood booths) are covered with linens, oil lamps and flowers in small carafes. The lamps cast flickering shadows on dark beamed ceilings, and old prints adorn the white walls. Chef-owner Chris J. Balcer refers to his cuisine as "creative contemporary" with French, continental and international accents. Meals are prix-fixe for appetizer, salad and main course. The soup of the day could be billi-bi or Moroccan lentil, the pasta perhaps ravioli stuffed with smoked duck and ricotta cheese, and the pâté Vermont pheasant teamed with orange chutney. The six entrées range from grilled ahi tuna with Vietnamese sweet and sour sauce to roast duckling with a sauce of kiwi and rum. The specialty is boneless rack of lamb royale. Desserts might be a fabulous raspberry tart with white chocolate mousse served with raspberry-cabernet wine sauce or homemade Jack Daniels chocolate-chip sorbet. A bistro menu is available in the elegant lounge. Hearth-baked pizzas, grilled rainbow trout and lamb shanks osso buco are typical offerings.

(802) 457-1818. www.princeandpauper.com. Prix-fixe, $43. Dinner nightly, 6 to 9 or 9:30; jackets requested. Bistro, entrées, $12.95 to $20, nightly 5 to 10 or 11.

Barnard Inn Restaurant, 5518 Route 12.

Innovative new American cuisine is the forte of this dining landmark under new owners Will Dodson and Ruth Schimmelpfennig, Culinary Institute of America graduates who operated two neighborhood restaurants in San Francisco. They sold their restaurants and moved into this landmark 1796 brick house with a 50-seat restaurant on twelve rural acres. The husband-and-wife team lightened up the decor in four cozy, elegantly Colonial dining rooms and added a tavern menu to the charming tavern in back. Dinner is prix-fixe ($45 for three courses) in the main dining rooms and à la carte in the tavern. From the kitchen comes the inn's longtime specialty, roast duckling, the presentation varying but on a recent winter menu pairing medium-rare breast of muscovy duck and a duck leg confit with a classic glace de volaille accented with maple syrup. Other entrées included pan-seared escolar with lemon-caper-herb butter, sesame-seared ahi tuna with ginger-soy glaze and filet of beef with cabernet demi-glace. The first course could be a butternut squash soup with crabmeat and herbs, a Greek salad, Asian pork dumplings, soft-shell crab with cilantro-lime mayonnaise or duck pâté on toast points. Finish with Ruth's signature Tahitian vanilla crème brûlée, frozen grand marnier soufflé with blackberry sauce, or a trio of grapefruit-campari, lemon zest and mango sorbets. Dinner in the cozy tavern is a pleasant mix of the innovative and comfort food, from crab and scallop cakes with jalapeño mayo to yankee pot roast ("the real deal") and von Schimmelpfennig wiener schnitzel.

(802) 234-9961. www.barnardinnrestaurant.com. Prix-fixe, $45. Dinner by reservation, Tuesday-Saturday from 6, Thursday-Saturday in off-season. Tavern, entrées, $12 to $17, Tuesday-Saturday 5 to 8:30.

Simon Pearce Restaurant, The Mill, Quechee.

This special restaurant has as much integrity as the rest of Irish glass-blower Simon Pearce's mill complex. The chefs train at Ballymaloe in Ireland, and they import flour from Ireland to make their great Irish soda and Ballymaloe brown breads.

The decor is spare but pure: sturdy ash chairs at bare wood tables topped with small woven mats by day and white linens at night. The heavy Simon Pearce glassware and the deep brown china are made at the mill. Through large windows you have a view of the river, hills rising beyond. An enclosed terrace with retractable full-length windows opening to the outside is almost over the falls and offers the tables of choice year-round. The menu changes frequently but there are always specialties like the delicious beef and Guinness stew, a generous lunch serving of fork-tender beef and vegetables, served with a small salad of julienned vegetables. Hickory-smoked coho salmon with potato salad and a skewer of grilled chicken with a spicy peanut sauce and a green salad with vinaigrette also are extra-good. The walnut meringue cake with strawberry sauce, a menu fixture, is crisp and crunchy and melts in the mouth. At night, a candlelight dinner might start with a trio of smoked fish, crispy ginger calamari with wasabi drizzle or grilled portobello mushrooms with shaved parmesan, fennel and watercress. Main courses could be grilled swordfish with lime hollandaise, crisp roast duck with mango chutney sauce and juniper-seared venison loin with cherry molasses jus. Naturally, you can get beers and ales from the British Isles.

(802) 295-1470. www.simonpearce.com. Entrées, $23 to $38. Lunch daily, 11.30 to 2:45. Dinner nightly, 6 to 9.

Parker House Inn, 1792 Quechee Main St., Quechee.

Walt and Barbara Forrester traded life in Chicago for running a New England inn and restaurant. Each is a trained chef, taking turns in the kitchen while the other hosts in a house-party atmosphere out front. The atmosphere is elegant in two dining rooms and a delightful cocktail lounge opening onto a balcony overlooking the Ottauquechee River out back. Dinner begins with an amuse-gueule, in our case roasted eggplant, red peppers and garlic pickled with fennel. A sampler of three appetizers produced a stellar seafood crêpe, a mushroom cap stuffed with an escargot and a Vermont goat cheese tart. Among main courses, the pork normandy sauced with apples, leeks, cider and applejack, and the pan-seared Long Island duck breast marinated with soy sauce, garlic and ginger lived up to advance billing. Other possibilities ranged from sea bass provençal to rack of lamb with rosemary-lingonberry sauce. Cappuccino accompanied a couple of Barbara's desserts, apple crisp with vanilla ice cream and chocolate-almond torte. Upstairs in the inn are seven guest rooms with private baths renting for $125 to $150 a night, but the Parker House priorities clearly lie with the restaurant.

(802) 295-6077. www.theparkerhouseinn.com. Entrées, $17 to $25. Dinner nightly except Tuesday, 5:30 to 9.

Mangowood Restaurant, 530 Woodstock Road (Route 4 West), Woodstock.

The newly styled restaurant at the old Lincoln Inn at the Covered Bridge conveys a distinct Asian accent, thanks to co-owner and chef Teresa Tan from Singapore. Her specialties are dumplings, among them crispy pork and shrimp with three dipping sauces, and grilled sirloin steak with a garlic marinade and sautéed Asian greens. You also might try Teresa's Singapore laska, chicken and prawns in a spicy coconut cream broth, or the tender rack of pork confit with lychee-mango sauce. Expect starters like Asian lobster bisque and roast duck quesadilla with cilantro crème fraîche. Sweet endings are maple-ginger crème brûlée, bittersweet chocolate grand marnier pot de crème and a trio of sorbets, including lychee-ginger and mango-passion fruit. Dinner is served in two royal blue and white dining rooms, one bearing a wall of paintings of crazed chefs. Drinks and appetizers are available in a comfy living-room-style bar with a fireplace and seasonally on the Mango's Terrace bar outside. The restaurant is their priority, but Teresa and co-owner Amy Martsolf offer six guest rooms with private baths, $125 a night.

(802) 457-3312. www.lincolninn.com. Entrées, $24 to $28. Dinner, Tuesday-Saturday 6 to 9, nightly in foliage season.

Casual Choices

Bentleys Restaurant, 3 Elm St., Woodstock.

This casual, engaging and often noisy place at the prime corner in Woodstock packs in the crowds at all hours. On several levels, close-together tables are set with small cane mats, Perrier bottles filled with flowers, and small lamps or tall candles in holders. Old floor lamps sport fringed shades, windows are framed by lace curtains, the plants are large potted palms, and walls are covered with English prints and an enormous bas-relief. The international menu is as interesting as the decor. For lunch, we enjoyed the specialty French tart, a hot puff pastry filled with vegetables in an egg and cheese custard, and a fluffy quiche with turkey, mushrooms and snow peas, both accompanied by side salads. From the dessert tray came a delicate chocolate mousse cake with layers of meringue, like a torte, served with the good Green Mountain coffee in clear glass cups. Appetizers, salads, sandwiches and light entrées such as sausage crespolini and cold sliced marinated flank steak make up half the dinner menu. The other side offers more hearty fare from fillet of Alaskan salmon with a dill-aioli crust to maple-mustard chicken to pepper-crusted sirloin steak flamed tableside with Yukon Jack bourbon.

(802) 457-3232. www.bentleysrestaurant.com. Entrées, $13.95 to $19.95. Lunch. Monday-Saturday 11:30 to 3 (late lunch menu 3 to 5). Dinner nightly, 5 to 9:30 (late dinner to 11). Sunday brunch, 11 to 3.

Tuscan Treat

Osteria Pane e Salute, 61 Central St., Woodstock.

This true little osteria got its start as an Italian bakery. But the weekend dinners that Caleb Barber and his wife Deirdre Heekin offered as a supplement proved to be the tail that wagged the dog. They gradually phased out the bakery and stopped serving lunch to expand their dinner business to five nights a week. Caleb, who apprenticed at a bakery south of Florence, does the baking and cooking, while his wife manages the front of the house and sells fresh breads and pizzas to go. The menu of Italian country fare changes weekly, offering a handful of choices for each of four courses (prix-fixe, $36, or à la carte). A meal typically begins with assorted vegetable antipasti and perhaps grilled onions with ricotta cheese and toast or an endive salad with gorgonzola and walnuts. The main course could be tiger shrimp steamed with zucchini, Sicilian veal and pork stew or handmade pasta with portobello and porcini mushroom sauce. Dinner might end with pears poached in pernod, an apple-almond tart, profiteroles or the house selection of three cheeses. Fifteen versions of Tuscan pizzas are available, as are beer and wine. The couple were thinking of reinstituting lunch on summer weekends.

(802) 457-4882. Prix-fixe, $35. Entrées, $18 to $20. Dinner, Thursday-Monday 6 to 9.

FOR MORE INFORMATION: Woodstock Chamber of Commerce, 18 Central St., Woodstock, Vt. 05091, (802) 457-3555 or (888) 496-6378. www.woodstockvt.com.

Meredith with its new inns and restaurants lies at western end of Lake Winnipesaukee.

Lake Winnipesaukee, N.H.
Getaway Lake Playground

There are people for whom a lake represents the best of all possible getaway destinations.

Make it a big lake. Give it inlets and bays stretching mysteriously in multiple directions. Surround it with forests and mountains. Punctuate its shore with sandy beaches and clusters of civilization.

Such a lake is Winnipesaukee, the dominant player in the Lakes Region and the largest lake in New Hampshire. The lake is big enough and its surroundings varied enough that it appeals to visitors of all types. Here is a true getaway lake playground, the biggest and busiest in New England.

Beaches, swimming, boating, sailing, amusement parks – you name it, Winnipesaukee offers it in spades. Countless lodging facilities, eateries and attractions court visitors and their wallets.

Since most of the shoreline is privately owned and developed, there's little access to the lake except in certain areas and through public facilities. Indeed, you often cannot even see the lake – much less get to it – from the main routes that loop 97 miles around the lake in what the state labels a New Hampshire Scenic and Cultural Byway.

You do get views of the lake and access to it from pockets of development, particularly along the busy southwestern shore around Laconia, Gilford and Weirs Beach.

More appealing for adult getaways are choice areas at either end of the lake. Beside a bay at the far eastern end, quaint Wolfeboro developed in the 18th century as America's first "summer resort." And it has stayed much the same, an icon of the past, basically off by itself – in spirit as well as geography – from the rest of Winnipesaukee.

More conveniently and centrally located at the western end of the lake, sleepy Meredith emerged as an up-and-coming resort town in the late 20th century. Inns and restaurants took belated advantage of its lakefront to accommodate sophisticates who had found the area wanting.

The Winnipesaukee area is really too big to cover in one getaway. So pick either Wolfeboro or Meredith as your base, depending on your preferences, and enjoy.

Wolfeboro

Wolfeboro has laid claim to being America's oldest summer resort ever since its last English Colonial governor, John Wentworth, built in 1768 the country's first summer home, a palatial mansion on the shore of the nearby lake that bears his name. Today it's a classic, all-American village of 3,000 year-round residents, sequestered between Lake Wentworth and Wolfeboro Bay, the eastern end of Lake Winnipesaukee. Wolfeboro has resisted well the honky-tonk that mars some other sections of Lake Winnipesaukee.

Seeing and Doing

Wolfeboro maintains its sedate, small-town atmosphere, but visitors find plenty to do. You can get out onto the lake on the Winnipesaukee Belle or the M/S Mount Washington excursion boat, which stops here four days a week (see Meredith). Brewster Academy opens its beach to the public in summer. Museums attract just enough visitors to make opening worthwhile. Frequent concerts are presented in summer. There are benches for relaxation in the waterfront Cate Park and along Main Street. Shopkeepers know their customers by name, and everyone on the street seems to know everyone else.

Molly the Trolley makes its rounds hourly from 10 to 4 in summer, showing off the town and providing transportation to the downtown area from outlying parking lots. Narrated tours leave the town docks on the hour. All-day fares: adults $3, children $1.

BOAT RIDES. Ninety-minute narrated cruises around the nearby portion of the lake are offered two or three times daily from the Wolfeboro Town Dock by the **Winnipesaukee Belle,** (603) 569-3026 or (800) 451-2389. The riverboat-style side paddlewheeler shows one of the oldest boatyards on the lake, a loon refuge, the former Chiang Kai-shek estate and islands with interesting histories; adults $10, children $5. The **Millie B,** a ten-passenger antique speedboat owned by the Wolfeboro Trolley Co., (603) 569-1080, offers half-hour rides on demand from 10 a.m. to sunset from the Wolfeboro Town Dock; adults $15, children $7. **Wet Wolfe Rentals,** (603) 569-3200, rents paddle boats and pleasure boats in the Wolfe Town complex along Back Bay at 19 Bay St. **Winnipesaukee Kayak** at 17 Bay St., (603) 569-9926, has everything for the kayaker.

RECREATION. Cate Park, a pleasant little waterfront park beside the town dock, is the site of Wednesday evening concerts by the Cate Park Community Band, and dances and art shows throughout the summer. Back Bay Recreation Area has four tennis courts that are lighted until 10 p.m. Golfers are welcome at the eighteen-hole Kingswood Golf Club and at Perry Hollow Golf and Country Club. The Wolfeboro

Croquet Club offers English-style croquet in the traditional all-white attire on the Clarke Plaza Green. Hikers of modest endurance enjoy the Abenaki Tower Walk. A gradual, one-third-mile climb through the woods off Route 109 north in Tuftonboro leads to the abandoned fire tower, which yields a panoramic view of northern Lake Winnipesaukee and the Ossipee Mountains.

MUSIC. Since 1995, the **Great Waters Music Festival** has presented the Portland Symphony Orchestra and other musical attractions on several summer Saturday nights in its new lakeside performance tent on the Brewster Academy Field. **The Friends of the Wolfeboro Community Bandstand** has augmented the traditional Wednesday evening band concerts with a series of free Saturday evening concerts by visiting bands, from jazz to bluegrass. Since 1937, **Wolfeboro Friends of Music** has sponsored visiting entertainers in ten concerts throughout the year. In 2004, the **Heifetz International Music Institute** occupied the Brewster Academy campus and presented a series of Friday evening concerts in St. Cecelia Church.

Americana Personalized

Wright Museum, 77 Center St., Wolfeboro Falls.

A small tank seems to be crashing onto the street through the front brick wall of this fairly new museum devoted to the World War II era. The sight attracts passersby into a "museum of American enterprise," which showcases the nation's enterprising spirit as everyone rallied to the call to arms at home and abroad. The front building houses the "home front" exhibits, which recreate life in America during the 1940s. Life magazine covers, an old kitchen with a single-door refrigerator and a Ford V-8 evoke nostalgia for anyone from the era, as does the dental office with a long-forgotten pulley drill and side rinse basin. A victory garden flanks the pathway to the rear building, which houses the founding Wright family's collection of upwards of 40 military vehicles, including the largest American tank of World War II. Volunteers from town, all veterans clad in red, white and blue, help tell the story at this very personal place.

(603) 569-1212. www.wrightmuseum.org. Open Monday-Saturday 10 to 4, Sunday noon to 4, May-October; weekends April and November. Adults $5, students $3.

Clark House Museum Complex, South Main Street at Clark Road, Wolfeboro.

Earlier eras are on display in the Wolfeboro Historical Society's cluster of three historic museums on the village green. The Clark House (1778), a Revolutionary farmhouse, contains the first piano in Wolfeboro, an applewood four-poster bed, a dining room table from the Wentworth mansion, outstanding pewter, clocks and kitchenware. The one-room Pleasant Valley Schoolhouse (circa 1820) exhibits old school paraphernalia plus a replica of the Wentworth mansion (it burned to the ground in 1820, and there's considerable debate over what it was like). The Monitor Engine Co. Firehouse Museum, a replica of an 1862 firehouse, holds various pieces of fire apparatus.

(603) 569-4997. Museums open Monday-Friday 10 to 4, Saturday 10 to 2, July 5 to Labor Day, or by appointment. Adults $4, students $2.

The Libby Museum, Route 109 North, Wolfeboro.

The town-operated Libby Museum was started in 1912 by retired dentist Henry Forrest Libby to house his natural history collections. His original collection includes an alligator, a human skeleton, mummy hands, old surgeon's equipment and paintings from the campaigns of General Wolfe (for whom Wolfeboro was named). There are nearly 600 animals, birds, fish and reptiles in its natural history collection, plus 350 Native American artifacts. The section on Northern New England country living includes farm machinery, household items, pottery and Shaker implements.

(603) 569-1035. Open Tuesday-Saturday 10 to 4, Sunday noon to 4, June to mid-September. Adults $2, children $1.

SHOPPING. Wolfeboro has tasteful shops along its Main Street, the Wolfeboro Marketplace, Mill Street and Railroad Avenue. Free half-hour factory tours are conducted at the **Hampshire Pewter Co.** factory and showroom. Stop at **Cornish Hill Pottery** to see fine stoneware pottery, from lamps to tableware, and you usually can watch the potters at work. **Made on Earth** showcases artisans from around the world. Handcrafts and collectibles are shown at **The Straw Cellar. Finely Crafted** offers home accents. Jewelry and works of more than 200 artisans are shown at **Kalled Gallery.** For clothing and sportswear, head to **Wolfeboro Casuals. Milligan's Pendleton Shop** is New Hampshire's only licensed Pendleton specialist, outfitting "ladies and gentlemen." **The Country Bookseller** offers books, as does the **Camelot Book and Gift Shop**. **Black's Paper Store & Gift Shop** has paper goods, newspapers and magazines, as well as a gift shop and an interior accessories section upstairs.

The **Wolfeboro League Shop** of the League of New Hampshire Craftsmen at 64 Center St. is outstanding. Nearby, small wooden houses on the front lawn identify the **American Home Gallery,** which specializes in vintage items for home and garden.

Where to Stay

The Wolfeboro Inn, 90 North Main St., Wolfeboro 03894.

This venerable inn, built in 1812, was greatly expanded in 1988 to produce a total of 44 rooms, five with patios or balconies but, strangely for the location, very few with a good lake view. The layout is such that most rooms overlook the parking lot or village. Three end suites and three balconied rooms on the second floor view the water. The main-floor suite we saw had a large, angled living room, a kingsize four-poster in the bedroom, Lord & Mayfair toiletries and a hair dryer in the bathroom, a desk, two phones, TV in the armoire and a door to a small patio outside with a glimpse of the lake beyond a gazebo. Some of the original 1812 bedrooms retain their fireplaces and a sprightly country look. Although a bit removed from the lake, the inn has its own sand beach, docks, windsurfers and rowboats. It also runs the Winnipesaukee Belle excursion boat. Room rates include continental breakfast.

Meals are offered in two distinctly different venues – one formal, one historic – but the same menu serves both. That menu has been downscaled lately, the former 1812 Steakhouse menu giving way to the more casual fare traditionally offered in the atmospheric Wolfe's Tavern. The something-for-everyone menu now features sandwiches, burgers, "munchies," pizzas, pastas and basic entrées, from fish and chips, fried shrimp and broiled salmon to barbecued pork ribs, chicken fingers, sirloin steak and slow-roasted prime rib.

(603) 569-3016 or (800) 451-2389. www.wolfeboroinn.com. Forty-four rooms and suites with private baths. July and August: doubles $185 to $245, suites $265 to $305. Spring and fall: doubles $135 to $245, suites $205 to $305. November to mid-May: doubles $90 to $175, suites $155 to $195.

Entrées, $9.95 to $19.95. Tavern daily, 7 a.m. to 10 or 11 p.m. Dinner nightly in dining room, from 5:30.

Topsides Bed & Breakfast, 209 South Main St., Box 416, Wolfeboro 03894.

Virginians Dennis and Cynthia Schauer retired to their favorite summer vacation spot to open this deluxe B&B in 2004 in a restored dentist's home and office next door to St. Cecilia Catholic Church and Brewster Academy. Five guest rooms with queen beds and TVs are on two floors. Three in the rear yield lake views in the distance, as does a great L-shaped porch full of wicker furniture in the back. The main-floor Nantucket Room, fashioned from a former sun porch, and the second-floor Martha's Vineyard Room, light and airy with windows on three sides, sport a seashore theme. The main-floor Governor's Room testifies to the Schauers' former residence in a Virginia manor house, as does the Hunt Country Room, a private hideaway up a rear staircase with the largest bedroom and a small sitting room. Cynthia puts out breakfast on a counter made of a boat's top side between her kitchen and the dining room. The fare might be an egg casserole or pancakes.

(603) 569-3834. Fax: (603) 569-3835. www.topsidesbb.com. Five rooms with private baths. Doubles, $175 to $195, off-season $120 to $135.

The Lake Motel, 280 South Main St. (Route 28), Wolfeboro 03894.

Its spacious grounds alongside tiny Crescent Lake commend this family-owned motel of 1950s vintage. Situated well back from the road on sixteen acres, the motel has 30 rooms, half facing the water. All have two double beds, two upholstered chairs and cable TV. Our room was quite comfortable, but the best part was just outside: a broad lawn sloping toward a busy little beach, various lawn games, a tennis court and boats for rent. Five housekeeping apartments rented weekly are located away from the water. **Bailey's Restaurant,** open for three meals daily in season at the entrance to the grounds, serves the most for the money in town, according to motel owners Allan and Julie Bailey, who run their operation more like an inn than most motel keepers do.

(603) 569-1100 or (888) 569-1110. Fax (603) 569-1258. www.thelakemotel.com. Thirty rooms and five apartments with private baths. Doubles, $119 to $139. Apartments, $655 weekly. Closed mid-October to mid-May.

Where to Eat

Mise en Place, 96 Lehner St., Wolfeboro.

This first-rate French bistro is hidden in the front of a nondescript building along a side street. There are a handful of tables on the sidewalk, but most of the dining takes place at well-spaced tables in a plain but pleasant room inside, where the bleached pine tables are dressed with white linens at night. Sconces on walls wainscoted in taupe and burgundy, a few pictures and a hutch holding wine and liqueur bottles set the scene. From a kitchen out of sight in back comes some of Wolfeboro's most sophisticated fare. For lunch, we sampled a crab cake with mustard sauce over mixed greens and a baby spinach salad with sea scallops, portobello mushrooms and bacon. Profiteroles with caramel-chocolate sauce and a lemon curd tart testified to the kitchen's prowess with desserts. At night, chef-owners Terry Adrignola and Siobhan Magee offer such entrées as pine nut-encrusted halibut with roasted red pepper pesto, baked shrimp stuffed with lump crab and smoked gouda, and grilled sirloin steak with blue cheese butter.

(603) 569-5788. Entrées, $12 to $24. Lunch, Monday-Friday 11:30 to 2. Dinner, Monday-Saturday 5 to 9. Closed Sunday and Monday in off-season.

Rumba, 14 Union St., Wolfeboro.

This 40-seat Latin-American bistro offers flavorful fare in convivial surroundings. Colombia native Fabio Rojas does some of the cooking but prefers to defer to his chef and play the genial host in a dining room best described as lively. Lively, too, is the food, especially the day's ceviche and the Madagascar shrimp appetizer sautéed in garlic and smoked paprika. Fabio suggests starting with the Latin-inspired New England clam chowder laced with chorizo, jalapeño and cilantro. He also recommends the serrano-fired paella laden with seafood, chicken and chorizo and the garlicky rack of lamb for main courses. The braised veal shank with chocolate madeira sauce and the grilled flatiron steak with chimichurri sauce are not for the faint-hearted. Cool off with one of the refreshing desserts, perhaps the brandy-flavored fig tart served with white cheese and dulce leche or the sliced pineapple sautéed with dark rum topped with homemade coconut-ginger ice cream.

(603) 569-4833. Entrées, $17 to $25. Dinner, Tuesday-Saturday 5 to 9, Sunday 5 to 8:30. Closed Sunday-Tuesday in winter.

East of Suez, 775 South Main St. (Route 28 South), Wolfeboro.

Although food and travel writer Charles Powell and his family, some from the Philippines, have operated this restaurant for 37 summers, it seems to be almost a secret except to devotees of Asian food. Housed in a building that once was part of a camp, it looks the part – an almost rickety house with a big screened side porch that serves as a dining room, set in a field south of Wolfeboro. Decor is spare oriental, with simple black or yellow tables and chairs, rough wood flooring and paper globe lamps. From the huge kitchen comes a procession of interesting dishes. Among starters and tapas, poached scallops with crab in miso sauce and the Philippine egg rolls known as lumpia are standouts. Half a dozen entrées are offered and all sound so good that it's hard to choose. Salads with extravagant and original dressings (ginger, creamy garlic, sweet peanut) come with. Our tempura included a wide variety of vegetables and many large shrimp; the batter was perfect. And the Szechwan shrimp and cashews, stir-fried with snow peas, was great. On another visit, we liked the Philippine pancit, curly noodles sautéed with morsels of shrimp and pork with oriental vegetables, and the Philippine national dish, adobo pork and chicken stewed in soy, vinegar and garlic and then broiled and served with sliced bananas. Everything comes with shiny crackers that arrive sizzling from a pan. The Philippine "sans rival," a cashew and meringue torte, is a worthy send-off.

(603) 569-1648. www.eastofsuez.com. Entrées, $13 to $15. Dinner, Tuesday-Sunday 5:30 to 9 or 10, June through early September. No credit cards. BYOB.

The Cider Press, 10 Middleton Road, Wolfeboro.

There's a cider press at the door, and apple trees are out back. Hence the name for this rustic restaurant that has been expanded several times in its twenty years by Robert and Denise Earle. They now seat 165 diners by candlelight in three country-pretty barnwood rooms and a lounge with a three-sided open hearth. Chef Bob, who runs the kitchen almost single-handedly, considers baby back ribs and golden fried tempura shrimp the specialty; they're listed on the menu as "the odd couple." The dinner menu is nicely priced for items like seafood pie, shrimp scampi, grilled Atlantic salmon, strip sirloin and steak béarnaise that would command twice the tab in metropolitan areas. Baked haddock, halibut oscar and steak au poivre might be blackboard specials. A fellow restaurateur said the best lamb chops he ever ate were served here. Most of the desserts are baked on the premises. The Boston cream pie, the ice cream crêpes, and the parfaits and sundaes are the downfall of many.

(603) 569-2028. www.theciderpress.net. Entrées, $13.95 to $19.95. Dinner nightly except Monday, 5 to 9, Sunday to 8. Abbreviated schedule in winter.

Waterside in Wolfeboro

Wolfetrap Grill & Rawbar, 19 Bay St., Wolfeboro.

Two red lobsters standing tall on the roof identify this popular seasonal place along Back Bay. Barbara and John Naramore borrowed the locally appropriate name from the Wolf Trap performing arts center outside Washington, D.C., where they used to live, and patterned it after a Maryland crab house, minus the emphasis on crabs. Here you'll find a stylish yet casual establishment with a large interior bar decked out in baseball caps, bar stools emblazoned with a wolf logo, an L-shaped dining room with butcher paper clipped to large tables, and a screened porch overlooking the water. On busy nights, upwards of 200 people are on the waiting list for one of the 98 seats. They wolf down raw bar items – from peel 'n eat shrimp to oysters on the half shell – the specialty lobster roll, served with fries and slaw, and a variety of fresh seafood from the Naramores' adjacent **Wolfecatch** fish market. Not to mention the clam boil, the soft-shell crab dinner, the blue-plate special, the sundried tomato pesto with vegetables over pasta and the hand-cut steaks. Desserts run to homemade pies and ice creams. The wines and microbrewed beers are as eclectic as the rest of the place, all part of a marina complex called the Wolfetown Marketplace.

(603) 569-1047. www.wolfetrap.com. Entrées, $10.95 to $21.95. Lunch, Thursday-Sunday from 11. Dinner nightly, 4 to 11. Seasonal.

Meredith

Except for a few predictable tourist trappings, Meredith (population 1,800) long languished in relative obscurity at the western end of Lake Winnipesaukee. That began to change in the 1980s, when the Inn at Mill Falls, a 54-room hotel, opened as the final phase of Mill Falls Marketplace, a shopping and restaurant complex across the road from the lake.

Gradually, the Meredith waterfront has been cleared and redeveloped, with three more inns joining the Mill Falls compound. Restaurants were provided by Alex Ray of the state's growing Common Man restaurant chain, headquartered in nearby Ashland.

Now Meredith makes a comfortable base for enjoying the busy western end of Lake Winnipesaukee, plus the quiet charms of Squam Lake nearby.

Seeing and Doing

For the visitor, the best way to see and experience the lake – other than being a house guest at a friend's cottage – is by tour boat.

M/S Mount Washington, Weirs Beach.

The hulk of this three-level excursion boat is far larger than you'd expect as it cruises ever so carefully up to the Meredith dock, an occasional stop on its itinerary. With a capacity of 1,250 passengers, the ship boards most passengers at its base in

Weirs Beach. The nearly three-hour cruise covers 50 miles and visits Wolfeboro and occasionally Meredith, Center Harbor and Alton Bay, boarding and disembarking passengers at each stop. The narrated cruise takes you through "The Broads," twelve miles long and five miles wide, beneath the Ossipee, Sandwich and Squam mountain ranges on the north, the Belknap Mountain range on the south and the White Mountains in the distance to the northeast. The ship seldom gets close to shore, though you do get a good view of the rocks known as Witches Island and the exclusive Governor's Island community that housed the German Embassy prior to World War I. You also get to see lots of powerboats that come up close to ride the wake.

Shorter cruises around Meredith Bay aboard the smaller **M/V Doris E** depart from Meredith at 11, 1, 3 and 5 daily except Monday (the day of the big boat's stop). The two-hour cruise is priced at $16 for adults, $8 for children.

(603) 366-5531 or (888) 843-6686. www.cruisenh.com. Cruise leaves Meredith Mondays at 12:15 (2:45 in July and August). It departs Weirs Beach daily at 10 and 12:30 (also at 3:15 in July and August). Operates Memorial Day to late October. Adults $19, children $9.

SHOPPING. The **Mills Falls Marketplace** in Meredith contains nearly twenty enterprises from **The Country Carriage** with country gifts and accessories to **Northern Air** for cottage fashions and accessories. We liked the birdhouses, garden benches and the cans labeled "Grow Your Own Forest" at **Upcountry Pastimes.** Handcrafted jewelry and accessories are featured at **Adornments.** Absent are the souvenir shops indigenous to much of the Lakes Region. We overheard one customer ask if a shop had any T-shirts with "Meredith" printed on the front. No, was the reply – you have to go to Weirs Beach to find that kind of thing. Lamented the customer: "But then it won't say 'Meredith.'"

The League of New Hampshire Craftsmen runs the **Meredith-Laconia Arts & Crafts,** 279 Daniel Webster Highway (Route 3) in Meredith and **Sandwich Home Industries** in Center Sandwich.

Annalee Doll Museum and Gift Shop, 50 Reservoir Road, is a gift shop, a museum, a "Factory in the Woods" and more, attracting sightseers by the carload. From humble beginnings, the late Annalee Thorndike built quite an operation in her Meredith complex. Although we're not crazy about these dolls, we must be in the minority because the Annalee Doll Society has more than 23,000 members. There are dolls for all occasions and seasons, especially Christmas, with Santas and Mrs. Santas and elves galore. Mice are dressed as Pilgrims for Thanksgiving, bunnies for Easter and kids in costume for Halloween. Little frogs surround a pond in one corner of the shop. Although commercial, it's fun – especially for collectors and youngsters. Museum open daily 9:30 to 5, Memorial Day to Halloween; free. Shop open daily year-round, 9 to 6.

Where to Stay

The Inns at Mill Falls, 312 Daniel Webster Hwy., Route 3, Meredith 03253.

The Inns at Mill Falls began with a restored nineteenth-century linen mill, a covered bridge and a 40-foot waterfall. Where it ends is anyone's guess. With two Bostonians as partners, Edward "Rusty" McLear developed the first Inn at Mill Falls, a 54-room hotel, as the final phase of Mill Falls Marketplace, a shopping and restaurant complex fashioned from the old mill site at the western end of Lake

Winnipesaukee. "We couldn't understand why a beautiful resort area like this had nothing more than a couple of cottages in which to stay," Rusty explained.

That was back in 1983, and now – three inns later under the name the Inns at Mill Falls – comes the crowning touch. **Church Landing at Mills Falls** on the site of a former Catholic church includes a 58-room inn, restaurant, conference center and health club on a 3.5-acre peninsula jutting into the lake with two sandy beaches and water on three sides. The three-story inn includes five suites and 53 rooms reflecting Adirondack style, all with gas fireplaces and all but three with balconies. Four suites and ten rooms include whirlpool tubs. The site also holds the Common Man chain's 200-seat **Lakehouse** restaurant and lounge (see Where to Eat). The health club includes the Cascade Spa, jacuzzi and sauna area, and an indoor/outdoor pool.

Also facing the waterfront around the corner is the four-story **Inn at Bay Point,** fashioned from an office structure that previously housed a bank. Guest rooms are on the three upper floors and all face the lake. Nineteen come with private balconies. Thirteen of the balconied rooms have queensize beds with a queen sofabed in the sitting area. Three substitute leather wing chairs for the sofabeds and two premium rooms contain kingsize beds, jacuzzi tubs and fireplaces. The spacious, front-corner penthouse on the fourth floor has a king bed, a queen sofabed in the sitting area, jacuzzi, fireplace, wet bar and balcony. The main floor contains the Common Man chain's full-service restaurant called **Lago** (see Where to Eat).

The Chase House at Mill Falls is across Route 3 from the lake and Church Landing on the site of a former restaurant. It has twenty rooms and three suites with king or queen beds and gas fireplaces. Some have in-room double jacuzzi tubs and balconies facing the lake. **Camp,** another restaurant in the Common Man chain, serves dinner nightly here (see Where to Eat).

All these somewhat upstage the original **Inn at Mill Falls,** a white frame structure on five levels set back from the lake and connecting with the marketplace. It has 54 rooms of varying size and color schemes, decorated in contemporary French country style with matching draperies and bedspreads, plush chairs and spacious baths. Old samplers on the walls, framed pictures of 19th-century Meredith, plants in an old sleigh and antique headboards lend a bit of history.

(603) 279-7006 or (800) 622-6455. www.millfalls.com. In-season rates for each inn are from mid-May to mid-October. Rates include continental breakfast.

Inn at Church Point: Fifty-three rooms and five suites. Doubles $189 to $279, suites $379; off-season, doubles $169 to $249, suites $329.

Inn at Bay Point: Twenty-four rooms. Doubles $179 to $249, penthouse $319; off-season, doubles $129 to $179, penthouse $249.

Chase House: Twenty rooms and three suites. Doubles $179 to $239, suites $249 to $309; off-season, doubles $129 to $179, suites, $209 to $259.

Inn at Mill Falls: Fifty-four rooms. Doubles, $109 to $269; off-season, $99 to $189.

The Meredith Inn, 2 Waukewan St., Meredith 03253.

This Victorian "Painted Lady" on a Meredith hilltop was refurbished from top to bottom in 1997 by the former owners of the Rangeley Inn in Maine. Janet Carpenter wanted a smaller inn when her parents retired, so they helped get her started in the handsome Hawkins-Deneault House. Coming from an inn background in a resort area, they knew exactly what they wanted: jacuzzi tubs, king or queen beds, a couple of fireplaces, TVs and telephones, lace curtains and a light Victorian feeling in a house full of 19th-century embellishments. Rooms are spacious and handsomely furnished. The premier room comes with a king bed, gas fireplace and an enormous bathroom, including a bidet. There are removable newel posts on several beds ("for hiding your jewels," Janet said as she pulled one open to show), etched brass doorknobs with matching plates, beautiful hardwood floors, shellacked southern yellow pine woodwork and turrets with window seats. Janet serves a full breakfast, culminating perhaps with french toast, omelets or apple-filled crêpes with ricotta cheese.

(603) 279-0000. Fax (603) 279-4017. www.meredithinn.com. Eight rooms with private baths. Doubles, $125 to $175 May-October, $109 to $159 rest of year.

Where to Eat

The Lakehouse Grille, 281 Daniel Webster Hwy., Meredith.

Lake views, Adirondack mountain lodge decor and contemporary American fare are what you get at this expansive new restaurant in the Church Landing at Mill Falls inn complex. It's the high-end restaurant of the Common Man group locally. From an open kitchen comes some of the area's more sophisticated fare. Expect starters like sherried lobster and corn chowder, lobster quesadilla and grilled duck sausage with an apple and fig compote. Main courses range from grilled swordfish and crab cakes with chipotle rémoulade to pecan-crusted grilled tenderloin and rack of lamb with minted demi-glace. Hearty eaters go for the cowboy steak or the mixed grill of filet mignon, swordfish and chicken breast. Typical desserts are white chocolate crème brûlée, chocolate truffle cake and pecan-praline pie.

(603) 279-5221. Entrées, $12 to $22. Breakfast, 7 to 10. Lunch, Monday-Saturday 11:30 to 3. Dinner nightly, 5 to 9.

Lago, 1 Route 25, Meredith.

Area restaurateur Alex Ray leased the main floor of the Inn at Bay Point to develop this waterfront prize, first known as the Boathouse Grille and converted in late 2003 into an Italian trattoria. Lago, Italian for lake, offers authentic "Old World Italian" fare and "bella" lake views in a redesigned and refurbished space. A bar in front opens to a dining area appointed in cocoa and taupe colors with rustic farm-style pine tables, black and white photographs, hand-painted murals of Italian scenery on the walls, a partly open corner kitchen, and an idyllic dining deck beside the lake. Lago's traditional Italian menu features fare from crusty ciabatta bread, polenta and gnocchi to flat-bread pizzas, house-made pastas and crêpes filled with ricotta and spinach. Typical entrées are grilled tuna with tomato and kalamata olives, chicken cooked under a brick, roast duck stuffed with sausage and wrapped in pancetta, and florentine porterhouse steak sauced with spinach and gorgonzola. Dessert could be homemade cannoli or tiramisu. Robust Tuscan wines are featured.

(603) 279-2253. Entrees, $15 to $21. Lunch daily, 11:30 to 3. Dinner nightly, 5 to 9 or 9:30. Sunday brunch, 10:30 to 2:30.

Mame's, 8 Plymouth St., Meredith.

Restaurateur John Cook takes pride in the fine restoration of the brick house and barn once owned by a 19th-century physician. A meandering series of small dining rooms on the main floor is topped by a large lounge on the second. The extensive menu is traditional steak and seafood with a continental flair, from seafood diane and lobster-scallop divan to prime rib and veal sautéed with crabmeat and scallops. Baked stuffed shrimp, Southwest chicken alfredo, veal marsala and steak au poivre are other favorites. The prices are reasonable, and the atmosphere intimate and romantic. Mud pie, bread pudding and black-bottom cheesecake are among desserts. A tavern menu is available in the lounge daily from 11:30 to 10.

(603) 279-4631. www.mamesrestaurant.com. Entrées, $12.95 to $21.95. Lunch daily, 11:30 to 3. Dinner, 4:30 to 9 or 9:30. Sunday brunch, 11 to 2.

Abondánte, 30 Main St., Meredith.

This Tuscan charmer offers serious Italian fare in a trattoria setting inside and out in what passes as downtown Meredith. The extensive menu features such pasta dishes as gorgonzola and walnut ravioli and penne with sausage and veal ragu. Typical main courses are pan-seared scallops with crispy artichokes, pork cutlets with mushrooms in a balsamic-marsala sauce and veal served with pears in a sage cream sauce. Antipasti could be a portobello mushroom stuffed with shrimp, spinach and feta cheese or saffron ravioli filled with lobster. Homemade desserts, an Italian wine list and an espresso bar round out the offerings. To accompany, there's live jazz on Thursday nights.

(603) 279-7177. Entrées, $11.95 to $19.95. Dinner nightly, 5 to 9, May-October; Wednesday-Sunday rest of year.

Bring On the S'mores

Camp at the Chase House, 300 Daniel Webster Hwy., Meredith.

Remember the summer camps of your youth? Those days are recreated in the cozy Adirondack-style camp dining room run by the Common Man chain in the Chase House inn. It features a fieldstone fireplace, tin ceilings, camp relics and comfort food, from baked macaroni and cheese to s'mores. Of course, most of the fare is a cut above the camp food you remember. Typical main courses include rainbow trout, baked scallops, chicken kiev, twin filets and a full rack of barbecued spare ribs. Not your typical camp fare are the seafood sauté served over orecchiette pasta or the mixed grill of filet mignon with béarnaise sauce, chicken with blueberry-balsamic vinegar sauce and crab cake with lemon-herb mayonnaise. For comfort, seek out "Mom's meatloaf," pot roast or chicken pot pie. Although desserts vary from four-layer chocolate cake to Indian pudding, happy campers opt for the s'mores.

(603) 279-3003. www.thecman.com. Entrées, $12.95 to $19.95. Dinner nightly from 5, closed Monday in off-season.

FOR MORE INFORMATION: Wolfeboro Chamber of Commerce, 32 Central Ave. in the Railroad Station, Box 547, Wolfeboro, NH 03894, (603) 569-2200 or (800) 516-5324. www.wolfeborochamber.com.

Meredith Area Chamber of Commerce, 272 Daniel Webster Hwy., Meredith, NH 03253, (603) 279-6121 or (877) 279-6121. www.meredithcc.org.

Mountains are backdrop for Sunset Hill House atop 1,700-foot-high ridge in Sugar Hill.

Franconia/Bethlehem, N.H.

A Notch Above

Perhaps no name other than Mount Washington better conjures up the essence of the Granite State than Franconia Notch. Here, receding glaciers from the Ice Age cut an eight-mile-long swath between the Franconia and Kinsman mountain ranges. Their legacies of beauty and adventure have stirred visitors for two centuries.

The Flume, the Basin, Echo Lake, the Cannon Mountain aerial tramway, the late Old Man of the Mountains – these are the best-known attractions of New Hampshire's best-known notch, which would be called a gap or a pass in other mountain regions. They make up Franconia Notch State Park, ranked among the nation's best by Money magazine.

Travelers often give the notch short shrift, pausing only to tour the Flume and get a distant look at what's left of the Old Man's profile etched in granite. Then they turn around and head back south to join the hordes around Lake Winnipesaukee or North Conway.

Too bad for them. For beyond the notch is an island of serenity away from the crowds. It's a different world, one of spectacular vistas, relatively few people and fewer signs of contemporary civilization. This is the world epitomized by the words of poet Robert Frost, written when he lived beneath Cannon Mountain: "Two roads diverged in a wood, and I – I took the one less traveled by, and that has made all the difference."

Frost was drawn by the serenity of small-town Franconia (population 950), so named because of its resemblance to the Franconia Alps in Germany. Grand summer hotels proliferated in the 19th century across the hillsides of Franconia and neighboring Sugar Hill. The nation's first ski school was established at Peckett's-on-Sugar Hill in 1929, and within a decade skiers were riding the nation's first aerial tramway lift to the top of Cannon.

Beyond Franconia and Sugar Hill lies Bethlehem, which claims to be the highest incorporated town east of the Rockies. The town of 2,300 perches along a mountain ridge 1,500 feet above sea level. Thousands of hay fever sufferers came here for its pollen-free air in the late 1800s; by the turn of the last century the early resort village boasted four railroad stations and 30 hotels. Today it is billed as the nation's smallest town with two PGA-rated golf courses.

The large hotels are long gone. The crowds and the condos stop at the south side of Franconia Notch, leaving Franconia, Sugar Hill and Bethlehem for those who appreciate them as vestiges of the past. The small city of Littleton adds a dash of urbanity nearby.

Mountain scenery, rural and village life, peaceful inns, hiking and other outdoors activities – these are the attributes that draw folks for getaways north of the notch. If you like tranquility, venture beyond. You'll be well rewarded.

Seeing and Doing

The most celebrated mountain gap in the East, Franconia Notch contains more scenic spots than any other in New Hampshire or Vermont.

Franconia Notch State Park

One of the nation's most spectacular parks, the 6,440-acre flagship of New Hampshire's state park system, is traversed by the magnificent Franconia Notch Parkway, a two-lane federal parkway linking four-lane portions of I-93 on either side of the notch. The parkway allows no stopping or left turns, and parking only in designated areas, but it gives passersby a glimpse of the treasures on either side.

Start at the Flume Visitor Center at the south entrance to the park. Here you'll see a fifteen-minute orientation movie that gives worthwhile background on the notch, which you learn was 400 million years in the making. "Remember, when you see it today, it will never be quite the same again," the narrator intoned – a premonition that became all too true when the Old Man of the Mountains collapsed in 2003. The visitor center contains historical displays, a cafeteria, a gift shop and, in front, a trout pond where fish leap for bread crumbs tossed by youngsters. Picnic groves are scattered around the center, as they are throughout the park. We picked blackberries for dessert along the path from the parking lot to a picnic table not far from the car.

The Flume. A bus shuttles visitors to within 1,500 feet of a natural gorge extending more than 700 feet along the flank of Mount Liberty at the south end of Franconia Notch. Granite walls rise 70 to 90 feet high. A boardwalk allows a close-up look at the luxurious growth of flowers, mosses and ferns. A two-mile gravel nature walk displays waterfalls, glacial boulders, mountain vistas and two covered bridges. Open daily, 9 to 5:30 in July and August, 9 to 5 in May-June and September through late October. Adults $8, children $5.

The **Basin** is a granite pothole twenty feet across at the foot of a waterfall. Its sides have been smoothed by sand and small stones whirled around by the Pemigewasset River. Below the Basin is a rock formation called the Old Man's Foot.

What's left of the Old Man of the Mountains hovers 1,200 feet above Profile Lake. Yes, they did look like an old man, those five granite ledges formed horizontally to resemble a human profile and keeping vigil southward through the notch through the centuries. Today you can make out the rock croppings where the Old Man used to be. Directly below the Old Man and nicknamed the Old Man's Washbowl is Profile Lake, the headwaters of the Pemigewasset River and a favorite of fly fishermen.

The **Cannon Mountain Aerial Tramway** gives up to 70 passengers at a time a seven-minute ride 2,022 feet up Cannon, a legend among skiers. The state-of-the-art cable car replaces the nation's first, a smaller model born in 1938 and retired in 1979. The tram operator points out Artists' Bluff and the adjacent Indian Head that looks like the face on an old nickel, as well as such salient sights as Mount Lafayette, the highest peak (5,249 feet) in the Franconia Range, which is second in height only to the Presidential Range. At the 4,160-foot summit are a cafeteria of the ski lodge variety and the well-maintained Rim Trail. The quarter-mile trail leads through spruce trees and along a ledge with a sheer drop to an observation platform yielding panoramic views in all directions. Summit barbecues are available on summer Saturdays from 4:30 to 7 p.m. (adults $7, children $5). The tram runs every fifteen minutes, 9 to 5 daily mid-May to late October, to 7:30 Saturdays in summer. Adults $10, children $5.

Echo Lake, a sand and spruce-ringed beauty at the north end of the notch at the foot of Cannon Mountain, offers swimming, fishing and boating. There's a fine beach, plus grassy areas for picnicking. Canoes, kayaks, paddleboats and rowboats are rented for $10 an hour at the beach. Beach admission $3, under 12 free.

Lafayette Place, just west of the parkway in the center of the park, is the camping and hiking hub of the notch. A lodge serves as a hiking information center, offering advice and guides to miles of hiking trails. The Lafayette Campground provides 97 wooded tent sites.

HIKING. Park officials recommend four hikes in particular. A 1.5-mile loop from Cannon's Peabody Base Lodge goes to Artists Bluff, where artists used to set their easels to paint the notch, and on to the open summit of Bald Mountain, a great place to watch the sunset. Another 2.5-mile round trip rises from Lafayette Place to Lonesome Lake, an undeveloped alpine lake some 1,000 feet above. There, a lakeside trail leads to the Appalachian Mountain Club's hut at the lake's far end and passes an active beaver lodge. The 2,557-foot summit of Mount Pemigewasset (Indian Head) can be reached via a 1.4-mile trail from the Flume Visitor Center or the Indian Head Trail, which starts one mile south off Route 3. The views from the summit, both to the north and south, are awesome. The easiest and an often overlooked hike is a half-mile walk along the Basin-Cascades Trail beside Cascade Brook from the Basin to Kinsman Falls. The brook's basins and ledges make for a pleasant half-hour diversion.

BIKING. One of the little-known treasures of the park is a paved, eight-mile bicycle path running from the Flume Visitor Center north to the Skookumchuk trailhead. It's reasonably level, which makes it popular with walkers as well. A concession at the Cannon Mountain parking lot rents mountain bikes for $10 an hour.

Other Attractions

Cannon Mountain, Franconia State Park, Franconia.

In an era of plasticized, free-wheeling skiing and snowboarding, the serious ski areas with character are few and far between. One of the last and best is Cannon, which considers itself the first major ski mountain in the Northeast (1937). Operated as a state park, it remains virginal and free of commercialism. The setting is reminiscent of the Alps, when you view the sheer cliffs and avalanche country across Franconia Notch on Lafayette Mountain and the majestic peaks of the Presidential Range beyond. A 70-passenger tramway, three quadruple chairlifts and three triple chairlifts serve 55 trails. From the 4,186-foot summit, there's a 2,146-vertical drop. Much of the skiing varies from tough to frightening, as befits the site of America's first racing trail and the first World Cup competition. But there's plenty of intermediate and novice skiing as well.

(603) 823-8800. www.cannonmt.com. Open weekends and holidays, 8:30 to 4; weekdays, 9 to 4. Lift tickets: adults, $49 weekends, $38 midweek; juniors, $29 weekends, $25 midweek.

New England Ski Museum, next to the tram station at Cannon Mountain, Franconia.

Skiers in particular enjoy this small museum that houses the most extensive collection of historic ski equipment, clothing, photography and literature in the Northeast. The maroon parka belonging to the founder of the National Ski Patrol is shown, as is a photo of him taken at Peckett's-on-Sugar-Hill. One of the more fascinating exhibits traces the evolution of ski equipment, with a wall of old skis built around the turn of the last century and the antiquated ski boots that resemble the hiking boots of today. Of special interest were one of the chairs from the original single chairlift at Stowe and the old red car from the Mount Cranmore Skimobile, both of which we used in our early skiing days. "Ski Tracks" is an informative and impressive, thirteen-minute audio-visual show with 450 slides tracing the development of skiing in New England.

(603) 823-7177 or (800) 639-4181. www.nesm.org. Open daily noon to 5, Memorial Day- Columbus Day and December-March. Free.

The Frost Place, Ridge Road off Route 116, Franconia.

The farmhouse in which poet Robert Frost lived from 1915 to 1920 and in which he summered through 1938 is a low-key attraction not to be missed. The house remains essentially unchanged from the 1920s. So do the sites that inspired him to write some of his best-loved poems. Each summer a different visiting poet occupies most of the house, but the front room and a rear barn are open with displays of Frost memorabilia, including his handwritten "Stopping by Woods on a Snowy Evening" and a rare, large photo of Frost at age 40 working at his desk in the room. Out back, plaques along a half-mile nature trail bear Frost's poems appropriate to the site; in two cases, the poems are on the locations where he wrote them. As if the poetry and setting weren't awesome enough, the stand of woods happens to contain every variety of wildflower indigenous to Northern New England.

(603) 823-5510. www.frostplace.com. Open daily except Tuesday 1 to 5, July to Columbus Day; also weekends, Memorial Day through June. Adults $3, children $1.25.

Sugar Hill Historical Museum, Sugar Hill.

Sugar Hill people advise not to miss this, and they're right. Established by proud descendants of Sugar Hill founders, this choice place displays an excellent collection in a modern, uncluttered setting. It gives a feel for the uncommon history of a unique hilltop town, named for the sugar maples that still produce sap for syrup. The life of the community is chronicled in photographs and artifacts. The Cobleigh Room recreates a stagecoach tavern kitchen from nearby Lisbon. The Carriage Barn contains a working blacksmith's shop as well as mountain wagons and horse-drawn sleighs, including one from the Butternut estate that used to belong to actress Bette Davis.

(603) 823-8142. Open July to mid-October, Thursday-Saturday 1 to 4. Free.

Sugar Hill Sampler, 71 Sunset Hill Road, Sugar Hill.

A horse may be grazing in front of this quirky store and museum, where commercialism gives way to personality and history. The large dairy barn, with nooks and crannies full of New England items for souvenir shoppers, is literally a working museum of Sugar Hill history. Owner Barbara Serafini is the sixth-generation descendant of one of Sugar Hill's founders and takes great pride in sharing her thoughts and possessions, even posting handwritten descriptions on the beams. In one rear section full of family memorabilia, she displays her grandmother's wedding gown, which she wore in a pageant written by her father and presented for President Eisenhower on the occasion of the Old Man of the Mountain's birthday in 1955. Amid all the memorabilia is an interesting selection of quaint and unusual merchandise, including maple syrup made by the Stewart family on Sugar Hill, and a special spiced tea mixture called Heavenly Tea. Many New Hampshire foods are featured, and you can taste samples of several. Toys, collectibles, quilts and Christmas decorations are displayed in nooks off the main barn.

(603) 823-8478. www.sugarhillsampler.com. Open daily, 9:30 to 5, mid-May through October, 10 to 4 in November and December, weekends mid-April to mid-May.

Sunset Hill Golf Course, Sunset Hill Road, Sugar Hill.

Atop a ridge that lives up to its name, this 1,977-yard golf course put into play in 1897 is the oldest nine-hole layout in New Hampshire. The clubhouse is also the oldest extant clubhouse for any course in the state (built in 1899 for the 1900 season) and remains virtually unchanged today. The owners of the Sunset Hill House across the street saved the property from development and had both the course and the clubhouse accepted for the state historic registry in 2002. By today's standards the 3,954-yard course is short (six par 4s and three par 3s), but in the days of hickory clubs and leather balls, "it was a much different beast," according to innkeeper Lon Henderson. "Today our motto is family fun. It's just hard enough to give an expert golfer a challenge and forgiving enough to give a beginner a boost of confidence." With greens fees at $15 to $25 for nine to eighteen holes, depending on day of the week, it's the least expensive golf course in the area. The price is right and the views are stupendous.

Aspects of Bethlehem

Picturesque but somewhat down-at-the-heels Bethlehem is the center of the area's golfing activity. The town is the smallest in New Hampshire to have two eighteen-hole courses (both designed by Donald Ross), and the smallest in the country with two PGA-rated courses. The golf cart is the town's most popular summertime vehicle, locals say.

The major presence along Route 302 at 2692 Main St. is **Maplewood Country Club & Hotel,** (603) 869-3335 or (877) 869-3335, site of a grand hotel that burned (like most others around here) in 1963. The clubhouse occupies the hotel's activity building and casino, nicely restored in 1988 and now offering twenty guest rooms and suites (doubles, $109 to $199). Basic golf-club lunches are served at the lounge, inside and out. The ball returns of what once was the bowling alley are still prominent in the long, narrow pro shop. Greens fees for the 6,001-yard championship course are $45 weekends, $35 midweek. Less of a presence than the Maplewood, but also eighteen holes, is the town-owned **Bethlehem Country Club** layout at 1901 Main St., (603) 869-5745; greens fees $33 weekends, $28 midweek. Near the Maplewood along

Route 302 is a roadside retreat that locals call the **Caddy Shrine,** erected by former Maplewood caddies and dedicated "to the traveler along this way."

Another summertime presence in Bethlehem are Hassidic Jews, who are much in evidence at a couple of old hotels in the center of town and in seasonal motels on the west side. Mainly from metropolitan New York and New Jersey, they come and go in large cars throughout July and August, relax on the lawns and walk along Main Street in their distinctive (and quite unsummery) attire. Otherwise Bethlehem, whose name was changed from Lloyd's Hills on Christmas Day in 1799, has an interfaith Bethlehem Christian Center, a Catholic church, a Methodist church, an Episcopal chapel and a small Hebrew Congregation synagogue not used by the Hassidic visitors.

The Rocks Estate, Glessner Road off Route 302, Bethlehem.

Boulders left by Ice Age glaciers yielded stone walls and rolling fields on this 1,300-acre property left by the grandchildren of Chicago industrialist John Glessner west of town. Six miles of self-guided trails, picnic areas, working woodlands and a variety of entertainment and educational events can be enjoyed. Strollers and hikers give way to cross-country skiers in winter. The Rocks Christmas Tree Farm offers fresh-cut and cut-your-own trees and horse-drawn sleigh rides in December.

(603) 444-6228 or (800) 639-1931. www.therocks.org. Open daily, dawn to dusk; free.

Bethlehem Flower Farm, Route 302 east, Bethlehem.

Owners Joan and Bob Schafer grow more than 100 varieties of day lilies, with names like Precious One, Christmas Carol and Gentle Shepherd. They're at peak bloom during July and August. To purchase, pick those that you like and Joan will dig them straight from the fields. Also on the premises are a woodland walk that takes about twenty minutes, The Gift Barn and Abigail's Country Collectibles, and Lily's Café where you may get a light lunch or ice cream. Bob says "we have the world's best chili," served with a corn muffin.

(603) 869-3131. Open Thursday-Sunday 10 to 5, Memorial Day to Labor Day, weekends to Columbus Day.

Shopping

In Sugar Hill, **Harman's Cheese and Country Store,** a tiny place with a large mail-order business, proclaims "the world's greatest cheddar cheese." Many of its food and local items are one of a kind, according to owner Maxine Aldrich, who with daughter Brenda is carrying on the late Harman family tradition. **Sugar Hill Antiques** and **P.C. Anderson Handmade Furniture** appeal to special interests.

In Franconia, the **Garnet Hill** factory store at 279 Main St. stocks firsts and seconds of fine bedclothes (English flannel sheets, comforters and the like), as well as pricey children's clothing, all in natural fibers. Stop at the **Quality Bakery** (home of Grateful Bread) for a loaf of soy-sesame bread. Two dozen varieties of breads and rolls are made; "we mill our own flour and our sourdough starter came from Germany 50 years ago," said the owner. We liked the local handcrafts displayed by volunteers at **Noah's Ark,** a shop run by the Church of Christ.

Antiquing is the main shopping attraction in Bethlehem, which calls itself Antiques Alley North. About a dozen shops are scattered along Main Street. Surrounding one unnamed house in the center of town was such a mishmash of junk, both inside and out, that only the intrepid would venture in. We know a couple who did and turned up a few prizes amid someone else's trash. A better bet is **Checkered Past,** the area's only multi-dealer shop, a kaleidoscope of antiques and collectibles displayed in an 1820s barn at 154 Guider Road. **WrenOvation!** at 2011 Main St. is a nifty store featuring the work of more than 100 artisans and crafters, from pottery and textiles to jewelry and specialty foods.

Littleton's Main Street has developed into an interesting shopping area, one that gained national recognition as one of five Great American Main Street Communities in 2003. The expanded **Village Bookstore** is one of the best in northern New England. **Duck Soup** is a good gift and kitchen shop, purveying everything from Christmas ornaments to coffee grinders. In the same Parker's Marketplace building are **The Elephant's Trunk** for clothing and **The Healthy Rhino** for everything that's good for you. You can try on funky clothing and look at antiques at **All That Jazz.** **Deacon's Bench Furniture** purveys beautiful home furnishings, accessories and gifts, and is known for its potpourri and scent items. Stop at **Bishop's Ice Cream Shoppe,** 183 Cottage St., for carrot cake ice cream, a banana split or a "Chill Out" T-shirt. There are those who think Bishop's homemade ice creams and frozen yogurts are the best anywhere. Take a break for the best lunch in Littleton at **Miller's Fare Café and Bakery,** in a restored mill beside the Ammonoosuc River at 16 Mill St.

Where to Stay

Inns and B&Bs

Adair, 80 Guider Lane, Bethlehem 03574.

This hilltop mansion on a 200-acre estate off Route 302 was built in 1927 as a wedding gift for Dorothy Adair Hogan from her father, nationally famous Washington trial lawyer Frank Hogan. The early guest list included presidents, governors, senators, judges, sports figures and actors. Today Judy and Bill Whitman host guests in eight large bedrooms (six with fireplaces), a suite with fireplace and a recently converted, private fireplaced cottage with two bedrooms and a full bath. They lease their dining operation to Tim and Biruta Carr, owners of our favorite **Tim-Bir Alley,** who moved their restaurant lock, stock and name from an alley in Littleton to the main floor of Adair (see Where to Eat). The country-estate-style guest rooms on the second and third floors, all with king or queen beds, are stylishly decorated and comfortable and named after nearby mountains, which is fitting considering their fabulous setting. We enjoyed the front Lafayette Room, a commodious affair including a queensize poster bed, a large sitting area with a gas stove and a bath with oversize soaking tub. Another prime accommodation is the Kinsman, with a kingsize sleigh bed, gas fireplace, a bath with the biggest double jacuzzi we've seen and a separate shower, and a deck for taking in the mountain view. Guests enjoy a grand, fireplaced living room with several sitting areas and a remarkable, all-granite (from walls to ceiling) basement taproom with TV/VCR, an imposing old Oliver Briggs Boston pool table and a small bar with setups. Out back is a large flagstone patio, terraced gardens and a rear lawn sloping down to a tennis court and a water garden beside a gazebo. Tea and sweets are offered in the afternoon. Breakfast could culminate in spinach and artichoke frittata or lemon chiffon pancakes.

(603) 444-2600 or (888) 444-2600. Fax (603) 444-4823. www.adairinn.com. Eight rooms, one suite and one cottage with private baths. Doubles, $175 to $250. Suite, $295. Cottage, $355. Add $50 during foliage. Deduct $35 midweek, November-May.

Sunset Hill House, 231 Sunset Hill Road, Sugar Hill 03585.

The landmark annex building that was all that was left of a famous hotel straddling the 1,700-foot-high ridge of Sugar Hill has been nicely transformed into an urbane country inn with an awesome view of the Presidential Range. Hospitable owners Lon and Nancy Henderson offer 21 stylish guest accommodations containing king or queen beds. Nearly half the rooms have a fireplace, whirlpool tub or both. At one visit, we could see the sun both rise and set from our second-floor north corner bedroom with windows on three sides. More recently, we luxuriated in one of two master suites, each with a king bed, living room with TV, fireplace, double whirlpool tub and separate shower. Ours had an enormous four-poster bed with a hidden jewelry compartment, a wood stove, a wet bar/kitchenette and a private balcony overlooking the mountains. The inn's adjacent Hill House is more like a B&B. Six oversize rooms are decorated in spiffy country inn style, some with separate sitting areas, two with porches and all with mountain views. The best room here comes with a kingsize bed, fireplace and a two-person whirlpool tub. Along the front of the main inn is a succession of three open, airy living rooms with fireplaces and splashy floral arrangements. Strung along the back are four elegant dining rooms with windows onto one of the best fall foliage views in New England (see Where to Eat). Outside in front is the oldest nine-hole golf course in New Hampshire, with a skating pond and cross-country trails in the winter. Behind the inn is a most attractive rock-rimmed swimming pool. Rates include a full breakfast.

(603) 823-5522 or (800) 786-4455. Fax (603) 823-5738. www.sunsethillhouse.com. Twenty-six rooms and two suites with private baths. Doubles $100 to $195, suites $275 and $325. Foliage: doubles $145 to $365, suites $349 to $599.

Sugar Hill Inn, Route 117, Box 954, Franconia 03580.

Nestled into the side of Sugar Hill is this old white farmhouse-turned-inn, its wraparound porch sporting colorfully padded wicker furniture and a telescope for viewing Cannon Mountain. All nine guest quarters in the main building have been reconfigured and restored. They exude upscale country charm with four-poster and canopy beds, hand stenciling, delicate wall coverings, heirloom coverlets and antiques. The newest are five luxury rooms and suites with gas fireplaces and whirlpool or two-person soaking tubs. Two have private decks. Six cottage rooms in back have been remodeled and winterized with new picture windows (for enjoying the mountain views), gas fireplaces and king or queen beds. Each has its own front porch with wicker chairs and flower boxes. Two living rooms in the main inn are available for guests. A cozy pub contains a three-stool bar, fireplace and tables with games to play. Innkeeper Judy Coots offers facials and massage therapy in the inn's new spa room.

Her husband Orlo, a professional chef, offers prix-fixe dinners by reservation Thursday-Sunday in a country-pretty dining room. The mushroom-dill soup, a signature item on the menu, is renowned, as is the mustard-crusted rack of lamb. Other choices could be cornbread-crusted cod, roast pork loin with spiked applesauce, and grilled brace of quail with peppery balsamic syrup. Chocolate pâté is the dessert favorite.

(603) 823-5621 or (800) 548-4748. Fax (603) 823-5639. www.sugarhillinn.com. Four rooms, five suites and six cottages with private baths. Rates, B&B: doubles $100 to $155, suites $175 to $225. Foliage, MAP: doubles $255 to $320, suites $345 to $380.

Dinner by reservation, Thursday-Sunday 6 to 8, nightly in foliage season. Prix-fixe, $40.

The Beal House Inn, 2 West Main St., Littleton 03561.

Built in 1833, the Beal House Inn has been serving travelers since Mrs. Beal opened the doors of her Colonial home smack up against the main street to overnight lodgers in 1938. The inn has undergone countless changes and upgrades under a succession of owners (four in the last decade alone), so it reveals the patina as well as the quirks of age and different personalities. It has been improved lately by Jose Luis and Catherine Pawelek, he an Argentine chef of some renown and she raised in the Netherlands. They offer three rooms and five suites, the latter enhanced with queensize poster beds topped with down comforters, sitting rooms with porcelain gas stoves, satellite TVs and mini-refrigerators. The rooms vary from the Rose Chamber, a large first-floor space with a queen sleigh bed with a lush fabric spread and matching swag draperies, a glowing antique rose chandelier and a bath with soaking tub, to the cozy Blue Room with a full-size pencil-post bed in an intimate nook at the top of the stairs. The pine-paneled Notchway beneath the eaves on the third floor is a two-bedroom suite likened to having "your own private camp." It includes a sitting room with a wall of windows onto the back yard, bedrooms with queensize and double beds, a private deck, a refrigerator and coffeemaker, and a bath with clawfoot tub. Another favorite is the Garden Suite with a front living room and a rear bedroom with queen poster bed and a double jacuzzi tub. Guests enjoy a couple of common rooms and a three-course gourmet breakfast. Dinner is served Wednesday-Sunday in the inn's café and martini bar (see Where to Eat).

(603) 444-2661 or (888) 616-2325. www.bealhouseinn.com. Three rooms and five suites with private baths. Doubles, $120 to $150. Suites $160 to $215. Closed first three weeks of November.

Angel of the Mountains, 2007 Main St., Box 487, Bethlehem 03574.

Pink with white trim, this handsome gabled Victorian B&B has a wraparound porch and two elegant sitting rooms and a dining room full of rich wood paneling. Up a majestic center staircase are three bedrooms with queensize beds, private baths and panoramic views of Mount Washington and the Presidential Range. A side carriage house with queen bedroom, kitchen, living room, TV/VCR and full-length deck overlooks a swimming pool and tennis courts on the site of what had been a hotel. Wine and cheese are offered in the late afternoon. Breakfast might culminate in an entrée like eggs florentine, frittata or french toast. Innkeepers Sally and Ben Gumm lead "mystery lantern walks" around historic Bethlehem on summer weekends. The 75-minute walking tour, lit by kerosene lanterns, illustrates the people and events that once made Bethlehem a premier tourist destination.

(603) 869-6473 or (888) 704-4004. www.angelofthemountains.com. Three rooms and a carriage house with private baths. Doubles, $98 to $110. Carriage house, $159 for two, $199 for four.

The Balmoral, 2533 Main St., Bethlehem 03574.

This Colonial home built in 1820 is named for the vacation home in Scotland of the British royal family. Owners Mark and Elizabeth Morrison, descendants of original Scottish settlers in Bethlehem, operate it as a B&B, treating guests as though they were visiting the home of old friends. The couple offer three guest rooms upstairs, all with TV/VCRs and two with queen beds and the other with a double bed. The largest, Burgundy, has a private bath in the hall, while the Forest Room, a favorite of honeymooners because of its fireplace, has a bath downstairs. It's reached by a servant's stair that some find quaint but, the Morrisons concede, others shun because of its steepness and low roof line. A separate entrance leads to a two-story suite, with a fireplaced living room on the main floor and a queen bedroom and full bath upstairs. The elegant house is full of antiques and reproductions, and the grounds are substantial. A full breakfast is served in the dining room, or at small tables in the guest rooms.

(603) 869-3169 or (800) 898-8980. Fax (603) 869-5462. www.thebalmoral.com. Three rooms and one suite. Doubles, $110. Suite, $175.

A Place for Romance

Rabbit Hill Inn, off Route 18, Lower Waterford, VT 05848.

If you have an iota of romance in your soul, you'll love this white-columned "inn for romantics" in a tiny hillside hamlet just across the Connecticut River from Littleton. Where else would you find, upon retiring to your room after a candlelight dinner, the bed turned down, the radio playing soft music, the lights turned off, a candle flickering in a hurricane chimney, and a small stuffed and decorated heart on the bed to use as a "do not disturb" sign and yours to take home? Innkeepers Leslie and Brian Mulcahy make guests feel at home in a cozy parlor, where afternoon tea and pastries are served. Next to it is the Snooty Fox pub, a comfortable place for libations and board games. Each of the seventeen guest rooms is decorated to a theme and all but four have working fireplaces with andirons in the shape of rabbits. Among the more prized accommodations is the Tavern's Secret, with kingsize canopy bed. Pull forward what appears to be a floor-to-ceiling bookcase opposite the fireplace and the secret is revealed: a gleaming bathroom with brass fixtures and a double jacuzzi. The grandest suite is the Jonathan Cummings, a fireplaced bedroom with queen canopy bed and a spacious dressing/sitting room with another fireplace facing a 44-jet hydro-massage tub for two. Cedar Glen, a new luxury room with a rustic Vermont cabin theme, features a handmade cedar-log kingsize bed and a whirlpool tub for two, both facing a sitting area in front of the fireplace.

Fine food and romantic ambiance are the hallmarks of the inn's charming dining rooms, which are lit by candles and lanterns. Silver gleams on burgundy mats on the polished wood tables, and napkins fold into pewter rings shaped like rabbits. Porcelain bunnies and oil lamps are on each table, and a fireplace adds warmth in chilly weather. A spinning wheel is on display in a second dining room added behind the original to accommodate the growing following attracted by the magical atmosphere. Longtime chef Russell Stannard offers the area's most exciting New American fare, available prix-fixe in three or five courses. Our dinner began with cream of celery soup with pimento and chives and smoked pork tenderloin with roasted garlic aioli and mustard greens, delicate salads with a creamy dressing, and a small loaf of piping-hot whole wheat bread. Sorbet drenched in champagne cleared the palate for the main courses: a very spicy red snapper dish and sautéed chicken with bananas, almonds and plums, served with an asparagus-leek tart and garnished with baby greens. Homemade peanut-brittle ice cream in an edible cookie cup and double chocolate-almond pâté with crème anglaise were fabulous finales. A harpist played, service was polished and the ambience serene.

(802) 748-5168 or (800) 762-8669. Fax (802) 748-8142. www.rabbithillinn.com. Ten rooms and nine luxury rooms and suites with private baths. Doubles, $185 to $225. Luxury rooms and suites, $295 to $310. Add $35 for foliage and Christmas Week.

Dinner nightly by reservation, 6 to 9. Prix-fixe, $40 for three courses, $50 for five.

Resorts and Motels

Lovett's Inn By Lafayette Brook, 1474 Profile Road (Route 18), Franconia 03580.
Twenty scenic acres and Cannon Mountain are the backdrops for this venerable inn, which dates to 1794 and is listed in the National Register of Historic Places. Innkeepers Jim and Janet Freitas are maintaining the reputation built over 70 years by the Lovett family as they upgrade the facilities and decor. The main house holds a candlelit dining room (see Where to Eat) and a pleasant lounge with a curved marble bar. Across the foyer are an old-fashioned Victorian parlor with beamed ceiling and a sunken TV room with a wood stove and an antique radio. We're partial to the sixteen units in seven cottages scattered around the lawns and beside the pool. Each has a wood-burning fireplace and a small patio with chairs for gazing upon Cannon Mountain. Some have kingsize beds and three have whirlpool tubs. All come with sitting areas and small television sets. Their elongated narrow bathrooms are ingenious as well as serviceable. The inn also offers a three-bedroom cottage with all the amenities of home. A full breakfast is included in the rates.

(603) 823-7761 or (800) 356-3802. www.lovettsinn.com. Three rooms, two suites and sixteen cottage units with private baths. Doubles, $115 to $235. Cottage, $435. Add $40 for foliage and holidays. Closed in early November and April.

Franconia Inn, Easton Road, Franconia 03580.
Situated amid 107 acres in the Easton valley with Cannon Mountain as a backdrop, this rambling white structure looks the way you think a country inn should look. It is the area's largest and busiest, and offers a variety of activities. Brothers Alec and Richard Morris have upgraded the 32 rooms and suites on three floors since acquiring the inn in 1980. Rooms vary in size and beds; some connect to become family suites. Corner rooms are best in terms of size and view. The newly renovated Kinsman Cottage next to the inn offers a loft apartment with queen bedroom and kitchen as well as a ground-floor suite with kingsize bed and jetted tub. The inn's main floor has an attractive dining room, a living room and oak-paneled library with fireplaces, a pool room, a game room with pinball machines, and a screened porch with wicker furniture overlooking a large swimming pool. Downstairs is the spacious **Rathskeller Lounge** with entertainment at night and, beyond, a hot tub in a large room paneled in redwood. Outside are four tennis courts and a glider/biplane facility. Trail rides are offered in season; in winter, the barn turns into a cross-country ski center. Breakfast is included in the rates. The attractive dining room, open to the public, features a short contemporary menu. Typical entrées are Maine crab cakes with chipotle mayonnaise, seared duck breast with pear and ginger marmalade, and mozzarella-crusted lamb loin with a raspberry-horseradish sauce.

(603) 823-5542 or (800) 473-5299. www.franconiainn.com. Twenty-nine rooms and three suites with private baths. Doubles, $125 to $155. Suites, $180 to $205. Add $30 for foliage and Christmas. Closed April to mid-May.
Entrées, $16.95 to $25.95. Dinner, 6 to 8:30 or 9. Closed Monday-Thursday in off-season.

Wayside Inn, Route 302 at Pierce Bridge, Box 480, Bethlehem 03574.
This is a homey inn of the old school, nicely located alongside the banks of the Ammonoosuc River. Fourteen rooms in the rambling main building contain period furniture, double, queen or king beds, and hardwood floors and trim. Some have whirlpool tubs. We prefer the newer motel out back, its twelve units on two floors each having sliding doors onto private balconies beside the river. Decor is standard motel, although one second-floor end unit departs with a queensize bed, a sofabed

and a Laura Ashley look that owner Kathe Hofmann likens to that of a city condo. The main inn also houses the **Riverview Restaurant** (see Where to Eat), a Victorian parlor, a second parlor with games and TV, plus a large lounge with TV. Outside are a swimming hole, a sandy beach, tennis court, and volleyball and basketball facilities.

(603) 869-3364 or (800) 448-9557. Fax (603) 869-5765. www.thewaysideinn.com. Fourteen inn rooms and twelve motel rooms with private baths. Doubles, $88 to $138.

Stonybrook Motel & Lodge, 1098 Profile Road (Route 18), Franconia 03580.

Nicely situated on eight landscaped acres beside Lafayette Book and beneath the Franconia Range, this is one of the area's more attractive motels. Tom and Pauline Palmer offer five pine-paneled rooms of varying sizes in the hand-timbered lodge and eighteen more modern, motel-style rooms. There are indoor and outdoor pools, a streamside picnic area with grills and a stocked trout pond. The lodge contains a large game room and fireplace.

(603) 823-8192 or (800) 722-3552. Fax: (603)823-5888. www.stonybrookmotel.com. Twenty-three rooms. Doubles, $80 to $95 in summer, $65 to 75 rest of year.

Franconia Hotel & Resort, 87 Wallace Hill Road, Franconia 03580.

This newish motor inn, just above I-93 and overlooking the village, offers the most modern (and expensive) motel facilities in the area. The 60 rooms on two floors contain kingsize or two double beds, some with poster headboards and TVs hidden in armoires. Each room is outfitted with a microwave, refrigerator and coffeemaker. Facilities include a large indoor pool with a whirlpool spa, sauna and exercise room. **The Pub with Mexican Grub** serves modest Mexican and American fare for dinner nightly and for lunch on weekends. Continental breakfast is included in the rates.

(603) 823-7422 or (888) 669-6777. Fax (603) 823-5638. www.franconiahotel.com. Sixty rooms. Doubles, $79 to $145, $89 to $155 in fall, $69 to $99 in spring.

─Extra-Good Value─

Eastgate Motor Inn, 335 Cottage St. (Route 302), Littleton 03561.

Up a hill not far off I-93 is this brick motel complex that started in the 1950s and grew to 55 ground-level units. Don't be deceived by the tiny room windows beside the entrances from the parking lot. The modern, well-kept rooms we saw opened to the rear with oversize windows and sliding doors onto attractive grounds. Beds come in a variety of configurations, from two doubles to queen or kingsize. The large and elegant white-linened dining rooms offer an extensive menu, priced from $9.95 for fish and chips to $16.95 for New York strip steak. The pool and on-site restaurant and cocktail lounge make this a good choice for visitors who want to stay put. Rates include continental breakfast.

(603) 444-3971 or (866) 640-3561. Fax: (603) 444-3971. www.eastgatemotorinn.com. Fifty-five rooms. Doubles, $79.70 June-September, $109.70 foliage, $69.70 rest of year.

Where to Eat

Fine Dining

Tim-Bir Alley, Old Littleton Road, Bethlehem.

For ten years, this little establishment named for its owners, Tim and Biruta Carr, was a culinary landmark in the basement of a building down an alley in downtown

Littleton. It moved a decade later into two small and elegant dining rooms in Adair, the high-style country inn, where the Carrs continue to serve some of the area's most sophisticated and inventive food. After optional cocktails with snacks served in the inn's basement Granite Tavern or outside on the flagstone terrace, patrons adjourn to the dining room for a meal to remember. Our latest began with fabulous chicken-almond wontons with coconut-curry sauce and delicate salmon pancakes on a roasted red-pepper coulis. From the selection of eight main courses on a menu that changes weekly, we enjoyed the breast of chicken with maple-balsamic glaze and plum-ginger puree and the pork tenderloin sauced with red wine, grilled leeks and smoked bacon. Follow this assertive fare with, perhaps, peach ricotta strudel with caramel sauce or white chocolate-strawberry tart with mango puree. The well-chosen wine list is affordably priced.

(603) 444-2600. Entrées, $18.95 to $24.95. Dinner by reservation, Wednesday-Saturday 5:30 to 9, also Sunday in summer and foliage. Closed in November and April.

Sunset Hill House, Sunset Hill Road, Sugar Hill.

Four elegant dining rooms seating a total of 100 are strung along the rear of this refurbished inn, their tall windows opening onto the Franconia, Kinsman and Presidential ranges. Veteran chef Joe Peterson's contemporary fare and the staff's flawless service are the match for a mountain view unsurpassed in the area. Broiled rainbow trout with horseradish-apple cream, cider-brined Iowa pork and duckling Bombay are signature dishes. We were impressed by starters of grilled boar sausage, served sliced with a soothing maple crème fraîche, and the seared ahi tuna steak with spicy mango-habañero and sweet ruby grapefruit sauces. The unusual house salad was tossed with a tequila-jalapeño dressing. Main courses included a superb filet mignon with a lemon-spinach peanut sauce, served with shiitake mushrooms and roasted new potatoes, and baked chicken stuffed with goat cheese. White chocolate cheesecake, iced lemon soufflé cake and bananas foster were sweet endings. The wine list is ranked among the best in the state. After dinner, if the timing is right, you'll want to head outside. Says innkeeper Lon Henderson: "It's not unusual for the inn to empty out at sundown to applaud one of our absolutely spectacular sunsets."

(603) 823-5522 or (800) 786-4455. Entrées, $17 to $27. Dinner nightly except Monday, 5:30 to 9, Memorial Day to foliage; nightly in foliage and holiday weeks. Rest of year: Thursday-Sunday 5:30 to 9.

Beal House Inn Restaurant, 2 West Main St., Littleton.

The former carriage house at the side of the Beal House Inn has been converted into a winning café by Jose Luis Pawelek, an Argentine chef of some renown, and his wife Catherine, who was raised in the Netherlands. Oriental rugs dot the polished wood floors of the intimate dining room seating a total of 40. Musical instruments pose with artworks on the sienna-colored walls above the original tin wainscoting in an elegant, white-tablecloth setting. A jazzy upstairs lounge decked out in white lights has a glistening wood floor and a copper-topped martini bar ranked as New Hampshire's best (252 martinis listed at last count). Jose does the cooking, offering a fairly extensive menu of superior "global cuisine without boundaries," every item so tempting it makes choosing difficult. Appetizers range from a medley of wild mushrooms in puff pastry to wood-grilled scallops and shrimp served on a buttermilk corn cake in a pool of smoky hot chipotle butter. Main courses include potato-crusted haddock with a roasted red-pepper sauce, duckling sauced with crème de cassis, and black angus tenderloin with a trio of sauces. The house specialty is cioppino in a spicy marinara sauce over linguini. Interesting sauces are the chef's forte: the snapper tropical is sautéed with mango, banana, grapes and dark rum, and the salmon with strawberries, balsamic vinegar and a cabernet reduction. The treats continue for dessert, perhaps the dream terrine (frozen white-chocolate mousse with chambord-infused raspberry mousse served with warm bittersweet chocolate sauce) and Catherine's signature tarte tatin, enhanced with peach or mango and served with French vanilla ice cream and a warm ginger-caramel sauce.

(603) 444-2661 or (888) 616-2325. www.bealhouseinn.com. Entrées, $19 to $27. Dinner, Wednesday-Saturday 5:30 to 9, Sunday 5:30 to 8.

The Grand Depot Café, 62 Cottage St., Littleton.

The restored railroad depot was gutted to produce this handsome restaurant, known for refined contemporary continental cuisine. The high-ceilinged dining room in the old waiting room looks like a French salon, dressed with white-clothed tables, shaded oil lamps and fine paintings and French posters. Several more tables are available in a small lounge, which has an ornate gold mirror and quite a collection of hats around the bar. Well-known local chef-owner Frederick Tilton has a loyal following. Typical main dishes range from potato-crusted Atlantic salmon with a lemon-mustard sauce and grilled yellowfin tuna with a sundried tomato and kalamata olive sauce to chicken cubano and grilled venison steak with a red currant sauce. The big-spender's favorite is the filet mignon served on a potato pancake garnished with roasted mushroom caps and finished with a parslied garlic butter. Appetizers could be the house chicken liver pâté, escargots bourguignonne or blackened carpaccio of barbary duck marinated in armagnac and fennel. Desserts include key lime cheesecake, apple crisp and quite a choice of unusual sorbets and gelatos. Global fare is featured on the eclectic bar menu. Chef Rick is especially proud of the extensive wine list and his roster of single-malt scotches.

(603) 444-5303. Entrées, $14.95 to $32, bar menu $6.95 to $14.95. Dinner, Monday-Saturday 5 to 9.

Lovett's Inn By Lafayette Brook, 1474 Profile Road, Franconia.

A little concrete fisherman sits with his pole at the end of the diving board over a pond formed by Lafayette Brook across the road. Illuminated at night, he attracts the curious to this inn's well-known restaurant, a fixture in the area since the days of legendary Charlie Lovett. People usually gather for cocktails around the curved marble bar (obtained from a Newport mansion) in the renovated lounge for socializing. Dinner is served in a country elegant, beamed dining room, with oriental carpets on the refinished hardwood floors. Chef-owner Janet Freitas has the cooking down to a routine, changing only the presentations and sauces occasionally on a menu that lists nine entrées. Typical are pan-seared Chilean sea bass with a red pepper coulis, chicken florentine, roast duck with a raspberry-vinaigrette sauce, veal genovese and herb-crusted rack of lamb with a red wine-dijon sauce. Shrimp cocktail, goat cheese strudel and crab cakes with tomato salsa make good starters. Desserts are extravagant, from hot Indian pudding with ice cream to flourless chocolate torte and crème brûlée.

(603) 823-7761 or (800) 356-3802. Entrées, $18 to $22. Dinner, Wednesday-Sunday 6 to 8 or 8:30.

More Casual Dining

Riverview Restaurant, Route 302, Bethlehem.

The place to eat at the Wayside Inn is on the enclosed porch opening off the dining room onto lovely gardens beside the Ammonoosuc River. Tables covered with red and white checked cloths and oil lamps are the setting for chef-owner Victor Hofmann's American and Swiss fare. His extensive menu mixes sea bass cacciatore, grilled duck breast with orange sauce, rack of lamb provençal, rahm schnitzel and pork Victor, the chef's favorite, doused with wild mushrooms. The mixed grill called "Beef and Bird" pairs grilled quail with beef tenderloin. Entrées start at $10.75 for chicken oriental and most are under $15.

(603) 869-3364 or (800) 448-9557. Entrées, $10.75 to $19.95. Dinner, Tuesday-Sunday 6 to 9; hours vary in winter.

Gallery of Good Eats

Cold Mountain Café & Gallery, 2015 Main St., Bethlehem.

Some of the area's most interesting fare emanates from the kitchen of this quirky, 34-seat storefront establishment. It's also served up at prices from yesteryear by chef-owners David Brown and Jack Foley. Imagine, bouillabaisse for dinner for $14.95, or rack of lamb for $15.95. The entrée price includes a house salad as well as starch and vegetable. Expect the likes of baked salmon with tamari-ginger glaze, chicken breast with a Thai curry sauce and pork medallions with mango chutney. Interesting salads, quesadillas, quiches and sandwiches are featured on the lunch menu. Cappuccino, beer and wines are the beverages of choice. Dining takes place in a spare room with pale yellow walls hung with changing local art, halogen lights and votive candles on bare wood tables.

(603) 869-2500. Entrées, $10.95 to $15.95. Lunch, Monday-Saturday 11 to 3:30. Dinner, Monday-Saturday 5:30 to 9 or 9:30. No credit cards.

Dutch Treat Restaurant, Main Street, Franconia.

The family-style dining room and the large bar and lounge aren't anything to write home about, but the food is. A quick lunch produced a turkey navy bean soup, a fine spinach and artichoke salad, and a croque monsieur. These were impressive enough to suggest a return for dinner, perhaps for seafood en papillote, Japanese-crusted porterhouse pork chops or top round of lamb with port wine and peppercorn gravy. Appetizers such as mussels marnière, fried calamari tossed with pineapple curry, crab-stuffed portobello mushroom and sesame pork dumplings with ponzu dipping sauce also tempted.

(603) 823-8851. Entrées, $7.95 to $15.95. Breakfast, lunch and dinner daily, 7 a.m. to 8 or 9 p.m.

Rosa Flamingo's, Main Street, Bethlehem.

This is not the Mexican eatery that we expected, but rather an Italian-American restaurant in a contemporary gray wood building with dining on the main floor, a bar below and a wraparound outdoor deck. The menu is large and varied to attract families and the younger set. We can vouch for the tortellini carbonara (a house specialty) and the chicken with garlic and artichoke hearts, both $9.95 and both of which lived up to their advance billing from a local innkeeper. The rest of the extensive dinner menu ranges from $6.25 for manicotti and baked ziti to $16.95 for steak and scampi. Pizzas, nachos and sandwiches are among the possibilities. Burgers and sandwiches in the $4 to $5 range are featured at lunch.

(603) 869-3111. Lunch. Friday-Sunday 11:30 to 4. Dinner nightly, 5 to 10.

A 'True' Place

Polly's Pancake Parlor, Hildex Maple Sugar Farm, Route 117, Sugar Hill. Only in a "true" place like Sugar Hill would a pancake house be a restaurant of note. Folks pour in from all over for down-home pancakes, sandwiches, salads and such in a rustic 1820 building that once was a carriage shed and now has louvered windows opening onto a glorious view of the Mount Lafayette range. Polly and Wilfred "Sugar Hill" Dexter opened the place in 1938. The tradition is carried on by their daughter, Nancy Dexter Aldrich, her husband Roger and their daughter and son-in-law. Red-painted kitchen chairs flank bare tables sporting red mats shaped like maple leaves, topped with wooden plates that Nancy hand-painted with maple leaves. You can watch the pancakes being made in the open kitchen. The batter is poured from a contraption that guarantees each will measure three inches in diameter. An order of six costs $5.40 for pancakes made with buckwheat, whole wheat cornmeal or oatmeal-buttermilk. All are available with blueberries, walnuts or coconut for $6.70. The coffee, made with spring water, is excellent and a glass of the spring water really hits the spot (no liquor is served). The shop at the entry sells pancake packs, maple syrup and sugar, jams and even the signature maple-leaf painted wooden plates.

(603) 823-5575. Pancakes/Light Fare, $5 to $9. Open daily, 7 to 3, mid-May to mid-October. Open weekends, early spring and late fall. Closed December-March.

FOR MORE INFORMATION: Franconia Notch Chamber of Commerce, Box 780, Franconia, NH 03580, (603) 823-5661. www.franconianotch.org

Bethlehem Visitors Center, 2182 Main St., Box 748, Bethlehem, NH 03574, (888) 845-1957. www.bethlehemwhitemtns.com.

Mount Washington Hotel is reflected in water with Presidential Range in background.

Mount Washington Valley, N.H.

Peak Experiences

What is it that attracts so many people to the Mount Washington Valley? The lure of scaling the Northeast's highest peak by foot, rail, car or snow coach? The rugged and spectacular scenery? The chance to stay in some of the mountain resort hotels of yesteryear? The opportunity to shop in tax-free discount outlets?

All these and more are attractions, but the main draw is legendary Mount Washington, king of the Presidential Range. The Native Americans called it Agocochook and didn't climb it, believing its ominous summit was the home of the Great Spirit (a phenomenon readily imaginable when it's shrouded in storm clouds today). Early settler Abel Crawford and son Ethan Allen Crawford blazed the first path to the summit in 1819, and people have followed ever since – by foot, auto or railway. These days, the summit is visited by tens of thousands of visitors a year. From there, on a clear day, it's possible to see five states and Canada, and nearly freeze in the process.

Like everyone else, you will probably want to conquer Mount Washington – at least once in your life. But there's much more to occupy you in this mountain wonderland of dramatic scenery, hiking trails, ski centers and mountain retreats from the lofty to the rustic – plus all the accoutrements of tourism that grew up around them.

The heart of the valley is congested North Conway, an elongated sliver of a place whose center looks more like a western frontier town than a New England village. Unless you're into outlet shopping, you may want to stay away (know that you can detour around on the West Side Road and avoid it altogether).

From the flatlands flanked by cliffs and foothills around North Conway, the valley floor narrows as it rises in a Y-shape from Glen through mountain notches around Mount Washington. The best bases for getaways are on either side of Mount Washington: rugged Crawford Notch and the more refined, quaint village of Jackson.

West of Mount Washington, Crawford Notch – named for the men who blazed the first trail to the summit – cuts through the heart of the rugged White Mountain National Forest. After the grand Mount Washington Hotel opened nearby in 1902, 50 trains arrived daily, depositing well-heeled city-dwellers in the midst of the mountains to escape summer's heat and partake of nature. The East's largest mountain resort developed at Bretton Woods, a name that left a bigger mark in international history than it did in travel circles.

East of Mount Washington, the road north to Pinkham Notch leads past Jackson, a European-style mountainside village of 600 residents. Here is one of the nation's earliest year-round destination resorts, dating to pre-Civil War days – and not much changed since its heyday around the turn of the last century when grand hotels turned it into an exclusive resort area. Mountain pursuits, golf and cross-country skiing are the draws in Jackson. Fine lodging and dining options make for indulgent getaways.

Seeing and Doing

The rugged mountains of the Presidential Range march in a rising crescendo toward Mount Washington, the highest peak (6,288 feet) in the Northeast. Nearly half the 86 mountains exceed 4,000 feet and reflect New Hampshire's calling as the Granite State.

The **White Mountain National Forest** here covers more than 770,000 acres, roughly the size of Rhode Island. Its rocky, forested terrain embraces not only mountains but also scores of backcountry lakes, miles of cascading streams and more than 100 waterfalls – the area crisscrossed by 1,200 miles of hiking trails. It's a virtual playground for mountaineers, rock climbers, skiers, mountain bikers, kayakers, fishermen, birdwatchers and especially hikers.

Getting to the Top

Mount Washington, the center of the region in spirit if not geography, is a brooding peak that's often obscured in clouds and capped in snow. The 52-acre Mount Washington State Park is at the top and – given all way ways that people can reach it – rather crowded. Here you'll find the restored Tip Top House, the oldest building on the mountain (1858). The Summit Stage Office, held down by iron chains, is where the world's highest wind gust (231 miles an hour) was recorded in April 1934. The Sherman Adams Summit Building offers a 360-degree view of the northern Presidential Range. The Mount Washington Observatory's summit museum displays exhibits about the mountain's geology and weather, including a new Weather Discovery Room in which visitors explore the summit's weather conditions and how they are recorded. The weather at the summit rivals that of Antarctica, with an average annual temperature below freezing. The museum is open daily 9 to 6, weather permitting, mid-May to mid-October. Adults $2, children $1.

The blustery peak can be reached by car via the Auto Road off Route 16 in Pinkham Notch and by the Mount Washington Cog Railway from Bretton Woods. Or you can hike or ski.

THE EASY WAY. The Mount Washington Auto Road, Route 16, Pinkham Notch. "This Car Climbed Mt. Washington," proclaim the ubiquitous bumper stickers, and you can sport one, too, if you care. The eight-mile ride up the narrow, winding road with an average grade of twelve percent travels through four different climate zones and multiple changes in terrain. It takes half an hour to drive up, and nearly that long to get down. The "Road to the Sky" is not for the faint of heart (low gear is recommended both ways) or for anyone with a fear of heights (no guardrails), but the views from the frequent turnouts compensate for the downsides. An audio cassette that comes with the hefty vehicle fee tells of the road's legends and lore. Guided tours in Auto Road vans called Stages (after the horse-drawn wagons that hauled tourists and took all day when the road opened in 1861) are available from 8:30 to 5, and include a half-hour stop at the summit. In winter, the nine-passenger SnowCoach (which looks like a van on bulldozer "wheels") gives sightseeing tours up the Auto Road to just above the tree line at the 4,600-foot mark (adults $40, children $25).

(603) 466-3988. www.mtwashingtonautoroad.com. Open daily, mid-May to mid-October, 7:30 to 6 mid-June to Labor Day, 8 to 4 or 5 rest of season. Driving tour, car and driver $18, adult passengers $7, children $4. Guided tour, adults $24, children $10.

THE FUN WAY. The Mount Washington Cog Railway, Route 302, Bretton Woods. The world's first mountain-climbing cog train makes a scenic three-hour round trip to the summit along its western face. Sylvester Marsh was told he might as well build "a railway to the moon," but his cog railway was a marvel of engineering when it opened in 1869 and remains so today. Its smoky, coal-fired steam engine has a toothed cogwheel that engages a cog rack between the traditional rails along a 3.5-mile trestle track, noisily pushing a 70-passenger coach at the questionable "I think I can, I think I can" speed of four miles an hour – which was just fine with early travelers, who found the relatively short trip in enclosed cars preferable to the all-day journey in open wagons on the forerunner to the Auto Road. The average grade is 25 percent, but you may get a rush of adrenalin when the train traverses Jacob's Ladder, a roller-coaster-style trestle 25 feet high that angles upward at a 37 percent grade. The three-hour trip includes breaks to add water to the steam engine, to check the track switches and to permit trains to pass in the opposite direction, as well as a twenty-minute stop at the summit. The train operated in the winter of 2004-05 for the first time to haul skiers and snowboarders a third of the way to the summit. Mile-long groomed trails on either side of the railway trestle give them 1,100 vertical feet of schussing on the way down.

(603) 846-5404 or (800) 922-8825. www.thecog.com. Trains depart daily, 9 to 4 mid-June through July, 8 to 5 in August, 9 to 3 rest of season. Adults $49, children $35. Winter ski train, day ticket $59, $25 per ride.

THE HARD WAY. Mount Washington has a fierce reputation as the "most dangerous small mountain in the world." Hurricane-force winds and sub-freezing temperatures have been recorded every month of the year. Yet more than 70,000 climbers and hikers ascend Tuckerman and adjacent Huntington ravines each year. Thousands more trudge the 1,200 miles of hiking and backpacking trails – from easy to difficult – elsewhere on the mountain and around the White Mountain National Forest. Exactly which are the best for your desires and capabilities can be determined from the Appalachian Mountain Club's official *White Mountain Guide.*

HIKING. The best place to begin a back-country adventure is the AMC's **Pinkham**

Notch Visitor Center, Route 16, Pinkham Notch, (603) 466-2725, about eight miles north of North Conway at the eastern base of Mount Washington. Here you will find up-to-date trail information, guided hikes, a cafeteria for buffet breakfast and lunch and family-style dinners, and the Trading Post retail store selling maps, books, outdoor clothing and supplies. Next door is the **Joe Dodge Lodge,** a rustic but comfortable place for hikers to stay, with snug bunkrooms and a few family rooms with a double and three bunk beds. The AMC also offers spartan bunks and meals in eight mountain huts (reservations essential) and a number of three-sided lean-to shelters for backpackers on a first-come basis. A hiker's shuttle bus links Pinkham Notch Visitor Center and the Highland Center at Crawford Notch, and stops at popular trailheads throughout the White Mountains, (603) 466-2727; fee, $12.

The most popular hiking trail to the top of Mount Washington, the 4.21-mile **Tuckerman Ravine Trail,** takes about six and one-half hours round trip. It climbs 4,300 feet to the summit via Tuckerman Ravine. The first half is wide and relatively easy, but becomes really steep as it attacks the ravine headwall. The last portion, up the summit cone, involves a steep ascent over large boulders and more rock hopping than trail walking. It meets the Auto Road in the lower parking lot on the mountaintop and officially ends just beyond a long wood staircase by the old Stage Office. At the top of the Tuckerman headwall, you can detour on the **Alpine Garden Path** across the grassy flats east of the summit, view the delicate wildflowers and alpine vegetation, and also connect with the Auto Road.

Less crowded trails are available from Pinkham Notch. The **Lion's Head Trail,** about the same length as the Tuckerman, is steeper and rougher, but you find better views and fewer crowds. The most difficult trail, the **Huntington Ravine Trail,** veers northwest off the Tuckerman Ravine Trail. It climbs straight up the smooth headwall of Huntington Ravine, continues across the Alpine Garden Trail and ends at the Auto Road below its 7-mile mark.

Ski Tuckerman's

Tuckerman Ravine on the southeast shoulder of Mount Washington is where the hardy ski when the snows elsewhere have long since melted, if they're up to the climb (a 1,500-foot vertical rise for a half-mile run down). The large, glacial bowl collects snow blowing off the Presidential Range. Snow averages 55 feet in the deepest spot. Access to skiing in Tuckerman Ravine requires hiking from the Pinkham Notch Visitor Center on Route 16. Scores of hikers congregate on the north side of the ravine in a jumble of boulders known as "Lunch Rocks" to watch the skiers (and sometimes icefalls and avalanches).

Highland Center at Crawford Notch. This is the other best place for hikers and backpacking expeditions, especially beginners and those interested in short day hikes with great views. The center is based in the historic 1891 railroad depot at the head of Crawford Notch, across from Saco Lake. It is a major stop on the Conway Scenic Railroad's excursions from North Conway and offers displays on the natural environment and the local railroad and hotel history.

Two trails approach Mount Washington from the west, both starting from the same trailhead off Route 302 on the Base Road leading to the Cog Railway Station. The trailhead is 500 feet higher than Pinkham, so hikers save that much elevation gain. Go up the Ammonoosuc/Crawford and down the Jewell to complete what hikers call the classic Mount Washington loop.

The **Ammonoosuc Ravine Trail,** combined with the **Crawford Path** at the top, is the shorter of the two (four-and-one-half miles up and six and one-half hours round trip), steeper and more scenic. Blazed in 1819 by the Crawford family, the Crawford is the oldest continuously maintained hiking trail in the country. From Mount Clinton Road parking area, the trail follows a ridge northeastward along the Presidentials, over Mounts Eisenhower, Franklin and Monroe, passing the Lake of the Clouds hut with views over the vast, 5,500-acre Great Gulf Wilderness Area. The Crawford Path climbs over rocks from the hut to the summit cone. Along the way, several good trails split off in either direction.

The least difficult footpath to the summit is the **Jewell Trail,** heading northeast to the Cog Railway Base Station, climbing through a series of switchbacks and among rocks to the Gulfside Trail, where hikers turn right to complete the ascent to the summit or left to explore the northern Presidentials. That hike is 5.1 miles up and takes about six and three-quarter hours.

For other recreation activities, a good base is the **Great Glen Trails Outdoor Center,** part of the recently renovated Mount Washington Auto Road Stage Office Building at Pinkham Notch, (603) 466-2333, www.greatglentrails.com. The center offers hiking and mountain biking on rolling carriage roads and challenging trails at the base of Mount Washington. In winter, cross-country skiers and snowshoers can find trails and terrain to match their skills. Guided kayak and canoe tours are offered on nearby lakes and rivers.

TOURING. If fun for you doesn't involve scaling rocky cliffs or taking dips in chilly mountain streams, you can still enjoy the mountain scenery by car. Route 302 takes travelers northwest through Crawford Notch. Route 16 slices north through Pinkham Notch. The most scenic drive is the famed **Kancamagus Highway** just south of the area, which links Conway and Lincoln. It provides frequent roadside turnouts for admiring waterfalls, sweeping mountain views and picnicking beside streams. You can reach it via Bear Notch Road (closed in winter) off Route 302 in Bartlett, which has the only midpoint access to the Kancamagus.

Conway Scenic Railroad, Route 16/302, North Conway.

Relive railroad history and enjoy spectacular scenery on the route of the first train through Crawford Notch 130 years ago. At the Victorian train station in downtown North Conway, board the modern "Notch Train" as it traverses Crawford Notch, passing sheer cliffs, steep ravines, cascading streams and mountain panoramas and crosses the famed Frankenstein Trestle and Willey Brook Bridge en route to Crawford Depot or Fabyan Station and back. Live commentary includes history and folklore of the railroad and the area, as well as points of interest. You can ride in an open coach car, an enclosed first-class car or a recently inaugurated observation "Dome Car" built in the 1950s for transcontinental rail service. There are one-way trips in summer, but most are round trips from and to North Conway. The outfit offers shorter trips and lunch and dinner trips on dining cars from North Conway to Bartlett or Conway. The round trip through Crawford Notch takes five hours to Crawford Depot, with an extra half hour to Fabyan Station during foliage season.

(603) 356-5251 or (800) 232-5251. www.conwayscenic.com. Trains leave Tuesday-Thursday and Saturday at 11, June 21 through Labor Day; daily at 11, Sept. 13 to Oct. 14. Round trips: adults $37 to $52, children $21 to $30.

Bretton Woods

For those of a certain age, Bretton Woods rings a bell. History was made here when delegates gathered at the Mount Washington Hotel for the Bretton Woods International Monetary Conference in 1944. The gold standard was established and the U.S. dollar chosen as the backbone of international exchange.

The summer hotel was showing its age when four Littleton families purchased it at a bank auction in 1991 and turned it into a world-class, four-season resort. Sportsmen are lured by New Hampshire's largest ski area and two golf courses, one a 27-hole course at the Mount Washington Resort. The Bretton Woods Cross-Country Center offers a spectacular new lodge for ski tourers and snowshoers.

Lodging and Dining

The Mount Washington Resort at Bretton Woods, Route 302, Bretton Woods 03575.

Recently restored to its original glory, the majestic white Mount Washington Hotel with red roof is beautifully situated on lush grounds backing up to the west face of Mount Washington. A mile-long driveway through some of the resort's 2,600 acres leads to the National Register landmark hotel, built in 1902 by railroad tycoon Joseph Stickney in the Spanish Renaissance style. Some 250 European artisans spent two years crafting the detailed plaster work and installing the Tiffany glass in the lobby of the five-story behemoth, whose construction was one of the most ambitious projects of its time. But the timing was right – it quickly became one of the best-known grand resorts, favored by city dwellers who enjoyed socializing on its 900-foot-long veranda with a panoramic view of the Presidential Range. With stately public rooms and spacious bedrooms, the "Grande Dame of the White Mountains" retains a turn-of-the-last-century formality. The refurbished hotel's airy rooms have twelve-foot-high ceilings, king or queen beds, and TVs in armoires. Many of the baths contain their original clawfoot tubs. Some deluxe rooms have double whirlpool tubs and fireplaces. Three Tower Suites come with sitting room, kingsize sleigh bed and bath with double whirlpool tub (one suite has a rooftop deck). The compound includes the 34-room **Bretton Arms Country Inn,** the 50-room **Lodge at Bretton Woods** (a motor inn), and a variety of rental condominiums of one to five bedrooms known as **The Townhomes at Bretton Woods**. Facilities include the expanded Bretton Woods Ski Area (lately billed as New Hampshire's largest), 27 holes of golf on two courses, twelve clay tennis courts, two heated pools, a health and fitness center, an equestrian center and miles of trails for horseback riding, jogging and mountain biking.

Guests and the public may dine in any of the resort's restaurants. The hotel's vast 730-seat, octagon-shaped, two-story-high main dining room was originally designed as a circle so that no one would end up in a corner. Tables in the middle lack the close-up mountain views of those near the windows. Crystal chandeliers, tuxedoed waiters and an orchestra for dancing turn dinner into a festive occasion. The meal here is prix-fixe, available from a changing, multi-choice American/ continental menu that's printed daily on an antique water-powered press. In addition to the formal dining room, the resort complex offers a variety of dining venues including **Stickney's Restaurant,** the **Bretton Arms Dining Room, Fabyan's Station,** the **Presidential Grille** and **Darby's Diner.** Nightly entertainment is provided in the granite-walled **Cave Lounge.**

(603) 278-1000 or (800) 314-1752. www.mtwashington.com. One hundred ninety-five rooms and five suites. Hotel rates, MAP. Doubles, $260 to $1,050. Suites, $910 to $1,550. Inn, doubles $130 to $398 B&B. Lodge, $99 to $199 B&B.

Hart's Location

⎯ *A Sumptuous Wilderness Retreat* ⎯⎯⎯

The Notchland Inn, Route 302, Hart's Location 03812.

This choice, small, self-contained inn is spectacularly situated off by itself in the White Mountain National Forest, blessed with 400 acres of woods and gardens and 8,000 feet of frontage on the Saco River, which has been dammed to create a nifty pond with two private swimming holes. The many-gabled stone manor house, built in 1862, holds an acclaimed dining room and eleven guest accommodations, each with king or queen bed and wood-burning fireplace. Ex-New Yorkers Les Schoof and Ed Butler offer guests deluxe creature comforts and then some. A couple of suites with double whirlpool tubs come with balconies for taking in the surroundings. Laura Ashley wallpapers and fabrics are among the stylish decorative accents. The old Schoolhouse building behind the inn has two recently renovated suites. We were happily ensconced in the one upstairs, whose large sitting area with a loveseat and plump chair faced the fireplace and an arched window looking onto Mount Hope. Also available is a two-bedroom Riverview Cottage, and two more cottages were planned to open in 2005. Back in the inn, the wonderful front parlor with large fireplace was designed by Arts and Crafts pioneer Gustav Stickley, the noted furniture maker. Other common areas are a music room with piano and stereo, and a summer sunroom with wicker furniture overlooking the property, where the owners raise llamas and miniature horses. A gazebo next to a small pond behind the inn houses a hot tub. A lavish breakfast is included in the rates.

Excellent dinners are served to inn guests and the public in a charming wing that was once the tavern in Abel Crawford's early White Mountain Hotel – the tavern was moved to this site in the 1920s. The fireplaced dining room, a sunken room that once served as the tavern's stage and a conservatory sun room look onto the pond and gazebo on one side and gardens and Mount Hope on the other. The chef creates a new five-course, prix-fixe menu nightly, but there's always a choice of two appetizers and two soups, three entrées, salad and three desserts. Our leisurely, two-hour dinner began with a couple of masterful soups, two-color tomato and squash and a Creole fish chowder, whose delicacy masked assertive tastes – a phenomenon that held true throughout the meal. Appetizers were Mediterranean goat cheese wrapped in grape leaves and a suave corn custard served on a pool of red bell pepper coulis. Roast chicken breast topped with crispy prosciutto and grilled rib lamb chops with herbed mint sauce followed. Perfect mixed green salads refreshed the palate for a couple of exceptional desserts, bread pudding with a spiced peach sauce and a cornmeal peach tart with ginger crème anglaise.

(603) 374-6131 or (800) 866-6131. Fax (603) 374-6168. www.notchland.com. Seven rooms, six suites and three cottages with private baths. Doubles, $195. Suites, $230 to $260. Add $50 for foliage and holidays.

Prix-fixe, $35; $40 to $45 for the public. Dinner by reservation, Tuesday-Sunday at 7.

Crawford Notch State Park, Route 302, Harts Location.

Crawford Notch is a six-mile-long, rugged mountain valley wilderness that angles through the heart of the White Mountains. The headwaters of the Saco River form in the notch, where Abel Crawford left his legacy. A plaque marks the site of the Willey House, immortalized by Nathaniel Hawthorne in his short story about a real-life tragedy in 1826. The Willey family fled their home in fear of an advancing avalanche. The avalanche divided above their homestead and spared the structure, but the seven who fled were killed in the onslaught.

Tumbling through the notch are a number of picturesque waterfalls accessible by trail. **Arethusa Falls** has the highest single drop of any waterfall in New Hampshire, and the 1.3-mile trail to the falls passes several attractive smaller cascades. Near the Willey House site, an easy one-mile round trip leads to **Ripley Falls,** where inviting swimming holes have formed at the top of the cascades. Other swimming holes are found just off the highway in the Saco River.

Bartlett and Glen

Tiny Glen is the access point from the south for Jackson and Pinkham Notch on the east side of the Presidential Range and Bretton Woods and Crawford Notch on the west side.

The major presence in Bartlett is the **Attitash Bear Peak Ski Area** and related ventures.

Heritage-New Hampshire and **Storyland** are side-by-side destinations in Glen. The former lets visitors walk through stage sets in which dioramas, costumed guides and talking figures depict 30 events in state history. Storyland is a fairytale village with buildings, themed rides and performances for children. Nearby is the **Grand Manor,** a museum of antique automobiles.

Lodging and Dining

The Bernerhof, Route 302, Box 240, Glen 03838.

This turreted and gabled Victorian began life in the 1880s as Pleasant Valley Hall, a way-station for travelers on their way through Crawford Notch to the Mount Washington Hotel. It took on a Swiss name and something of a European ambiance in the 1950s and became a restaurant destination with upgraded accommodations in the last two decades. Now under new owners for only the third time in 50 years, it offers a variety of lodgings beside busy Route 302. Three rooms in a recent addition feature kingsize brass beds and jacuzzi tubs in window alcoves, where you can gaze at the stars as you soak. Rooms that formerly shared baths were converted into two-room suites with sofabeds in the sitting rooms and more jacuzzis. All nine accommodations now have private baths, six with jacuzzis. One suite includes a sauna. Guests have use of a second-floor sitting room with cable TV and VCR. They can walk to a secluded swimming hole in summer. A full breakfast is included in the rates.

The main floor is devoted to things culinary, including the Taste of the Mountains Cooking School, an old-Swiss-turned-contemporary-American restaurant called **The Rare Bar Bistro** and a convivial lounge called the **Black Bear Pub.** Chefs Scott and Teresa Stearns, who met in culinary school, lease the premises and retained a touch of the past with holdovers like cheese fondue and wiener schnitzel.

But the couple have broadened the horizons to appeal to a more adventurous clientele, the kind who appreciate a five-course tasting menu that changes nightly. Otherwise, dinner might start with a rich lobster, corn and smoked bacon risotto, rabbit "coq au vin" or a warm duck salad with a sherry-truffle vinaigrette. Typical entrées are oven-roasted haddock with brown butter-citrus sauce, seared scallops on a fresh pea risotto and applejack-glazed venison served on wild rice cakes. Desserts could be flourless chocolate cake with coconut sorbet and warm apple galette with caramel sauce and vanilla ice cream. Meals are served in a warren of dining rooms amidst elegant mirrored walls, beamed ceilings, crisp white linens, a piano and a Swiss stove. The casual pub has an oak-paneled bar and an appealing light menu, with more than 90 beers from micro-breweries.

(603) 383-9132 or (800) 548-8007. www.bernerhofinn.com. Seven rooms and two suites with private baths. Doubles, $99 to $199.

Rare Bear, (603) 383-4414. www.rarebearbistro.com. Entrées, $22 to $29; pub, $12 to $19. Dinner, Tuesday-Sunday 6 to 9, pub 5 to 9:30.

The Red Apple Inn, Route 302, Glen 03838.

Just a short path away through the pines and birches from the Bernerhof is The Red Apple, a nice-looking motel. New Bernerhof owners George and June Phillips bought the neighboring property as well in 2003. Here they offer sixteen motel units and a suite. The property includes picnic tables and a barbecue grill, and shares a backyard pool and playground with the Bernerhof. An expanded continental breakfast is included in the rates.

(603) 383-9680 or (800) 826-3591. www.theredappleinn.com. Sixteen rooms and one suite with private baths. Doubles, $124 to $139.

The White Mountain Hotel and Resort, West Side Road, Box 1828, North Conway 03860.

Nicely located beneath Whitehorse and Cathedral Ledges in a scenic mountain setting at Hales Location is this low-profile small hotel. It's away from the fray in North Conway and closer to Glen, surrounded by the White Mountain National Forest and directly adjacent to Echo Lake State Park. Rooms in the three-story hotel come with mountain views as well as TV and coffeemaker. The property includes a nine-hole golf course, tennis court, a high-tech fitness center and Finnish saunas. The outdoor pool is heated for use year-round. The circular **Ledges Dining Room,** known for its $24.95 Friday night seafood buffet and the all-you-can-eat $15.95 Sunday brunch, offers views of gardens and mountains. The updated American menu ranges from the signature Atlantic citrus salmon to filet mignon and veal oscar.

(603) 356-7100 or (800) 533-6301. www.whitemountainhotel.com. Sixty-nine rooms and eleven suites. Rates, EP. Doubles, $169 to $219. Suites, $209 to $259. Off-season, doubles $79 to $149, suites $89 to $199.

Entrées, $17.95 to $24.95. Dinner nightly, 5:30 to 9. Sunday brunch, 10 to 1:30.

Red Parka Pub, Route 302, Glen.

This legendary steakhouse is the perfect spot for après-ski, from the "wild and crazy bar" with a wall of license plates from across the country (the more outrageous the better) to the "Skiboose," a 1914 flanger car that pushed snow off the railroad tracks and now is a cozy dining area for private parties. Somehow the rest of this vast place remains dark and intimate, done up in red and blue colors, red candles and ice cream-parlor chairs. A canopied garden patio offers outdoor dining in summer.

The menu, which comes inside the Red Parka Pub Tonight newspaper, features hearty steaks, barbecued ribs, teriyakis and combinations thereof, and homemade desserts like mud pie and Indian pudding. Start with nachos, Buffalo wings, spudskins or spare ribs. Snack from the soup and salad bar. Or go all out on prime rib or a 22-ounce porterhouse steak. The full menu is offered in the downstairs pub.

(603) 383-4344. www.redparkapub.com. Entrées, $10.95 to $29.95. Dinner nightly, 3:30 to 10.

Jackson

Drive through the old red covered bridge into Jackson and you enter a different world – a world isolated from the hubbub and congestion of the lower Mount Washington Valley. It's an upland valley of pristine air, scenic beauty, and peace and quiet, surrounded on all sides by mountains tiptoeing toward the mighty peak.

One of the nation's earliest year-round destination resorts, Jackson is a village of spirited tradition and pride, from the local book based on recipes used in Jackson's early lodges to the Jackson Resort Association's claim that "nowhere else in the world will you find a more concentrated area of diverse recreational opportunities."

Hikes and Drives. For more than a century, visitors have been "strolling the mile," a mile-long village loop around Jackson. The **"Village Mile"** is one of nine walks and hikes outlined in a handy guide published by the Jackson Resort Association. A good overview is offered by the **Five-Mile Circuit Drive** up Route 16B into the mountains east of Jackson, a loop worth driving both directions for different perspectives. Look for spectacular glimpses of Mount Washington, and stop for a picnic, a swim or a stroll through the picturesque cascades called Jackson Falls, part of the Wildcat River just above the village.

Golfers can play the scenic **Wentworth Golf Resort** eighteen-hole course, (603) 383-9641, whose fairways and greens wind their way around the village of Jackson and add tranquility and open space to the village's character. You cross a miniature covered bridge to reach the seventh hole. Greens fees are a bargain $20 to $45. Golf is also available in the upland valley spread out in a nine-hole course in front of the Eagle Mountain House, (603) 363-9111 or (800) 966-5779, a short drive from Jackson up that part of the Circuit Loop called Carter Notch Road.

┌─*Great Trails and a Run for Your Money*─────

Jackson Ski Touring Foundation, Route 16A, Jackson.

Jackson is considered the best place in the East and one of the four best places in the world for cross-country skiing. That's due in large part to the efforts of the non-profit Jackson Ski Touring Foundation, founded in 1972 and now offering 100 miles of well-groomed and marked trails starting in the village of Jackson and heading across public and private lands into the White Mountain National Forest. They interlace the village and link restaurants and inns, as well as connecting with 40 miles of Appalachian Mountain Club trails in Pinkham Notch. Cross-country lessons are available, as are ski and snowshoe rentals. For an unusual and exhilarating run, cross-country skiers can take the gondola to the summit of Wildcat and tour downhill via a twelve-mile trail to the village of Jackson 3,200 feet below.

(603) 383-9355 or (800) 927-6697. www.jacksonxc.org. Open daily, 8 to 4:30, December-March. Rates: Adults $15, children under 10 free.

Although known for cross-country touring, the area offers plenty of downhill skiing. Looming across Pinkham Notch from Mount Washington is **Wildcat,** a big mountain with plenty of challenge, a 2,112-foot vertical drop from its 4,100-foot summit, top-to-bottom snowmaking, five chairlifts and a gondola. Summer visitors enjoy riding the **Wildcat Gondola,** a 25-minute round trip to the summit to see some of the Northeast's most spectacular scenery. Gondolas leave daily, mid-June to mid-October; adults $9.50, children $4.50.

Closer to Jackson, **Black Mountain** is half Wildcat's height and far smaller in scope. Its sunny exposure and low-key, self-contained nature appeal to families.

Lodging and Dining

The Inn at Thorn Hill, Thorn Hill Road, Box A, Jackson 03846.

The Presidential Range is on full view from this handsome yellow hilltop structure, designed in 1895 by architect Stanford White and grandly reborn in 2003 following a major fire. The rebuilt inn was reconfigured in an L-shape and enlarged to nearly double the size of the original, so its deeper north side now faces a broad sweep of mountains to include the weather station atop Mount Washington. The main floor holds a library, a 60-seat dining room, a 40-seat lounge in a newly added turret and a grand wrap-around veranda. In the basement are an exercise room and spa facility and a private dining room in a 10,000-bottle wine cellar. Owners Jim and Ibby Cooper also raised the bar in the inn's sixteen large guest rooms and suites on the second and third floors. Each has a king or queen bed, sitting area, gas fireplace, concealed TV with DVD player and private telephone line with data port. Bathrooms gleam with white tile and marble vanities. Each has a two-person jacuzzi tub and separate shower, and some have steam showers. All are sumptuously furnished with antiques and oriental rugs. Sachet pillows are scattered about the plump beds, and there are many special touches. Tuckerman's Suite is stunning with a kingsize bed and a two-way fireplace also visible in the living room, which has a window seat and a wet bar with mini-refrigerator. The Mount Jefferson has a corner fireplace with a TV above and a bath with a jacuzzi tub in the window for taking in the view. Before the fire, the Coopers had added a deck and an outdoor hot tub to the carriage house, which shed its earlier ski-chalet ambiance. Five rooms and a suite were redone in a North Country look with Adirondack furnishings and new baths (four with jacuzzis). We enjoyed a getaway in one of three outlying cottages with gas fireplaces and double jacuzzis. The Notch View was a two-room affair equipped with a queensize bed and a front porch that caught the evening breeze. Breakfast, served formally on white china, lives up to the inn's culinary reputation. The main course could be the inn's spicy chicken hash with poached eggs and peppered hollandaise sauce or grand marnier french toast with peach conserve, both excellent.

Some of New Hampshire's best meals are served in the country-elegant dining room, a beauty in mauve and white, relocated for a northern exposure to take in the view of Mount Washington. Chef Richard Schmitt, the owners' son-in-law, and their daughter, his wife McKaella, the pastry chef, offer contemporary regional fare with international flair. Their seasonal menu starts with the likes of warm lobster vichyssoise, a giant prawn pad thai with wasabi caviar, and pheasant enrobed with white asparagus and dried cherries in port dressing. Main courses might be sake-marinated halibut on crispy soba noodles, paella, Peking duck and grilled veal chop on foraged mushrooms and arugula. Richard's version of surf and turf – called "steak and potato two ways" – pairs Hawaiian tuna and New York sirloin. McKaella's dessert repertoire is full of surprises: a honey-roasted pear with gorgonzola-dulce ice cream and a balsamic syrup, sautéed chioga beets with clotted cream, and blue Hawaiian sorbet with toasted coconut. Her "warm chocolate cake sundae" features root beer ice cream. A tapas and bento box menu is offered in the expanded pub/lounge. There also are a chef's table for eight in the kitchen for special culinary occasions, as well as a dining area for two to twenty-four in the showy wine cellar.

(603) 383-4242 or (800) 289-8990. Fax (603) 383-8062. www.innatthornhill.com. Seventeen rooms, five suites and three cottages with private baths. Rates, MAP. Doubles, $195 to $360, suites and cottages $320 to $360. Foliage and holidays, $245 to $410..

Entrées, $22.95 to $29.95. Dinner nightly, 6 to 9. Lounge menu, 5 to 10.

The Wentworth, Route 16A, Jackson 03846.

Built in 1869, the Wentworth was the grand hotel of Jackson at the turn of the last century when Jackson had 24 lodging establishments. It remains so today, its accommodations and resort facilities having been upgraded by Swiss-born hotelier Fritz Koeppel and his wife Diana, an area native. The turreted, yellow and green Victorian structure plus annexes and outbuildings contain a total of 55 guest rooms. Plushly carpeted halls lead to twenty spacious rooms on the second and third floors of the main building. All are beautifully restored in different shapes and sizes, most with refinished Victorian clawfoot tubs with showers and French Provincial furnishings. Fireplaces were added in nine rooms, three with jacuzzi tubs. Top of the line is the ground-floor Thornycroft Suite with king canopy bed, Victorian settee in front of the fireplace, and a three-room bath area with marble floors, a vanity with wet bar and a jacuzzi beside a fireplace. Several outbuildings have been upgraded as well. There are three new suites in the Arden, each with kingsize sleigh bed, whirlpool tub and fireplace, and four in the Sunnyside with similar amenities, except for one with a hot tub on its balcony. Other suites in the Amster emerged around an inner courtyard with a hot tub. The eighteen-hole golf course behind the hotel is part of the Jackson Ski Touring Center layout in the winter. Other facilities include a pool and clay tennis courts.

Regional American cuisine is featured in the hotel's candlelit dining room, its decor enhanced with sponge-painted walls, upholstered French Provincial chairs and skirted tables with floral prints. The concise dinner menu opens with appetizers like scallops ceviche with crispy tortilla chips and duck confit tartlet with wilted pepper cress salad. Main courses range from pan-seared halibut with tomato aioli to herb-crusted Australian rack of lamb with cider reduction. Dessert could be peaches and cream pie or blueberry napoleons served on vanilla anglaise.

(603) 383-9700 or (800) 637-0013. Fax (603) 383-4265. www.thewentworth.com. Fifty-five rooms and suites with private baths. Rates, MAP. Doubles, $185 to $325, foliage and holidays $215 to $355.

Entrées, $23 to $28. Dinner nightly, 6 to 9 or 10. Closed in April and November.

Eagle Mountain House, Carter Notch Road (Route 16B), Jackson 03846.

Good values and resort amenities are offered at this grand old hotel off by itself above Jackson Village. A picturesque row of high-backed rockers is lined up on the veranda that's as long as a football field, as they have been since the hotel opened in 1879. The interior was restored in 1986 into a 92-room hotel and condominium center run by Colony Hotels & Resorts. Although the establishment has an institutional air and caters to the group trade, there's no denying the location – up in the mountains, facing a beautiful nine-hole golf course and a colorful little pool and tennis court. Many rooms have sitting areas with sturdy mountain furniture, TVs hidden in armoires and queensize beds. Off a rambling front lobby are the **Eagle Landing Tavern,** a health club, the **Veranda Café** and a huge vintage dining room called **Highfields.** The fare ranges from baked haddock with lobster sauce and filet of ostrich to venison sauté and rack of lamb.

(603) 383-9111 or (800) 966-5779. Fax (603) 383-0854. www.eaglemt.com. Seventy-two rooms and 24 suites with private baths. Rates, EP. Doubles $89 to $159. Suites, $109 to $199. Entrées, $14.95 to $24.95. Dinner nightly from 6.

A Victorian Mountain Fantasyland

Nestlenook Farm Resort, Dinsmore Road, Box Q, Jackson 03846.

Gingerbread and romance reach the ultimate in this 65-acre Victorian fantasyland built around the oldest house in Jackson. Local condominium developers Robert and Nancy Cyr transformed a rustic B&B specializing in horseback riding into a deluxe playground brimming with nostalgia. The focus of the venture is the Victorian B&B. Behind front doors of beveled glass lie a lovely living room with beamed ceiling and fireplace, a tin-ceilinged breakfast room, an intimate taproom and a bird cage full of finches in the lobby. Upstairs are five bedrooms and two suites, each named for the Jackson artist whose paintings hang in the room. All are decorated to the hilt and have two-person therapy spa tubs and 19th-century parlor stoves or fireplaces. The prized William Paskell Room has a hand-carved four-poster kingsize bed with a crocheted canopy, cherry and mahogany furnishings and french doors opening onto a small balcony. Complimentary wine and cheese are offered in the afternoon. A low-fat country breakfast is served in the dining room at seven tables set with high-back chairs and fine English china. The landscaped grounds are outfitted with statuary, gardens and even a big pond into which a waterfall trickles beneath a curving bridge. Music is piped into a huge gazebo, complete with a fireplace, park benches, a ceiling fan and a red sleigh in the middle. A riverside chapel (for making or renewing marriage vows), a heated pool, sleigh or horse-drawn trolley rides and daily massages are among the offerings. Nestlenook Farm's new Victorian Village includes twelve villas containing deluxe rooms and suites.

(603) 383-9443 or (800) 659-9443. Fax (603) 383-4515. www.luxurymountaingetaways.com. Five rooms and two suites with private baths. Foliage and winter: doubles $190 to $320, suites $240 to $544. April to mid-September and mid-October to mid-December: doubles $145 to $235, suites $195 to $408. Off-season: doubles $125 to $220, suites $175 to $384.

Snowflake Inn, Main Street, Jackson 03846.

Quite a presence in the center of town – and rather un-Jackson-like – is this inn built for adult getaways on a prime piece of property that formerly housed the famed Jack Frost Shop and the Jackson Ski Touring Foundation. The shop went bankrupt, the foundation relocated and the six-acre parcel was eventually acquired by Sue and Gary Methot, who owned three motels in Hampton Beach before moving to the mountains for this venture. They built a long and handsome, two-story structure that includes a large lobby, an indoor jetted spa that looks like a small swimming pool and twenty hotel-style guest accommodations. The Snowflake is mainly about the latest in rooms – or suites, as they are called here. The typical one has a small, window-less sitting area inside the door, separated by a bathroom from the kingsize bedroom beyond. Each has a flick-on gas fireplace, flat-screen TV and

DVD/VCR player, a two-person whirlpool tub in the bedroom and a shower with two heads and two seats in the bathroom. Spa services are available in the privacy of one's guest room as part of the inn's spa packages. The two-story lobby includes a soaring stone fireplace and a second-floor billiards area. The lobby also serves as the site for evening coffee and cookies and morning continental breakfast.

(603) 383-8250 or (888) 383-1020. www.snowflakeinnjackson.com. Twenty suites with private baths. Doubles, $175 to $350 summer and winter, $165 to $325 rest of year.

The Crowes' Nest, Thorn Mountain Road, Box 427, Jackson 03846.

After traveling around the world on business, Christine and Myles Crowe settled here to pamper B&B guests with what she calls "refined country" charm in a house and restored barn on a hillside a stone's throw above Jackson Village. They offer two rooms in the main house, where guests enjoy a living room with a grand piano, a dining room and a sun porch with a view, where breakfast is served. For their premier accommodations, the Crowes gutted a barn that was built in 1922 entirely from wood cut on the property. They saved floors and rebuilt the interior from scratch. A two-story high foyer/common room with a gas fireplace leads to three rooms and two suites, all comfortably furnished with antiques and artworks from around the world. The main floor holds a large premier room with kingsize bed and fireplace and two rooms with queen beds and sunporch sitting areas. The second floor consists of two premier suites with fireplaces, whirlpool tubs, balconies and enclosed sun porches that double as sitting rooms or extra bedrooms for children. Breakfast is a three-course treat, as you'd expect from a woman who published a 270-page cookbook entitled *Friends and Family,* written for her career-bound daughters and distributed privately to those for whom the book was named. Specialties include florentine frittata and a baked apple pancake she calls a johnny jump-up. Pears in mascarpone custard, cheddar cheese and chive biscuits and specially blended chicory coffee might accompany.

(603) 383-8913 or (800) 511-8383. Fax (603) 383-8241. www.crowesnest.net. Seven rooms with private baths. Doubles, $105 to $175, foliage $135 to $225.

Carter Notch Inn, Carter Notch Road (Route 16B), Box 269, Jackson 03846.

The century-old owners' residence for the Eagle Mountain House hotel has been converted into a personal B&B by hotelier Jim Dunwell and his wife Lynda. A light and airy look prevails in seven comfortable guest rooms of various sizes and bed configurations, ranging from queensize to double with twin. Quilts, straw hats, dried flowers, oak and wicker are the norm. Two with fireplaces, double jacuzzi tubs and balconies are most in demand. There's a rear deck with a communal hot tub off the second floor. The main floor holds an oversize living room and a dining room with a table for eight overlooking the wraparound porch. Jim serves an elaborate breakfast that might culminate in grand-marnier french toast one day, scrambled eggs with brie and mushrooms in puff pastry the next. The location is quiet and the view from the wraparound front porch is of a golf course and mountains.

(603) 383-9630 or (800) 794-9434. www.carternotchinn.com. Seven rooms with private baths. Doubles, $99 to $159, foliage $129 to $199.

Thompson House Eatery, Route 16A at 16, Jackson.

A red farmhouse dating from the early 19th century holds an expanded restaurant full of cozy rooms and alcoves and floral-bedecked canopied patios. "Handcrafted food presented in an artful manner" has been the byword since 1977 of chef-owner

Larry Baima, who offers original fare with Italian and oriental influences. He's created so many unusual sandwiches and salads that, legend has it, he had no room on the menu for hamburgers or french fries. A frequent dinner offering is "Baked Popeye," a remarkable spinach casserole with mushrooms, bacon and cheese and an option of scallops. Other artful choices could be cinnamon bay shrimp and scallops with ginger and grilled lamb chops on Mediterranean pesto garnished with feta cheese. The ginger-cured pork tenderloin and a special of scallops with spinach, plum tomato sauce and ziti made a fine dinner by candlelight on the rear deck enveloped in flowers. Swiss chocolate truffle and wild berry crumble are great desserts.

(603) 383-9341. www.thompsonhouseeatery.com. Entrées, $18.95 to $26.95. Lunch, Wednesday-Sunday 11:30 to 3:30. Dinner, Wednesday-Monday 5:30 to 9 or 10. Closed in April and November.

Wildcat Inn and Tavern, Route 16A, Jackson.

Some of the best food in the area is what this inn is best known for. The old front porch had to be converted into dining space to handle the overflow from the original two dining rooms, as cozy and homey as can be. There's also patio dining at tables scattered around the prize-winning gardens, an idyllic setting in summer. The exceptional cream of vegetable soup is chock full of fresh vegetables; that and half a reuben sandwich made a hearty lunch. We also liked the delicate spinach and onion quiche, served with a garden salad dressed with creamy dill. Dinner entrées range widely from lasagna to beef oscar. You can get mondo chicken with Italian sausage and apricot brandy, shrimp and scallop scampi and "the extravaganza" – shrimp, lobster and scallops sautéed with vegetables and served with linguini or rice pilaf. Desserts like chocolate silk pie and frozen lemon pie slathered with whipped cream are memorable. A pub menu offers lighter fare. Upstairs on the second and third floors, owners Marty and Pam Sweeney offer fourteen B&B guest rooms (doubles, $109 to $139).

(603) 383-4245 or (800) 228-4245. www.wildcattavern.com. Entrées, $16.95 to $23.95. Lunch daily in season, 11:30 to 3, weekends in winter. Dinner nightly, 6 to 9 or 10. Pub, Sunday-Friday 4 to 9.

Red Fox Bar & Grille, Route 16, Jackson.

"Woodfire grilling" is the theme of the Red Fox, which relocated in 2003 from a building beside the Wentworth Golf Club in Jackson Village to a more visible spot in a huge new lodge-style facility across Route 16 from Jackson's covered bridge. Seasoned woods fire the brick oven beside the main entry, from which come handmade pizzas in countless varieties. Other specialties are pasta dishes, at least eight kinds. Also featured are "woodfire grill specialties," from grilled salmon to baby back ribs to filet mignon. There are sandwiches and burgers, as well as all-American appetizers such as chicken wings and nachos. Prices are down to earth, and the atmosphere is casual in a variety of dining rooms seating 250. They're usually packed for the all-you-can-eat Sunday jazz breakfast buffet – at $6.95 the best bargain around. .

(603) 383-4949. www.redfoxbarandgrille.com. Entrées, $12.95 to $19.95. Lunch, Saturday and Sunday from noon. Dinner nightly, from 4. Sunday breakfast, 7:30 to 1.

FOR MORE INFORMATION: Mount Washington Valley Chamber of Commerce, Box 2300, North Conway, NH 03860, (603) 356-5701 or (800) 367-3364. www.mtwashingtonvalley.org. Jackson Chamber of Commerce, Box 304, Jackson, NH 03846, (603) 383-9356 or (800) 866-3334. www.jacksonnh.com.

Reborn Wentworth by the Sea hotel rises behind Little Harbor Marina at water's edge.

Portsmouth

A Dynamic Past and Present

Settled in 1623, barely three years after the Pilgrims landed at Plymouth Rock, Portsmouth is the third-oldest city in the nation and wears the title proudly. It grew up along the tidal Piscataqua River, whose watery shores produced such a profusion of wild berries that its British founders called their new home Strawbery Banke and their neighborhood Puddle Dock.

The early seaport and shipbuilding center developed around a protected harbor four miles inland from the river's mouth – which prompted its name change in 1653 to Port's-mouth to reflect its growing stature as a port and as the Colonial capital of New Hampshire. Grand residences spread along the harbor from Puddle Dock and their owners' cargo warehouses were reputed to be the tallest buildings in the United States at the time. The ancient houses, restored warehouses, cobblestone streets and soaring church spires cast a patina of history across the heart of town to this day.

Now a small city of 23,000, Portsmouth retains its sense of place as well as its scale. Rather than lose its heritage in the name of urban renewal, Portsmouth preserved the original settlement at Strawbery Banke. More than 45 historic buildings in a ten-acre urban neighborhood comprise an outdoor history museum that calls to visitors to savor the past.

Portsmouth's pride in its past also manifests itself in the six museum homes of the Historic Portsmouth Trail, the creative reuse of old buildings around the harbor, and even the restoration of the old Wentworth by the Sea hotel on the adjacent island of New Castle. The past is present, too, in the rocky Isles of Shoals six miles out to sea.

In this city that knows how to restore and recycle rather than raze, dated buildings like the old Merchants Row warehouses have been converted into retail shops and restaurants. Lofts above downtown storefronts provide the young and entrepreneurial with space for living and for high-tech startups. The Seacoast is now the E-Coast in local lingo. The city is consistently ranked as one of the nation's most livable.

This lively town has a noticeable joie de vivre. You can sense it in its flourishing downtown, virtually unsullied by chain stores, fast-food outlets or traffic lights. You can experience it in its thriving restaurants whose quality and scope surpass those of cities many times its size. You can see it in its lively Seacoast Repertory Theater and new Music Hall. You can feel it in its Prescott Park Arts Festival, the Ceres Street Crafts Fair, the Seacoast Jazz Festival.

Portsmouth's mix of living past and lively present makes for a rewarding getaway.

Seeing and Doing

Most of Portsmouth's attractions are clustered along the riverfront and around the downtown area. Their proximity to each other makes this a good place for walking. The free **Seacoast Trolley,** (603) 743-5777, shuttles people between the key historic sites from July to early September. Board it at Market Square, Strawbery Banke or Prescott Park. Another way to tour is by horse and carriage with **Portsmouth Livery Co.,** (603) 427-0044. The talkative guide, in beard and top hat, adds dimension to the city's history as he gives sightseeing tours for $20 to $40. The tours leave from the Market Square carriage stand from noon into the evening, daily Memorial Day through Labor Day and weekends in the off-season.

Living History

More than 70 points of scenic or historic significance are visible along the **Portsmouth Harbour Trail.** Along the way are ten buildings listed on the National Register, ten national historic landmarks and three homes maintained by the Society for the Preservation of New England Antiquities. The trail is detailed in a 32-page map and guide (available for $2 from the Chamber of Commerce visitor center and the downtown Market Square information kiosk). Marked by bright blue signs, the trail is divided into three loops. One covers the Ceres Street waterfront and another the downtown area south of Market Square. The longest loop covers the historic East Side around Strawbery Banke. Guided walking tours leave from the Market Square information kiosk, Thursday-Monday at 10:30 and 5:30 (Sunday at 1:30 p.m.), July 4 through Columbus Day; adults $8, children $4.

A favorite area is along Ceres Street, site of the wharves and early warehouses lately converted into shops and restaurants. When they're not out guiding ships up the tricky tidal river, red and black tugboats – local icons – may be tied up at the docks. Walk up and around Bow Street to the Strawbery Banke museum complex (see below).

Across Marcy Street is **Prescott Park,** a generally tranquil waterfront retreat graced in summer by showy and prolific flowerbeds. New floral varieties are tested in the formal gardens, a joint venture between the park and the University of New Hampshire's Cooperative Extension Service. Benches are scattered about for taking in the scene and the waterfront activity. The park contains the 1705 Sheafe Warehouse, where John Paul Jones outfitted his warship Ranger. It now houses the **Folk Art Museum**, which has a small boat building exhibit as well as hand-carved mastheads and ship models (open daily in summer, 9 to 6; free). The park is the site for frequent special events, from the month-long Prescott Park Arts Festival to the Seacoast Jazz Festival, the Chowder Fest and the Piscataqua Faire – A Renaissance on the Waterfront. Picnicking is permitted in Prescott Park, but an even better place is **Four Tree Island**, within walking distance of the park. Nearly in the middle of the river, it is reached across a short bridge from the end of Mechanic Street to Pierce Island and then via a causeway. There are picnic tables under shelters, all with views of the water.

SHOPPING. Many of the restored warehouses and chandleries from Portsmouth's early mercantile seaport days now harbor shops and galleries on the ground floor and high-tech startups or residential quarters above. They are concentrated around Market Square and the Merchants Row area along Bow and Ceres streets.

In one of its stores, **Macro Polo Inc.** carries retro-chic gifts, gadgets and inventive children's toys; we were transported back to our childhood while gazing at the assortment of marbles in the window. **Wholly Macro!** stocks handmade Texas boots among its wares. **Macroscopic** struck us as rather New Agey. The colorful glass shown in the prominent windows draws us into **Not Just Mud! Craft Gallery,** which stocks fabulous hand-blown art glass, kaleidoscopes, pottery, jewelry and titanium clocks among its contemporary crafts. **Salamandra Glass Studio** is another favorite of glass lovers. We did some Christmas shopping at the contemporary **N.W. Barrett Gallery**, which carries Sabra Field's woodcuts and fantastic jewelry, glassware, crafts and more. The **Robert Lincoln Levy Gallery,** operated by the New Hampshire Art Association, features fine art produced by New Hampshire artists. **Worldly Goods** purveys birdhouses, oil lamps, interesting baskets and adorable cat pins. The **Paper Patch** is the shop for whimsical cards. Among its treasures, **Les Cadeaux** stocks exotic bath salts, fancy stationery, boxes of decorated sugar cubes from Kentucky, chocolate spoons to dip in hot chocolate, lovely china casseroles with different fruits on top for handles, and preserves and mustards from Le Cordon Bleu in France. You'd have to see them to believe the high-heeled shoes made of papier-mâché and trimmed with jewelry at **Gallery 33;** we also liked the hand-carved whimsical animals here. Wearing a T-shirt urging "squeeze me, crush me, make me wine," jovial proprietor David Campbell brings a sense of fun along with expertise to his wines, specialty foods and gift baskets at the **Ceres Street Wine Merchants.** More good art and gift destinations are **Lovell Designs, Pierce Gallery, The Blue Frog** and **City & Country** home accessories. **The Cultured Garden** is "where home and garden meet." **The Gardener's Cottage,** a charming cottage with its own pocket garden at the foot of State Street beside Prescott Park, specializes in tools and accessories for the garden enthusiast. **Strawbery Banke's Museum Shop** at the Dunaway Store on Marcy Street is a good gift shop. **Strawbery Banke's** working crafts shops offer the wares of potters, a cabinetmaker, a weaver, and dories made in the boat shed.

Upscale shops are moving out Congress Street. Look for the block containing **Magnifico** (hand-crafted imports), **Celtic Crossing, Runner's Alley, Chaise Lounge** ("distinctive furnishings") and **Nahcotta** ("cool goods").

Historic Restorations

Strawbery Banke, Marcy Street, Portsmouth.

Billed as "an American original," this walk-through museum is the careful restoration of one of the nation's oldest neighborhoods – Puddle Dock, the waterfront site where Portsmouth was settled. Saved from urban redevelopment in the 1950s, the site offers a glimpse into the everyday lives of the early settlers and others who left their mark on Portsmouth's history. Some 45 structures across ten acres date from the late 1600s to the 1950s and depict four centuries of cultural and architectural change. Ten have been restored and furnished to particular periods to show Strawbery Banke's collection of local arts and furniture and how the occupants lived. Among them is the 19th-century home of author Thomas Bailey Aldrich, the first house in Portsmouth — and one of the first in the country — to be restored to a specific period in the past. The 1795 Drisco House epitomizes the museum's mission to show how life in urban neighborhoods evolves and how houses adapt to the times. Half the house shows the domestic setting of its first occupants in the 1700s. The other half shows the lives of the last families to live there in the 1950s.

Six of the structures have simply been preserved and only their exteriors can be viewed. Still others serve as working crafts shops (independent of the museum, potters, coopers and boat builders are earning their living as well as re-enacting history). Others are used for educational exhibits including archaeology, architectural styles and construction techniques. Award-winning period gardens show the connection between inside and outside living spaces, and represent a living history of the New England landscape. Paul Revere, George Washington, Daniel Webster, John Hancock, John Paul Jones all visited here. Yet these are not all homes of the rich or famous, but rather of ordinary people. The mix is one of its most compelling factors.

(603) 433-1100. www.strawberybanke.org. Open May-October, Monday-Saturday 10 to 5, Sunday noon to 5; adults $15, children $10, families $35. Open November-April for 90-minute guided walking tours on the hour, Thursday-Saturday 10 to 2 and Sunday noon to 2; adults $10, children $5, families $25. Closed in January.

Portsmouth Historic House Associates. Six of Portsmouth's restored house museums are open individually under different auspices and linked by a walking tour. Considered the one not to miss is the 1763 **Moffatt-Ladd House,** a replica of an English manor house located at 154 Market St., just above the Ceres Street restaurants and shops. It is set amid terraced English gardens on a lawn that once swept down to the harbor. Rooms on three floors display 18th-century furnishings and architectural details. The 1716 **Warner House,** 150 Daniel St., is perhaps the finest illustration of a brick urban mansion from the 18th century left in New England. The 1760 **Wentworth-Gardner House,** 50 Mechanic St., is a perfect example of the Georgian style. Once owned by New York's Metropolitan Museum, it narrowly escaped being torn apart and rebuilt in Central Park. The Portsmouth Historical Society Museum displays its collections at the 1758 **John Paul Jones House,** 43 Middle St., where the "father of the U.S. Navy" resided while supervising construction of his sloop Ranger (see below). George Washington described the imposing Georgian-style **Governor John Langdon House** (1784), 143 Pleasant St., as "the finest house in Portsmouth." The Federal-style **Rundlet-May House** (1807), 364 Middle St., reflects varying lifestyles of four generations of the same merchant family until 1971. Most houses are open six or seven days a week from June to mid-October and charge $5 or $6 each. Admission to one house entitles the participant to a "Portsmouth Passport" good for $1 off the admission price at all other member sites.

A seventh structure, the 1664 **Jackson House** at 76 Northwest St., is the oldest surviving wood frame house in northern New England. On a two-acre site on North Mill Pond, it is open the first Saturday of the month, June-October.

The **Ranger Trail,** a self-guided walking tour, traces the footsteps of John Paul Jones and the sites linked to the naval hero and his sloop-of-war Ranger, the first ship to carry America's new Stars and Stripes flag into battle overseas. His raid on English ports in 1778 helped win foreign support for the Revolution and gave credibility to the fledgling Continental Navy. The trail details fifteen sites, from the John Paul Jones House to the Sheafe Warehouse in Prescott Park to a couple of taverns in Strawbery Banke. The trail is sponsored by the local Ranger Foundation, (603) 433-3221, which is restoring the vessel.

Wentworth Coolidge Mansion, 375 Little Harbor Road, Portsmouth.

This enormous yellow house dating to 1720 served as the residence for New Hampshire's first royal governor. It overlooks Little Harbor, just off Route 1-A on the way to New Castle. The tour of the 42-room structure includes a look at the only French stewing kitchen in New England, built for the governor's French chef. Visitors may explore the grounds and shoreline to see evidence of a 19th-century swimming pool, remnants of the Wentworths' wharf along the seawall and the oldest purple lilacs in North America, imported in the 1750s. Parking and admission to the grounds are free and picnicking is encouraged.

(603) 436-6607. Open mid-May through Labor Day, Wednesday-Saturday 10 to 3, Sunday 1 to 4; Saturday and Sunday to mid-October. Guided tour, $3.

Out to the Seacoast

New Hampshire claims America's smallest seacoast – a mere eighteen miles – but makes the most of it. The southern half around Seabrook and Hampton Beach are chock-a-block beachy and touristy. The northern half around Rye and New Castle are less developed and more refined, as in affluent.

The Town of New Castle, quaint islands reached by short bridges and causeways east of Portsmouth, are part of the original settlement established in 1623. The meandering roads and treed residential properties, many with water frontage, mix contemporary-style houses with those of days gone by. You can view a couple of forts that were built to defend Portsmouth harbor and visit the seacoast park at **Great Island Common,** where there are waterfront picnic tables, a playground and views of the Isles of Shoals ten miles offshore. If you can't stay, at least take a look at the lately restored Wentworth-by-the-Sea, a majestic seaside resort hotel if ever there was one.

Fort Constitution, a state historic site beside the U.S. Coast Guard station off Route 1-B in New Castle, originated in the early 1600s but reflects today the Revolutionary, War of 1812 and Civil War periods. A 1774 raid by local patriots was the first overt act against England and predated the Revolution's outbreak by four months. Beside the fort is the Fort Point Lighthouse and just offshore, the Whaleback Lighthouse. The fort is open daily year-round, 10 to 5; free.

Fort Stark, Wild Rose Lane, off Route 1-B, New Castle, is another state historic site. The fort dates to 1746, but reflects its service in protecting the Portsmouth Naval Shipyard in World War II. A walking trail traverses the ten-acre fort site and yields spectacular ocean views. It's open weekends and holidays 10 to 5, May-October; free.

Odiorne Point State Park, 570 Ocean Blvd (Route 1-A) in Rye, is part of the first settlement in New Hampshire in 1623. The largest undeveloped stretch of the state's seacoast, the 137-acre park at the northernmost point of the state's seacoast harbors walking trails, picnic tables by the ocean and vestiges of Fort Dearborn, built for coastal defense during World War II. Trails lead through seven distinct coastal habitats.

Located in the park is the recently renovated and expanded **Seacoast Science Center,** which offers exhibits on the area's natural history and nature programs. Visitors touch tidal pool creatures in indoor touch tanks and watch ocean fish swim in the 1,000-gallon Gulf of Maine tank. Exhibits portray nearly four centuries of local history.

Park: (603) 436-7406. Admission $3, children under 12, free. Open daily, 8 to dusk. Science Center: (603) 436-8043. www.seacentr.org. Open daily 10 to 5, April-October; Saturday-Monday 10 to 5, rest of year. Adults $3, children $1.

Fuller Gardens, 10 Willow Ave., North Hampton.

One of the last remaining estate gardens of the early 20th century, these were part of Runnymede-by-the-Sea, erected by former Massachusetts Gov. Alvan T. Fuller, whose family members still live in nearby mansions. The house was razed in 1961, but the grounds and gardens – designed in the early 1930s and typical of Colonial Revival estate gardens – are maintained for visitors. An extensive tulip display opens the season in early May. Wisteria, azaleas and rhododendrons in a Japanese garden follow. Two thousand rose bushes burst into bloom in late June and some continue through October. Perennials and annuals are interspersed among fountains and statuary, all within sculpted hedges. A greenhouse contains tropical and desert plants.

(603) 964-5414. www.fullergardens.org. Open mid-May to mid-October, daily 10 to 5:30. Adults $6, children $2.

The Isles of Shoals. Six miles off the coast from Rye is this group of nine stark, rocky islands beloved by naturalists and bird-watchers. Charted by Capt. John Smith when he sailed past in 1614, the barren islands originally drew European fishermen for their "shoals" or schools of fish. A large fishing community thrived here during Colonial times. By the mid-1800s, resort hotels entertained famous guests on the two largest islands, Appledore and Star. Today, Star Island is home to a conference center operated by the Unitarian-Universalist and Congregational churches, whose week-long summer retreats are based at the Victorian-era Oceanic Hotel. Appledore is home to the Shoals Marine Laboratory, North America's largest undergraduate marine field station, as well as celebrated poetess Celia Thaxter's cottage and garden. Except for a few summer cottages and homes of lobstering families, the Isles are populated mostly by a host of sea birds and marine life.

On Wednesdays in summer, **Celia Thaxter's Garden Tour** offers the only public access to Appledore Island. The Victorian poetess, daughter of a lighthouse keeper at White Island, was known for the cottage and garden that inspired her famous little book, "An Island Garden." Up to 50 tour participants are shuttled to Appledore Island from neighboring Star Island, now reached aboard vessels operated by Eastman's Docks, River Street, Seabrook Beach (603) 474-3461. Reservations are required through the Shoals Marine Laboratory, (607) 255-3717, run by Cornell University in cooperation with the University of New Hampshire.

For years, the public accessed Star Island on daytrips via the Isles of Shoals Steamship Co., a family-owned passenger ferry service that shuttled conference guests and staff. That service was ended in 2005 in part because of homeland security concerns. The Star Island Corp., which owns Star and Appledore islands, made arrangements to ferry conference participants only. The only public access as this edition went to press was a chartered harbor cruise out to Star Island for a brief walking tour and dinner at the historic Oceanic Hotel, arranged by Northeast Charter, (207) 439-0990. As in the past, two-hour sightseeing cruises around the Isles aboard a lobster boat are scheduled daily at noon and 2:30 in July and August by **Island Cruises,** Rye Harbor State Marina, Rye, (602) 964-6446.

From Portsmouth, sightseeing cruises out to the Isles are run by two outfits:

Isles of Shoals Steamship Co., 315 Market St., Portsmouth.

The 348-passenger replica Victorian steamship M/V Thomas Laighton gives a variety of excursions. Among them are three-hour cruises twice daily in summer out through the harbor and around the Isles of Shoals. They are the traditional lighthouse and historical cruises, the only difference being they no longer stop at Star Island. The harbor portion of the tour passes the nation's oldest working naval yard and its closed castle-like prison called "the Alcatraz of the East," five forts and three lighthouses.

(603) 431-5500 or (800) 441-4620. www.islesofshoals.com. Cruises daily at 9:55 and 1:55, mid-June to Labor Day; fewer in spring and fall; hours vary. Isles/Harbor tours, adults $24, children $14.

Portsmouth Harbor Cruises, Ceres Street Dock, Portsmouth.

The 49-passenger Heritage takes passengers on cruises around the fourteen islands of the harbor, up the Piscataqua River as far as Dover and Great Bay, along the shore at sunset and, three times a week, out to the Isles of Shoals. The basic 90-minute harbor tour shows nearly 400 years of history from the area's settlement in 1623 to the harbor's modern-day role in the nation's economy and defense.

(603) 436-8084 or (800) 776-0915. www.portsmouthharbor.com. Harbor cruises, mid-June to mid-September, daily at 10 and 3, also Saturday-Monday at noon and Friday-Sunday at 4:30; adults $14, children $9. Isles of Shoals cruises in summer leave Wednesday-Friday at noon; adults $18, children $10. Hours vary in spring and fall.

Where to Stay

All kinds of motor inns and motels of the chain variety are available around the Portsmouth Traffic Circle west of town beside Interstate 95. Those who seek a complete Portsmouth experience are advised to stay in or near downtown.

Downtown Locations

Sheraton Harborside Portsmouth, 250 Market St., Portsmouth 03801.

A prime downtown location is claimed by this red-brick hotel and conference center of recent vintage that curves around a circular courtyard and blends into the historic architecture along the Portsmouth waterfront. Mahogany furniture enhances the airy lobby, and a curving stairway sweeps gracefully to the second-floor function rooms. Guest rooms are typical hotel style, with kingsize or two double beds. Some yield views of the harbor. The fourth floor, added in 1997, consists of deluxe club-level rooms. Here, continental breakfast and afternoon hors d'oeuvres are put out in two small lounge areas. Seven Ports of Call penthouse suites atop the hotel feature gas fireplaces, kitchens and balconies overlooking the harbor. The hotel also offers two-story, two-bedroom Market Wharf townhouse suites. Facilities include an indoor pool, sauna, fitness center and two restaurants.

Harbor's Edge serves a traditional dinner menu of grilled seafood and meats, ranging from shrimp and scallops provençal to chicken dijonnaise and rack of lamb. Lobster is offered in various guises, from an award-winning lobster chowder to sautéed lobster cakes, lobster and scallops tarragon and lobster scampi in the shell. A pianist entertains on weekends.

(603) 431-2300 or (877) 248-3794. Fax (603) 431-7805. www.sheratonportsmouth.com. One hundred eighty-five rooms and 17 suites. Doubles, $259 to $299. Suites, $425 to $875. Entrées, $16.95 to $28.95. Dinner nightly, 5:30 to 10.

The Bow Street Inn, 121 Bow St., Portsmouth 03801.

This conveniently located downtown riverfront establishment is a cross between a motel and a small hotel. It occupies the second floor of a restored four-story brick brewery warehouse that also houses condominiums, the Seacoast Repertory Theatre and a café. Guest rooms go off either side of a center hallway. Rather small, they are furnished simply but attractively in light pastel colors with queensize brass beds (except for one with a king/twins), thick carpeting, TV and a single chair. One room, billed as a mini-suite for extended stays, contains a sofa and a small dining table. Juice, cereal, muffins, bagels and breads for toasting are put out in a pleasant brick dining room with three tables and a small refrigerator for guests' use. The owner "tries to make people feel at home," said one of the assistants on duty at our visit. Because the condominium blocks the view of the river except from Room 6, any views are of rooftops or the street. Parking is on the street or in a municipal garage.

(603) 431-7760. Fax (603) 433-1680. www.bowstreetinn.com. Ten rooms with private baths. Doubles, $140 to $175 May-October, $109 to $160 rest of year.

The Inn at Strawbery Banke, 314 Court St., Portsmouth 03801.

For those seeking both history and convenient location, this B&B is close to both downtown and the Strawbery Banke museum complex. The 1800 ship captain's house is situated right up against the street, as so many in Portsmouth are. The seven guest rooms vary in size and style, but have their own baths, though one is in the hall. Strawberry stenciling, strawberry comforters and strawberry candies on the pillows accent the prevailing green and white color scheme. Three guest rooms on the main floor share a common room with telephone and TV. Four more bedrooms go off an upstairs common room, also with TV. One with windows on three sides contains a double and a single bed and three ice-cream-parlor chairs around a glass table. Innkeeper Sally Glover O'Donnell serves a full breakfast in a skylit breakfast room with an abundance of hanging plants. The main course at our visit was sourdough blueberry pancakes with sausages, supplemented by oatmeal, cold cereals and homemade pastries. The room looks onto a strawberry patch, bird feeders and the trellised rose garden of the historic Governor Langdon House just behind. Sally keeps cookie jars stocked for afternoon or evening snacks in the two cozy common rooms, both outfitted with television sets.

(603) 436-7242 or (800) 428-3933. www.innatstrawberybanke.com. Seven rooms with private baths. Doubles, $145 to $150 mid-May through mid-October, $100 to $115 rest of year.

Nearby Choices

The Governor's House, 32 Miller Ave., Portsmouth 03801.

Artistry and amenities mix nicely in this stately 1917 white Georgian Colonial that was the former home of a governor and reopened as a B&B in 2002 under new owners Bob Chaffee and Barbara Trimble. The artistry is evident in the framed doilies made by the owner's grandmother displayed suavely on the living room walls and in the "carpet" hand-painted on the floor of the side sun porch, and especially in the murals hand-painted on the tiles of the guest bathrooms. The amenities include Bose radios and TV/DVD players in the guest rooms, luxurious bedding, evening wine and cheese, personalized breakfasts and an outdoor hot tub. There's even a backyard tennis court that's lighted for play at night. The Prescott is the largest and fanciest of the four spacious guest rooms, each with an antique queensize bed dressed in Frette linens and down comforter. A life-size mermaid on the shower wall carries out the nautical theme in the Captain's Room. Around the double whirlpool tub in the Prescott Room are lovebirds with phrases for affection written in French. A butler painted on the wall of the shower in the Governor's Room is "at the governor's service." Guests gather in the spacious living room, the adjacent sun porch or on the leafy patio, enveloped by rhododendrons overlooking the tennis court in the hidden back yard. Breakfast is delivered at the time and place of the guests' choosing from a check-off menu offering a selection of fruit, baked goods, cereal and perhaps quiche.

(603) 431-6546 or (866) 427-5140. Fax (603) 427-5145. www.governors-house.com. Doubles, $195 to $245 May-October, $165 to $215 rest of year.

Martin Hill Inn, 404 Islington St., Portsmouth 03801.

This B&B in a handsome yellow 1820 house comes with a deep and nicely landscaped back yard, a shady retreat where 400 plants thrive and a water garden is illuminated at night. Afternoon tea is served here by innkeepers Jane and Paul Harnden, who have been enhancing the property ever since they opened Portsmouth's first B&B in 1978. The Harndens offer three spacious guest rooms in the main house, plus a room and three suites in the adjacent Guest House. All have queensize beds, modern baths, loveseats or comfortable chairs, good reading lamps, writing desks, armoires, and nice touches like potpourri in china teacups and the inn's own wildflower glycerin soaps. We're partial to the Greenhouse Suite in the spiffy side annex, which contains a small solarium furnished in wicker looking onto the water garden, rattan furniture in an interior sitting room and a bedroom with a spindle bed and a full bath. Breakfast is served on a gleaming mahogany table in the antiques-filled dining room, whose walls display three coordinated English wallpapers and paints. Paul makes dynamite french toast with Italian sourdough bread, slathered with almonds and accompanied by Canadian bacon and homemade cranberry relish. Our scrambled eggs with cheese and chervil were served with cranberry bread, and the coffeepot was bottomless.

(603) 436-2287. www.martinhillinn.com. Four rooms and three suites with private baths. Doubles, $125 to $165 July-October, $98 to $130 rest of year.

Sise Inn, 40 Court St., Portsmouth 03801.

Stay in Victorian comfort in this Queen Anne home built in 1881 for the John E. Sise family as remodeled and expanded with great taste by a Canadian-based hotel group called Someplace(s) Different Ltd. The 34 rooms and suites on three floors and in a carriage house vary in bed configuration, size and decor. All are elegantly furnished in antiques and period reproductions with striking window treatments and vivid wallpapers. Geared to the business traveler, they have queen or twin beds, vanities outside the bathrooms (the larger of which contain whirlpool baths), writing desks, clock radios, telephones, and remote-control television and VCRs, often hidden in armoires. The stylish main-floor living room is much like an English library with several conversation areas and fresh flowers all around. An extensive help-yourself continental breakfast is available amidst much ornate wood in the dining room.

(603) 433-1200 or (877) 747-3466. Fax (603) 433-0200. www.siseinn.com. Twenty-five rooms and nine suites with private baths. Mid-May through October: doubles $189, suites $229 to $269. Rest of year: doubles $129, suites $159 to $199.

A Storied Resort Reborn

Wentworth by the Sea, 588 Wentworth Road, New Castle 03854.

Perhaps no grand oceanfront hotel in northern New England was better known than the storied Wentworth, poised on a rise at the tip of the island of New Castle and host to the rich and famous for more than a century. It was saved from the wreckers' ball after becoming the first hotel to be placed on the National Trust for Historical Preservation's list of America's Eleven Most Endangered Places. Closed in 1982, the rebuilt Wentworth reopened in 2003 as a Marriott hotel and spa, bearing the Wentworth's exterior look and heritage but with an interior reflecting typical Marriott motifs and amenities. The sparkling-white hotel with red roof appears squeezed between new front and back access roads and residential development where open lawns had been, with showy landscaping and a gazebo providing lush pastoral relief. The elongated, four-story hotel contains 143 guest rooms, some with french doors onto Juliet balconies facing the harbor and ocean in front and the meandering Piscataqua River in back – those on the third floor are most in demand. Rooms generally are on the small side, but are equipped with marble baths and the usual Marriott attributes. The best rooms (and views) are in eighteen bi-level suites at water's edge in the Little Harbor Marina. Formerly called the "Ship Building" for its vague resemblance to early ocean liners, the four-story building is a short hike downhill from the hotel. Its suites have one or two bedrooms, full kitchens, sitting/dining areas and private balconies. Resort activities include a full-service spa, tennis and guest access to the Wentworth by the Sea Country Club and Marina.

Three meals a day are served in two side-by-side hotel dining rooms, one with pillars and a frescoed domed ceiling. Executive chef Daniel Dumont's contemporary, seafood-oriented menu ranges from tournedos of yellowfin tuna and smoky bacon-crusted "filet mignon" of lobster to a pot au feu of pheasant with toasted barley truffle flan and pine nut-crusted rack of lamb. Across the street in the marina, **Latitudes** offers informal dining inside beside floor-to-ceiling windows or near the fireplace in the bar and outside on a teak deck overlooking the waterfront.

(603) 422-7322 or (866) 240-6313. Fax (603) 422-7329. www.wentworth.com. One hundred forty-three rooms and eighteen suites. Doubles, $200 to $400. Suites, $500 up. Dining room, entrées, $28 to $36. Latitudes, entrées, $18 to $29. Serving daily, 11 to 10.

The Inn at Christian Shore, 335 Maplewood Ave., Portsmouth 03801.

An abundance of antiques, rather lavishly decorated guest rooms with television and an inviting dining room with a fireplace are attractions in this 1800 Federal house, located in the historic Christian Shore area in the western part of town. Across from the Jackson House, Portsmouth's oldest, this structure was renovated and decorated by three antiques dealers, who sold to Mariaelena Koopman. The first and second floors contain five guest rooms, three with queensize beds. Two rooms have fireplaces. All contain handsome furnishings, antiques and crocheted afghans. A harvest table dominates the beamed breakfast room, which is the heart of the house with its large brick fireplace. Three smaller dining tables with upholstered wing chairs are beside windows on the sides. Accessories here include textiles from around the world, Argentine silver, pre-Columbian ceramics and African art. A full breakfast is served by the European-born innkeeper. Omelets, a Spanish tortilla, caramelized french toast and even porridge with "a tot of whiskey" could be the fare.

(603) 431-6770. Fax (603) 431-7743. Five rooms with private baths. Doubles, $100 to $120 mid-May through October, $95 to $100 rest of year.

Where to Eat

Pesce Blue, 103 Congress St.
Portsmouth's hottest restaurant is this contemporary Italian seafood grill with a California twist. The 70-seat dining room is a drop-dead, knockout space fashioned from a former bookstore. It's long, narrow and mod, dark in a palette of blacks and taupes and illuminated by day from windows onto a side street and at night by striking lamp spheres dangling from the high ceiling. Chef Mark Segal's seafood dishes draw knowing diners day and night. The choices change daily, but you might find sautéed Icelandic char with lemon-caper emulsion, sautéed Maine skate with orange-ginger sauce or grilled yellowfin tuna with green peppercorn sauce. Some go for the house specialty, mixed grill – an assortment of five of the day's freshest fish with grilled vegetables. Others go for "the whole thing" – another specialty of crispy whole local mackerel, perhaps, or Mediterranean branzino (sea bass), salt-crusted and grilled or oven roasted. The treats begin with such appetizers as a crispy baccala fritter, swordfish carpaccio, a salad of grilled octopus and fried calamari with three dipping sauces. Five seafood pastas and risottos are available as small plates or large. The night's menu holds only two items called "landfood," usually pan-roasted "flattened" chicken and grilled ribeye steak alla fiorentina. Desserts include a selection of sorbets, Italian crêpes and crème brûlée served with fresh berries. A sidewalk patio is open seasonally.

(603) 430-7766. www.pesceblue.com. Entrées, $16.75 to $26.50. Lunch, Monday-Friday 11:45 to 2. Dinner nightly, 5 to 9:30 or 10.

Anthony Alberto's, 59 Penhallow St.
The most elegant food and service in town are found in this atmospheric establishment, a local institution hidden in the Custom House Cellar. Tod Alberto and Massimo Morgia renovated the space and named it after Tod's father. It's elegant, dark and grotto-like with stone and brick walls, arches, exposed beams on the ceiling and oriental rugs on the slate floors. Aqua upholstered chairs, mauve fanned napkins and white tablecloths add a Mediterranean look. The menu is high Italian, as in lobster poached in sauternes and herbed butter and served with handmade lemon-pepper fettuccine, grilled veal chop with a currant-balsamic demi-glace and rosemary-marinated grilled beef tenderloin in a dijon-green peppercorn cream sauce. Expect such antipasti as veal tenderloin carpaccio, pheasant ravioli, pan-seared crab cake with a garlic-cilantro aioli, and potato blini with smoked salmon and caviar. Desserts include fruit tarts, bananas flambé, tiramisu and crème caramel.

(603) 436-4000. www.anthonyalbertos.com. Entrées, $17.95 to $29.95. Dinner, Monday-Saturday 5 to 9:30 or 10:30.

43° North, 75 Pleasant St.

A former chef from Anthony Alberto's opened his own restaurant in the space known earlier as The Grotto. No more grotto, this. Geno Gulotta christened it a kitchen and wine bar, hung its aqua brick walls with fine paintings and furnished it with Hungarian antique sideboards for an elegant continental look. The contemporary international menu ranges widely. Among "small plates and bowls" are wonderful Maine mussels steamed in chardonnay, garlic, fennel and tomato and served with grilled olive focaccia. The crisp duck spring rolls and a pan-seared Maine crab cake with slivered endive and watercress salad come highly recommended. For "large plates," consider the pumpkin seed-crusted haddock with tomato-balsamic syrup, porcini-dusted john dory with oven-dried tomato vinaigrette, the roast breast and confit of duck with caramelized apple jus or the grilled bourbon-molasses rubbed elk chops with dried blueberry jam. Dessert could be crème brûlée or chocolate hazelnut ganache.

(603) 430-0225. www.fortythreenorth.com. Entrées, $19 to $27. Dinner, Monday-Saturday from 5.

Jumpin' Jay's Fish Café, 150 Congress St.

Fresh seafood from around the country is featured at this mod new place that started small and quickly quadrupled in size. Jay McSharry, co-owner with chef John Harrington, named it to convey a lively and unpretentious atmosphere. "Fish with an attitude" is how he describes the fare. One day's catch included sable fish from Alaska, wahoo from Florida, john dory from Gloucester and yellowfin tuna from Baja. Each came with a choice of sauces, among them roasted red pepper relish, lobster velouté and spicy poblano-chipotle coulis. Lobster risotto is a signature dish. Others are haddock piccata and jonah crab and vegetable lasagna. Each night, you can order mussels, scallops, shrimp or chicken served puttanesca or provençal style over linguini. Starters range widely from rock shrimp and wonton napoleon and Maine crab cake with chipotle aioli to smoked salmon tartare and a sashimi tuna and avocado salad. Dessert could be crème brûlée or chocolate-kahlua mousse cake. Well-spaced white tables with black chairs are situated beneath string lights in a mod red and white, high-tech setting. A circular, stainless steel bar is in the center.

(603) 766-3474. www.jumpinjays.com. Entrées, $14.95 to $23.95. Dinner nightly, 5 or 5:30 to 9:30 or 10.

Victory 96 State Street, 96 State St.

An aura of history surrounds this three-story brick Federal townhouse known for more than 50 years as the home of the Victory Spa Diner and later Victory Antiques. Chef Duncan Boyd and manager George Frangos worked together in Washington, D.C., restaurants before their wives' Portsmouth connections lured them here. The restaurant on two floors is a beauty, with brick walls and tables spaced well apart from which to enjoy the glow from six fireplaces. The tables were made with planks from the wide-board floors found in the building's attic during the restoration. The setting is casual near the bar on the main floor and more formal upstairs. The New England seafood-oriented menu ranges from cedar-planked Maine salmon and pork and clams Portuguese style to hunter-style rabbit and grilled beef sirloin with pinot noir sauce. The "Victory mac 'n cheese" teams lobster with Vermont cheddar, aged gruyère, crimini mushrooms and roasted red peppers. Starters include seared foie gras with brandied peaches, steamed mussels with chorizo sausage and sweet peppers, and a salad of smoked trout and frisée with potato croutons and a poached egg. Dessert could be a selection of farmstead cheeses, peach upside-down cake with buttermilk ice cream or warm chocolate soufflé cake with caramel anglaise.

(603) 766-0960. www.96statestreet.com. Entrées, $22 to $27. Dinner, Tuesday-Sunday 5:30 to 10.

Lindbergh's Crossing, 29 Ceres St.

This bistro and wine bar with obscure references to Charles Lindbergh is across the street from the harbor in space long occupied by the famed Blue Strawbery restaurant. A propeller hangs on one wall of the brick and beamed downstairs bistro in a 200-year-old former ship's chandlery. A representation of Lindbergh's flight across the Atlantic flanks the stairway to the casual upstairs wine bar, where dinner also is available and no reservations are taken. The contemporary Mediterranean fare receives high marks from locals. Expect eclectic variety in such main courses as seafood bourride with saffron aioli, pan-fried trout with crabapple chutney, a smoked lobster croque monsieur, coq au vin or beef tenderloin au poivre. Typical starters are mussels marinière, frog's legs over spicy rémoulade, escargots with raclette and coriander-crusted rare tuna with provençal sauce. Desserts include a signature "medium rare chocolate cake" (whose center is described as the consistency of chocolate pudding), blueberry-lemon crème caramel and bing cherry clafoutis with whipped cream.

(603) 431-0887. www.lindberghscrossing.com. Entrées, $17 to $28. Dinner nightly, from 5 or 5:30. Wine bar from 4.

The Wellington Room, 67 Bow St.

A waterfront setting is enjoyed by diners in this small restaurant backing up to the river. Also enjoyed is some of the best food in town – and, an added fillip, a British-style afternoon tea. New Zealand-born chef-owner David Robinson apprenticed in restaurants in Australia, Europe, Cincinnati and Boston before taking over the intimate, 38-seat dining room, hidden from view above and behind a downtown storefront. The most romantic tables are a pair of deuces in an alcove, with windows onto the harbor. The chef's global travels impart Asian, Italian and French accents to his creative American cuisine. Typical entrées are oven-roasted haddock with chardonnay-tomato broth, roasted duck breast with a watercress and Australian shiraz reduction, and, of course, New Zealand rack of lamb, with minted blackberry-honey drizzle. Starters include a mushroom and cheese crêpe, pan-seared foie gras over sautéed cranberries and apples, Caribbean grilled shrimp and szechuan peppercorn-crusted tuna with a sesame-seaweed salad.

Afternoon tea service is the chef's tribute to his late British grandmother, for whom a proper British tea was a ritual. The à-la-carte menu offers nine loose-leaf teas from around the world as well as scones with Devonshire cream, fruit tarts and a choice among six elegant tea sandwiches.

(603) 431- 2989. www.thewellingtonroom.com. Entrées, $17 to $28. Tea, Friday-Sunday 3:30 to 4:30. Dinner, Wednesday-Friday 5 to 9, Saturday 5 to 9:30, Sunday 4 to 9.

Café Mirabelle, 64 Bridge St.

French chef Stephan Mayeux and his wife Chris claim theirs is one of the longest continuously owned restaurants on the New Hampshire Seacoast, going into its fifteenth year in what had been the Fish Shanty. Now very un-shantyish, it's crisp and contemporary on two floors, with a handful of tables downstairs in a café near the bar. Upstairs is a cathedral-ceilinged room with beams and interesting angles, mission-style chairs at burgundy-linened tables up against tall windows, shelves of country artifacts along sand-colored walls and twinkling lights on ficus trees. Stephan offers the pure cooking of the French countryside, unsullied by contemporary conceits. Bouillabaisse and chicken mirabelle (with prosciutto, lobster and asparagus) are menu fixtures. So are things like salmon épernay with sea scallops in champagne-shallot cream sauce, roasted pork tenderloin calvados, magret of duck roasted in a tangy raspberry-vinegar sauce and filet au poivre. Start with baked brie with walnuts and thyme in puff pastry, a mushroom crêpe or mussels muscadet. Finish with a profiterole, white and dark chocolate mousse, the French clafouti, homemade sorbet or a thin pear-almond tart with crème anglaise.

(603) 430-9301. Entrées, $17.95 to $22.95. Dinner, Wednesday-Sunday from 5:15.

Blue Mermaid World Grill, 409 The Hill.

Two restaurateurs from Boston gave the old Codfish restaurant an arty and whimsical decor, installed the town's first wood grill and started dispensing spicy foods of the Caribbean, South America, California and the Southwest. Partners Jim Smith and Scott Logan added embellishments like a fascinating abstract mural of the Portsmouth Farmers' Market and iron animals atop some chandeliers, and identified the rest rooms with mermaids and mermen. A super lunch testified to their success. As we sat down, tortilla strips with fire-roasted vegetables and salsa arrived in what otherwise might be a candle holder. These piqued the taste buds for a cup of tasty black bean soup, a sandwich of grilled Jamaican jerk chicken with sunsplash salsa and a sandwich of grilled vegetables with jarlsberg cheese on walnut bread. These came with sweet-potato chips and the house sambal. We also sampled a side order of thick grilled vidalia onion rings with mango ketchup. A generous portion of ginger cheesecake, garnished with the hard candy-like topping of crème brûlée, was a sensational ending. The signature dinner dish is grilled lobster with mango butter, served with grilled vegetables and cornbread. Other treats include Caribbean pan-seared cod with coconut cream sauce, lobster and shrimp pad thai and Southwestern skirt steak with roasted corn and red pepper salsa.

(603) 427-2583. Entrées, $15.95 to $20.95. Lunch daily, 11:30 to 5. Dinner, 5 to 9 or 10.

The Oar House, 55 Ceres St.

One of the best of the touristy choices along the waterfront is this veteran of 30 years, situated across the street from the harbor and adding a deck beside the water in summer. The dining room and lounge are housed on the lower floor of an old warehouse building in which goods used to be unloaded directly from ships and raised by elevators to the upper floors. Today, the space contains appropriate mementos of the city's long maritime heritage. Artworks trace the history of prominent ships built here, and the models are all of Portsmouth-built vessels. The dinner menu features the traditional, as in broiled or baked stuffed haddock, grilled salmon, broiled sea scallops and filet mignon. Bouillabaisse, roast duckling with apricot-peppercorn glaze and rack of lamb are specialties. Appetizers range from brie in puff pastry and escargots to pizza margarita and lobster spring rolls. There's also a raw bar. The jaunty deck across the street beside the harbor is the venue of choice in summer.

(603) 436-4025. Entrées, $20 to $34. Lunch, Monday-Saturday 11:30 to 3. Dinner nightly, 5 to 9 or 9:30. Sunday brunch, 11:30 to 3.

Local Color and Casual

Café Brioche, 14 Market Square.

Lately expanded into an old stationery store to twice its original size, this large sidewalk café and meeting spot provides a taste of Paris on Market Square. Run by longtime owner Paul Norton, a baker and pastry chef of note, it's a good place to stop for a light breakfast, say a scone or a ham and cheese croissant with cappuccino. It's also popular for lunch, with several kinds of quiche, salads and great soups (caldo verde and curried crab bisque at one visit). The sandwich bar ($4.25 to $5.50) offers everything from hummus and tofu to PB&J, honey-baked ham and roast beef. The café puts up box lunches to go – one involves brie in puff pastry, chilled chicken jardinière on fresh spinach, Mediterranean rice salad, a baguette, strawberries and sacher torte. Come in the evening for espresso and a fancy European-style dessert pastry, sometimes served up with live jazz.

(603) 430-9225. www.cafebrioche.com. Open daily, from 6:30, to 6 or 9 in the winter, to 11 in summer and weekends.

The Stockpot, 53 Bow St.

Homemade soups are the hallmark at this popular spot overlooking the water. The upstairs bar and lounge has a few tables beside big windows onto the harbor, while the downstairs Riverview Dining Room adds an outside deck. Soups, of course, are the specialty and can be ordered with half a sandwich. The fare ranges widely: burgers, Syrian bread sandwiches including an artichoke and tomato melt, salads like hummus plate or crab salad, steamed mussels and peel-and-eat shrimp. The homemade meatloaf sandwich is considered a great value, as is the meatloaf dinner platter including fries and coleslaw. Paella valencia is the signature dish. The kitchen gets creative with such dinner entrées as coconut-encrusted tuna with pineapple salsa, cajun haddock with pesto-tartar sauce and grilled strip steak with zinfandel marinade.

(603) 431-1851. Entrées, $12.95 to $17.95. Open daily, 11 a.m. to 11:30 p.m.

BG's Boat House Restaurant, 191 Wentworth Road.

Lobster and down-home surroundings lure the locals to this little restaurant with outdoor decks and a marina out past the Wentworth resort in New Castle. Windows look onto an ocean inlet officially known as Sagamore Creek. The walls are paneled, the floors bare and tables have captain's chairs and paper mats. It's a perfect backdrop for devouring the lobsters delivered by boat to the back door by BG's own lobstermen. Last we knew, you could get a lobster roll with french fries for under $10. A seafood platter commands top dollar at $15.95. BG's also offers sandwiches, hamburgers, potato skins and mozzarella sticks, but most people go here for lobster and seafood, plain and simple.

(603) 431-1074. Entrées, $8.95 to $15.95. Lunch, daily in summer, 11 to 4. Dinner nightly, 5 to 9. Closed Monday and Tuesday in spring and fall and October to mid-March.

FOR MORE INFORMATION: Greater Portsmouth Chamber of Commerce, 500 Market St., Portsmouth, NH 03801, (603) 436-1118. www.portsmouthchamber.org. Other informative websites are www.portsmouthnh.com and www.seacoastnh.com.

Patio of Yachtsman Lodge & Marina looks onto Kennebunk River out toward ocean.

Kennebunkport, Me.

The Most and Best of Everything

For a high-end getaway in Maine, the small coastal area known as the Kennebunk Region has the most and best of everything: the best beaches, the most inns, the best shops, the most eating places, the best scenery, the most galleries, the best sightseeing, the most diverse appeal.

All combine to create a Kennebunk mystique that has strong appeal for a getaway. Actually, there are at least three Kennebunks. One is the town of Kennebunk and its inland commercial center, historic Kennebunk. The second is Kennebunkport, the coastal resort community that was one of Maine's earliest summer havens for the wealthy, and adjacent Kennebunk Beach. A third represents Cape Arundel around the George Bush family compound at Walker Point, the fishing hamlet of Cape Porpoise and Goose Rocks Beach, whose rugged coastal aspects remain largely unchanged by development in recent years.

Even before the first George Bush's election as president, Kennebunkport and its Dock Square and Lower Village shopping areas had become so congested that tourists were shuttled by bus from parking areas on the edge of town. Although some of the lustre faded during the Clinton years, visitors were still drawn, much as they are by the Kennedy name to Hyannis Port, Mass. – and all the more so since George W. Bush became president.

The nice thing about Kennebunkport is that, although small, it's spread out and much of it is not overly developed. So it's easy to escape the congestion. Stay at a luxury inn or a choice B&B away from the crowds – some are so nicely located or so self-contained that you may have little reason to leave.

If you do: walk, bike or drive out Ocean Avenue around Cape Arundel past Walker Point to Cape Porpoise. Head out Beach Avenue to Lord's Point, Strawberry Island or Kennebunk Beach, and explore the Rachel Carson Wildlife Preserve. Savor times gone by among the historic homes of Summer Street in Kennebunk or along the beach at Goose Rocks.

One of the charms of the Kennebunks is that the crowded restaurants, shops and art galleries co-exist with events like the annual Unitarian Church blueberry festival and the Rotary Club chicken barbecue, and the solitude of Parson's Way.

Watercolorist Edgar Whitney proclaimed the Kennebunks "the best ten square miles of painting areas in the nation." What the artists paint, you can enjoy.

Seeing and Doing

The picturesque coast, which varies here in a relatively short stretch from sandy beach to rugged and rockbound, offers a variety of recreational activities. The interior has attractions as well.

In Kennebunkport, the **Intown Trolley** offers a 45-minute narrated tour on the hour daily from Memorial Day to Columbus Day from the main trolley stop on Ocean Avenue, around the corner from Dock Square next to the Landing Restaurant. It makes a circle tour out Ocean Avenue and back through town to Kennebunk Beach. The fare (adults $10, children $5) is good all day, and you can get on or off the trolley at any stop.

Walks, Drives and Wildlife

Parson's Way Shore Walk. A marker opposite the landmark Colony Hotel notes the land given to the people of Kennebunkport so that "everyone may enjoy its natural beauty." Sit on the benches, spread a blanket on a rock beside the ocean, or walk out to the serene little chapel of St. Ann's Episcopal Church by the sea. On a clear day you can see Mount Agamenticus on the horizon beyond Ogunquit.

Ocean Avenue. Continue past Parson's Way to Spouting Rock, where the incoming tide creates a spurting fountain as waves crash between two ragged cliffs. Blowing Cave is another roaring phenomenon within view of Walker Point and the Bush family's impressive eleven-acre vacation compound, which has been in the family for more than 100 years. Here you might see his speedboat when the former president is in residence (you'll know from all the passersby stopped with binoculars). The road turns inland and winds its way to Cape Porpoise, dating to the early 1600s. It's the closest thing to a fishing village hereabouts, with a working lobster pier (up to 50 lobster boats come and go daily), a picturesque harbor dotted with islands and some interesting art galleries.

Rachel Carson National Wildlife Refuge, 321 Port Road (Route 9), Wells. Seemingly far removed from the surrounding resort and beach scene is this 4,800-acre reserve near the Kennebunkport-Wells town line. It's named for the environmental pioneer who summered in Maine and conducted research in the area for several of her books. A mile-long interpretive trail through saltwater marshes and adjacent grasslands covers an area rich in migratory and resident wildlife. The trail, "paved" with small gravel, and boardwalks head through tranquil woods until – just when you begin to wonder what all the fuss is about – the vista opens up at the sixth marker and a boardwalk takes you out over wetlands and marsh. Cormorants, herons and more are sighted here, and benches let you relax and take in the scene. An even better view of the ocean in the distance is at Marker 7, the Little River overlook. The widest, best view of all is near the end of the loop at Marker 11. If you don't have time for the entire trail, ignore the directional signs and go counter-clockwise. You'll get the best view first.

(207) 646-9226. Refuge headquarters open Monday-Friday 8 to 4:30. Trail open daily, dawn to dusk; donation.

Wells National Estuarine Research Reserve, 342 Laudholm Farm Road, Wells.

Abutting the Carson wildlife refuge to the south is one of 26 protected estuarine reserves in the country, based at Laudholm Farm off Route 1, north of Wells Corner. Its 1,600 acres of salt marshes, sand dunes and tidal rivers include seven miles of nature trails and a wide variety of wildlife. Guided tours, education programs, and a slide show and exhibits are offered in the stately, rambling Greek Revival Laudholm Farm visitor center. Interesting nature walks are scheduled throughout the reserve. Varied exhibits are shown in the new Maine Coastal Ecology Center, a research and education facility opened in late 2004.

(207) 646-1555. www.wellsreserve.org. Visitor center open Monday-Saturday 10 to 4, Sunday noon to 4, May-October; weekdays rest of year; closed mid-December to mid-January. Grounds open daily 8 a.m. to dusk, year-round. Adults $2, children $1 daily in summer and weekends May-October.

┌─ *Main(e)ly in the Plains* ─

The **Kennebunk Plains,** on either side of Route 99 four miles west of Kennebunk, are a little-known trove of rarities in Maine for walkers and nature lovers. The 1,900-acre grasslands habitat, the largest in New England and uncommon in a region so forested and hilly, is home to several rare and endangered species. Paths through the grassland pass ponds and stands of pitch pine and scrub oak. Birders spot dozens of species, including uncommon grassland nesting birds such as the grasshopper sparrow, horned lark and upland sandpiper. Wild blueberries grow in the plains in late July. In late August, the plains turn a brilliant pinkish purple with the blooming of the Northern blazing star, an extremely rare flower – 90 percent of its global population lies in the Kennebunk Plains, according to the Nature Conservancy, which manages the site with the Maine Department of Inland Fisheries and Wildlife. Two other unusual plants, white-topped aster and upright bindweed, grow nearby. A rare reptile, the Northern black racer snake, also may be found here. A pair of small parking lots, one on either side of Route 99, lead into the plains. Recently, the partnership protected 673 adjacent acres along the Mousam River for hiking, bird watching, blueberry picking and cross-country skiing.

Historic Attractions

Kennebunkport "literally begs for an exploratory walk," according to the Kennebunkport Historical Society, caretaker of the town's history. The society offers hour-long walking tours from its in-town landmark, the Nott House. Guides point out pristine examples of Colonial, Federal, Greek Revival and Victorian homes along village streets. Tours are scheduled Thursday and Saturday at 11 in July and August, and Saturday at 11 in September; adults, $3.

The society is headquartered at the **History Center of Kennebunkport,** a complex of five buildings at 125-135 North St. Here you will find the **Pasco Exhibit Center** with changing historical exhibits and the 1899 one-room **Town House School,** now the society's research center. On one side of the school, the **Clark Shipwright's Office** of a former Kennebunk River shipyard displays artifacts from the shipping era. On the other side are the town's old jail cells.

The Nott House, 8 Maine St., Kennebunkport.

Nicknamed White Columns for its majestic Doric colonnade, this 1853 Greek Revival house recreates the era when shipbuilding thrived and the shipping trade made Kennebunkport one of the wealthiest towns in New England. The house was left to the historical society by Elizabeth Nott, a past president, who had no heirs. The original wallpaper, carpets, furnishings and collections remain, reflecting the evolving tastes of four generations of Perkins and Nott families from the late 1700s to the mid-1900s. Especially prized is the large collection of Victorian pieces. The gardens have been restored recently and are open free.

(207) 967-2751. House tours, Tuesday-Friday 1 to 4 and Saturday 10 to 1, mid-June to mid-October. Adults, $5.

Inland Kennebunk is more obviously historic, especially along Summer Street (Route 35) between Kennebunkport and Kennebunk. Running south from downtown Kennebunk, Summer Street is considered one of the architecturally outstanding residential streets in the nation. The 1803 **Taylor-Barry House** is open for tours, and the aptly named yellow-with-white-frosting Wedding Cake House (1826) is a sight to behold. Architectural walking tours of the National Register Historic District, Maine's first, are offered by the Brick Store Museum around the corner.

The Brick Store Museum, 117 Main St., Kennebunk.

There's a treasure behind every door on the block at this 1825 museum, which occupies four restored 19th-century commercial buildings at the edge of downtown. The museum was founded in 1936 by Edith Cleaves Barry, who created a repository for her family's local history collection in her great-grandfather's brick dry goods store. The museum's excellent collection of decorative and fine arts, Federal period furniture, ship models, ship building tools, artifacts, costumes and textiles illustrates the area's history from the earliest settlements to the present. The museum mounts a couple of major exhibits each year (photos of the great fire of 1947 were shown at one visit). Ninety-minute walking tours around the Summer Street historic district are scheduled seasonally Friday at 11; adults $5.

(207) 985-4802. www.brickstoremuseum.org. Open Tuesday-Friday 10 to 4:30, Saturday 10 to 1. Donation, $3.

Material Pursuits

ART GALLERIES. Its picturesque coastal location has turned Kennebunkport into a mecca for artisans. The Art Guild of the Kennebunks numbers more than 50 resident professionals as members and claims the Kennebunks are the largest collective community of fine art on the East Coast.

Art and galleries are everywhere, but are concentrated around Kennebunkport's Dock Square and the wharves to the southeast. The **Ebb Tide Gallery** shows more than twenty artists in a stylish setting overlooking the Kennebunkport River basin, just across the bridge from Dock Square. Local, regional and national artists are represented across the street at the **Gallery on Chase Hill.** More than 105 artists show at **Mast Cove Galleries,** a lovely Greek Revival home and barn next to the library on Route 9. Spectacular contemporary American glass is shown at **Silica,** a knockout gallery in Cape Porpoise. Also in Cape Porpoise is **The Wright Gallery,** where 31 artists display on two floors of a 19th-century post and beam house.

For a change of pace, visit the grounds of the **Franciscan Monastery** (where, as some budget-savvy travelers know, spare and inexpensive bedrooms are available) and St. Anthony's Shrine. The shrines and sculpture include the towering piece that adorned the facade of the Vatican pavilion at the 1964 New York World's Fair.

SHOPPING. Dock Square and, increasingly, Kennebunk's Lower Village across the river are full of interesting stores. Expect anything from the **Lavender Creek Trading Co.** for Provence-inspired gifts and home accessories to the **Port Canvas Co.,** with all kinds of handsome canvas products. Crowning the main corner of Dock Square is the decidedly upscale **Compliments,** "the gallery for your special lifestyle." It features lots of glass, including lamps and egg cups, trickling fountains and cute ceramic gulls, each with its own personality. Admire the prolific flowers on the riverside deck of the **Kennebunk Book Port,** where you can take a book outside to browse on benches or deck chairs above the water. We liked the contemporary crafts at **Kennebunkport Arts** and **Plum Dandy,** the nature-inspired jewelry and tableware at **Lovell Designs,** and the Asian ceramics at **East and Design.** Check out the birdhouses made of hats along with clothing and whimsical gifts at **Carrots & Co.,** whose theme is "because life's too short for boring stuff." **Digs, Divots and Dogs** has gifts for gardeners, golfers and, yes, dogs. **Alano Ltd.** and **Carla's Corner** have super clothes. Lilly Pulitzer designs are featured at **Snappy Turtle. Dock Square Clothiers** stocks casual resort apparel for men and women. **Abacus,** the **Good Earth Pottery**, the **Sheepscot River Pottery, The Whimsy Shop, Maison et Jardin** and the shops at Union Square and Village Marketplace are other favorites. **Keys to the Kitchen** is an excellent kitchen store and gift gallery on two floors.

Water Activities

THE BEACHES. Gooch's Beach, a curving half-mile crescent, and **Kennebunk Beach** are two sandy strands with surf west of town (parking by permit, often provided by innkeepers, otherwise $10 daily). When not occupied or when at low tide, the hard-packed sands of Gooch's are great for walking, a Florida-style treat for occupants of the substantial summer homes across the road. The "Kennebunk workout" involves walking the 1.5-mile stretch of beach from Gooch's out to Lord's Point and back. The fine silvery white sand at three-mile-long **Goose Rocks Beach** (parking by permit, $5 daily) looks almost tropical and the waters are protected. At low tide, you can barely see offshore a barrier reef rock formation known as "Goose Rocks," which migrating geese use as a navigational point. Children paddle in the warm tidal pools that form in depressions along the beach. Beachcombers find starfish and sand-dollar shells here in early morning. More secluded is **Parson's Beach,** set among the tall grasses next to the Rachel Carson Wildlife Refuge.

BOAT CRUISES AND WHALE WATCHES. Kennebunkport is another departure point for spotting the whales that feed seasonally twenty miles offshore at Jeffrey's Ledge. Sighted frequently are finbacks, humpbacks, minkes and Atlantic white-sided dolphins.

Whale watch excursions aboard the double-decker Nick's Chance are available from **First Chance Whale Watch,** 4 Western Ave., (207) 967-5507 or (800) 767-2628. Trips leave from the downtown bridge daily at 9 and 2:30; adults $32, children $20. The First Chance outfit also offers five 90-minute scenic lobster cruises daily aboard the 65-foot Kylie's Chance at 10, noon, 2, 4 and 6 (adults $15, children $10).

Cape Arundel Cruises, (207) 967-5595 or (877) 933-0707, offers whale watching cruises aboard the 100-passenger Nautilus daily at 10 (also at 4 in summer) from the Landing Restaurant, 192 Ocean Ave. (adults $32, children $20). It also gives 90-minute scenic cruises aboard the Deep Water II daily at 11 and 1 (adults $15, children $7.50).

For a virtual scuba diver experience in the comfort of a 49-passenger boat, check out **Atlantic Exposure Cruises,** (207) 967-4784. Capt. Michael Day gives two-hour scenic eco-cruises aboard the Atlantic Explorer three or four times a day in season from the Nonantum Resort marina out the Kennebunk River and along the coast to Goat Island Light and Cape Porpoise. Passengers watch live underwater video through a remotely operated camera (adults $20, children $10).

Two-hour sailing trips aboard the gaff-rigged schooner **Eleanor** are offered several times daily by Capt. Rich Woodman from the docks at the Arundel Wharf Restaurant, (207) 967-8809. He built the 55-foot schooner in 1999 and gives up to twenty passengers what he calls "the feel of yachting in the 1930s." The rate is $38 per person.

Capt. Jim Jannetti takes up to six passengers on his 37-foot ocean racing yacht, **Bellatrix**, from the Nonantum Resort on Ocean Avenue, (207) 967-8685. The rate is $40 each for a two-hour trip.

Kayaking is good along the Kennebunk River. Rentals are available from the **Kennebunkport Marina,** 67 Ocean Ave., (207) 967-3411.

Where to Stay

The White Barn Inn, 37 Beach Ave., Kennebunkport 04046.

In terms of sybaritic comforts, here is Maine's classiest act. Australian owner Laurence Bongiorno took a restaurant in a great white barn and elevated its dining and lodging experience to Relais & Chateaux status. An oasis of elegance and calm awaits in accommodations dispersed among a cluster of classic Maine-style structures including an 1860s homestead, a carriage house and cottages. The inn's 25 rooms and suites vary, as their price range indicates. A renovated cottage beside the elegant, stone-rimmed pool area is the ultimate in plush privacy with a living room, porch, kingsize bedroom, double-sided fireplace and two-person jacuzzi. Almost its equal is a loft suite, adjacent to the main inn with a king bed, fireplace and oversize marble bath with whirlpool and separate steam shower. Suites in the carriage house offer Queen Anne kingsize four-poster beds and secretary desks, library-style sitting areas, wide-screen plasma TVs, dressing rooms, spacious marble bathrooms with jacuzzis and separate showers, chintz-covered furniture and plush carpeting. The fireplace in the Blue Suite here was laid with real wood and we were enveloped in luxury with a personal note of welcome from the innkeeper, a bowl of fresh fruit, much closet and drawer space and no fewer than four three-way reading lights (plus a portable book light delivered with a plate of cookies at turndown). Four large rooms with cathedral ceilings in the Garden House also claim fireplaces and jacuzzis, as well as queensize sleigh beds, sitting areas with wing chairs and fine art on the walls. Smaller rooms upstairs in the main inn are less regal, but all are refurbished with whimsical trompe-l'oeil decorative accents painted by a local artist. The newest accommodations are four cottage units fashioned from fish shanties beside the Kennebunk River. They are furnished more like cabins in Arts & Crafts style, each with a snug queen bedroom, kitchenette, living room with fireplace and TV/VCR. The inn's handsome main floor contains sitting rooms with plush furniture and an inviting sun porch. An elaborate afternoon tea spread is set out in one room. In the morning a substantial continental buffet breakfast is offered in an elegant Colonial dining room. An inviting 50-foot swimming pool nestled in birches and pines invites guests to spend the day, as do spa treatments in the poolside cabanas. A light bistro menu is available here at lunchtime.

(207) 967-2321. Fax (207) 967-1100. www.whitebarninn.com. Sixteen rooms, eight suites and five cottages with private baths. Doubles $280 to $540. Suites and cottages, $565 to $785.

The Captain Lord Mansion, Pleasant Street, Box 800, Kennebunkport 04046
This beautifully restored 1812 mansion – one of the finest examples of Federal architecture in the country – boasts an octagonal cupola, a suspended elliptical staircase, blown-glass windows, trompe-l'oeil hand-painted doors, an eighteen-foot bay window and a hand-pulled working elevator. Not to mention a gas fireplace in every guest room – a feature for which the pace-setting B&B is widely known. Chocolates are placed every evening in the bedrooms, which are elegantly furnished in antiques, most with four-poster or canopied beds. The prime quarters seem to change with every upgrade, of which peerless innkeepers Rick Litchfield and his wife Bev Davis never seem to tire. Lately they have made remarkable enhancements, particularly in terms of bath facilities. The first-floor Merchant Suite with king canopy bed and fireplace gained two bathrooms, one with a heated marble floor, a ten-jet hydro-massage waterfall shower and a bidet and the other carpeted with twin granite vanities and a double whirlpool tub in front of a gas fireplace. The Dana, Mary Lord and Excelsior rooms on the second floor gained renovated baths with heated Italian tiled floors and double whirlpool tubs. The Champion added a mini-bar and a large bath with twin vanities and double whirlpool tub. The Lincoln acquired a king bed and a bath with heated marble floor, marble shower and oversize antique vanity. The third-floor Mousam became a two-room suite with queen canopy bed and a new bath with a heated black granite floor and double-headed shower for two. Guests gather beneath crystal chandeliers in the richly furnished parlor for herbal tea or Swedish glögg, or beside the fire in the Gathering Room. Downstairs in what was once the summer kitchen is another common room with a fireplace. An ample breakfast is served family-style at large tables in the kitchen.

(207) 967-3141 or (800) 522-3141. Fax (207) 967-3172. www.captainlord.com. Eighteen rooms and two suites with private baths. June-October and weekends through December: doubles $248 to $375, suites $248 to $475. Rest of year: doubles $116 to $329, suites $123 to $375.

Old Fort Inn, Old Fort Avenue, Box M, Kennebunkport 04046
This well-established B&B with an inviting swimming pool and a tennis court is a quiet retreat on fifteen acres of immaculately maintained grounds and woodlands, away from the tourist hubbub, but within walking distance of the ocean. At night, the silence is deafening, says David Aldrich, innkeeper with his wife Sheila. The couple cosset guests in fourteen large and luxurious rooms in a stone and brick

carriage house, plus two suites upstairs in the main lodge in a converted barn. They are furnished with style and such nice touches as velvet wing chairs, stenciling on the walls and handmade wreaths over the beds. Each air-conditioned room has a deluxe wet bar with microwave, since this is a place where people tend to stay for some time. In the most luxurious rooms, of which there seem to be more at every visit, the TV may be hidden in a handsome chest of drawers, the kingsize four-poster beds are topped with fishnet canopies, and the baths are outfitted with jacuzzis, Neutrogena amenities and heated tile floors. The main lodge holds an antiques shop and a large common room with enormous beams, weathered pine walls and a massive brick fireplace. It's the site for the daily breakfast buffet. Guests help themselves to bowls of fruit and platters of pastries, and sit around the lodge or outside on the sun-dappled deck beside the pool. The pool area and tennis court are such attractions that many stay around for the day.

(207) 967-5353 or (800) 828-3678. Fax (207) 967-4547. www.oldfortinn.com. Fourteen rooms and two suites with private baths. Doubles, $160 to $375 mid-June to late October, $99 to $295 rest of year. Closed mid-December to mid-April.

Cape Arundel Inn, Ocean Avenue, Kennebunkport 04046.

"Bold ocean views" and an excellent restaurant are features of Kennebunkport's only oceanfront inn. Veteran restaurateur Jack Nahil, who formerly owned the White Barn Inn, has upgraded the accommodations in the 1895 shingle-style mansion perched on a landscaped knoll above the crashing surf. He added queen and kingsize beds, enhanced the decor with some of his paintings and those of fellow artists, and completely refurbished the adjacent 1950s motel building in a country inn motif. Renamed Rockbound, each room here has a full bath and TV, and a small balcony with a head-on view of the ocean beyond wild roses in front. Our end room with a fireplace had a queen bed with a sturdy white wood headboard crafted by a local artisan, angled from the corner to take in the view. Occupants in a rear carriage-house suite called Ocean Bluff enjoy a gas fireplace along with spectacular vistas from a deck. The inn's wraparound porch is a super place to curl up with a good book or enjoy a cocktail or a nightcap, all with that bold ocean view taking in a presidential estate at the side. Breakfast is a hearty continental buffet. Ours included toasted basil-parmesan bread and a small spanakopita, prepared by the chef's wife and "presented" in the dinner style on an oversize plate.

(207) 967-2125. Fax (207) 967-1199. www.capearundelinn.com. Thirteen rooms and one suite with private baths. Doubles, $275 to $345 mid-June to mid-October, $150 to $295 rest of year. Closed January and February.

The Breakwater Inn & Hotel, 127 Ocean Ave., Kennebunkport 04046.

This two-part hostelry – an inn dating to the 1800s and a hotel built in 1986 – took on a new look under owner Laurie Bongiorno of Kennebunkport's stylish White Barn Inn. The inn's two restored buildings containing twenty guest rooms, fifteen with water views, were refurbished in the contemporary coastal style to which guests at his other inns are accustomed, most of these in robin's-egg blue. Rooms vary widely from kingsize with sitting areas to small with a double bed. All have TVs and most have refrigerators. The public rooms, Victorian parlor, breakfast room, wraparound porches and restaurant afford panoramic vistas of the water, garden courtyard and lawns sloping to the inn's private pebble beach. The best views are enjoyed by the relocated **Stripers,** a waterfront restaurant and raw bar, serving lunch and dinner in season (see Where to Eat).

In 2004 the Breakwater was joined in name to a more recent acquisition, the former Schooners Inn, which is now billed as a boutique hotel. Facing the Kennebunk River just north of the inn, the seventeen hotel rooms are crisply decorated in a high-tech look amid prevailing colors of creams and taupes. Beds are king or queensize, crafted by furniture maker Thomas Moser, who also did the cupboards that hold the flat-screen TVs. White satin robes, in-room refrigerators and Molton Brown toiletries from London are among the amenities. The prime accommodation is the Savannah Suite, with a kingsize bed enveloped in a sheer white canopy beneath a raised sitting area in a large bay window opening onto an idyllic deck. The curving main-floor lounge is the setting for afternoon tea and cookies, as well as a complimentary cocktail hour. The baked goods for tea and the continental-plus breakfast are prepared at the White Barn Inn.

(207) 967-5333. Fax (207) 967-2040. www.thebreakwaterinn.com. Thirty-seven rooms with private baths. July and August: doubles $199 to $359 in inn, $239 to 389 in hotel. Rest of year: $149 to $289 in inn, $179 to $359 in hotel.

Small and Choice

Bufflehead Cove Inn, Gornitz Lane, Box 499, Kennebunkport 04046.

Down a long dirt road and past a lily pond is this hidden treasure: a gray shingled, Dutch Colonial manse right on five wooded acres beside a scenic bend of the Kennebunk River, the kind of summer home you've always dreamed of. Owners Harriet and Jim Gott offer six stylish accommodations, each bright and cheerful and embellished with arty touches. The walls and ceilings are hand-painted with vines in the Cove Suite, two rooms with lots of wicker, a gas fireplace and a jacuzzi tub. The Garden Room in back has its own entrance and patio, a wicker sitting area, gas fireplace, a handcrafted queensize bed and grapevine stenciling that echoes the real vines outside the entry. The spacious Balcony Room with kingsize bed, fireplace and corner jacuzzi for two offers a wicker-filled balcony overlooking the river. The secluded Hideaway suite in the adjacent riverside cottage – mostly glass and windows – holds a kingsize bed, a central fireplace open to both bedroom and living room, two couches and a bathroom with a double jacuzzi. Outside is a private deck almost at water level. The latest treat is the deluxe River Cottage with cathedral-ceilinged living room/bedroom, fireplace, small kitchen, a loft with a library and entertainment center, and a soaring palladian window onto the water. The common rooms, porches and decks in the main house are made for enjoying the riverfront setting. Wine and cheese are served in the early evening, and there are decanters of sherry plus bottles of Bufflehead Cove sparkling water in each room. Harriet serves a memorable breakfast, perhaps asparagus strata or soufflés with popovers. Guests may not see much of Jim, a lobster fisherman, unless they join his fishing expedition at 4:30 a.m. He provides the lobster incorporated in the breakfast quiche and omelets.

(207) 967-3879. www.buffleheadcove.com. Three rooms, one suite and two cottages with private baths. June-November: doubles $165 to $295, suite and cottages $210 to $350. Rest of year: doubles $115 to $245, suites $175 to $350. Closed December-March.

The Inn at Harbor Head, 41 Pier Road, Kennebunkport 04046.

The tranquil setting of this rambling shingled home on a rocky knoll right above the picturesque Cape Porpoise harbor is an attraction at this small B&B. Another is the artistry inside the house. The four guest quarters, each with king or queensize canopy bed, are decorated with hand-painted murals. The entrance to the main-floor Garden Room is paved with stones and a little fountain, and original drawings of peach and plum blossoms float on the wall. The Greenery in which we stayed has a mural of fir trees by the shore, a bathroom with hand-painted tiles and jacuzzi tub, and a view of the front gardens. Painted clouds drift across the ceiling of the Summer Suite, which offers the best view of the harbor from its balcony. It also has a gas fireplace and a cathedral-ceilinged bathroom with skylight, bidet and jacuzzi tub. Innkeepers Eve and Dick Roesler serve breakfast in the elegant dining room that's the heart of the house. Crabmeat and bacon quiche, zucchini frittata or honey-pecan french toast could be the main course. Afterward, you may have neither the energy nor the will to leave the premises. Enjoy the colorful gardens beyond the rear terrace or relax on the lawn sloping to the shore, where you can swim from the floats or loll in an oversize rope hammock, watching the lobster boats go by.

(207) 967-5564. Fax (207) 967-1294. www.harborhead.com. Three rooms and one suite with private baths. Mid-June to mid-October: doubles $195 to $270, suite $325. Rest of year: doubles $160 to $245, suite $245 to $275. Closed November-April.

1802 House, 15 Locke St., Kennebunkport 04046.

Relax at this B&B on the side deck or broad lawns open to the 15th fairway of the Cape Arundel golf course and you feel you're out in the country. Inside the restored 1802 farmhouse on a quiet residential street, all is comfortable and thoroughly up-to-date. Innkeepers Marc and Susan Trottier offer six queensize guest rooms furnished in a Colonial motif that suits the house. Four have gas fireplaces and double whirlpool tubs and the other rooms have one or the other. The ultimate is the three-room Sebago Suite in a separate wing of the house. Its cozy living room comes with a fireplace, wet bar, refrigerator and TV/VCR. The bedroom has a canopy bed draped in white organza and an adjoining marble bathroom with a dual-head shower and heated tile floor. The third space is the "Roman Garden tub room," appointed with Italian tiles and containing a two-person whirlpool tub. From it, french doors open onto a private deck overlooking the golf course. Guests gather in an open common room, where a fire in a cast-iron potbelly stove on a brick platform warms the air on chilly days. Adjacent is a cheerful breakfast room, where intimate tables for two flank a large and convivial family table favored by many. The fare could be vegetable frittata or lemon-ricotta pancakes.

(207) 967-5632 or (800) 932-5632. Fax (207) 967-5632. www.1802inn.com. Five rooms and one suite with private baths. Doubles, $159 to $279, suite $299 to $379. Off-season, doubles $139 to $239, suite $259 to $299. Children over 12.

The Captain Fairfield Inn, Pleasant and Green Streets, Kennebunkport 04046.

This circa-1813 Federal sea captain's mansion, overlooking the River Green, wears its National Register listing proudly. Upgraded by recent owners, it offers nine air-conditioned guest quarters with new full baths, queensize beds dressed with pretty linens and lots of pillows, and comfortable sitting areas for two. Six have fireplaces and flat-panel TVs. Both are attributes of the prized main-floor Library Suite, which has a fishnet canopy queen bed, a bath with a double whirlpool tub and its own porch with two rocking chairs. Guests gather in an elegant living room or a music room with an ebony grand piano. French doors open from the music room onto the garden and a large side lawn. Tea and cookies are offered in the afternoon, and a decanter of port awaits in the living room. Breakfast, a highlight here, is served in a fireplaced gathering room and a sun room.

(207) 967-4454 or (800) 322-1928. Fax (207) 967-8537. www.captainfairfieldinn.com. Nine rooms with private baths. Doubles, $150 to $310 late June to late October, $120 to $250 rest of year.

'Escape from the 21st Century'

The Tides Inn By-the-Sea, 252 Kings Hwy., Goose Rocks Beach, Kennebunkport 04046.

You want to get away from the beautiful people and let your hair down in style? "Escape from the 21st century," innkeeper Marie Henriksen urges, to her yellow shingled Victorian charmer, barely a stone's throw from Goose Rocks Beach. She used to bill it as "a casual, crazy place with a true Maine air." After years of upgrades, it's still casual but nicely so, and not so crazy nor primitive as it used to be. All but three of the 22 refurbished guest rooms on the second and third floors now have modern baths (some of them admittedly small), and all but the shared-bath rooms contain king or queensize beds. Eleven yield ocean views. Plush carpeting and floral fabrics co-exist with antiques. There are whimsical and arty touches, from flowers painted on the doorways to faux designs atop bureaus. A mural of Teddy Roosevelt, who signed an early guest book, graces the third-floor stairwell, and Marie likes to show off a surprise visitor lurking behind one doorway. A large Victorian living room/lobby contains the inn's TV set. Continental breakfast is served in the sun porch overlooking the beach.

Dinner is offered in the richly paneled **Belvidere Club,** a vintage Victorian dining room and bar. The menu begins with the likes of Timber Island crab cake with roasted garlic and corn salad, mussels steamed in ale and a signature salad of spinach, toasted walnuts and herbed goat cheese. Main courses range from braised Chilean sea bass with chive sauce to grilled hanger steak with foie gras butter. Still etched in our memories is a sensational dinner here of grilled lamb with a side of salsa containing the proper amount of cilantro and a delectable grilled shrimp and fettuccine with green onions, sundried tomatoes, basil and garlic cream.

(207) 967-3757. www.tidesinnbythesea.com. Nineteen rooms with private baths and three with shared bath. Doubles, $195 to $325 mid-June to Labor Day, $145 to $325 rest of year. Closed mid-October to mid-May.

Lodges and Cottages

The Yachtsman Lodge & Marina, Ocean Avenue, Box 2609, Kennebunkport 04046.

Savor the sun and shore at the most luxurious "motor lodge" quarters you're likely to see. Laurence Bongiorno of the nearby White Barn Inn took over the old Yachtsman motel beside the Kennebunk River, parked his 44-foot yacht in the marina and transformed the interior into an inn-like lodge of distinction. Each spacious room with vaulted ceiling is the same, done in understated style to resemble a yacht with cream-colored, bead-board walls accented with sailing prints and mahogany trim. The kingsize bed is dressed in a fluffy white goose-down duvet covered in Egyptian cotton and the TV is hidden in an armoire. Furnishings include two cushioned rattan chairs, a round table and a writing desk. The closet lights automatically to reveal terrycloth robes, a mini-refrigerator chills bottled water, and the bathroom has a granite vanity bearing all kinds of toiletries. The front of the room is screened from the parking area and road by lush landscaping. The back opens through french doors onto private patios with lounge furniture facing a swath of lawn about fifteen feet from river's edge. Quacking ducks that paraded by made more noise than the sleek yachts passing the marina at our visit. A common terrace between the two lodge buildings has plenty of lounge furniture, the better for enjoying the afternoon spread of beverages and pastries. A huge, push-button coffee machine produces cappuccino and espresso. The sunny breakfast room holds a complimentary array of fruit, cereals and baked goods including, at our stay, a savory quiche prepared by the White Barn Inn kitchen.

(207) 967-2511. Fax (207) 967-5056. www.yachtsmanlodge.com. Thirty rooms with private baths. Doubles, $289 to $315 in July and August, $149 to $299 rest of year. Closed January-March.

The Seaside Inn & Cottages, 80 Beach Ave., Box 631, Kennebunkport 04046.

Varied and comfortable accommodations at the head of the Kennebunk River on a twenty-acre oceanfront peninsula with your own beach. That's what you get at this appealing establishment beside Gooch's Beach. Sandra and Michael Severance run the place that his Gooch family forebears founded twelve generations ago in 1667. Six extra-spacious oceanfront rooms on the second floor of the 22-room motor inn are most in demand, although the rest are no slouches. Each has two queensize beds, TVs recessed in Queen Anne highboys, two leather armchairs, a small refrigerator in a wet bar area, and deck chairs on a private balcony or patio. Six ground-floor rooms face the ocean, although occupants must stretch to see it over the dunes. The terrace-side rooms look out onto attractive grounds. Ten efficiency cottages of one to four bedrooms, most with river or ocean views, are scattered about the property and rent by the month in summer, weekly in the off-season. Closest to the beach is a year-round two-bedroom beach house aptly called The Dunes. Guests enjoy a complimentary continental-plus breakfast in an 1850 boathouse room.

(207) 967-446 or (800) 967-4461. www.kennebunkbeachmaine.com. Twenty-two rooms, ten cottages and one beach house with private baths. Doubles, $229 to $245 in summer, $105 to $185 rest of year. Cottages, from $995 weekly in off-season to $9,250 monthly in summer. House, $12,999 monthly in summer, $1,000 to $3,100 weekly rest of year.

Where to Eat

The White Barn Inn, 37 Beach Ave., Kennebunkport.

If fine food is your priority, know that some of the best dining in New England takes place in this white barn against a breathtaking backdrop of flowers rising on tiers outside a twenty-foot-high rear window, all dramatically illuminated at night. Two barnwood dining rooms are filled with understated antiques and oil paintings dating to the 18th century, and the loft holds quite a collection of wildlife wood carvings. Leather chairs from Italy are at white-linened tables set with silver, Schottsweizel crystal and Villeroy & Boch china. Swiss-trained British chef Jonathan Cartwright's food is in the vanguard of contemporary regional cuisine. Dinner is prix-fixe in four courses, with eight to ten choices for most courses. Our latest dinner, the highlight of several over the years, began with a glass of Perrier-Jouët extra brut (complimentary for house guests) and the chef's "welcome amenity," an herbed goat cheese rosette, a tiny onion tart and a tapenade of eggplant and kalamata olives. A lobster spring roll with daikon radish, savoy cabbage and hot and sweet glaze, and seared Hudson Valley foie gras on an apple and celeriac tart with a calvados sauce were sensational appetizers. Champagne sorbet in a pool of Piper Heidsieck extra-dry cleared the palate with a flourish for the main courses.

One was a duo of Maine rabbit: a grilled loin with roasted rosemary and pommery mustard and a braised leg in cabernet sauvignon, accompanied by wild mushrooms and pesto-accented risotto. The other was pan-seared tenderloin of beef topped with a horseradish gratin and port-glazed shallots on a pool of potato and Vermont cheddar cheese, with a fancy little side of asparagus. Dessert was anything but anti-climactic: a classic coeur à la crème with tropical fruits and sugared shortbread and a trio of pear, raspberry and mango sorbets, served artistically on a black plate with colored swirls matching the sorbets and decorated with squiggles of white and powdered sugar. A tray of petits-fours gilded the lily.

(207) 967-2321. Prix-fixe, $89. www.whitebarninn.com. Dinner nightly, 6 to 9:30, Friday-Sunday from 5:30. Closed two weeks in mid-January. Jackets required.

Cape Arundel Inn, Ocean Avenue, Kennebunkport.

What could be more romantic than dining at a window table at the Cape Arundel, watching wispy clouds turn to mauve and violet as the sun sets, followed by a full golden moon rising over the darkened ocean? That the food is so good is a bonus. The sea and sky provide more than enough backdrop for owner Jack Nahil's simple but stylish dining room that's a study in white and cobalt blue. Chef Rich Lemoine's changing repertoire runs the gamut of regional American fare. Crusty basil-parmesan-rosemary bread got our latest dinner here off to a good start. Appetizers were a composed spinach salad with prosciutto and oyster mushrooms and an artfully presented chilled sampler of ginger poached shrimp, a crab-filled spring roll and tea-smoked sirloin with wasabi citrus rémoulade. Main courses were a superior sliced leg of lamb teamed with cavatelli pasta and wilted arugula, and a mixed grill of duck sausage, veal london broil and loin lamb chop. Seafood choices ranged from pan-fried halibut with a russet and sweet potato crust to a broiled seafood sampler served over saffron fettuccine with spicy rouille. The dessert of cinnamon ice cream with strawberries over lady fingers was enough for two to share.

(207) 967-2125. Entrées, $24 to $36. Dinner, Monday-Saturday 5:30 to 8:30 or 9. Closed January to mid-April.

Grissini Italian Bistro, 27 Western Ave., Kennebunkport.

Spirited Tuscan cooking with a New England accent emanates from this glamorous bistro owned by Laurie Bongiorno of the White Barn Inn. It's a stunning space, with vaulted beamed ceilings three stories high and a tall fieldstone fireplace. Sponged pale yellow walls, large tables spaced well apart, comfortable lacquered wicker armchairs, and fancy bottles and sculptures backlit in the windows create a thoroughly sophisticated feeling. On warm nights, crowds spill onto a tiered outdoor courtyard that rather resembles a grotto. Opera music played in the background as a plate of tasty little crostini, some with pesto and black olives and some with gorgonzola cheese and tomato, arrived to start our dinner. Among antipasti, we loved the wood-grilled local venison sausage on a warm caramelized onion salad and the house-cured Maine salmon carpaccio with olive oil, herbs and lemon juice and topped with pasta salad. Secondi range from pan-seared lobster tail with olive oil, smashed potato and herbs to osso buco. The wood-grilled leg of lamb steak with Tuscan white beans, pancetta, garlic and rosemary was sensational. A sampler plate of tiramisu, a chocolate delicacy and strawberries in balsamic vinegar with mascarpone cheese wound up a memorable dinner.

(207) 967-2211. www.restaurantgrissini.com. Entrées, $20.95 to $26.95. Dinner nightly, 5:30 to 9 or 9:30.

Hurricane Restaurant, 29 Dock Square, Kennebunkport.

The old family-style seafood restaurant that inspired owner Brooks MacDonald to think about the restaurant business is now Hurricane No. 2, an offshoot of the Ogunquit trend-setter. In place of the soda fountain where he hung out as a teenager is a hand-crafted mahogany bar serving 60 wines by the glass to patrons in a 90-seat restaurant set on pilings over the Kennebunk River. The contemporary American menu features Hurricane's signature dishes and a few items unique to Dock Square. Seafood and lobster are the specialties on a roster ranging from pan-roasted arctic char served over black quinoa to the signature lobster cioppino. Fire-roasted Chilean sea bass served over a crispy duck confit and fingerling potato hash, oven-roasted Alaskan halibut with grilled apples and papaya coulis, and fennel-crusted rack of lamb finished with preserved lingonberry sauce are typical. A bento box of shrimp, scallop and salmon lumpia, Maine lobster rangoon, vegetable nori rolls and marinated beef is a specialty appetizer to be shared. The pastry chef's desserts could be warm rum-raisin bread pudding with orange sabayon or chocolate-grand marnier crème brûlée.

(207) 967-9111. www.hurricanerestaurant.com. Entrées, $18 to $39. Lunch daily, 11:30 to 3. Dinner nightly, 5:30 to 10:30, to 9:30 in winter.

Pier 77, 77 Pier Road, Cape Porpoise, Kennebunkport.

This is the trendy successor to our favorite Seascapes restaurant, the latest incarnation of a landmark building that's been a restaurant at the edge of Cape Porpoise Harbor for more than 70 years. Chef-owner Peter Morency renovated the place to reflect his New England roots and wife Kate's sense of San Francisco laid-back flair. "Contemporary American fine dining without attitude" is their hallmark. That and an unbeatable view of the harbor through floor-to-ceiling windows on two sides, with a stylish, less-is-more decor that capitalizes on the outdoor scene. The harbor waters lap at the door of the walkout lower-level **Ramp Bar & Grill,** where you can drink at outdoor tables or order from an appealing grill menu amid sports memorabilia inside. We sampled the creative kitchen's fare at an autumn lunch. The clam chowder, though tasty, contained far more potatoes than clams. The roasted chicken taquito with guacamole and salsa fresca was delicious, and the star of the show was succulent fish and chips, paired with superior coleslaw. Desserts were pumpkin cheesecake with caramel sauce and warm banana cake with milk chocolate ganache. At night, the chef shines with the likes of cioppino, seafood mixed grill, grilled hanger steak, grilled pork chop and lamb kabobs.

(207)967-8500. www.pier77restaurant.com. Entrées, $20 to $30. Lunch daily in summer, 11:30 to 3. Dinner nightly, 5 to 10. Closed Tuesday and Wednesday in off-season.

Stripers, 127 Ocean Ave., Kennebunkport.

This stylish newcomer began life as Stripers Fish Shack and dropped the "fish shack" from its name in 2004 when it relocated from an outbuilding behind the former Schooners Inn to the main waterfront dining room of the Breakwater Inn. It's now Stripers, "a waterfront restaurant and raw bar." Here is White Barn Inn owner Laurence Bongiorno's shrine to seafood, still something of a "fish shack" in terms of food concept but stylish as all get-out in its stunning new digs at the rear of the inn. Atop each elegantly set table is a mini-aquarium harboring a tropical fish inside, mirroring the giant aquarium at the entry. Also on the table is a stash of appropriate sauces for what amounts to the original fish shack fare. The menu is short and deceptively straightforward, but eons removed in delivery from the clam shack and fish fry idiom. Look for the day's catch (swordfish, Atlantic salmon, halibut, yellowfin tuna), available chargrilled, broiled or pan seared and served – as are most entrées – with fries and what the menu calls "mushy" peas, a mix of mashed and whole peas in a rich buttery and creamy mash. Also look for lobster, bouillabaisse and blackboard specials. Perhaps the best fish and chips you ever ate comes in the form of ale-battered haddock with fries, garnished with wedges of lemon and lime. Other favorites are the seafood platter – an array of oysters, shrimp, clams, mussels and cracked lobster – and the bento box. Soups, stews, salads and appetizers are offered to begin. The only other "fishless options" are grilled chicken, filet mignon and rack of lamb. Desserts include peanut butter pie, apple crumble and vanilla bean crème brûlée. Just off the porch is a spacious raw bar with seating for dining and cocktails.

(207) 967-3625. Entrées, $17.50 to $32.50. Lunch daily in summer, 11:30 to 2:30. Dinner, Monday-Thursday 5:30 to 9, Friday-Sunday 5 to 9:30. Closed January-March.

Windows on the Water, 12 Chase Hill Road, Kennebunkport.

The windows are architecturally interesting at this expansive restaurant on a hilltop above the Kennebunk River, although their views have been obstructed by the Federal Jack's Restaurant & Brew Pub complex below. Chef-owner John Hughes has earned quite a collection of awards for his lobster-stuffed baked potato, lobster ravioli, lobster bisque and free-range chicken tortellini alfredo in what he markets as "bold cross-cultural cuisine." The dinner menu ranges from Portuguese fisherman's stew and coriander-crusted tuna with lime rémoulade to pan-seared duck breast with peppercorn-armagnac sauce and grilled filet mignon topped with brandy-infused foie gras and a marsala demi-glace. Typical starters are prosciutto-wrapped sea scallops, a duo of lobster and crab cakes with distinctive sauces, and beef satay with a trio of dipping sauces. Dessert could be lemon cheesecake, chocolate oblivion torte and charlotte au chocolat. Dining is in a variety of different-windowed venues, plus a two-level Garden Room at the side, half enclosed and half screened. Upstairs is a lounge with a cathedral ceiling and a Palladian window overlooking the river.

(207) 967-3313 or (800) 773-3313. www.windowsonthewater.com. Entrées, $24 to $38. Lunch daily, 11:45 to 2:30. Dinner, 5:30 to 9:30 or 10:30. Closed Monday in winter.

On the Marsh, 46 Western Ave. (Route 9), Lower Village, Kennebunk.

The soaring, barn-like interior of the former Salt Marsh Tavern is chicly elegant, thanks to new owner Denise Rubin, an interior designer. Here she offers diners "a feast for the eyes as well as the palate," changing the decor with the seasons. All the artworks on the walls, most of the antiques adorning the lofts and even the chairs and the silverware are for sale. Tables are flanked by fancy padded chairs that the owner designed and are draped to the floor in white-over-emerald cloths. Large rear windows look onto a salt marsh stretching toward Kennebunk Beach. With an eye for the dramatic, the owner and her chefs categorize their menu by "prologue" and "performance." Warm up with a foie gras torchon with dried cherries or lobster ravioli with leeks and peas. Typical main courses are oven-roasted halibut with herb butter, muscovy duck breast and confit, and seared filet mignon with béarnaise sauce. Desserts include dark chocolate pâté with rum crème anglaise and, the owner's favorite, blueberry-raspberry sorbet with Belgian chocolate spears.

(207) 967-2299. www.onthemarsh.com. Entrées, $19 to $30. Dinner nightly, from 5:30. Closed Monday and Tuesday in off-season and month of January.

Bandaloop, 2 Ocean Ave., Kennebunkport.

This lively new restaurant overlooking Dock Square is a favorite with the late-night crowd, but it also earns plaudits for its assertive contemporary cuisine at down-to-earth prices. Chef-owner Scott Lee, who came to town to open On the Marsh, moved on to his own place in 2004. He named it for the fictional tribe that claimed to know the secret to eternal life, which he celebrates here with good food and wine – make that healthy food, for he serves organic, natural and local products whenever possible. You don't often see tofu skewers or three-grain organic tempeh on a menu hereabouts. He offers those and more, pairing half a dozen entrée selections with an equal number of sauces, all vegan or vegetarian. You could order haddock fillet, pork medallions or hanger steak and pair them with Thai green curry sauce, ginger-red plum glaze or creamy roasted garlic gravy – whatever turns you on. If those don't appeal, try the night's specials, perhaps Scottish salmon with a grapefruit beurre blanc or free-range Australian lamb loin medallions with an ouzo and roasted garlic sauce. Warm up with crab and avocado cakes, steamed mussels or "egg rolls." Finish with the blueberry and apple crisp, "vegan and flourless until we add vanilla ice cream." The bar swings with live music some evenings.

(207) 967-4994. www.bandaloop.biz. Entrées, $17 to $23. Dinner nightly from 6. Closed Tuesday in off-season.

Arundel Wharf Restaurant, 43 Ocean Ave., Kennebunkport.

The expansive deck at this riverfront landmark affords 125 outdoor diners the best waterfront setting in town. Another 75 can be seated inside at shiny nautical chart tables amidst wooden ship models, mahogany accents and a distinct yacht-club feel. Happily, the food is equal to the setting. The lobster club sandwich, the meaty lobster stew and the avocado stuffed with crabmeat made a fine lunch one day. The extensive dinner menu ranges from charbroiled swordfish and roasted fillet of sole to the Passamaquoddy clambake – a pottery crock filled with steamers and mussels and topped with a lobster. Lobster comes seven ways. "Other interests" are served by chicken diablo, prime rib or venison sauté. Or you can settle for fried seafood or a basic hamburger. Save room for dessert, perhaps bread pudding with whiskey sauce, mixed four-berry pie or blueberry-apple crisp.

(207) 967-3444. www.arundelwharf.com. Entrées, $15.50 to $34.95. Lunch daily, 11:30 to 2:30. Dinner nightly, 5 to 9 or 9:30. Closed late October to mid-April.

Mabel's Lobster Claw, 124 Ocean Ave., Kennebunkport.

George and Barbara Bush sometimes eat lobsters here, as do locals partial to Mabel Hanson's small, personal place across the street from the water. The interior is fancier than you might expect from the name or the exterior. You sit at booths or tables with leather chairs amid knotty pine paneling, and citronella candles flicker at night. For more than 30 years, Mabel has done all the cooking and baking – quite a feat considering the size of her menu. Seafood and lobster reign, of course, from seafood newburg to lobster savannah. Start with Mabel's homemade soup or chowder. End up with her famous peanut-butter ice cream pie.

(207) 967-2562. Entrées, $15.95 to $27.95. Lunch daily, 11:30 to 3. Dinner, 5 to 9. Closed November-March.

FOR MORE INFORMATION: Kennebunk and Kennebunkport Chamber of Commerce, 17 Western Ave., Box 740, Kennebunk, ME 04043. (207) 957-0857. www.visitthekennebunks.com.

Casco Bay and islands are on view from park along Portland's Eastern Promenade.

Portland, Maine

Maine(ly) City

They call Portland the "Forest City," but it is not the greens or the density of the trees that catch the eye of visitors. Rather it is the blues of the ocean and its tidal inlets and bays on all sides. This is, as native son Henry Wadsworth Longfellow famously described it, "the beautiful town that is seated by the sea."

The sea defines Maine's largest city. Although actually beside Casco Bay, the city is a peninsula ringed on all flanks by water, and the proximity of the water on every side is the first thing a visitor notices. The second may be the city's height. The downtown is on a crest that gives it something of the look of an old European town – it is one of few cities in this country where the downtown is located higher than its surroundings.

The height is fortuitous. On a clear day, the view of the shimmering waters of Casco Bay from the Eastern Promenade is breathtaking. From no other Eastern city do the blues of the water, the greens of the islands and the whites of the sailboats seem quite so pristine. From the Western Promenade, you can see New Hampshire's White Mountains.

Portland, variously described as a big town or a little city (population, 65,000), is the rejuvenated urban center of the largest state in northern New England. Portland slumbered longer than many New England cities, so it is perhaps a surprise that it has come farther and faster than most. Faced with a dying port in the 1950s, business interests gave the city a new downtown with mini-skyscrapers and plazas, landscaping and monuments, kiosks and élan. They also gave it a thriving cultural and entertainment life, including the Portland Performing Arts Center, the Portland Symphony Orchestra and the expanded Museum of Art with its collection of paintings by Winslow Homer, the pride of Portland. The city's professional teams consistently set attendance records for minor-league baseball and hockey.

A lively group known as Greater Portland Landmarks Inc. is responsible for 45 years of restoration efforts that are turning Portland into what some call, on a lesser scale, "the Savannah of the North."

The crowning restoration achievement is the Old Port, an edge-of-downtown historic district fashioned from a decaying waterfront where restaurants, boutiques and galleries flourish side by side with sailmakers and ship's chandlers.

Some of the city's best restaurants and most interesting shops are located here. The working waterfront nearby is the hub of fishing and boating activity. It is the port of call for ocean liners and the departure point for cruises around Casco Bay's 365 Calendar Islands, four of them occupied by year-round residents who commute to Portland.

Savor this rejuvenated city, which is compact enough to get around in and enjoy in a day. But know that you also can easily get out of the city. Head south through Cape Elizabeth to Two Lights, Scarborough and the coastal beaches. Head north along Route 88 through suburban Falmouth Foreside and old Yarmouth. And head east, out onto the Casco Bay islands.

Portland offers a little of everything for an urban getaway.

Seeing and Doing

Sightseeing

Old Port. The restored port district southeast of downtown between Monument Square and the waterfront is at once the city's oldest and newest neighborhood. Settled in the 1600s, the area was ravaged by the British during the Revolution and by the Great Fire of 1866. It was rebuilt, but was going downhill until Greater Portland Landmarks began revitalizing the area in the 1960s. An old-town restoration like those out West, Portland's is particularly successful and well done, although the accoutrements of a sophisticated city tend to overshadow what boosters describe as "a working harbor full of the sights, sounds and smells of the sea."

Exquisite architecture, landscaping, colorful signs, benches, mini-parks and a lifelike trompe-l'oeil mural on a building at Middle and Exchange streets make this a fine place in which to stroll as well as partake of scores of shops and restaurants. Exchange, Fore and Middle streets are the core, but don't overlook the side streets in this approximately five-block-square area stretching between Congress and Commercial streets.

Guided walking tours of the Old Port area are offered in summer by Greater Portland Landmarks, (207) 774-5561. Tours leave Monday-Saturday at 10:30, mid-June to Columbus Day, from the Portland Convention and Visitors Bureau, 245 Commercial St.; adults $8, children free.

WALKING TOURS. Congress Street, the city's main thoroughfare from historic Stroudwater to the Eastern Promenade, is also the main business street and is noteworthy for its landmark buildings, from the old Romanesque public library at

619 to the French Renaissance City Hall at 389. A Greater Portland Landmarks brochure guides the way, as do others to the Old Port, Western Promenade and the State and High street area, which was added in 1971 to the National Register of Historic Places in recognition of its architectural examples. These were the grand homes of old Portland, many of them Federal and Greek Revival. On the other side of Congress Square is Deering Street, an enclave of notable Victorian residences only a block removed from the city's business heart.

SHOPPING. With the distinctive sound of seagulls all around, the shops in the Old Port draw their share of browsers and buyers, and more good stores open every year. **The Stein Gallery** at 30 Milk St. showcases perfectly stunning glass pieces by more than 100 artists from across the country. A Los Angeles couple staying at our B&B were about to buy a spectacular large vase for $650 and considered it a bargain. Original jewelry by top Maine designers is showcased at **Fibula.** The stunning paintings in the window at **Lyn Snow Watercolors** caught our eye. At **Portmanteau** you can watch colorful handbags and totes of canvas and tapestry being made. We've bought a couple of tapestry handbags here over the years – they are distinctive and sold nowhere else. **Casco Bay Wool Works** is the retail outlet for its handcrafted blankets and elegant capes and shawls of Merino wool and cashmere, plus the slick-looking Casco Bay "rain wrap." **Serendipity** offers lovely sweaters, mohair throws and Geiger clothes, while **Abacus** stocks unusual and very contemporary jewelry, pottery and other craft items. For years, **Amaryllis** has been the place to go for unique and trendy clothing, with a competitor emerging lately in **Betsy's.** The **Paper Patch** carries cards for all occasions and we stock up every year. **The Foreside Company** has interesting accessories for the home, many from Indonesia, at factory prices. **Covent Garden** has especially nice soaps and Caswell-Massey items, as well as MacKenzie-Childs pottery. The selection of pottery at **Maxwell's Pottery Outlet** at 384 Fore St. is outstanding. The **Maine Potters Market,** a co-op just across the street, is also a worthwhile stop. European antiques, art and accessories are featured on the main floor of **The Clown,** while the downstairs showcases Maine's largest wine cellar. Check out the earth-friendly housewares, clothing and gifts at **The Resourceful Home.**

Uptown at 542 Congress St. is a new **L.L. Bean Factory Store.**

The Ultimate Downtown Farm Market

Portland Public Market, Preble Street and Cumberland Avenue, Portland.

New England's biggest farm market was built from scratch at the edge of downtown in 1998 by Maine philanthropist Elizabeth Noyce. A block long and half as wide, it's an architectural marvel of timbered beams, walls of windows and soaring ceilings. A granite central fireplace is flanked by stone benches, where you can rest your weary bones after navigating the aisles. More than two dozen selected Maine food growers and high-end vendors purvey everything from elk to eels. We often stop here to pick up an interesting cheese or two, plus some of the state's famed Borealis Breads (the apple-nut bread is especially good for french toast). A couple of butcher shops sell exotic meats raised on nearby farms. Besides all the market stalls, there's a steakhouse restaurant called **Maverick's** and the casual **Scales** seafood shack, opened by top local restaurateurs Dana Street and Sam Hayward.

(207) 228-2000. www.portlandmarket.com. Open Monday-Saturday 9 to 7, Sunday 10 to 5.

DRIVING TOURS. Although downtown and the Old Port are for walking, cars are a necessity for most Portland visitors, and the city and surroundings are extraordinarily easy to traverse by car (with a good map). Drive out Congress Street past the landmark Portland Observatory to the **Eastern Promenade,** an aptly named residential street along the crest overlooking Casco Bay. It's bordered by parkland with a municipal pool, benches where you can enjoy a panoramic view and the occasional picnic table. Fort Allen Park possesses a cannon from the USS Maine and overlooks old Fort Gorges in the harbor. Continue your tour to Route 1 and Baxter Boulevard around the Back Cove, past more water and parks and a bayside trail frequented by walkers and joggers. Eventually you get to the **Western Promenade** and its Reed Monument. From here on a clear day you can see Mount Washington in New Hampshire and tour another area of imposing, architectural-landmark residences.

To the north is Falmouth Foreside, home of the Portland Country Club, Portland Yacht Club and waterfront estates. Beyond, Yarmouth has some of the area's earliest buildings, plus the **Cousins Island Beach,** which is excellent for swimming.

To the south is suburban Cape Elizabeth, with fine residential sections beside Casco Bay. A favorite stop is **Fort Williams Park** and the Portland Head Light and museum. Farther on are **Two Lights State Park** and the Lobster Shack at Two Lights, where you can feast on lobster at picnic tables with a spectacular view of the open Atlantic. Still farther are **Crescent Beach State Park, Higgins Beach** and the exclusive summer colony of **Prouts Neck,** whose rugged cliffs inspired artist Winslow Homer and where his studio is to become part of the Portland Museum of Art.

Cultural and Historic Sites

Portland Museum of Art, 7 Congress Square, Portland.

This is widely considered northern New England's most important art museum, although it has been upstaged lately by the Farnsworth Museum and Wyeth Center in mid-coast Rockland. Philanthropist and summer resident Charles Shipman Payson not only sparked the museum's expansion with his gift of seventeen Winslow Homer paintings, but provided the funding for a showcase addition bearing his name. The magnificent I.M. Pei-designed structure (1983) joins the original Federal-style McLellan-Sweat House (1800) and L.D.M. Sweat Memorial (1911) museum buildings and provides five times as much space. The four-story structure with its enormous elevator, a staircase that makes you feel as if you're floating upstairs and portholes through which you look outside is intriguing. So are Payson's Homer collection, the works of Andrew Wyeth and Rockwell Kent, the American Galleries, the decorative arts galleries, the Pepperrell Silver Collection and changing exhibitions. The Joan Whitney Payson Collection is a remarkable group of Impressionist and Post-Impressionist works by Picasso, Monet, Degas, Renoir, Van Gogh and others. In 2004, the museum launched a capital campaign to acquire and preserve the Winslow Homer Studio in nearby Prouts Neck.

(207) 775-6148. www.portlandmuseum.org. Open daily 10 to 5, Friday to 9, Memorial Day to Columbus Day; closed Monday rest of year. Adults $8, children $2.

Wadsworth-Longfellow House, 489 Congress St., Portland.

Henry Wadsworth Longfellow wrote much of his early poetry in Portland's first brick building (1785), the oldest surviving residence on the Portland peninsula. A beauty it is, with virtually all of its furnishings and contents original to the illustrious

Wadsworth and Longfellow families. The poet's grandfather, General Peleg Wadsworth, built the house with bricks shipped by barge from Philadelphia. Within its walls lived three generations of one remarkable family that made significant contributions to the political, literary and cultural life of the nation. Deeded to the Maine Historical Society upon the death of the poet's younger sister in 1901, it is the only single-family residence to survive downtown Congress Street's evolution from mixed-use to urban business district. Guided tours of the house, restored to the 1850s period when Longfellow had become a national literary figure, offer a glimpse into the life of his family as well as the cultural and social history of 19th-century Portland. Behind the house and its lovely garden is the Center for Maine History Museum, with changing exhibitions and an outstanding research library.

(207) 879-0427. www.mainehistory.com. Open May-October, Monday-Saturday 10 to 5, Sunday noon to 5; also holiday hours in November and December. Adults $7, children $3. Price includes admission to museum, which is open year-round.

Victoria Mansion, 109 Danforth St., Portland.

This 1860 brownstone edifice, one of the nation's most opulent Italian villas, is considered the finest example of residential design from the pre-Civil War era in America. Its interior was among the most lavish and sophisticated of its era, reflecting what one scholar described as "an encyclopedia of mid-19th-century decoration, domestic life and determined elegance." The mansion was built in the downtown area with a view of the harbor below for hotel magnate Ruggles Morse. Drawing on his experience in the luxury hotel trade, Morse incorporated such ahead-of-their-time amenities as a master bedroom with adjoining bathroom, a billiards room and a Turkish smoking room – the last is the first documented smoking room in a private house in America, though such rooms were common in hotels at the time. The house retains most of the original contents, including a remarkable, six-by-25-foot stained-glass skylight atop the soaring, three-story stair hall. Notable are the richly carved woodwork, colorful frescoes, trompe-l'oeil walls and ceilings, carved marble fireplaces and etched glass. New York interior designer Gustave Herter created the sumptuous interiors, coordinating everything from the elaborate plasterwork and gas lighting fixtures to the plush carpets, upholstery fabrics and window treatments. An important collection of furniture, designed and manufactured in his New York workshops, represents his only surviving commission. Guided tours of the house leave every half hour and last 45 minutes.

(207) 772-4841. www.victoriamansion.org. Open May-October, Tuesday-Saturday 10 to 4, Sunday 1 to 5; also in December for Christmas at Victoria Mansion. Adults $10, children $3.

Portland Observatory, 138 Congress St., Portland.

Built in 1807 atop Munjoy Hill, this is not a lighthouse but rather the last surviving maritime signal tower in the country. The octagonal, 86-foot-high tower served as a communication station for the busy Portland Harbor for more than 100 years. From his lofty perch, sea captain-turned-entrepreneur Lemuel Moody used a powerful telescope to identify incoming vessels and then signaled downtown merchants with coded signal flags. "Signalizing" allowed merchants time to reserve a berth on the wharves and to hire stevedores before the vessel docked. Now the tower contains exhibits detailing its history and preservation. Climb its 102 steps for a panoramic view of the city, Casco Bay and the White Mountains.

(207) 774-5561. www.portlandlandmarks.org. Open daily 10 to 5, Memorial Day to Columbus Day. Adults $5, children $4.

The Museum at Portland Head Light, 1000 Shore Road, Cape Elizabeth.

The East's oldest operating lighthouse, commissioned in 1791 by George Washington, is said to be the Atlantic coast's most photographed. The lighthouse at the entrance to Portland Harbor was occupied continuously until 1989, when it was automated. The main floor of the lighthouse keepers' quarters is now a museum. Exhibits chronicle the history of Portland Head Light and Fort Williams, a military outpost that developed for coastal defense next to the lighthouse. Included are original artifacts and documents, navigational aids, lenses, models and video displays. The 90-acre fort property is an appealing town park with trails, picnic tables, a pebble beach and great views of the ocean. A small museum shop is housed in an adjacent garage.

(207) 799-2661. www.portlandheadlight.com. Museum open daily 10 to 4, June to mid-October; weekends, mid-April-May and mid-October to mid-December. Adults $2, children $1. Park open daily, dawn to dusk. Free.

Tate House, 1270 Westbrook St., Portland.

Built in 1755 by George Tate, mast agent for Britain's Royal Navy, this house in the historic Stroudwater neighborhood is maintained by the National Society of Colonial Dames of America in Maine. With gambrel roof, eight fireplaces and the parlor table set for tea, it reflects an 18th-century London townhouse. Out back, a raised-bed herb garden of 18th-century plants overlooks the Stroudwater River. Saturday afternoon architectural tours show the cellar, servants' quarters and attic.

(207) 774-9781. www.tatehouse.org. Open Tuesday-Saturday 10 to 4 and Sunday 1 to 4, mid-June through September, Friday-Sunday through October. Adults $5, children $2.

On the Water

Swimming is offered at Crescent Beach State Park, where sand dunes lead to a gentle beach with locker rooms, concession stand and picnic grills. Higgins Beach in Scarborough is fine, but parking is limited; beyond is Scarborough State Beach with good surf. Far less crowded and free, to boot, is the delightful Cousins Island Beach across the causeway from Yarmouth. There's no surf and it's a bit of a climb down (stairs provided), but the bay waters are warmer (65 degrees, compared with the ocean's 58) and the beach far less populated.

Scarborough Marsh Nature Center, Pine Point Road, Scarborough.

The Maine Audubon Society center covers 3,000 acres of salt marsh rich in plant and animal life. Although naturalists lead tours, a favorite pursuit is paddling a canoe through the marshes to see wildlife on your own. Canoe rentals are $15 an hour. Guided sunrise, sunset and full moon tours are offered periodically. You can go on a guided bird walk or wildflower walk. The center has rotating exhibits, aquariums and a nature store.

(207) 883-5100. Open daily, 9:30 to 5:30, mid-June to Labor Day, weekends in June and September.

BOAT TOURS. Several daily cruises are offered from its ferry terminal at Commercial and Franklin streets by **Casco Bay Lines,** (207) 774-7871. These are the sidelines to a working ferry service – said to be America's oldest – transporting residents, school children, mail and necessities along with visitors to and from the Calendar Islands. The mail boat stops twice daily at Cliff, Chebeague, Long, and Little and Great Diamond islands, giving visitors dockside views of island life (see below). The premier cruise (adults $18, children $8) is a six-hour trip to Bailey Island, where you get off for lunch. Shorter cruises go to Diamond Pass or involve sunset and moonlight excursions.

The smaller **Bay View Cruises**, 184 Commercial St. on Fisherman's Wharf, (207) 761-0496, offers seal watch, island, harbor, cocktail, brunch, lobster bake and sunset cruises from 10:30 to 6:30 daily in summer; adults $10, children $7. **Olde Port Mariner Fleet,** 170 Commercial St., (207) 775-0727 or (800) 437-3270, offers daily whale watches, harbor cruises, dinner cruises and assorted other options, daily in July and August and weekends in June and September. Six-hour whale watch cruises out to Jeffrey's Ledge depart at 10; adults $38, children $28. Ninety-minute harbor cruises leave at 11, 12:45 and 2:30; adults $10, children $7. Walking tours of fishing operations and the working waterfront leave daily at 10; adults $10, children $8.

Narrated lighthouse cruises are offered up to five times daily by **Mainely Tours,** 163 Commercial St., (207) 774-0808, in conjunction with its sightseeing tours by trolley; land and sea combination, adults $22, children $13. The cruise portion is run by **Eagle Island Tours,** 1 Long Wharf, (207) 774-6498, adults $10, children $7. Its four-hour narrated tour at 10 a.m. daily goes to Eagle Island and Admiral Robert E. Peary's summer home; adults $24, children $13.

Up to 48 passengers board the 72-foot schooner *Bagheera* for two-hours cruises on Casco Bay. They're offered four times daily by the **Portland Schooner Co.,** (207) 766-2500 or (877) 246-6637, leaving from the Maine State Pier on Commercial Street except Tuesdays when it leaves from Peaks Island; adults $25 to $35, children $12.

The 58-foot ocean racer **Palawan,** (207) 773-2163 or (888) 284-7251, gives morning, afternoon and all-day sails through the Calendar Islands from Long Wharf for $20 to $95 per person.

Cruise to the Casco Bay Islands

One of the joys of being in Portland is its proximity to the 365 Calendar Islands just offshore in Casco Bay – a scene not unlike that of the Puget Sound islands near Seattle. Several thousand people live on four main islands, many commuting to jobs and school in Portland. The islands are rustic, even primitive. Although partly within view of the city, Portlanders say, "it's a different world out there."

Visitors can get onto the islands via the Casco Bay Lines mail boats and working ferries, which in summer run as frequently as hourly. Peaks Island, the closest major island to the city, has a year-round population of 1,500 and up to 6,000 in summer. Mainly residential and accessible by car ferry, it offers three small restaurants, stores, the Island Bike Rental, a sea kayaking outfit and Keller's B&B. It is a good destination for those with limited time or budget (the passenger ferry runs every hour or so, and you can walk around the entire island in an hour or two).

Long Island recently separated from the city to run its own affairs. It offers a fine public state beach on the ocean side, a fifteen-minute walk across the island from the ferry landing. The year-round population of 300 swells to 1,500 in the summer.

Great Chebeague, the largest island in the bay, is six miles long and has 400 permanent residents. It's the destination of choice for those who can take a day (and a bicycle) to explore. You can play nine holes of golf, eat at the Nellie G Cafe and stay overnight at the Chebeague Inn or a couple of B&Bs. Cliff Island is the smallest of the major inhabited islands (273 acres).

Great Diamond Island offers a "cocktail cove" favored by boaters and a residential community called Diamond Cove with condo rentals and a good restaurant.

The twice-daily mail boat run is the best way to see all the major islands. With a couple of blasts on the ferry horn ("cover your ears," the loudspeaker warns), the ferry starts on its leisurely, three-hour journey from the Casco Bay Lines ferry terminal at Commercial and Franklin streets. The visitor's first impression is that these islands are surprisingly densely populated, especially along the shore and especially Peaks Island, the first major island you see (but the mail boat doesn't visit). Also you soon realize this differs from the usual ferry, in that it's used primarily by islanders rather than tourists, which explains why there's little or no narration. You have to guess what you're looking at or overhear the regulars pointing out favorite sights. At the dock at Long Island, we watched as an older couple arrived with a child's wagon to pick up a delivery of groceries. The crew gingerly lowered a pallet of soft drinks, perhaps destined for the Spa Marina and Restaurant alongside. At Chebeague, a mother directed a bevy of youngsters unloading a pallet of roofing materials into a pickup truck. That and a Dodge van that got stuck as it tried to get up a makeshift ramp off the ferry provided twenty minutes of entertainment. Cliff Island proved the busiest stop on our tour as passengers debarked and boarded and what little there was of the day's outgoing mail was picked up. The return trip was enlivened by a couple of performing seals, a passing Russian freighter, and a frenzied flock of gulls chasing a fishing boat back to Portland.

Mail boat leaves Portland daily at 10 and 2:15, also Monday-Friday at 7:45, mid-June to Labor Day. Rest of year, daily at 10 and 2:45. Adults $12.50, children $6.

Where to Stay

Hotels and Motels

Portland Harbor Hotel, 468 Fore St., Portland 04101.

The brick facade and residential-style lobby spell elegance at this new boutique hotel in the Old Port district. From Fore Street, you'd never guess that it was built atop an existing three-level parking garage – a creative use of otherwise wasted space. At the entry, an elevator and stairs rise to the second-floor lobby, where the day's newspapers await guests in comfortable sitting areas and the unobtrusive Lobby Bar. The four-story hotel offers 100 accommodations with views of the city, Casco Bay or a courtyard garden. Cheery in pale yellows and blue-grays, rooms have king or queen beds dressed with 250-thread count linens, duvet coverlets and down feather pillows. Custom-made furnishings include armoires with his and her sections. Granite surrounds enhance soaking tubs and enclosed showers, and jacuzzis are available in deluxe rooms and suites. A chocolate treat accompanies evening turndown service.

Beside the lobby is **Eve's at the Garden,** an elegant but casual-looking mix between coffee shop and dining room serving inspired, highly rated fare. It opens through large windows and french doors to a large rooftop courtyard terrace, where umbrellaed tables are set for al fresco dining. Chef Jeff Landry's contemporary American menu covers the gamut from grilled yellowfin tuna with wasabi vinaigrette to pancetta-wrapped filet mignon.

(207) 775-9090 or (888) 798-9090. Fax (207) 775-9990. www.theportlandharborhotel.com. Ninety-seven rooms and three suites. Doubles, $269 to $379 July-October, $189 to $299 rest of year.

Eve's: (207) 523-2045. Entrées, $20 to $32. Lunch, Monday-Friday 11 to 2, weekends noon to 2. Dinner nightly, 5:30 to 9 or 10.

Portland Regency Hotel, 20 Milk St., Portland 04101.

This downtown hotel is superbly situated in the Old Port area, which justifies the extra charge for valet parking. The fact that it's in the restored 1895 armory, providing some unusual architectural treatments, is a bonus. It wears its designation as a member of the Historic Hotels of America proudly. Most of the 95 guest and suites go off a three-story atrium above the dining room. Rooms are plush, many with kingsize four-poster beds and mini-bars. Corner rooms come with gas fireplaces, sitting areas and recently added whirlpool tubs. Complimentary coffee and newspapers are placed at the door with your wakeup call. The health club is up-to-date, and the Armory Lounge offers complimentary hors d'oeuvres with cocktails and nightly entertainment in a warren of downstairs rooms. The **Armory Restaurant** has a traditional menu for breakfast, lunch and dinner.

(207) 774-4200 or (800) 727-3436. Fax (207) 775-2150. www.theregency.com. Ninety-five rooms. Doubles, $209 to $269 July-October, $159 to $219 rest of year.

Holiday Inn By the Bay, 88 Spring St., Portland 04101.

A good location, just across the street from the Civic Center and within walking distance of the Old Port, is one reason to stay in this eleven-story, 239-room motor hotel that used to be called simply the Holiday Inn-Downtown. Another is the view from the higher floors. We especially enjoyed watching the Scotia Prince ferry, lit up like a Christmas tree, dock at her berth around 8 one night from our room overlooking the Fore River. If you pay a bit extra, you might get an end room with two big windows instead of one. The indoor pool room is windowless, which is fine for a rainy day, but if it's sunny and warm, you might prefer the attractive **Holiday Inn-West** out Brighton Avenue with its nicely landscaped outdoor pool and garden courtyard. The downtown inn's lobby and refurbished **Port of Call** restaurant and lounge are large and ornate. A plus for a city hotel is free in-and-out covered parking.

(207) 775-2311 or (800) 345-5050. Fax (207) 761-8224. www.innbythebay.com. Two hundred thirty-nine rooms. Doubles, $172 to $182 June-October, $109 to $143 rest of year.

Bed and Breakfasts

Pomegranate Inn, 49 Neal St., Portland 04102.

Two exotic plant sculptures (holding live plants, no less) often welcome guests at the entrance to this exceptional in-town B&B. The art theme continues inside the handsome 19th-century house in Portland's residential West End. The antiques collections and contemporary artworks of owner Isabel Smiles make it a cross between a museum and a gallery. The seven bedrooms on the second and third floors, all with modern tiled baths, televisions and telephones, are a kaleidoscope of design. Their walls were hand-painted by a local artist and are themselves works of art, bearing no resemblance to other inns' folksy stenciling or sprigged wallpapers. Each room is unique, blending antique rugs, colorful fabrics, antique and contemporary furnishings, charming eccentricities and prized artworks. Even the bed configuration is mixed: five rooms come with queensize beds, another with kingsize and one has twins. Four have gas fireplaces. A deluxe suite has been added upstairs in the renovated carriage house across a terrace beside the main inn. We happily splurged for the downstairs garden room in the carriage house. It had two plush chairs and a puffy duvet on the bed, a marble bathroom and walls painted with riotous flowers. It opened onto a secret courtyard, so quiet and secluded it was hard to imagine we were in the midst of a city. A full breakfast is served at a long communal table or a couple of smaller ones in one of the eclectic parlors. The fare might be creamy quiches, pancakes with sautéed pears or, in our case, tasty waffles with bananas and raspberries.

(207) 772-1006 or (800) 356-0408. Fax (207) 733 4426. www.pomegranateinn.com. Seven rooms and one suite with private baths. Doubles, $175 to $265 Memorial Day through October, $95 to $165 rest of year..

The Danforth, 163 Danforth St., Portland 04102.

The landmark 1821 mansion that had been the rectory for the Roman Catholic Archdiocese of Portland has been converted into an urbane B&B. Owner Barbara Hathaway offers nine deluxe guest rooms and a number of intriguing common areas. The latter range from a basement billiards room to a main-floor library to a third-floor solarium and an enclosed rooftop widow's walk, which yields one of the best wraparound views in town. The nine accommodations (one a two-bedroom suite) on the second and third floors are spacious, light and airy with tall windows and thick off-white carpeting. They're outfitted with queensize beds bearing pillow-top mattresses, television, telephones, loveseats or wing chairs, antique armoires, writing desks with data-port terminals and all the accoutrements of the good B&B life. Indian shutters cover the windows and Baccarat crystal knobs open the doors. All have wood-burning tiled fireplaces. Breakfast is served in the formal dining room or in an adjacent sun porch. The menu posted at our visit listed baked apple and scrambled eggs in puff pastry. Late afternoon brings cookies and tea or lemonade. Decanters of port, brandy and sherry await in the evening.

(207) 879-8755 or (800) 991-6557. Fax (207) 879-8754. www.danforthmaine.com. Eight rooms and one suite with private baths. Doubles, $139 to $329 mid-May through October, $119 to $249 rest of year.

The Percy Inn, 15 Pine St., Box 8187, Portland 04104.

Travel writer Dale Northrup transformed a vacant 1830 Federal-style brick townhouse in his hometown into the kind of B&B he finds travelers want. Renovations produced four upstairs guest rooms with queen beds, a main-floor living room with fireplace and library, and a second-story breakfast room and wet bar, which remains open 24 hours for snacks and board games. The same schedule prevails for a top-floor pantry called the Poet's Corner and containing a coffee and tea station. Beyond, a rooftop deck yields a view of Portland roofs and, in the distance, Mount Washington and the Presidential Range. Room decor and designer fabrics vary, but common amenities include wet bars, stocked refrigerators, TVs, CD players, weather radios and candles. "I paid attention to what I'd miss if I stayed here," says Dale. Lately, he bought an adjacent section of the row house and added two studio suites and a fifth guest room. He also rents three rooms and suites in buildings around the neighborhood.

(207) 871-7638 or (888) 417-3729. Fax (207) 775-2599. www.percyinn.com. Five rooms and two suites with private baths. Doubles, $129 to $209 Memorial Day through October, $89 to $209 rest of year.

Resorts by the Sea

The Inn by the Sea, 40 Bowery Beach Road, Cape Elizabeth 04107.

Handsomely designed in the Maine shingle style to blend with its oceanfront setting, this contemporary, luxury resort has 25 one-bedroom suites in the angular main building and eighteen condo-style units of one or two bedrooms in four attached cottages. All have living rooms with reproduction Chippendale furniture, TVs hidden in armoires, kitchenettes, and balconies or patios looking onto manicured lawns, a pleasant pool and the ocean beyond Crescent Beach. We liked our first stay in a garden suite facing the lawn and ocean on the first floor, its living room opening through sliding doors onto an outside patio. Its small bedroom with a four-poster queen bed was quite adequate, though the windows opened onto the parking lot. Next time we reveled in the extra space of one of the loft suites on the second floor, which offered a better water view from its balcony and a three-section bathroom even bigger than the kingsize bedroom. Furnishings are most comfortable and the decor understated in a Maine woods theme, as executed by owner/innkeeper Maureen McQuade.

Meals are available in the serene **Audubon Room,** a harmonious space striking in white, with comfortable chairs and an enclosed porch around two sides. We hear the rack of lamb is to die for, but were quite content at one visit with a couple of salads (spinach with grilled portobello mushrooms and caramelized walnuts, and fanned breast of duck on baby spinach and arugula) and main dishes of grilled medallions of jerk-spiced pork on a papaya and sundried-cherry relish, and shrimp szechuan, tossed with broccoli rabe, snow peas and a zesty orange-ginger sauce on cellophane noodles. Another occasion produced a fabulous seafood fettuccine, loaded with lobster, diver scallops and tiger shrimp in an ethereal seaweed and saffron cream sauce, and a rich seafood strudel, highlights of a memorable meal.

(207) 799-3134 or (800) 888-4287. Fax (207) 799-4779. www.innbythesea.com. Forty-three one and two-bedroom suites with private baths. Doubles, $359 to $679 late spring to early fall, $149 to $299 rest of year.

Audubon Room: (207) 767-0888. Entrées, $24 to $29. Lunch daily, noon to 2, to 4 in summer. Dinner nightly, 6 to 9.

Black Point Inn Resort, 510 Black Point Road, Prouts Neck 04074.

But for the elegant antique car parked out front, this grand old, gray shingled inn built in 1925 is not all that imposing – although attractive in a traditional Maine way and impeccably kept up. The location not far south of Portland on Prouts Neck is smashing, with Sand Dollar Beach on one side and Scarborough Beach on the other. The delightful public rooms include an old-fashioned lobby, porches, a library and a salon with grand piano. They're notable for overstuffed chairs, fireplaces, game tables and books to read, and many are the guests who seem to hang out here from morning to night. Staying in one of the 48 homey inn rooms or 26 rooms in four outlying guest houses is one way to get to see the exclusive summer community of Prouts Neck. The famous Cliff Walk passes Winslow Homer's studio, and the pine woods between inn and ocean are a national bird sanctuary. Guests enjoy an adjacent eighteen-hole golf course and fourteen tennis courts hidden in the woods. The ambiance is low-key social – "steeped in tradition," as the inn calls it – and jackets are required in all public areas in the evening, as they always have been.

Breakfast and dinner are served in a big, pine-paneled dining room. Five-course dinners with several choices for each course are offered to guests and the public by reservation, and the formerly prix-fixe menu has been changed to à la carte. On good days a buffet lunch is set out beside the large saltwater pool overlooking the ocean.

(207) 883-4126 or (800) 258-0003. Fax (207) 883-9976. www.blackpointinn.com. Eighty-four rooms and cottages with private baths. Rates, MAP: doubles $480 to $660 in summer, from $229 off-season. Closed mid-February to late April.

Dinner by reservation, nightly 6:30 to 9. Entrées, $17.95 to $29.95. Jackets required.

Where to Eat

Portland's dining scene has improved markedly in the last two decades. It now claims more restaurants per capita than any American city after San Francisco.

Fine Dining

Fore Street, 288 Fore St., Portland.

"Refined peasant food" is how veteran Brunswick chef Sam Hayward describes the fare at one of New England's most celebrated restaurants. He and Portland restaurateur Dana Street transformed a former tank-storage warehouse at the edge of the Old Port into a soaring, loft-like space of brick and windows with assorted booths and tables on two levels, all overlooking a large and busy open kitchen in the midst of it all. The menu, printed nightly, offers about a dozen main courses categorized as roasted, grilled or braised. Expect understated treats such as wood-oven roasted Maine lobster, seafood misto, spit-roasted pork loin, penne and polenta with wild mushroom ragout, grilled duckling breast with pancetta and roasted shallots, grilled hanger steak and grilled venison steak. That's it – no highfalutin language, just a few surprises like an autumn mixed grill of lamb sirloin, game sausage, duck confit and farm-raised elk liver, teamed with a chestnut-garlic mash and wild Maine chanterelles. Start with a grilled garlic and mushroom sandwich or a pizzetta with roasted garlic, shiitakes and taleggio cheese. Finish with roasted banana mousse or a trio of mango, blackberry and peach sorbets. The mix of seasonal ingredients, true tastes and sense of place ranked Fore Street tops in New England and sixteenth in the country in a recent Gourmet magazine lineup of America's 50 best restaurants.

(207) 775-2717. Entrées, $14.95 to $28.95. Dinner nightly, from 5:30.

Hugo's, 88 Middle St., Portland.

New owners took over Hugo's Portland Bistro, shortened the name, upgraded the decor and refined the menu. Chef-owner Rob Evans, who cooked at the Inn at Little Washington in Virginia and the French Laundry in California's Napa Valley, and partner Nancy Pugh not only won local acclaim, but he was anointed one of the nation's ten best new chefs in 2004 by Food & Wine magazine. The menu is prix-fixe, $55 for four multiple-choice, over-the-top courses exploding with exotica. The first course might involve a choice of Atlantic fluke sashimi, salt-cured foie gras panini or soft-shell lobster and foraged local mushrooms. Continue with Scottish salmon tartare or cider-braised rabbit stew. The third course could be "Maine surf and turf" (roasted monkfish and beef tataki) or three versions of "duck explored." The signature dessert is flourless chocolate cake and shake with smoked maple ice cream. These or similar items turn up individually on the nightly bar menu, which is both affordable and appealing. The special chef's menu of ten to twelve courses, booked ahead, is the ultimate experience in dining here.

(207) 774-8538. www.hugos.net. Prix-fixe, $55. Bar menu, $8 to $14. Dinner, Tuesday-Saturday 5:30 to 9 or 9:30.

Five Fifty-Five, 555 Congress St., Portland.

Some of the most exciting fare in the city is served up by Steve and Michelle Corey, who moved from California wine country with a couple of stops in top Maine coastal restaurants before taking over the downtown space formerly occupied by the French bistro Aubergine. Chef Steve's food concept is innovative, divided into five "plate" sub-sections, some with whimsical names and offbeat pairings but all tasty and well received. Small plates include a dynamite lobster risotto, a carpaccio and reggiano-parmigiano treat called "steak and cheese," and "popkins," crispy pockets of curried lamb. "Green plates" are salads and "savory plates" are main dishes, among them peppercorn-crusted dayboat scallops, chimichurra-spiked hanger steak with sweet pepper mayonnaise and pork "every which way" – a star-anise crispy pork belly and pan-seared tenderloin with soft whole-grain mustard dumplings, braised rainbow chard and date-fennel compote. Eleven exotic cheese-plate choices were part of a recent menu. You also could finish with the pastry chef's "sweet plate," perhaps a goat cheese beignet with house-churned sugar plum ice cream or a truffle martini of chocolate-infused vodka. All this good eating takes place in a converted firehouse with a hip main-floor dining area augmented by loft seating on a wraparound mezzanine. The wine list carries a Wine Spectator award.

(207) 761-0555. www.fivefifty-five.com. Entrées, $17.95 to $23.95. Dinner nightly except Tuesday, 5 to 10. Sunday brunch, 10:30 to 2:30.

Back Bay Grill, 65 Portland St., Portland.

This 34-seat dining room with a fanciful, twenty-foot-long mural along one wall is the city's most urbane restaurant, one that would be at home in Boston's Back Bay or New York's SoHo. It's at the edge of downtown Portland, as reflected by the mural's rendering of restaurant scenes and characters indigenous to the Back Bay Grill. Veteran executive chef Larry Matthews Jr., who purchased the restaurant from owner Joel Freund, tinkers with the menu seasonally. To begin, consider the crab cake with lemon-pepper crème fraîche, the house-smoked arctic char with rémoulade sauce or the crisp fried veal sweetbreads with smoked bacon. Entrées range from pecan-crusted salmon on sweet potato sauce and swordfish with sundried tomato-basil vinaigrette to grilled free-range chicken with cilantro-sour cream sauce and rack of lamb with burgundy sauce. A dessert like pecan puff pastry napoleon with cannoli cream and toasted almond anglaise makes a fitting finale. A short bar menu is offered in the recently revamped lounge.

(207) 772-8833. www.backbaygrill.com. Entrées, $22 to $35. Dinner, Monday-Saturday 5:30 to 9:30 or 10, also Sunday 5 to 9 in July and August.

Bibo's Madd Apple Café, 23 Forest Ave., Portland.

Some of the best cooking and best values among serious restaurants in town are found at this reborn favorite. Chef Bill Boutwell added the opening letters of his first and last names to an established café next to the Portland Performing Arts Center. A memorable lunch showed his flair: a shrimp and avocado sandwich on toasted rye bread and a juicy lamb burger, each flanked by abundant mesclun salad, roasted potatoes and garnishes of garlic-marinated cucumbers. For dinner, expect the likes of seared rare tuna loin wrapped in leeks and prosciutto, braised leg of rabbit with a juniper-infused red wine reduction, and roasted loin of lamb dusted with cornmeal spices and served with a sweet corn broth. Starters could be shrimp and vegetable maki rolls with a spicy peanut sauce or smoked salmon shaped like a rose, stuffed with goat cheese and drizzled with a raspberry-horseradish crème fraîche. Among desserts are chocolate-macadamia pâté and chocolate-banana-coconut dumplings with coconut and chocolate sauces.

(207) 774-9698. Entrées, $14.95 to $18.95. Lunch, Wednesday-Friday 11:30 to 2. Dinner, Wednesday-Saturday from 5:30. Sunday, brunch 11 to 3, dinner from 4.

Blue-Plate Special

Blue Spoon, 89 Congress St., Portland.

You'd have to know about this tiny gem of a place to find it, hidden up Munjoy Hill in the East End. But the locals who keep its 25 seats filled liken it to eating in someone's dining room. That's the way owner David Iovino, a New Jersey native who trained at the French Culinary Institute in New York, wanted it. The sign outside announces "food from friends, family and travels," featuring American, European, Mediterranean and Latin cuisines. But the sign doesn't prepare you for food that is both first-rate and reasonably priced, let alone the choice beers and wines served in burgundy stemware and the polished but friendly service. The changing menu might start with prosciutto-wrapped sea scallops or a goat cheese gratin. Two people could sample the mezzi plate, an antipasti platter bearing the likes of peppered sausage, olives, roasted red peppers, a fish roe spread, fresh mozzarella and flatbread wedges. Main courses might be trout stuffed with Tuscan greens over a bed of brown rice, chicken roasted under a brick or skirt steak with a smoked paprika aioli, plus vegetarian and vegan options. A slice of apple and pear pie or carrot cake might finish a meal that won't begin to break the bank.

(207) 773-1116. Entrées, $10 to $15. Lunch and dinner, Tuesday-Saturday noon to 9. Sunday brunch, 9:30 to 2.

Street & Company, 33 Wharf St., Portland.

Seafood, pure and simple, is the staple of this Old Port restaurant that's wildly popular with the locals. Owner Dana Street stresses the freshest of fish on his blackboard menu. An open grill and kitchen are beside the door. Beyond are 60 seats in an ancient room with bare pegged floors and strands of herbs and garlic hanging on brick walls and in a smaller room adjacent. Outside are twenty more seats along Wharf Street during good weather. The tables might turn four times on a busy night, which seems to be the norm. Half a dozen varieties of seafood fresh from the nearby docks can be grilled, blackened or broiled. Or you can order mussels marinara, clams or shrimp with garlic, all served over linguini. The only other entrées at our latest visit were scallops in pernod and cream, sole française and lobster fra diavolo ($34.95 for two). The wine list is affordable, and there are great homemade desserts.

(207) 775-0887. Entrées, $16.95 to $20.95. Dinner nightly, 5:30 to 9:30 or 10.

Walter's Café, 15 Exchange St., Portland.

Noisy and intimate, this "now" kind of place has been packed to the rafters since it was opened by Mark Loring in partnership with Walter Loeman. The two have since parted, Mark holding onto this and becoming involved in a pair of waterfront restaurants in South Portland as well. The emphasis on spirited food at pleasant prices continues here. We faced a twenty-minute wait for a weekday lunch in July, but thoroughly enjoyed a BOLT – bacon, lettuce, tomato and red onion sandwich with sweet cajun mayonnaise, served in a pita with a pickle and gnarly fries. The "chilling pasta salad" yielded a zesty plateful tossed with chicken, avocado and red peppers. From our table alongside a brick wall in the long and narrow high-ceilinged room the cooks could be seen splashing liberal amounts of wines into the dishes they were preparing in the open kitchen. Typical dinner entrées are Thai spice-rubbed shrimp with lobster nori rolls, grilled chile-rubbed salmon over corn risotto cakes with jicama slaw, and pan-seared chicken with pancetta in a whole-grain mustard cream over pappardelle pasta. Dessert might be Irish cream cheesecake or orange mousse with wild blueberries.

(207) 871-9258. www.walterscafe.com. Entrées, $17 to $23. Lunch, Monday-Saturday 11 to 3. Dinner nightly, 5 to 10.

Cinque Terra, 36 Wharf St, Portland.

This former ship chandlery was converted into a restaurant by an Italian restaurateur who named it for his family's home region of the Cinque Terra, five remote fishing villages on the Italian Riviera. It's a dramatic, 80-seat dining room on two levels with brick walls, high skylit ceilings and a cheery decor of celadon green and sunflower yellow. A grand staircase leads to a balcony bordered by a wrought-iron railing, from which diners get a bird's-eye view of the open kitchen. The chefs produce rustic Italian country fare with local ingredients, including produce from new owner Dan Kary's organic farm. Diners are encouraged to share several courses, and half portions are available. Start with the bruschetta with lobster and tomato or the semolina-encrusted calamari and shrimp with basil, hot peppers and caper aioli. Consider some of the homemade pastas, perhaps the daily ravioli or the risotto with Maine lobster. Save room to sample such main courses as king salmon with arugula and two-olive tapenade and the veal scaloppine with radicchio, pancetta and gorgonzola. Finish with a typical Italian dessert, such as panna cotta, a chocolate and biscotti plate or homemade gelato.

(207) 347-6154. www.cinqueterramaine.com. Entrées, $17 to $21. Dinner nightly, 5:30 to 9:30 or 10.

Natasha's, 82 Exchange St., Portland.

Starting small at the edge of downtown, this restaurant moved into the thick of the action in the heart of the Old Port. Its sleek and urbane setting is eclectic, just like the food dispensed by Natasha and Steve Durham, a fusion of Asian, American and Italian styles amalgamated here into "new world cuisine." Chef Natasha's menu is full of assertive flavors, unpronounceable ingredients and pleasant surprises. She gives international twists to local favorites, as in appetizers of Casco Bay mussels roasted in chipotle adobe broth and Maine crab rangoon with ginger and scallions. Typical main courses include a "Cambodian hot bowl" with tofu or pork over crackling sushi rice, toasted with Asian vegetables, fried bananas, ginger and scallions, and a lobster and couscous "hot pan" – lobster, mussels and shrimp served over spiced saffron couscous. Natasha might offer a northern Italian white fish pie or muscovy duck breast with fried blue oysters and smoky vinaigrette. Even the rack of New Zealand lamb is livened up with minted poblano pepper jelly.

(207) 541-3663. Entrées, $18.95 to $27.95. Lunch, Monday-Friday 11 to 3. Dinner, Monday-Saturday from 5.

Old Port Sea Grill and Raw Bar, 93 Commercial St., Portland.

This dramatic fishbowl of a new restaurant lures a young crowd for the raw bar and the freshest of seafood – wood-grilled, sautéed and fried. The menu is like that of the owner's Falmouth Sea Grill in Falmouth Foreside, while the electric decor here mimics the habitat of its primary menu theme. Chef Jeff Leeber gives minimalist treatment to the likes of boneless rainbow trout, salmon, sea scallops and arctic char cooked in a custom-built hardwood grill. You can get lobster steamed or baked stuffed or as lobster primavera. Start with local and West Coast oysters on the half shell. Finish with a delicate key lime mousse or praline cheesecake. The dining room and bar each seat 60 and look out through large windows onto the downtown harborfront.

(207) 879-6100. Entrées, $16.95 to $24.95. Lunch daily, 11:30 to 5. Dinner nightly, 5 to 10 or 11.

┌─ *Worldly and Colorful* ──────────────

Pepperclub, 78 Middle St., Portland.

Among the players on Portland's Restaurant Row is this organic-vegetarian-seafood establishment, billed as a smoke-free environment and colorful as can be. It's the inspiration of artist Jaap Helder, Danish-born chef-artist who owned the late, great Vinyard (Portland's earliest gourmet restaurant) nearby. He re-emerged here with his paintings and a new partner, former art editor Eddie Fitzpatrick, to produce a showplace of quirky culinary design. A crazy paint job with many colors on the walls, fresh flowers on the tables and a bar made of old Jamaican steel drums, painted and cut in half, create a vivid setting. The food is colorful as well. The blackboard menu lists starters like curried corn chowder, Caribbean shrimp cakes and vegetarian samosas. Main dishes range from an organic pepper burger to ginger-lime chicken with mango salsa and Moroccan lamb with zatat bread and couscous. Main dishes include Maine shrimp with pasta and pesto, Greek lamb with minted green beans, Mongolian cashew chicken, Tunisian couscous and pinto bean burrito with salsa. Dessert could be orange chiffon cake or mocha-hazelnut dacquoise.

(207) 772-0531. Entrees, $10.95 to $14.95. Dinner nightly, 5 to 9 or 10.

Food with a View

Saltwater Grille, 231 Front St., South Portland.

The area's best waterfront setting is claimed by this sleek, contemporary grill run by Mark Loring of Walter's Café in Portland. The view is toward the city skyline from South Portland across the harbor, and a large waterfront deck takes full advantage. The open and airy interior dining room with a two-sided fireplace, saltwater fish tank and open display kitchen seats 150. The lobster and roasted corn bisque is a favorite starter, as are the lobster cakes with a tomato-horseradish aioli. Main courses run from lobster sauté with a marsala cream sauce served over bow-tie pasta to grilled filet mignon with port wine and blue cheese butter. About the most creative dish on the printed menu is scallops carbonara, a fixture at both lunch and dinner. The nightly specials from the grill are more interesting: perhaps grilled swordfish with anaheim peppers and peach salsa. The pastry chef is known for treats such as a tri-berry torte, lemon chiffon cheesecake and English pudding with caramel and white chocolate.

(207) 799-5400. www.saltwatergrille.com. Entrees, $16.95 to $24.95. Lunch daily, 11 to 3. Dinner nightly, 5 to 9.

Joe's Boathouse, 1 Spring Point Drive, South Portland.

Here's one of those rarities where the food is equal to the view. The view is of boats bobbing in the marina where Portland Harbor opens into Casco Bay and, beyond, the enchanting islands out in the bay itself. The food offered by co-owners Joe Loring and Nate Chalaby is sophisticated and first-rate. An eat-at bar popular with single diners is just inside the main entrance. Beyond are a couple of simple, low-slung dining rooms, the main one with a fireplace and large windows. The tables of choice in summer are outside by the harbor, where torches are lit at night. Lunch here was a festive treat as 1950s music played in the background. The portobello and asiago club sandwich was a knife-and-fork whopper, paired with homemade chips and served on the restaurant's colorful Fiestaware. The orange-ginger crispy salmon salad was a masterpiece of contrasting flavors. It took desserts of chocolate-kahlua mousse and homemade sorbets to clear the palate. Dinner entrées range from lobster fettuccine and mango chicken to hickory-smoked pork ribs with a blueberry barbecue sauce. Best of the starters is a dish of crab cakes drizzled with rémoulade over fried potatoes and greens.

(207) 741-2780. Entrées, $13.95 to $21.95. Lunch, Monday-Saturday 11 to 3. Dinner nightly, 5 to 9:30. Sunday brunch, 9 to 3.

Lobster, Two Ways

DiMillo's Floating Restaurant, 25 Long Wharf, Portland.

The old DiMillo's Lobster House now occupies the 206-foot-long ship Newport, a car ferry converted for $2 million into one of the largest floating restaurants in the nation and probably "the busiest restaurant in Maine," according to a member of the DiMillo family. Nearly 900 people can be accommodated at once in two outdoor café lounges fore and aft, a side deck, the Quarterdeck Dining Room and three private rooms, plus a very long bar, which helps those with endurance tolerate the one-hour (or more) wait on weekends. The sign at the gangplank saying "browsers welcome" and the gift shop at the entry set the theme. From the rare albino and orange lobsters in the tank at the reception desk to the blue and red linens, the place is incredibly nautical. The emphasis is on seafood, steaks and Italian dishes: lobster in various sizes and presentations, baked stuffed haddock, mixed seafood broil, chicken cacciatore, veal chop, prime rib and filet mignon.

(207) 772-2216. www.dimillos.com. Entrées, $18 to $28. Lunch daily, 11 to 5. Dinner nightly, 5 to 11.

Two Lights Lobster Shack, 225 Two Lights Road, Cape Elizabeth.

Here is a no-frills place within the shadow of two lighthouses south of Portland. You can eat inside, but the picnic tables on the bluff at ocean's edge are where we like to dig into a boiled lobster dinner or a fisherman's platter. This is a great place to bring youngsters because they can clamber around on the rocks while waiting for dinner and because the Lobster Shack offers hot dogs, hamburgers and fried chicken as well as fried seafood, chowder, clam cakes and steamers.

(207) 799-1677. Entrées, $7.95 to $16.95. Open daily, 11 to 8 or 8:30, April to mid-October.

FOR MORE INFORMATION: Visitor Information Center of the Convention and Visitors Bureau of Greater Portland, 245 Commercial St., Portland, ME 04101, (207) 772-5800. www.visitportland.com.

Old-time Maine prevails around Mackeral Cove on Bailey Island.

Freeport and the Harpswells, Me.

Main Street and More

Every year, nearly four million people from around the world make the pilgrimage to the big, plain building with the canoes and kayaks out front in the center of Freeport.

Many are supposedly in search of nostalgia, of simpler times, of basic virtues and values. Their destination is the legendary, 24-hour-a-day retail store of L.L. Bean, purveyor of goods for the outdoorsman and symbol to many of the Maine mystique. They are coming to mecca – seeking to get back to the earth, if only through Bean boots or a Bean jacket

And what a shopping mecca it is. Not only have all those pilgrims turned Bean's into the second most frequented tourist destination in the state (after Acadia National Park). They also have helped lure more than 125 outlet stores to town – not discount stores gathered in strip centers, mind you, but high-style outlets, many housed in free-standing buildings restored or erected for the purpose. They make up a new kind of downtown, turning Freeport into *the* outlet shopping village of New England. In their wake have popped up two dozen inns and B&Bs, a dozen restaurants, and assorted peripheral services and attractions in a village of fewer than 2,000 residents.

But there's more to Freeport than Bean's and its expanding, Disneyesque-look Main Street – a fact overlooked by most visitors bent on bargains. Head down to gracious South Freeport and a picturesque working harbor far removed in place and spirit from what the rest of us call Freeport and old-timers know as Freeport Square or Freeport Corner. Explore the byways of Porter's Landing, Lower Mast Landing and the other settlements along Freeport's hidden coastline. Enjoy the waterside walking trails at Wolfe's Neck Woods State Park, the wildlife at Mast Landing Sanctuary, the swimming and camping at Winslow Memorial Park.

If that piques your interest, head a few miles east to the Harpswells, rural fingers of land stretching south from Brunswick into northern Casco Bay. Great, Orr's and Bailey islands, connected by bridges, make up one finger. Harpswell Neck forms another. This is Maine as it used to be, the natural state you find far Down East but not along the southwestern coast. Hidden coves, ocean vistas, quaint hamlets and lobster pounds portray the Maine you came for, the one you suspected lies far beyond the portals of L.L. Bean.

But it is here, just outside. In close proximity lie two different worlds, one old and one new. You can experience the best of both, the Maine that's in the vanguard and the Maine that used to be.

Freeport

Once a thriving shipbuilding center and later a mill town, 200-year-old Freeport had fallen on hard times in the mid-20th century. It harbored L.L. Bean's eccentric factory and mail-order house, where hunters would stop on their way to the woods, but that was about all. The Bean retail store emerged from relative obscurity only in the 1970s, and began inflating into its current gargantuan state in the 1980s.

Freeporters point to 1981 as the start of the village's latter-day boom, which some consider a mixed blessing. Fire had destroyed Leighton's 5 & 10, and into its rebuilt quarters across from L.L. Bean moved a Dansk outlet center. Scores more were to follow. Their situation in Freeport, however, was determined by a two-year legal battle involving McDonald's, which sought to install golden arches in place of one of Freeport's finest remaining 19th-century mansions. Opponents, united in what they called a Mac Attack, forged a compromise: McDonald's could sell its fast food, but only if it restored the interior and retained the facade of the 1855 William Gore House. So it is that thousands of Big Macs are consumed in Freeport in a Colonial setting, that Banana Republic occupies a most un-Banana-Republic-like, two-story Federal brick edifice, and The Gap is located in a white contemporary colossus. Tight zoning and management helped the town spurn the typical outlet-strip look in favor of a village downtown appearance.

Where shoppers converge, food and lodging are sure to follow. Jameson Tavern, where the papers were signed making Maine a separate state in 1820, was turned into a restaurant next door to L.L. Bean – a happenstance its owner likened to having the hot dog franchise at Boston's Fenway Park. Two native Maine sisters who had a thriving lodging operation in Connecticut recognized the opportunities in Freeport and expanded a five-room B&B into the first-class Harraseeket Inn and restaurant. Small B&Bs and more restaurants emerged as well.

Seeing and Doing

The draw for most visitors is shopping, specifically L.L. Bean. Beyond Main Street is another Freeport with often-bypassed attractions.

Shopping

L.L. Bean, 95 Main St., Freeport.

Leon Leonwood Bean's legacy is the stuff of retailing legends. From his brother's clothing store across the street from what is now the Bean retail store, late-blooming outdoorsman "L.L.," as he was called, invented at age 40 the Maine hunting shoe. It was a practical boot with rubber bottoms and leather uppers that's still Bean's best-seller (about a quarter million pairs a year). Bean was an early master at mail order, promising unconditional guarantees and free delivery along with value, the assurance of personal testing and plenty of homespun charm. He designed many of the goods himself and tried them out personally on the trails. Although mail order remains a major component of the business, it is retailing that is most evident in Freeport. The early factory/mail-order business located conveniently above the local post office developed a retail adjunct when sportsmen would stop for licenses and equipment at all hours. That prompted L.L. to throw away the key in 1951 and stay open for business 24 hours a day.

Following his death in 1967, the Bean enterprise prospered under grandson Leon Gorman, spurting from sales of $4 million to $600 million a year. The original Bean building was removed in 1977 for parking space, but the various additions L.L. built over the decades comprise half of today's 125,000-square-foot, three-level structure that includes skylights, atriums and a stocked trout pond beneath the main staircase. Although goods for the outdoorsman remain foremost, Bean's now carries 75,000 items – far more than are pictured in the catalogs mailed annually to millions of customers. Totes, books, Adirondack chairs, Maine foods, clothing, footwear, sports equipment, bicycles – you name it, and if it fits L.L.'s vision, Bean's carries it. Never more so than after Lisa Birnbach's *The Official Preppy Handbook* made L.L. Bean the bearer of preppy tidings. Bean's sales increased a record 42 percent the next year. But as Leon Gorman noted, Bean's had suddenly become fashionable at the expense of function. While new customers were buying Bean's products, he said, they were buying them for the wrong reasons. Threatened with being passed by as last year's fashion house, Bean rededicated itself to the family and to the outdoors. Besides its flagship store in Freeport, Bean's has a hunting and fishing store and a factory store in Freeport as well as a downtown "branch" in big-city Portland.

(877) 552-3268. www.llbean.com. Open 24 hours a day, 365 days a year.

OTHER RETAILING. Freeport's recent advertising as Maine's answer to Rodeo Drive is a stretch. More credible is its claim to be "the Maine village quality goods made famous." Downtown Freeport avoided the strip mentality of Kittery, Ellsworth and North Conway, though a bit of that is evident on the outskirts along Route 1 south. It also shunned the outlet image of its counterparts. Twenty percent of the 125 (and growing) retailers here aren't factory outlets at all. These include **Abacus** for outstanding crafts, **Edgecomb Potters** for fine pottery, the **Claire Murray Store** for fabulous hand-hooked rugs and the **Thos. Moser Cabinetmakers Furniture Showroom & Art Gallery,** displaying Maine-made items in an old house. Most of the others feature first-quality items (no seconds) at prices that aren't particularly bargains. Some have outlet corners or floors (Bean's factory store is tucked away off Depot Street). Ten to fifteen new retailers enter the Freeport market every year and five to ten leave as the merchandising mix evolves, according to the Freeport Merchants Association. A **Brooks Brothers** factory store occupies a prime space along Bow Street. Among the biggest along Main Street are **The Gap, Banana Republic, Jones New York** and **Polo Ralph Lauren.** We also like the **Patagonia, Cuddledown, Coach, Cole Haan** and **Burberry** stores.

Appropriately for Maine, the **Mangy Moose** branch of a Jackson Hole outfit carries more items with moose on them than we knew existed, from swizzle sticks to tea towels to golf balls to $5,000 moose antler chandeliers to leather jackets and, of course, T-shirts for the entire family. Next door is the new **Cool as a Moose.** A surprise for Maine is **Bridgham and Cook, Ltd.,** which offers hard-to-find British goods, from apparel and tableware to groceries and gifts. Another is the new **Trip Trap Denmark,** which carries teak furniture and accessories with a maritime flair.

If you suffer from crowds, avoid Freeport at peak hours on busy shopping days. We happened by on a cloudy, non-beach weekday in early August to find ourselves embroiled in what at the time was Freeport's biggest day ever – an estimated 25,000 people. Vehicles were bumper-to-bumper along Main Street between exits from I-95. Cars cruised for parking spaces blocks away from downtown.

Other Attractions

South Freeport. The focal point of a 19th-century boom in shipbuilding and still a working harbor, this is now a fashionable residential area and yachting center. We first discovered there was more to Freeport than Main Street a few years ago when we set out for a lobster roll at Harraseeket Lunch & Lobster Co. The surprises yielded by the rural route there were exceeded only by the sights of the gracious homes and the picturesque harbor at the end. Other than the harbor, the town's best known landmark is Casco Castle, a 100-foot-high stone tower – all that remains of a large summer hotel destroyed by fire in 1914.

Atlantic Seal Cruises, 25 Main St., South Freeport.

An old, 28-passenger Coast Guard cruiser departs from the town wharf on a variety of daily excursions. Most popular are three-hour tours out seven miles to **Eagle Island**, a state park where the boat pauses for an hour to let passengers explore the seventeen-acre island and visit the fascinating museum/home of Admiral Robert E. Peary, the first man to reach the North Pole. Photos and artifacts from his Arctic explorations are displayed in his summer home along with a collection of mounted Arctic and Maine birds. Capt. Tom Ring hauls his lobster traps on the return voyage. The Atlantic Seal also offers seal and osprey watches in summer daily at 6 and trips to view foliage in fall.

(207) 865-6112 or (877) 285-7325. Eagle Island cruises, daily at 9:30 and 1:30, Memorial Day through September. Adults $24, children $18.

Wolfe's Neck Woods State Park, 426 Wolfe's Neck Road, Freeport.

Barely a five-minute drive from the center of Freeport lie five miles of hiking trails and secluded picnic sites on 233 acres along the Harraseeket River and Casco Bay. "To the uninitiated, all of this may appear as nothing more than a collection of trees and brush," notes the display board. You learn that the forests of Wolfe's Neck represent a unique collection of ecological and local climatic conditions. Some of the white pine trees are thought to have been used by the British Navy as masts for their sailing ships. That led to the name for nearby Mast Landing and gave the unusual shape to Freeport Square, the triangle opposite L.L. Bean, where the logs were given extra turning room as they were hauled to the waterfront. People can swim off the Casco Bay trail, spot the pair of osprey that make the Googins Island sanctuary their home, and dig up to a peck of clams from the salt marsh when the tide is out. The park is open daily from 9 to sunset, Memorial Day through Labor Day; fee for parking. Upon leaving, drive farther down Wolfe's Neck Road through huge pines that resemble a redwood forest to the University of Southern Maine's working farm and Smith Stone House, whose landscaped grounds yield a view of Casco Bay on one side and South Freeport's Casco Castle on the other.

(207) 865-4465. Open daily from 9 to sunset, April-October. Adults $3, children $1.

Mast Landing Sanctuary, Upper Mast Landing Road, Freeport.

The Maine Audubon Society operates this 140-acre sanctuary along the tidal salt marshes of the Harraseeket River estuary, where Maine lumber used to be delivered. More than seven miles of marked trails lead past streams and through fields, alder lowlands and pine and hemlock forests. A favorite attraction is a mill stream cascading over a dam into the salt marshes beside the ruins of an old mill. Visitors see shorebirds, beavers, minks, deer and porcupines. In winter, the trails are open to cross-country skiers.

(207) 781-2330. Open daily, dawn to dusk. Free.

Other choice spots include **Winslow Memorial Park,** Staples Point Road, South Freeport, a 90-acre municipal park with a good sandy beach (the area's nine-foot tides are such that there's swimming at high tide only), a grassy picnicking area and a 100-site coastal campground; day-use charge, $1.50. The park also hosts the annual "Lobsterman Triathlon" in early September, featuring a 1.5-kilometer swim in Casco Bay, a 40-kilometer bike ride along hills and coastline and a 10-kilometer run through South Freeport.

The Freeport Historical Society operates the **Harrington House** at 45 Main St., (207) 865-3170. The 1830 Greek Revival house museum includes exhibits on Freeport history dating from the late 18th century and a period perennial garden in the courtyard. Personnel there can provide directions for a scenic walk at the society's **Pettingill Farm & Gardens,** an 1810 saltbox farmhouse on a saltwater farm with 140 acres of gardens, fields and hiking trails. Mildred Pettingill, who lived in the primitive house until 1970, transplanted wild roses, lilacs, cedars and other plants from the area into the gardens and grounds. Some are native American species that were among the flowers colonists found upon arrival.

Top entertainers are featured in free **Summer Concerts in the Park,** a weekly series sponsored by L.L. Bean in Bean's Discovery Park, situated just off Main Street between its flagship store and its hunting and fishing store. Concerts begin at 7:30 every Saturday from July 4 through Labor Day weekend.

Where to Stay

Harraseeket Inn, 162 Main St., Freeport 04032.

Nancy Gray and Jody Dyer, two sisters from South Portland who built the thriving Inn at Mystic complex in Connecticut, foresaw the budding Freeport boom and started here with an elegant five-room B&B in 1984. Five years later, they added a three-story, 49-room inn and restaurant and followed that with an expanded tavern, an enclosed swimming pool and 30 more guest rooms. Standard rooms contain two double beds or one queensize with blue and white fabric half-canopies and a single wing chair. Our deluxe third-floor room offered a kingsize bed with a partial-canopy headboard and botanical prints, a sofa and wing chair beneath a palladian window, a working fireplace, a wet bar and a small refrigerator, a TV hidden in an armoire, and an enormous bath with a jacuzzi. Turndown service produced chocolates at night. The newest wing holds a mix of luxury units with fireplaces and jacuzzis and others with two double beds for traveling families. All told, the inn offers 41 accommodations with whirlpool tubs, 23 of those with fireplaces. Excellent meals are available in the **Maine Dining Room** and the **Broad Arrow Tavern** (see Where to Eat). A full breakfast buffet and an elaborate afternoon tea in the inn's attractive living room are included in the rates.

(207) 865-9377 or (800) 342-6423. Fax (207) 865-1684. www.stayfreeport.com. Eighty-two rooms and two suites with private baths. Doubles, $199 to $279. Suites, $279. Off-season, $110 to $245.

Brewster House Bed & Breakfast, 180 Main St., Freeport 04032.

One of Freeport's early B&Bs occupies a handsome 1888 Queen Anne house built by local merchant Jarvis Brewster, whose store was on the block where L.L. Bean stands today. It was converted from three-family apartment status during a year-long renovation by a young couple whose four children outgrew their inn quarters after ten years. Lester and Nikki Evans took over and redid the formerly kid-friendly living room in more formal style. They are known for their ample breakfasts, offering guests a daily choice of made-to-order omelets or blueberry pancakes one day and french toast the next. The dining room with deep blue walls and a pressed tin-ceiling opens into a parlor with fireplace and TV. The main floor also has a cozy guest room with twin beds. The second floor adds four larger bedrooms with queen beds and wicker sitting areas, several colorful in Laura Ashley or Ralph Lauren linens and fabrics. On the third floor are two suites, each consisting of a master bedroom with king bed connected via a bathroom to a smaller room with a double bed. Nicki Evans wasn't happy with the commercial soaps available, so she makes rose-shaped bars of all-natural, scent-free avocado-cucumber soaps for each bathroom. They proved so popular that she now makes several hundred at a time, and most guests buy a batch to take home.

(207) 865-4121 or (800) 865-0822. Fax (207) 865-4221. www.brewsterhouse.com. Five rooms and two suites with private baths. Mid-May through November: doubles $105 to $175, suites $140 to $295. Rest of year: doubles $95 to $160, suites $125 to $275.

Kendall Tavern Bed & Breakfast, 213 Main St., Freeport 04032.

Big bucks went into the 1991 renovation of this old farmhouse, recently enhanced by new owners Richard and Wendy Conroy. The landscaped grounds and the attractive yellow house with white trim are welcoming, as are the two small common rooms, both with fireplaces. One serves as a library/reading room and the other as a TV room. Wonderful paintings adorn a breakfast room set with seven tables for two, where the Conroys might serve apple-cheddar quiche, cheese and tomato-basil omelets or strawberry-stuffed french toast. On the second floor are four snug guest rooms with queensize beds and one with twins. Two larger rooms are on the third floor. One has a king bed and a twin bed, and the other has a queen bed, a fireplace and a sitting area.

(207) 865-1338 or (800) 341-9572. Fax (207)(865-3544. www.kendalltavern.com. Seven rooms with private baths. Doubles, $140 to $175, off-season $110 to $140.

The James Place Inn, 11 Holbrook St., Freeport 04032.

Only one house separates this newly renovated, 1880 cottage-style stick Victorian edifice from the busy Main Street shopping area, which makes it especially convenient for those who want to drop off their goodies and rest a bit between rounds. Maine natives Darcy and Bill James offer a comfortable and quiet refuge in seven guest rooms with queen beds and TVs. Four rooms have whirlpool tubs. The main-floor Pine Room features a wood-burning fireplace and private deck. Guests gather in a common room or on a jaunty café-style side deck. Served in a pine-furnished sunroom or on the deck, breakfast could be crabmeat quiche or belgian waffles.

(207) 865-4486 or (800) 964-9086. www.jamesplaceinn.com. Seven rooms with private baths. Doubles, $135 to $155 May-October, $110 to $145 rest of year.

White Cedar Inn, 178 Main St., Freeport 04032.

This historic Victorian residence was once the home of Arctic explorer Donald B. MacMillan, second-in-command to Robert E. Peary, who in 1909 was the first man to reach the North Pole. MacMillan was the designer and captain of the schooner, Bowdoin, which is now the official State of Maine sailing vessel. White Cedar has been a B&B in the elongated Maine farmhouse style for two decades. New innkeepers Monica Kissane and Rock Nadeau offer seven guest rooms, most with queen beds and two with fireplaces. Rooms are generally spacious and furnished with antiques and period pieces. A suite with a spiral staircase is named Bowdoin for the MacMillan schooner. Guests relax in the common room and enjoy a country breakfast in a sun room overlooking the landscaped grounds.

(207) 865-9099 or (800) 853-1269. Fax (207) 865-6636. www.whitecedarinn.com. Seven rooms with private baths. Doubles, $120 to $170 Memorial Day through October, $95 to $165 rest of year.

Atlantic Seal Bed & Breakfast, 25 Main St., Box 146, South Freeport 04078.

Freeport's only B&B on the water, this is the lifelong home of Tom Ring, a tugboat captain by trade. His is an 1850s Cape Cod-style house full of nautical memorabilia and antiques, among them an ancient sextant, an original clipper ship painting over the fireplace and old ship models made by his grandfather and showcased in a lighted corner cabinet. Tom offers three bedrooms with views of the Harraseeket River and harbor. Largest is the Dash, with windows on three sides, a balcony overlooking the harbor, a queensize and a double bed, TV and a bath with a deep, oversize jacuzzi and a separate shower. The old-fashioned Heart's Desire room has a kingsize cannonball bed and a Rumford fireplace, while the cozy Glen has a queen bed, two windows onto the harbor and a hall bath. The rear deck overlooking the water holds some of the striking modern wood slat chairs made by Tom's father. Tom lets guests use a rowboat at high tide, and offers a discount on his morning Atlantic Seal excursions to Eagle Island. He traps the lobsters that go into the trademark lobster omelets for breakfast.

(207) 865-6112 or (877) 285-7325. Three rooms with private baths. Doubles, $125 to $200.

┌─ *A Motel for Bargain Seekers* ─

Coastline Inn, 537 U.S. Route 1 South, Freeport 04032.

Shoppers who are bargain hunters go for the prices at this motel, part of a small Maine chain. It has 108 rooms with two double, one double or one kingsize bed and standard motel furnishings. The rooms are air-conditioned, have no balconies and the windows unfortunately don't open. (In the off-season, these would be quite adequate but in summer, we wonder who wants to be in Maine in a place where you can't sit outside or open the windows?) At least the room configuration puts guests away from the highway noise, which is more than can be said for the Super 8 squashed between Route 1 and I-95 across the street. Continental breakfast is included in the rates.

(207) 865-3777 or (800) 470-9494. Fax (207) 865-4678. One hundred eight rooms. Doubles, $60 to $150 May-October, $50 to $70 rest of year.

Where to Eat

Harraseeket Inn, 162 Main St., Freeport.

Excellent meals are available at this much-expanded inn near the center of Freeport Its stylish **Maine Dining Room,** divided into three sections and warmed by two fireplaces, is pretty as a picture. Substantial black windsor chairs and a few banquettes flank tables set formally with white linens, heavy silver, silver service plates and pink stemware. From a state-of-the-art kitchen, executive chef Theda Lyden oversees some highly rated new American fare. The stress is on products from area farmers and growers, all of whom are nicely credited on a page at the back of the menu. Main courses range from organic chicken stuffed with mushrooms and spinach to "tableside classics" for two – tamarind-glazed rack of lamb and all-natural châteaubriand. Recent choices included seared halibut with littleneck clams in pesto broth, filet mignon with chianti syrup and duck breast with morel mushrooms, blackberries and foie gras. Lobster often turns up in such starters as sherried lobster stew, lobster risotto and lobster bruschetta or in a main course of lobster fricassee. Finish with a flourish: rum-flamed Jamaican bananas, chocolate overdose flamed with grand marnier, a choice of crêpes, the evening's soufflé or one of the exotic homemade ice creams and sorbets. The **Broad Arrow Tavern** offers more casual dining, an open kitchen, a wood-fired oven and grill and a remarkably extensive menu.

(207) 865-9377 or (800) 342-6423. www.stayfreeport.com. Entrées, $24 to $34. Lunch daily, 11:30 to 2:30. Dinner nightly, 5:30 to 9 or 9:30. Sunday brunch, 11:45 to 2. Tavern, daily from 11:30.

Azure Café, 123 Main St., Freeport.

Freeport locals and visiting shoppers welcomed with open arms this new endeavor by Jonas and Kate Werner bringing "a taste of Italy to the coast of Maine." The couple provide a pleasant ambiance in a handsome dining room with white-clothed tables set amid grotto-style columns and arches. They hung local art on the walls and installed elegant umbrella-topped tables on a garden patio for outdoor dining. Chef Christopher Bassett raised the Freeport culinary bar a notch with innovative fare in the contemporary Italian idiom. His chowders and pasta dishes are first-rate, as is the Azure salad starring lobster over mixed field greens. The lunch menu is the most interesting in town. At night, the fare ranges from haddock stuffed with crabmeat and fennel and served with four-cheese risotto and herb-roasted vegetables to beef tenderloin grilled with applewood-smoked sea salt in a port wine reduction. Veal saltimbocca and Tuscan-roasted pork tenderloin glazed with chianti-currant butter were recent winter hits. San Francisco-style cioppino is touted as the house specialty and measures up. A house-made trio of aioli accompanies the frito misto or Maine crab cake to start. Azure features live jazz several nights a week and hosts monthly wine dinners.

(207) 865-1237. www.azurecafe.com. Entrées, $18 to $28. Open daily, 11 to 9 or 10, to 8 or 9 in winter.

Jameson Tavern, 115 Main St., Freeport.

With a location next to L.L. Bean and an historic setting in a 1779 residence proclaimed as the birthplace of Maine, how could this place miss? A plaque outside denotes it as the site in 1820 of the signing of the papers that separated Maine from

Massachusetts. A selection of menus steers hundreds of patrons on a busy day to the dark and intimate dining rooms, the rear taproom and the large outdoor deck alongside. This is not a place for leisurely dining, and the menu encourages turnover of tables by limiting appetizers and desserts. Dinner entrées run from seafood-stuffed haddock to filet mignon topped with crabmeat. Salmon oscar, brandy-glazed roast duckling and veal piccata reflect a continental bent. Burgers and lighter fare are offered in the taproom, where shrimp stew is a highlight.

(207) 865-4196. www.jamestontavern.com. Entrées, $15.95 to $27.95. Open daily, 11 to 10 or 11.

The Muddy Rudder, 1335 U.S. Route 1, Yarmouth.

Just across the narrow Cousins River from Freeport is this large and spiffy restaurant and lounge where the first-thing-you-see bar gives little hint of the cut-above food to come. We like the jaunty outdoor deck overlooking the Great Salt Marsh and the dining areas with large windows beside. The 125-item menu is one of those something-for-everyone encyclopedias. It offers for dinner a range from Italian-style broiled haddock and shrimp scampi over linguini to grilled halibut, swordfish kabob and fisherman platter. The teriyaki steak and chicken combo was being touted at a recent visit. The lobster cobb and crabmeat caesar salads star on the lunch menu, and seafood benedict is a highlight of the weekend brunch. Desserts run to ice cream puff and blueberry pie, but we'd try the pineapple-walnut bread pudding with bourbon sauce. Live piano music is played in the bar at night.

(207) 846-3082. www.muddyrudder.com. Entrées, $11.99 to $18.99. Open daily, 11 to midnight.

A Budget Choice

The Corsican Restaurant, 9 Mechanic St., Freeport.

Plain as plain can be but ever-popular is this offshoot of a Brunswick pizza and vegetarian eatery. For lunch, you might choose a veggie and avocado sub, a lobster pizza for $9.95 or any number of salads or sandwiches. Dinnertime adds such entrées as haddock florentine, scallops and red peppers sautéed in garlic butter, and chicken and lobster and scallop aioli. There are no beef dishes beyond penne and meatballs. Beer and wine are available.

(207) 865-9421. www.corsicanrestaurant.com. Entrées, $12.95 to $16.95. Lunch and dinner daily, 11 to 9. Closed Sunday in off-season.

Seafood by the Shore

Harraseeket Lunch & Lobster Company, Town Wharf, South Freeport.

Family-run and astride the fishing pier, this serves typical lobster-pound and seafood fare inside and out. It's at its best for lunch, when you can sit outside and watch the harbor goings-on (though you might have to wait in a long line for a table); evenings are apt to get too buggy to eat outdoors. A recent lunch included a delicious clam chowder, a clam roll on a toasted bun and a clam burger for under $15. The two weighty lobsters we took home for dinner in a special icebox cost an additional $22. Last we knew, you could get a fish sandwich for $5.25, a specialty basket of fried clams for $13.50 and a lobster dinner with corn and steamers for $15.95.

(207) 865-3535. Entrées, $12,95 to $21.50. Open daily in summer, 11 to 8:45, to 7:45 in off-season. BYOB. No credit cards. Closed mid-October to May.

The Harpswells

Diametrically opposed to Freeport's Main Street and what it represents are the Harpswells, the collective name for the peninsular fingers of land stretching ten miles into Casco Bay south of Brunswick. They embrace Harpswell Neck and Great Island, Orr's Island and Bailey Island. The three islands are attached one to the other and the mainland by short bridges and, because of their narrowness, cast a thoroughly watery aspect to 150 miles of shoreline. Bailey, the most seaward of the islands, is said to be the most popular of Casco Bay's 365 Calendar Islands because of its accessibility by auto, though relatively few venture down there. Harpswell Neck is a peninsula leading from Brunswick and, because it is wider, has less of a watery feeling except at the ends of roads leading off Route 123 or at the neck's far end near South Harpswell.

The Harpswells – with their solitude, their scenery and their stability reflecting Maine as it used to be – are the perfect antidote to the frenzy of Freeport. Anyone partial to being near the water would be advised to make them their base for exploring the area.

Seeing and Doing

What's there to do? Not much, which is precisely the lure for those in the know. A few inns, motels and B&Bs of the old school offer lodging, the restaurants called lobster houses provide sustenance, the fishing villages and working harbors add charm, the seaside air is exhilarating, and rockbound coves and inlets pop up at almost every turn.

You can take a boat cruise, thanks to the Casco Bay Lines out of Portland, which runs a six-hour cruise to Bailey Island. As round-trip passengers lay over for lunch here, others board for a 90-minute **nature cruise** through Potts Harbor, past Eagle Island and Haskell Island, and into Mackerel Cove (noon daily from Cook's Marina; adults $11.50, children $5).

Explore the shoreline, dig clams, walk or bike along the back roads, browse at one of the Harpswell Craft Guild's member galleries or shop for seasonal produce at the Vegetable Corner in North Harpswell, a rustic stand that seems to be the busiest enterprise along Harpswell Neck. If you want more, the shops of Freeport are less than 45 minutes' drive away.

You'll notice that during an early-morning walk, many others are out walking, too. Folks exchange pleasantries, and even wave to the occasional motorist with out-of-state license plates who happens by. You marvel at the piles of lobster traps, some stunning seaside homes interspersed between the prevailing weather-beaten cottages, the old fishing boats that give Mackerel Cove the look of Nova Scotia, and the passing lobster boats hauling in their bounty.

You stop outside All Saints By the Sea, a tiny Episcopal chapel that is most un-chapel-like, a shingled cottage without so much as a steeple. A sign points the way to **Giant Stairs,** a five-minute walk past wild rose and bayberry bushes along a bluff like that of Ogunquit's Marginal Way. Just when you think you won't find the stairs, a family who preceded say that you've arrived. Their youngsters are scrambling on the massive stone steps that march down to the open ocean. A plaque at the top relates that these were given to their native town in 1910 by Capt.

William Henry Sinnett and his wife Joanna. The preceding family, who have summered for years on Bailey Island, point out the jagged Pinnacle Rock, advise of Thunder Hole and Pirate's Cove and Land's End beyond, and tell how the locals go out by small boat to trade with Russian fishermen on trawlers just beyond the lighthouse.

You drive down to **Land's End,** where a statue of a lobsterman rises outside an unlikely-looking gift shop.

All this is the genuine Maine for you.

Where to Stay

Log Cabin – An Island Inn, Route 24, Box 410, Bailey Island 04003.

This started as a restaurant in a large log summer house, but you'd never know it following its continuing upgrades. Downsizing and ultimately closing (to the public) their popular restaurant to add lodging, Sue and Neal Favreau offer nine comfortable, home-like accommodations, each with its own deck upon which to savor the water views. The bright and airy second-floor York Room has a queen bed, TV, kitchenette, jacuzzi tub and separate shower. The Mount Washington suite atop a former garage comes with a full kitchen, separate kingsize bedroom, two TVs, stereo and a deck with its own hot tub, from which you can see New England's tallest peak 90 miles away on a clear day. The new Harpswell Suite has a living room with a gas fireplace and a hot tub on the deck, plus a kingsize bedroom with a whirlpool bath and a second balcony. Along with the TV/VCR standard in all rooms, the Sunset and Westview rooms offer gas fireplaces as well as jacuzzi tubs and queensize beds topped with duvets. Guests make lots of use of a large, pleasant swimming pool. They also enjoy a complimentary breakfast of eggs or french toast with meats and home fries. Dinner is available for inn guests in a cozy, lodge-like room with a moosehead above the fireplace, in an intimate front bar and on enclosed porches with water views. Sue, who has been in the food business since she was 13 and originally ran the late Rock Ovens restaurant nearby, oversees the kitchen. A typical menu includes honey-glazed scallops, shrimp scampi, boiled lobster, teriyaki chicken and filet mignon, plus a couple of appetizers and dessert of the day.

(207) 833-5546. Fax (207) 833-7858. www.logcabin-maine.com. Seven rooms and two suites with private baths. Summer: doubles $149 to $199, suites $269 to $299. Off-season: doubles $99 to $189, suites $189 to $249. Closed mid-October to April.

Harpswell Inn, 108 Lookout Point Road, Harpswell 04079.

A handsome 1761 structure that once served as the cookhouse for the famed Lookout Point Shipyard has been renovated into an up-and-coming B&B with twelve stylish rooms full of antique furnishings. The prized main-floor Rackliffe Room is all blue and yellow with peacock wallpaper. The Lilac Suite has Laura Ashley print wallpaper and draperies and a loveseat. The rear Bowdoin Room resembles a college dorm haunt and bears all sorts of memorabilia from Bowdoin College in Brunswick. The Texas Room on the third floor sports a queensize bed with longhorns above in honor of the innkeepers' years in Houston. Youngsters like to pull the chain at the top of the staircase to ring the rooftop bell that summoned hungry shipbuilders to their meals back in the 1860s. The carriage house was expanded and rebuilt to produce three light and airy luxury units with kitchen facilities, gas-fired stoves, queen beds and decks with views of Middle Bay. Much of the main floor in the inn is given over to a "great" room, which has a huge fieldstone fireplace, a grand piano, comfortable seating and windows almost to the floor. Breakfast in a large dining room might yield Swedish pancakes, waffles with caramelized strawberry sauce, omelets or sausage and cheese casserole. In 2005, longtime owners Bill and Susan Menz had the inn under contract to local purchasers, a chef/culinary instructor and his wife who planned to keep things the same the first year before possibly adding a restaurant.

(207) 833-5509 or (800) 843-5509. www.harpswellinn.com. Seven rooms and three suites with private baths; two rooms with shared baths. Doubles, $89 to $150. Suites, $175 to $230.

Little Island Motel, 44 Little Island Road, Orr's Island 04066.

"Please drive slowly – duck crossing," advises the sign at the entrance to the spit of land jutting into the water off Lowell's Cove Road. Beyond is an inviting small complex billed by owner Jo Atlass as "the intimate resort." It includes a seven-room, chalet-style motel with decks right over the water and two more private units at either end of her house opposite. A carved duck and a lobster trap are outside each door. The rooms we saw had small sitting areas with TV and mini-refrigerators and one had an efficiency kitchenette, but most appealing were the decks, granted privacy by canvas screens between each unit. Ducks emerged from under the trees and waddled up to a shady sitting area with a barbecue and picnic tables beside the water. Jo puts out a complimentary buffet breakfast in her home: lots of homemade muffins, ham and cheese biscuits, bacon or sausage, and often smoked salmon and cream cheese. Her small shop called the Gull's Nest stocks Maine handicrafts and rather suave gifts.

(207) 833-2392. www.littleislandmotel.com. Nine rooms with private baths. Doubles, $136 to $140, $116 to $120 midweek in May, June and October. Closed mid-October to mid-May. No credit cards.

Tower Hill Bed & Breakfast, 1565 Harpswell Islands Road, Orr's Island 04066.

The stone foundation of what had been a 1,000-gallon water and observation tower greets visitors to this farmhouse built in the early 19th century and claiming several subsequent additions. Bill Whiteside, a retired Bowdoin College history professor, and his wife Susan, past president of the local Chamber of Commerce, share their home with guests in three rooms that Susan calls demi-suites. Theirs is a much lived in house – "a work in progress," she calls it – full of the couple's collections. Hats take over part of the living room and stunning Western Chinese ceremonial costumes line the walls of one of the stairways. The East Suite is masculine, paneled in bead board and yellow pine, its queen bed outfitted with an array of sheets that change depending on the guests and the whim of the hostess. The Iris Suite includes a sitting room with a day bed and rattan chairs and a paneled bedroom with kingsize bed, colorful quilt and big TV. Its bath contains a clawfoot tub and all kinds of iris prints. Lilacs are the decorative theme in the dining room, where Bill might serve his specialty pancakes, strata, quiche or eggs. Breakfast also can be taken in the rear "greenhouse," if you can find a place to sit amid all the plants and what-not.

(207) 833-2311 or (888) 833-2311. www.towerhillb-b.com. One room and two suites with private baths. Doubles, $130 to $160.

Bailey Island Motel, Route 24, Box 4, Bailey Island 04003.

This small, lovingly tended motel is idyllically located on a grassy, shady waterside property beside the landmark cribstone bridge at the entrance to Bailey Island. Ralph Black Jr., a lifelong island resident, has upgraded the accommodations and added helpful books of visitor information in each room. There are several places from which to enjoy the views of Casco Bay: from the balcony off the second-floor rooms, on a brick terrace off the ground-floor rooms, or on chairs right beside the water. We like to take the complimentary continental breakfast of homemade strawberry muffins to a picnic table on a shady knoll affording views of both bay and Harpswell Sound beyond the cribstone bridge. The bridge was built with granite blocks laid in honeycomb fashion without cement to let the area's nine-foot tides flow through.

(207) 833-2886. Fax (207) 833-7721. www.baileyislandmotel.com. Eleven rooms with private baths. Doubles, $120 in summer, $90 to $105 off-season. Closed late October to May.

Back to Basics

The Driftwood Inn, Washington Avenue, Bailey Island 04003.

If you really want to get away from it all, consider this simple, old-fashioned place at a rocky point known as Land's End. The complex of gray-shingled buildings perched beside the water at the tip of the outermost island in Casco Bay has been around for more than 100 years and looks it. The Charles Conrad family offers six housekeeping cabins and sixteen double and eight single guest rooms in three houses, most sharing one bathroom per floor. Four rooms in one house contain half-baths. Each house includes a common room and a porch that yields a view toward the open ocean. A saltwater swimming pool is set in the rocks. Meals are served at a single seating in an open-timbered dining room with windows onto the water on two sides. Outside diners may come for breakfast ($6.50) at 8 or dinner ($15.50) at 6. The two-choice menu usually offers fish of the day and roast pork on Monday, veal parmesan on Wednesday, steak or lobster on Friday and turkey dinner on Sunday. The rustic rooms are sparsely furnished and there are few 20th-century amenities, let alone 21st, out here – just a smashing oceanfront setting and a primitive lifestyle, the way Maine used to be. People love the place or hate it, returning year after year or vowing never to return. You get what you pay for.

(207) 833-5461. www.thedriftwoodinnmaine.com. Doubles, $75 to $120, EP. Housekeeping cabins, $625 to $660 weekly. No credit cards. Closed mid-October to Memorial Day.
Dinner by reservation, nightly at 6. Prix-fixe, $15.50; Friday, $18 for lobster or steak.

Where to Eat

Cook's Lobster House, 68 Garrison Cove Road, Bailey Island.

Folks come from all over the Harpswells for the fresh seafood and lobster at this old-timer in a marina on a point surrounded by water. With windows on three sides, the main dining room is an expanse of low pine booths with a lamp on every table. Every seat gets a view of Garrison Cove and the famed cribstone bridge. Outside is Moby's Deck, a raw bar serving light food and drinks. The dinner menu ranges from broiled haddock, shrimp scampi and seafood newburg, to sautéed lobster, baked stuffed lobster, lobster newburg, steaks, and four shore dinners. Blackboard specials when we were there were grilled swordfish and fried oysters.

(207) 833-2818. www.cookslobster.com. Entrées, $14.95 to $32.95. Open daily, 11:30 to 9, to 10 in summer.

Estes Lobster House, Route 123, South Harpswell.

Here is a huge, two-story barn of a place on a spit of land with water on both sides. You order at a large counter near the entrance, pick up your meal served on paper plates with wimpy plastic implements, and take a seat in a couple of long, nondescript dining rooms or, our choice, at picnic tables outside. The mosquitoes were fierce only for ten minutes around dusk, and the manager obliged by providing a couple of citronella candles (well, we *were* the only ones outside on a slow night and the inside was nearly empty). Estes was pushing its original triple lobster plate, but we stuck with the lobster pie (lots of lobster, topped with stuffing) and a really good seafood medley (broiled halibut, swordfish, salmon and scallops), both with french fries. A bottle of wine, candlelight and a gorgeous sunset made for quite a picnic, but next time we'd bring our own cutlery. Lately, Estes has opened offshoots called Estes II at 1945 Harpswell Island Road (Route 24) on Bailey Island and at 956 Cundy's Harbor Road, Holbrook Wharf.

(207) 833-6340. Entrées, $14.95 to $23.95. Daily, 11:30 to 9. Closed mid-October to mid-April.

The Dolphin Chowder House, 515 Basin Point, Harpswell.

Local folks pour in for lunch and dinner at this small, pine-paneled restaurant with a counter, eight tables, two booths, an attempt at a store and the best fish chowder around. We can vouch for the chowder, absolutely delectable and containing more fish than broth. Also great was the lobster stew, accompanied, rather strangely, by a blueberry muffin that we took home for breakfast the next day. Although it was lunchtime, the value enticed one of us to try the complete dinner of clam strips, chowder, salad (with pepper-parmesan dressing on the side), french fries, rainbow sherbet and coffee, ending up thoroughly sated. No wonder the old-timers come here for midday dinner. At night, the menu offers fried clams, haddock, Casco Bay scallops, Maine shrimp and steak. There's beer and wine, but iced tea seems to be the beverage of choice. The windows also don't open, and one of us found the air so stifling she thought she was going to faint. Imagine, all that sea air and those water views and you're stuck behind storm windows. But is it ever popular!

(207) 833-6000. Entrées, $12.95 to $19.95. Open daily, 11 to 8, May-October.

FOR MORE INFORMATION: The Freeport Merchants Association, 23 Depot St., Box 452, Freeport, ME 04032, (207) 865-1212 or (800) 865-1994. www.freeportusa.com. It operates a small visitor center at the foot of Mill Street in downtown Freeport. The state-run Yarmouth Information Center along U.S. Route 1 at Exit 17 off I-95 has considerable information on Freeport and environs.

Information on the Harpswells is available from the Harpswell Business Association, www.harpswellmaine.org.

Back porch of Main Street gift shop looks onto Camden Harbor.

Camden/Rockland, Me.

Where Mountains Meet Sea

"Where the Mountains Meet the Sea" is how its boosters bill this part of Mid-Coast Maine. The rocky coast veers sharply to the north here. The shoreline becomes hilly, even mountainous as the ocean creates the broad and deep Penobscot Bay. Behind are the "three long mountains and a wood" that native poet Edna St. Vincent Millay described famously in 1910. Ahead are "three islands in a bay."

Between mountains and sea lie two towns. Rockland, population 8,000, is a working fishing port and the up-and-coming commercial heart of the Mid-Coast area. Eight miles to the north is Camden, a sophisticated resort enclave long favored by tourists. The two towns are separated from each other by Rockport, a mainly residential community.

The mountains distinguish the area from others along the Maine coast. They give residents and visitors the opportunity to enjoy traditional mountain pursuits – hiking, biking and skiing, among them – in close proximity to activities and attractions associated with the sea.

Mount Battie, one of the highest mountains along the East Coast, is the focal point for the area's mountain activities. Penobscot Bay, studded with islands and seemingly endless vistas, offers myriad water pursuits, most having to do with sailing. The bay is the home of the world's largest windjammer fleet, and many visitors come here simply to see or sail the windjammers.

Leafy Camden, one of the most stylish and affluent communities in Maine, retains a small-town charm that belies its 5,000 population. Its posh inns, restaurants, shops and cultural activities lure visitors who crave the good life.

Hard-scrabble Rockland lately has undergone remarkable rejuvenation, thanks to the Wyeth family's connection with the much-expanded Farnsworth Art Museum and an improved harborfront area. Having laid claim to Camden's title as the windjammer capital of Maine, it also is becoming a competitor in terms of art galleries, shops and restaurants.

The two towns eye each other somewhat suspiciously as rivals, and each has its own Chamber of Commerce. Camden bills itself as "the Jewel of the Maine Coast." Rockland counters with "The Real Maine."

Together they make a great getaway for those who crave urban amenities and a dose of the good life amid mountains and sea.

Seeing and Doing

The area's museums and attractions vie for the visitor's attention as much as its ocean and mountain activities.

Museums and Attractions

Farnsworth Art Museum and the Wyeth Center, 16 Museum St., Rockland.

One of the nation's leading regional art museums is a must-see for visitors – indeed it's a primary destination for many of its more than 250,000 visitors a year. With America's first family of art, the Wyeths, deciding to make it the repository for their Maine-related works and major benefactors reaching into deep pockets, the Farnsworth doubled its size in 1998 and again in 2000. It has sprawled across five new or restored buildings into a "campus" covering two and one-half city blocks, requiring four entrances and making it one of the country's most spread-out museums. The heart of the complex remains the original Georgian-style brick museum and library funded in 1948 by the estate of Lucy Copeland Farnsworth, which grew to the point where it now holds one of the best collections of Maine art in the world. The opening of the Wyeth Center in 1998 in the former Pratt Memorial Methodist Church across Union Street put Rockland on the art map nationally. The Morehouse Wing honoring the late artist Jamien Morehouse in 2000 was the icing on the cake. Occupying the site of a former five-and-dime store, it offers more gallery space for the growing collection (now more than 13,000 objects spanning four centuries) as well as an excellent museum shop fronting on Main Street.

Such leading artists as Gilbert Stuart, Fitz Hugh Lane, Thomas Sully, Frank Benson, Childe Hassam and Maurice Prendergast are represented in the museum's permanent collection, "Maine in America." The museum also houses the nation's second-largest collection of works by premier 20th-century sculptor Louise Nevelson and has opened four new galleries to showcase contemporary art.

The Wyeths, of course, touch the essence of Maine. The family's history in the Rockland area dates back to N.C. Wyeth, but it was son Andrew who incorporated the people and places of the nearby Cushing peninsula as his subjects for more than three decades. Outside the Olson House there he painted *Christina's World,* an American classic. Despite rapid growth, the Farnsworth retains a sense of the personal. It is reflected in the exhibit descriptions and catalogs and is obvious in the tours of the museum's Olson House (see below), led daily at 2 by 91-year-old curator Dudley Rockwell, Andrew Wyeth's brother-in-law, who summers in Cushing. Included in the museum admission in season is the adjacent **Farnsworth Homestead,** considered one of the most beautiful Greek Revival houses in the country. Its Victorian interior is furnished as it was when the Farnsworths lived there.

(207) 596-6457. www.farnsworthmuseum.org. Open daily, 9 to 5, Wednesday-Friday to 7, mid-June to Columbus Day; Tuesday-Sunday 10 to 4 or 5 rest of year. Adults $9, children free.

Visit the Olson House

Olson House, Hathorn Point Road, Cushing.

The people and places of the Cushing peninsula provided some of the most enduring images for Andrew Wyeth. The evocative Olson house near the bay, once the home of Christina Olson and her brother Alvaro, had magnetic appeal for Wyeth, who found it the essence of Maine and spent more than 30 years nearby. "I just couldn't stay away from there," he once remarked. It's open to the public following its donation to Rockland's Farnsworth Art Museum by Apple Computer founder John Sculley. Try to catch the 2 p.m. daily lecture by Dudley Rockwell, longtime Olson neighbor and Andrew Wyeth's brother-in-law. Quite the raconteur, he volunteers fascinating tidbits about the history of the house, the Olson family and how Wyeth had come to paint here. After the talk, venture upstairs to see the rooms in which Wyeth produced *Christina's World, Wind from the Sea* and *End of Olsons* and other drawings, watercolors and tempuras featuring the house and its residents. Then walk out through the field to the Olson family gravesite overlooking the bay. Christina and Alvaro share a headstone, where people sometimes leave flowers.

(207) 354-0102. Open Memorial Day to Columbus Day, daily 11 to 4. Adults, $4.

The Island Institute, 386 Main St., Rockland.

Maine's island and coastal preservation movement is headquartered in a former department store restored in an effort led by Philip Conkling, co-founder and president of the Island Institute. The restoration coincided with the opening of the addition to the Farnsworth Art Museum honoring his late wife, artist Jamien Morehouse. The main floor holds interesting island displays, lobstering exhibits, revolving shows and the terrific institute store, **Archipelago.** It showcases works by more than 200 island artists and artisans, "all inspired by our beautiful coastal setting."

(207) 594-9209. www.islandinstitute.org. Open Monday-Saturday 9 to 7, June-September; Tuesday-Saturday 10 to 5:30, rest of year.

The Owls Head Transportation Museum, Route 73, Owls Head.

One of the country's largest collections of working antique aircraft, autos, motorcycles, bicycles and carriages is shown at this establishment, located next to the Knox County Airport and known for its special auto and air shows. The exhibition hall covers the evolution of transportation over nearly two centuries. The Aircraft Collection contains replicas and originals representing the first century of flight, from Cayley's unmanned glider (1804) to the legendary Curtiss Jenny of the barnstorming era. Among the more than 150 exhibits are a full-scale replica of the Wright brothers' Kitty Hawk Flyer, World War I bi-planes, an extensive collection of

Woodie wagons, luxury autos from the Silent Film era, and the largest motorcycle ever made. Highlights are a 1935 Stout Scarab (called the world's first minivan, one of only six ever made) and the 1963 prototype of the Ford Mustang.

(207) 594-4418. www.ohtm.org. Adults $6, children $4, family rate $16. Open daily 10 to 5, April-October, 10 to 4 rest of year.

Maine Lighthouse Museum, One Park Drive, Rockland.

Opened in 2005 in the new Gateway Visitor Center overlooking the Rockland breakwater is this expanded museum, an amalgamation of the fledgling lighthouse museum and the Shore Village Museum, which relocated from Limerock Street. Housed in a former newspaper printing plant, it contains the largest collection of lighthouse lenses and U.S. Coast Guard artifacts on display in the country. Flashing lights, clanging bells and groaning foghorns add a little excitement to the exhibits of lighthouse equipment and ship models. The Coast Guard exhibits include lighthouse machinery, buoys, lifesaving gear and search and rescue boats, many of them collected by Kenneth Black, who came to town to serve in the Coast Guard office. He spearheaded a 30-year drive to create a lighthouse museum in the heart of the area where fourteen of the state's 68 lighthouses are located.

(207) 594-3301. www.mainelighthousemuseum.com. Open Monday-Friday 9 to 4:30, Saturday-Sunday 10 to 4. Adults $3, children free.

Relive local history at the **Conway Homestead-Cramer Museum,** Route 1, Rockport, (207) 236-2257. It includes a restored 18th-century farmhouse, a barn displaying antique carriages and sleighs, a working blacksmith shop, a Victorian privy, an herb garden and an 1820 maple sugar house. The Mary Meeker Cramer Museum displays ship models, quilts, period clothing and other memorabilia. The complex run by the Camden-Rockport Historical Society is open Monday-Thursday 10 to 4 in July and August, by appointment in June and September; adults $5, children $2.

Merryspring, 30 Conway Road, Camden, (206) 236-2239, is a 66-acre nature park and horticultural center founded in 1974 by horticulturalist Mary Ellen Ross of the mail-order plant business Merry Gardens. It includes walking trails and herb, rose and perennial gardens, an arboretum and three greenhouses. Open daily, dawn to dusk; free.

A Haven of Tranquility

Vesper Hill Chapel, Calderwood Lane, Rockport, (207) 236-4594.

A terrific view of Penobscot Bay is afforded from this non-denominational outdoor chapel, built of pine and resembling a Swiss chalet, atop a rock ledge along the shore. It's the legacy of Helene Bok, who fulfilled a dream of building a chapel that would open out onto the world on the site of a summer estate-turned-hotel that was destroyed by fire in 1954. Mrs. Bok and friends created a garden showplace and a chapel sanctuary for the ages. Up to 50 people can be seated for informal meditation on Sunday mornings. Not wanting to intrude on the Quaker Meeting we came upon, we bided our time in the formal perennial and Biblical herb gardens below. More than 60 wedding ceremonies take place here annually, but the casual visitor can stop by to enjoy peace, quiet and beauty any other time from mid-April through October.

CULTURE. Summer entertainment, from band concerts to vaudeville, is provided periodically in Camden in the outdoor **Bok Amphitheater** next to the town library, just a few hundred feet from the harbor. The **Camden Civic Theatre,** (207) 236-2281, produces five plays from April into December at the restored brick Camden Opera House, 29 Elm St. Classical music and jazz concerts are offered Thursday and Friday in summer and monthly the rest of the year at the Rockport Opera House at 10 Summer St. on the harbor by **Bay Chamber Concerts,** (207) 236-2823 or (888) 707-2770.

ART GALLERIES. The sea and the varied landscape inspire local and visiting artists, whose galleries abound, especially in Camden and Rockport. The **Center for Maine Contemporary Art,** 162 Russell Ave., Rockport, displays changing exhibits of contemporary works by established and emerging Maine artists in a large, renovated 19th-century livery stable. It's open June-September, Tuesday-Saturday 10 to 5 and Sunday 1 to 5; adults, $3. Famed Rockport artist **Anne Kilham** displays her distinctive Maine seaside designs in her home gallery at 142 Russell Ave., Rockport. You can watch the glass blower at work in the **Prism Glass Studio & Gallery,** 297 Commercial St., Rockport, which also serves good food at the Gallery Café (see Where to Eat). In Camden, the **Camden Falls Gallery** occupies a priceless location beside a waterfall with a view of the harbor. Other galleries worth a visit include the **Bearse Art Gallery** on U.S. Route 1 between Camden and Lincolnville, featuring Jan Bearse's watercolors and oils, and the **H. Swanson Studio & Gallery,** Route 1, Lincolnville Beach, showing the paintings of Harry Swanson. The most extensive selection of wildlife carvings in Maine is available at **Duck Trap Decoys,** Duck Trap Road, Lincolnville Beach. A gallery of a different kind is the showroom and workshop of **Windsor Chairmakers,** U.S. Route 1, just north of Lincolnville Beach.

SHOPPING. Rockland's Main Street has been entered in the National Register of Historic Places for its fine examples of Italianate, Mansard, Greek Revival and Colonial Revival architecture. Recent renovations of commercial buildings have produced new restaurants, espresso bars, galleries and shops. Among the galleries near the Farnsworth Museum along Main and Elm Streets are **Élan Fine Arts**, **Caldbeck Gallery, Huston Tuttle & Gallery One, Playing with Fire Glassworks and Gallery** and **Nan Mulford Gallery. Harbor Square Gallery** showcases its paintings and fine art jewelry amid the arches and vaulted ceiling of an old bank. **The Store** is a gourmet kitchen shop that also sells cards and children's toys. **Meander** is a gift shop stocking "elegant necessities and practical indulgences." **Saltwater Trading Co.** features Maine and nautical items.

Interesting specialty shops and boutiques pop up every year in Camden, where sophisticated stores predominate. **Planet** is a world marketplace with a trendy selection of gifts, clothing, housewares, accessories, toys and more, many with a nature or planetary theme. Its related **Emporium** store across the street features contemporary women's apparel with a worldly theme. More traditional favorites for clothing and gifts are the **House of Logan** and **Margo Moore. The Admiral's Buttons** has preppy clothing and sailing attire. **Surroundings** offers "durable goods" for home and garden, while **Maine Gathering** specializes in fine Maine crafts. **Wild Birds Unlimited** has an amazing collection of bird feeders, carved birds, birdsong tapes and the like. A large carved gull wearing a windjammer tie drew us into the **Ducktrap Bay Trading Co.,** a wildlife and Maine art gallery showing things from decoys to paintings. We bought a handcrafted Maine wooden bucket for use as a planter from **Once a Tree,** which also has great clocks, toys, bracelets and everything else made from wood.

Shoppers in search of snacks seek out **Boynton-McKay Food Co.** at 30 Main St. for espresso, fruit smoothies and old-fashioned ice cream prepared in the original art deco soda fountain of an 1890s pharmacy. It also offers sandwiches, salads and prepared foods, as does the upscale grocer **French & Brawn Marketplace. Cappy's Bakery & Coffee House** at 1 Main St. purveys cappuccino, wine, panini sandwiches and home-baked goods.

Active Pursuits

TOURING. A scenic drive is out Route 52 to Megunticook Lake, an island-studded lake that emerged eerily from the fog the first time we saw it. A walking tour of Camden and a bicycle or car tour of Camden and adjacent Rockport are available through the Camden-Rockport Historical Society. A favorite drive or bicycle tour heads southeast out of Camden on Bay View Street to Beauchamp Point and curves along Mechanic Street into Rockport. It returns to Camden via Chestnut Street. Some of the area's estates may be seen, along with belted Galloway cows grazing at Aldermere Farm.

HIKING. Some of the East Coast's most scenic hiking is available in **Camden Hills State Park,** where eighteen trails of varying lengths and difficulty are detailed in a trail guide. With an elevation of 1,380 feet, Mount Megunticook is the highest of the three mountains that make up the park and the second highest point on the Eastern Seaboard. If you're not up to hiking, drive the toll road up Mount Battie to the 790-foot summit. The view over village and bay is worth the $1-per-person toll. More rugged hiking is available on the trails of Camden Snow Bowl.

WINTER SPORTS. Skiing takes over in the off-season at the **Camden Snow Bowl,** John Street, Camden, (207) 236-3438. Ten trails are served by a double chairlift and two T-bars, one of them the longest in the state at 4,088 feet. Night skiing is offered Tuesday-Friday. Adult lift tickets cost $29 weekends, $18 midweek. The Snow Bowl, incidentally, is the only area in Maine to have a public toboggan chute, a 400-foot-long run ending on frozen Hosmer Pond (rides, $1 each). The U.S. National Toboggan Championships are held here each February. Cross-country skiing is available on the golf course at the Samoset Resort in Rockport. Indoor skating is offered at the ice arena at the Midcoast Recreation Center, Route 90, Rockport, (207) 236-9400. It also has four indoor tennis courts.

Water Activities

Although Rockland claims the title of "Schooner Capital of Maine" and a number of windjammers set sail from Rockland harbor, no major regularly scheduled boat tours are offered here, this being essentially a working harbor. Pleasure craft gravitate to Camden harbor.

A boat launch and picnic tables are available at **Rockport Marine Park,** André Street, Rockport, (207) 236-4404. The harborside park is known for its statue of André the seal, the legendary harbor seal who cavorted here. Three restored lime kilns date to the early 1900s when Rockport was one of the greatest lime producing towns in the nation. There's a replica of the locomotives that transported lime rock to waiting ships in the harbor. Open daily, dawn to dusk. Free.

BOAT TRIPS. A variety of cruises on Penobscot Bay leave from the Camden harbor, where there are benches for viewing the passing boat parade. The famed windjammers are generally booked for five-day sails, but lately some have been giving daily two-hour trips, lunch or dinner cruises and even an overnight excursion.

Two-hour cruises priced at $20 to $28 each are offered by at least three schooners from Camden Harbor. The area's biggest daysailer is the 86-foot **Appledore,** (207) 236-8353, a tall ship that has sailed around the world. It takes up to 49 passengers three times a day from Bayview Landing. Sailing from the adjacent Camden Public Landing are the smaller schooners **Surprise,** (207) 236-4687; **Lazy Jack,** (207) 230-0602, and **Olad,** (207) 236-2323. Passengers sail past islands and lighthouses and see seals, porpoises, eagles and osprey.

The Wooden Boat Company's 65-foot schooner yacht **Heron** offers three trips daily from Rockport Harbor, (207) 236-8605 or (800) 599-8605. They are a lobster lunch sail, an Indian Island lighthouse tour and a gourmet sunset sail.

The **M/V Betselma,** (207) 236-4446, a 38-foot powerboat, gives scenic coastal and island tours of one or two hours each from Camden Public Landing. One-hour trips (adults $10, children $5) between Camden and Rockport show harbor lighthouses and oceanfront estates. Two-hour trips ($20 and $10) reveal more lighthouses, islands, sea birds and seals, as well as some of the famed summer mansions on the island of Islesboro.

A former biology teacher, Capt. Alan Philbrick, runs two-hour lobster fishing and ecotours through the islands from Bayview Landing on the lobster boat **Lively Lady, Too,** (207) 236-6672; adults $20, children $5. By reservation, he offers a four-hour sunset cruise to an uninhabited island for a lobster bake ($50).

SEA KAYAKING. Because of its relatively protected waters, Penobscot Bay and its coves and islands are good for kayaking and canoeing. Several outfits offer rentals and guided tours. The biggest is **Maine Sport Outfitters,** (207) 236-7120 or (800) 722-0826, whose colorful facility is a landmark along Route 1 in Rockport. Others are **Ducktrap Sea Kayak,** 2175 Atlantic Highway, Lincolnville Beach, (207) 236-8608, and **Breakwater Kayak** out of Rockport, (207) 596-6895 or (877) 559-8800.

SWIMMING. The Lincolnville Beach is good for swimming in Penobscot Bay. A more secluded, picturesque setting is Camden's little-known Laite Memorial Beach with treed lawns sloping down to the water, a small beach, picnic tables and old-fashioned fireplaces off Bay View Street. Lake swimming is available at Hosmer Pond and Lake Megunticook.

Where to Stay

Rockland Area

The Berry Manor Inn, 81 Talbot Ave., Rockland 04841.

Original signed wallpaper and a water downspout are encased in glass here to indicate the meticulous restoration of one of Rockland's larger residences, built by merchant Charles Berry in 1898 and located in a quiet residential section. Michael LaPosta and his wife, Cheryl Michaelsen, installed seven gas fireplaces, five jacuzzi tubs and several hundred rolls of wallpaper to turn it into mid-coast Maine's first AAA four-diamond B&B. They offer eight spacious corner bedrooms on the second and third floors. Each comes with a king or queensize bed, comfortable sitting area, and full closet with built-in chest of drawers. All enveloped in luxury, some are feminine and manifestly Victorian. Others are masculine and quite un-Victorian. Three high-end rooms and a suite, all with fireplaces and three with jacuzzi tubs, were added in the side carriage house. The entire main floor is turned over to guests: a formal sitting room, a more casual living room with big-screen TV, a dining room with individual tables and a guest pantry stocked with everything from evening pies baked by Mike's mother to soft drinks and beer. Cheryl's multi-course breakfasts are big deals and feature blueberries in some form every day. The main course might be shirred eggs with havarti, vegetable strata or blueberry-stuffed french toast.

(207) 596-7696 or (800) 774-5692. Fax (207) 596-9958. www.berrymanorinn.com. Eleven rooms and one suite with private baths. Mid-June to mid-October: doubles $145 to $215, suite $310. Rest of year: doubles $95 to $155, suite $210.

A Resort to Get Happily Lost In

Samoset Resort, 220 Warrenton St., Rockport 04856.

You can be as active as you want or simply hide out in a variety of accommodations at this golf and conference resort, which occupies a 230-acre peninsula stretching into Penobscot Bay. The place dates to 1889, although you'd never know it today. The original turreted hotel, destroyed by fire in 1972, was rebuilt from the old timbers of an abandoned Portland granary. Three wings off the main resort building contain large guest rooms, most with ocean views across the golf fairways and all with a terrace or balcony. A new extension to one wing offers 28 deluxe rooms and suites. These have larger baths with floors and walls of marble, a feature going into existing rooms as they are renovated. Suites on the fourth floor enjoy the best water views, a living room with wet bar, bath with a double vanity and larger balcony. The idyllic Flume Cottage, a two-bedroom house with a large deck off the living room and master bedroom, is on a rocky spit of land off the fifteenth fairway (it comes complete with its own four-passenger golf cart). The resort also rents 72 time-share units of one and two bedrooms in three separate, freestanding buildings, for $419 to $499. A fitness center offers an indoor pool, hot tubs and saunas as well as Nautilus equipment and a racquetball court. There are four tennis courts, an outdoor pool and an eighteen-hole championship golf course with seven oceanside holes.

Tableside service by a tuxedoed staff and an award-winning wine list are featured in the fancy ocean-view dining room, **Marcel's.** A pianist accompanies on busy nights. The contemporary continental menu begins with appetizers like seared foie gras with grilled brioche and escargots in puff pastry. Caesar salad is prepared tableside for two, as are châteaubriand and rack of lamb. Other entrée possibilities range from Atlantic salmon roasted on a cedar plank to chipotle-dusted beef tenderloin with red wine demi-glace. A more casual menu is available across the foyer in the **Breakwater Café,** with a tavern look and an appealing outdoor deck and terrace.

(207) 594-2511 or (800) 341-1650. Fax (207) 594-0722. www.samoset.com. One hundred fifty-six rooms and 22 suites. Rates, EP. July to mid-October: doubles $258 to $499, suites $299 to $549. Rest of year: doubles $99 to $209, suites $229 to $319.

Entrées, $17 to $34. Dinner nightly, 6 to 9. Café open daily from 11:30; entrées, $16.95 to $24.95.

Captain Lindsey House Inn, 5 Lindsey St., Rockland 04841.
Self-styled a "small luxury hotel," this occupies an 1837 sea captain's home one

building away from Rockland's busy Main Street. Its mustard yellow façade with green awnings conveys the look of an older hotel, but the interior is smartly up-to-date. Ken and Ellen Barnes, both sea captains, opened the inn in 1995 to help spark Rockland's rejuvenation as well as provide land-based accommodations for their windjammer travelers. Stylishly furnished with maritime pieces, the main floor harbors a handsome living room with fireplace, an adjacent library and a snug breakfast room where a continental buffet is put out each morning, followed by pastries, sherry and port in the afternoon. A rear courtyard provides a pleasant retreat in summer. Urbane rooms on three floors come with a variety of bed configurations from twins and doubles to kingsize. TVs are hidden in armoires and hotel-style amenities are abundant. Adjacent in what used to be the town's water works is the casual **Waterworks Restaurant & Pub,** a microbrewery and pub offering a limited menu day and night.

(207) 596-7696 or (800) 523-2145. www.lindseyhouse.com. Nine rooms with private baths. Doubles, $140 to $190 Memorial Day to mid-October, $85 to $125 rest of year.

Camden

Norumbega, 61 High St., Camden 04843.

Want to stay in a castle overlooking Penobscot Bay? This elegant B&B is ensconced in an opulent cobblestone and turreted mansion, one of the great late-19th-century villas built along the Maine coast. The exterior is said to be Maine's most photographed piece of real estate. Inside are endlessly fascinating public rooms (the woodwork alone is priceless), ten bedrooms and two suites, all with sitting areas and telephones and some with TVs. Most have fireplaces and canopy beds, all kingsize except for a queen in the smallest garden-level room. The ten in back have breathtaking views of Penobscot Bay. Guests have the run of the common areas including a formal parlor, a small library, an intimate retreat for two beside a fireplace on the landing of the ornate staircase, as well as flower-laden rear porches and balconies on all three floors overlooking expansive lawns and the bay. Manager JoAnne Reuillard and staff pour tea or wine in the afternoon. Breakfast is a feast of juices and fruits, all kinds of breads and muffins, and, when we stayed, the best french toast ever, topped with sliced oranges and a dollop of sherbet.

(207) 236-4646 or (877) 363-4646. Fax (207) 236-4990. www.norumbegainn.com. Ten rooms and two suites with private baths. Doubles, $160 to $340. Suites, $365 to $475.

The Inn at Sunrise Point, U.S. Route 1, Lincolnville (Box 1344, Camden 04843).

Here is the inn of an inn reviewer's dreams. After critiquing others across the country, California-based travel writer Jerry Levitin opened his own B&B on four forested acres at the foot of a private lane descending from Route 1 to Penobscot Bay. "I built what I'd like to stay at," said Jerry, who eventually tired of innkeeping and sold to Stephen Tallon from Ireland and his wife Deanna from Australia. They converted the seasonal operation into a year-round endeavor, offering three rooms in the shingle-style main house plus four cottages and two suites. A new suite, just twenty feet from water's edge, is the former owner's quarters with a queen bedroom, living/dining room, kitchen and deck. The Tallons named the suite for Jerry Levitin and decorated it in a travel theme. The Winslow Homer Cottage that we occupied right beside the water contains a kingsize bed, a fireplace, TV/VCR, wet bar and an enormous bathroom with a jacuzzi for two and a separate shower. Also close to the water and with the same attributes is the Fitz Hugh Lane Cottage. Two smaller cottages possess queen beds, as do three snug rooms upstairs in the main inn. Each has a fireplace, music system, built-in desk, double whirlpool tub, armoire holding TV and VCR, and a private balcony overlooking the water. The new Loft Suite has a king bed, polished hardwood floors, clawfoot soaking tub and a steam shower. Guests are welcomed in the main inn with afternoon beverages. The main floor harbors a wonderful living/dining room that's mostly windows onto Penobscot Bay, an English hunting-style library with a fireplace and a small conservatory for tête-à-tête breakfasts. We feasted here on pecan coffeecake, a terrific frittata with basil, bay shrimp and jack cheese, potatoes dusted with cayenne, crisp bacon and hazelnut coffee.

(207) 236-7716. Fax (207) 236-0820. www.sunrisepoint.com. Three rooms, two suites and four cottages with private baths. Doubles, $310 to $330. Suites and cottages, $350 to $495. Off-season: doubles $225 to $245, suites and cottages $250 to $300.

Inn at Ocean's Edge, U.S. Route 1, Lincolnville (Box 704, Camden 04843).

The waves lull you to sleep at this deluxe lodging establishment housed in two contemporary gray buildings, one above the other, on seven acres along the shore of Penobscot Bay. All guest rooms but one face the water, although only the twelve newest rooms in the higher Hilltop Building have private balconies for taking in the view. Outfitted with different wallpapers and linens, each extra-spacious room has a kingsize four-poster bed, wing chairs facing a corner gas fireplace, a TV/VCR in an armoire, an open jacuzzi flanked by pillars at the end of the bedroom, and a separate bathroom. Guests gather in a couple of large common areas in the main building. One is a Great Room with vaulted ceiling and two levels of atrium windows and a set of french doors onto an oversize oceanfront deck. Another is the front pub with a full bar. There's also a garden-level lounge and patio beside a heated pool, plus a tennis court. At our visit, the oceanfront deck was the setting for a memorable breakfast of poached pears, homemade granola, applesauce-raisin muffins and cranberry-orange zest pancakes with bacon. The nicely landscaped back lawn leads to 250 feet of ocean frontage. New owners Tim and Joan Porta also run Migas Lodge in the Sebago Lake region.

(207) 236-0945. Fax (207) 236-0609. www.innatoceansedge.com. Twenty-six rooms and one suite with private baths. Doubles, $239 to $295, off-season $159 to $265. Closed early December to April.

Lord Camden Inn, 24 Main St., Camden 04843.

Deluxe accommodations are offered in this recently upgraded and expanded establishment in the center of town. On three floors above an 1893 brick storefront and the old Masonic Temple, it's really more like a small hotel than an inn – but a plush and welcoming one, following renovations in 2004 and 2005. Six premier rooms on the fourth floor have canopied decks yielding panoramic ocean views over the rooftops across the street. Partial harbor views are available from third-floor front rooms, and eight rooms in the rear offer decks and views of the passing Megunticook River and hills behind the inn. Six new deluxe rooms on the second floor come with gas fireplaces, marble baths and large recessed balconies with views of the downtown scene. Fireplaces and balconies were added to six front rooms on the third floor in 2005. Most rooms offer large flat-screen TVs, DVD players, hair dryers, ironing boards and free high-speed internet wireless access. New innkeeper Philip Woodland is proud of the luxurious bedding, including plush-top mattresses and 400 thread-count sheets. Besides a new fitness room on the fourth floor, an expanded dining room offers a complimentary gourmet breakfast. Choices range from eggs benedict to make-your-own belgian waffles.

(207) 236-4325 or (800) 336-4325. Fax (207) 236-7141. www.lordcamdeninn.com. Thirty rooms and six suites with private baths. Doubles, $179 to $269, off-season $90 to $159.

A Little Dream, 66 High St., Camden 04843.

This lacy valentine of a B&B is "a little dream" as envisioned and executed by innkeeper Joanne Fontana and her husband Bill, a sculptor. They offer three spacious bedrooms and a suite in the turreted Victorian house, each comfortably furnished and accented with Victorian clothing, lace, ribbons and at least eight pillows on each bed. Three deluxe accommodations in the carriage house offer seclusion and bay views. The Isle Watch here is a huge room with kingsize iron canopy bed, a chintz sofa and wing chair, and a window seat looking onto an idyllic private porch. The top level of the carriage house holds a Loft room and Treetops, a suite with living room, queen bedroom and a front balcony with an island view. Joanne pampers guests in a parlor furnished in wicker and chintz, an elaborate dining room beside a conservatory and a wraparound porch, the side portion of which has lately been enclosed in glass for year-round use. Breakfast is served amid much lace and silver. The choice might involve lemon-ricotta soufflé pancakes with raspberry sauce, banana-pecan waffles with maple country sausage, or a smoked salmon omelet.

(207) 236-8742 or (800) 217-0109. www.littledream.com. Four rooms and three suites with private baths. Doubles, $159 to $225. Suites, $215 to $295. Closed in March.

Hartstone Inn, 41 Elm St., Camden 04843.

After toiling for gourmet restaurants in luxury hotel chains around the world, Mary Jo and Michael Salmon wanted to pamper guests in their own place and on a smaller scale. They do it very nicely in this inn complex headquartered in an 1835 house at the edge of Camden's business district. In the main house they offer eight elegant bedrooms, two with fireplaces and all with queen beds covered with feather duvets, CD players, tiled-floor baths and triple-paned windows to muffle street noise. A restored carriage house in the rear offers two bi-level suites done in contemporary barn style, with fireplaced living rooms, TVs hidden in armoires and private entrances overlooking the gardens in which the Salmons grow herbs and vegetables for their dining room (see Where to Eat). Tucked away in a flower garden are two new suites with sitting rooms created when the Salmons vacated their quarters and moved to an adjoining property they now call the Manor House on Free Street. The Cottage Suite has a queen poster bed, fireplace and bath with whirlpool tub. The Manor House contains two more large guest rooms, one the summery, cathedral-ceilinged Arbor with kingsize mahogany sleigh bed, gas fireplace and TV/VCR. Back in the main inn, guests enjoy a formal parlor with a fireplace, a rear library, a small game room and a formal dining room and adjacent enclosed porch. The latter is the site for an extravagant breakfast that might culminate in a prosciutto baked egg with spinach tortilla or a lobster and asparagus quiche.

(207) 236-4259 or (800) 788-4823. Fax (207) 236-9575. www.hartstoneinn.com. Ten rooms and four suites with private baths. Late June through October: doubles $125 to $190, suites $235 to $245. Rest of year: doubles $100 to $175, suites $175 to $195.

Camden Maine Stay, 22 High St., Camden 04843.

Started rather simply by doting innkeepers whose skills were the envy of their colleagues, the Maine Stay expanded, upgraded and lured a repeat clientele to the point where it was the one B&B in Camden that always seemed to be fully booked when others hung out "vacancy" signs. Retired business executive Bob Topper and his Austrian-born wife Juanita inherited a going concern when they took over the rambling 1802 farmhouse that started with nine bedrooms sharing three baths. The Maine Stay now has eight bedrooms and suites, all with updated baths (some with Corian tiled showers), and some with gas fireplaces or wood stoves. All are comfortably furnished and decorated with style and charm. The former Room 3, upstairs front, is typical of the accommodations as they have evolved. Formerly two small rooms with a shared bath, it is now the Christina Topper Suite with a sofabed and gas fireplace in the front sitting room, a queen brass bed in back and a private deck. The attached carriage house harbors a delightful downstairs room, cheery in white with blue trim and yellow accents, with queen bed, gas stove and private stone patio – who would guess it was once a root cellar with no windows and a dirt floor? Another favorite is the large Common Ground Room decorated with agricultural fair posters. It has a vaulted ceiling, tall windows, queen bed, Maine cottage furniture and a Vermont Castings stove, plus an outside deck. Guests enjoy two fireplaced parlors and a library, a rear sun porch and seating areas in a two-acre backyard backing up to Camden Hills State Park. Breakfast is served at a convivial harvest table in the dining room or at tables for two on the sun porch overlooking the garden. The main course might be quiche or peach french toast.

(207) 236-9636. Fax (207) 236-0621. www.camdenmainestay.com. Six rooms and two suites with private baths. Doubles, $125 to $205 June-October, $100 to $160 rest of year.

Cottage Hideaways

Cedarholm Garden Bay, U.S. Route 1, Lincolnville Beach (Box 345, Camden 04843).

Looking for a modern oceanfront cottage all to yourselves, surrounded by woodlands and some spectacular gardens? Barry and Joyce Jobson oblige with four secluded cottages he built amid the trees along the Penobscot Bay shore, part of a small and personal cottage colony dating to the 1950s. Each has a queen or king bedroom, wet bar with mini-refrigerator, TV and telephone and a waterside deck. Two have a living room with vaulted ceiling and stone fireplace as well as a bath with double whirlpool tub and separate shower. The ceilings are finished in cedar and the furnishings are of the upscale lodge variety. Two renovated cottages are located at the top of the sixteen-acre property, where guests enjoy continental breakfast in the cedar-paneled breakfast room in the Jobsons' house. Joyce bakes muffins with blueberries, blackberries and gooseberries that grow on the property, and oversees the showy gardens all around.

(207) 236-3886. www.cedarholm.com. Six cottages with private baths. Doubles, $275 to $340 on the waterfront, others $165.

The Hawthorn, 9 High St., Camden 04843.

Elegance and comfort are the hallmarks of this 1894 Queen Anne-style beauty, one of the few in Camden with glimpses of the Camden harbor. Well-traveled owner Maryanne Shanahan offers ten guest quarters in the main house and a rear carriage house, plus a nicely landscaped back yard sloping toward Camden Harbor and a gate opening onto the town amphitheater. All rooms have telephones and queensize beds (except one with twins). The four prime accommodations, three with double jacuzzis and three with gas fireplaces, are in the carriage house. Each has a private deck or patio and a TV/VCR. The inn's main floor contains a double parlor with not one but two turrets and a formal dining room. Healthful breakfasts are served at individual tables there or on a spacious rear deck. The fare the morning of our visit included coffeecake, homemade granola and a raspberry blintz soufflé.

(207) 236-8842 or (866) 381-3647. Fax (207) 236-6181. www.camdeninn.com. Eight rooms and two suites with private baths. Doubles, $149 to $289 May to mid-November, $99 to $199 rest of year.

Where to Eat

Rockland Area

Primo, 2 South Main St. (Route 73), Rockland.

Foodies from across the country flock to Rockland to try celebrity chef Melissa Kelly's sparkling restaurant. Cited by the James Beard Foundation as the best chef in the Northeast in 1999 when she was cooking in New York's Hudson Valley, she teamed here with Price Kushner, her fiancé and a baker and pastry chef of note. Named for her Italian grandfather, Primo Magnani, the chic hot spot occupies a century-old Victorian residence. The pair installed a wood-fired brick oven and imparted a cozy, elegant country look to three small, white-tablecloth dining rooms with deep mustard-colored walls on the main floor and a large, more casual upstairs bar area where a bar menu, pizzas and paninis are available. Melissa's menu draws its roots from the Mediterranean and its ingredients from Maine, some from the lavish herb and vegetable gardens the pair planted outside. A complimentary amuse-bouche of smooth duck liver mousse on brioche followed by crusty, rustic sourdough breads with choice of olive oil or butter got our dinners off to an auspicious start. Scallops with risotto were a tasty appetizer. Main courses were pork saltimbocca, served on mashed potatoes and spinach, and venison fanned around cabbage and wild rice studded with huckleberries. Desserts were assorted homemade ice creams and a stellar pear tarte tatin with ginger-almond ice cream. Though Primo is open year-round, the owners spend part of the off-season at their new Primo, the signature restaurant in the J.W. Marriott Grande Lakes Hotel in Orlando, Fla.

(207) 596-0770. www.primorestaurant.com. Entrées, $19 to $32. Dinner by reservation, nightly from 5:30. Closed Tuesday and Wednesday in off-season.

Café Miranda, 15 Oak St., Rockland.

The beige and green colors of the exterior are repeated inside the trendy cafe at the edge of downtown. Chef-owner Kerry Altiero cooks almost everything – even the fish of the day – in a wood-fired brick oven in an open kitchen, going through a cord of wood a month. His enormous menu ranges widely, from pasta with sundried tomatoes, ricotta and artichoke hearts to chicken mole, lamb steaks and braised rabbit. North African and Thai influences show up in such dishes as grilled salmon with mandarin oranges and cilantro, served with couscous, and pork with gorgonzola, polenta and three chiles with avocado salsa. You could make a meal of small plates like fried oysters over arugula or shrimp tossed with avocado-corn salsa on roasted romano grits. Wife Evelyn Donnelly's artistic talents are evident in the desserts, perhaps chocolate-kahlua torte or frozen lemon mousse pie.

(207) 594-2034. www.cafemiranda.com. Entrées, $17 to $22. Dinner nightly, from 5:30. Closed Monday in off-season.

Amalfi, 421 Main St., Rockland.

When a Maine coast restaurant is launched in the dead of winter and acquires a wide reputation before summer arrives, visitors know it's worth seeking out. Chef-owner David Cooke converted a downtown storefront into a colorful, 35-seat Mediterranean eatery with purple runners and pink napkins on the tables and a mural of a Tuscan vineyard painted on the wall. A Culinary Institute of America graduate, the Chicago native turns out such dishes as a signature paella, fish stew, duck risotto, Moroccan chicken kabob, braised lamb shanks and grilled strip steak. Tempting starters are mussels steamed in cilantro and garlic, a caramelized onion and goat cheese tart or a trio of tapas. Dessert could be a crème brûlée, a specialty chocolate soup with berries, lemon tart, or a homemade ice cream or sorbet.

(207) 596-0012. www.amalfi-tonight.com. Entrées, $13.95 to $20.95. Dinner, Tuesday-Saturday 5 to 9, Sunday 5 to 8.

— A Secluded Lobster Find —

Waterman's Beach Lobster, 343 Waterman Beach Road, South Thomaston.

Rockland may be the lobster capital of the world, but the best place to eat lobster hereabouts is about five miles south at this off-the-beaten-path seasonal lobster shack that won a James Beard award in 2001 as an American classic – "just a regional award, not fancy gourmet or anything," owners Anne and Lorri Cousens assured. Order a lobster roll ($9.95), steamed clams or a one-pound lobster dinner ($11.95), or splurge for the lobster and steamed clam combo ($21.95). The only non-seafood item is a hotdog and chips for $1.75. The owners also bake superior rhubarb, lemon sponge and blueberry pies. Take your meal to one of the cloth-covered picnic tables on an open deck overlooking a jetty and watch lobster being unloaded from lobster traps or arriving from the Spruce Head lobster pound nearby. No buildings are in sight to mar the tranquil setting.

(207) 596-7819 or (207) 594-7518. Lobster dinners, $11.95 to $35.95 depending on size. Open mid-June to Labor Day, Thursday-Sunday 11 to 7. BYOB.

The Gallery Café, 297 Commercial St. (Route 1), Rockport.

"Art of food" is the theme of this café at the new Prism Glass Studio & Gallery. Patrons enjoy watching resident glass blower/owner Patti Kissinger at work in the adjacent barn before dining in the house containing the café and Lisa Sojka's Glass Gallery shop. Sip a glass of wine as you view the work of more than 100 glass artists, then settle down for a meal. Chef Tim Pierre Labonte's dinner menu might start with lobster velouté topped with crème fraîche, five-spiced quail with lemon-dressed orzo or a dish called "3X Duck," chilled roulade of mallard duck breast stuffed with duck confit and foie gras. "Maine courses" range from swordfish pomodoro and grilled free-range chicken with poblano cream to "beef in a blanket," filet layered with roasted corn-golden raisin duxelles baked in puff pastry. Sweet endings include frozen lemon parfait, macadamia-key lime pie and vanilla malt crème brûlée.

(207) 230-0061. www.prismglassgallery.com. Entrées, $19 to $33. Lunch, Wednesday-Saturday 11 to 3. Dinner, Wednesday-Saturday 5 to 9. Sunday brunch, 10 to 3.

Camden

Atlantica, 1 Bay View Landing, Camden.

The food is innovative, the surroundings convivial and the contemporary ambiance nautical at chef-owner Ken Paquin's bustling restaurant on the Camden waterfront. Dining is on two floors, plus a much-coveted upstairs turret with a table for five, as well as outdoors on an upper deck and a covered terrace beneath. One of us made a dinner of two appetizers: the Maine crab and shrimp tower with mustard-mango vinaigrette and basil-caper tartar sauce, and pan-fried oysters with a sweet corn salad. The other enjoyed the caesar salad that came with the entrée, one of the best seafood pasta dishes we've had, brimming with clams, mussels and scallops with lemon pasta in a Thai curry broth. Other choices on the seafood-oriented menu might be pan-seared ahi tuna with green peppercorn vinaigrette and roasted monkfish stuffed with shrimp and wrapped in prosciutto. Typical desserts are orange crème brûlée, chocolate cake with a hollow center filled with ganache and our choices, ginger ice cream and red raspberry sorbet.

(207) 236-6011 or (888) 507-8514. www.atlanticarestaurant.com. Entrées, $19 to $27. Lunch seasonally, Tuesday-Sunday 11:30 to 2:30. Dinner, Tuesday-Sunday 5:30 to 9:30, Thursday-Monday 5 to 8 in winter.

Francine Bistro, 55 Chestnut St., Camden.

Hidden on a side street, this funky newcomer serves some of the most innovative food in town. Lisa Dorr and her husband, Luke Eder, moved from New York to convert a former bicycle shop into a casual, L-shaped, European-style bistro that's deliberately shabby chic with church pews for benches, chocolate brown walls and a linoleum floor, four stools at the bar and a small sidewalk patio. At lunch, they had run out of many of the offerings, so we settled for an oyster po-boy sandwich and a goat cheese salad with fried almonds and pears. Great warm French bread with sweet butter preceded and was reordered because of desultory service and small portions, said salad amounting to little more than a mound of goat cheese, four almonds and about a quarter of a pear. Locals advise the dining experience is at its best at night. A new chef who worked with Todd English in Boston offers a handful of changing entrées. You might find seared halibut with mustard greens, roast chicken with chanterelles, grilled lamb with mint sauce and that bistro staple, steak frites. Appetizers one summer night included crispy sweetbreads with Jerusalem artichokes and sherry-shallot glaze, and a trio of briny local oysters with black pepper mignonette for a cool $4 each. The bistro has a beer and wine license, and seems to be a daytime hangout for coffee and espresso.

(207) 230-0083. Entrées, $20 to $26. Lunch, Tuesday-Saturday noon to 3. Dinner, Monday-Saturday 5:30 to 10. Closed mid-February through March.

Natalie's at the Mill, 43 Mechanic St., Suite 200, Camden.

A section of the old Knox Mill building that formerly housed the MBNA credit card company was transformed into an elegant restaurant in late 2004 by Abby Alden, former manager at the Lord Camden Inn. The atmospheric place seats 80 in a dining room with windows on three sides and a partly open kitchen. The splashy waterfall outside the soaring windows adds to the effect. The large outside patio facing the millpond and falls of the Megunticook River is the icing on the mix. It's a dramatic, elegant backdrop for high-end fare that may upstage the scenery outside. Lunch offerings are exotic, perhaps a warm fallen chèvre soufflé over salad or a Maine lobster BLT. The opening dinner menu offered appetizers like chilled local oysters with a ginger-melon mignonette, caramelized diver scallops in a parsley broth, and lobster-coconut bisque with coriander crème fraîche. Main courses ranged from local halibut with morels in orange-brown butter sauce and marinated big-eye tuna with pulped avocado, daikon and lemon vinaigrette to slow-roasted organic duck breast with a huckleberry reduction and beef sirloin with foie gras and madeira jus. Desserts included grand marnier crème brûlée with orange-cardamom butter cookies, warm chocolate espresso cake with a frozen sour cherry mousse, and coconut panna cotta with a pomegranate gelee and blood orange sorbet.

(207) 236-7008. Entrées, $22 to $32. Four-course prix-fixe, $60. Lunch, Monday-Saturday 11:30 to 2. Dinner, Tuesday-Saturday 5:30 to 9.

Hartstone Inn, 41 Elm St., Camden.

Prix-fixe dinners of distinction are served in the pretty dining room and enclosed side porch of this small inn that has become a destination for gourmands. Chef-owner Michael Salmon's cuisine is cutting-edge and his presentations artistic. A typical dinner might begin with a mosaic of Maine seafood, followed by chilled gazpacho with herbed cream. Peach sorbet refreshes the palate for the main course, which could be Maine lobster with angel-hair pasta and asparagus, veal saltimbocca with mushroom-thyme couscous, or potato-crusted filet mignon with portobello-merlot butter. Individual warm soufflés are usually the dessert, variously featuring blueberry-hazelnut, chocolate, chambord and macadamia nut flavors.

(207) 236-4259 or (800) 788-4823. Prix-fixe, $42.50. Dinner by reservation, Wednesday-Sunday at 7, June-October; Thursday-Sunday, rest of year.

The Waterfront Restaurant, Harborside Square off Bay View Street, Camden.

This old-timer might not get the critics' accolades, but it sure draws the crowds. Its popularity is due, no doubt, to its expansive outdoor deck shaded by a striking white canopy resembling a boat's sails, right beside the windjammers on picturesque Camden Harbor, and for its affordable international menu. The Waterfront is a great spot for lunch, when seven good salads in glass bowls are dressed with outstanding dressings. Dinner offerings turn more eclectic, although chef Charles Butler – named Maine lobster chef of the year – offers four lobster entrées. Among appetizers are calamari and shrimp, mussels marinière and an award-winning clam chowder or chilled raspberry soup accented with grand marnier. The superlative smoked seafood sampler was our choice for sharing. For main courses, we've been well satisfied by Maine crab cakes with creamy mustard sauce, an assertive linguini with salmon and sundried tomatoes, shrimp with oriental black beans over angel-hair pasta, and grilled chicken with lime, cilantro and olives. Mint chocolate-chip pie with hot fudge sauce and whipped cream proved to be the ultimate dessert. All sorts of shellfish and light fare are available at the oyster bar and outdoor grill.

(207) 236-3747. www.waterfrontcamden.com. Entrées, $14.95 to $21.95. Lunch daily, 11:30 to 2:30. Dinner, 5 to 10. Raw bar, 2 to 11.

Frogwater Café, 31 Elm St., Camden.

Innovative, healthful cuisine at modest prices is offered by Erin and Joseph Zdanowicz, who moved across the country from Tacoma, Wash., to open this homey storefront café in the former Galloway's, a diner. They named it for Frogwater Lane on their favorite Bainbridge Island and stress Oregon and Washington wines on a select wine list. Chef Joseph presents a far-ranging menu, from vegetarian shepherd's pie to pan-seared halibut with a cool cucumber and red onion sauce. Among the choices are jerk-marinated monkfish served over dirty rice with mango chutney and grilled pork with honey-garlic sauce. Start with some of the signature Spanish onion rings, sweet potato cakes topped with shrimp or lobster, potato-cheddar pierogies or one of the grilled flatbreads. Finish with Erin's caramel shortcake with peaches and strawberries or a creamy lemon-lime tart splashed with gin. For lunch, we enjoyed a hearty bacon-leek-potato soup, an open-faced grilled baguette with feta cheese, tomato, cucumber, black olives and sundried tomato pesto, and a "BLT and Then Some Club" sandwich adding onions, cucumber and cheddar cheese on Texas toast. Sides of zesty macaroni and vegetable salads came with each, and the meal indicated the style that the couple added to the Camden dining scene.

(207) 236-8998. www.frogwatercafe.com. Entrées, $15 to $19. Lunch daily, 11 to 3. Dinner nightly, 5 to 9.

Cappy's Chowder House, 1 Main St., Camden.

"The Maine you hope to meet" is one of the catchy slogans surrounding Cappy's, and local color is its strong point. The scene is barroom nautical: lobster traps hang above the bar, and green billiards-room lamps illuminate the bare wood tables. The upstairs Crow's Nest, dark and very pubby, offers a glimpse of the harbor. The something-for-everyone menu is Down East cutesy: Maine pigskins, burgers on the bounty, Camden curly fries, mussel beach pasta and deserted islands. The place packs in the crowds for clam chowder, a lobster pizza, "cakes of crab" on a bed of wild greens, seafood pie, baked stuffed haddock, baby back ribs, sirloin steak "and all the latest gossip." Main courses come with French bread from Cappy's Bakery & Company Store below, rice pilaf and salad with a good house dressing. Burgers, sandwiches, salads and lighter fare are available day and night. Oysters and shrimp by the bucket are served from the raw bar during happy hour in the Crow's Nest.

(207) 236-2254. www.cappyschowder.com. Entrées, $12.95 to $19.95. Open daily, 11 a.m. to midnight; winter hours vary.

The Camden Deli, 37 Main St., Camden.

"The best view in town" is offered from the new upper deck at this casual spot on two floors backing up to the harbor. There's waitress service in the upstairs dining area with a wine bar, lounge and rooftop deck, but many prefer to head for the downstairs deli cases to select their soups, salads and sandwiches. No fewer than 41 varieties of sandwich were offered when we were there, making the eventual choices of an albacore tuna sandwich and a BLT all the more difficult. The seafood chowder and the Greek salad were fine, too; the lemon bars for dessert were not. Light meals are available for dinner.

(207) 236-8343. www.camdendeli.com. Sandwiches $4.95 to $6.50; light fare, $3 to $10. Breakfast, lunch and dinner daily, 7 a.m. to 9 p.m.; shorter hours in winter.

Bayview Lobsters, Bay View Landing, Camden.

You can't get much closer to the water in Camden than at this dockside establishment with a mostly canopied deck beside the harbor and a rustic dining room inside. The lobster steaming in pots alongside captures passing strollers. They stop for a lobster roll ($10.25), lobster stew, sandwiches with fries and more substantial fried chicken or lobster dinners. Beer and wine are available, as are espresso and ice cream from a stand beside.

(207) 236-2005. Entrées, $10.25 to $21.50. Open daily in season, 11 to 10.

FOR MORE INFORMATION: Camden-Rockport-Lincolnville Chamber of Commerce, Public Landing, Box 919, Camden, ME 04843, (207) 236-4404 or (800) 223-5459. www.visitcamden.com.

Rockland-Thomaston Area Chamber of Commerce, Harbor Park, Box 508, Rockland, ME 04841, (207) 596-0376 or (800) 562-2529. www.therealmaine.com.

Blue Hill Bay presents peaceful sight from Water Street in Blue Hill village.

Blue Hill Peninsula/Deer Isle, Me.

Treasures of Tranquility

Between the chic of Camden and the bustle of Bar Harbor lies a picturesque, largely unspoiled peninsula jutting into East Penobscot Bay. Turn south off busy U.S. Route 1 and prepare for a different pace in a timeless place.

Of all Maine's peninsulas stretching out to sea, this is one of the most appealing. From the scenic lookout atop Caterpillar Hill as you head down Route 15 in Sedgwick is one of the more spectacular vistas in all New England. Blue waters, green islands and small mountains meld into one astonishing panorama as far as the eye can see.

Roughly at the center of the peninsula is tranquil Blue Hill. So small that the unknowing traveler could pass it by, the village lies between the 940-foot-high hill from which it takes its name and an inlet of Blue Hill Bay. It is the focal point of an area long known for fine handicrafts, especially pottery, and for summer chamber music.

The little finger of the Blue Hill Peninsula leads to Castine, a tiny but historic town – one of the oldest in Maine, and one with considerable cachet. The town slopes downhill from Revolutionary War fortifications to a picturesque harbor. Visitors are well cared for in four summery inns. Castine is a haven for rest and relaxation, blessedly off by itself and away from the mainstream.

At the foot of the Blue Hill Peninsula lies a bigger "finger" stretching farther into Penobscot Bay. Cross the high, unexpectedly imposing suspension bridge over the fine sailing waters of Eggemoggin Reach to Little Deer Isle and, across a causeway,

Deer Isle, the second largest island off the Maine coast. Here is another world: one of little traffic, no neon, no fast food, few residents and fewer tourists. The area's beauty and remoteness make it a favorite of artists and craftsmen. At the end of the isle is the rough-edged fishing village of Stonington, the area's second biggest population center after Blue Hill.

The peninsula has no large beaches or marinas, no shopping plazas or chain motels. What it does have are nationally known potteries and crafts cooperatives, art studios and galleries, a handful of exceptional inns and restaurants, and rural byways that remain much the way they were a generation ago and invite aimless exploration. Best of all is an aura of serenity that draws the knowing few back time after time for the utter peace and quiet of it all.

Blue Hill Peninsula

A few roads and streets converge from different directions and, suddenly, here is the center of Blue Hill, population 2,400. The knob of a "mountain" called Blue Hill is a backdrop for the town. Hiking trails lead to the top, where you can climb up a fire tower for an even higher view of the islands in Blue Hill Bay and, across the way, the mountains of Acadia National Park on Mount Desert Island.

Seeing and Doing

Not the hill but pottery "put Blue Hill on the map," according to Sheila Varnum, owner of the first and largest, **Rowantrees Pottery.** Inspired in 1934 by Adelaide Pearson through her friend Mahatma Gandhi, Rowantrees is still going strong out Union Street in a rambling house and barn reached by a pretty brick path through gardens. Inside, you may be able to see potters at work; veteran employees in the upstairs shop might recall for you the days when as children they joined the story hours and pottery classes run by Miss Pearson and her protégé, Laura Paddock. Rowantrees is especially known for its jam jar with a flat white lid covered with blueberries, as well as for unique glazes. Items are attractively displayed for sale.

Rackliffe Pottery at the other end of town is an offshoot of Rowantrees, Phil Rackliffe having worked there for twenty years. He and his family make all kinds of handsome and useful kitchenware in a work area next to their shop on Route 172. The soup tureens with blueberry, strawberry or cranberry covers are especially attractive.

A culturally rich year-round community, Blue Hill supports a volunteer FM radio station, WERU (We Are You), with a down-home cultural programming mix.

Blue Hill is also known for the **Kneisel Hall Chamber Music Festival,** Pleasant Street, (207) 374-2203. The festival is part of the summer session of the Kneisel Hall School of Music, founded by Dr. Franz Kneisel and called "the cradle of chamber music teaching in America." Concerts by well-known faculty members are given Friday evenings and Sunday afternoons from late June to mid-August in a rustic concert hall off upper Pleasant Street. Concert tickets, $30; veranda seats, $20.

The 1814 **Jonathan Fisher House,** just south of the village on Route 15, offers a glimpse of early American life as lived to the utmost by the town's first minister, a scholar and artist who brought culture to the frontier village in the wilderness. The Federal house testifies to the versatile talents of the Renaissance man who built the house himself, painted it with paint he made himself and furnished it with furniture he also made. The house is filled with his paintings, furniture and a collection of his unusual inventions, plus maps that he surveyed and copies of books that he wrote, bound and illustrated. Tours are available daily 2 to 5, July to mid-September.

The 1815 **Holt House** on Water Street, home of the Blue Hill Historical Society, is a restored Federal house with period furnishings and outstanding stenciling. It's open Tuesday and Friday 2 to 5 in July and August; admission, $1.

GALLERIES AND SHOPS. Along Blue Hill's Main Street, big spenders are drawn to the famed **Jud Hartmann Gallery.** Here, sculptor Hartmann shows spectacular paintings by artist-friends along with the exceptional bronze sculptures – many depicting the woodland Indian tribes of the Northeast – he crafts at his studio in nearby Brooklin. Everything is artfully arranged at **The Handworks Gallery,** which shows super contemporary crafts. Artist Judith Leighton's **Leighton Gallery** off Parker Point Road is considered one of the best in Maine, and her backyard is a garden of art punctuated with sculpture. Other favorites include **Liros Gallery, Blue Hill Bay Gallery** and **Mark Bell Pottery.** Birdhouses, carved birds, hooked fish hangings, tables with driftwood bases and Victorian twig furniture appeal at **Belcher's Country Store,** an offshoot of the main store in Deer Isle. **North Country Textiles** offers wonderful throws, rugs, table linens, wicker and wooden furniture, pottery and more. **Asian World Imports** is a remarkable trove of treasures from trinkets to garments to crafts to jewelry, all gathered personally by owner Jeff Kaley during trips to Southeast Asia where he deals personally with his craftspeople. **The Blue Hill Wine Shop** claims the largest selection in Down East Maine, along with teas and tobaccos. **SaraSara's** offers fun and funky apparel for women. Blue Hill also supports two good bookstores, **Blue Hill Books** and **North Light Books**.

If you time it right, stop at the **Blue Hill Farmer's Market,** Route 172, at the Blue Hill Fairgrounds. Each Saturday in July and August from 9 to 11:30 a.m., local farmers and artisans gather here for a real down-home event. Horse-drawn wagons give youngsters hayrides, while residents and visitors browse through a small but interesting display of everything from local produce to goat cheese, jellies, handmade gifts, lamb's wool and patterned ski sweaters.

Elsewhere on the Blue Hill Peninsula, in the Brooksville area check out **Bagaduce Forge**, a blacksmith shop, for hand-forged fireplace tools, andirons, pot racks, bird feeders and weather vanes. **Island Soap Gifts and Gallery** makes and sells more than a dozen varieties of homemade soap. The **Sow's Ear Winery** produces organic wines from apples, rhubarb, blueberries and cranberries as well as grapes. Above the rustic winery is **The Silk Purse,** a weaving studio featuring hand-woven rag rugs.

Take a break at the **Holbrook Island Sanctuary** along Penobscot Bay at 172 Indian Bar Road, Brooksville. The 1,345-acre state wildlife preserve on Cape Rosier offers hiking trails, bird watching and picnic tables in a scenic area of upland forests, rocky shores and a 115-acre island accessible by private boat. Stop nearby at **Bagaduce Lunch** for a snack or ice cream and watch the nearby reversing falls.

Where to Stay

Blue Hill Inn, Union Street, Box 403, Blue Hill 04614.

This trim white Colonial inn with dark green shutters looks more like a stately Maine house than an historic inn. Inside are twelve guest accommodations nicely appointed with 19th-century antiques and traditional pieces as well as plush carpeting, new wallpaper and modernized bathrooms. Four have fireplaces. Our rear bedroom – occupied the previous night by Peter of Peter, Paul and Mary fame following a concert for Paul Stryker's hometown fans at the Blue Hill Fairgrounds – was comfortable with a kingsize bed, two wing chairs, colorful bed linens, plump towels and windows on three sides to circulate cool air. The luxurious Cape House efficiency suite comes with a kingsize canopy bed, fireplace, living room with TV, kitchen and a rear deck for enjoying the back yard. Guests enjoy a small library/ game room furnished in antiques. The larger main parlor, notable for a ten-candle Persian chandelier, is where innkeepers Mary and Don Hartley serve hors d'oeuvres (perhaps smoked bluefish or local goat cheese) during a nightly reception for inn guests. Breakfast is a culinary event culminating in an omelet with avocado and smoked salmon or belgian waffles with fresh strawberries.

(207) 374-2844 or (800) 826-7415. Fax (207) 374-2829. www.bluehillinn.com. Ten rooms and two suites with private baths. Mid-June to mid-October: doubles $158 to $195, suites $205 and $285. Off-season: doubles $138 to $175, suites $165 and $235. Closed November to mid-May.

Blue Hill Farm, Route 15, Box 437, Blue Hill 04614.

Situated out in the country north of Blue Hill, this B&B really has a farm feeling – from the rambling farmhouse and the barn exterior of a newer addition to the goats grazing outside to the garden, stone wall, trout pond and 48 acres of woods and brooks out back. The barn, full of fanciful touches and furnishings, includes a spacious and lofty main floor where meals are served and where there are all kinds of sitting areas – perfect for the occasional summer jazz concerts to which the inn plays host. Upstairs are seven modern, smallish guest rooms with private baths and double beds. Seven more guest rooms with double or twin beds and shared baths are in the original farmhouse to which the barn is attached. It offers a cozy, old-fashioned parlor for those who prefer more seclusion. From an ample kitchen, innkeepers Marcia and Jim Schatz serve what they call a Maine continental breakfast: fresh orange juice, a plate of fruit and cheese, homemade granola, yogurt, cereals and, every third or fourth day, a treat of lox and bagels. Dinners are served by advance request in what the Schatzes call their "Barn Appetit" dining room. A typical meal might be poussin with Sicilian barbecue sauce, seafood wellington or peasant bouillabaisse plus salad and a dessert of homemade ice cream for $25, BYOB.

(207) 374-5126. www.bluehillfarminn.com. Seven rooms with private baths and seven rooms with shared baths. Doubles, $85 to $99, June-October; $75 to $85 rest of year.

First Light Bed & Breakfast, 821 East Blue Hill Road, Blue Hill 04614.

How about an overnight in a former lighthouse? Book the Lighthouse Suite at this waterfront B&B. It's part of a house connected to a lighthouse tower descending to the rocks and pebbly beach beside McHeard Cove. Owner Beverly Bartlett's most popular offering is the round bedroom on the main floor of the lighthouse tower. It has a private bath, dressing area and queen bed from which you can see the cove, and side windows yield a view of tidal waters flowing in and out of a saltwater pond. The Seaside Garden Room and Maine Room, located on the second floor of the main part of the house, share a bath. The former has a queen bed and views of the water as well as the innkeeper's gardens. The Maine Room, which also overlooks the gardens, has a double bed and a twin. Guests relax in a great room with a view of the cove. In the early morning, many like to climb the spiral stairs to the top of the tower to experience dawn's "first light." Finnish oven pancakes or blueberry-stuffed french toast might be served for breakfast.

(207) 374-5879. wwwfirstlightbandb.com. One room with private bath and two rooms with shared bath. Doubles, $105 to $175. Two-night minimum stay.

Where to Eat

Arborvine, Main Street, Blue Hill.

Veteran chef John Hidake, who launched Blue Hill's late Fire Pond restaurant in 1977 and led it through its glory years, converted a rambling, 200-year-old Maine house on Tenney Hill into this fine-dining restaurant. The house also is headquarters for his Moveable Feasts catering service and the Vinery, a piano bar and bistro, open daily for lunch and light fare. Three dining areas, each with a fireplace, convey the ambiance of an early 1800s house and are stylishly furnished to the period. Mismatched tables and chairs in the Shaker, Heppelwhite and Windsor styles are set with antique linens, flowers and votive candles. The short dinner menu features local seafood as well as heartier fare. Seasonal dishes might be broiled halibut with mushrooms and scallions in a green curry sauce, grilled yellowfin tuna with mango-red onion chutney, crispy roast duckling with blood orange glaze and noisettes of lamb chasseur. Typical appetizers are brie in puff pastry with figs and toasted almonds and a medley of smoked scallops and trout with horseradish cream. Desserts could be grand marnier chocolate mousse, plum napoleon with orange sabayon and mocha crème caramel. The **Vinery,** a brick-floored conservatory, offers appetizers, pizzettes and light fare such as baby back ribs or a medley of sausages.

(207) 374-2119. www.arborvine.com. Entrées, $18 to $22. Dinner, Tuesday-Sunday 5 to 9:30, Friday-Sunday in winter, 5:30 to 8:30. Vinery, lunch in season, Wednesday-Saturday noon to 2; supper, Wednesday-Sunday 5 to 9.

The Brooklin Inn, Main Street (Route 175), Brooklin.

"We try to know who raised, grew, picked or caught all the food you eat here," advises the menu at this inn's restaurant in a small coastal village along Eggemoggin Reach. Chef Elaine Randell features local organic food and some unusual offerings on a menu that changes daily. Dinner might start with a lobster and smoked fish plate or crab cakes on mizuna leaves with basil aioli. Main courses could be bouillabaisse, finnan haddie, potato-crusted halibut with a chardonnay-caper beurre blanc, chicken cooked under a brick or pan-seared sirloin steak with mushroom sauce and burgundy butter. Baked haddock, meatloaf and Guinness beef stew are light-fare options, available in the country-elegant, salon-style dining room or in the Irish Pub. The wine list covers an unusually broad price range. Inn owners Gail and Chip Angell offer five guest rooms, two with private baths; doubles, $95 to $145.

(207) 359-2777. Fax (207) 359-2225. www.brooklininn.com. Entrées, $18 to $29. Dinner nightly in summer, Wednesday-Sunday rest of year.

Castine

Poised at the end of its own peninsula jutting into East Penobscot Bay, Castine is a picturesque enclave of peace and quiet.

Therein lies a certain irony, for this charming little town with such an admirable waterside location was forged from a military heritage and a maritime disposition.

Founded in 1613 as a French trading colony that evolved into the first European permanent settlement in New England, Castine was a major battlefield through the French and Indian wars, the American Revolution and the War of 1812 as four countries sought to possess its strategic location. No fewer than sixteen fortifications have been built on the peninsula since 1635, so it's appropriate that the town's only through street is named Battle Avenue.

Castine's maritime bent is evident in the windjammers in its deep-water harbor and by the Maine Maritime Academy, as dominant a physical presence on the steep Castine hillside today as its enormous training vessel State of Maine is in the harbor when in port.

Located well away from the mainstream, Castine became a summer colony for big-city "rusticators." They built well-tended Federal-style houses – dressed in what appears to be the local uniform, pristine white with black shutters – in town as well as shingled, Victorian-era mansions on the outlying shores. History is more noticeable here than in most such places, if only because there's a large historical marker at nearly every turn.

Seeing and Doing

WALKING TOURS. "Welcome to Castine," a Castine Merchants Association brochure you find everywhere, with maps and a history, gives specifics for a walking tour of most of Castine. You can stick to the central area, which covers Main and Water streets and the quaint, out-of-the-way village common that's as picturesque as any in New England. The Castine Historical Society, located facing the green in a former Italianate school building topped by a cupola, is open Tuesday-Sunday in July and August. You can drive, though it's preferable to poke along on foot or bicycle, to see a larger area embracing Perkins Street and Battle Avenue. Included are the major fortifications (Fort Madison consists of a few embankments with a couple of picnic tables beside the water; Fort George is larger with earthen ramparts and ditches), historic sites, a public path to the water from Dyces Head Lighthouse, tree-shaded Georgian and Federalist houses, buildings of the Maine Maritime Academy, and such unexpected sights as a tiny circular shorefront house and the enormous stucco summer home, Guerdwood.

The Wilson Museum, Perkins Street, Castine.

Built in 1921 to house the extensive collections of anthropologist and geologist J. Howard Wilson, this is a highly personal place reflecting the tastes of Dr. and Mrs. Wilson and their world travels. "There's a bit of the whole world here," said the woman on duty. "The way it's laid out tells you the history of mankind back to Cyprus in 3000 B.C." Included are everything from remarkable beaded Indian moccasins and ceremonial leggins, ship models, an Indian pueblo model, firearms, stone artifacts and pottery to modern paintings by 21 artists. The Wilsons' daughter, Ellenore Wilson Doudiet, is the museum director and guiding force. The property also contains a working blacksmith shop, a hearse house with Castine's funeral vehicles from a century ago, and the 1763 **John Perkins House**, the area's oldest house, which was moved to the site and restored in 1970.

(207) 326-9247. www.wilsonmuseum.org. Museum open Tuesday-Sunday 2 to 5, Memorial Day through September; free. Perkins House open Sunday and Wednesday 2 to 5 in July and August; tours $5.

Swimming and Other Sports. Swimming off a long, stony beach known as Backshore Beach is available to the public at Wadsworth Cove. The Castine swimming pool provides saltwater swimming in a pool nearby. A nine-hole golf course is open for a fee at the private Castine Golf Club, one of America's earliest (1897); its first five holes were originally on the site of adjacent Fort George. The club also has four tennis courts. The Maine Maritime Academy offers its gymnasium, pool, weight room, and squash and racquetball courts for a daily fee.

SHOPPING. Downtown Castine consists of few but select stores. **Four Flags Gifts** offers nautical equipment as well as gifts from around the world, books, jewelry, Gordon Fraser cards and, just arrived one time when we were there, a novelty scent called Eau de Low Tide. At the **Water Witch,** tall, dark and striking Jean de Raat, the water witch herself when not hawking real estate, sells a variety of fine clothing (placemats, napkins and pillows, too) made of cotton Dutch wax batiks and Java prints; check out her silk caps and hats. Artist Greg Dunham sells his watercolors as well as other artworks at the **McGrath Dunham Gallery.** Another stop for art is **Fay's One Gallery.** Former Castine Patriot editor John Vernelson runs the expanded **Compass Rose Bookstore,** while his wife Ruth Heffron serves up espresso, smoothies, sandwiches and snacks in the **Linger Longer Café** out back. **Leila Day Antiques** and **Oakum Bay Ltd.** combine to offer antique furniture and accessories along with contemporary crafts and collectibles.

Lodging and Dining

Pentagoet Inn, 26 Main St., Box 4, Castine 04421.
International accents prevail at this turreted 1894 inn, carefully being returned to its roots as a steamboat inn by Jack Burke and his wife, Julie VandeGraaf. The couple scoured the countryside to find antique headboards for the beds and steamboat-era prints and lithographs for the walls of eleven guest rooms in the main inn and five in the adjacent 200-year-old cottage (called 10 Perkins Street). All have antique furnishings, an historically authentic feeling and mementos from Jack's twenty years' service with the United Nations in Africa. The couple turned the inn's former Victorian library into Passports Pub, a playful hodgepodge of vintage photos and foreign memorabilia that's appropriate for an international town that has flown the flags of four countries. Besides the atmospheric pub, guests relax in a parlor area with a nifty turret window seat looking toward the harbor, on shaded verandas made for rocking and on a garden patio off the expanded dining room. Julie's background as owner of a pastry shop in Philadelphia is evident at breakfast, which might feature featherbed eggs or baked apple french toast, muffins and scones.

Dinner is served to guests and the public at widely spaced tables in two elegant dining rooms and outside on a wraparound veranda. Chef Gina Melita's menu features starters as simple as "a big ol' bowl of Blue Hill mussels" steamed in wine, basil and lavender and as complex as a salad of lobster escabèche with avocado and goat cheese. Entrées range from the signature bouillabaisse in a rich saffron broth to anise-dusted duck breast in marsala jus. Desserts could be a plum crisp with vanilla ice cream and double chocolate torte with espresso cream.

(207) 326-8616 or (800) 845-1701. www.pentagoet.com. Sixteen rooms with private baths. Doubles, $85 to $195, $70 to $135 off-season. Closed November-April.

Entrées, $15 to $24. Dinner, Monday-Saturday 5:30 to 8; off-season, Tuesday-Saturday 6 to 8.

Castine Inn, 33 Main St., Box 41, Castine 04421.

A wraparound porch overlooking prized gardens and the harbor beyond welcomes guests to the Castine Inn, built in 1898 and operated continuously since. Chef-owner Tom Gutow has elevated its reputation for some of the finest, most creative food in Maine. He and his wife Amy are gradually upgrading the accommodations, which open hotel-style off long, wide corridors on the second and third floors. All rooms are carpeted and comfortable with queensize or twin beds. Decor is modest yet stylish, with understated floral fabrics and window treatments. The Gutows turned two small rear rooms into a large room with a queen poster bed, an armchair and two club chairs, the first of a number of planned upgrades. On the main floor is a guest parlor hung with local artworks. Across the spacious front hall is hidden a dark and cozy pub with hand-painted tables and a fireplace. A side deck overlooks the spectacular gardens. Chef Tom's breakfast menu generally offers three entrées: an omelet with goat cheese and herbs, corned beef hash topped by a poached egg and homemade apple bread french toast.

The serene, 60-seat dining room is graced by stunning murals of Castine painted by the former innkeeper, an artist. Tom's fare changes weekly. The basic menu is prix-fixe, $55 for three courses. Available for the entire table are a six-course tasting menu ($85 per person) and a twelve-course grand tasting menu ($125). One night's prix-fixe offerings illustrate the refined, sophisticated style. They began with a choice of potato and ramp soup with littleneck clams, local crab cake with mustard vinaigrette or braised beef short rib with red pepper gnocchi. Following a mixed green salad, main courses were poached salmon with cold pickled onions and finnan haddie foam, goat cheese agnolotti with roasted root vegetables and a sweet vermouth sauce, and pork with spinach, butter chard and fingerling potatoes. Sorbet and petit-fours accompanied the dessert course, a choice among chocolate breton, lavender crème brûlée and caramel tea financier.

(207) 326-4365. Fax (207) 326-4570. www.castineinn.com. Nineteen rooms with private baths. Doubles, $90 to $225. Closed Dec. 20 through April.

Prix-fixe, $55. Dinner nightly, 5:30 to 8:30 Memorial Day to Labor Day, 6 to 8 to Columbus Day, weekends only rest of season.

The Manor Inn, Battle Avenue, Box 873, Castine 04421.

The sprawling Victorian summer cottage designed by Mead, McKim and White looks the way a big old Maine lodge should. A long driveway ascends to an edifice of brown wood and stone, a flower-bedecked terrace and an entry porte cochere tunneling between the main house and a wing with the second floor overhead. Owners Tom Ehrman and Nancy Watson reconfigured the dining room and pub and converted the main floor of the West Wing into a guest lounge with billiards table, TV and stone fireplace, a conference room and a yoga studio. Overhead is the Pine Tree Suite, an enormous space with king canopy bed, a sitting area with fireplace and a sun porch with a day bed. Four guest rooms and five common rooms have fireplaces. With five acres of lawns near the end of a dead-end street, the inn is so quiet that the only sound we heard all night was that of a melodic harbor bell in the distance. A full breakfast, perhaps waffles or pancakes, is included in the rates.

Dinner is served in an enclosed, two-level wraparound porch with front windows looking toward the harbor, and in an adjacent library with a fireplace. Typical starters are Dyces Head chowder, calamari with wasabi-sake dipping sauce, a trio of potstickers and a classic caesar salad. Entrées could be the signature crab cakes with mustard and chile aioli sauces, cedar plank-roasted salmon, India-style curried chicken and charbroiled strip steak with blue cheese topping. Seasonal desserts include strawberry-rhubarb pie and chocolate oblivion torte with blackberry-raspberry sauce. A light menu is available in the intimate pub.

(207) 326-4861. Fax (207) 326-0891. www.manor-inn.com. Twelve rooms and two suites with private baths. Doubles, $110 to $230 in summer, $95 to $170 spring and fall. Closed late December to mid-February..
Entrées, $18 to $29. Dinner seasonally, Tuesday-Saturday 6 to 8; pub from 5.

Castine Harbor Lodge, 147 Perkins Street, Box 215, Castine 04421.

Water access and views are assets at this laid-back establishment – complete with a boat dock for mooring, a new wine bar on the wraparound porch and a new waterside patio. Paul and Sara Brouillard, who got their innkeeping start at the Manor (the home in which she grew up), have slowly furnished and upgraded the Edwardian mansion built in 1893 directly on the harbor. All but one of the sixteen accommodations have water views – even from some of the bathrooms. Rooms have been repainted in bold colors. Furnishings are stylish yet homey and unpretentious, like the inn itself. Four simpler rooms in an attached annex share two baths. The inn also has an L-shaped efficiency cottage, with queensize bed and private deck, right on the water.

The recently enclosed, wraparound porch curving for 250 feet around the side and back of the house holds Paul's pride and joy, the **Bagaduce Oyster Bar** and wine bar where the sometime chef serves dinner by whim or reservation. He offers a selection of local seafood and shellfish, specializing in locally raised oysters. The ambitious menu ranges from mixed Japanese grill (tuna, scallops and salmon with cucumber and seaweed salad) to veal flank steak and grilled venison loin. Besides a blue-flecked granite bar with stools facing the water, the porch has sofas and chairs around a gas fireplace and an open porch with banquette seating and tables taking full advantage of the harbor view. So do a couple of enormous open common areas, which begin with a billiards table in the foyer. Included are a living room with a gigantic sectional sofa facing the fireplace, a library with TV and a dining room. A continental-plus breakfast is included in the rates.

(207) 326-4335 or (866) 566-1550. www.castinemaine.com. Eleven rooms and one cottage with private baths and four rooms with shared bath. Doubles, $85 to $245. Cottage, $1,250 weekly.
Dinner by reservation, no set schedule. Entrées, $17.50 to $28.50.

Dining

Dennett's Wharf & Oyster Bar, 15 Sea St., Castine.

Peripatetic local chef Paul Brouillard started this seafood emporium and lobster pound right on the water below Sea Street. The former sail and rigging loft built in the early 1900s has been upscaled a bit under the ownership of his brother Gary and Carolyn Brouillard. A shoulder-high partition divides what had been the world's longest oyster bar from the dining area. We prefer to eat outside at the hexagonal or regular picnic tables on a large deck right over the water. The twenty or so dinner entrées range from broiled haddock to scallops chardonnay and five versions of steak. Seafood linguini is a house specialty. Look for nightly specials like bouillabaisse, rack of New Zealand lamb and sirloin steak au poivre. There are plenty of options for appetizers and light fare. The dessert list includes white chocolate-macadamia nut cheesecake, chocolate truffle torte, apple spice cake and piña colada cake. At a recent lunch, we enjoyed a clam roll with a side of potato salad and a crab roll with pasta salad, washed down with a pint of Dennett's own Wharf Rat Ale. On a sunny day the deck is glorious – alas, it usually gets too buggy for use at night. In season, there's a busy schedule of live entertainment.

(207) 326-9045. www.dennettswharf.com. Entrées, $13.95 to $26.95. Lunch daily, 11 to 5. Dinner, 5 to 9. Closed November-March.

Bah's Bakehouse, Main and Water Streets, Castine.

Hidden down an alley and reached from either street is this funky bakehouse and café, where Bah ("it's a childhood nickname that stuck") Macomber from New Orleans packs in the locals for great sandwiches, pastries and the like. She works in an open kitchen, the better to view (and interact with) her customers, many of whom are pictured on the walls. Dining is on a porch and deck with a harbor view and in a small dining room. The food is foremost. Consider one day's soups – tomato-cognac bisque, haddock chowder, whole bean and garlic, and Thai coconut shrimp and lobster. Sandwiches range from vegetarian to meatloaf to liverwurst to pâté with chutney, served on French or lavasch breads in small or large sizes. The dessert pastries are to die for.

(207) 326-9510. Sandwiches, $3.95 to $6.95. Open Monday-Saturday 7 to 5, Sunday 8 to 5.

Deer Isle/Stonington

Deer Isle, the second largest island off the Maine coast, is far different from its better-known and larger neighbor across the way, Mount Desert Island.

Back in the mid-18th century, Deer Isle ranked second only to Gloucester, Mass., as a fishing port. Later, it was the source of granite for New York's major bridges, Rockefeller Center and the John F. Kennedy Memorial in Arlington National Cemetery. At its height, Stonington, its biggest village, had 3,500 people, steamer service, a theater/opera house and something of a boomtown atmosphere.

Today, the commercial fishing fleet remains active, and lobster traps are piled all around a village occasionally permeated by the odor of fish. Granite is still quarried, but Stonington's population has dwindled to fewer than 1,300 hardy souls who, they say, rise with the sun and retire when darkness sets in.

The appeal of Deer Isle lies in the endearing charms of tiny hamlets like Deer Isle (the name of the second biggest community, as well as of the island). Two hamlets on either side of the island are called simply Sunrise and Sunset. Scenic views appear at every turn of roads that meander hither and yon around bays and inlets. The world-famous Haystack Mountain School of Crafts at Sunshine is worth the drive for the breathtaking view from its unsurpassed setting on a steep, forested slope with stairs down to Jericho Bay. It has attracted many craftsmen to the area and inspired others to stay.

Boating, nature walks, and art and craft galleries are the main attractions of this quiet, unspoiled area where "the people are gentle and strong, the sea water cool...and the rest of the hectic world seems removed for awhile," as Chamber of Commerce president Jean Wheeler advised in the helpful Island Guide.

Crafts and Shopping

Haystack Mountain School of Crafts, Sunshine Road, Deer Isle, (207) 348-2306. A long gravel road brings you finally to this crafts school, clinging to a hillside with wondrous views through deep green spruce trees of the sparkling blue waters below. The hardy can descend what seem like endless wooden stairs to the rocky shore. We found the various artists' studios and the school's layout interesting but were disappointed not to find any crafts on display. This is a working school, however, and no items are for sale. Three-week sessions attract top craftsmen from all over. Visitors are welcome to join campus tours at 1 p.m. Wednesdays in summer.

Ronald Hayes Pearson, whose jewelry is exhibited across the country, has a studio and gallery in his striking home at 29 Old Ferry Road in North Deer Isle. Pearson works in silver and gold; his twist earrings are especially in demand. He and his wife Carolyn Hecker, executive director of the growing Maine Crafts Association that started locally, welcome visitors Monday-Saturday from 10 to 5.

Farther along Reach Road, which parallels Eggemoggin Reach, is the home and studio of potter **William Mor,** designer of handsome functional stoneware. Lately, he has been selling stunning, reasonably priced oriental rugs made by Afghan refugees living in Pakistan. Wife Carolyn has been known to offer delicious fresh-baked cookies to browsers in the sheltered outdoor sales area surrounded by gardens and a pond, open daily from 10 to 5.

Harbor Farm, which started in 1985 as a Christmas shop featuring its own wreaths, has blossomed into a nationally known mail-order operation with a delightful store and showroom in an 1850 schoolhouse beside the causeway in Little Deer Isle. From trout pottery to Silesian stoneware to wooden hay forks to wrought-iron hooks to walking sticks, it sells fascinating furnishings for the person and home.

In Deer Isle, which claims more galleries per capita than any other small village in Maine, the **Deer Isle Artists Association** shows works by members. Mary Nyburg's **Blue Heron Gallery** exhibits American crafts, featuring works by the Haystack School faculty. Elena Kubler's wonderful **Turtle Gallery** has changing exhibits of watercolors, oils, drawings, photographs and crafts. **Greene-Ziner Gallery** features the owners' decorative clay and sculptural metalwork. **Dockside Quilt Gallery** is known for colorful island-made quilts. **The Periwinkle** stocks books, cards, knit goods, stuffed animals and local crafts

---

Sweet Whimsy

Nervous Nellie's Jams and Jellies, 598 Sunshine Road, Deer Isle.

The whimsical sculptures on the grounds draw passersby into this place that's well worth a visit. Peter Beerits and company put up 40,000 jars of jam each year in the little house with a big kitchen. So many people began stopping in that Peter decided to serve refreshments as well. His Mountainville Café offers morning coffee and afternoon tea with homemade breads and pastries, including a frozen drink called a Batido, a refreshing but caloric mix of cream cheese, freezer jam and crushed ice cubes. The jam business that Peter started because he could not find employment as an artist has enabled him to work full-time producing sculptures – many made from found objects. We were intrigued by a sculpture of a lobsterman with huge red wooden claws for arms. Lately, Peter cleared the surrounding woods to be peopled with sculptures from his studio, which he fashioned from an abandoned store that he moved to the site. Look for witches, woodsmen and owls among the trees.

(207) 348-6182 or (800) 777-6845. www.nervousnellies.com. Open daily 9 to 5, mid-May through Christmas; rest of year, by chance.

Stonington's Main Street has been enhanced by **The Clown,** an exceptional seasonal venture combining European antiques and furniture, contemporary art and Italian ceramics with Italian wines and specialty foods like fabulous Italian olive oil. It proved such a success that owners Kyle Wolfe and Martin Kolk opened a larger, year-round establishment of the same name in Portland. Farther along Main Street is the **Eastern Bay Gallery,** showing works of local artists. Other galleries caught our eye: **D. Mortenson Gallery, Isalos Fine Art** and the **Hoy Gallery,** displaying Jill Hoy's vibrant paintings of coastal Maine. The charming **Dockside Bookstore,** right beside the water with chairs for reading on a little deck, specializes in Maine and marine books and nautical gifts. **Bayside Antiques & Gifts** features period and country furniture. **The Dry Dock** and **The Grasshopper Shop** offer creative and eclectic gifts and miscellany. The Fish Shop at the **Stonington Sea Products** facility on Route 15 outside Stonington features hickory-smoked salmon, smoked slowly and naturally in a kiln imported from Glasgow. It has been rated the finest Scottish-style smoked salmon outside Scotland.

Other Attractions

Penobscot Bay cruises and passenger ferry service out to Isle au Haut are offered by **Isle au Haut Co.,** 27 Sea Breeze Ave., Stonington. Most are on mailboats, so they operate seasonally and generally on postal schedules. An exception is the hour-long sightseeing cruise aboard Miss Lizzie. The boat's captain relates island folklore and history as passengers watch seals, seabirds and fishing boats and view the Mark Island Lighthouse and the Deer Isle granite quarry at Crotch Island. Five mailboat trips daily out to Isle au Haut take about 45 minutes each way, with about a fifteen-minute stop on the island. The 10 a.m. trip goes on to Acadia National Park at Duck Harbor, on the protected southwest shore of Isle au Haut at the base of Duck Harbor Mountain. The adventurous may want to disembark, hike or bike the park's trails, and catch the late boat at 5:45 p.m. for the return trip.

(207) 367-5193. www.isleauhaut.com. Sightseeing cruise, Monday-Friday at 9 and 2 and Saturday at 2, June 14-Sept. 11; adults $14, children $6. Mailboat to Isle au Haut, Monday-Saturday at 7, 10, 11:30, 3:15 and 4:30, also Sunday at 10:30 and 3, June 20-Sept. 12, fewer trips in off-season. Duck Harbor trip, Monday-Saturday 10 and 4:30, June 12-Sept. 9. Fares are one-way: adults $16, children $8; return on same trip for half price. Ride all day on any combination of trips for $32, children $16.

Crockett Cove Woods Preserve, Crockett Cove, Stonington, is among attractions for nature lovers. It's hard to find, off Whitman Road at Burnt Cove on the Stonington-Sunset Road. The persistent will be rewarded with a pleasant quarter-mile walk through part of a 100-acre coastal rain forest maintained by the Maine Nature Conservancy. The self-guided tour is enhanced by a brochure that helps the already knowledgeable identify what they're seeing. Even the uninitiated will be impressed by the beautiful shades of greens, the exotic mosses, a bog, the lush growth and huge rocks. It really is like a rain forest.

A self-guiding nature trail passes through spruce forests and freshwater and saltwater marshes in the **Holt Mill Pond Preserve** off Airport Road, Stonington. Nearly 50 species of birds have been identified in the preserve, which is maintained by the Stonington Conservation Commission.

The Island Country Club on Sunset Road, Deer Isle, (207) 348-2379, welcomes visitors for "friendly golf and tennis," according to an advertisement. It has a nine-hole golf course and a tennis court.

Lodging and Dining

The Pilgrim's Inn, 20 Main St., Deer Isle 04267.

This striking, dark red 1793 house occupies a grand location on a spit of land between Northwest Harbor in front and the Mill Pond in back. Listed on the National Register of Historic Places, the inn exudes an aura of history, although new innkeepers Rob and Cathy DeGennaro added contemporary comforts and amenities in an effort to "take the inn to the next level." Most rooms now have king or queensize beds topped with down pillows and duvet comforters. Each has a wood stove and some of the updated baths have vanities topped with Deer Isle granite. A vintage house next door contains two efficiency suites with TVs and gas stoves, sharing a large deck overlooking the water. The deluxe Rugosa Rose cottage is a two-level affair with kitchenette, dining/sitting area and water-view deck on the main floor and a queen bedroom with gas fireplace on the upper level. New for 2005 was a secluded loft suite in the barn with queensize bedroom, kitchen and a living room with a sofabed and a super view of the grounds and the Mill Pond. Inn guests have use of a main-floor library-turned-game room and a cozy common room on the lower level with a bay window overlooking the Mill Pond and a new rear deck. For breakfast, smoked salmon benedict or piña colada-stuffed french toast might be the main course.

Some of the island's best meals have long attracted the public as well as inn guests for dinner at the Pilgrim's Inn. In 2005, the new owners renamed the restaurant the **Whale's Rib Tavern,** added a second dining room next to the inn's taproom and augmented their traditional offering with an upscale tavern menu. The former goat barn has been refurbished to resemble a 1793 tavern, with windsor chairs at white-clothed tables. Well-known Maine chef Jonathan Chase has presided in the Pilgrim's Inn kitchen since he sold his namesake Blue Hill restaurant in 2002. He and two other chefs offer up to 40 entrées nightly. Their tavern menu includes the likes of baby back ribs, meatloaf, bangers and mash, and shepherds pie. The traditional menu might start with Scandinavian-style borscht, parmigiano-reggiano flan with tomato-basil coulis and a smoked seafood sampler of mussels, Maine shrimp and Scottish salmon. Entrées range from a signature seafood stew and tuna niçoise to pan-seared venison medallions with a shiitake mushroom-red wine sauce. Desserts include chambord cheesecake and mocha mousse.

(207) 348-6615 or (888) 778-7505. www.pilgrimsinn.com. Twelve rooms and four suites with private baths. Summer: doubles, $129 to $229, suites, $249 to $269. Off-season: doubles $99 to $179, suites $179 to $239. Closed mid-October to mid-May. Cottage suites open all year. Entrées, $11.95 to $34.95; tavern menu, $8.95 to $14.95. Dinner nightly, 4:30 to 10:30. Closed early January to early May.

Goose Cove Lodge, Goose Cove Road, Box 40, Sunset 04683.

A 1.5-mile long dirt road leads to the End of Beyond – the loveliest sight in the world, according to the lodge brochure. The secluded, 70-acre preserve marked by trails, tree-lined shores and sandy beaches is a paradise for nature lovers. At low tide, you can walk across a sand bar to Barred Island, a nature conservancy full of birds and wildlife. Lodge owners Joanne and Dom Parisi have updated many of the formerly rustic accommodations and now offer "gracious lodging and fine dining" that more than live up to their billing. They accommodate 90 guests in cabins, rooms and suites and offer two meals a day, plus sandwich lunches from the gift shop. Two luxurious suites are upstairs in the main lodge and eight more suites and rooms are in the nearby East and North annexes. Most in demand are the nine secluded cottages and four duplex cabins, each with ocean view, sun deck, kitchenette or refrigerator and fireplace. The epitome of a Maine lodge includes a lobby with an enormous fieldstone fireplace and stylish sofas, chairs, benches and bookcases. Breakfast is included in the rates.

The food here is some of the island's most inspired, and the waterside setting is without peer. The **Point Dining Room,** paneled in pine with wraparound windows onto the water, is augmented by an expansive dining deck almost at water's edge. The innovative, much-acclaimed dinner menu changes weekly. At a recent visit the entrées included twin peeky-toe crab cakes with roasted tomato-vodka sauce, Mediterranean seafood stew, pan-seared duck breast with raspberry demi-glace and grilled butterflied lamb with rosemary demi-glace. The vegetarian entrée showed the kitchen's reach: seared tofu with quinoa, grilled butternut disk and wilted greens served with a roasted portobello mushroom and vegan pesto. Among starters were tuna tartare with wasabi cream and rosemary-skewered Maine diver scallops on polenta with wilted greens. Typical desserts are peach bread pudding on caramel sauce, chocolate decadence with raspberry sauce and poached pear on a flourless chocolate pâté with vanilla crème anglaise.

(207) 348-2508 or (800) 728-1963. Fax (207) 348-2624. www.goosecovelodge.com. Twenty-two rooms, suites, cottages and cabins with private baths. Doubles, $225 to $525 B&B. Cottages rented weekly in summer; other rooms, two-night minimum. Closed late-October to mid-May.

Entrées, $15 to $27. Dinner by reservation, Tuesday-Sunday 5:30 to 8:30. Closed mid-October to mid-June.

Lodging

The Inn at Ferry Landing, 108 Old Ferry Road, RR 1, Box 163, Deer Isle 04627.

The wide waterfront location – at a point along Eggemoggin Reach where the ferry from Sargentville once landed – is the draw for this B&B in a restored 1850s farmhouse. Owners Jean and Gerald Wheeler offer four guest quarters, two up and two down, all with water views and furnished with family antiques. The Blue Room at the rear of the main floor has twin beds, a clawfoot tub and a private entrance from the yard. We're partial to the second-floor suite with a brass queensize bed, a huge tub and walk-in shower, a pullout sofa and chair, a wood stove and skylights in the pitched ceiling. Families go for the two-bedroom housekeeping apartment called the Mooring in the rear annex, which has a waterfront deck. The real showplace is the large, contemporary-style great room, white with mauve trim, airy and open with expansive windows on three sides. It holds lots of seating plus two grand pianos (Gerald formerly was music director of Christ Church Cathedral in Montreal). His wife serves exotic breakfasts at a mahogany table in the dining room. The fare might be omelets, pain au chocolate or french toast made with oatmeal bread and orange slices.

(207) 348-7760. Fax (207) 348-5276. www.ferrylanding.com. Three rooms, one suite and a two-bedroom apartment with private baths. Doubles, $110 to $120. Suite, $165. Annex, $1,300 weekly, EP.

Inn on the Harbor, Main Street, Box 69, Stonington 04681.

Four 19th-century buildings joined by a flower-laden common deck overlooking the harbor have been transformed into comfortable guest quarters named after schooners that sail into Stonington harbor. A New Yorker who has a summer home nearby, owner Christina Shipps produced larger rooms with sitting areas, many queen or kingsize beds, updated bathrooms and new overstuffed furnishings interspersed with antiques and family heirlooms. All different, rooms vary from small and cozy to suites that are rather substantial. All have TVs and telephones. Three on the village side compensate for lack of harbor views with extra space. In those facing the water, you're lulled to sleep by the sounds of gulls and foghorns. A continental breakfast buffet is put out in the reception room, which also operates as an espresso bar open to the public from 11 to 6. The inn also offers the adjacent Stephen Taber cottage with queen bed and private deck and a two-bedroom sea-view suite in the owner's residence out West Main Street.

(207) 367-2420 or (800) 942-2420. Fax (207) 367-5165. www.innontheharbor.com. Eleven rooms, two suites and a cottage with private baths. Doubles, $115 to $140. Suites and cottage, $135 and $195.

Près du Port, West Main Street and Highland Avenue, Box 319, Stonington 04681.

This gray house on a hill overlooks Stonington harbor and takes full advantage of its view. Rockers in a semi-circle face the water in a side sun porch; Adirondack chairs do the same on an upstairs sundeck. Charlotte Casgrain, a Connecticut resident who has summered on the island since 1955, offers three guest rooms, each with its own bath. Beau Rivage is a large room with a panoramic view of the harbor, old oak furniture and a small vanity sink to match. It has a double bed, as does Beau Ciel, also with a vanity and a view, and done in pale azure; note the tiny silver-plated faces on the Victorian drawer pulls. Beau Sejour has twin beds, a loft with futons, a kitchenette and a garden view. Breakfast, served buffet style, consists of fruit, cereals, yogurts, muffins and breads, sometimes with bacon or sausage and eggs.

(207) 367-5007. www.presduport.com. Three rooms with private baths. Doubles, $125. Open mid-June to mid-October.

Dining

Maritime Café, 27 Main St., Stonington.

The former Café Atlantic gave way in 2004 to this with-it establishment, run by an Austrian by way of Colorado and offering some interesting twists. Rudi Newmayr, a contractor who built many a restaurant but said this is the first he ever owned, dispenses typical Maine fare, of course. But he also has an espresso and crêpe bar geared to the after-theater crowd from the Stonington Opera House and a barbecue grill outside serving up spicy German sausages. The regular menu ranges widely from grilled Atlantic salmon with lemon-dill butter, seafood crêpes or sea scallops with snap peas and tomatoes over capellini to sautéed chicken breast with prosciutto, fontina and sage, herb-rubbed pork loin with caramelized onion sauce and grilled sirloin steak. Lobster is offered in three versions. You might start with steamed mussels in a spicy tomato broth or an Alsatian onion tart. Finish with one of the specialty dessert crêpes. With windows onto the water, the 28-seat dining room is simple but stylish with white paneling, flooring and benches imported from Colorado. An outdoor deck is put into service at lunchtime.

(207) 367-2600. www.maritimecafe.com. Entrées, $15 to $21. Lunch daily, 11:30 to 2:30. Dinner, 5 or 5:30 to 8:30. BYOB. Closed November-April.

Bayview Restaurant, Sea Breeze Avenue, Stonington.

There's not much in the way of decor – pressed-tin ceiling and walls, linoleum floor and mismatched Scandinavian cutlery, raspberry-colored paper mats and an arrangement of wildflowers at each table. And, despite the name, there's not much of a water view except, perhaps, from the rear kitchen. Service can be so slow as to be exasperating, moreover. But, rest assured, the signs proclaim this is Stonington's oldest continuously operated restaurant and shout values like "meat loaf special, $5.99" and nuances like "always smoke-free." The food is fresh and reasonably priced, ranging from chicken kiev to Nellie's sautéed lobster à la Nova Scotia, "an old family recipe served on toast points." Chef-owner Robert Dodge loves to cook and is doing this "out of the goodness of his heart," according to regulars. He's at his best with his evening specials – "whatever I feel like doing," he says. At our latest visit that meant grilled arctic char with lemon-butter sauce, baked halibut provençal, charbroiled venison medallions with cranberry game sauce and Maine-raised black angus steak. Pretty good for a place that serves a range from hot dogs to seafood pie. "We still have fresh fish," Bob says. "You can't get away from that around here."

(207) 367-2274. Entrées, $8.50 to $12.75. Breakfast daily, 9 to 11. Lunch, 11 to 3. Dinner, 5 to 8:30. BYOB.

Lily's Café, Route 15, Stonington.

This inauspicious looking little house across the cove from South Deer Isle offers consistently good, interesting food. Chef-owner Kyra Alex has a steady following for eclectic fare that ranges from antipasto salad to cold Chinese noodles to crab cakes to crispy baked haddock sandwich to albacore tuna melt to veggie sandwich and Lily's nutburger. That's a sampling of the all-day fare. At night, Kyra adds a couple of specials that she decides about around 3 p.m. and are "ready at 5." One recent night's choices were steamed mussels in red wine and tomato broth, chicken pot pie and Italian pot roast on pasta. The main floor of the house holds six tables, most topped with glass and dolls or shells. More tables in the eclectic **Chef's Attic** shop upstairs are pressed into service at busy times. The restaurant hews to limited hours, never on weekends and closing at 8 p.m. on nights dinner is served. We know, because we were running late and nearly didn't make it. But our innkeeper guests pulled rank and got us in for a convivial meal of delectable lamb chops, topped off with bread pudding.

(207) 367-5936. Entrées, $12.95 to $16.95. Open Monday, Tuesday and Friday 7 to 4, Wednesday and Thursday 7 to 8 p.m. in summer, to 7 p.m. in winter. BYOB.

FOR MORE INFORMATION: Deer Isle-Stonington Chamber of Commerce, Box 490, Deer Isle, ME 04627, (207) 348-6124. www.deerislemaine.com.

East Penobscot Bay Association, www.penobscotbay.com.

Blue Hill Peninsula Arts, Lodging and Business Guide, www.bluehillmaine.com.

Canopied deck at Thurston's Lobster Pound overlooks picturesque Bass Harbor.

Mount Desert and Bar Harbor, Me.

The Cadillac of Islands

With the first torrid heat wave of every summer, all you can think of is chilling out. The mind wanders to the coast of Maine, reviving memories of cooler temperatures, misty fogs and sparkling blue waters, noble rocks, thundering surf and succulent lobsters to be eaten on a wharf.

The epitome of this vision for us is Mount Desert (pronounced "dessert"), Maine's largest island, home of Bar Harbor and Acadia National Park. Although seemingly a long way from just about anywhere, the trip is worth the effort – for a day, a weekend, a week or longer (the four million who make the trek annually make Acadia the nation's second most-visited national park after the Great Smokies).

Mount Desert has just about everything we love in Maine. It is the kind of place where you can be as active or as idle as you like.

The draw for most visitors is Acadia, the first national park east of the Mississippi. Situated where northern and temperate zones overlap, the park has sea and mountains and an amazing variety of flora and fauna – including plants of the Arctic tundra – on its 40,000 acres of unspoiled beauty.

When Samuel de Champlain encountered the island in 1604, he named it L'Isle des Monts Deserts for its barren mountains (for years it was part of the French province of Acadia, which gives the park its name). The fifteen rounded peaks of the Mount Desert Mountains are mostly bare and rocky at their summits, with evergreen forests below. The 1,530-foot-high Cadillac Mountain is the tallest along the East Coast. At sea level, majestic cliffs rise above the pounding surf and, in Somes Sound, form the East's only natural fjord. There are fresh-water lakes, sandy beaches, and wetlands and forests full of wildlife.

The national park encompasses some of the most scenic and rugged portions of the island. That is not to denigrate the rest. Bar Harbor, the largest and best-known town on Mount Desert Island, is a focal point. It is of strollable size, with many shops and restaurants and activities to investigate. In mid-summer, it's crammed with tourists.

More rewarding for a feel of old Maine are visits to Seal Harbor, Northeast Harbor, Southwest Harbor, Manset, Bass Harbor and Somesville, all of which have singular charms.

The on-the-water opportunities are endless, ranging from canoeing and kayaking to lobster fishing and whale-watch expeditions. Fascinating nature cruises are led by park naturalists. The park offers hiking, nature trails, carriage roads, campground talks, scenic spots, beaches and picnic areas. It's hard to find time to take advantage of everything available. And don't think that because Mount Desert is a fairly small island, it's easy to explore. Roads are convoluted, driving times between towns are longer than you might think, and there is much to see along the way.

Whether you stick to the main roads of the park and Bar Harbor, or strike off to the less crowded, "quiet side" of the island, Mount Desert Island offers rewards to those of all ages and inclinations.

Seeing and Doing

Acadia National Park

The largest national park in the East is Mount Desert Island's big draw. Acadia encompasses 44 miles of dramatic coastline, all the island's major mountains, part of the Somes Sound fjord, all or part of every major lake shore, 120 miles of hiking trails and bike paths, and a scenic 27-mile Park Loop Road that reveals the highlights.

Your first stop should be the main **Park Visitor Center,** three miles northwest of Bar Harbor at Hulls Cove. A two-minute walk from the parking area leads to a rustic contemporary building where a huge picture window yields a panoramic view of Frenchman Bay. A fifteen-minute movie, "Search for Acadia," is shown on the half hour.

Here you can find out about the current park naturalist tours and programs, from boat cruises to mountain hikes to nature walks to evening activities. They follow a set daily schedule, usually starting with a three-hour birder's walk at 7 a.m. and ending at 9 p.m. with a Seawall Amphitheater program. Among the more appealing titles are Birds of Prey, Green Kingdom, Mr. Rockefeller's Bridges Walk, Life Between the Tides, Trees along the Trail and Secrets of the Summit. The park naturalists and their assistants are engaging and enlightening, and we've enjoyed every tour and program we've tried.

(207) 288-3338. Visitor Center open daily 8 to 6, July-August; 8 to 4:30, May-June and September-October. Park open year-round. Admission by weekly pass, $20 per car. Annual pass, $40.

The Park Loop Road

Starting from the Visitor Center, the 27-mile loop winding through the eastern half of the island can take three hours (with stops) or up to a day. The two-lane, limited-access roadway can be entered or exited at several locations, but the Ocean Drive segment is one-way outbound. The first two overlooks provide good views of Frenchman Bay, Bar Harbor and the area burned in a disastrous 1947 fire.

Sieur de Monts Spring, covered by a small octagonal structure but still bubbling water from a fountain in the adjacent nature center, is a favorite stop. Here is the original **Abbe Museum** (there's a newer branch in downtown Bar Harbor), whose

Native American artifacts span 12,000 years (adults $2, children 50 cents). The wonderful **Wild Gardens of Acadia** has more than 500 plants indigenous to the area's forests, mountains and shores. They're labeled and grouped in thirteen sections, from deciduous weeds to dry heath and bog. Well-maintained gravel paths lead past some rare specimens, with benches placed strategically along the way.

The 1.4-mile **Precipice Trail,** sometimes closed when peregrine falcons are nesting in its ledges, rises sharply from the Champlain Mountain overlook. The males in our family climbed it and returned with the report that it took 90 minutes to get up, 40 minutes to come down, and that there were two tunnels and countless firemen-type ladders to traverse, with sheer drops to contemplate. The wild blueberries along the way and the view from the barren summit made the effort worthwhile.

Going from the sublime to the ridiculous, cool off after your climb at **Sand Beach,** the only saltwater beach in the park and an arc of sand between two cliffs. You may notice lots of people on the beach and only a few in the ocean. Feel it and you'll know why; the water temperature rarely tops 55 degrees. If you don't like to get numb, simply soak up some sun on the beach or hike the easy 1.8-mile **Ocean Path** along the water.

Thunder Hole is where the waves rush into a small cave and roar out with a thunderous sound, when tides and surf coincide – the best time to hear it is at three-quarter rising tide when the sea is rough. At the 100-foot-high **Otter Cliffs,** look out to sea from the highest headlands on the East Coast. Beyond is **Otter Point,** a rocky place good for sunning and picnicking. Marked by wooden stairs leading to the water, **Little Hunters Beach** is a steeply pitched cove lined with cobblestones polished by the pounding surf.

Leaving the ocean, the Park Loop Road turns inland toward **Jordan Pond.** Stop for lunch or tea at the venerable Jordan Pond House (see Where to Eat) and admire the view of the two rounded mountains known as the **Bubbles** (named long ago by a youth for the bosom of his amour). At the end of Jordan Pond is a huge boulder balancing atop a cliff.

Pass beautiful **Eagle Lake,** which gets smaller and bluer as you drive the 3.2-mile side trip up **Cadillac Mountain,** at 1,530 feet the highest point on the Atlantic Seaboard. The road is excellent and gradual (an eight percent grade, not bad for bicycling) and the view from the top is incredible in all directions. A short summit trail has interesting interpretive markers. The Sunset Parking Area near the top is where everyone gathers to watch the sunset – the mountains and waters to the west a changing rainbow of greens, blues, oranges and reds. It's an enlightening sight for anyone who thinks Key West or Carmel sunsets are the ultimate. It's also exhilarating at dawn, for those hardy enough to get up and be among the first in the United States to see the rising sun.

Descend Cadillac Mountain and you've completed the loop. Follow the signs to Bar Harbor or other destinations.

Hiking, Walking and Biking

The Park Loop Road has shown you only a portion of the park, albeit the most popular part. There are many other drives and cycling routes on the island. Take **Sargent Drive,** which borders the fjord-like Somes Sound, out of Northeast Harbor to Somesville for some of the best views. Across the sound is **Echo Lake,** with a fine beach and water far warmer for swimming than the ocean. Head down the west side of Echo Lake for a short hike up to **Beech Cliff,** which has a great view down to the lake below (holler and you can hear your echo).

Farther down the peninsula they call the Quiet Side, past Southwest Harbor, is a section of the park containing **Seawall, Wonderland,** the **Ship Harbor Nature Trail** (which is well worth taking), and the landmark **Bass Harbor Light.** Visit **Bass Harbor** and **Bernard,** across an inlet from each other and the most authentic fishing communities on the island.

Other sections of the park are off-island on Isle au Haut and on the mainland **Schoodic Peninsula.,** which is a long way around, but should not be missed. Drive around fashionable **Winter Harbor** to see how the other half lives before heading down the six-mile, one-way loop around **Schoodic Point,** where the crashing surf is awesome. We could spend hours here watching gulls, ogling passing lobster boats, climbing rocks, viewing Mount Desert Island across the way and generally chilling out. This part of the park offers plenty of space for picnics and privacy.

You can also get to Schoodic Point via the passenger-only **Bar Harbor Ferry Co.,** which offers up to ten round trips daily from the Bar Harbor Inn pier to Winter Harbor, where you can ride your bicycle or board a free Island Explorer bus that runs seasonally out to Schoodic Point. The trip costs $24 for adults, $15 for children, $5 for bicycles.

CARRIAGE PATHS. Fifty-seven miles of scenic, tranquil carriage paths were planned and built in the 1920s by John D. Rockefeller Jr., a summer resident of Seal Harbor, to provide a refuge for carriages from the intrusions of the automobile. The ten-foot-wide paths follow the land's contours, protected by stone culverts and retaining walls and notable for thirteen interesting, hand-cut stone bridges. About eighteen miles of the cut-stone paths have been specially surfaced for bicycles; the rest are better for hikers, mountain bikers and horseback riders.

BIKING. Although the terrain is hilly, biking opportunities abound. The park visitor center provides detailed maps of roads and trails through the park. Cyclists can take the same routes as listed above on the Park Loop and other drives. They can get away from cars and trailers on the park's carriage paths. The Eagle Lake-Witch Hole Loop is a five-hour carriage park ride with spectacular views of lakes, mountains and ocean. For shore viewing, bike the road to Seawall and Wonderland. A longer excursion is to take the 40-minute ferry ride from Bass Harbor to **Swan's Island.** We picnicked in an eerie fog at deserted Hockamock Head Lighthouse high on a cliff with a bell buoy ringing off shore and an abundance of raspberries, blueberries and gooseberries waiting to be picked. Bicycles are available for rent in Bar Harbor at Bar Harbor Bicycle Shop, 141 Cottage St., and Acadia Bike, 48 Cottage St., and in Southwest Harbor at Southwest Cycle, Main Street.

HIKING. In addition to the carriage paths, 120 miles of hiking trails await the hiker. They vary from mountain climbs (naturalists lead hikes up Beech and Gorham mountains and Huguenot Head) to self-guided walks for casual strollers – the Jordan Pond nature path and the Ships Harbor nature trail. A favorite is the gently rolling **Ocean Trail,** a 3.6-mile footpath along the rocky shore beside Frenchman Bay from Sand Beach to Otter Cliffs.

Walk the Bar. For two hours on either side of low tide, you can walk across a bit of Frenchman Bay on a sand bar from Bar Harbor to Bar Island, where there are trails and shoreline to explore and the clear water is considerably warmer than at Sand

Beach. Bring a bathing suit and a picnic, but don't tarry too long or you'll have to swim back across the current. The bar surfaces at the foot of Bridge Street. If the tide's in, settle for a walk along the quarter-mile-long **Shore Path** from the Town Pier to Hancock Street, passing shorefront mansions from Bar Harbor's Golden Age.

Gorgeous Gardens

Asticou Terraces and Thuya Gardens, Route 3, Northeast Harbor.

It's a ten-minute hike up a steep but well-maintained switchback trail to the prized gardens surrounding Thuya Lodge, former home of landscape artist Joseph Henry Curtis. The intrepid are rewarded with a spectacular hilltop spread combining English flowerbeds with informal natural Japanese effects, some common and uncommon annuals plus hardy rhododendron and laurel that you don't expect to see so far north. Other attractions are a gazebo, a free-form freshwater pond, a shelter with pillowed seats and deck chairs in the shade – just as you'd find in the gardens of a private estate, which this once was. A plaque relates that Curtis left this "for the quiet recreation of the people of this town and their summer guests."

(207) 276-3344. Open daily in July and August, 7 to 7. Free.

Asticou Azalea Gardens, Junction of Routes 3 and 198, Northeast Harbor.

You can walk amid azaleas in early summer here. Twenty species were moved from the former Rife Point gardens of Beatrice Farrand in Bar Harbor, and new varieties are added each year in this showplace funded by John D. Rockefeller Jr. Around a free-form pond are azaleas and rhododendrons at their showy best in June, a Sand Garden with an arrangement of sand and stones as in Kyoto, Japanese-style evergreens and bonsai. There are gravel paths raked into lovely patterns to walk and stone benches for contemplation in this, one of the most perfect gardens anywhere.

Open daily April-October, 7 a.m. to 9 p.m. Free.

On the Water

Park naturalists conduct cruises aboard privately owned boats, and these are among the most informative of all the island's cruises. Typical tours:

Sea Princess Cruises, Northeast Harbor, (207) 276-5352, has naturalists aboard its three-hour morning and afternoon nature cruises around Great Harbor and Somes Sound Fjord, each with a stop in Islesford on Little Cranberry Island; adults $18, children $12. The Sea Princess also has a late-afternoon Somes Sound Fjord cruise and a three-hour sunset cruise around the Cranberry Isles with optional dinner (adults $15, children $10). In the middle of the sunset cruise, dinner at the Islesford Dock Restaurant on the wharf is a waterside treat not to be missed.

The **Dive-In Theater Boat,** 55 West St., Bar Harbor, (207) 288-3483, gives three-hour cruises with a ranger around Frenchman Bay looking for seals, porpoises and coastal birds three times daily. Passengers watch a real-time underwater video as a diver searches the sea bottom for marine life to bring aboard the boat for discussion; adults $33.50, children $23.50.

The **Lulu,** a traditional Downcast lobster boat, offers lobster fishing and seal watching rides daily from 55 West St., Bar Harbor, (207) 963-2341 or (866) 235-2341; adults $25, children $15.

Island Cruises, Little Island Way, Bass Harbor, (207) 244-5785, schedules a daily cruise to the fishing village of Richboro on Long Island, including a guided walking tour and optional lunch (adults $25, children $15). There's also a two-hour afternoon nature tour around the islands of Blue Hill Bay (adults $20, children $15).

WHALE WATCH CRUISES. Bar Harbor Whale Watch Co., 1 West St., (207) 288-2386 or (800) 942-5374, offers three-hour whale watching and 3½-hour combination puffin and whale watching excursions aboard the jet-powered, 112-foot catamaran Friendship V, daily early June to mid-October; whale trips, adults $45, children $25.

Acadian Whale Adventures, 55 West St., (207) 288-9800 or (888) 533-9253, gives approximately three-hour tours two or three times daily aboard a 100-foot catamaran, billed as the fastest and most luxurious jet-powered boat of its type in North America; adults $45, children $25.

CANOEING AND KAYAKING. The lakes of Mount Desert Island are paradise for canoeists and kayakers. Locals recommend Long Pond, the island's largest with three access points, as well as secluded Seal Cove Pond, Echo Lake, Eagle Lake and Jordan Pond. Tidal currents in Somes Sound are dangerous for light craft; you also might be surprised by frolicking porpoises. Canoeing the Bass Harbor Marsh at high tide is quite an experience, especially on a moonlit night when you may hear and see herons, owls, beavers and deer. Canoes and kayaks may be rented in Bar Harbor from **Acadia Outfitters** at 106 Cottage St. and **Cadillac Mountain Sports** at 26 Cottage St. or **National Park Canoe & Kayak Rentals** at Pond's End in Somesville. **Coastal Kayaking Tours** at 48 Cottage St. is the oldest among nearly a dozen outfits offering sea kayak tours.

SWIMMING. The only ocean beach is **Sand Beach** in Acadia National Park. Lifeguards staff it and the park's **Echo Lake.** Outside the park, there's saltwater swimming at the pleasant little town beach in Seal Harbor. Explore or ask around and you may come upon a little beach or swimming area on other of the numerous freshwater lakes. If you're adventurous, you can swim off the rocks or in the coves of Frenchman Bay.

Museums

Everything you might want to know about lobsters and other sea life is revealed at the **Mount Desert Oceanarium,** now at two locations on the island. The original Oceanarium in a former ship's chandlery along the working waterfront off Clark Point Road, Southwest Harbor, (207) 244-7330, offers much of interest to young and old. It consists of a marine aquarium with a touch tank and a fisherman's museum. The newer **Bar Harbor Oceanarium** is off Route 3 at the entrance to Mount Desert Island, (207) 288-5005. Here visitors can board a lobster boat, see harbor seals in a 50,000-gallon tank, explore the Maine Lobster Museum, tour a lobster hatchery and study the ecosystem along the Thomas Bay Marsh Walk. Both facilities are open Monday-Saturday 9 to 5, Memorial Day to mid-October. Bar Harbor: adults $9.95, children $6.95. Mount Desert: adults $6.95, children $4.75. Combination ticket: adults $13, children $9.65.

The **George B. Dorr Museum of Natural History** on the College of the Atlantic campus at 105 Eden St., Bar Harbor, (207) 288-5015, contains exhibits depicting the island's marine mammal, seabird and plant life. Visitors are encouraged to disassemble and reassemble the backbone of a twenty-foot whale skeleton and to walk nature trails. Open Monday-Saturday 9 to 5, mid-June to Labor Day; Thursday-Sunday 1 to 4 and Saturday 10 to 4 rest of year. Adults $3.50, children $1.

The **Wendell Gilley Museum,** Main Street and Herrick Road, Southwest Harbor, (207) 244-7555, honors the late nationally known bird carver from Southwest Harbor. The life-size wood carving of a bald eagle in the entry rotunda looks like a mounted bird, but it and the other 200 bird carvings in the museum's collection were created by Wendell Gilley. Changing wildlife exhibits, carving demonstrations and an excellent shop are among the attractions; open Tuesday-Sunday 10 to 5, July and August, 10 to 4 in June and September; Friday-Sunday 10 to 4 in May and November-December; adults $5, children $2.

Shopping

In Bar Harbor, the sidewalks are crowded and everyone appears to be shopping – or at least window-shopping. Stores are concentrated along Main, Cottage and Mount Desert streets. **Island Artisans,** a co-op, is owned by the two dozen artists who are represented in the handsome shop by a variety of wares. The Bar Harbor headquarters of the **Acadia Shops,** which also are located in the national park and at the Jordan Pond House, features the crafts, gifts and foods of Maine. Natural gifts and accessories, from rock vases to porch rockers, are available at **Window Panes. The Happy Clam** carries nifty accents for the home and garden. **Cool as a Moose** is where to get a bathing suit or a T-shirt. Tons of clocks are sold at **Get Clocked,** or pick up a gift for man's best friend at **Bark Harbor. Sunrise Clothing and Jewelry** speaks for itself. **Domus Isle** combines music, gifts and wines. **Porcupine Island Co.** at 4 Cottage St. claims the state's largest selection of made-in-Maine specialty foods. **J.H. Butterfield Co.** is a gourmet grocery store of the old school.

In tony Northeast Harbor, two perennial favorites are the **Kimball Shop and Boutique,** with room after room of housewares and clothing and anything else that's in, and **Smart Studio and Gallery,** featuring Wini Smart's evocative paintings of Maine. **The Romantic Room** carries a range from Lilly Pulitzer and straw hats to wicker furniture and brass beds. Margaret Hammond at **Local Color** offers hand-painted woven clothing, soft and elegant in jewel-like colors and like nothing we've seen elsewhere.

Of special appeal in Southwest Harbor are **Hot Flash Anny's** for stained-glass pieces and the **Little Notch Bakery** for superb breads. **The Sand Castle Ocean & Nature Store** features the works of more than 60 Maine artisans. **MDI Sportswear** carries clothing and accessories.

Where to Stay

Dozens of motels and cottage colonies line Route 3 heading into Bar Harbor. The choicest accommodations are generally off the main roads, with a concentration in and around Bar Harbor and Southwest Harbor. The best are generally booked far in advance in mid-summer, although you may find openings available for spur-of-the-moment getaways.

Hotels, Large Inns and Resorts

Bar Harbor Inn, Newport Drive, Bar Harbor 04609.

The prime downtown location in Bar Harbor is occupied by this large and totally renovated complex that began as a hotel and motor inn. Now it better reflects owner David Witham's vision for luxurious accommodations on eight shady landscaped acres with the sea on two sides. Rebuilt in 2000, the main inn features a wing with 43 deluxe jacuzzi rooms, all with king or queen beds and most with fireplaces and bayfront balconies. We're partial to the 64-room oceanfront lodge, closest to the shore and constructed on the site of the original motel. The lodge was totally refurbished in 1999 and offers rooms with kingsize or two queen beds, sitting areas and private balconies with stunning views of rocks, water and islands. The original motel was moved uphill, later to be razed and rebuilt. Now known as the Newport Building, it has 38 rooms with king or queen beds and patios or decks overlooking the grounds, but lacking water views. There's a large heated pool, and a small public beach is adjacent. Continental breakfast is complimentary.

The inn's circular, many-windowed restaurant called the **Reading Room** claims the finest ocean panorama in town. Harp or piano music plays as you consider a choice of five lobster specialties. Other entrées range from seared halibut topped with sautéed fiddleheads and scallions to roast Long Island duck with a port wine-cherry sauce. Start with a lobster and cilantro spring roll or a local chèvre and vegetable strudel. Finish with bananas foster bread pudding or a triple chocolate dessert called chocolate trillium. The **Terrace Grille,** situated at harbor's edge with yellow umbrella-covered tables, is lovely for waterside meals. It's known for a Down East lobster bake, and serves light fare and lunch.

(207) 288-3351 or (800) 248-3351. www.barharborinn.com. One hundred forty-two rooms and eleven suites with private baths. Doubles, $199 to $369 late June to Labor Day, $99 to $329 rest of year. Closed Thanksgiving to late March.

Entrées, $21 to $31. Dinner nightly, 5:30 to 9:30. Sunday brunch, 11:30 to 2:30. Grill open Monday-Saturday, 11:30 to 9:30, entrées $7.95 to $18.95. Closed mid-November to mid-April.

Harborside Hotel & Marina, 55 West St., Bar Harbor 04609.

The legendary Bar Harbor Club has been incorporated into this showy new hotel and resort complex at water's edge in downtown Bar Harbor. Tom Walsh, who numbers the Bar Harbor Regency among his growing empire, spent many millions converting the aging Golden Anchor Motel complex into an urbane oceanfront resort worthy of the site. It now stretches along the waterfront from The Pier Restaurant to the spa, fitness and meeting facility in the old Bar Harbor Club. The half-timbered Tudor look of the historic club and casino has been incorporated into the architecturally interesting, three-story hotel, which sprawls in long corridors opening from a mahogany paneled lobby with a marble floor. All 185 hotel-style rooms and suites have full or partial water views, best enjoyed from good-looking balconies or patios laden with colorful plantings. Suites come with fireplaces, kitchens and whirlpool tubs. A heated pool and hot tub are stunningly located in a courtyard area between the hotel and the casual **Pier Restaurant,** overlooking the marina. A fine-dining restaurant was planned in the former Bar Harbor Club property in 2005.

(207) 288-5033 or (800) 328-5033. Fax (207) 288-3089. www.theharborsidehotel.com. One hundred eighty-five rooms. Doubles, $209 to $469 in summer, $119 to $369 off-season. Closed November to early May.

Bar Harbor Regency/Holiday Inn Sunspree Resort, 123 Eden St. (Route 3), Bar Harbor 04609.

Erected in 1986 in a semi-residential section along the bay on the outskirts of town, the luxury Regency structure became a Holiday Inn franchise in 1990 and later was made a Sunspree resort, which accounts for the long-winded name. The four floors of its main building contain 180 rooms, all rather sophisticated for Downeast Maine (there's even a glass-enclosed elevator from which to view Frenchman Bay). The Tiki Bar in a gazebo beside the pool at water's edge offers lunch and drinks. **Stewman's Lobster Pound** claims to be Bar Harbor's only waterfront lobster pound. The **Edenfield** dining room, with windows onto the water, offers a standard seafood menu. The waterfront grounds include a large and angular pool beside the water, two hot tubs and a sauna, a fitness center, a walking path, two lighted tennis courts, a putting green and docking facilities.

(207) 288-9723 or (800) 234-6835. Fax (207) 288-3089. www.barharborholidayinn.com. Two hundred nineteen rooms and two suites. Doubles, $139 to $300, off-season $99 to $275. Closed November to early May.

Atlantic Oakes By-the-Sea, 119 Eden St. (Route 3), Bar Harbor 04609.

This good-looking resort complex is located beside the Nova Scotia ferry terminal on the estate that belonged to Sir Harry Oakes. It includes 42 ocean-view rooms in a four-story building and the restored **Willows Mansion at the Oakes,** which operates as a B&B with seven guest rooms, four with oceanfront porches, and a two-bedroom suite. We prefer the older, low-slung, brown-shingled motel buildings right beside Frenchman Bay, their private balconies or patios enjoying privacy as well as quiet. The attractive grounds include five tennis courts (two of them lighted and with a tennis pro in residence), a heated pool and a pebbly beach with a float and a pier, where boats may be rented and sailing lessons are given. There's also an indoor pool. B&B guests are served a complimentary breakfast in the mansion each morning. Lobster cookouts and clambakes are available several nights a week.

(207) 288-5801 or (800) 336-2463. Fax (2207) 288-8402. www.barharbor.com. One hundred fifty-one rooms and two suites. July to Labor Day: doubles $162 to $198, mansion $159 to $305. Rest of year: doubles, $62 to $178. Mansion and some small buildings closed in winter.

Asticou Inn, Route 3, Northeast Harbor 04662.

A classic old resort hotel favored by Northeast Harbor socialites and wannabes, the Asticou dates to 1883 but is updated and elegant in an understated, old-fashioned way. The setting high above the harbor is exceptional, with a swimming pool, tennis court and well-tended lawns and gardens sloping toward the sea. Cheerful, pleasant common rooms with oriental rugs and wingback chairs welcome guests, some of whom have been coming here for extended stays for the last 50 years. They stay in the inn's 30 simple rooms and suites on the second, third and fourth floors (four with private balconies viewing the water) or in outlying rooms in Cranberry Lodge, guest houses and the circular Topsider cottages – six of the most contemporary and deluxe accommodations, with water views. A deluxe continental breakfast buffet is included in the rates.

The outdoor deck off the cocktail lounge is a great place for lunch or dinner al fresco, or simply to enjoy drinks while viewing the harbor goings-on in the distance. The MAP Meal plan is no longer required – nor are jackets and ties in the dining room – as the inn continues to evolve with the times. The pillared dining room is notable for oriental rugs and hand-painted murals of trees and flowers on the buttercup yellow walls. Most coveted seating (and generally reserved for regulars) is in the adjacent enclosed porch, with views onto the harbor beyond. The menu features the traditional lobster chowder and baked stuffed lobster, as well as more contemporary fare like grilled swordfish with cucumber-dill sauce and grilled veal chop with wild mushroom demi-glace.

(207) 276-3344 or (800) 258-3373. www.asticou.com. Thirty-three rooms and fifteen suites with private baths. Doubles, $225 to $350; off-season, $130 to $230. Closed mid-October to mid-May.
Entrées, $19 to $33. Lunch, Monday-Saturday in July and August, 11:30 to 2. Dinner nightly, 6 to 9, mid-June to mid-September. Sunday jazz brunch, 11:30 to 2:30.

The Claremont Hotel, Clark Point Road, Box 137, Southwest Harbor 04679.

The broad lawns sloping down to Somes Sound outside the island's oldest hotel invite relaxation. And relax the guests do – in Adirondack chairs scattered about, in a rope hammock tied between two trees, on the championship croquet layout and on the wraparound porch overlooking it all. The main yellow building holds 24 guest rooms, most recently renovated with heat and full baths; furnishings remain simple yet comfortable. Seven more rooms and two suites are offered in two guest houses and the Cole Cottage. Available for longer stays are thirteen housekeeping cottages with living rooms, franklin stoves or stone fireplaces and decks, and two guest houses. Besides croquet, boating and tennis are offered, and the hardy can swim from the dock in Somes Sound.

Every table in the inn's dining room enjoys a water view. Arrive early for drinks on the decks surrounding the Boathouse (which also offers sandwiches and salads for lunch). The short dinner menu ranges from pan-seared yellowfin tuna and soy-seared darne of salmon to duck breast and grilled sirloin steak. Typical starters are smoked salmon torta and grill-roasted oysters. Homemade desserts include cheesecake and lemon ice with Claremont cookies.

207) 244-5036 or (800) 244-5036. Fax (207) 244-3512. www.theclaremonthotel.com. Thirty-one rooms, two suites and thirteen cottages with private baths. Doubles, $229 to $245 MAP, $175 B&B. Cottages, $180 to $250 EP, three-night minimum. Closed mid-October to Memorial Day.
Entrées, $20 to $24. Lunch at the Boathouse, noon to 2, July and August. Dinner nightly, 6 to 9, late June through Labor Day. No credit cards.

Small Inns and B&Bs

The Inn at Bay Ledge, 1385 Sand Point Road, Bar Harbor 04609.

Away from the fray, this rural hideaway overlooks Frenchman Bay from a perch on a cliff. Jack and Jeani Ochtera offer king or queen featherbeds in seven guest rooms, three with jacuzzis. All have picture windows or french doors and balconies yielding vistas of the bay. A veranda full of Bar Harbor wicker and an expansive deck stretch along the back of the inn overlooking the water. Here are umbrellaed tables and twig chairs where you may read and relax at this, a truly relaxing place. A small swimming pool and a whirlpool are on a lower level of the deck. Rolling lawns and gardens lead to a sheer cliff, where a staircase descends to the stony beach. The inn's main floor contains a sauna and steam shower, a living room decorated with Jeani's baskets and a sun porch where she offers a lavish breakfast of, perhaps, smoked turkey hash, blueberry buckle or cheese strata. Farewell boxes of Bay Ledge candies are given to guests upon departure. The inn also offers three cottages, all stylishly redone in wicker and oak, hidden in the trees across the road. Next to the inn is the two-bedroom Summer House, which has an expansive deck 25 feet from the shore and rents by the week.

(207) 288-4204. Fax (207) 288-5573. www.innatbayledge.com. Seven rooms and three cottages with private baths. Doubles, $180 to $375. Cottages, $160 to $185. Summer House, $2,500 to $3,000 weekly. Closed November-April.

The Bass Cottage Inn, 14 The Field, Box 242, Bar Harbor 04609.

Stylish accommodations and gourmet breakfasts are the hallmarks of this deluxe B&B, grandly reborn in 2004 after a year's renovations. Teri and Jeffrey Anderholm offer an uncommon amount of common space and ten spacious guest rooms, all suavely decorated by Teri in her vision of "grand cottage style." Antiques and 19th-century architectural elements blend comfortably with light colors, stunning art and contemporary amenities for a refined 21st-century look. Rooms on four floors vary from a queen bedroom with a fireplace on the main floor to a skylit "penthouse retreat" in the old attic with a kingsize bed, whirlpool tub and separate shower. The largest is a second-floor corner room with kingsize poster bed, a white chaise lounge beside the fireplace and a whirlpool tub for two. Five rooms have partial water views. All have TV/DVDs, telephones, Poland Spring bottled water and abundant toiletries. The main-floor common areas include a rattan-furnished front atrium/sun porch, a large parlor that doubles as a library and music room with a baby grand piano, a clubby lounge and a well-stocked guest pantry off the professional kitchen. The dining room section of the wraparound sun porch is the setting for a breakfast to remember. Egg and crab strata was featured the morning of our visit. Complimentary wine and hors d'oeuvres are offered in the afternoon.

(207) 288-4234 or (866) 782-9224. www.basscottage.com. Ten rooms with private baths. Doubles, $225 to $340, off-season $185 to $275. Closed mid-December to mid-May.

Ullikana Bed & Breakfast, 16 The Field, Bar Harbor 04609.

Tucked away in the trees between the Bar Harbor Inn and "the field," a meadow of wildflowers, is this substantial, Tudor-style cottage built in 1885. Transplanted New Yorkers Roy Kasindorf and his Quebec-born wife, Hélène Harton, have imbued it with a warm, easygoing personality. Ten bedrooms in the main house hold lots of chintz, wicker, good artworks and antiques. Some come with balconies, fireplaces or both. We were happily ensconced in the second-floor Room 5, a majestic space outfitted in country French provincial fabrics with king bed, two wing chairs in front of the fireplace and a water-view balcony upon which to relax and watch the passing parade. The main floor harbors a wicker-furnished parlor with lots to look at. It's the site for a convivial wine and cheese hour in the late afternoon. Breakfasts are an event, served in the dining room or outside on a pleasant terrace with a glimpse of the water. Roy is the waiter and raconteur, doling out – in our case – cantaloupe with mint sauce, superior cinnamon-raisin muffins with orange glaze, and puff pancakes yielding blueberries and raspberries. Lately the couple added six more guest rooms – lighter and more airy in the style of a simple summer home – in the Yellow House across the street.

(207) 288-9552. Fax (207) 288-3682. www.ullikana.com. Sixteen rooms with private baths. Doubles, $165 to $305, off-season $125 to $240. Closed November-April.

Balance Rock Inn, 21 Albert Meadow, Bar Harbor 04609.

Facing the ocean across a pool and an acre of lawns and gardens, this century-old mansion has evolved from a B&B into an urbane small hotel. It's run by the owner of the rather glitzy Ledgelawn Inn in town. The glitz continues here with double whirlpool tubs, steam baths, a gym and health club, and a small poolside Veranda Bar featuring cigars as well as drinks. "Definitely the fanciest place to stay in Bar Harbor – no question about it," claims owner Michael Miles, who made it so. The gray-shingled mansion contains thirteen guest rooms, all but three with water views. A $700,000 wing with an elevator holds three sumptuous suites. Rooms with reproduction furniture include king or queen beds, twelve working fireplaces, fancy wing chairs, TV/VCRs, and a few private decks. A third-floor hideaway has a sauna overlooking the ocean and, up a boat ladder, a private rooftop deck. An elaborate buffet draws early-risers to a cozy breakfast room with six tables. In summer, most take it on trays to the terrace beside the pool.

207) 288-2610 or (800) 753-0494. Fax (207) 288-2610. www.barharborvacations.com. Thirteen rooms and three suites. July and August: doubles $255 to $525, suites $495 to $625. Off-season: doubles $115 to $425, suites $195 to $595. Closed November-April.

Bar Harbor Tides B&B, 119 West St., Bar Harbor 04609.

This in-town, 1887 Greek Revival mansion beside Frenchman Bay has only four guest quarters, but what quarters they are! Three suites each have an oceanfront bedroom with kingsize bed and a sitting room with TV. Two on the second floor have fireplaces. We stayed in the master suite where the massive four-poster bed looks onto the water through a picture window and the ample bath has a clawfoot tub and oversize shower. Every room in the Ocean Suite has a water view, even the bathroom; other attributes are a tiny balcony and a living room of Victorian oak. The third-floor Captain's Suite has the best view of the bay. Common areas include a fabulous wraparound veranda, complete with its own fireplace, where afternoon refreshments are offered. Guests also have use of a formal living room and an upstairs sitting room with a huge sofa in front of a fireplace. Owners Ray and Loretta Harris serve elaborate breakfasts amid much linen, crystal and silver. Cheese blintzes with strawberries and vegetable omelets might be the fare. The one-and-a-half-acre property, with lovely rolling green lawns and landscaped with old lilac trees and Japanese maples, has 150 feet of bay frontage.

(207) 288-4968. www.barharbortides.com. One room and three suites with private baths. Double, $225. Suites, $375 to $395. Off-season, $225 to $275. Two-night minimum.

Manor House Inn, 106 West St., Bar Harbor 04609.

Listed on the National Register, this striking mustard yellow 1877 Victorian mansion with green trim occupies a prime residential location across from the old Bar Harbor Club. Innkeepers Stacey and Ken Smith offer ten comfortable guest rooms and suites in the main house, three in a rear chauffeur's cottage and two in small gingerbread cottages at the side of the property. All have queen or kingsize beds, seven have fireplaces and a few have whirlpool tubs. The main house is outfitted with colorful Victorian wallpapers, period antiques and a decidedly Victorian theme. Each of the romantic, rustically elegant cottages with bow windows has rattan furniture, a corner gas fireplace, TV and a front deck. The new Acadia Cottage contains three luxury rooms with queen beds, gas fireplaces, whirlpool tubs, TV and wet bars. A full buffet breakfast, including a main dish like quiche or eggs florentine, is offered in the formal dining room. Guests enjoy a fireplaced parlor with grand piano and a wraparound porch with a neat wicker swing on the side, overlooking an acre of elaborately landscaped grounds.

(207) 288-3759 or (800) 437-0088. Fax (207) 288-2974. www.barharbormanorhouse.com. Eighteen rooms and suites with private baths. Doubles, $135 to $235 late June to Labor Day, $77 to $200 off-season. Closed November to mid-April.

Grey Rock Inn, Harbourside Road, Northeast Harbor 04662.

Remarkable gardens greet visitors to this venerable B&B, said to have been a gathering place for Northeast Harbor socialites after it was built in 1910 as a private residence. Inside the inviting large fieldstone and shingled mansion is a veritable showcase for British owner Janet Millet's decorating tastes: an array of wicker like you've never seen, fans and paintings from the Orient, fringed lamps and masses of exotic flowers. Wicker serves as furniture and art, from table lamps to loveseats, from desk to plant stand. Guest rooms are equally exotic. The huge main-floor corner room with canopied four-poster bed, oriental screen and private balcony could not be more romantic. The upstairs rooms are lacy, frilly and flowery, with much pale pink and green, all kinds of embroidered towels, and porches all around. Some have fireplaces, and all have views of the trees or gardens on this wooded hilltop above and back from the road. Assisted by sons Adam and Karl, Janet serves a continental-plus breakfast, including a fruit compote with eight to ten kinds of fresh fruit, assorted baked goods and bacon, occasionally eggs, and what she states is "a good cup of coffee for a British lady."

(207) 276-9360. Fax (207) 276-9894. www.greyrockinn.com. Seven rooms and one suite with private baths. Doubles, $185 to $375 July-October, $110 to $275 mid-May through June. Closed November to mid-May.

Lindenwood Inn, 118 Clark Point Road, Box 1328, Southwest Harbor 04679.

Towering linden trees shade this turn-of-the-century sea captain's home, grandly refurbished by owner Jim King. Call it different, call it eclectic, call it cosmopolitan. With a decorator's eye and international tastes, Jim positioned Lindenwood to be "in the vanguard of the new look." You'll find palm trees on the front veranda, Italian chairs and glass tables in a dining area, a collection of shells and stones in each bedroom, sleek black modern lights, potted cactus plants on the tables, and pottery from Mexico and Indonesia here, a contemporary mission bed there. Upstairs are eight guest quarters of varying sizes, several with fireplaces and six with private decks with ocean views. The ultimate is the penthouse suite with a curved sofa and gas fireplace, opening onto an enormous rooftop deck holding an oversize spa. We stayed in the poolside bungalow, with a TV and gas fireplace in the cathedral-ceilinged living room, an efficiency kitchen and a queensize bedroom. Just outside was a heated gunite pool and a separate spa topped by a sculptured mask spraying a stream of water. Elaborate breakfasts, perhaps herbed omelets or fruit crêpes, are served in the main dining room furnished in what Jim calls "tropical primitive."

(207) 244-5335 or (800) 307-5335. Fax (207) 244-3643. www.lindenwoodinn.com. Four rooms, three suites and one cottage with private baths. Doubles, $105 to $275 mid-June to mid-October, $95 to $225 off-season. Closed mid-December to mid-March.

The Kingsleigh Inn, 373 Main St., Box 1426, Southwest Harbor 04679.

A wraparound porch full of wicker and colorful pillows embellishes this B&B with glimpses of water in the distance. Taking over the B&B in which Lindenwood Inn owner Jim King got his start (and left his name), Dana and Greg Moos redecorated the common rooms with an eclectic mix of antiques and contemporary furnishings. More antiques and artworks enhance the eight bedrooms, many with harbor views. One has a balcony with chairs overlooking the water, and another a deck. The Turret Suite on the third floor offers a kingsize poster bed, fireplace, television and a great view from a telescope placed on a tripod between two cozy wicker chairs. Port wine and homemade truffles are in each room. Afternoon tea and homemade cookies are served on the porch or in cool weather by the fireplace. Breakfast by candlelight, considered by Dana "a special occasion," is taken at tables for two in the dining room. Her repertoire includes individual egg soufflés with roasted red pepper sauce, baked eggs in ham crisps and bananas foster-stuffed french toast.

(207) 244-5302. Fax (207) 244-0349. www.kingsleighinn.com. Seven rooms and one suite with private baths. Mid-June to mid-October: doubles $135 to $165, suite $260. Rest of year: doubles $110 to $130, suite $175.

Harbour Cottage Inn, 9 Dirigo Road, Box 258, Southwest Harbor 04679.

Perched atop Dirigo Hill with a view of the harbor in the distance, this restored B&B dates to 1852 when it was built as an annex to the island's first summer hotel. Owners Don Jalbert and Javier Montesinos lend an international flair to their seven queensize or kingsize bedrooms and a pair of two-bedroom suites. All are bright and airy, stylishly decorated in generally bold colors. All except one have jacuzzi tubs or steam showers. TVs, telephones and data ports are standard. Adjacent to the inn is the Southwester, a three-bedroom house with a great sundeck and full facilities. Another deck enhances the Carriage House, a fireplaced cottage with kitchen. Guests are partial to the breakfast pizzas and blueberry-stuffed french toast, served in the dining room or on the porch. The partners also operate four rental units known as Pier One on the harbor.

(207) 244-5738 or (888) 843-3022. Fax (207) 244-5731. www.harbourcottageinn.com. Seven rooms, two suites and two cottages with private baths. Doubles, $149 to $159 in summer, $110 to $120 off-season. Suites and cottages $199 to $245 summer, $135 to $165 off-season. Closed November-March.

Budget Choices

The Moorings Inn & Cottages, Shore Road, Southwest Harbor 04679.

Calling itself the "Little Norway of America," the Moorings claims one of the island's more dazzling locations at the entrance to Somes Sound in Manset, not far from Southwest Harbor and next to the famed Hinckley boatyards. It's a quirky, down-home, old-fashioned place with ten bedrooms, all named for sailing ships built in Maine. The complex also has three rooms with decks, refrigerators and microwaves in a motel wing out back, the two-bedroom Pilot House and three efficiencies in the Lookout Cottage. Five of the upstairs inn rooms offer waterfront balconies, and the view from the end motel unit is billed as "probably the finest on the coast." We called our inn room the Agatha Christie, as several of her paperbacks were on the bureau, and a candle rested in a china holder beside the bed. Towels are large and fluffy and the mostly double or twin beds bear colorful patterned sheets. The fireplace glows on cool summer mornings in the inn's living room, which has a color TV and abundant books and magazines. The coffee pot is on all day in the inn's office, where complimentary orange juice and donuts are served in the morning. Longtime owners Leslie and Betty King have turned over day-to-day operations to son Storey, who runs a tour boat service, and his wife Candy. They provide charcoal for the grills beside the shore, a spectacular place to cook your steak or seafood dinner. You can rent canoes, rowboats and sailboats, and borrow clamming equipment. The beach is stony; the water cold but swimmable. The Moorings is most unpretentious and the prices are, too.

(207) 244-5523 or (800) 596-5523. www.mooringsinn.com. Ten rooms and four cottage units with private baths. July to mid-September: doubles $87 to $120, cottages $105 to $150. Rest of year: doubles $60 to $100, cottages $95 to $135.

Anne's White Columns Inn, 57 Mount Desert St., Bar Harbor 04609.

Bar Harbor's early "guest house row" acquired yet another when a Christian

Science church was converted into as contemporary a Victorian B&B as you could find. The ten spacious guest rooms have modern baths, queensize beds and cable TVs; three on the second floor come with private balconies. Wine and cheese are served in the fireplaced parlor, where a buffet breakfast including three kinds of cereal is put out in the morning. Owner Anne Bahr blends her own hazelnut coffee.

(207) 288-5357 or (800) 321-6379. www.anneswhitecolumns.com. Ten rooms with private baths. Doubles, $100 to $150, off-season $75 to $135. Closed December-April.

Island Watch, 73 Freeman Ridge Road, Southwest Harbor 04679.

Floor-to-ceiling windows and a couple of spacious decks take full advantage of the panoramic view of islands and water at this stunning contemporary ranch house atop a high ridge west of town. Maxine Clark rents six homey guest rooms (one a single), plus an efficiency suite for longer rentals in a separate building. Guests enjoy TV and stereo in the spacious living/dining room, where breakfast is served in the morning. We managed to rouse ourselves from the great rear deck long enough to enjoy Maxine's french toast with ricotta stuffing and strawberry-raspberry sauce at a festive table in the dining room. There's a greenhouse at the end of the dining room so folks can enjoy both breakfast and plants with an island view.

(207) 244-7229. www.islandwatch.info. Six rooms and one suite with private baths. Doubles, $95 in summer, $85 off-season. Two-night minimum required. Closed late October to late May.

Where to Eat

When you think of eating in Bar Harbor, you think of lobsters. But Bar Harbor isn't all lobster, nor are all the restaurants in Bar Harbor.

Lobster Pounds

The cheapest lobsters are at the tiny shacks lining Route 3 on the way onto the island from Ellsworth. Large signs tell what the going price is, and most have picnic tables where you can dig in. Considered the best is **Trenton Bridge Lobster Pound** at 1237 Bar Harbor Road, (207) 667-2977, a rustic, family-owned affair with dining inside and out beside the Narrows between Frenchman and Western bays. Lobster is served here all day except Sunday from 8:30 to 8, Memorial Day to mid-October.

Abel's Lobster Pound, Route 103, Mount Desert.

This widely promoted icon is favored by traditionalists (and reviewers) who remember it as a simple, outdoors-oriented place in the evergreens beside Somes Sound. Something was lost when it enlarged the indoor dining facility, added a bar and waitress service, catered to the hordes and lost the rustic outdoor feeling – the waterfront views marred by industrial-looking boatyard ventures beside. There are a few non-seafood choices, but lobster is clearly the specialty. Six versions of lobster dinner, served with rolls and baked potato or french fries, range from $22 for a one-pounder to $37 for a biggie with steamed clams. Blueberry pie is the favored dessert.

(207) 276-5827. Entrées, $18 to $27. Lunch daily, noon to 4. Dinner, noon to 9.

Thurston's Lobster Pound, Steamboat Wharf Road, Bernard.

From the canopied upstairs deck, you can look below onto Thurston's Wharf and see where the lobstermen keep their traps. This is a real working lobster wharf beside picturesque Bass Harbor. And if you couldn't tell from all the pickup trucks parked along the road, one taste of the lobster will convince you. You can get a lobster dinner for $9.75 to $10.75 a pound, plus $4.75 for extras like corn on the cob, coleslaw, a roll and blueberry cake. We also sampled the chock-full lobster stew, a really good potato salad, steamers and mussels and, at our latest visit, a fabulous crab cake but a not so fabulous scallop chowder. You place your order at the counter, wait for one of the tables on the covered deck above or on the open deck below, and settle down with a bottle of beer or wine (from a choice selection). Little wonder that the island lobster cognoscenti consider this place the best around.

(207) 244-7600. Open daily, 11 to 8:30. Closed October to Memorial Day.

Head of the Harbor Restaurant, 433 Main Street, Southwest Harbor.
Lobsters are steaming and steaks are grilling outside at the entrance as you place your order at a side window. Waitresses deliver meals to picnic tables on an expansive canopied deck or two multi-windowed dining rooms looking down toward Somes Sound. Although you can get all the usual suspects, you'll also find sautéed crab cakes, chargrilled salmon, fried chicken tenders ("'cause not everyone wants seafood"), Italian dinners (chicken or scallops parmigiana) and sirloin steak. Blueberry pie and root-beer float are the favored desserts. The food is affordable and adequate, and the setting is good for families.

(207) 244-3508. Entrées, $9.99 to $17.99. Open daily, 11:30 to 9, late June to Columbus Day.

Beal's Lobster Pier, 182 Clark Point Road, Southwest Harbor.
Things are more rustic here beside the Coast Guard Station, and the feeling is rather commercial. You can eat on the pier at picnic tables, and lobsters, mussels and steamers are sold inside. Lobsters are about $9.95 to $10.95 a pound boiled, but boiling often ends early, between 6:30 and 8. At the casual **Captain's Galley** out front, they had plenty of dessert pastries but were strangely out of most flavors of ice cream when we were last there.

(207) 244-3202. Open daily in season, 9 to 8, to 5 off-season.

Bar Harbor Choices

George's, 7 Stevens Lane, Bar Harbor.
A tradition in Bar Harbor, this Southern-style house hidden off a parking lot behind a bank offers some of the island's more imaginative food in a glamorous setting. When longtime owner George Demas retired, he turned the restaurant over to two of his staff, Adeena and Christopher Fisher. The menu is unusual in that all appetizers are $10 or $12 and all entrées $25. You can graze or order a prix-fixe meal (appetizer, main course and dessert) for $37 to $40. At one dinner, hot crusty French bread and the best little Greek salads ever preceded the entrées, distinctive smoked scallops on fettuccine and a special of shrimp on a fresh tomato sauce with feta cheese, rice pilaf and New Zealand spinach with orange juice and orange zest. Most recently, we loved the appetizer of salmon quesadilla, the lobster strudel and a special of elk medallions. Desserts range from chilled champagne sabayon with figs to peach crème brûlée.

(207) 288-4505. www.georgesbarharbor.com. Entrées, $25. Dinner nightly, 5:30 to 10. Open late May through October.

Thrumcap, 123 Cottage St., Bar Harbor.
The Porcupine Grill gave way to this with-it café and wine bar – same owner, but new concept. Proprietor Tom Marinke said he had tired of eating large, formal meals

at hefty prices and figured his clientele had, too. He changed the name, made more casual the ambiance, and offered a prix-fixe menu "of smaller courses and more of them." The four-course menu with multiple choices might begin with a watercress and mahogany clam bisque or a green salad with pears and manchego croutons. The next course could be fried oysters with creamed spinach, a roasted beet and feta tart or a salad of pheasant confit, endive and fiddleheads. Third courses range from pan-roasted lobster fricassee with corn and mushroom flan to grilled flatiron steak with burgundy reduction. For dessert, go for the sublime peach ice cream and ginger shortbread if they're on the docket. Up to 40 wines are offered by the glass or flight, or you can select your own from the 1,000-bottle exhibition wine room. The name, incidentally, comes from Thrumcap Island, a small island adjacent to the Porcupine Islands for which the grill was named.

(207) 288-3884. Prix-fixe, $39. Dinner nightly from 6, July-October; weekends, rest of year. Closed March and April.

Havana, 318 Main St., Bar Harbor.

Innovative, Latin-inspired fare is served in stylish surroundings at this sophisticated establishment, where white-clothed tables tone down mandarin red walls that glow in the candlelight. Typical appetizers are shrimp stuffed with jícama and coconut and a succulent crab and roasted corn cake served with red pepper purée and cilantro sour cream. Winning main dishes run from sweet and sour tuna and shrimp with jalapeños and poblano peppers in a ginger-coconut sauce to pork medallions sautéed in bourbon and served with saffron rice and grilled zucchini. The filet mignon is finished with chimichurri sauce, topped with blue cheese and served with chorizo sausage. Typical desserts are guava mousse in a chocolate-dipped waffle cone and a mango and tuaca chocolate truffle torte.

(207) 288-2822. www.havanamaine.com. Entrées, $16 to $25. Dinner nightly, 5 to 10..

Café This Way, 14 Mount Desert St., Bar Harbor.

The food is first-rate and the interior somewhat theatrical at this pleasant, laid-back café down a side street with a sign pointing the way. Local chefs Julie Harris and Julie Berberian from Bar Harbor's former Fin Back Restaurant and partner Susanne Hathaway turned the old Unusual Cabaret dinner theater space into a casual mélange of tables and bookcases surrounding a circle of sofas in the center. But for the theater lights overhead, the dining area looks like a large living room. The contemporary menu features seafood, as in entrées of lemon vodka lobster served over fettuccine, grilled tuna with sautéed apples and smoked shrimp, and crab cakes with tequila-lime sauce. Several main dishes also are available as appetizers on the mix-and-match menu. Folks rave about the salads, perhaps watercress, caesar or baby spinach with grated asiago cheese and prosciutto, or warmed endive with grilled shrimp over greens with citrus vinaigrette. Chocolate turns up in most of the desserts. Some of the best and most reasonable breakfasts in Bar Harbor are offered here.

(207) 288-4483. www.cafethisway.com. Entrées, $16 to $22. Breakfast, Monday-Saturday 7 to 11, Sunday 8 to 1. Dinner nightly, 6 to 9. Closed November to mid-April.

McKay's Public House, 231 Main St., Bar Harbor.

A lovely gravel patio and front porch draw diners to this homey new restaurant in a house moved from the site of the new Bar Harbor Grand Hotel and bearing quite a history. Ask your server to tell you some of its past as you consider whether to have pub fare or go full bore, knowing that the prices won't break the bank. The former yields things like bangers and mash, shepherd's pie, corned beef and cabbage and a lamb burger. The dinner menu typically offers porcini-encrusted halibut, crispy duck breast with a champagne-curry sauce, bistro steak and the signature rack of lamb. Shrimp bruschetta and mussels steamed in coconut-curry broth make good starters.

(207) 288-2002. Entrées, $15.95 to $21.95. Lunch in summer, 11:30 to 3. Dinner nightly, 5 to 10.

124 Cottage Street, 124 Cottage St., Bar Harbor.
"Downeast fare, creatively prepared" is the theme of this restaurant, one of Bar Harbor's most popular. The crowded scene and the 50-item gourmet salad bar attract many. You'll likely wait for a table in the rear courtyard or on the enclosed front porch, even on weeknights, but a new lounge may mitigate any delays. The extensive, something-for-everyone regional/continental menu specializes in seafood (including bouillabaisse and four versions of shrimp), pastas and such house favorites as haddock amandine, tamari-ginger scallops, Mediterranean chicken and New York sirloin. The appetizer cheesecake, served with fruit and crostini, is a favorite appetizer. Sweet finales include double chocolate fudge cake, varying cheesecakes, roulades and crème brûlée.

(207) 288-4383. www.124cottagestreet.com. Entrées, $19 to $28. Dinner nightly, from 5. Sunday jazz brunch, 9 to noon. Closed November and March-April.

Galyn's, 17 Main St., Bar Harbor.
You can watch half the world go by from four white-clothed tables on the tiny front porch beside the sidewalk or catch a view of the harbor from the glassed-in upstairs room in the rear of this establishment sandwiched between storefronts a half block from the pier. Seafood is the specialty, outside or in several nautical dining rooms, and lunch is said to be particularly good here. The food is a cut above most restaurants of its ilk: fresh fish specials like pan-baked tuna, plus bouillabaisse, Mediterranean scallops, mixed seafood grill, peppercorn chicken, slow-roasted prime rib and filet mignon. Lobster bisque, shrimp and scallop skewer, dijon mussels and lobster cocktail are among starters. Dessert could be truffle mousse cake, Mississippi mud pie or blueberry-apple crisp. Light fare is offered at the mahogany bar in the **Galley Lounge,** where you might find live jazz on Saturday or Sunday night.

(207) 288-9706. Entrées, $14 to $22. Lunch daily, 11:30 to 2:30. Dinner nightly, 4 to 10. Closed December-February.

The Parkside, 185 Main St., Bar Harbor.
Seemingly every table gets a view and every diner seems to be on display to passersby at this aptly named, Victorian-styled restaurant across from the village green. There are shady outside patios, tables by full-length windows inside and even a second-story deck. Come here for lunch, when you'll find a crab melt, lobster roll and french dip sandwich. Burgers start at $4.50 and a lobster roll goes for $10.95. Assorted lobster dinners were featured the noontime we stopped by. The dinner menu gets a bit more innovative: almond-crusted salmon fillet with champagne beurre blanc and rack of lamb with cilantro-mint chutney. You can get a traditional shore dinner, or splurge for filet mignon with béarnaise sauce.

(207) 288-3700. Entrées, $16.95 to $24.95. Lunch daily, 11 to 3. Dinner nightly, 5 to 10. Closed November-April.

Around the Island

The Burning Tree, Route 3, Otter Creek.

A long screened front porch and a couple of small dining rooms cast a summer-cottage feel to this "pure" restaurant in a rural setting, off the beaten path between Bar Harbor and Northeast Harbor. Those in the know beat a path to the front door for what chef-owners Allison Martin and Elmer Beal Jr. call gourmet seafood with organic produce and a vegetarian sideline. The seafood ranges from basic (as in oven-poached codfish in a seafood wine broth) to lofty (pan-seared yellowfin tuna over lemony blue-cheese croustades). Our party was impressed with starters of mussels with mustard sauce, grilled scallops and an excellent vegetarian sushi. The cioppino was so highly rated that two of us ordered it. The others chose baked monkfish with clams and artichokes on saffron orzo and the cajun crab and lobster au gratin, a fixture on the menu. The garden out back provides vegetables and herbs, and Elmer buys his fish direct from the boat. Strawberry pie, nectarine mousse cake and a rich chocolate-kahlua cheesecake finish off an entirely satisfying meal.

(207) 288-9331. Entrées, $19.50 to $23.75. Dinner nightly except Tuesday, 5 to 10. Open mid-June to mid-October.

⌐ Tea and Tradition ─────────────────────

Jordan Pond House, Park Loop Road, Acadia National Park.

Tea on the lawn at this landmark in the national park is a Bar Harbor tradition. Green lawns sloping down to Jordan Pond and the Bubbles mountains in the background are the spectacular backdrop for a steady stream of visitors who start arriving at 2:30 for tea (two popovers with butter and strawberry preserves, $7) and, more recently, cappuccino and popovers ($8) and Oregon chai and popovers ($8.25). The restaurant itself is contemporary with cathedral ceilings, huge windows and open porches onto the lawn. Dinners feature grilled salmon, baked haddock, crab cakes with green onion sauce, prime rib and, of course, steamed lobster. Most of the menu is available day and night, meaning you can come anytime for a lobster roll, crab and havarti quiche or sirloin steak. For lunch on the porch, the seafood pasta and curried chicken salad proved satisfying. Don't try to fill up on the popover – it's huge, but hollow.

(207) 276-3316. www.jordanpond.com. Entrées, $14 to $20. Lunch daily, 11:30 to 2:30. Tea on the lawn, 11:30 to 5:30. Dinner nightly, 5:30 to 8 or 9. Closed mid-October to mid-May.

La Matta Cena, 5 Firehouse Lane, Northeast Harbor.

Spirited Tuscan cuisine is the theme of this jolly newcomer that debuted in 2004 in a former beauty shop. The rehabbed interior is done in rustic trattoria style, but the dining venue of choice in season is the leafy umbrellaed patio. Proprietor Cheryl Shields named the place for the Tuscan village medieval midnight potluck feast translated as "the mad supper." Here she recreates the vibrancy and conviviality of the custom with an array of robust crostini platters, best ordered in combinations of six or nine. Otherwise, look for appetizers like haddock cakes with sundried tomato-caper rémoulade or grilled portobello mushroom layered with mozzarella. Main courses could be pan-seared salmon with purple basil jelly, lavender-rubbed chicken or filet mignon prepared with bay salt and oregano-pine nut compound butter.

(207) 276-3305. Entrées, $23 to $27. Lunch daily, noon to 3. Dinner nightly, 5:30 to 9 or 9:30.

151 Main St., 151 Main St., Northeast Harbor.

Occupying a site that has seen many a restaurant, this venture's setting is as simple as its name. Dining is dark and intimate at small bistro tables with a bar in back. The extensive, Mediterranean-inspired menu offers thin-crust pizzas, house-made pastas and quite a selection of small plates and large plates in the contemporary idiom. You might start with peekytoe crab cakes with citrus aioli, mussels roasted in the brick oven or the trio of house-smoked salmon, scallops and mussels, served with three sauces. Large plates range from pork and beef meatloaf and chicken piccata to bouillabaisse and rack of lamb. The chef's award-winning catfish roulade is stuffed with a crab cake and served over mixed greens with jasmine rice.

(207) 276-9898. Entrées, $14 to $22. Dinner, Tuesday-Saturday from 5. Closed mid-December to March.

Red Sky, 14 Clark Point Road, Southwest Harbor.

Red sky at night, sailor's delight. Red sky in morning…"we don't serve breakfast," says James Lindquist, owner of this new restaurant that shines at night with delightful dinners. Folks sit at the deep bar made from a tree in Camden as well as at white-clothed tables to enjoy a panoply of changing contemporary treats. You might start with an appetizer like Maine sea scallops sautéed with tequila and lime juice, served with an avocado puree; Maine shrimp dumplings with tamari-ginger sauce, or lollipop lamb chops dusted with bitter chocolate and sweet mint. Main courses run from panko-crusted halibut to dry-aged New York strip steak with a tamarind and roasted jalapeño steak sauce. Lobster risotto with green and white asparagus and porcini mushrooms is a signature dish. Finish with a cheese course, four kinds served with fruit. Or sample desserts like belgian bittersweet chocolate pudding, sour lemon tart with strawberry sauce and raspberries, or the Red Sky's ice cream sandwich with belgian chocolate and madagascar vanilla bean ice cream.

(207) 244-0476. Entrées, $19 to $27. Dinner, Monday-Saturday 5:30 to 10.

Fiddlers' Green, 411 Main St., Southwest Harbor.

Chef Derek Wilber, son of a local boat builder, gutted an aging family eatery to create a stylish restaurant with windows onto the ocean and a side deck. A short menu itemizes changing choices in the new regional idiom. To start, sample a blueberry martini among the twenty or so choices from the martini bar. Pair it with treats from the cold seafood bar, perhaps lobster timbale or sashimi martini or the Elysian sampler of several. Main courses could be wok-fried salmon and crab with a citrus-peanut sauce, bacon-wrapped saddle of rabbit, steak frites or venison chops with a black cherry-port wine sauce. Pheasant, elk and rabbit are offered in game season. Typical desserts are honey-mango crème brûlée, cream puffs and maple-nut tart.

(207) 244-9416. www.fiddlersgreenrestaurant.com. Entrées, $18 to $26. Dinner, Tuesday-Sunday from 5:30; Thursday-Saturday in off-season, 5:30 to 9. Closed January-April.

Seaweed Café, 146 Seawall Road, Manset.

"Natural seacoast cuisine" is featured at this diminutive newcomer, tucked away in a charming Cape Cod-style house in the Manset section of Southwest Harbor. Chef-owner Bill Morrison, whose fare we first sampled at the Lindenwood Inn when it was serving dinner, specializes in the fare of "Asian islands – Japan, Hawaii, Thailand" – as well as China. From an open kitchen comes a changing array of flavorful fare. Sample the signature Japanese maki sushi rolls, perhaps crab with cilantro and lobster with avocado, or the Thai mussels steamed in sake. You can make a meal of the dinner chowder or seafood stew. Or indulge in tuna steak au poivre with wasabi béarnaise or five-spiced duck with grand marnier and green peppercorn demi-glace. Bourbon ice cream with chocolate biscotti and a strawberry tart with mascarpone are refreshing counterpoints to such assertive dinner flavors.

(207) 244-0572. Entrées, $15 to $23. Dinner nightly in summer, 6 to 9; Tuesday-Saturday in off-season. Closed mid-February to spring. BYOB. No credit cards.

Nautilus Restaurant, Route 102A, Bass Harbor.

This summery place bears a new look and vibrancy under the tutelage of a most unlikely proprietress – a Texan who coaches the Harvard debate team during the academic year and looked for "something creative" to do in the summer. Sherry Hall found it in her reincarnation of the former Keenan's seafood restaurant/shack where Route 102A meets Flat Iron Road at "the Triangle" in Bass Harbor. The shack look has given way to an arty tropical scene that her sister-in-law painted on the walls and ceiling of the screened porch, the dining venue of choice (even though the cozy interior has been spruced up). Sherry gives Southwest, tropical and Italian accents to Maine ingredients to produce a memorable meal. Lunch here on a spicy Nogales chicken soup, a dainty scallop taco and a fabulous lobster quesadilla and you'll probably come back for more. The smoked chicken quesadilla recommended as an encore was equally arresting, and the lemon crème brûlée was masterful. These were from the cantina menu. We'd happily return for dinner to try the Down East ceviche or the Southwest sampler to start, and the lobster risotto or the grilled mojito chicken for the main event. The Maine lobster comes two ways: grilled with chile butter, or baked and stuffed with crab, both accompanied by grilled corn and roasted red potatoes. Try which ever – there's no debate, this cook knows her stuff.

(207) 244-0699. www.nautilusrestaurant.com. Entrées. $19 to $28. Cantina menu, Tuesday-Sunday noon to 4. Dinner, Tuesday-Sunday from 5:30.

──*Dining, Plus...*──

The Deck House Restaurant & Cabaret Theater, 11 Apple Lane, Southwest Harbor.

An island tradition since 1970 at Bass Harbor, this moved to grand new quarters upstairs in the loft of an old canning factory in the Hinckley Great Harbor Marina complex in Southwest Harbor. It's a much larger and more substantial venue for cabaret theater presented, as always, by the singing wait staff. The dining room opens at 6:30 for dinner. The menu is as extensive as any in the area, and all the entrées are priced the same, from Maine lobster to prime rib and from pecan-crusted halibut to tenderloin steak chasseur. At 8:15, the servers become players, singing solos, duets, quartets and ensemble numbers in the round. No customer is more than four tables from the action. The emphasis is on Broadway show tunes, but barbershop quartet, mime numbers and dance also have been featured. Some attendees consider the event the highlight of their visit to Down East Maine.

(207) 244-5044. www.thedeckhouse.com. Entrées, $21.95. Dinner nightly, from 6:30; show at 8:15. Open mid-June to mid-September.

FOR MORE INFORMATION: Bar Harbor Chamber of Commerce, 93 Cottage St., Box 158, Bar Harbor, ME 04609, (207) 288-5103 or (800) 288-5103. www.barharbormaine.com.
Southwest Harbor/Tremont Chamber of Commerce, Route 102 at Seal Cove Road, Box 1143, Southwest Harbor 04679, (207) 244-9264 or (800) 423-9264. www.acadia.net/swhtrcoc.

Moosehead Lake, Me.
The Great North Woods Experience

The drive through interior Maine on Route 6 and 15, the only road into the Moosehead Lake region, seems endless. You want to get away, but hey, isn't this a bit much? Suddenly, the road crests atop a hill and now, before you in all its glory, unfolds the majesty of Moosehead, the Northeast's largest lake.

And yes, just ahead lies Greenville (population 2,200), the region's only town of note at the near end of the lake. It's the beginning of the end of the line. On all sides are mountains – small ones, to be sure, but enough to alter the landscape of what to the south had been essentially rolling flatlands. Beyond lies Maine's tallest mountain, Katahdin, and the wilds of Baxter State Park. The sky-blue glacier lake spreads its tentacles like the antlers of a moose head around islands and into coves. Picture an inland sea stretching into a forest of green, Maine's legendary Great North Woods.

The pristine lake, shaped vaguely like a moose head, is 40 miles long and twenty miles across at its widest. It's up to 300 feet deep at the base of the arresting landmark Mount Kineo cliffs, which rise 800 feet straight out of the lake. Most of the 400 miles of shoreline, owned by paper companies more interested in lumber than in resorts, is undeveloped. Forestry and recreation are the area's industries.

A century ago, fashionable visitors arrived in Greenville on a train direct from New York to spend the summer away from the heat and crowds, at grand hotels along the shores of Moosehead Lake. The hotels and railroad are long gone, their place taken by hunters and fishermen who revel in a sportsman's paradise in the North Woods wilderness. Lately, eco-tourism has been on the rise. Increasingly, Moosehead's lure is broadening to embrace nature and wildlife lovers, hikers, rafters and kayakers in summer, and cross-country skiers, downhill skiers and snowmobilers in winter.

A handful of luxury inns provide creature comforts for those who can't bear to get away from everything. True, much of the area remains raw and primeval. But its virgin veneer is leavened by a gentleness that the great lake imparts to the mountains, by a subtle sophistication that evades other north woods destinations.

Moose-watching is a mania, and few visitors leave without spotting at least a couple – front and center during a moose cruise or safari or unexpectedly, as they feed beside the road. The region stages the annual Moosemania, a month of moose-related activities in late spring. Several shops convey a moose theme.

This is the natural state of "the Maine you remember," as the Moosehead Lake Region Chamber of Commerce bills it – the Maine that Maine people remember, that is. For it's the Maine that most others never know, let alone remember. Just you and the moose, and a few others who like to get away from the crowds.

Seeing and Doing

The Sporting Life

Fishing and hunting have traditionally been the leading outdoor activities here, although neither is quite as good in terms of take as in days gone by. "Overkill," explained a Maine Guide matter-of-factly. To compensate, some of the old sporting camps have altered their focus to appeal to nature lovers and wildlife watchers.

Front lawn of Blair Hill Inn yields scenic view of Moosehead Lake.

Myriad opportunities offer the sportsman a variety of game fish. Guides can lead you to salmon and trout on Moosehead Lake or you can venture to a remote pond for a day of fly-fishing for brook trout. Abandoned logging roads give hunters easy access to the uninhabited back country where whitetail deer, partridge and black bears abound.

The nearby Kennebec and Penobscot rivers offer some of the best whitewater rafting in the East.

Although Mount Katahdin beckons nearby at the end of the Appalachian Trail, less ardent hikers enjoy three trails leading up **Mount Kineo** to a renovated fire tower, which yields a panoramic view of Moosehead Lake and environs. One of the prime waterfront spots is occupied by **Lily Bay State Park,** an uncrowded favorite of swimmers, picnickers and campers.

"Come Play the Rock," advertises the **Mount Kineo Golf Course,** (207) 534-9012. For $15, you can play golf on a scenic nine-hole course, built in the 1880s and said to be the second oldest course in New England. The most picturesque hole on the 3,000-yard course is the fourth, 138 yards over water to a green nestled at the base of Mount Kineo.

In winter, skiing at **Big Squaw Mountain,** (207) 695-1000 or (800) 754-6246 is improving under new owners (from Florida, of all places). Just outside Greenville on Route 15 north, Squaw has a triple chairlift, a surface lift, 33 trails and a 1,750-foot vertical rise facing Moosehead Lake. Best of all, there are rarely lift lines. It offers plenty of skiing for a remarkably low $19 for everyone – adults and juniors, on weekdays, weekends, even holidays – except for children under 5 and seniors over 70, who ski free. The slopeside Big Squaw Mountain Motel has 52 rooms that rent for $89 a night in ski season. The ski area is open daily, 9 to 4.

Cross-country skiing also is popular, but tends to get overshadowed by the snowmobilers who make this their noisy base.

Moose Watching

Everyone looks for moose, and local promoters say more moose reside in the Moosehead area than anywhere in the East. You'll likely spot them feeding in ponds and rivers shortly after dawn and just before dusk. They're said to be at their most numerous halfway up the lake around the roads and waterways near Rockwood and Kokadjo. A brochure outlines "moose safari" packages by land, sea and air.

One of the best ways to see moose and understand their habitat is to take the moose cruise offered by the **Birches Resort and Wilderness Expeditions** in Rockwood, (207) 534-7588 or (800) 825-9453. Plush seats accommodate up to sixteen passengers on a 24-foot-long pontoon boat. Moose were spotted on 96 of 100 excursions in the previous summer, resort co-owner Bill Willard advised. We thought we were going to be among the four percent failure rate until, at the end of our two-hour cruise up and down a jungle-like river, a lone moose suddenly obliged up close. "Every trip is different," our laconic boat pilot-guide acknowledged. Two more moose were spotted from a distance on the return trip to the resort. We also encountered two moose along Route 15 on the drive back to Greenville after dinner. Next morning we took a half-hour sightseeing flight, and the pilot pointed out a moose feeding in an inlet. That was it for moose of the live variety on one four-day visit. As we were leaving town on Route 15 south, however, a highway sign warned: "High rate of moose crashes next three miles."

The Birches Resort and Wilderness Expeditions moose cruise departs daily at 7 a.m. from the Birches marina (adults $28, children $15). The "scenic moose safari" at 4 p.m. is a three-hour sightseeing eco trip that concludes with a pass beside the Mount Kineo cliffs (adults $40, children $25). Other Wilderness Expeditions offerings are whitewater rafting on the Penobscot, Kennebec and Dead rivers, guided kayak and mountain bike eco-tours, seaplane rides and guided Jeep eco-tours. The Birches Resort facilities include a restaurant and lounge, a beach, a hot tub, sauna and fitness center. Lodging is in four lodge rooms ($55 to $90 a night), fifteen waterfront log cabins, private vacation homes, rustic cabin tents and wilderness "yurts" along cross-country ski trails. Most takers are sportsmen and families. Except for campers, getaway couples are few and far between.

Sightseeing Trips

AIR ADVENTURES. Almost as much as moose, seaplanes define the Moosehead area, and the sheer numbers of seaplanes taking off and landing on Moosehead convey a different look and feel to the lake. Indeed, the lake is so favored by backwoods pilots that they converge every September on Greenville for the International Seaplane Fly-In, the largest of its kind in the Northeast. Since much of the Moosehead Lake shoreline and many sporting camps are not accessible by road, seaplanes get quickly where motor vehicles and boats cannot.

Two commercial air services, **Currier's Flying Service,** (207) 695-2778, and **Folsom's Flying Service,** (207) 695-2821, offer sightseeing excursions. A half-hour flight around the lower half of the lake with Malcolm Folsom proved a good way to appreciate the vastness of both lake and wilderness.

Other airplane sites may be of interest. The last operating DC-3 seaplane, an ark of an Army Air Force plane fitted with pontoons, is based at Greenville's tiny municipal airport. The curious also may view remnants of the wreckage of a B-52, which crashed due to air turbulence against Elephant Mountain during the Cuban missile crisis in January 1963, killing seven crewmen. Access is via a logging road maintained by Scott Paper Co.

BOAT TRIPS. Another good way to see this area is by boat, and a variety of craft seems to be everywhere for rent or hire around Moosehead and its tributaries. Experience a bygone era with a cruise on the 1914-era **Katahdin,** the last of 50 steamboats that plied the lake, ferrying cargo and people to resorts and sporting camps before cars and trucks reached the area. Upon retirement it became the star floating exhibit of the tiny **Moosehead Marine Museum,** beside the lake at Greenville's municipal parking lot, (207) 695-2716. In summer and foliage season, the diesel-powered Katahdin gives three-hour cruises on the lower third of the lake Tuesday, Thursday, Saturday and Sunday at 12:30; adults $25, children $15. A six-hour cruise up the lake to Mount Kineo, with a stop at the site of the old landmark Kineo House hotel on Kineo Island, departs Wednesdays at 10; adults $31, children $18. A small ship's galley sells hot dogs, candy and the like.

One of the most rewarding, peaceful ways to experience Moosehead Lake is by kayak or canoe. Listen to the cry of the loon as you paddle. Miles of unspoiled shoreline, dozens of islands and secluded beaches invite exploration, picnicking and camping. Campsites on islands and mainland are available on a first-come, first-served basis. Equipment rentals and information are available from **Northwoods Outfitters,** one of Maine's larger sporting goods outfits in downtown Greenville, (207) 695-3288 or (866) 223-1380. Owner Mike Boutin stocks everything the sportsman needs in his store, where his partner serves up fancy coffees, baked goods and Internet services in the **Hard Drive Café.**

┌─ *Get Away to Kineo Island* ─

You want to get away from the "crowd?" A nostalgic place to visit on a sunny day is Kineo Island, distinguished by the distinctive, straight-edge cliffs along the southeast face of Mount Kineo, which rises 800 feet right above the center of the lake opposite Rockwood, about twenty miles north of Greenville. Kineo is actually a peninsula attached to the mainland by a 500-foot stone causeway on the far side of the lake. You can play a round of golf on a scenic nine-hole course. Or rent a golf cart to poke along three miles of bumpy roads around the island. Swim at the secluded and picturesque Pebble Beach beside the causeway, where knowing boaters often tie up for the afternoon. Observe moose, deer, loons and eagles in the wildlife sanctuary. Hike up Mount Kineo or scale a portion of the rocky cliffs. Take a peak at the abandoned yacht club building known as the Breakers on the point. It might call to you as a potential site for a restaurant or a B&B to fill part of the void left by the late Kineo House resort, which in its heyday was the largest inland waterfront hotel in America. Enjoy lunch or a drink or even an overnight stay at the Oak Lodge, which opens on an intermittent basis.

The island is reached by pontoon boat (Kineo Shuttle, hourly from 9 a.m. to 5 p.m. from the state boat ramp in Rockwood, 534-8812, $8 round trip). Another Kineo shuttle leaves by reservation or on demand from Rockwood Cottages, 534-7725.

Shopping

Greenville's compact downtown is of interest to browsers. Moose are the pervasive theme at **Moosehead Traders,** a general store on Main Street. A moose motif also prevails, from banners to tea towels, at **Moosin' Around Maine. The Blushing Moose** carries eclectic clothing, jewelry, gifts and what-not, plus cards and coasters that might cause a moose to blush. If you're in the mood for a little nosh, it's good to know that **The Stress Free Moose,** a casual restaurant and bar, offers late-night food to accompany its libations.

At **Mud Puddle Mercantile,** a small country store and gift shop, proprietor Helen Schacht touted a tapestry shopping bag on wheels for $7.99 as her "best-seller." In addition to its namesake items, **Maine Mountain Soap and Candle Co.** carries baskets, pottery and home accessories. Look for jams and jellies, cards, baskets, books, Hummel figurines, Christmas villages and more at **The Corner Shop.** Across the street, former chef Claudine Dallam, who closed her prized Blue Moose Café nearby, runs **Claudine's Gourmet Kitchen Shop.** A canoe hangs overhead in the **Great Eastern Clothing Co**. Rustic lamps with carved bears for the base, carved birds, prints and moose, of course, are available at **The Woodcarver's Place.**

Just south of town, the **Indian Hill Trading Post** is the local version of a mall. If you can't find what you're looking for here, locals say, you don't need it.

Where to Stay

The Lodge at Moosehead Lake, Lily Bay Road, Greenville 04441.

High up Blair Hill overlooking Squaw Mountain and Moosehead Lake, this 1917 shingle-style Cape Cod Colonial summer home sets a standard for low-key luxury in the wilds. The foyer with its artful arrangement of fishing creels and other piscatory accessories indicate this is no ordinary inn. Windows in a long living room open onto a full-length deck. Beside is a smaller parlor/library and beyond is a summery dining room where breakfast and, at certain times, dinner are served to houseguests. Opening onto a patio on the lower level is a large game room with English darts and a billiards table. Sumptuous comfort prevails in the guest accommodations, each ingeniously outfitted in a different wildlife motif. Each has a hand-carved four-poster queensize bed dressed with fine linens, sitting areas with loveseats and wing chairs richly upholstered in woodsy fabrics, plush carpeting and twig stenciling – twigs running around the tops of walls in intricate patterns. Small black climbing bears are carved upon each bedpost in the Bear Room. There are loon books and a loon-patterned table in the Loon Room, pillows in the shape of fish in the Trout Room, and antlers holding the valances in the Moose Room. Each provides a TV/VCR in a cabinet above a gas-lit fireplace outlined in stone and a bath with whirlpool tub for two. The ultimate accommodations are three fireplaced "retreat suites" in an adjacent structure, a converted boathouse. On two levels, they have sunken living rooms with lake views through sliding glass doors that open onto a deck and, below, a landscaped patio set into rocks and gardens along the hillside. Two have unique queensize beds hung on boom chains from the ceiling and swaying lengthwise to rock occupants to sleep. The Katahdin in which we stayed has a step-up kingsize bed with a moose antler canopy and a large bathroom with double vanity, fireplace and a two-person whirlpool bath in a mirrored corner illuminated by a flicker chandelier and candles. Birch branches formed decorative molding around the vaulted ceiling. A deer bounded across the back lawn during breakfast the next morning in the Lakeview Dining Room. The fare included a choice of souféed eggs or stuffed french toast with cream cheese and fruits. Traditionally, innkeepers Bruce and Sonda Hamilton offer dinner for houseguests on Sunday in summer and Saturday in winter. The night's menu is recited, and the five-course meal is prix-fixe ($50).

(207) 695-4400 or (800) 825-6977. www.lodgeatmooseheadlake.com. Five rooms and three suites with private baths. Early June to mid-October: doubles, $275 to $375, suites $425 to $475. Rest of year: doubles, $205 to $250, suites, $350 to $375.

The Blair Hill Inn, Lily Bay Road, Greenville 04441.

Blessed with the most majestic lake views around, this hillside house was built in 1891 by Chicago socialite Lyman Blair at the heart of a 2,000-acre working farm that became the largest in Maine. Ruth and Dan McLaughlin surround themselves with fifteen acres of lovely grounds and offer eight guest rooms, some of them quite sumptuous and all conveying laid-back luxury. Four have wood-burning fireplace and all but one enjoy lake views. Beds are king or queensize, topped with feather mattress pads and pillows, and dressed with 300-plus count sheets and down comforters. Terrycloth robes and soaps and bath products from the local Maine Mountain Soap and Candle Co. are standard. On the main floor is an elegant, 43-seat dining room and summery enclosed side porch (see Where to Eat). Available for inn guests are a stylish formal living room with a fireplace and a baby grand piano as well as a cozy library/game room. Other attributes are a side sun porch with a stocked guest pantry, an exercise facility, a hot tub and a fabulous, 90-foot-long front veranda with wicker chairs looking down the lawn toward Moosehead Lake. In the inn's summer concert series, guest musicians perform on the lawn surrounded by gardens that have been featured in the Downeast book, *Gardens, Maine Style.* The hospitable McLaughlins prepare lavish breakfasts. Lobster benedict with fresh fiddleheads or waffles with bananas and toasted pecan sauce might be the main course.

(207) 695-0224. Fax (207) 695-4324. www.blairhill.com. Eight rooms with private baths. June-October: doubles, $275 to $425. Rest of year: $250 to $350. Two-night minimum weekends. Children over 10.

Greenville Inn, 40 Norris St., Greenville 04441.

An aura of old money pervades this established inn, built as a summer home in 1895 by a wealthy lumber baron. Carved mantels, mosaics and English tiles surround the fireplaces. Embossed Lincrusta walls and gas lights convey an air of antiquity in the hallways, and a large spruce tree painted on a leaded glass window adorns the stairway landing. New innkeepers Terry and Jeff Johannemann from New Jersey have restored the mansion to its original Victorian era and refreshed the decor. Four bedrooms with king or queen beds and two suites are available in the inn and attached carriage house. Some of the beds are draped in canopies and covered with plush comforters, and all now have TVs. Our room had a king bed and a fireplace, but had only one chair and a clawfoot soaking tub without a shower. Indulge in the master suite with its canopied king bed awash in pillows, a sitting room with wood-burning fireplace and an English-tiled bathroom with a soaking tub and marble spray shower. Or escape to the private tower suite in a new building, where you'll find a king bed draped in soft scarves, a fireplace, a TV/DVD, a two-person jacuzzi and a balcony/veranda. Other hideaways are six pine-paneled cottages clustered off to the side of the inn. Each has a sitting area, TV and front porch with a lake view.

The Johannemanns serve a hearty breakfast of quiche, omelets, cheese blintzes with cranberry coulis or baked stuffed french toast.

(207) 695-2206 or (888) 695-6000. www.greenvilleinn.com. Four rooms, three suites and six cottages with private baths. Doubles, $160 to $205. Suites, $240 to $350. Cottages, $160 to $205.

Pleasant Street Inn, 26 Pleasant St., Greenville 04441.

An unusual spired turret on the fourth floor tops this rambling Victorian house built in 1889 by one of Maine's original outfitters on a residential side street. Now called "The Tower," it offers windows on four sides and chairs around a small games table in the center, and is the venue of choice for watching the sun go down over the lake and mountains in the distance. The Tower is one of several common areas spruced up by owners Tim Shelep, John Cusick and Dan Turek, who call themselves "The Three Bears." The pump organ at one end of the front dining room, the photo-realistic oil paintings done by Tim, the eclectic decor, and the cooking of John and Dan belie the inn's website visuals that this might be run by a trio of lumberjacks. A masculine motif of plush leather prevails in the large main-floor living room. A second sitting room at the head of the stairs on the second floor is for TV watching. More sitting areas are available on the 150-foot-long porch that wraps around the front and side. Guest rooms vary in size and style. Most have queen beds and original bath fixtures, including vintage soaking tubs and marble showers. Dan made the draperies by hand for a two-bedroom suite, each room with a queen bed. John prepares the breakfasts of perhaps three-cheese omelets or buttermilk pancakes with blueberries. He turns over cooking duties at night to Dan, who offers prix-fixe dinners for guests by reservation.

(207) 695-3400. Fax (207) 695-2004. www.pleasantstreetinn.com. Five rooms and one two-bedroom suite with private baths. Doubles, $110 to $175. Two-bedroom suite, $260.

Evergreen Lodge, Route 15, HCR 76, Box 58, Greenville 04441.

Five miles south of town is this attractive, all-cedar structure, built as a physician's home and set back from the road amid evergreens and birches and showy flower gardens on 30 acres. Hank and Janice Dyer offer six comfortable guest rooms, each strikingly paneled in varieties of cedar. Colorful quilts and lots of pillows enhance the contemporary lodge-style decor. Gas-log stoves have been added to the first-floor Bear and Loon rooms, each with kingsize bed. The Moose Room is done with a moose theme, incorporating blue quilts with a moose design on the queen bed and on an extra twin bed in an alcove. Guests gather in two cheery sitting rooms with TVs and fireplaces. Breakfast is served in a sunroom with a greenhouse section overlooking the perennial gardens. The fare includes fresh fruit, pastries, breakfast meats, pancakes, eggs or puffed french toast. Moose and deer are sighted occasionally on the property.

(207) 695-3241 or (888) 624-3993. www.evergreenlodgemoosehead.com. Six rooms with private baths. Doubles, $110 to $150. Children over 12.

Where to Eat

Greenville Inn, 40 Norris St., Greenville.

Among Greenville folk, this restaurant is "the toast of the town," in one innkeeper's words. Since 1988, it has been known for some of northern Maine's fanciest fare, served in manorial surroundings. Two dining rooms are clad in white linens amid rich wood paneling, ornate fireplaces, embossed Lincrusta walls and distant views of Moosehead Lake's East Cove Harbor. The traditional heavy, European fare has been lightened up and updated by chef Curtis "Bear" Hillard from Atlanta. To begin, he offers the likes of Maine lobster cake with mango-citrus coulis and an escargot and foie gras vol-au-vent. Main courses could be salmon fillet wrapped in parma ham with a preserved lemon aioli, breast of free-range chicken stuffed with foie gras mousseline and rack of Maine venison with zinfandel sauce. Chocolate profiteroles and berries romanoff make flamboyant finales.

(207) 695-2206 or (888) 695-6000. Entrées, $25 to $35 Dinner by reservation, Monday-Saturday 5 to 9, June to mid-October.

The Blair Hill Inn, Lily Bay Road, Greenville.

A spectacular view of lake and mountains draws the public to this hilltop inn's seasonal restaurant. Diners take in the sunset as they enjoy cocktails and a complimentary amuse-bouche on the 90-foot-wide front veranda before adjourning to the big-windowed dining room, a picture of understated elegance, or the summery enclosed side porch. Executive chef Jack Neal, a Culinary Institute of America graduate, takes a break from his landscaping business to prepare exceptional contemporary international fare on weekends. The meal is prix-fixe, $50, with a modest choice among five courses that change weekly. A typical dinner opens with the option of a crispy smoked shrimp roll over a tatsoi salad with chile-lime dressing or a golden pineapple and lobster salad tossed in miso-honey vinaigrette. A chilled red pepper and tomato soup and a green salad follow. Main courses could be crab-stuffed salmon roulade with a scallion risotto cake over Sicilian tomato ragu, wood-grilled duck breast with cherries and merlot on a mulled sweet potato mash, and Asian barbecued hanger steak with a sweet soy drizzle. Finish with chocolate espresso cake with crème anglaise or tahitian vanilla ice cream with gingered plums.

(207) 695-0224. Prix-fixe, $50. Dinner by reservation, Friday-Saturday 6 to 8:30, mid-June through mid-October, Saturday in winter for house guests.

The Black Frog, Pritham Avenue, Greenville.

For casual dining with a water view, there's no better place in downtown Greenville than this. It's a sprawl of a place oriented toward the water, with tables around a bar, in a solarium and outside on a pier with a tiki bar. The setting is such that the inconsistency of the food may not matter. Local restaurateur Leigh Turner continues to lampoon what he calls "the pretensions of fine dining" made infamous in his short-lived Road Kill Café chain. His current version of "North Woods Cuisine" is detailed on an irreverent menu that opens with "Canadian nachaux: Not bad for being 3,000 miles from Tiajuana." Soups, salads, burgers and "sammiches" continue the theme. Entrées are strips, fips, ribs and balls: "chish and fips, faddock hilet with satyr toss," seafood platter, froggy's famous fried chicken, barbecued ribs, steaks and mooseballs, "unquestionably the tenderest cut of the moose. Requires 48-hour advance notice and 25% deposit, $1,495." The menu makes for fun reading, if not the most appetizing eating. Upstairs, the Black Frog offers two lakefront housekeeping suites for $110 to $150 a night.

(207) 695-1100. www.theblackfrog.com. Entrées, $12.95 to $21.95. Open daily, 11:30 to 11:30.

Flatlander's, 36 Pritham Ave., Greenville.

Billed as "a country place for food and drink," this small downtown emporium is a cut above, thanks to its specialty of broasted chicken. You can order a three-piece chicken dinner ($6.95), including french fries and coleslaw, to eat here or take out to a picnic table in the pocket-size town park facing the harbor across the street. If broasted chicken is not your thing, Flatlander's offers other options, from appetizers to burgers, soups to salads. Among main courses, expect a few basics like a spaghetti dinner, baked haddock, shrimp scampi with linguini, fish and chips, country ribs and ribeye steak. Decor in the long, narrow room with a bar at the back and a shiny wood counter down the center is minimal. The handsome bare wood tables are made of Maine pine – "you can hardly find trees like this any more," their maker advised.

(207) 695-3373. Entrées, $5.95 to $12.95. Lunch and dinner daily in summer, 11 to 8 or 9; reduced hours in off-season.

Rod-N-Reel Café, 44 Pritham Ave., Greenville.

The best food in downtown Greenville is served at this unassuming café across the road from the lake. The place is known for its prime rib (the huge slab goes for a bargain $20.95). It also supplements the standard fried seafood and pasta fare with things like charbroiled salmon, baked scallops, a variety of chicken dishes and New York sirloin steak. Fried Maine shrimp, haddock chowder, nachos and mozzarella sticks are among the starters. Desserts include homemade pies.

(207) 695-0388. Entrées, $9.95 to $20.95. Open daily except Tuesday, 11 to 8 or 9. Winter, Wednesday-Saturday from 11, Sunday 11 to 3.

A North Woods (Re)Treat

Northern Pride Lodge, 3405 Lily Bay Road, Kokadjo.

A pleasant dining porch and an inspired-for-the-area menu draw folks from Greenville for dinner at this small lodge built in 1896 by a logging baron as his summer home in out-of-the-way Kokadjo (whose sign says Population; Not Many). It's eighteen miles northeast of Greenville, just before the paved road ends on the back way to Baxter State Park and Mount Katahdin. Visitors receive a royal welcome from lodge owners Barbara and Wayne Plummer, registered Maine guides who don't exactly get hordes of visitors out here in the semi-boondocks. They seat guests for cocktails in the living room opposite a huge fieldstone fireplace. The meal is served in an enclosed porch, part of a long screened porch that wraps around the front and sides and looks onto the waterfront property at the end of First Roach Pond. The short menu starts with a choice of spicy chicken wings and a longtime favorite, a baked brie cheese wheel with warm caramel sauce, fruit and french bread. Seasonal greens embellish the Mediterranean and smoked shrimp salads that come with the meal. Main courses include baked salmon with raspberry-maple glaze, roast duckling with orange sauce and grilled ribeye steak smothered with sautéed mushrooms. A daily homemade dessert supplements the hot fudge sundae on the menu. To complete the North Woods experience, the Plummers put up overnight guests in five bedrooms sharing two baths (doubles, $90 to $125).

(207) 695-2890. www.northernpridelodge.com. Entrées, $17.95 to $19.95. Dinner nightly by reservation (by noon), seasonally 5 to 9.

FOR MORE INFORMATION: Moosehead Lake Region Chamber of Commerce, Indian Hill Plaza, Greenville, ME 04441. (207) 695-2702 or (888) 876-2778. www.mooseheadlake.org.

Index

G

H